ASSESSMENT ITEM LISTING
FOR
BIOLOGY: PRINCIPLES
AND EXPLORATIONS © 2001

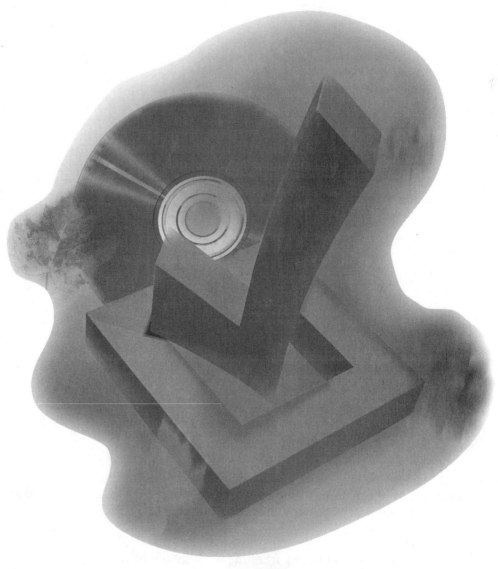

HOLT, RINEHART AND WINSTON

A Harcourt Classroom Education Company

Austin • New York • Orlando • Atlanta • San Francisco • Boston • Dallas • Toronto • London

Cover design: Morgan-Cain & Associates
Cover Photography: HRW, Sam Dudgeon

Printed in the United States of America

ISBN 0-03-054358-4

3 4 5 6 095 04 03 02

Table of Contents

Introduction

The *Biology: Principles and Explorations* Test Generator and *Assessment Item Listing*

The *Biology: Principles and Explorations* Test Generator consists of a comprehensive bank of test items and the ExamView® Pro 3.0 software, which enables you to produce your own tests based on the items in the Test Generator and items you create yourself. Both Macintosh® and Windows® versions of the Test Generator are included on the *Biology: Principles and Explorations* One-Stop Planner with Test Generator. Directions on pp. vi–viii of this book explain how to install the program on your computer. This *Assessment Item Listing* is a printout of all the test items in the *Biology: Principles and Explorations* Test Generator.

ExamView Software

ExamView enables you to quickly create printed and on-line tests. You can enter your own questions in a variety of formats, including true/false, multiple choice, completion, problem, short answer, and essay. The program also allows you to customize the content and appearance of the tests you create.

Test Items

The *Biology: Principles and Explorations* Test Generator contains a file of test items for each chapter of the textbook. Each item is correlated to the chapter objectives in the textbook and by difficulty level.

Item Codes

As you browse through this *Assessment Item Listing,* you will see that all test items of the same type appear under an identifying head. Each item is coded to assist you with item selection. Following is an explanation of the codes.

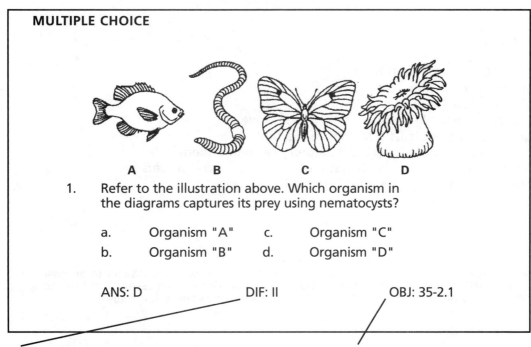

MULTIPLE CHOICE

1. Refer to the illustration above. Which organism in the diagrams captures its prey using nematocysts?

   a. Organism "A"   c. Organism "C"
   b. Organism "B"   d. Organism "D"

   ANS: D   DIF: II   OBJ: 35-2.1

DIF defines the difficulty of the item.
 I requires recall of information.
 II requires analysis and interpretation of known information.
 III requires application of knowledge to new situations.

OBJ lists the chapter number, section number, and objective. (21-2.2 = Chapter 21, Section 2, Objective 2)

Installation and Startup

The Test Generator is provided on the One-Stop Planner. The Test Generator includes ExamView and all of the questions for the corresponding textbook. ExamView includes three components: the Test Builder, Question Bank Editor, and Test Player. The Test Builder includes options to create, edit, print, and save tests. The Question Bank Editor lets you create or edit question banks. The Test Player is a separate program that your students can use to take on-line* (computerized or LAN-based) tests. Please refer to the ExamView User's Guide on the One-Stop Planner for complete instructions.

Before you can use the Test Generator, you must install ExamView and the test banks on your hard drive. The system requirements, installation instructions, and startup procedures are provided below.

System Requirements
To use ExamView, your computer must meet or exceed the following hardware requirements:

Windows®

- Pentium processor
- Windows 95®, Windows 98®, Windows 2000® (or a more recent version)
- color monitor (VGA-compatible)
- CD-ROM and/or high-density floppy disk drive
- hard drive with at least 7 MB space available
- 8 MB available memory (16 MB memory recommended)
- an Internet connection (if you wish to access the Internet testing features)*

Macintosh®

- PowerPC processor, 100 MHz
- System 7.5 (or a more recent version)
- color monitor (VGA-compatible)
- CD-ROM and/or high-density floppy disk drive
- hard drive with at least 7 MB space available
- 8 MB available memory (16 MB memory recommended)
- an Internet connection with System 8.6 or a more recent version
  (if you wish to access the Internet testing features)*

* You can use the Test Player to host tests on your personal or school Web site or local area network (LAN) at no additional charge. The ExamView Web site's Internet test-hosting service must be purchased separately. Visit www.examview.com to learn more.

Installation

Instructions for installing ExamView from the CD-ROM:

Windows®

Step 1
Turn on your computer.
Step 2
Insert the One-Stop Planner into the CD-ROM drive.
Step 3
Click the Start button on the taskbar, and choose the Run option.
Step 4
In the Open box, type "d:\setup.exe" (substitute the letter for your drive if it is not d:)
and click OK.
Step 5
Follow the prompts on the screen to complete the installation process.

Macintosh®

Step 1
Turn on your computer.
Step 2
Insert the One-Stop Planner into the CD-ROM drive. When the CD-ROM icon appears
on the desktop, double-click the icon.
Step 3
Double-click the ExamView Pro Installer icon.
Step 4
Follow the prompts on the screen to complete the installation process.

*Instructions for installing ExamView from the Main Menu of the One-Stop Planner
(Macintosh® or Windows®):*

Follow steps 1 and 2 from above.
Step 3
Double-click One-Stop.pdf. (If you do not have Adobe Acrobat® Reader installed on
your computer, install it before proceeding by clicking Reader Installer.)
Step 4
To advance to the Main Menu, click anywhere on the title screen.
Step 5
Click the Test Generator button.
Step 6
Click the appropriate Install ExamView button.
Step 7
Follow the prompts on the screen to complete the installation process.

Getting Started

After you complete the installation process, follow these instructions to start ExamView. See the ExamView User's Guide on the One-Stop Planner for further instructions on the program's options for creating a test and editing a question bank.

Startup Instructions

Step 1
Turn on the computer.

Step 2
Windows®: Click the Start button on the taskbar. Highlight the Programs menu, and locate the ExamView Pro Test Generator folder. Select the ExamView Pro option to start the software.
Macintosh®: Locate and open the ExamView Pro folder. Double-click the ExamView Pro icon.

Step 3
The first time you run the software, you will be prompted to enter your name, school/institution name, and city/state. You are now ready to begin using ExamView.

Step 4
Each time you start ExamView, the Startup menu appears. Choose one of the options shown.

Step 5
Use ExamView to create a test or edit questions in a question bank.

Technical Support

If you have any questions about the Test Generator, call the Holt, Rinehart and Winston technical support line at 1-800-323-9239, Monday through Friday, 7:00 A.M. to 6:00 P.M., Central Standard Time. You can contact the Technical Support Center on the Internet at http://www.hrwtechsupport.com or by e-mail at tsc@hrwtechsupport.com.

TRUE/FALSE

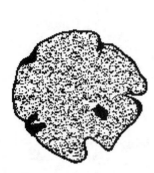

1. Refer to the illustration above. Unlike the sand dollar, the paramecium does not have to maintain a stable internal environment.

   ANS: F   DIF: II   OBJ: BPE 1-1.1

2. Refer to the illustration above. The sand dollar and the paramecium both exhibit organization.

   ANS: T   DIF: II   OBJ: BPE 1-1.1

3. Refer to the illustration above. Both species are multicellular.

   ANS: F   DIF: II   OBJ: BPE 1-1.1

4. Refer to the illustration above. Reproduction ensures the ongoing success of both species.

   ANS: T   DIF: II   OBJ: BPE 1-1.1

5. Refer to the illustration above. Both species have DNA in their cells.

   ANS: T   DIF: II   OBJ: BPE 1-1.2

6. A paramecium is a multicellular organism.

   ANS: F   DIF: I   OBJ: BPE 1-1.3

7. Cells are highly organized, tiny structures.

   ANS: T   DIF: I   OBJ: BPE 1-1.3

8. All living things are able to reproduce.

   ANS: T   DIF: I   OBJ: BPE 1-1.4

9. The passing of traits from offspring to parents is called heredity.

   ANS: F   DIF: I   OBJ: BPE 1-1.4

10. Homeostasis is the maintenance of constant internal conditions in spite of changes in the environment.

    ANS: T   DIF: I   OBJ: BPE 1-1.4

11. In 1999, the world's human population passed 6 billion people.

    ANS: T   DIF: I   OBJ: BPE 1-2.1

12. Genetically engineered crops will increase the need for insecticides.

    ANS: F   DIF: I   OBJ: BPE 1-2.2

13. Genetic engineers are trying to create crops that are less resistant to insects and microorganism

    ANS: F   DIF: I   OBJ: BPE 1-2.2

14. Genetic engineers are trying to create plants that are more resistant to frost damage.

    ANS: T   DIF: I   OBJ: BPE 1-2.2

15. Cystic fibrosis is a growth disorder of cells that occurs when cells divide uncontrollably within the body.

    ANS: F   DIF: I   OBJ: BPE 1-2.3

16. Since amphibians have been on Earth for about 370 million years, scientists have concluded tha they are not very sensitive to their environments.

    ANS: F   DIF: I   OBJ: BPE 1-3.1

17. A scientist who performs an experiment has no idea what the outcome of the experiment is goir to be.

    ANS: F   DIF: I   OBJ: BPE 1-3.1

18. Scientific investigations always follow a series of rigidly defined steps.

    ANS: F   DIF: I   OBJ: BPE 1-3.1

19. Acid rain has a pH above 8.5.

    ANS: F   DIF: I   OBJ: BPE 1-3.2

20. The control and experimental groups are designed to be identical.

    ANS: F   DIF: I   OBJ: BPE 1-3.3

21. The independent variable is the variable that changes in an experiment.

    ANS: T   DIF: I   OBJ: BPE 1-3.3

22. A theory is a hypothesis that has been proven true.

    ANS: F   DIF: I   OBJ: BPE 1-3.4

23. A theory is an assumption made by scientists and implies a lack of certainty.

    ANS: F   DIF: I   OBJ: BPE 1-3.4

MULTIPLE CHOICE

1. Biology is the study of
    a. minerals.   c. the weather.
    b. life.   d. energy.

    ANS: B   DIF: I   OBJ: BPE 1-1.1

2. Which of the following is characteristic of all living things?
    a. reproduction   c. cellular organization
    b. metabolism   d. All of the above

    ANS: D   DIF: I   OBJ: BPE 1-1.1

3. chemical reactions : metabolism ::
    a. cell membrane : cells   c. reproduction : living
    b. heredity : homeostasis   d. experimentation : verifying a prediction

    ANS: D
    (is/are part of the process of)

    DIF: III   OBJ: BPE 1-1.1

4. Living things
    a. require energy to carry on life processes.   c. are composed of cells.
    b. have the ability to reproduce.   d. All of the above

    ANS: D   DIF: I   OBJ: BPE 1-1.2

5. A group of genetically similar organisms that can produce fertile offspring is called a
    a. species.   c. mutation.
    b. gene.   d. paramecium.

    ANS: A   DIF: I   OBJ: BPE 1-1.2

6. All living organisms are composed of
   a. diatoms.
   b. cellulose.
   c. cells.
   d. None of the above

   ANS: C   DIF: I   OBJ: BPE 1-1.3

7. Cell membranes
   a. are only found on a small number of cells.
   b. contain genes.
   c. are made of DNA.
   d. are thin coverings that surround cells.

   ANS: D   DIF: I   OBJ: BPE 1-1.3

8. As a characteristic of all living things, homeostasis relates most directly to which of the following biological themes?
   a. interacting systems
   b. stability
   c. evolution
   d. scale and structure

   ANS: B   DIF: I   OBJ: BPE 1-1.4

9. All living things maintain a balance within their cells and the environment through the process o
   a. growth.
   b. development.
   c. homeostasis.
   d. evolution.

   ANS: C   DIF: I   OBJ: BPE 1-1.4

10. Homeostasis means
    a. a change over long periods of time.
    b. keeping things the same.
    c. rapid change.
    d. the same thing as evolution.

    ANS: B   DIF: I   OBJ: BPE 1-1.4

11. The energy that drives metabolism in animals comes from
    a. homeostasis.
    b. food.
    c. water.
    d. heredity.

    ANS: B   DIF: I   OBJ: BPE 1-1.4

12. The process by which organisms make more of their own kind is called
    a. heredity.
    b. mutation.
    c. gene.
    d. reproduction.

    ANS: D   DIF: I   OBJ: BPE 1-1.4

13. In what direction does energy flow?
    a. sun→plants→plant eater→meat eater
    b. plants→sun→plant eater→meat eater
    c. plant eater→plants→sun→meat eater
    d. sun→plants→meat eater→plant eater

    ANS: A   DIF: I   OBJ: BPE 1-1.4

14. Children tend to resemble their parents due to
    a. metabolism.
    b. mutation.
    c. heredity.
    d. homeostasis.

    ANS: C   DIF: I   OBJ: BPE 1-1.4

15. The destruction of rain forests leads to
    a. a lessening of the world's biological diversity.
    b. the extinction of many species of plants.
    c. the extinction of many species of animals.
    d. All of the above

    ANS: D   DIF: I   OBJ: BPE 1-2.1

16. Which of the following statements is correct?
    a. Biologists are seeking new crops that grow more efficiently in tropical soils.
    b. Genetic engineers are transplanting genes into plants to create crops that are more
       resistant to insects.
    c. As the population continues to grow, the demand for food is going to strain our ability to
       feed all of the people.
    d. All of the above

    ANS: D   DIF: I   OBJ: BPE 1-2.2

17. The leading cause of death among American males between the ages of 24 and 44 is
    a. cancer.
    b. heart disease.
    c. AIDS.
    d. accidents.

    ANS: C   DIF: I   OBJ: BPE 1-2.3

18. Cystic fibrosis and muscular dystrophy are examples of
    a. viral infections.
    b. genetic disorders.
    c. sexually transmitted diseases.
    d. None of the above

    ANS: B   DIF: I   OBJ: BPE 1-2.3

19. Scientists are using gene therapy to manage
    a. deforestation.
    b. population growth.
    c. cystic fibrosis.
    d. measles.

    ANS: C   DIF: I   OBJ: BPE 1-2.3

20. A scientist noticed that the number of salamanders in ponds in the Rocky Mountains were
    declining. This was a(n)
    a. hypothesis.
    b. theory.
    c. observation.
    d. control.

    ANS: C   DIF: I   OBJ: BPE 1-3.1

21. Acid rain
    a. has a low pH.
    b. may fall in the form of snow.
    c. may contain sulfuric acid.
    d. All of the above

    ANS: D   DIF: I   OBJ: BPE 1-3.1

22. Most typically, the order in which the steps of scientific investigations are applied is
    a. observations, predictions, hypothesis, controlled testing, conclusions, questions.
    b. predictions, observations, hypothesis, conclusions, controlled testing, questions.
    c. observations, questions, hypothesis, predictions, controlled testing, conclusions.
    d. observations, hypothesis, predictions, controlled testing, questions, conclusions.

    ANS: C   DIF: I   OBJ: BPE 1-3.1

23. Scientists usually design experiments
    a. with a good idea of the expected experimental results.
    b. based on wild guesses.
    c. in order to develop new laboratory tools.
    d. All of the above

    ANS: A   DIF: I   OBJ: BPE 1-3.1

24. frogs : acid rain ::
    a. wind : smoke
    b. salamanders : hot weather
    c. theories : predictions
    d. rain forests : fire

    ANS: D
    (are destroyed by)

    DIF: II   OBJ: BPE 1-3.1

25. A hypothesis is a
    a. definite answer to a given problem.
    b. testable possible explanation of an observation.
    c. proven statement.
    d. concluding statement.

    ANS: B   DIF: I   OBJ: BPE 1-3.2

26. A hypothesis that is not supported by the data that has been collected and analyzed
    a. is known as an inaccurate forecast.
    b. often predicts a different observation.
    c. is rejected.
    d. None of the above

    ANS: C   DIF: I   OBJ: BPE 1-3.2

27. The English physician Ronald Ross wanted to try to find the cause of malaria. Based on his observations, Dr. Ross suggested that the *Anopheles* mosquito might spread malaria from person to person. This suggestion was a
    a. prediction.
    b. hypothesis.
    c. theory.
    d. scientific "truth."

    ANS: B   DIF: I   OBJ: BPE 1-3.2

28. observation : hypothesis ::
    a. theory : observation
    b. guess : hypothesis
    c. hypothesis : prediction
    d. certainty : investigation

    ANS: C
    (leads to a(n))

    DIF: II   OBJ: BPE 1-3.2

29. Dr. Ross knew that the parasite *Plasmodium* was always found in the blood of malaria patients. He thought that if the *Anopheles* mosquitoes were responsible for spreading malaria, then *Plasmodium* would be found in the mosquitoes. This ideas was a
    a. prediction.
    b. hypothesis.
    c. theory.
    d. scientific "truth."

    ANS: A   DIF: I   OBJ: BPE 1-3.3

30. Scientific hypotheses are most often tested by the process of
    a. communicating.
    b. inferring.
    c. experimenting.
    d. analyzing data.

    ANS: C   DIF: I   OBJ: BPE 1-3.3

31. A planned procedure to test a hypothesis is called a(n)
    a. prediction.
    b. experiment.
    c. control.
    d. variable.

    ANS: B   DIF: I   OBJ: BPE 1-3.3

32. The variable that is measured in an experiment is the ____ variable.
    a. independent.
    b. dependent.
    c. control.
    d. experimental.

    ANS: A   DIF: I   OBJ: BPE 1-3.3

33. A unifying explanation for a broad range of observations is called a
    a. hypothesis.
    b. theory.
    c. prediction.
    d. controlled experiment.

    ANS: B   DIF: I   OBJ: BPE 1-3.4

34. A scientific theory
    a. is absolutely certain.
    b. is unchangeable.
    c. may be revised as new evidence is presented.
    d. is a controlled experiment.

    ANS: C   DIF: I   OBJ: BPE 1-3.4

35. The word *theory* used in a scientific sense means
    a. that of which the scientist is most certain.
    b. a guess made with very little knowledge to support it.
    c. an absolute scientific certainty.
    d. None of the above

    ANS: A   DIF: I   OBJ: BPE 1-3.4

COMPLETION

1. Molecules of _____ inside cells encode information to direct their growth and development.

   ANS: DNA   DIF: I   OBJ: BPE 1-1.2

2. Change in inherited _____ over time is called evolution.

   ANS: traits   DIF: I   OBJ: BPE 1-1.2

3. The study of the interactions of living organisms with one another and with the nonliving part of their environment is called _____.

   ANS: ecology   DIF: I   OBJ: BPE 1-1.2

4. Every living organism is composed of one or more _____.

   ANS: cells   DIF: I   OBJ: BPE 1-1.3

5. All cells have the same basic _____.

   ANS: structure   DIF: I   OBJ: BPE 1-1.3

6. Some organisms are _____ -celled, while others are multicellular.

   ANS: single   DIF: I   OBJ: BPE 1-1.3

7. _____ is the sum of all chemical reactions carried out in an organism.

   ANS: Metabolism   DIF: I   OBJ: BPE 1-1.4

8. The energy used by living organisms originates from the _____.

   ANS: sun   DIF: I   OBJ: BPE 1-1.4

9. To function properly, all living things maintain a constant internal environment through the process of _____.

   ANS: homeostasis   DIF: I   OBJ: BPE 1-1.4

10. An animal's traits are determined by its _____.

    ANS: genes or DNA   DIF: I   OBJ: BPE 1-1.4

11. Genetic engineers are transplanting plant _____ into other plants to create crops that are resistant to frost damage.

    ANS: genes or DNA   DIF: I   OBJ: BPE 1-2.2

12. _____ is a virus that destroys the immune system, causing AIDS.

    ANS: HIV   DIF: I   OBJ: BPE 1-2.3

13. Frogs, toads, and salamanders are all examples of _____.

    ANS: amphibians   DIF: I   OBJ: BPE 1-3.1

14. Stating in advance the result that may be obtained from testing a hypothesis is called _____.

    ANS: predicting   DIF: I   OBJ: BPE 1-3.2

15. An educated guess, or _____, may be tested by experimentation.

    ANS: hypothesis   DIF: I   OBJ: BPE 1-3.2

16. A(n) _____ experiment is one in which a group that receives some experimental treatment is compared to a group that does not receive the experimental treatment.

    ANS: controlled   DIF: I   OBJ: BPE 1-3.3

17. In a controlled experiment, the _____ group is the group that receives some type of experimental treatment.

    ANS: experimental   DIF: I   OBJ: BPE 1-3.3

18. The _____ group receives no experimental treatment.

    ANS: control   DIF: I   OBJ: BPE 1-3.3

19. A unifying explanation for a broad range of observations is a(n) _____.

    ANS: theory   DIF: I   OBJ: BPE 1-3.4

ESSAY

1. Name five characteristics that are considered distinct properties of all living things.

   ANS:
   Each organism is composed of one or more cells. All living things carry out metabolic reactions that involve the use of energy. Reproduction is characteristic of all living things, as is homeostasis, the maintenance of a constant internal environment. All organisms pass on genetic information to offspring. All living organisms respond and adjust to their environment, as well as grow and develop.

   DIF: II   OBJ: BPE 1-1.1

2. Toads that live in hot, dry regions bury themselves in the soil during the day. How might this be important to the toad?

   ANS:
   The toad must maintain a constant internal environment (homeostasis) in order to function properly. Burying themselves in the soil is a way to keep their body temperature from rising too high and to keep their bodies from drying out.

   DIF: II   OBJ: BPE 1-1.1

3. Evaluate the role biologists play in saving our tropical forests.

   ANS:
   Biologists study the plants and animals in the rain forests in order to better understand how we can maintain a balance between people's growing need for land and the need to protect these plants and animals.

   DIF: II   OBJ: BPE 1-2.1

4. The results of an experiment do not support the hypothesis that the experiment was designed to test. Was the experiment a waste of time? Explain.

   ANS:
   No, the experiment was not a waste of time. A scientist works by systematically showing that certain hypotheses are not valid when they are not consistent with the results of experiments. The results of experiments are used to evaluate alternative hypotheses. An experiment can be successful if it shows that one or more of the alternative hypotheses are inconsistent with observations.

   DIF: II   OBJ: BPE 1-3.1

5. What are the predicted consequences of sulfuric acid being released into the environment from a coal plant?

ANS:
The sulfuric acid released from the burning of high-sulfur coal will fall back to the Earth as rain and snow. This will result in decreased pH levels in streams and ponds when the snow melts. The pH will fall to acidic levels in the spring.

DIF: II   OBJ: BPE 1-3.2

TRUE/FALSE

1. Atoms have a positive charge.

    ANS: F   DIF: I   OBJ: BPE 2-1.1

2. An element is made up of more than one kind of atom.

    ANS: F   DIF: I   OBJ: BPE 2-1.1

3. Hydrogen and oxygen atoms have an equal number of electrons.

    ANS: F   DIF: I   OBJ: BPE 2-1.1

4. A molecule is an atom that has gained or lost an electron.

    ANS: F   DIF: I   OBJ: BPE 2-1.2

5. An atom that gains or loses one or more electrons is called an ion.

    ANS: T   DIF: I   OBJ: BPE 2-1.3

6. An atom with more electrons than protons has a positive charge.

    ANS: F   DIF: I   OBJ: BPE 2-1.3

7. Ionic bonds form between two negatively charged particles.

    ANS: F   DIF: I   OBJ: BPE 2-1.3

8. A covalent bond forms between two atoms that share electrons to form a molecule.

    ANS: T   DIF: I   OBJ: BPE 2-1.3

9. Adhesion is an attraction between different substances.

    ANS: T   DIF: I   OBJ: BPE 2-2.1

10. The ability of water to retain heat helps cells maintain homeostasis.

    ANS: T   DIF: I   OBJ: BPE 2-2.1

11. Nonpolar molecules dissolve well in water.

    ANS: F   DIF: I   OBJ: BPE 2-2.2

12. Water molecules attract nonpolar molecules such as oil.

ANS: F   DIF: I   OBJ: BPE 2-2.2

13. Your body cannot adjust the pH of body fluids.

ANS: F   DIF: I   OBJ: BPE 2-2.3

14. Organic compounds contain carbon atoms that are covalently bonded to other elements—typically hydrogen, oxygen, and other carbon atoms.

ANS: T   DIF: I   OBJ: BPE 2-3.1

15. A nucleotide has four parts.

ANS: F   DIF: I   OBJ: BPE 2-3.3

16. RNA is made up of a double strand of nucleotides.

ANS: F   DIF: I   OBJ: BPE 2-3.3

17. DNA stores hereditary information that can be used to make proteins.

ANS: T   DIF: I   OBJ: BPE 2-3.3

18. When a person uses food as a source of energy to run a race, energy is converted from chemical energy to mechanical energy.

ANS: T   DIF: I   OBJ: BPE 2-4.1

19. The amount of energy needed to cause a chemical reaction to start is called activation energy.

ANS: T   DIF: I   OBJ: BPE 2-4.2

20. Without enzymes, chemical reactions necessary for life would not occur at a rate sufficient to sustain life.

ANS: T   DIF: I   OBJ: BPE 2-4.3

21. Enzymes speed up a chemical reaction by increasing the activation energy of the reaction.

ANS: F   DIF: I   OBJ: BPE 2-4.3

22. When an enzyme binds with its substrate, the activation energy needed for the chemical reaction to occur is increased.

ANS: F   DIF: I   OBJ: BPE 2-4.3

23. Chemical reactions that occur in cells are called biochemical reactions.

ANS: T   DIF: I   OBJ: BPE 2-4.3

MULTIPLE CHOICE

1. Atoms are composed of
   a. protons.   c. electrons.
   b. neutrons.   d. All of the above

   ANS: D   DIF: I   OBJ: BPE 2-1.1

2. The electrons of an atom
   a. are found in the nucleus along with the protons.
   b. occupy the space surrounding the nucleus.
   c. have a positive charge.
   d. are attached to the positive charge of neutrons.

   ANS: B   DIF: I   OBJ: BPE 2-1.1

3. The smallest particle of matter that can retain the chemical properties of carbon is a(n)
   a. carbon molecule.   c. carbon atom.
   b. carbon macromolecule.   d. element.

   ANS: C   DIF: I   OBJ: BPE 2-1.1

4. A substance that is composed of only one type of atom is called a(n)
   a. nucleus.   c. element.
   b. cell.   d. molecule.

   ANS: C   DIF: I   OBJ: BPE 2-1.1

5. All matter is composed of
   a. cells.   c. atoms.
   b. molecules.   d. carbon.

   ANS: C   DIF: I   OBJ: BPE 2-1.1

6. A molecule that has a partial positive charge on one side and a partial negative charge on the other side is called a
   a. nonpolar molecule.   c. charged molecule.
   b. polar molecule.   d. bipolar molecule.

   ANS: B   DIF: I   OBJ: BPE 2-1.2

7. A chemical formula shows the
   a. kinds of bonds found in the molecule.
   b. kinds of bonds found in the compound.
   c. kinds of elements found in the compound.
   d. arrangement of the elements found in the compound.

   ANS: C   DIF: I   OBJ: BPE 2-1.2

8. Ionic bonds form between molecules that have
   a. opposite charges.   c. no charges.
   b. the same charge.   d. neutral charges.

   ANS: A   DIF: I   OBJ: BPE 2-1.3

9. The bond formed when two atoms share a pair of electrons is called a(n)
   a. hydrogen bond.   c. covalent bond.
   b. ionic bond.   d. water bond.

   ANS: C   DIF: I   OBJ: BPE 2-1.3

10. Sharing of electrons in the outer energy levels of two atoms
    a. results in ion formation.
    b. occurs in covalent bonds.
    c. only occurs if both are atoms of the same element.
    d. is found only among carbon atoms.

    ANS: B   DIF: I   OBJ: BPE 2-1.3

11. Nonpolar molecules have
    a. no negative or positive poles.   c. only a negative pole.
    b. both negative and positive poles.   d. only a positive pole.

    ANS: A   DIF: I   OBJ: BPE 2-2.1

12. Water is important to life because it
    a. surrounds all cells.
    b. is found inside cells.
    c. influences the shape of the cell membrane.
    d. All of the above

    ANS: D   DIF: I   OBJ: BPE 2-2.1

13. When placed in the same container, oil and water do not mix because
    a. they are both polar.   c. they are both nonpolar.
    b. water is polar and oil is nonpolar. d. water is nonpolar and oil is polar.

    ANS: B   DIF: I   OBJ: BPE 2-2.2

14. Water is a polar molecule because
    a. it contains two hydrogen atoms for each oxygen atom.
    b. it has a charge.
    c. different parts of the molecule have slightly different charges.
    d. it does not have a charge.

    ANS: C   DIF: I   OBJ: BPE 2-2.2

15. Due to the polarity of water, compounds that dissolve best in water contain
    a. nonpolar bonds.   c. polar bonds.
    b. ionic bonds.   d. Both (b) and (c)

    ANS: D   DIF: I   OBJ: BPE 2-2.2

16. Acidic solutions have a pH that is
    a. less than 7.   c. a negative number.
    b. between 7 and 14.   d. more than 7.

    ANS: A   DIF: I   OBJ: BPE 2-2.3

17. Hydrogen ions, H^+, react with hydroxide ions, OH^-, to form
    a. water.   c. a base.
    b. an acid.   d. None of the above

    ANS: A   DIF: I   OBJ: BPE 2-2.3

18. Which of the following is *not* an organic macromolecule?
    a. carbohydrate   c. lipid
    b. ice   d. nucleic acid

    ANS: B   DIF: I   OBJ: BPE 2-3.1

19. All organic compounds contain the element
    a. carbon.   c. calcium.
    b. nitrogen.   d. sodium.

    ANS: A   DIF: I   OBJ: BPE 2-3.1

20. Which of the following is a carbohydrate?
    a. DNA   c. wax
    b. insulin   d. sucrose

    ANS: D   DIF: I   OBJ: BPE 2-3.2

21. Which organic molecules below are classified as carbohydrates?
    a. amino acids   c. nucleotides
    b. fatty acids   d. sugars

    ANS: D   DIF: I   OBJ: BPE 2-3.2

22. Animals store glucose in the form of
   a. cellulose.
   b. glycogen.
   c. wax.
   d. lipids.

   ANS: B   DIF: I   OBJ: BPE 2-3.2

23. Carbohydrates and lipids have many carbon-hydrogen bonds; therefore, they both
   a. store energy in these bonds.
   b. are easily dissolved in water.
   c. dissolve only in vinegar.
   d. exist only in cells of plants.

   ANS: A   DIF: I   OBJ: BPE 2-3.2

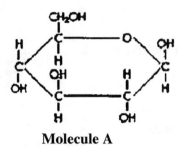

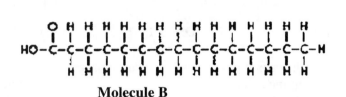

Molecule A   **Molecule B**

24. Refer to the illustration above. Molecules like Molecule B are found in
   a. carbohydrates.
   b. lipids.
   c. nucleic acids.
   d. proteins.

   ANS: B   DIF: II   OBJ: BPE 2-3.2

25. Polysaccharides are
   a. carbohydrates.
   b. lipids.
   c. proteins.
   d. unsaturated fats.

   ANS: A   DIF: I   OBJ: BPE 2-3.2

26. Lipids are
   a. polar molecules.
   b. similar to water molecules.
   c. water soluble.
   d. nonpolar molecules.

   ANS: D   DIF: I   OBJ: BPE 2-3.2

27. Which organic molecules below are most closely related to proteins?
   a. amino acids
   b. fatty acids
   c. nucleotides
   d. sugars

   ANS: A   DIF: I   OBJ: BPE 2-3.2

28. Long chains of amino acids are found in
   a. carbohydrates.
   b. lipids.
   c. proteins.
   d. sugars.

   ANS: C   DIF: I   OBJ: BPE 2-3.2

29. All of the following are examples of lipids *except*
    a. saturated fats.   c. cholesterol.
    b. starch.   d. earwax.

    ANS: B   DIF: I   OBJ: BPE 2-3.2

30. Liquid fats called oils contain
    a. mostly unsaturated fatty acids.   c. many glucose molecules.
    b. mostly saturated fatty acids.   d. amino acids.

    ANS: A   DIF: I   OBJ: BPE 2-3.2

31. Lipids are soluble in
    a. water.   c. oil.
    b. salt water.   d. All of the above

    ANS: C   DIF: I   OBJ: BPE 2-3.2

32. Which organic molecules below are most closely related to lipids?
    a. amino acids   c. nucleotides
    b. fatty acids   d. sugars

    ANS: B   DIF: I   OBJ: BPE 2-3.2

33. The shape of a protein is primarily determined by
    a. the type and sequence of its amino acids. c. its cell location.
    b. its size.   d. None of the above

    ANS: A   DIF: I   OBJ: BPE 2-3.2

34. Which organic molecules below are most closely related to nucleic acids?
    a. amino acids   c. nucleotides
    b. fatty acids   d. sugars

    ANS: C   DIF: I   OBJ: BPE 2-3.3

35. A molecule shaped like a spiral staircase (double helix) is typical of
    a. deoxyribonucleic acid.   c. lipids.
    b. ribonucleic acid.   d. carbohydrates.

    ANS: A   DIF: I   OBJ: BPE 2-3.3

36. The two types of nucleic acids are
    a. chlorophyll and retinal.   c. lipids and sugars.
    b. DNA and RNA.   d. glucose and glycogen.

    ANS: B   DIF: I   OBJ: BPE 2-3.3

37. DNA stores
   a. fat.
   b. carbohydrates.
   c. protein.
   d. heredity information.

   ANS: D   DIF: I   OBJ: BPE 2-3.3

38. The two strands of a DNA molecule are held together by
   a. ionic bonds.
   b. covalent bonds.
   c. hydrogen bonds.
   d. None of the above

   ANS: C   DIF: I   OBJ: BPE 2-3.3

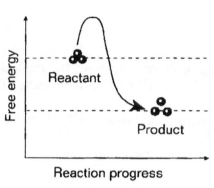

Graph A

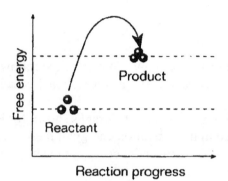

Graph B

39. Refer to the illustration above. Which graph illustrates what happens during an energy-releasing reaction?
   a. Graph A
   b. Graph B
   c. Both graphs; they each show a different stage of an energy releasing reaction
   d. None of the above

   ANS: A   DIF: II   OBJ: BPE 2-4.2

40. Refer to the illustration above. Which graph illustrates a reaction during which energy is released?
   a. Graph A
   b. Graph B
   c. Both graphs, because all chemical reactions release energy
   d. None of the above

   ANS: A   DIF: II   OBJ: BPE 2-4.2

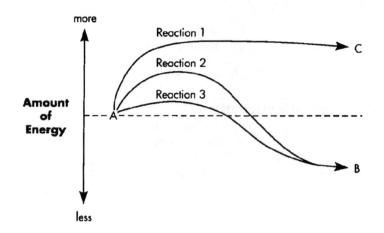

41. Refer to the illustration above. Which of the following statements regarding the graph is true?
    a. Reaction 2 occurs faster than Reaction 3 because Reaction 2 requires more energy than Reaction 3.
    b. The difference between the graphs shown for Reaction 2 and Reaction 3 is because of a difference in the activation energy of these reactions.
    c. Reactant A contains more energy at the beginning of the reaction than product C has after the reaction.
    d. All of the above

    ANS: B   DIF: II   OBJ: BPE 2-4.2

42. Refer to the illustration above. Reaction 3 in the graph
    a. probably occurred in the presence of a catalyst.
    b. requires more activation energy than Reaction 2.
    c. is the same as Reaction 1, but faster.
    d. is slower than Reaction 2.

    ANS: A   DIF: II   OBJ: BPE 2-4.3

43. The molecule on which an enzyme acts is called a(n)
    a.   active site.   c.   organic molecule.
    b.   inactive site.   d.   substrate.

    ANS: D   DIF: I   OBJ: BPE 2-4.3

44. An enzyme
    a. is not used up when catalyzing a reaction.
    b. lowers the activation energy of a reaction.
    c. bonds with a substrate molecule at the enzyme's active site.
    d. All of the above

    ANS: D   DIF: I   OBJ: BPE 2-4.3

45. Enzymes
    a. are able to heat up molecules so that they can react.
    b. always provide carbon dioxide for chemical reactions.
    c. are biological catalysts.
    d. absorb excess heat so that reactions occur at low temperatures.

    ANS: C   DIF: I   OBJ: BPE 2-4.3

46. Which of the following conditions affects the function of enzymes?
    a. pH   c. enzyme concentration
    b. heat   d. All of the above

    ANS: D   DIF: I   OBJ: BPE 2-4.3

47. A cell contains
    a. thousands of different kinds of enzymes, each promoting a different chemical reaction.
    b. one kind of enzyme that promotes thousands of different chemical reactions.
    c. approximately 100 kinds of enzymes, each promoting a different chemical reaction.
    d. one enzyme that promotes photosynthesis and one enzyme that promotes cellular respiration.

    ANS: A   DIF: I   OBJ: BPE 2-4.3

48. Reducing activation energy
    a. is a violation of the laws of nature.
    b. requires higher temperatures than those found within cells.
    c. occurs only when reactants are quickly added to the reaction mixture.
    d. is accomplished by the action of catalysts on reactants.

    ANS: D   DIF: I   OBJ: BPE 2-4.3

COMPLETION

1. _____ are the negatively charged particles in an atom.

    ANS: Electrons   DIF: I   OBJ: BPE 2-1.1

2. Protons and neutrons are found in the _____ of an atom.

    ANS: nucleus   DIF: I   OBJ: BPE 2-1.1

3. A(n) _____ is a group of atoms held together by covalent bonds.

    ANS: molecule   DIF: I   OBJ: BPE 2-1.2

4. Sodium chloride, NaCl, is an example of a(n) _____.

    ANS: compound   DIF: I   OBJ: BPE 2-1.2

5. A(n)_____ bond forms between two atoms sharing electrons.

    ANS: covalent   DIF: I   OBJ: BPE 2-1.3

6. _____ bonds are weak chemical attractions between polar molecules.

    ANS: Hydrogen   DIF: I   OBJ: BPE 2-1.3

7. The attraction between oppositely charged ions results in the formation of a(n)
    _____ _____.

    ANS: ionic bond   DIF: I   OBJ: BPE 2-1.3

8. Water heats and cools _____.

    ANS: slowly   DIF: I   OBJ: BPE 2-2.1

9. _____ is the attraction that causes water and other liquids to form drops and
    thin films.

    ANS: Cohesion   DIF: I   OBJ: BPE 2-2.1

10. _____ is the medium in which most cellular events take place.

    ANS: Water   DIF: I   OBJ: BPE 2-2.1

11. Substances with a pH lower than 7 are _____.

    ANS: acidic   DIF: I   OBJ: BPE 2-2.3

12. Substances with a pH greater than 7 are _____.

    ANS: basic   DIF: I   OBJ: BPE 2-2.3

13. The pH scale measures the concentrations of _____ ions in solutions.

    ANS: hydrogen   DIF: I   OBJ: BPE 2-2.3

14. Lipids are _____ molecules because they have no negative and positive pole

    ANS: nonpolar   DIF: I   OBJ: BPE 2-3.2

15. Long chains of nucleotides are called _____ _____.

    ANS: nucleic acids   DIF: I   OBJ: BPE 2-3.3

16. Chromosomes are made of _____ and proteins.

    ANS: DNA   DIF: I   OBJ: BPE 2-3.3

17. _____ is defined as the ability to move or change matter.

   ANS: Energy   DIF: I   OBJ: BPE 2-4.1

18. All living things require a source of _____ to carry out their life activities.

   ANS: energy   DIF: I   OBJ: BPE 2-4.1

19. The starting materials for chemical reactions are called _____, while the new substances that are formed are called _____.

   ANS: reactants, products   DIF: I   OBJ: BPE 2-4.1

20. All living things require a source of _____ to carry out their life activities.

   ANS: energy   DIF: I   OBJ: BPE 2-4.1

21. The energy needed to start a chemical reaction is called _____ _____.

   ANS: activation energy   DIF: I   OBJ: BPE 2-4.2

22. A chemical reaction can be sped up by adding a substance called a(n) _____, which lowers the amount of activation energy required to start the reaction.

   ANS: catalyst (enzyme)   DIF: I   OBJ: BPE 2-4.3

23. The portion of an enzyme molecule into which a specific substrate can fit is called the _____ _____.

   ANS: active site   DIF: I   OBJ: BPE 2-4.3

PROBLEM

1. The following statements are about the molecule ATP (adenosine triphosphate). For each statement, first determine whether it is true or false. Then, if it is false, rewrite the statement so that it is correct. Write your answers in the space below.
   a. ATP is chemically similar to a carbohydrate.
   b. Cells require ATP to function.
   c. None of the energy in food molecules is stored in ATP.
   d. ATP is the primary source of energy for chemical reactions occurring in all cells of all living organisms.

   ANS:
   a. False, ATP is chemically similar to nucleotides.
   b. True.
   c. False, Energy in carbohydrates and fats, for example, is stored in ATP.
   d. True.

   DIF: III   OBJ: BPE 2-3.3

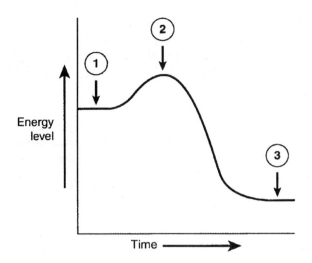

2. Refer to the illustration above. The graph depicts the relative energy levels of the products and reactants for the following chemical reaction: $A + B \leftrightarrow C + D$.
    a. Which substances, A, B, C, and/or D, are present at point 1 on the graph?
    b. Which substances, A, B, C, and/or D, are present at point 3 on the graph?
    c. Why is point 2 at a higher energy level than point 1?
    d. Why is point 3 at a lower energy level than point 1?
    e. Draw a dashed line on the graph indicating how the energy level of this reaction over time would be different if the enzyme that catalyzes the reaction were not present.

    ANS:
    a. A and B
    b. C and D
    c. An input of energy, called the activation energy, is required in order to get the reaction going.
    d. This is an energy-releasing reaction. The products contain less energy than the reactants, and energy is given off in the reaction.
    e. The graph should be the same except that the energy level at point 2 should be higher.

    DIF: III   OBJ: BPE 2-4.2

Enzymes catalyze a variety of biological reactions. The extent to which they can speed up the rate of a reaction is dependent on a number of factors. Draw a graph for the following condition(s), showing the effect of altering one factor on the relative rate of a reaction. Use "0" to indicate no activity, and "1" through "10" to indicate increasing rate of reaction from very low to very high. Include a label for your graph(s).

3. Refer to the paragraph above, and then draw your graph in the space below. Enzyme #1 is inactive between 0°C and 10°C. It is active above 10°C, with the rate increasing steadily until the temperature reaches 40°C. At 40°C, the rate of the reaction is very high. Above 40°C, the rate decreases steadily until the temperature reaches 60°C, at which point the enzyme is no longer active.

ANS:
The graph should look similar to the following:

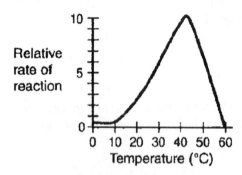

Effect of temperature on the
rate of the reaction catalyzed
by enzyme #1

DIF: III   OBJ: BPE 2-4.3

4. Refer to the paragraph above, and draw your graph in the space below. Enzyme #2 is inactive at a pH of 1–4. It is active above a pH of 4, with the rate increasing slowly until the pH reaches 6. Above a pH of 6, the rate increases sharply until the pH reaches 7. Above a pH of 7, the rate decreases sharply until the pH reaches 8. Above a pH of 8, the rate decreases gradually until the pH reaches 10, at which point the enzyme is no longer active.

ANS:
The graph should look similar to the following:

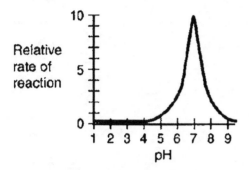

Effect of pH on the rate
of the reaction catalyzed
by enzyme #2

DIF: III   OBJ: BPE 2-4.3

5. Refer to the paragraph above, and draw your graph in the space below. Enzyme #3 is inactive when the concentration of the substrate it acts upon is zero. The enzyme is active when the substrate concentration is above zero, with the rate increasing only very slightly until the concentration reaches 30%. Above 30%, the rate increases very sharply, to a high level, until the concentration reaches 60%. Above a concentration of 60%, the rate increases very little. The rate does not increase when the substrate concentration is above 80%.

ANS:
The graph should look similar to the following:

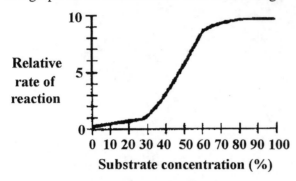

Effect of substrate concentration on the rate of the reaction catalyzed by enzyme #3

DIF: III   OBJ: BPE 2-4.3

ESSAY

1. Describe how an enzyme can function in speeding up a chemical reaction within a cell.

ANS:
Enzymes are biological catalysts. They are usually proteins with specific three-dimensional shapes that allow them to bind to particular substrate molecules. Once attached, the enzymes allow substrates to interact, lowering the activation energy that would otherwise be required for the reaction to occur.

DIF: II   OBJ: BPE 2-4.3

CHAPTER 3—CELL STRUCTURE

TRUE/FALSE

1. Scientists always take measurements using the International System of Measurements (SI).

    ANS: T   DIF: I   OBJ: BPE 3-1.1

2. Robert Hooke observed cork cells under a microscope.

    ANS: T   DIF: I   OBJ: BPE 3-1.1

3. Anton van Leeuwenhoek concluded that all plants are composed of cells.

    ANS: F   DIF: I   OBJ: BPE 3-1.1

4. Resolution is a microscope's power to increase an object's apparent size.

    ANS: F   DIF: I   OBJ: BPE 3-1.2

5. Viewing details of extremely small objects requires a microscope with both good magnification and good resolution.

    ANS: T   DIF: I   OBJ: BPE 3-1.2

6. A light microscope magnifies an object 20,000 times its actual size.

    ANS: F   DIF: I   OBJ: BPE 3-1.2

7. Using a 10× ocular lens with a 10× objective lens, an object will be magnified 20× its actual size.

    ANS: F   DIF: I   OBJ: BPE 3-1.3

8. The light microscope uses a beam of electrons to magnify a specimen.

    ANS: F   DIF: I   OBJ: BPE 3-1.3

9. Light microscopes have a lower magnifying power than electron microscopes, but light microscopes can be used to view living organisms.

    ANS: T   DIF: I   OBJ: BPE 3-1.4

10. The scanning tunneling microscope can be used to view living specimens.

    ANS: T   DIF: I   OBJ: BPE 3-1.5

11. The scanning tunneling microscope can be used to view objects as small as individual atoms.

    ANS: T   DIF: I   OBJ: BPE 3-1.5

12. Inside small cells, materials and information can be transported to all parts of the cells more quickly than inside larger cells.

     ANS: T   DIF: I   OBJ: BPE 3-2.2

13. As a cell gets larger, its surface-area-to-volume ratio decreases.

     ANS: T   DIF: I   OBJ: BPE 3-2.2

14. Two different structures that all cells have are a cell membrane and a cell wall.

     ANS: F   DIF: I   OBJ: BPE 3-2.3

15. Most living prokaryotes are multicellular protists.

     ANS: F   DIF: I   OBJ: BPE 3-2.3

16. Organelles enable eukaryotic cells to carry out specialized functions.

     ANS: T   DIF: I   OBJ: BPE 3-2.3

17. The cells of animals are prokaryotic.

     ANS: F   DIF: I   OBJ: BPE 3-2.3

18. All living things that are not bacteria are eukaryotes.

     ANS: T   DIF: I   OBJ: BPE 3-2.3

19. Microtubules and microfilaments form the cytoskeleton of cells.

     ANS: T   DIF: I   OBJ: BPE 3-2.3

20. The only difference between a plant cell and an animal cell is that plant cells have chloroplasts.

     ANS: F   DIF: I   OBJ: BPE 3-2.3

21. Proteins in the cell membrane may serve as channels, receptors, or markers.

     ANS: T   DIF: I   OBJ: BPE 3-2.4

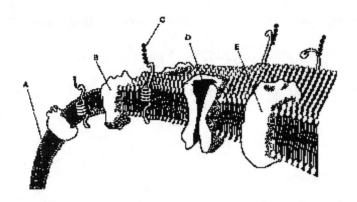

22. Refer to the illustration above. The diagram shows the lipid bilayer that forms the framework of the cell membrane.

ANS: T DIF: II OBJ: BPE 3-2.4

23. Cell surface marker proteins face the inside of the cell.

ANS: F DIF: I OBJ: BPE 3-2.4

24. The cell membrane contains DNA.

ANS: F DIF: I OBJ: BPE 3-2.4

25. A phospholipid is a lipid made of a phosphate group and two fatty acids.

ANS: T DIF: I OBJ: BPE 3-2.4

26. The nonpolar tails of a phospholipid are attracted to water.

ANS: F DIF: I OBJ: BPE 3-2.4

27. Receptor proteins bind to signal molecules outside the cell.

ANS: F DIF: I OBJ: BPE 3-2.4

28. Most functions of a prokaryotic cell are controlled by the cell's nucleus.

ANS: F DIF: I OBJ: BPE 3-3.1

29. DNA stores information that directs the activities of a cell.

ANS: T DIF: I OBJ: BPE 3-3.1

30. Substances made in the nucleus, such as RNA, move into the cytoplasm by passing through nuclear pores.

ANS: T DIF: I OBJ: BPE 3-3.1

31. Flattened, membrane-bound sacs that package and distribute proteins are called mitochondria.

    ANS: F   DIF: I   OBJ: BPE 3-3.2

32. Lysosomes contain digestive enzymes that break down proteins, nucleic acids, lipids, and carbohydrates.

    ANS: T   DIF: I   OBJ: BPE 3-3.2

33. Ribosomes are the sites of ATP production.

    ANS: F   DIF: I   OBJ: BPE 3-3.2

34. Lysosomes transfer energy from organic compounds to ATP.

    ANS: F   DIF: I   OBJ: BPE 3-3.2

35. Most of a cell's ATP is produced in the cell's mitochondria.

    ANS: T   DIF: I   OBJ: BPE 3-3.3

36. Mitochondria contain DNA.

    ANS: T   DIF: I   OBJ: BPE 3-3.3

37. Each animal cell contains one or more chloroplasts.

    ANS: F   DIF: I   OBJ: BPE 3-3.4

38. Chloroplasts have DNA different from nuclear DNA.

    ANS: T   DIF: I   OBJ: BPE 3-3.4

MULTIPLE CHOICE

1. The metric system of measurement is based on powers of
   a. 1.   c. 100.
   b. 10.   d. 1,000.

    ANS: B   DIF: I   OBJ: BPE 3-1.1

2. One meter is equal to
   a. 1,000 mm.   c. 0.001 km.
   b. 100 cm.   d. All of the above

    ANS: D   DIF: I   OBJ: BPE 3-1.1

3. The image produced by a microscope is called
   a. magnification.
   b. resolution.
   c. a micrograph.
   d. amplification.

   ANS: C   DIF: I   OBJ: BPE 3-1.2

4. Fuzzy images viewed with a microscope may be due to poor
   a. resolution.
   b. amplification.
   c. magnification.
   d. None of the above

   ANS: A   DIF: I   OBJ: BPE 3-1.2

5. A microscope with a 4× objective lens and a 10× ocular lens produces a total magnification of
   a. 14×.
   b. 40×.
   c. 400×.
   d. 4000×.

   ANS: B   DIF: I   OBJ: BPE 3-1.3

6. The most powerful light microscope can magnify an object about
   a. 500×.
   b. 2,000×.
   c. 50,000×.
   d. 200,000×.

   ANS: B   DIF: I   OBJ: BPE 3-1.4

7. Living specimens can be viewed using a(n)
   a. light microscope.
   b. electron microscope.
   c. scanning tunneling microscope.
   d. Both (a) and (c)

   ANS: D   DIF: I   OBJ: BPE 3-1.4

8. The smallest units of life are
   a. cells.
   b. mitochondria.
   c. chloroplasts.
   d. None of the above

   ANS: A   DIF: I   OBJ: BPE 3-2.1

9. When the volume of a cell increases, its surface area
   a. increases at the same rate.
   b. remains the same.
   c. increases at a faster rate.
   d. increases at a slower rate.

   ANS: D   DIF: I   OBJ: BPE 3-2.2

10. Surface area is an important factor in limiting cell growth because
    a. the cell can burst if the membrane becomes too large.
    b. materials cannot enter the cell if it is too large.
    c. the cell may become too large to take in enough food and to remove enough wastes.
    d. waste products cannot leave the cell if it is too small.

    ANS: C   DIF: I   OBJ: BPE 3-2.2

11. The size to which a cell can grow is limited by its
   a. location.   c. function.
   b. structure.   d. surface area.

   ANS: D   DIF: I   OBJ: BPE 3-2.2

12. As cell size increases, the surface-area-to-volume ratio
   a. decreases.   c. increases then decreases.
   b. increases.   d. remains the same.

   ANS: A   DIF: I   OBJ: BPE 3-2.2

13. To function most efficiently, a cell must be
   a. large.   c. small.
   b. medium.   d. None of the above

   ANS: C   DIF: I   OBJ: BPE 3-2.2

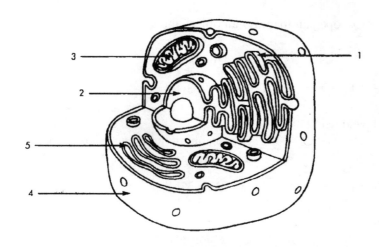

14. Refer to the illustration above. Which structure immediately identifies this cell as a eukaryote?
   a. structure 1   c. structure 3
   b. structure 2   d. structure 4

   ANS: B   DIF: II   OBJ: BPE 3-2.3

15. Refer to the illustration above. In eukaryotic cells, chromosomes are found in
   a. structure 1.   c. structure 3.
   b. structure 2.   d. structure 5.

   ANS: B   DIF: II   OBJ: BPE 3-2.3

16. Refer to the illustration above. Which structure produces vesicles filled with proteins?
   a. structure 1   c. structure 3
   b. structure 2   d. structure 5

   ANS: A   DIF: II   OBJ: BPE 3-3.2

17. Refer to the illustration. Structure 1 is
   a. rough endoplasmic reticulum.
   b. a Golgi apparatus.
   c. a mitochondrion.
   d. the nucleus.

   ANS: A   DIF: I   OBJ: BPE 3-3.2

18. Refer to the illustration above. Structure 5 is
   a. part of the endoplasmic reticulum.
   b. a Golgi apparatus.
   c. a mitochondrion.
   d. the nucleus.

   ANS: B   DIF: II   OBJ: BPE 3-3.2

19. Refer to the illustration above. Structure 2 is
   a. rough endoplasmic reticulum.
   b. a Golgi apparatus.
   c. a mitochondrion.
   d. the nucleus.

   ANS: D   DIF: II   OBJ: BPE 3-3.2

20. Refer to the illustration above. The cell uses structure 3
   a. to transport material from one part of the cell to another.
   b. to package proteins so they can be stored by the cell.
   c. as a receptor protein.
   d. to produce ATP.

   ANS: D   DIF: II   OBJ: BPE 3-3.3

21. Refer to the illustration above. The cell shown is probably an animal cell because it
   a. has mitochondria.
   b. does not have a cell wall.
   c. has a cell membrane.
   d. does not have a nucleus.

   ANS: B   DIF: II   OBJ: BPE 3-3.4

22. One difference between prokaryotes and eukaryotes is that
   a. nucleic acids are found only in prokaryotes.
   b. mitochondria are found in larger quantities in eukaryotes.
   c. Golgi vesicles are found only in prokaryotes.
   d. prokaryotes do not have a nucleus.

   ANS: D   DIF: I   OBJ: BPE 3-2.3

23. Which of the following is characteristic of prokaryotes?
   a. They have a nucleus.
   b. Their evolution preceded that of eukaryotes.
   c. The organelles in their cytoplasm are surrounded by membranes.
   d. None of the above

   ANS: B   DIF: I   OBJ: BPE 3-2.3

24. Which of the following is an example of a prokaryotic cell?
    a. amoeba
    b. virus
    c. bacterium
    d. liver cell

    ANS: C   DIF: I   OBJ: BPE 3-2.3

25. Only eukaryotic cells have
    a. DNA.
    b. membrane-bound organelles.
    c. ribosomes.
    d. cytoplasm.

    ANS: B   DIF: I   OBJ: BPE 3-2.3

26. A structure within a eukaryotic cell that performs a specific function is called a(n)
    a. organelle.
    b. organ tissue.
    c. tissue.
    d. biocenter.

    ANS: A   DIF: I   OBJ: BPE 3-2.3

27. Short hairlike structures that protrude from the surface of a cell and are packed in tight rows are called
    a. flagella.
    b. microtubules.
    c. microfilaments.
    d. cilia.

    ANS: D   DIF: I   OBJ: BPE 3-2.3

28. Which type of molecule forms a lipid bilayer within a cell membrane?
    a. protein
    b. phospholipid
    c. nucleic acid
    d. carbohydrate

    ANS: B   DIF: I   OBJ: BPE 3-2.4

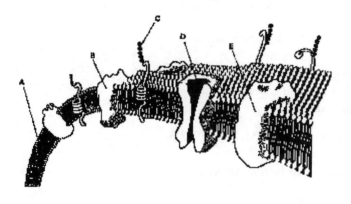

29. Refer to the illustration above. The structure labeled A is composed of
    a. lipids.
    b. carbohydrates.
    c. proteins.
    d. None of the above

    ANS: A   DIF: II   OBJ: BPE 3-2.4

30. Refer to the illustration above. The structure that acts as a gate to the cell's interior is labeled
    a. A.   c. C.
    b. B.   d. D.

    ANS: D   DIF: II   OBJ: BPE 3-2.4

31. Refer to the illustration above. Structure C is a
    a. carbohydrate chain.   c. fatty acid.
    b. glycerol molecule.   d. nucleic acid.

    ANS: A   DIF: II   OBJ: BPE 3-2.4

32. The cell membrane
    a. encloses the contents of a cell.
    b. allows materials to enter and leave the cell.
    c. is selectively permeable.
    d. All of the above

    ANS: D   DIF: I   OBJ: BPE 3-2.4

33. Phospholipids are molecules that
    a. contain phosphate.
    b. have nonpolar "tails" and polar "heads."
    c. form the lipid bilayer of the cell membrane.
    d. All of the above

    ANS: D   DIF: I   OBJ: BPE 3-2.4

34. Most of the food and waste materials that move into and out of a cell pass through
    a. receptor proteins.   c. enzymes.
    b. marker proteins.   d. channel proteins.

    ANS: D   DIF: I   OBJ: BPE 3-2.4

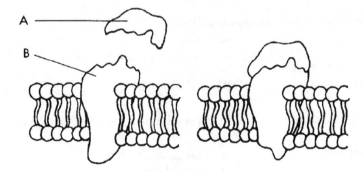

35. Refer to the illustration above. The structure labeled B in the diagram is an example of a
    a. channel protein.   c. receptor protein.
    b. marker protein.   d. None of the above

    ANS: C   DIF: II   OBJ: BPE 3-2.4

36. Refer to the illustration above. The structure labeled A is most likely a
   a. DNA molecule.   c. chromosome.
   b. signal molecule.   d. marker protein.

   ANS: B   DIF: II   OBJ: BPE 3-2.4

37. The structure that regulates what enters and leaves the cell is the
   a. nucleus.   c. nuclear membrane.
   b. cell wall.   d. cell membrane.

   ANS: D   DIF: I   OBJ: BPE 3-2.4

38. A protein that fits into the cell membrane
   a. has two polar ends that are attracted to water.
   b. floats in the cell membrane.
   c. has a nonpolar middle section.
   d. All of the above

   ANS: D   DIF: I   OBJ: BPE 3-2.4

39. Elongated proteins on the surface of a cell and that identify the cell are called
   a. marker proteins.   c. receptor proteins.
   b. channel proteins.   d. enzymes.

   ANS: A   DIF: I   OBJ: BPE 3-2.4

40. cell : cell membrane ::
   a. nucleus : chromosome   c. chromosome : DNA
   b. nucleus : nuclear envelope   d. cell : DNA

   ANS: B
   (is surrounded by)

   DIF: II   OBJ: BPE 3-3.1

41. The double membrane surrounding the nucleus is called the
   a. nucleolus.   c. ribosome.
   b. nuclear wall.   d. nuclear envelope.

   ANS: D   DIF: I   OBJ: BPE 3-3.1

42. One important organelle that helps maintain homeostasis by moving substances from one part of the cell to another is the
   a. endoplasmic reticulum.   c. Golgi apparatus.
   b. mitochondrion.   d. cytoplasm.

   ANS: A   DIF: I   OBJ: BPE 3-3.2

43. The Golgi apparatus is an organelle that
    a. receives proteins and lipids from the endoplasmic reticulum.
    b. packages molecules made in the endoplasmic reticulum.
    c. is involved in the distribution of proteins.
    d. All of the above

    ANS: D   DIF: I   OBJ: BPE 3-3.2

44. The packaging and distribution center of the cell is the
    a. nucleus.   c. central vacuole.
    b. Golgi apparatus.   d. nuclear envelope.

    ANS: B   DIF: I   OBJ: BPE 3-3.2

45. In a cell, proteins are made on the
    a. mitochondria.   c. nucleus.
    b. ribosomes.   d. cell membrane.

    ANS: B   DIF: I   OBJ: BPE 3-3.2

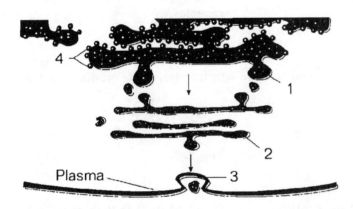

46. Refer to the illustration above. The structures labeled 4 are
    a. vesicles.   c. ribosomes.
    b. lysosomes.   d. chloroplasts.

    ANS: C   DIF: II   OBJ: BPE 3-3.2

47. Refer to the illustration above. Which structure packages and distributes proteins and lipids?
    a. structure 1   c. structure 3
    b. structure 2   d. structure 4

    ANS: B   DIF: II   OBJ: BPE 3-3.2

48. Refer to the illustration above. Structure 3 is a(n)
    a. mitochondrion.   c. ribosome.
    b. endoplasmic reticulum.   d. vesicle.

    ANS: D   DIF: II   OBJ: BPE 3-3.2

49. Refer to the illustration above. Structure 3 may contain
    a. proteins.
    b. carbohydrates.
    c. None of the above
    d. All of the above

    ANS: D   DIF: II   OBJ: BPE 3-3.2

50. A cell that requires a lot of energy might contain large numbers of
    a. chromosomes.
    b. vacuoles.
    c. mitochondria.
    d. lysosomes.

    ANS: C   DIF: II   OBJ: BPE 3-3.3

51. Which of the following pairs contains unrelated items?
    a. eukaryote-amoeba
    b. ribosomes-protein
    c. cell wall-animal cell
    d. mitochondria-ATP

    ANS: C   DIF: I   OBJ: BPE 3-3.4

52. The organelles associated with plant photosynthesis are the
    a. mitochondria.
    b. chloroplasts.
    c. Golgi apparatus.
    d. vacuoles.

    ANS: B   DIF: I   OBJ: BPE 3-3.4

53. Plant cells have a large membrane-bound space in which water, waste products, and nutrients can be stored. This space is called the
    a. mitochondrion.
    b. chloroplast.
    c. Golgi apparatus.
    d. vacuole.

    ANS: D   DIF: I   OBJ: BPE 3-3.4

54. How are chloroplasts similar to mitochondria?
    a. They can both use energy from sunlight.
    b. They are both found in prokaryotic cells.
    c. They both contain their own DNA.
    d. They are both found in animal cells.

    ANS: C   DIF: I   OBJ: BPE 3-3.4

55. All the following are found in both plant and animal cells, *except*
    a. a cell wall.
    b. a cell membrane.
    c. mitochondria.
    d. endoplasmic reticulum.

    ANS: A   DIF: I   OBJ: BPE 3-3.4

COMPLETION

1. Scientists use _____ units when taking measurements.

    ANS: metric   DIF: I   OBJ: BPE 3-1.1

2. A meter is a basic unit used when measuring _____.

   ANS: length   DIF: I   OBJ: BPE 3-1.1

3. In a(n) _____ microscope, light passes through one or more lenses to produce an enlarged image of a specimen.

   ANS: light   DIF: I   OBJ: BPE 3-1.2

4. The ability to make an image appear larger than its actual size is called _____.

   ANS: magnification   DIF: I   OBJ: BPE 3-1.2

5. _____ is a measure of the clarity of an image.

   ANS: Resolution   DIF: I   OBJ: BPE 3-1.2

6. A compound microscope is a type of _____ microscope.

   ANS: light   DIF: I   OBJ: BPE 3-1.3

7. Total magnification of a light microscope is calculated by _____ the magnification of the objective lens by the magnification of the ocular lens.

   ANS: multiplying   DIF: I   OBJ: BPE 3-1.3

8. Electron microscopes have _____ magnifying power than light microscopes do.

   ANS: higher   DIF: I   OBJ: BPE 3-1.4

9. While a light microscope uses light to visualize a specimen, electron microscopes use an _____ beam and a vacuum chamber.

   ANS: electron   DIF: I   OBJ: BPE 3-1.4

10. A(n) _____ microscope cannot be used to view living specimens.

    ANS: electron   DIF: I   OBJ: BPE 3-1.4

11. The scanning tunneling microscope uses a probe to measure differences in _____ caused by electrons that leak from the surface of an object or specimen.

    ANS: voltage   DIF: I   OBJ: BPE 3-1.5

12. All cells arise from _____ _____.

    ANS: existing cells   DIF: I   OBJ: BPE 3-2.1

13. The basic unit of structure and function in an organism is the _____.

ANS: cell   DIF: I   OBJ: BPE 3-2.1

14. The statement that "cells arise only from existing cells" is part of the _____ _____.

ANS: cell theory   DIF: I   OBJ: BPE 3-2.1

15. As a cell's size decreases, its surface-area-to-volume ratio _____.

ANS: increases   DIF: I   OBJ: BPE 3-2.2

16. The surface-area-to-volume ratio limits a cell's _____.

ANS: size   DIF: I   OBJ: BPE 3-2.2

17. Modern prokaryotes are generally known as _____.

ANS: bacteria   DIF: I   OBJ: BPE 3-2.3

18. Eukaryotic cells contain specialized structures called _____.

ANS: organelles   DIF: I   OBJ: BPE 3-2.3

19. A cell with a well-defined nucleus surrounded by a nuclear envelope is a(n) _____ cell.

ANS: eukaryotic   DIF: I   OBJ: BPE 3-2.3

20. The meshlike network of protein fibers that supports the shape of the cell is called the _____.

ANS: cytoskeleton   DIF: I   OBJ: BPE 3-2.3

21. Scientists think that _____ cells evolved about 1.5 billion years ago.

ANS: eukaryotic   DIF: I   OBJ: BPE 3-2.3

22. All substances that enter or leave a cell must cross the cell _____.

ANS: membrane   DIF: I   OBJ: BPE 3-2.4

23. _____ proteins on the surface of cells have carbohydrates attached to the protein.

ANS: Marker   DIF: I   OBJ: BPE 3-2.4

24. Proteins that aid in moving substances into and out of the cell are called _____ proteins.

ANS: transport   DIF: I   OBJ: BPE 3-2.4

25. A phospholipid is a molecule with a(n) _____ head.

ANS: polar   DIF: I   OBJ: BPE 3-2.4

26. The _____ houses a cell's DNA, which contains heredity information.

ANS: nucleus   DIF: I   OBJ: BPE 3-3.1

27. The organelles that are the site of protein synthesis in a cell are called _____.

ANS: ribosomes   DIF: I   OBJ: BPE 3-3.2

28. _____ cells have a system of internal membranes.

ANS: Eukaryotic   DIF: I   OBJ: BPE 3-3.2

29. Rough endoplasmic reticulum has _____ embedded on its surface.

ANS: ribosomes   DIF: I   OBJ: BPE 3-3.2

30. Photosynthesis takes place in the _____ of plant cells.

ANS: chloroplasts   DIF: I   OBJ: BPE 3-3.4

31. Both plant cells and animal cells have cell membranes. In addition, plant cells are surrounded by a(n) _____ _____.

ANS: cell wall   DIF: I   OBJ: BPE 3-3.4

ESSAY

1. Compare and contrast light microscopes with electron microscopes.

ANS:
Both microscopes are used to magnify small objects. A light microscope uses a light passing through one or more lenses to produce an enlarged image of a specimen. An electron microscope uses a beam of electrons to form an enlarged image of the specimen. A light microscope can be used to view living specimens. An electron microscope requires that the specimen be placed in a vacuum. Therefore, the electron microscope can only be used to view nonliving specimens.

DIF: II   OBJ: BPE 3-1.4

2. Small cells function more efficiently than large cells. Briefly explain why this is true using the concept of surface-area-to-volume ratio.

ANS:
All substances must cross the cell surface. A small cell has a high surface-area-to-volume ratio. This allows materials to pass readily into or out of the cell. As cells increase in size, the surface-area-to-ratio volume decreases. Large cells cannot take in, or get rid of, materials in numbers large enough to meet their needs. Also, materials have further to travel in large cells than in small cells.

DIF: II   OBJ: BPE 3-2.2

3. Relate the concept of surface-area-to-volume ratio to explain why many desert animals are often small in size. Include the term "homeostasis" in your explanation.

ANS:
Homeostasis is the maintenance of constant internal conditions. Homeostasis requires energy. Desert animals are often small because small body size produces a high surface-area-to-volume ratio. This allows small animals to get rid of excess heat and maintain a constant body temperature without using extra energy. Large animals with a low surface-area-to-volume ratio cannot get rid of body heat as readily as small animals can and spend a great deal of energy trying to maintain a constant internal temperature in such a warm climate.

DIF: II   OBJ: BPE 3-2.2

4. Describe the movement of proteins through the internal membrane system of a cell.

ANS:
Proteins are made by ribosomes on the surface of the rough endoplasmic reticulum. Once made, proteins move from the ribosomes to the endoplasmic reticulum where they are transported through the cell. Portions of the endoplasmic reticulum containing proteins pinch off forming vesicles. Vesicles containing newly made proteins move through the cytoplasm to the Golgi apparatus. The Golgi apparatus modifies the proteins received from the vesicles. New vesicles are formed from Golgi apparatus membrane repackaging the modified proteins. These new vesicles move to the cell membrane where the modified proteins are released outside the cell.

DIF: II   OBJ: BPE 3-3.2

TRUE/FALSE

1. Diffusion is an active process that requires a cell to expend a great deal of energy.

    ANS: F   DIF: I   OBJ: BPE 4-1.1

2. During diffusion, molecules diffuse from a region where their concentration is low to a region where their concentration is higher, until the particles are evenly dispersed.

    ANS: F   DIF: I   OBJ: BPE 4-1.1

3. When the concentration of dissolved particles outside a cell is equal to the concentration of dissolved particles inside the cell, the cell solution is isotonic.

    ANS: T   DIF: I   OBJ: BPE 4-1.1

4. Membranes are selectively permeable if they allow only certain substances to move across them.

    ANS: T   DIF: I   OBJ: BPE 4-1.1

5. A cell placed in a strong salt solution would probably burst because of osmosis.

    ANS: F   DIF: I   OBJ: BPE 4-1.2

6. Water will diffuse out of a cell when the cell is placed in a hypertonic solution.

    ANS: T   DIF: I   OBJ: BPE 4-1.2

7. To pass through a cell membrane, water requires carrier proteins.

    ANS: F   DIF: I   OBJ: BPE 4-1.2

8. Osmosis is the diffusion of starch molecules through a selectively permeable membrane.

    ANS: F   DIF: I   OBJ: BPE 4-1.2

9. The binding of specific molecules to ion channels controls the ability of particular ions to cross the cell membrane.

    ANS: T   DIF: I   OBJ: BPE 4-1.3

10. Diffusion through ion channels is a form of active transport.

    ANS: F   DIF: I   OBJ: BPE 4-1.3

11. In facilitated diffusion, carrier proteins require energy to transport substances across the cell membrane.

    ANS: F   DIF: I   OBJ: BPE 4-1.4

12. Facilitated diffusion moves molecules and ions against their concentration gradient, while active transport moves molecules and ions down their concentration gradient.

    ANS: F   DIF: I   OBJ: BPE 4-1.4

13. The transport of specific particles down their concentration gradient through a membrane by carrier proteins is known as facilitated diffusion.

    ANS: T   DIF: I   OBJ: BPE 4-1.4

14. Passive transport uses ATP to move molecules against their concentration gradient.

    ANS: F   DIF: I   OBJ: BPE 4-2.1

15. In active transport, energy is required to move a substance across a cell membrane.

    ANS: T   DIF: I   OBJ: BPE 4-2.1

16. The sodium-potassium pump requires energy to move ions across the cell membrane.

    ANS: T   DIF: I   OBJ: BPE 4-2.2

17. The sodium-potassium pump moves sodium ions and potassium ions against their concentration gradient.

    ANS: T   DIF: I   OBJ: BPE 4-2.2

18. The sodium-potassium pump transports sodium ions out of a cell while causing potassium ions to move into the cell.

    ANS: T   DIF: I   OBJ: BPE 4-2.2

19. The sodium-potassium pump uses ATP.

    ANS: T   DIF: I   OBJ: BPE 4-2.2

20. Exocytosis is a process that uses vesicles to capture substances and bring them into a cell.

    ANS: F   DIF: I   OBJ: BPE 4-2.3

21. Exocytosis helps the cell rid itself of wastes.

    ANS: T   DIF: I   OBJ: BPE 4-2.3

22. During the process of exocytosis, the cell membrane extends to engulf substances that are too big to pass through the cell membrane.

    ANS: F   DIF: I   OBJ: BPE 4-2.3

23. Exocytosis does not use energy to expel proteins from the cell.

    ANS: F   DIF: I   OBJ: BPE 4-2.3

24. Receptor proteins pump sodium ions into a cell.

    ANS: F   DIF: I   OBJ: BPE 4-2.4

25. Receptor proteins may cause the formation of a second messenger molecule inside a cell.

    ANS: T   DIF: I   OBJ: BPE 4-2.4

26. A receptor protein sends signals into a cell by transporting a specific molecule through the cell membrane.

    ANS: F   DIF: I   OBJ: BPE 4-2.4

MULTIPLE CHOICE

1. Which of the following does *not* require energy?
   a. diffusion
   b. endocytosis
   c. active transport
   d. sodium-potassium pump

    ANS: A   DIF: I   OBJ: BPE 4-1.1

2. As a result of diffusion, the concentration of many types of substances
   a. always remains greater inside a membrane.
   b. eventually becomes balanced on both sides of a membrane.
   c. always remains greater outside of a membrane.
   d. becomes imbalanced on both sides of a membrane.

    ANS: B   DIF: I   OBJ: BPE 4-1.1

Lump

3. Refer to the illustration above. The process shown is called
   a. osmosis.
   b. facilitated diffusion.
   c. active transport.
   d. diffusion.

   ANS: D   DIF: II   OBJ: BPE 4-1.1

4. Diffusion is the movement of a substance
   a. only through a lipid bilayer membrane.
   b. from an area of low concentration to an area of higher concentration.
   c. only in liquids.
   d. from an area of high concentration to an area of lower concentration.

   ANS: D   DIF: I   OBJ: BPE 4-1.1

5. The dispersal of ink in a beaker of water is an example of
   a. diffusion.
   b. osmosis.
   c. active transport.
   d. endocytosis.

   ANS: A   DIF: I   OBJ: BPE 4-1.1

6. The interior portion of a cell membrane forms a nonpolar zone that
   a. allows polar molecules to pass through the membrane.
   b. allows food to pass through the membrane.
   c. prevents ions and most large molecules from passing through the membrane.
   d. None of the above

   ANS: C   DIF: I   OBJ: BPE 4-1.1

7. The diffusion of water into or out of a cell is called
   a. solubility.
   b. osmosis.
   c. selective transport.
   d. endocytosis.

   ANS: B   DIF: I   OBJ: BPE 4-1.2

Concentration of Water and Solutes in Four Adjacent Cells

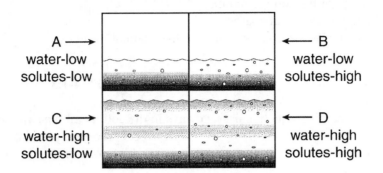

8. Refer to the illustration above. In this system, water molecules are most likely to diffuse in which direction?
    a. from A to B
    b. from B to D
    c. from D to C
    d. from C to A

    ANS: D   DIF: II   OBJ: BPE 4-1.2

9. Refer to the illustration above. Which cell is most likely to lose both water molecules and dissolved particles as the system approaches equilibrium?
    a. cell A
    b. cell B
    c. cell C
    d. cell D

    ANS: D   DIF: II   OBJ: BPE 4-1.2

10. Refer to the illustration above. In this system, dissolved particles in cell B are most likely to
    a. remain in cell B.
    b. adhere to cell B's membrane.
    c. diffuse into cell A.
    d. diffuse into cell D.

    ANS: C   DIF: II   OBJ: BPE 4-1.2

11. Osmosis is a type of
    a. active transport.
    b. passive transport.
    c. facilitated diffusion.
    d. endocytosis.

    ANS: B   DIF: I   OBJ: BPE 4-1.2

12. A cell will swell when it is placed in a(n)
    a. hypotonic solution.
    b. hypertonic solution.
    c. isotonic solution.
    d. None of the above

    ANS: A   DIF: I   OBJ: BPE 4-1.2

13. Ions move through ion channels by
    a. endocytosis.
    b. diffusion.
    c. passive transport.
    d. active transport.

    ANS: C   DIF: I   OBJ: BPE 4-1.3

14. Ion channel gates close the pores of some ion channels in response to
    a. stretching of the cell membrane.
    b. a change in electrical charge.
    c. the binding of specific molecules to the channel.
    d. All of the above

    ANS: D   DIF: I   OBJ: BPE 4-1.3

15. Proteins that act like selective passageways in the cell membrane are known as
    a. marker proteins.   c. receptor proteins.
    b. channel proteins.   d. None of the above

    ANS: B   DIF: I   OBJ: BPE 4-1.3

16. Transport proteins that allow ions to pass through the cell membrane are called
    a. receptor proteins.   c. ion channels.
    b. marker proteins.   d. None of the above

    ANS: C   DIF: I   OBJ: BPE 4-1.3

17. Sugar molecules cross the cell membrane by
    a. active transport.   c. osmosis.
    b. facilitated diffusion.   d. gated channels.

    ANS: B   DIF: I   OBJ: BPE 4-1.4

18. Proteins involved in facilitated diffusion are
    a. carrier proteins.   c. Both (a) and (b)
    b. receptor proteins.   d. None of the above

    ANS: A   DIF: I   OBJ: BPE 4-1.4

19. Sugar molecules can enter cells through the process of
    a. exocytosis.   c. osmosis.
    b. facilitated diffusion.   d. ion pumps.

    ANS: B   DIF: I   OBJ: BPE 4-1.4

20. Unlike passive transport, active transport
    a. requires energy.
    b. moves substances down their concentration gradient.
    c. does not involve carrier proteins.
    d. All of the above

    ANS: A   DIF: I   OBJ: BPE 4-2.1

21. Both active transport and facilitated diffusion involve
    a. ATP.
    b. movement against a concentration gradient.
    c. carrier proteins.
    d. All of the above

    ANS: C   DIF: I   OBJ: BPE 4-2.1

22. The sodium-potassium pump
    a. is a carrier protein   c. is located in the cytoplasm of a cell.
    b. uses passive transport.   d. transports sugar molecules.

    ANS: A   DIF: I   OBJ: BPE 4-2.2

23. The sodium-potassium pump usually pumps
    a. potassium ions out of the cell.   c. potassium ions into the cell.
    b. sodium ions into the cell.   d. only potassium ions and sugar molecules.

    ANS: C   DIF: I   OBJ: BPE 4-2.2

24. Which of the following is a form of active transport?
    a. osmosis   c. facilitated diffusion
    b. diffusion   d. sodium-potassium pump

    ANS: D   DIF: I   OBJ: BPE 4-2.2

25. The sodium-potassium pump
    a. increases the concentration of sodium ions inside a cell.
    b. decreases the concentration of sodium ions inside a cell.
    c. increases the concentration of potassium ions inside a cell.
    d. Both (b) and (c)

    ANS: D   DIF: I   OBJ: BPE 4-2.2

26. Proteins and polysaccharides that are too large to move into a cell through diffusion or active transport move in by
    a. exocytosis.   c. the sodium-potassium pump.
    b. endocytosis.   d. None of the above

    ANS: B   DIF: I   OBJ: BPE 4-2.3

27. Molecules that are too large to be moved through the membrane can be transported into the cell by
    a. osmosis.   c. exocytosis.
    b. endocytosis.   d. diffusion.

    ANS: B   DIF: I   OBJ: BPE 4-2.3

28. Molecules that are too large to be moved across a cell membrane can be removed from the cell by
  a. diffusion.
  b. exocytosis.
  c. endocytosis.
  d. osmosis.

  ANS: B   DIF: I   OBJ: BPE 4-2.3

29. Ridding the cell of materials by discharging the materials in vesicles is called
  a. osmosis.
  b. diffusion.
  c. exocytosis.
  d. endocytosis.

  ANS: C   DIF: I   OBJ: BPE 4-2.3

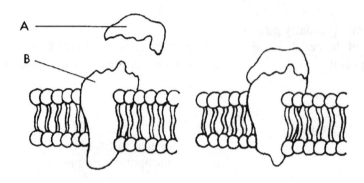

30. What happens when the structure labeled A binds to the structure labeled B?
  a. Information is sent into the cell.
  b. Proteins enter the cell.
  c. The cell begins to undergo mitosis.
  d. none of the above

  ANS: A   DIF: II   OBJ: BPE 4-2.4

31. Signal molecules bind to
  a. carbohydrates.
  b. marker proteins.
  c. receptor proteins.
  d. transport proteins.

  ANS: C   DIF: I   OBJ: BPE 4-2.4

32. When a signal molecule binds to a receptor protein, the receptor protein may
  a. change the permeability of the membrane.
  b. cause the formation of a second messenger molecule.
  c. speed up the chemical reactions in the cell.
  d. All of the above

  ANS: D   DIF: I   OBJ: BPE 4-2.4

33. Which of the following transmit information into a cell by binding to signal molecules?
  a. channel proteins
  b. receptor proteins
  c. marker proteins
  d. end proteins

  ANS: B   DIF: I   OBJ: BPE 4-2.4

COMPLETION

1. The random motion of particles of a substance that causes the substance to move from an area of high concentration to an area of lower concentration is called _____.

   ANS: diffusion   DIF: I   OBJ: BPE 4-1.1

2. A cell does not expend _____ when diffusion takes place.

   ANS: energy   DIF: I   OBJ: BPE 4-1.1

3. The diffusion of _____ through cell membranes is called osmosis.

   ANS: water   DIF: I   OBJ: BPE 4-1.1

4. Substances always flow from an area of high concentration to an area of _____ concentration.

   ANS: low   DIF: I   OBJ: BPE 4-1.2

5. When the concentration of free water molecules is higher outside a cell than inside the cell, water will diffuse _____ the cell.

   ANS: into   DIF: I   OBJ: BPE 4-1.2

6. If a cell is placed in a(n) _____ solution, water will flow out of the cell.

   ANS: hypertonic   DIF: I   OBJ: BPE 4-1.2

7. If a cell is placed in a(n) _____ solution, water will flow into the cell.

   ANS: hypotonic   DIF: I   OBJ: BPE 4-1.2

8. If a cell is placed in a(n) _____ solution, water flows into the cell at a rate that is equal to the rate at which water flows out of the cell.

   ANS: isotonic   DIF: I   OBJ: BPE 4-1.2

9. If the interior of a typical cell is negatively charged, _____ charged ions will not require energy to diffuse into the cell using an ion channel.

   ANS: positively   DIF: I   OBJ: BPE 4-1.3

10. Diffusion of ions through ion channels is a form of _____ transport.

    ANS: passive   DIF: I   OBJ: BPE 4-1.3

11. In facilitated diffusion, _____ proteins are used to transport substances down their concentration gradient.

ANS: carrier   DIF: I   OBJ: BPE 4-1.4

12. In _____ _____ carrier proteins do not require energy to transport amino acids into a cell.

ANS: facilitated diffusion   DIF: I   OBJ: BPE 4-1.4

13. Carrier proteins _____ shape to transport sugars to the interior of cells.

ANS: change   DIF: I   OBJ: BPE 4-1.4

14. Active transport requires the use of _____ by a cell.

ANS: ATP   DIF: I   OBJ: BPE 4-2.1

15. The _____ _____ pump transports ions against their concentration gradients.

ANS: sodium-potassium   DIF: I   OBJ: BPE 4-2.2

16. The sodium-potassium pump uses energy supplied by _____.

ANS: ATP   DIF: I   OBJ: BPE 4-2.2

17. The sodium-potassium pump prevents the accumulation of _____ ions inside the cell.

ANS: sodium   DIF: I   OBJ: BPE 4-2.2

18. The movement of a substance into a cell by a vesicle is called _____.

ANS: endocytosis   DIF: I   OBJ: BPE 4-2.3

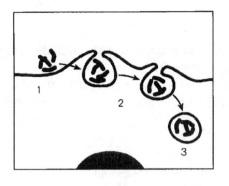

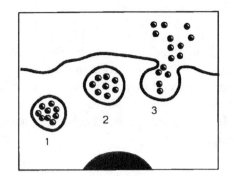

A   B

19. Refer to the illustration above. The process shown in figure B is called _____.

ANS: exocytosis   DIF: II   OBJ: BPE 4-2.3

20. Refer to the illustration above. Cells often engulf extracellular particles and fluid, as shown in figure A. This is called _____.

ANS: endocytosis   DIF: II   OBJ: BPE 4-2.3

21. Receptor proteins can change the _____ of the cell membrane.

ANS: permeability   DIF: I   OBJ: BPE 4-2.4

22. Receptor proteins may act as _____, speeding up the chemical reactions inside the cell.

ANS: enzymes   DIF: I   OBJ: BPE 4-2.4

23. In the cell membrane, proteins that transmit information into the cell by responding to signal molecules are called _____.

ANS: receptors   DIF: I   OBJ: BPE 4-2.4

PROBLEM

Paramecia are unicellular protists. They have a number of characteristics also found in animals, such as the need to ingest food in order to obtain energy (they are heterotrophs), and they are surrounded by a cell membrane but not by a rigid cell wall. They have organelles found in animal cells, including a nucleus, mitochondria, ribosomes, and cilia. In addition, they have star-shaped organelles, called contractile vacuoles, that expel excess water. The picture below depicts a paramecium.

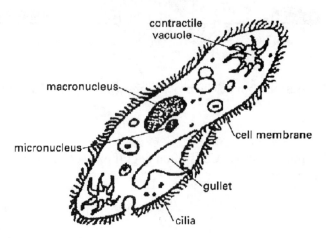

1. Refer to the illustration above. The data presented in the table below were obtained in an experiment in which paramecia were placed in different salt concentrations and the rate at which the contractile vacuole contracted to pump out excess water was recorded.

Salt	Rate of contractile vacuole contractions/minute
Very high	2
High	8
Medium	15
Low	22
Very low	30

a. How can you explain the observed relationship between salt concentration and rate of contractile vacuole contraction?

b. If something happened to a paramecium that caused its contractile vacuole to stop contracting, what would you expect to happen? Would this result occur more quickly if the paramecium was in water with a high salt concentration or in water with a low salt concentration? Why?

Write your answer in the space below.

ANS:

a. The contractile vacuole maintains water balance by pumping water out of the cell. When the salt concentration outside of the cell is very high, water will move from inside the cell to outside the cell—little or no pumping action is required. When the salt concentration outside of the cell is low, the tendency is for water to move from outside the cell to inside the cell, necessitating increased pumping action by the vacuole to move excess water out of the cell.

b. If the contractile vacuole were to stop contracting, the cell would burst because water would collect in excess inside of it and the cell membrane would not be strong enough to resist rupturing. This result would be expected to occur more quickly if the organism were placed in water with a low salt concentration than it would if the organism were placed in water with a high salt concentration. This is because water accumulates inside the paramecium more rapidly when it is placed in a low salt environment.

DIF: III   OBJ: BPE 4-1.2

2. A biologist conducts an experiment designed to determine whether a particular type of molecule is transported into cells by diffusion, facilitated diffusion, or active transport. He collects the following information:
1. The molecule is very small.
2. The molecule is polar.
3. The molecule can accumulate inside a cell, even when its concentration inside the cell initially is higher than it is outside the cell.
4. Cells use up more energy when the molecule is present in the environment around the cells than when it is not present.
The biologist concludes that the molecule moves across cell membranes by facilitated diffusion. Do you agree with his conclusion? Why or why not? Write your answer in the space below.

ANS:
Students should disagree. The information that cells can accumulate the molecule against a concentration gradient is compelling evidence that active transport is the mechanism of transport. This is the only mechanism among those named that allows movement against a concentration gradient. Active transport also requires energy consumption, which was also found to be a property of transport of this molecule.

DIF: III   OBJ: BPE 4-2.1

ESSAY

1. Why do dissolved particles on one side of a membrane result in the diffusion of water across the membrane?

ANS:
Dissolved particles reduce the number of water molecules that can move freely on that side. Water then moves by osmosis from the side where the free water molecule concentration is high to the side where the concentration is lower.

DIF: II   OBJ: BPE 4-1.2

2. Why is it dangerous for humans to drink sea water?

ANS:
The concentration of salt in sea water is higher than the concentration of salt in the fluids that surround the cells in the human body. Drinking sea water increases the concentration of salt in the body's fluids. This causes water to leave the cells by osmosis, and without the proper amount of water the cells will be harmed or will die.

DIF: II   OBJ: BPE 4-1.2

3. Distinguish between facilitated diffusion and active transport.

ANS:
In facilitated diffusion, carrier proteins assist the diffusion of substances down their concentration gradient. Active transport, on the other hand, is the movement of substances against their concentration gradient.

DIF: II   OBJ: BPE 4-2.1

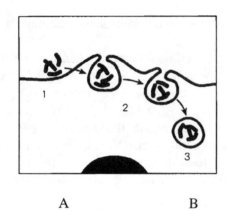   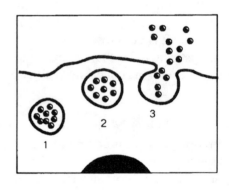

A   B

4. Refer to the illustration above. Identify and explain the processes taking place in figure A and figure B.

ANS:
Endocytosis is the process taking place in figure A. Endocytosis is the process by which cells engulf substances that are too large to enter the cell, by enclosing the substances in vesicles. Exocytosis is the process taking place in figure B. Exocytosis is the process by which cellular wastes are discharged from vesicles at the cell's surface.

DIF: II   OBJ: BPE 4-2.3

5. Describe three ways in which the binding of a signal molecule to a receptor protein can change the functioning of a cell.

ANS:
1. The receptor can act as an enzyme.
2. The receptor may cause the formation of a second messenger that will have an effect in another part of the cytoplasm.
3. The receptor can open a channel through the membrane.

DIF:　　II　　　　　　OBJ:　BPE 4-2.4

TRUE/FALSE

1. Heterotrophs obtain the chemical energy used in metabolism from autotrophs or from other heterotrophs.

    ANS: T   DIF: I   OBJ: BPE 5-1.1

2. All organisms require energy to carry out life processes.

    ANS: T   DIF: I   OBJ: BPE 5-1.1

3. Heterotrophic organisms use light energy to make organic compounds.

    ANS: F   DIF: I   OBJ: BPE 5-1.1

4. Some of the energy in sunlight is captured and used to make inorganic compounds.

    ANS: F   DIF: I   OBJ: BPE 5-1.1

5. Energy moves through food chains from heterotrophs to autotrophs.

    ANS: F   DIF: I   OBJ: BPE 5-1.1

6. Autotrophs make their own organic molecules by using energy from inorganic materials or sunlight.

    ANS: T   DIF: I   OBJ: BPE 5-1.2

7. Most plants are heterotrophic.

    ANS: F   DIF: I   OBJ: BPE 5-1.2

8. Animals that live exclusively by eating other animals are unable to use carbohydrates to fuel their life processes.

    ANS: F   DIF: I   OBJ: BPE 5-1.2

9. ATP is a portable form of "energy currency" inside cells.

    ANS: T   DIF: I   OBJ: BPE 5-1.3

10. ATP is a nucleotide with two carbohydrate groups.

    ANS: F   DIF: I   OBJ: BPE 5-1.3

11. In ATP, three phosphate groups branch from a five-carbon sugar, ribose.

ANS: T   DIF: I   OBJ: BPE 5-1.4

12. The phosphate "tail" of an ATP molecule is unstable because the bonds between the phosphate groups are strong.

ANS: F   DIF: I   OBJ: BPE 5-1.4

13. Photosynthesis is a process that takes place in autotrophs.

ANS: T   DIF: I   OBJ: BPE 5-2.1

14. The major light-absorbing pigment in plant photosynthesis is chlorophyll.

ANS: T   DIF: I   OBJ: BPE 5-2.1

15. When light hits a plant, all of the wavelengths of light are absorbed by chlorophyll.

ANS: F   DIF: I   OBJ: BPE 5-2.1

16. Plant cells use light energy to make ATP and NADPH.

ANS: T   DIF: I   OBJ: BPE 5-2.2

17. The "light reactions" of photosynthesis can occur only under light conditions, and the "dark reactions" occur only during the dark hours.

ANS: F   DIF: I   OBJ: BPE 5-2.3

18. The most common method of carbon dioxide fixation is the electron transport chain.

ANS: F   DIF: I   OBJ: BPE 5-2.3

19. During photosynthesis, carbon dioxide and water, in the presence of light, are used to form sugars and oxygen gas.

ANS: T   DIF: I   OBJ: BPE 5-2.3

20. The reactions that "fix" carbon dioxide are sometimes called dark reactions.

ANS: T   DIF: I   OBJ: BPE 5-2.3

21. Most of the three-carbon sugars formed during the Calvin Cycle are used to generate the initial five-carbon compounds.

ANS: T   DIF: I   OBJ: BPE 5-2.3

22. During photosynthesis, when electrons are transferred from one molecule to another, they are usually carried by hydrogen ions and NADP⁺.

ANS: T   DIF: I   OBJ: BPE 5-2.3

23. While the rate of photosynthesis is independent of temperature, it has been shown to be markedl affected by changes in light intensity.

ANS: F   DIF: I   OBJ: BPE 5-2.4

24. As light intensity increases indefinitely, the rate of photosynthesis increases indefinitely.

ANS: F   DIF: I   OBJ: BPE 5-2.4

25. As carbon dioxide concentration increases indefinitely, the rate of photosynthesis increases indefinitely.

ANS: F   DIF: I   OBJ: BPE 5-2.4

26. Glycolysis breaks down glucose into two pyruvates.

ANS: T   DIF: I   OBJ: BPE 5-3.1

27. Glycolysis occurs during the second stage of cellular respiration.

ANS: F   DIF: I   OBJ: BPE 5-3.1

28. During aerobic respiration, the breakdown of a molecule of glucose yields a net of two molecule of ATP.

ANS: F   DIF: I   OBJ: BPE 5-3.1

29. Glycolysis is carried out in the cytoplasm of cells.

ANS: T   DIF: I   OBJ: BPE 5-3.1

30. Aerobic respiration must follow glycolysis if a cell is to maximize its ATP production.

ANS: T   DIF: I   OBJ: BPE 5-3.2

31. Pyruvate produced during glycolysis enters a mitochondrion during the second stage of cellular respiration.

ANS: T   DIF: I   OBJ: BPE 5-3.2

32. Oxygen is *not* present during aerobic respiration.

ANS: F   DIF: I   OBJ: BPE 5-3.2

33. Fermentation and aerobic respiration both take place in the absence of oxygen.

    ANS: F   DIF: I   OBJ: BPE 5-3.3

34. Carbon dioxide production by yeast, which is used in the rising of bread and the carbonation of some beverages, takes place under aerobic conditions.

    ANS: F   DIF: I   OBJ: BPE 5-3.3

35. Under anaerobic conditions, electrons are transferred to oxygen in order to recycle NAD^+.

    ANS: F   DIF: I   OBJ: BPE 5-3.3

36. Lactic acid fermentation is a type of anaerobic process.

    ANS: T   DIF: I   OBJ: BPE 5-3.3

37. Fermentation enables glycolysis to continue as long as the glucose supply lasts.

    ANS: T   DIF: I   OBJ: BPE 5-3.3

38. Cellular respiration produces more ATP molecules than fermentation does.

    ANS: T   DIF: I   OBJ: BPE 5-3.4

39. The total amount of ATP that a cell gains for each glucose molecule that enters glycolysis depends on the presence of carbon dioxide.

    ANS: F   DIF: I   OBJ: BPE 5-3.4

MULTIPLE CHOICE

1. Most of the energy used by life on Earth comes from
   a. the sun.
   b. the rotation of the Earth.
   c. the moon.
   d. None of the above

    ANS: A   DIF: I   OBJ: BPE 5-1.1

2. Energy flows from the sun through the living world when
   a. plants capture sunlight and produce carbohydrates.
   b. animals eat plants.
   c. animals eat other animals that have eaten plants.
   d. All of the above

    ANS: D   DIF: I   OBJ: BPE 5-1.1

3. Heterotrophs get energy
   a. from organic molecules.
   b. through cellular respiration.
   c. from breaking down food molecules.
   d. All of the above

   ANS: D   DIF: I   OBJ: BPE 5-1.2

4. Heterotrophs are organisms that
   a. produce food from inorganic molecules or sunlight.
   b. can survive without energy.
   c. must consume other organisms to get energy.
   d. None of the above

   ANS: C   DIF: I   OBJ: BPE 5-1.2

5. Many autotrophs obtain the energy they need for metabolism through
   a. fermentation.
   b. photosynthesis.
   c. cellular respiration.
   d. eating food.

   ANS: B   DIF: I   OBJ: BPE 5-1.2

6. When cells break down food molecules, energy is
   a. released all at once.
   b. released entirely as body heat into the environment.
   c. temporarily stored in ATP molecules.
   d. None of the above

   ANS: C   DIF: I   OBJ: BPE 5-1.3

7. ATP is called a cell's "energy currency" because
   a. ATP catalyzes all metabolic reactions.
   b. ATP allows one organelle to be exchanged for another between cells.
   c. glucose is made of ATP.
   d. most of the energy that drives metabolism is supplied by ATP.

   ANS: D   DIF: I   OBJ: BPE 5-1.3

8. When living cells break down food molecules, energy is
   a. stored as ADP.
   b. stored as ATP.
   c. released as heat.
   d. Both (b) and (c)

   ANS: D   DIF: I   OBJ: BPE 5-1.3

9. Energy is required for a variety of life processes including
   a. growth and reproduction.
   b. movement.
   c. transport of materials across cell membranes.
   d. All of the above

   ANS: D   DIF: I   OBJ: BPE 5-1.3

10. Energy released from ATP
    a. contains five phosphate groups.
    b. drives most of a cell's activities.
    c. is found only in bacteria.
    d. All of the above

    ANS: B   DIF: I   OBJ: BPE 5-1.4

11. When a phosphate group is removed from an ATP molecule,
    a. a substantial amount of energy is released.
    b. an enzyme is formed.
    c. energy is stored.
    d. activation energy is increased.

    ANS: A   DIF: I   OBJ: BPE 5-1.4

12. Chemical energy stored in food molecules is released through
    a. fermentation.
    b. photosynthesis.
    c. cellular respiration.
    d. None of the above

    ANS: C   DIF: I   OBJ: BPE 5-2.1

13. Light energy is converted to chemical energy through the process of
    a. cellular respiration.
    b. fermentation.
    c. photosynthesis.
    d. glycolysis.

    ANS: C   DIF: I   OBJ: BPE 5-2.1

14. The major atmospheric by-product of photosynthesis is
    a. nitrogen.
    b. carbon dioxide.
    c. water.
    d. oxygen.

    ANS: D   DIF: I   OBJ: BPE 5-2.1

15. When electrons of a chlorophyll molecule are raised to a higher energy level,
    a. they become a photon of light.
    b. they form a glucose bond.
    c. they enter an electron transport chain.
    d. carotenoids are converted to chlorophyll.

    ANS: C   DIF: I   OBJ: BPE 5-2.1

16. Chlorophyll is green because
    a. it absorbs green wavelengths of light.
    b. it absorbs blue and yellow wavelengths, which make green.
    c. it reflects green wavelengths of light.
    d. of an optical illusion caused by transmitted light.

    ANS: C   DIF: I   OBJ: BPE 5-2.1

17. The process in which plants capture energy and make organic molecules is known as
    a. homeostasis.
    b. evolution.
    c. photosynthesis.
    d. development.

    ANS: C   DIF: I   OBJ: BPE 5-2.1

18. Because of photosynthesis,
    a. the atmosphere is rich in oxygen gas.
    b. animals can get energy directly from the sun.
    c. plants produce carbon dioxide.
    d. All of the above

    ANS: A   DIF: I   OBJ: BPE 5-2.1

19. Based on the cycle of photosynthesis and cellular respiration, one can say that the ultimate original source of energy for all living things on Earth is
    a. carbohydrates.   c. the sun.
    b. water.   d. carbon dioxide.

    ANS: C   DIF: I   OBJ: BPE 5-2.1

20. photosynthesis : oxygen ::
    a. oxygen : carbon dioxide   c. cellular respiration : oxygen
    b. cellular respiration : carbon dioxide   d. cellular respiration : enzymes

    ANS: B
    (produces)

    DIF: II   OBJ: BPE 5-2.1

21. Which of the following enables plants to convert light energy to chemical energy?
    a. the sodium-potassium pump   c. sugar channels
    b. coupled channels   d. proton pumps

    ANS: D   DIF: I   OBJ: BPE 5-2.2

22. The source of oxygen produced during photosynthesis is
    a. carbon dioxide.   c. the air.
    b. water.   d. glucose.

    ANS: B   DIF: I   OBJ: BPE 5-2.2

23. Electrons that have been excited by light energy absorbed by a chlorophyll molecule
    a. attach to two protons and an oxygen atom to form a water molecule.
    b. jump to molecules in the membrane of the thylakoid.
    c. are absorbed to the interior of a thylakoid.
    d. are transformed to protons by a proton pump.

    ANS: B   DIF: I   OBJ: BPE 5-2.2

24. While one type of electron transport chain is used to form molecules of ATP, a second electron transport chain is used
    a. in forming molecules of NADPH.
    b. to migrate to another proton pump.
    c. to produce water.
    d. as a fuel for forming another chlorophyll molecule.

    ANS: A   DIF: I   OBJ: BPE 5-2.2

25. Proton pumps found in the thylakoid membranes are directly responsible for
    a. moving hydrogen nuclei out of the thylakoid.
    b. providing the energy to produce ATP molecules.
    c. producing NADP⁺.
    d. generating glucose molecules.

    ANS: B   DIF: I   OBJ: BPE 5-2.2

26. NADPH is important in photosynthesis because it
    a. becomes oxidized to form NADP.
    b. is needed to form chlorophyll.
    c. provides additional oxygen atoms.
    d. carries high-energy electrons needed to produce organic molecules.

    ANS: D   DIF: I   OBJ: BPE 5-2.2

27. At a proton pump of the thylakoid membrane,
    a. electrons return to their original energy levels.
    b. electrons are pushed out of the thylakoid.
    c. energy from electrons is used to make ATP.
    d. the thylakoid bursts, releasing energy.

    ANS: C   DIF: I   OBJ: BPE 5-2.2

28. light energy : boosting electrons ::
    a. entropy : potential energy
    b. proton : electron
    c. ATP and NADPH : carbon dioxide fixation
    d. energy : food

    ANS: C
    (is/are needed for)

    DIF: II   OBJ: BPE 5-2.2

29. During the third stage of photosynthesis, sugars are produced from
    a. ADP.
    b. glucose.
    c. carbon atoms from carbon dioxide in the air and hydrogen atoms from water.
    d. carbon atoms from carbon dioxide in the air and hydrogen atoms from NADPH.

    ANS: D   DIF: I   OBJ: BPE 5-2.3

30. Products of the light reactions of photosynthesis that are required by the dark reactions are
    a. oxygen and ATP.   c. ATP and NADPH.
    b. water and oxygen.   d. oxygen and NADPH.

    ANS: C   DIF: I   OBJ: BPE 5-2.3

31. The dark reactions of photosynthesis
    a. require ATP and NADPH.
    b. are light-independent.
    c. generate sugars.
    d. All of the above

    ANS: D   DIF: I   OBJ: BPE 5-2.3

32. The energy used in the Calvin cycle for the production of carbohydrate molecules comes from
    a. ATP only.
    b. the Krebs cycle.
    c. ATP and NADH.
    d. carbon dioxide.

    ANS: C   DIF: I   OBJ: BPE 5-2.3

33. During photosynthesis, the series of reactions that create the complex carbohydrates needed for
    energy and growth is called
    a. the Calvin cycle.
    b. the Krebs cycle.
    c. the electron transport chain.
    d. None of the above

    ANS: A   DIF: I   OBJ: BPE 5-2.3

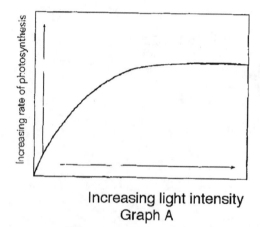

Increasing light intensity
Graph A

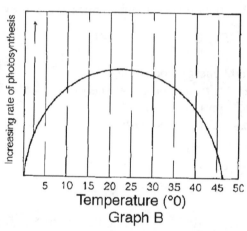

Temperature (°0)
Graph B

34. Refer to the illustration above. Graph A demonstrates that the rate of photosynthesis
    a. decreases in response to increasing light intensity.
    b. increases indefinitely in response to increasing light intensity.
    c. increases in response to increasing light intensity, but only to a certain point.
    d. is unaffected by changes in light intensity.

    ANS: C   DIF: II   OBJ: BPE 5-2.4

35. Refer to the illustration above. Taken together, these graphs demonstrate that
    a. photosynthesis is independent of environmental influences.
    b. increases in light intensity cause increases in temperature.
    c. as the rate of photosynthesis increases, the temperature of a plant eventually decreases.
    d. the rate of photosynthesis is affected by changes in the environment.

    ANS: D   DIF: II   OBJ: BPE 5-2.4

36. As light intensity increases, the rate of photosynthesis
    a. increases indefinitely.
    b. decreases indefinitely.
    c. increases until the light saturation point is reached.
    d. decreases until the light saturation point is reached.

    ANS: C   DIF: I   OBJ: BPE 5-2.4

37. Low temperatures may cause photosynthesis to occur
    a. more quickly.   c. at a constant rate.
    b. more slowly.   d. None of the above

    ANS: B   DIF: I   OBJ: BPE 5-2.4

38. CO_2 concentration : photosynthesis ::
    a. catalysis : inorganic molecule   c. organic molecule : respiration
    b. enzyme : coenzyme   d. enzyme activity : biochemical reactions

    ANS: D
    (affects the rate of)

    DIF: II   OBJ: BPE 5-2.4

39. When glycolysis occurs,
    a. a molecule of glucose is split.   c. some ATP is produced.
    b. two pyruvates are made.   d. All of the above

    ANS: D   DIF: I   OBJ: BPE 5-3.1

40. The process of cellular respiration
    a. is performed only by organisms that are incapable of photosynthesis.
    b. breaks down food molecules to release stored energy.
    c. occurs before plants are able to carry out photosynthesis.
    d. occurs only in animals.

    ANS: B   DIF: I   OBJ: BPE 5-3.1

41. Cellular respiration takes place in two stages:
    a. glycolysis and fermentation.
    b. electron transport chain, then fermentation.
    c. glycolysis, then aerobic respiration.
    d. None of the above

    ANS: C   DIF: I   OBJ: BPE 5-3.1

42. Which of the following is *not* part of cellular respiration?
    a. electron transport   c. Krebs cycle
    b. glycolysis   d. Calvin cycle

    ANS: D   DIF: I   OBJ: BPE 5-3.1

43. An important example of an electron acceptor that functions in glycolysis is
    a. ATP.
    b. oxygen.
    c. NAD⁺.
    d. water.

    ANS: C   DIF: I   OBJ: BPE 5-3.2

44. The final electron acceptor in aerobic respiration is
    a. water.
    b. ATP.
    c. NADPH.
    d. oxygen.

    ANS: D   DIF: I   OBJ: BPE 5-3.2

45. In cellular respiration, a two-carbon molecule combines with a four-carbon molecule as part of
    a. glycolysis.
    b. carbon dioxide fixation.
    c. the Krebs cycle.
    d. the electron transport chain.

    ANS: C   DIF: I   OBJ: BPE 5-3.2

46. Acetyl-CoA
    a. is formed from the breakdown of pyruvate.
    b. enters the Krebs cycle.
    c. combines with a four-carbon compound.
    d. All of the above

    ANS: D   DIF: I   OBJ: BPE 5-3.2

47. Water is an end product in
    a. lactic acid fermentation.
    b. alcoholic fermentation.
    c. the Krebs cycle.
    d. the electron transport chain.

    ANS: D   DIF: I   OBJ: BPE 5-3.2

48. Glycolysis and aerobic respiration are different in that
    a. glycolysis occurs on the cell membrane, while aerobic respiration occurs in mitochondria.
    b. glycolysis occurs only in photosynthesis, while aerobic respiration is part of cellular respiration.
    c. glycolysis occurs in the absence of oxygen, while aerobic respiration requires oxygen.
    d. None of the above

    ANS: C   DIF: I   OBJ: BPE 5-3.2

49. After proton pumps in mitochondria have depleted electrons of their energy during ATP production,
    a. the electrons are used in the formation of water.
    b. the electrons carried are used in the formation of ethyl alcohol.
    c. the electrons build up inside the mitochondria and diffuse back to a thylakoid.
    d. None of the above

    ANS: A   DIF: I   OBJ: BPE 5-3.2

The questions below refer to the following balanced chemical equation.

$$C_6H_{12}O_6 + 6O_2 + ADP + P \rightarrow 6CO_2 + 6\,H_2O + MOLECULE\ A$$

50. Refer to the equation above. The process summarized by the equation begins in the cytoplasm of a cell and ends in the
   a. cytoplasm.
   b. mitochondria.
   c. endoplasmic reticulum.
   d. cell membrane.

   ANS: B   DIF: II   OBJ: BPE 5-3.2

51. Which of the following is *not* formed during the Krebs cycle?
   a. CO_2
   b. $FADH_2$
   c. NADH
   d. NADPH

   ANS: D   DIF: I   OBJ: BPE 5-3.2

52. The name of the process that takes place when organic compounds are broken down in the absence of oxygen is
   a. respiration.
   b. oxidation.
   c. fermentation.
   d. All of the above

   ANS: C   DIF: I   OBJ: BPE 5-3.3

53. Fermentation enables glycolysis to continue under
   a. anaerobic conditions.
   b. aerobic conditions.
   c. photosynthetic conditions.
   d. None of the above

   ANS: A   DIF: I   OBJ: BPE 5-3.3

54. If oxygen is absent during the second stage of cellular respiration,
   a. fermentation will occur.
   b. the Krebs cycle begins.
   c. the electron transport chain works more efficiently.
   d. glycolysis stops.

   ANS: A   DIF: I   OBJ: BPE 5-3.3

55. Cells produce ATP most efficiently in the presence of
   a. water.
   b. carbon dioxide.
   c. oxygen.
   d. glucose.

   ANS: C   DIF: I   OBJ: BPE 5-3.4

56. The total amount of ATP that a cell gains for each glucose molecule depends on the presence of
   a. water.
   b. carbon dioxide.
   c. oxygen.
   d. glucose.

   ANS: C   DIF: I   OBJ: BPE 5-3.4

57. For each molecule of glucose that is broken down during aerobic respiration, the Krebs cycle produces
    a. 2 ATP.
    b. 4 ATP.
    c. 6 ATP.
    d. 8 ATP.

    ANS: A   DIF: I   OBJ: BPE 5-3.4

58. Which of the following is the best explanation for the presence of both chloroplasts and mitochondria in plant cells?
    a. In the light, plants are photosynthetic autotrophs. In the dark, they are heterotrophs.
    b. If plants cannot produce enough ATP in the process of photosynthesis to meet their energy needs, they can produce it in aerobic respiration.
    c. Sugars are produced in chloroplasts. These sugars can be stored in the plant for later use.
    d. The leaves and sometimes the stems of plants contain chloroplasts, which produce ATP to meet the energy needs of these plant parts. The roots of plants contain mitochondria, which produce ATP to meet the energy needs of these plant parts.

    ANS: C   DIF: III   OBJ: BPE 5-1.2

COMPLETION

1. The ultimate source of energy for all life on Earth is the _____.

    ANS: sun   DIF: I   OBJ: BPE 5-1.1

2. Energy from the sun enters living systems through _____ such as plants and certain bacteria.

    ANS: autotrophs   DIF: I   OBJ: BPE 5-1.1

3. Autotrophs are organisms that use energy from _____ or inorganic substances to make organic compounds.

    ANS: sunlight   DIF: I   OBJ: BPE 5-1.2

4. Heterotrophs get energy from food through the process of _____ _____.

    ANS: cellular respiration   DIF: I   OBJ: BPE 5-1.2

5. Organisms that harvest energy from sunlight or inorganic substances in order to make food molecules are called _____.

    ANS: autotrophs   DIF: I   OBJ: BPE 5-1.2

6. _____ is known as the energy currency of a cell.

    ANS: ATP   DIF: I   OBJ: BPE 5-1.3

7. ATP is an end product of the process of _____ _____.

   ANS: cellular respiration   DIF: I   OBJ: BPE 5-1.3

8. When a phosphate group is removed from an ATP molecule, a(n) _____ molecule is formed.

   ANS: ADP   DIF: I   OBJ: BPE 5-1.4

9. When a phosphate group is removed from an ATP molecule, energy is _____.

   ANS: released   DIF: I   OBJ: BPE 5-1.4

10. Plant pigments that absorb primarily red and blue light are _____ pigments, while pigments that absorb other wavelengths and appear yellow and orange are _____ pigments.

    ANS: chlorophyll, carotenoid   DIF: I   OBJ: BPE 5-2.1

11. During the first stage of photosynthesis, _____ _____ is absorbed by chlorophyll.

    ANS: light energy   DIF: I   OBJ: BPE 5-2.1

12. The abundance of oxygen in Earth's atmosphere is partly due to _____.

    ANS: photosynthesis   DIF: I   OBJ: BPE 5-2.2

13. The electron transport chain produces molecules that temporarily store _____ in the cell.

    ANS: energy   DIF: I   OBJ: BPE 5-2.2

14. The energy lost by electrons while in the electron transport chain is used to pump _____ ions into the thylakoid.

    ANS: hydrogen   DIF: I   OBJ: BPE 5-2.2

15. During the second stage of photosynthesis, the electron transport chain transfers light energy to two molecules, _____ and _____.

    ANS: ATP, NADPH   DIF: I   OBJ: BPE 5-2.2

16. The third stage of photosynthesis, in which carbohydrates are produced, is called _____ _____ fixation.

    ANS: carbon dioxide   DIF: I   OBJ: BPE 5-2.3

17. The transfer of carbon dioxide to organic compounds is called carbon dioxide
    _____.

    ANS: fixation   DIF: I   OBJ: BPE 5-2.3

18. Because of the enzyme-assisted reactions involved in photosynthesis, photosynthesis occurs be:
    within a certain _____ range.

    ANS: temperature   DIF: I   OBJ: BPE 5-2.4

19. Three factors affecting the rate of photosynthesis are light intensity, _____
    _____ concentration, and temperature.

    ANS: carbon dioxide   DIF: I   OBJ: BPE 5-2.4

20. Glucose is split into smaller molecules during a biochemical pathway called
    _____.

    ANS: glycolysis   DIF: I   OBJ: BPE 5-3.1

21. _____ is a biochemical pathway of cellular respiration that is anaerobic.

    ANS: Glycolysis   DIF: I   OBJ: BPE 5-3.1

22. During the first stage of cellular respiration, glucose is converted to _____.

    ANS: pyruvate   DIF: I   OBJ: BPE 5-3.1

23. Electrons that provide the energy for the production of most of a cell's ATP are carried to the
    electron transport chain by _____ and _____ molecules.

    ANS: NADH, $FADH_2$ DIF: I   OBJ: BPE 5-3.2

24. During the second stage of cellular respiration, pyruvate enters _____ where
    ATP will be produced.

    ANS: mitochondria   DIF: I   OBJ: BPE 5-3.2

25. Fermentation allows for the recycling of NAD^+ and production of ATP under
    _____ conditions.

    ANS: anaerobic   DIF: I   OBJ: BPE 5-3.3

26. In the absence of oxygen, instead of aerobic respiration following glycolysis, glycolysis is
    followed by _____.

    ANS: fermentation   DIF: I   OBJ: BPE 5-3.3

27. During fermentation, either ethyl alcohol and carbon dioxide or _____ is formed.

ANS: lactate   DIF: I   OBJ: BPE 5-3.3

28. Because oxygen is the final electron acceptor at the end of the electron transport chain, if oxygen were absent in aerobic respiration no _____ would be made.

ANS: ATP   DIF: I   OBJ: BPE 5-3.4

29. Hydrogen ions combine with electrons and oxygen forming _____ at the end of the electron transport chain.

ANS: water   DIF: I   OBJ: BPE 5-3.4

PROBLEM

1. Scientists have been able to induce chloroplasts to produce ATP in the dark. First, they remove intact chloroplasts from plants. Next, they soak the chloroplasts in a solution with a low pH (about 4) and keep them in the dark. After a period of time, the chloroplasts are removed from the low pH solution and placed in a higher pH solution (about 8), again in the dark. ATP is soon found to be present in the higher pH solution.
   a. Evaluate the results of this experiment. Include an explanation of what apparently happened to the chloroplasts while they were in the low pH solution and how this enabled them to produce ATP when they were placed in the higher pH solution.
   b. What occurs in chloroplasts exposed to light that was simulated in this experiment?

   ANS:

   a. In the low pH solution, the chloroplasts apparently take up hydrogen ions from the solution. The hydrogen ions move inside the thylakoid compartments of the chloroplasts and accumulate there. When the chloroplasts are placed in the higher pH solution, a pH gradient exists between the inside of the thylakoid compartments and the stroma of the chloroplasts. This drives the movement of hydrogen ions from the thylakoid compartments to the outside of the thylakoid. As the hydrogen ions move outside the thylakoid, they pass through the carrier protein that produces ATP from ADP.
   b. Chloroplasts exposed to light will have electrons passed along an electron transport chain. As they pass along this chain, they give off energy. Some of this energy is used to pump hydrogen ions into the thylakoid compartments. The resulting pH gradient drives the movement of hydrogen ions from the thylakoid compartments to the outside of the thylakoid. As the hydrogen ions move out of the thylakoid, they pass through the protein ATP synthetase. This enzyme is thereby induced to produce ATP from ADP.

   DIF: III   OBJ: BPE 5-2.2

Glycolysis:

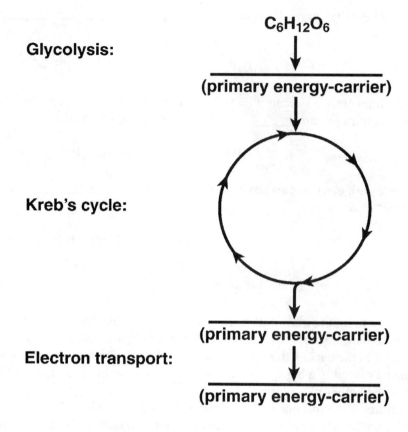

$C_6H_{12}O_6$

(primary energy-carrier)

Kreb's cycle:

(primary energy-carrier)

Electron transport:

(primary energy-carrier)

2. The summary equation for glycolysis and aerobic respiration is:
$C_6H_{12}O_6 + 6O_2 \rightarrow 6CO_2 + 6H_2O + ATP$

In the diagram above, the three major stages of aerobic respiration are indicated.
 a. In each of the blank spaces, write the name of the primary energy-carrying molecule that is produced at the end of each of these stages.
 b. Draw an arrow or arrows and write "O_2" to indicate where the oxygen required in aerobic respiration is used.
 c. Draw an arrow or arrows and write "CO_2" to indicate where the carbon dioxide released in aerobic respiration is produced.
 d. Circle the names of any and all of the stages of glycolysis and aerobic respiration that occur inside of mitochondria.

ANS:

 a. Pyruvate is the primary energy-carrying molecule at the end of glycolysis. NADH is the primary energy-carrying molecule at the end of the Kreb's cycle. ATP is the primary energy carrying molecule at the end of electron transport.
 b. A single arrow should be drawn indicating that oxygen is used in electron transport.
 c. Either one arrow or three arrows should be drawn indicating that carbon dioxide is released in the Krebs cycle.
 d. The Krebs cycle and electron transport should be circled. Glycolysis should not be circled.

DIF: III   OBJ: BPE 5-3.4

ESSAY

1. The relationship between photosynthesis and cellular respiration is usually described as a cycle. Briefly explain.

   ANS:
   The relationship between photosynthesis and cellular respiration is often described as cyclic because the products of one process are used as the reactants for the other. Photosynthesis produces carbohydrates from carbon dioxide and water, incorporating light energy into the bonds of the carbohydrates. Cellular respiration, on the other hand, releases energy from the bonds of carbohydrates, producing carbon dioxide and water.

   DIF: II   OBJ: BPE 5-1.2

2. Distinguish between autotrophs and heterotrophs.

   ANS:
   Organisms that acquire energy by making their own food are called autotrophs. Plants and certain unicellular organisms are autotrophs. Organisms that gain energy by eating other organisms are called heterotrophs. Some unicellular organisms, as well as all animals and fungi, are heterotrophs.

   DIF: II   OBJ: BPE 5-1.2

3. Why do the cells of plant roots generally lack chloroplasts?

   ANS:
   Chloroplasts contain chlorophyll, the pigment that absorbs sunlight. Because most roots are underground, they have no need for chlorophyll or chloroplasts.

   DIF: II   OBJ: BPE 5-2.1

4. Briefly explain how plants obtain energy from their environment and store it for later use.

   ANS:
   Plants use photosynthesis to convert light energy into chemical energy, creating energy-storing macromolecules.

   DIF: II   OBJ: BPE 5-2.1

5. Explain why the leaves of plants appear green to the human eye.

   ANS:
   When visible light strikes the leaves of a plant, red and blue wavelengths are absorbed by chlorophyll. Green wavelengths, however, are reflected. The observer perceives the leaves as being green.

   DIF: II   OBJ: BPE 5-2.1

TRUE/FALSE

1. Cell division in bacteria and eukaryotes takes place in precisely the same manner.

    ANS: F   DIF: I   OBJ: BPE 6-1.1

2. Asexual reproduction can occur by mitosis.

    ANS: T   DIF: I   OBJ: BPE 6-1.1

3. Binary fission is a form of sexual reproduction in bacteria.

    ANS: F   DIF: I   OBJ: BPE 6-1.1

4. A gene is a segment of DNA that directs the production of a specific protein.

    ANS: T   DIF: I   OBJ: BPE 6-1.2

5. The information needed by a cell to direct its activities and to determine its characteristics is contained in molecules of deoxyribonucleic acid (DNA).

    ANS: T   DIF: I   OBJ: BPE 6-1.2

6. After the replication of a cell's chromatids, there are twice as many centromeres as there are chromosomes.

    ANS: F   DIF: I   OBJ: BPE 6-1.2

7. Genes on chromosomes are the units of inheritance.

    ANS: T   DIF: I   OBJ: BPE 6-1.2

8. After cell division each new cell will contain the same genetic information as the original cell.

    ANS: T   DIF: I   OBJ: BPE 6-1.2

9. A male can produce sperm with either an X or a Y chromosome.

    ANS: T   DIF: I   OBJ: BPE 6-1.3

10. Each human somatic cell contains two copies of each chromosome for a total of 23 homologous chromosomes.

    ANS: F   DIF: I   OBJ: BPE 6-1.4

11. Human sperm and egg cells have 23 chromosomes.

    ANS: T   DIF: I   OBJ: BPE 6-1.4

12. Gametes are diploid so that when fertilization occurs, the resulting zygote will have the characteristic number of chromosomes for that species.

    ANS: F   DIF: I   OBJ: BPE 6-1.4

13. A somatic or body cell contains a haploid number of chromosomes.

    ANS: F   DIF: I   OBJ: BPE 6-1.4

14. The fusion of two diploid gametes produces a haploid zygote.

    ANS: F   DIF: I   OBJ: BPE 6-1.4

15. Down syndrome occurs as a result of nondisjunction of chromosome 21 during cell division.

    ANS: T   DIF: I   OBJ: BPE 6-1.5

16. It is possible that a fragment of DNA may become detached from a chromosome and then reattach in the reverse orientation, resulting in a mutation called inversion.

    ANS: T   DIF: I   OBJ: BPE 6-1.5

17. A karyotype is a type of gene.

    ANS: F   DIF: I   OBJ: BPE 6-1.5

18. Trisomy is the addition or removal of a single nitrogen-containing base.

    ANS: F   DIF: I   OBJ: BPE 6-1.5

19. Nondisjunction results from the failure of replicated chromosomes to separate during cell division.

    ANS: T   DIF: I   OBJ: BPE 6-1.5

20. Cells spend most of their lifetime in interphase.

    ANS: T   DIF: I   OBJ: BPE 6-2.1

21. After mitosis and cytokinesis, each new cell has a complete set of the parent cells' chromosomes.

    ANS: T   DIF: I   OBJ: BPE 6-2.1

22. The cell cycle has checkpoints that act to inhibit uncontrolled cell division.

    ANS: T   DIF: I   OBJ: BPE 6-2.2

23. Cancer is a disease characterized by uncontrolled cell division.

    ANS: T   DIF: I   OBJ: BPE 6-2.3

24. The immune system destroys all abnormal cells before they become cancerous.

    ANS: F   DIF: I   OBJ: BPE 6-2.3

25. Spindles move chromosomes during cell division.

    ANS: T   DIF: I   OBJ: BPE 6-3.1

26. During telophase, a nuclear envelope usually surrounds each new set of chromosomes.

    ANS: T   DIF: I   OBJ: BPE 6-3.2

27. Chromatids separate from each other during telophase.

    ANS: F   DIF: I   OBJ: BPE 6-3.2

28. Plant cells cannot undergo cell division because of their strong cell walls.

    ANS: F   DIF: I   OBJ: BVL 6-3.3

29. Cytokinesis can only occur during metaphase II.

    ANS: F   DIF: I   OBJ: BPE 6-3.3

30. In plant cells, cytokinesis results in the formation of a cell plate in the center of a dividing cell.

    ANS: T   DIF: I   OBJ: BPE 6-3.3

31. Animal cells form cell walls on either side of the cell plate during cytokinesis.

    ANS: F   DIF: I   OBJ: BPE 6-3.3

32. During cytokinesis in plant cells, the cell is pinched in half by a belt of protein threads.

    ANS: F   DIF: I   OBJ: BPE 6-3.3

MULTIPLE CHOICE

1. Binary fission
   a. occurs when two cells collide with each other.
   b. produces excess energy.
   c. creates new species.
   d. is the process by which bacteria reproduce.

   ANS: D   DIF: I   OBJ: BPE 6-1.1

2. The chromosome of a bacterium
   a. is wrapped around proteins.   c. occurs in multiple pairs within the cell.
   b. has a circular shape.   d. is found within the nucleus.

   ANS: B   DIF: I   OBJ: BPE 6-1.1

3. In a bacterium, cell division takes place when
   a. its nucleus divides.
   b. the cell splits into two cells, one of which receives all of the DNA.
   c. the DNA is copied, a new cell wall forms between the DNA copies, and the cell splits into two cells.
   d. None of the above

   ANS: C   DIF: I   OBJ: BPE 6-1.1

4. The point at which two chromatids are attached to each other in a chromosome is called a(n)
   a. chloroplast.   c. gamete.
   b. centromere.   d. centriole.

   ANS: B   DIF: I   OBJ: BPE 6-1.2

5. Chromatids are
   a. dense patches within the nucleus.
   b. bacterial chromosomes.
   c. joined strands of duplicated genetic material.
   d. prokaryotic nuclei.

   ANS: C   DIF: I   OBJ: BPE 6-1.2

6. The chromosomes in your body
   a. exist in 23 pairs in all cells but gametes.   c. form right before cells divide
   b. each contain thousands of genes.   d. All of the above

   ANS: D   DIF: I   OBJ: BPE 6-1.2

7. In order to fit within a cell, DNA becomes more compact by
   a. breaking apart into separate genes.
   b. extending to form very long, thin molecules.
   c. wrapping tightly around associated proteins.
   d. being enzymatically changed into a protein.

   ANS: C   DIF: I   OBJ: BPE 6-1.2

8. When a molecule of DNA is being used to direct a cell's activities,
   a. areas containing specific active genes are extended.
   b. the areas of the molecule containing active genes become shorter.
   c. the entire DNA molecule becomes tightly coiled.
   d. the molecule becomes a rod-shaped structure with two chromatids.

   ANS: A   DIF: I   OBJ: BPE 6-1.2

9. Normal human males develop from fertilized eggs containing which of the following sex chromosome combinations?
   a. XY   c. XO
   b. XX   d. OO

   ANS: A   DIF: I   OBJ: BPE 6-1.3

10. Homologous chromosomes are pairs of chromosomes containing genes that code for
    a. different traits.   c. DNA.
    b. same traits.   d. cytosol.

    ANS: B   DIF: I   OBJ: BPE 6-1.3

11. In humans, gametes contain
    a. 22 autosomes and 1 sex chromosome.   c. 45 autosomes and 1 sex chromosome.
    b. 1 autosome and 22 sex chromosomes.   d. 1 autosome and 45 sex chromosomes.

    ANS: A   DIF: I   OBJ: BPE 6-1.3

12. In humans, the male determines the sex of the child because males have
    a. two X chromosomes.   c. two Y chromosomes.
    b. one X and one Y chromosome.   d. 46 chromosomes.

    ANS: B   DIF: I   OBJ: BPE 6-1.3

13. The X and Y chromosomes are called the
    a. extra chromosomes.   c. sex chromosomes.
    b. phenotypes.   d. All of the above

    ANS: C   DIF: I   OBJ: BPE 6-1.3

14. female : XX ::
    a. female : gametes
    b. female : eggs
    c. male : YY
    d. male : XY

    ANS: D
    (has the sex chromosomes in chromosome pair)

    DIF: II   OBJ: BPE 6-1.3

15. Monosomy : nondisjunction ::
    a. chromatids : centromere
    b. XY chromosomes : male
    c. haploid cell : meiosis
    d. meiosis : diploid

    ANS: C
    (is the result of)

    DIF: II   OBJ: BPE 6-1.3

16. How many chromosomes are in the body cells of an organism that has a haploid number of 8?
    a. 4
    b. 8
    c. 12
    d. 16

    ANS: D   DIF: I   OBJ: BPE 6-1.4

17. The diploid number of chromosomes in a human skin cell is 46. The number of chromosomes found in a human ovum is
    a. 46.
    b. 92.
    c. 23.
    d. 12.5.

    ANS: C   DIF: I   OBJ: BPE 6-1.4

18. diploid : somatic cell :: haploid :
    a. body cell
    b. chromosome
    c. gamete
    d. zygote

    ANS: C   DIF: I   OBJ: BPE 6-1.4

19. A diploid cell is one that
    a. has two homologues of each chromosome.
    b. is designated by the symbol $2n$.
    c. has chromosomes found in pairs.
    d. All of the above

    ANS: D   DIF: I   OBJ: BPE 6-1.4

20. If nondisjunction occurs,
    a. there will be too many gametes produced.
    b. no gametes will be produced.
    c. a gamete will receive too many or too few homologues of a chromosome.
    d. mitosis cannot take place.

    ANS: C   DIF: I   OBJ: BPE 6-1.5

21. A mutation caused by a piece of DNA breaking away from its chromosome and becoming attached to a nonhomologous chromosome is called
a. deletion.
b. duplication.
c. inversion.
d. translocation.

ANS: D   DIF: I   OBJ: BPE 6-1.5

22. Trisomy is a mutation that results in a cell having an extra
a. nitrogen base.
b. codon.
c. chromosome.
d. gene.

ANS: C   DIF: I   OBJ: BPE 6-1.5

23. People with Down syndrome have
a. 45 chromosomes.
b. 46 chromosomes.
c. 47 chromosomes.
d. no X chromosomes.

ANS: C   DIF: I   OBJ: BPE 6-1.5

24. A student can study a karyotype to learn about the
a. cell cycle.
b. genes that are present in a particular strand of DNA.
c. medical history of an individual.
d. number and structure of the chromosomes in a somatic cell.

ANS: D   DIF: I   OBJ: BPE 6-1.5

25. The stage of the cell cycle that occupies most of the cell's life is
a. G_1.
b. M.
c. G_2.
d. S.

ANS: A   DIF: I   OBJ: BPE 6-2.1

26. Which of the following shows the correct sequence of the cell cycle?
a. $C \rightarrow M \rightarrow G_1 \rightarrow S \rightarrow G_2$
b. $S \rightarrow G_1 \rightarrow G_2 \rightarrow M \rightarrow C$
c. $G_1 \rightarrow S \rightarrow G_2 \rightarrow M \rightarrow C$
d. None of the above

ANS: C   DIF: I   OBJ: BPE 6-2.1

27. Cells that are not dividing remain in the
a. mitosis phase.
b. synthesis phase.
c. first growth phase.
d. cytokinesis phase.

ANS: C   DIF: I   OBJ: BPE 6-2.1

28. The synthesis (S) phase is characterized by
a. DNA replication.
b. cell division.
c. replication of mitochondria and other organelles.
d. the division of cytoplasm.

ANS: A   DIF: I   OBJ: BPE 6-2.1

29. Mitosis is the process by which
    a. microtubules are assembled.
    b. cytoplasm is divided.
    c. the nucleus is divided into two nuclei.
    d. the cell rests.

    ANS: C   DIF: I   OBJ: BPE 6-2.1

30. The first three phases of the cell cycle are collectively known as
    a. cellular respiration.
    b. telophase.
    c. mitosis.
    d. interphase.

    ANS: D   DIF: I   OBJ: BPE 6-2.1

31. cell growth : G_1 ::
    a. mitosis : C
    b. mitosis : meiosis
    c. mitochondria replication : S
    d. DNA copying : S

    ANS: D
    (occurs during)

    DIF: II   OBJ: BPE 6-2.1

32. metaphase : prophase ::
    a. photon : light particle
    b. G_2 : S
    c. thylakoid : grana
    d. autotroph : producer

    ANS: B
    (follows)

    DIF: II   OBJ: BPE 6-2.1

33. At the DNA synthesis (G_2) checkpoint, DNA replication is checked by
    a. receptor proteins.
    b. electron transport chains.
    c. repair enzymes.
    d. cell surface markers.

    ANS: C   DIF: I   OBJ: BPE 6-2.2

34. The cell cycle is monitored as each cell passes through
    a. cellular respiration.
    b. checkpoints.
    c. photosynthesis.
    d. homeostasis.

    ANS: B   DIF: I   OBJ: BPE 6-2.2

35. In eukaryotes, the cell cycle is controlled by
    a. proteins.
    b. carbohydrates.
    c. lipids.
    d. fats.

    ANS: A   DIF: I   OBJ: BPE 6-2.2

36. Normal cells become cancer cells when
    a.   regulation of cell growth and division is lost.
    b.   cells do not respond normally to control mechanisms.
    c.   cells continue to divide without passing through G_1.
    d.   All of the above

    ANS: D   DIF: I   OBJ: BPE 6-2.3

37. A spindle fiber is a specialized form of
    a.   microtubule.   c.   cilium.
    b.   flagellum.   d.   chromosome.

    ANS: A   DIF: I   OBJ: BPE 6-3.1

38. The phase of mitosis that is characterized by the arrangement of all chromosomes along the equator of the cell is called
    a.   telophase.   c.   anaphase.
    b.   metaphase.   d.   prophase.

    ANS: B   DIF: I   OBJ: BPE 6-3.2

39. As a result of mitosis, each of the two new cells produced from the parent cell during cytokinesis
    a.   receives a few chromosomes from the parent cell.
    b.   receives an exact copy of all the chromosomes present in the parent cell.
    c.   donates a chromosome to the parent cell.
    d.   receives exactly half the chromosomes from the parent cell.

    ANS: B   DIF: I   OBJ: BPE 6-3.2

1   2   3   4   5

40. Refer to the illustration above. The cell in diagram 1 is in
    a.   metaphase.   c.   anaphase.
    b.   telophase.   d.   prophase.

    ANS: C   DIF: II   OBJ: BPE 6-3.2

41. Refer to the illustration above. Mitosis begins with the stage shown in diagram
    a.   1.   c.   3.
    b.   2.   d.   4.

    ANS: B   DIF: II   OBJ: BPE 6-3.2

42. Refer to the illustration above. The cell shown in diagram 5 is in
    a. metaphase.   c. anaphase.
    b. telophase.   d. prophase.

    ANS: B   DIF: II   OBJ: BPE 6-3.2

43. Mitosis is a process by which
    a. DNA is replicated.   c. cells grow in size.
    b. cytokinesis occurs.   d. a cell's nucleus divides.

    ANS: D   DIF: I   OBJ: BPE 6-3.2

44. Refer to the illustration above. Which of the following correctly indicates the order in which these events occur?
    a. A, B, C, D   c. B, A, C, D
    b. C, B, A, D   d. A, C, B, D

    ANS: B   DIF: II   OBJ: BPE 6-3.2

45. Refer to the illustration above. During which stage do the centromeres divide?
    a. A   c. C
    b. B   d. D

    ANS: A   DIF: II   OBJ: BPE 6-3.2

46. 5 steps: the cell cycle ::
    a. 6 steps : prophase   c. 3 steps : meiosis
    b. 9 steps : cytokinesis   d. 4 steps : mitosis

    ANS: D
    (are in)

    DIF: II   OBJ: BPE 6-3.2

47. In plant cells, cytokinesis occurs
    a. immediately after the chromosomes make exact copies of themselves.
    b. immediately after the spindle fibers are formed.
    c. as mitosis ends.
    d. when osmotic pressure is too low.

    ANS: C   DIF: I   OBJ: BPE 6-3.3

48. Which of the following statements is *true?*
    a. Prokaryotes divide by mitosis.
    b. Eukaryotes have circular chromosomes.
    c. Animal cells form new cell walls when they divide.
    d. Plant cells and animal cells have different strategies for cytokinesis.

    ANS: D   DIF: I   OBJ: BPE 6-3.3

49. Cytokinesis in plant cells involves the formation of
    a. replicated chromosomes.   c. spindle fibers.
    b. a cell plate.   d. centrioles.

    ANS: B   DIF: I   OBJ: BPE 6-3.3

COMPLETION

1. _____ _____ is the process by which bacteria split
   asexually into two identical organisms.

   ANS: Binary fission   DIF: I   OBJ: BPE 6-1.1

2. In bacteria, cell division takes place in two stages. First the _____ is copied,
   and then the cell splits.

   ANS: DNA   DIF: I   OBJ: BPE 6-1.1

3. Growth occurs through cell enlargement and cell _____.

   ANS: division   DIF: I   OBJ: BPE 6-1.1

4. Following replication of its DNA, each chromosome contains two _____ ,
   which are attached to each other by a centromere.

   ANS: chromatids   DIF: I   OBJ: BPE 6-1.2

5. The DNA in eukaryotic cells is packaged into structures that are called _____

   ANS: chromosomes   DIF: I   OBJ: BPE 6-1.2

6. A _____ is a segment of a DNA molecule that carries the instructions for
   producing a specific trait.

   ANS: gene   DIF: I   OBJ: BPE 6-1.2

7. Chromosomes that are not involved in sex determination are called _____.

   ANS: autosomes   DIF: I   OBJ: BPE 6-1.3

8. The X and Y chromosomes are called the _____ chromosomes.

    ANS: sex   DIF: I   OBJ: BPE 6-1.3

9. In humans, the genotype XX results in a _____.

    ANS: female   DIF: I   OBJ: BPE 6-1.3

10. The diploid number of chromosomes is re-established through _____.

    ANS: fertilization   DIF: I   OBJ: BPE 6-1.4

11. A fertilized egg cell is called a(n) _____.

    ANS: zygote   DIF: I   OBJ: BPE 6-1.4

12. Fertilization of the haploid sperm and egg results in the restoration of the
    _____ number of chromosomes in the zygote.

    ANS: diploid   DIF: I   OBJ: BPE 6-1.4

13. Somatic cells containing two sets of 23 chromosomes are always _____.

    ANS: diploid   DIF: I   OBJ: BPE 6-1.4

14. The failure of replicated chromosomes to separate is called _____.

    ANS: nondisjunction   DIF: I   OBJ: BPE 6-1.5

15. A mutation in which a piece of a chromosome is lost during meiosis is called a(n)
    _____.

    ANS: deletion   DIF: I   OBJ: BPE 6-1.5

16. In humans, the specific condition caused by an extra chromosome 21 is called
    _____ _____.

    ANS: Down syndrome   DIF: I   OBJ: BPE 6-1.5

17. When a piece of chromosome attaches itself to a nonhomologous chromosome, the resulting
    mutation is called a(n) _____.

    ANS: translocation   DIF: I   OBJ: BPE 6-1.5

18. A picture of a cell's chromosomes is called a(n) _____.

    ANS: karyotype   DIF: I   OBJ: BPE 6-1.5

19. The sequence of events that occurs in a cell from one mitotic division to the next is called the
    _____ _____.

    ANS: cell cycle   DIF: I   OBJ: BPE 6-2.1

20. Collectively, the time spent in $G_1 + S + G_2$ is called _____.

    ANS: interphase   DIF: I   OBJ: BPE 6-2.1

21. A cell's DNA is copied during the _____ phase.

    ANS: synthesis.   DIF: I   OBJ: BPE 6-2.1

22. Cells that are not dividing remain in the _____ phase.

    ANS: G_1 (first growth)   DIF: I   OBJ: BPE 6-2.1

23. Normal cell growth and cell division is stimulated by _____.

    ANS: proteins   DIF: I   OBJ: BPE 6-2.2

24. The _____ checkpoint triggers the exit from mitosis.

    ANS: mitosis   DIF: I   OBJ: BPE 6-2.2

25. The cell cycle is controlled in eukaryotes at three principal _____.

    ANS: checkpoints   DIF: I   OBJ: BPE 6-2.2

26. DNA replication is checked at the _____ checkpoint.

    ANS: S (synthesis)   DIF: I   OBJ: BPE 6-2.2

27. Loss of control and regulation of the _____ _____ can
    result in the development of cancer.

    ANS: cell cycle   DIF: I   OBJ: BPE 6-2.3

28. Cancer is a disease of _____ _____.

    ANS: cell division   DIF: I   OBJ: BPE 6-2.3

29. "Cables" made of microtubules that extend from the poles of a cell to the centromeres during ce
    division are called _____ _____.

    ANS: spindle fibers   DIF: I   OBJ: BPE 6-3.1

30. Spindle fibers are made of hollow tubes of protein called _____.

    ANS: microtubules   DIF: I   OBJ: BPE 6-3.1

31. In mitosis, anaphase follows _____.

    ANS: metaphase   DIF: I   OBJ: BPE 6-3.2

32. Chromosomes coil up into short, fat rods during _____.

    ANS: prophase   DIF: I   OBJ: BPE 6-3.2

33. Chromosomes coil up and become visible during _____.

    ANS: prophase   DIF: I   OBJ: BPE 6-3.2

34. Chromatids migrate toward poles as spindle fibers shorten during _____.

    ANS: anaphase   DIF: I   OBJ: BPE 6-3.2

35. In many eukaryotic cells, _____ takes place after the nucleus divides.

    ANS: cytokinesis   DIF: I   OBJ: BPE 6-3.3

36. After a new nuclear membrane forms during telophase of mitosis or meiosis, the
    _____ divides, resulting in two cells.

    ANS: cytoplasm   DIF: I   OBJ: BPE 6-3.3

1. Refer to the illustration above. Identify the structure in the diagram and discuss its importance during eukaryotic cell division.

    ANS:
    This is a chromosome, the structure where the DNA in eukaryotic cells is found. The chromosome is formed right before a eukaryotic cell divides. Chromosomes are made of two chromatids attached at the centromere. During mitosis, the nucleus of a cell divides into two nuclei, each containing a complete set of the cell's chromosomes. Thus, each new cell formed during cell division contains identical DNA.

    DIF: II   OBJ: BPE 6-1.2

2. Explain the mechanism of sex determination in humans.

    ANS:
    A female parent donates one X chromosome. A male parent donates either an X or a Y chromosome. If an egg is fertilized by a sperm containing an X chromosome, the resulting zygo will be XX, and the new individual will be female. If an egg is fertilized by a sperm containing Y chromosome, the resulting zygote will be XY, and the new individual will be male.

    DIF: II   OBJ: BPE 6-1.3

3. What would happen if the chromosome number were not reduced before sexual reproduction?

ANS:
The number of chromosomes in the offspring would be double the number in the parents. The number and characteristics of chromosomes in cells determine the traits of the organism. The organism would almost certainly not survive the doubling of its chromosomes, and even if it did survive and reproduce, then the number of chromosomes would become unmanageably large after only a few generations.

DIF: II   OBJ: BPE 6-1.5

4. Describe Down syndrome and its cause.

ANS:
Down syndrome is a disorder characterized by mental retardation and weak muscles. This syndrome results from an extra copy of chromosome 21.

DIF: II   OBJ: BPE 6-1.5

5. Discuss how a karyotype can be used to diagnose Down syndrome.

ANS:
A karyotype is a photograph that shows the collection of chromosomes found in an individual's cells. Analysis of this collection of chromosomes can reveal abnormalities in chromosome number. Down syndrome is associated with trisomy 21—an extra chromosome # 21 in the cells of a person. Such an abnormality can be detected by observing a karyotype of an affected person.

DIF: II   OBJ: BPE 6-1.5

6. Briefly describe the five stages of the cell cycle.

ANS:
The G_1 stage of the cell cycle is the phase of cell growth. This is followed by the S stage, during which DNA is copied. G_2 involves the cell preparing for cell division. The nucleus of a cell is divided into two nuclei during the mitosis phase. The cell cycle concludes with cytokinesis, during which the cytoplasm divides. The newly formed cells then enter into a new cell cycle, repeating these stages again.

DIF: II   OBJ: BPE 6-2.1

TRUE/FALSE

1. While paired together during the second division of meiosis, two chromosomes may exchange segments of DNA.

   ANS: F   DIF: I   OBJ: BPE 7-1.1

2. Meiosis produces four nuclei that have different chromosome numbers from the parent cell.

   ANS: T   DIF: I   OBJ: BPE 7-1.1

3. Crossing-over is the exchange of corresponding portions of chromatids between homologous chromosomes.

   ANS: T   DIF: I   OBJ: BPE 7-1.2

4. At the conclusion of crossing-over, genetic recombination has occurred.

   ANS: T   DIF: I   OBJ: BPE 7-1.2

5. Independent assortment occurs when each pair of chromosomes segregates (separates) independently.

   ANS: T   DIF: I   OBJ: BPE 7-1.2

6. Random fertilization refers to the fact that gametes are produced independently.

   ANS: F   DIF: I   OBJ: BPE 7-1.2

7. The process by which sperm are produced in male animals is called spermatogenesis.

   ANS: T   DIF: I   OBJ: BPE 7-1.3

8. Oogenesis occurs in the female reproductive organs.

   ANS: T   DIF: I   OBJ: BPE 7-1.3

9. Gametogenesis occurs only in males.

   ANS: F   DIF: I   OBJ: BPE 7-1.3

10. Meiosis in female animals results in the same number of ova as sperm were produced by meiosis in the male.

    ANS: F   DIF: I   OBJ: BPE 7-1.3

11. The two cells produced during the first cytokinesis in female animals are approximately equal in size and contain the same amount of cytoplasm.

    ANS: F   DIF: I   OBJ: BPE 7-1.3

12. Some organisms look exactly like their parents.

    ANS: T   DIF: I   OBJ: BPE 7-2.1

13. In asexual reproduction two parents each pass copies of all of their cells to their offspring.

    ANS: F   DIF: I   OBJ: BPE 7-2.1

14. In sexual reproduction two parents each form haploid cells, which join to form offspring.

    ANS: T   DIF: I   OBJ: BPE 7-2.1

15. Some eukaryotes reproduce asexually, and some reproduce sexually.

    ANS: T   DIF: I   OBJ: BPE 7-2.1

16. Amoebas reproduce by fission.

    ANS: T   DIF: I   OBJ: BPE 7-2.2

17. In budding, new individuals develop from fragments of the original one.

    ANS: F   DIF: I   OBJ: BPE 7-2.2

18. Asexual reproduction provides for genetic diversity, the raw material for evolution.

    ANS: F   DIF: I   OBJ: BPE 7-2.3

19. The pairing of homologous chromosomes during meiosis may have originally been a way to repair damaged DNA.

    ANS: T   DIF: I   OBJ: BPE 7-2.3

20. Genetic diversity is the raw material for evolution.

    ANS: T   DIF: I   OBJ: BPE 7-2.3

21. In most animals, including humans, meiosis produces sperm and egg cells.

    ANS: T   DIF: I   OBJ: BPE 7-2.4

22. Alternation of generations is the simplest of the sexual life cycles.

    ANS: F   DIF: I   OBJ: BPE 7-2.4

23. During the haploid life cycle, the zygote is the only diploid cell.

    ANS: T   DIF: I   OBJ: BPE 7-2.4

24. During a diploid life cycle, all of the cells are diploid.

    ANS: F   DIF: I   OBJ: BPE 7-2.4

25. Plants, algae, and some protists have a life cycle that regularly alternates between a haploid phase and a diploid phase.

    ANS: T   DIF: I   OBJ: BPE 7-2.4

26. In plants, the diploid phase in the life cycle that produces spores is called a gametophyte.

    ANS: F   DIF: I   OBJ: BPE 7-2.4

27. In the life cycle of a plant, the gametophyte is the haploid phase that produces gametes by mitosis.

    ANS: T   DIF: I   OBJ: BPE 7-2.4

28. Unlike a gamete, a spore gives rise to a multicellular individual without joining with another cell.

    ANS: T   DIF: I   OBJ: BPE 7-2.4

29. Roses are examples of plants that have a life cycle called alternation of generations.

    ANS: T   DIF: I   OBJ: BPE 7-2.4

30. Moss plants have haploid life cycles.

    ANS: F   DIF: I   OBJ: BPE 7-2.4

MULTIPLE CHOICE

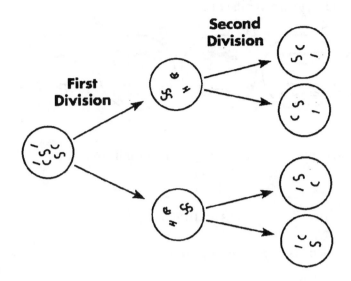

1. Refer to the illustration above. The process shown in the diagrams is
   a. mitosis.
   b. chromosomal mutation.
   c. meiosis.
   d. dominance.

   ANS: C   DIF: II   OBJ: BPE 7-1.1

2. Separation of homologues occurs during
   a. mitosis.
   b. meiosis I.
   c. meiosis II.
   d. fertilization.

   ANS: B   DIF: I   OBJ: BPE 7-1.1

3. The difference between anaphase of mitosis and anaphase I of meiosis is that
   a. the chromosomes line up at the equator in anaphase I.
   b. centromeres do not exist in anaphase I.
   c. chromatids do not separate at the centromere in anaphase I.
   d. crossing-over occurs only in anaphase of mitosis.

   ANS: C   DIF: I   OBJ: BPE 7-1.1

4. When crossing-over takes place, chromosomes
   a. mutate in the first division.
   b. produce new genes.
   c. decrease in number.
   d. exchange corresponding segments of DNA.

   ANS: D   DIF: I   OBJ: BPE 7-1.1

Using the information you have learned about cell reproduction, infer answers to the questions below about a cell with a diploid number of 4 chromosomes. Select from among the diagrams below, labeled A, B, C, D, and E, to answer the questions.

A   B   C   D   E

5. Which of the diagrams above depicts a cell at the beginning of mitosis?
    a. B   c. D
    b. C   d. E

    ANS: C   DIF: III   OBJ: BPE 7-1.1

6. Which of the diagrams above depicts a cell at the end of meiosis I?
    a. B   c. C
    b. C   d. E

    ANS: D   DIF: III   OBJ: BPE 7-1.1

7. Which of the diagrams above depicts a cell at the end of meiosis II?
    a. A   c. C
    b. B   d. D

    ANS: A   DIF: II   OBJ: BPE 7-1.1

8. Which of the diagrams above depicts a cell at the end of mitosis?
    a. A   c. C
    b. B   d. D

    ANS: B   DIF: II   OBJ: BPE 7-1.1

9. The exchange of segments of DNA between the members of a pair of chromosomes
    a. ensures that variations within a species never occur.
    b. acts as a source of variations within a species.
    c. always produces genetic disorders.
    d. is called crossing.

    ANS: B   DIF: I   OBJ: BPE 7-1.2

10. Crossing-over occurs
    a. during prophase II.   c. during prophase I.
    b. during fertilization.   d. at the centromere.

    ANS: C   DIF: I   OBJ: BPE 7-1.2

11. Which of the following does *not* provide new genetic combinations?
    a. random fertilization
    b. cytokinesis
    c. independent assortment
    d. crossing-over

    ANS: B   DIF: I   OBJ: BPE 7-1.2

12. During cytokinesis in the female, what divides unequally?
    a. the sperm cell
    b. the ovary
    c. the cytoplasm
    d. None of the above

    ANS: C   DIF: I   OBJ: BPE 7-1.3

13. The more common name for an ovum is a(n)
    a. egg.
    b. hormone.
    c. nutrient.
    d. polar body.

    ANS: A   DIF: I   OBJ: BPE 7-1.3

14. The process of producing offspring is called reproduction and can be
    a. eukaryotic or prokaryotic.
    b. asexual or sexual.
    c. cardiovascular or respiratory.
    d. None of the above

    ANS: B   DIF: I   OBJ: BPE 7-2.1

15. Which of the following is not a type of asexual reproduction?
    a. budding
    b. fragmentation
    c. fission
    d. fertilization

    ANS: D   DIF: I   OBJ: BPE 7-2.2

16. Types of asexual reproduction include
    a. budding.
    b. fragmentation.
    c. fission.
    d. All of the above

    ANS: D   DIF: I   OBJ: BPE 7-2.2

17. Hydras reproduce by
    a. budding.
    b. fragmentation.
    c. fission.
    d. None of the above

    ANS: B   DIF: I   OBJ: BPE 7-2.2

18. Budding is an example of
    a. endosymbiosis.
    b. asexual reproduction.
    c. meiosis.
    d. sexual reproduction.

    ANS: B   DIF: I   OBJ: BPE 7-2.2

19. The simplest and most primitive method of reproduction is
    a. sexual.   c. haploid.
    b. diploid.   d. None of the above

    ANS: D   DIF: I   OBJ: BPE 7-2.3

20. Which of the following is not a type of sexual life cycle?
    a. alternation of generations   c. diploid
    b. haploid   d. cellular

    ANS: D   DIF: I   OBJ: BPE 7-2.4

21. To create new haploid cells during the haploid life cycle, the zygote undergoes
    a. mitosis.   c. fusion.
    b. fertilization.   d. meiosis.

    ANS: D   DIF: I   OBJ: BPE 7-2.4

22. In alternation of generations, a diploid spore-forming cell gives rise to four
    a. zygotes.   c. haploid spores.
    b. sperm cells.   d. diploid spores.

    ANS: C   DIF: I   OBJ: BPE 7-2.4

23. During alternation of generations, cells reproduce by
    a. meiosis.   c. both meiosis and mitosis.
    b. mitosis.   d. None of the above

    ANS: C   DIF: I   OBJ: BPE 7-2.4

COMPLETION

1. The stage of meiosis during which homologues line up along the equator of the cell is called
   _____ _____.

   ANS: metaphase I   DIF: I   OBJ: BPE 7-1.1

2. Fertilization of the haploid sperm and egg results in the restoration of the
   _____ number of chromosomes in the zygote.

   ANS: diploid   DIF: I   OBJ: BPE 7-1.1

3. After a new nuclear membrane forms during telophase of mitosis or meiosis, the
   _____ divides, resulting in two cells.

   ANS: cytoplasm   DIF: I   OBJ: BPE 7-1.1

4. The cells resulting from meiosis in either males or females are called _____.

   ANS: gametes   DIF: I   OBJ: BPE 7-1.1

5. The process called _____ guarantees that the number of chromosomes in gametes is half the number of chromosomes in body cells.

ANS: meiosis   DIF: I   OBJ: BPE 7-1.1

6. A reciprocal exchange of corresponding segments of DNA is called _____ - _____.

ANS: crossing-over   DIF: I   OBJ: BPE 7-1.1

7. The four haploid cells formed in the male at the end of meiosis II develop a tail and are called _____.

ANS: sperm   DIF: I   OBJ: BPE 7-1.3

8. An individual produced by asexual reproduction that is genetically identical to its parent is called a(n) _____.

ANS: clone   DIF: I   OBJ: BPE 7-2.1

9. The separation of a parent into two or more individuals of about equal size is called _____.

ANS: fission   DIF: I   OBJ: BPE 7-2.2

10. The process in which sperm and egg cells join is called _____.

ANS: fertilization   DIF: I   OBJ: BPE 7-2.4

11. A spore is a haploid reproductive cell produced by _____.

ANS: meiosis   DIF: I   OBJ: BPE 7-2.4

12. The entire span in the life of an organism from one generation to the next is called a(n) _____ _____.

ANS: life cycle   DIF: I   OBJ: BPE 7-2.4

13. The diploid phase in the life cycle of plants is called the _____.

ANS: sporophyte   DIF: I   OBJ: BPE 7-2.4

ESSAY

1. What would happen if the chromosome number were not reduced before sexual reproduction?

   ANS:
   The number of chromosomes in the offspring would be double the number in the parents. The number and characteristics of chromosomes in cells determine the traits of the organism. The organism would almost certainly not survive the doubling of its chromosomes, and even if it did survive and reproduce, then the number of chromosomes would become unmanageably large after only a few generations.

   DIF: II   OBJ: BPE 7-1.1

2. Compare the features of mitotic metaphase, meiotic metaphase I, and meiotic metaphase II.

   ANS:
   During metaphase of mitosis, the diploid number of chromosomes of the cell line up single file across the equator of the cell. Meiotic metaphase I is characterized by the homologous chromosomes lining up as pairs (double file) along the equator. Metaphase II of meiosis appears similar to mitotic metaphase, except that the number of chromosomes is the haploid number rather than the diploid number. These chromosomes line up single file across the cell equator.

   DIF: II   OBJ: BPE 7-1.1

3. Identify three ways in which genetic recombination results during meiosis.

   ANS:
   Genetic recombination results when crossing-over occurs between homologous chromosomes, when homologous pairs separate independently in meiosis I, when sister chromatids separate independently in meiosis II, and when the zygote that forms a new individual is created by the random joining of two gamtes.

   DIF: II   OBJ: BPE 7-1.2

4. Explain why crossing-over is an important source of genetic variation.

   ANS:
   Crossing-over occurs when two homologous chromosomes exchange reciprocal segments of DNA during prophase I of meiosis. This results in chromosomes in which the two chromatids no longer have identical genetic material. When meiosis is completed, the resulting gametes carry new combinations of genes.

   DIF: II   OBJ: BPE 7-1.2

5. What are the two things that might happen to a bud?

    ANS:
    It may break from the parent and become an independent organism, or it may remain attached to the parent and eventually give rise to many individuals.

    DIF: II   OBJ: BPE 7-2.2

6. What are at least two advantages of asexual reproduction?

    ANS:
    1. It is less complex than sexual reproduction.
    2. In a stable environment it allows organisms to produce many offspring in a short period of time.
    3. Organisms do not need to use energy producing gametes or finding a mate.

    DIF: II   OBJ: BPE 7-2.3

TRUE/FALSE

1. Genetics is the branch of biology that involves the study of how different traits are transmitted from one generation to the next.

   ANS: T   DIF: I   OBJ: BPE 8-1.1

2. Mendel discovered predictable patterns in the inheritance of traits.

   ANS: T   DIF: I   OBJ: BPE 8-1.1

3. Garden peas are difficult to grow because they mature slowly.

   ANS: F   DIF: I   OBJ: BPE 8-1.2

4. The mating of garden-pea flowers can be easily controlled because the male and female reproductive parts are enclosed within the same flower.

   ANS: F   DIF: I   OBJ: BPE 8-1.2

5. When Mendel cross-pollinated two varieties from the P generation that exhibited contrasting traits, he called the offspring the second filial, or F_2, generation.

   ANS: F   DIF: I   OBJ: BPE 8-1.3

6. Mendel's initial experiments were monohybrid crosses.

   ANS: T   DIF: I   OBJ: BPE 8-1.3

7. In Mendel's experiments, the recessive traits appeared in the F_2 generation in approximately 25 percent of the plants.

   ANS: T   DIF: I   OBJ: BPE 8-1.4

8. A dominant allele masks the effect of a recessive allele.

   ANS: T   DIF: I   OBJ: BPE 8-2.1

9. Individuals must exhibit a trait in order for it to appear in their offspring.

   ANS: F   DIF: I   OBJ: BPE 8-2.1

10. The allele for a recessive trait is usually represented by a capital letter.

    ANS: F   DIF: I   OBJ: BPE 8-2.2

11. Heterozygous individuals have two of the same alleles for a particular gene.

    ANS: F   DIF: I   OBJ: BPE 8-2.2

12. In heterozygous individuals, only the recessive allele is expressed.   T+

    ANS: F   DIF: I   OBJ: BPE 8-2.2

13. The law of segregation states that two or more pairs of alleles separate independently of one another during gamete formation.

    ANS: F   DIF: I   OBJ: BPE 8-2.3

14. A Punnett square represents the phenotype of an organism.

    ANS: F   DIF: I   OBJ: BPE 8-3.1

15. If the offspring of a test cross all have the dominant trait, then the genotype of the individual being tested is homozygous.

    ANS: T   DIF: I   OBJ: BPE 8-3.2

16. Probability is the likelihood that a certain event will occur.

    ANS: T   DIF: I   OBJ: BPE 8-3.3

17. The expression of sex-linked genes is controlled by hormones.

    ANS: F   DIF: I   OBJ: BPE 8-3.4

18. An autosomal trait will occur with equal frequency in both males and females.

    ANS: T   DIF: I   OBJ: BPE 8-3.4

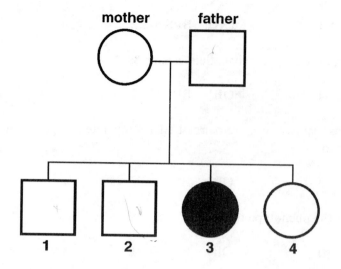

mother   father

1   2   3   4

19. Refer to the illustration above. The father listed in the pedigree is most likely heterozygous for the trait.

   ANS: T   DIF: II   OBJ: BPE 8-3.4

20. Refer to the illustration above. Child # 3 probably has a homozygous recessive phenotype.

   ANS: T   DIF: II   OBJ: BPE 8-3.4

21. Refer to the illustration above. The trait indicated in the pedigree is sex-linked.

   ANS: F   DIF: II   OBJ: BPE 8-3.4

22. In codominance, two dominant alleles are expressed at the same time.

   ANS: T   DIF: I   OBJ: BPE 8-4.1

23. All genes have only two alleles.

   ANS: F   DIF: I   OBJ: BPE 8-4.1

24. The only way a mutation in a recessive gene can show up in a child born to two normal parents i for both parents to be heterozygous.

   ANS: T   DIF: I   OBJ: BPE 8-4.2

25. Hemophilia is caused by a mutated allele that produces a defective form of the protein hemoglobin.

   ANS: F   DIF: I   OBJ: BPE 8-4.3

26. Cystic fibrosis is a genetic disorder caused by a defective chloride-ion transport protein.

    ANS: T   DIF: I   OBJ: BPE 8-4.3

27. Genetic counselors often help people with a family history of genetic disorders.

    ANS: T   DIF: I   OBJ: BPE 8-4.4

MULTIPLE CHOICE

1. The passing of traits from parents to offspring is called
   a. genetics.   c. development.
   b. heredity.   d. maturation.

    ANS: B   DIF: I   OBJ: BPE 8-1.1

2. The difference between Mendel's experiments in the area of heredity and those done by earlier researchers was that
   a. earlier researchers did not have microscopes.
   b. earlier researchers used detailed and numerical procedures.
   c. Mendel expressed the results of his experiments in terms of numbers.
   d. Mendel used pea plants with both purple and white flowers.

    ANS: C   DIF: I   OBJ: BPE 8-1.1

3. The scientific study of heredity is called
   a. meiosis.   c. genetics.
   b. crossing-over.   d. pollination.

    ANS: C   DIF: I   OBJ: BPE 8-1.1

4. The "father" of genetics was
   a. T.A. Knight.   c. Gregor Mendel.
   b. Hans Krebs.   d. None of the above

    ANS: C   DIF: I   OBJ: BPE 8-1.1

5. Mendel obtained his P generation by allowing the plants to
   a. self-pollinate.   c. assort independently.
   b. cross-pollinate.   d. segregate.

    ANS: A   DIF: I   OBJ: BPE 8-1.3

6. Step 1 of Mendel's garden pea experiment, allowing each variety of garden pea to self-pollinate for several generations, produced the
   a. F_1 generation.   c. P generation.
   b. F_2 generation.   d. P_2 generation.

    ANS: A   DIF: I   OBJ: BPE 8-1.3

7. $F_2 : F_1 ::$
   a. $P : F_1$
   b. $F_1 : F_2$
   c. $F_1 : P$
   d. dominant trait : recessive trait

ANS: C
(is produced by the)

DIF: II   OBJ: BPE 8-1.3

8. Mendel : ratio of traits ::
   a. monosomy : trisomy
   b. nondisjunction : prenatal testing
   c. XY : XX
   d. karyotype : numbers of chromosomes

ANS: D
(showed/shows)

DIF: II   OBJ: BPE 8-1.4

9. Mendel's law of segregation states that
   a. pairs of alleles are dependent on one another when separation occurs during gamete formation.
   b. pairs of alleles separate independently of one another after gamete formation.
   c. each pair of alleles remains together when gametes are formed.
   d. the two alleles for a trait separate when gametes are formed.

ANS: D   DIF: I   OBJ: BPE 8-2.1

10. Garden peas
    a. are difficult to grow.
    b. mature quickly.
    c. produce few offspring.
    d. are not good subjects for studying heredity.

ANS: B   DIF: I   OBJ: BPE 8-2.2

11. The phenotype of an organism
    a. represents its genetic composition.
    b. is the physical appearance of a trait.
    c. occurs only in dominant pure organisms.
    d. cannot be seen.

ANS: B   DIF: I   OBJ: BPE 8-2.2

12. If an individual possesses two recessive alleles for the same trait, the individual is said to be
    a. homozygous for the trait.
    b. haploid for the trait.
    c. heterozygous for the trait.
    d. mutated.

ANS: A   DIF: I   OBJ: BPE 8-2.2

13. A genetic trait that appears in every generation of offspring is called
    a. dominant.   c. recessive.
    b. phenotypic.   d. superior.

    ANS: A   DIF: I   OBJ: BPE 8-2.2

14. An individual heterozygous for a trait and an individual homozygous recessive for the trait are crossed and produce many offspring that are
    a. all the same genotype.   c. of three different phenotypes.
    b. of two different phenotypes.   d. all the same phenotype.

    ANS: B   DIF: I   OBJ: BPE 8-2.2

15. Tallness (T) is dominant to shortness (t) in pea plants. Which of the following represents a genotype of a pea plant that is heterozygous for tallness?
    a. T c. Tt
    b. TT d. tt

    ANS: C   DIF: I   OBJ: BPE 8-2.2

16. homozygous : heterozygous ::
    a. heterozygous : Bb c. dominant : recessive
    b. probability : predicting chances   d. factor : gene

    ANS: C
    (is different from)

    DIF: II   OBJ: BPE 8-2.2

17. Mendel's finding that the inheritance of one trait had no effect on the inheritance of another became known as the
    a. law of dominance.   c. law of separate convenience.
    b. law of universal inheritance.   d. law of independent assortment.

    ANS: D   DIF: I   OBJ: BPE 8-2.3

18. The discovery of chromosomes provided a link between Mendel's principles and
    a. pollination.   c. mitosis.
    b. inheritance.   d. meiosis.

    ANS: D   DIF: I   OBJ: BPE 8-2.3

19. A 3:1 ratio of tall to short pea plants appearing in the F_2 generation lends support to the law of
    a. recessiveness.   c. segregation.
    b. mutation.   d. crossing-over.

    ANS: C   DIF: I   OBJ: BPE 8-2.3

20. The law of segregation states that
    a. alleles of a gene separate from each other during meiosis.
    b. different alleles of a gene can never be found in the same organism.
    c. each gene of an organism ends up in a different gamete.
    d. each gene is found on a different molecule of DNA.

    ANS: A   DIF: I   OBJ: BPE 8-2.3

In humans, having freckles (*F*) is dominant to not having freckles (*f*). The inheritance of these traits can be studied using a Punnett square similar to the one shown below.

21. Refer to the illustration above. The child represented in box 1 in the Punnett square would
    a. be homozygous for freckles.   c. be heterozygous for freckles.
    b. have an extra freckles chromosome.   d. not have freckles.

    ANS: A   DIF: II   OBJ: BPE 8-3.1

22. Refer to the illustration above. The parents shown in the Punnett square could have children with a phenotype ratio of
    a. 1:2:1.   c. 3:1.
    b. 4:0.   d. 2:2.

    ANS: C   DIF: II   OBJ: BPE 8-3.1

23. Refer to the illustration above. Which box in the Punnett square represents a child who does not have freckles?
    a. box 1   c. box 3
    b. box 2   d. box 4

    ANS: D   DIF: II   OBJ: BPE 8-3.1

24. Refer to the illustration above. The child in box 3 of the Punnett square has the genotype
    a. *FF*.
    b. *Ff*.
    c. *ff*.
    d. None of the above

ANS: B   DIF: II   OBJ: BPE 8-3.1

In rabbits, black fur (*B*) is dominant to brown fur (*b*). Consider the following cross between two rabbits.

Bb x Bb

	B	b
B	1	2
b	3	4

25. Refer to the illustration above. The device shown, which is used to determine the probable outcome of genetic crosses, is called a
    a. Mendelian box.
    b. Punnett square.
    c. genetic graph.
    d. phenotypic paradox.

ANS: B   DIF: II   OBJ: BPE 8-3.1

26. Refer to the illustration above. Both of the parents in the cross are
    a. black.
    b. brown.
    c. homozygous dominant.
    d. homozygous recessive.

ANS: A   DIF: II   OBJ: BPE 8-3.1

27. Refer to the illustration above. The phenotype of the offspring indicated by box 3 would be
    a. brown.
    b. black.
    c. a mixture of brown and black.
    d. None of the above

ANS: B   DIF: II   OBJ: BPE 8-3.1

28. Refer to the illustration above. The genotypic ratio of the F_1 generation would be
    a. 1:1.
    b. 3:1.
    c. 1:3.
    d. 1:2:1.

ANS: D   DIF: II   OBJ: BPE 8-3.1

29. What is the expected genotypic ratio resulting from a homozygous dominant × heterozygous monohybrid cross?
    a. 1:0
    b. 1:1
    c. 1:2:1
    d. 1:3:1

    ANS: B   DIF: II   OBJ: BPE 8-3.1

30. What is the expected genotypic ratio resulting from a heterozygous × heterozygous monohybrid cross?
    a. 1:2:1
    b. 1:3:1
    c. 1:2
    d. 1:0

    ANS: A   DIF: II   OBJ: BPE 8-3.1

31. What is the expected phenotypic ratio resulting from a homozygous dominant × heterozygous monohybrid cross?
    a. 1:3:1
    b. 1:2:1
    c. 2:1
    d. 1:0

    ANS: D   DIF: II   OBJ: BPE 8-3.1

32. The unknown genotype of an individual with a dominant phenotype can be determined using
    a. a ratio.
    b. a dihybrid cross.
    c. probability
    d. a test cross.

    ANS: D   DIF: I   OBJ: BPE 8-3.2

33. What is the probability that the offspring of a homozygous dominant individual and a homozygous recessive individual will exhibit the dominant phenotype?
    a. 0.25
    b. 0.5
    c. 0.66
    d. 1.0

    ANS: D   DIF: I   OBJ: BPE 8-3.3

34. A trait that occurs in 450 individuals out of a total of 1,800 individuals occurs with a probability of
    a. 0.04.
    b. 0.25.
    c. 0.50.
    d. 0.75.

    ANS: B   DIF: II   OBJ: BPE 8-3.3

35. If a characteristic is sex-linked, it
    a. occurs most commonly in males.
    b. occurs only in females.
    c. can never occur in females.
    d. is always fatal.

    ANS: A   DIF: I   OBJ: BPE 8-3.4

36. Since the allele for colorblindness is located on the X chromosome, colorblindness
    a. cannot be inherited.
    b. occurs only in adults.
    c. is sex-linked.
    d. None of the above

    ANS: C   DIF: I   OBJ: BPE 8-3.4

37. A diagram in which several generations of a family and the occurrence of certain genetic characteristics are shown is called a
    a. Punnett square.
    b. monohybrid cross.
    c. pedigree.
    d. family karyotype.

    ANS: C   DIF: I   OBJ: BPE 8-3.4

38. In humans, the risks of passing on a genetic disorder to offspring can be assessed by
    a. analysis of a pedigree.
    b. genetic counseling.
    c. prenatal testing.
    d. All of the above

    ANS: D   DIF: I   OBJ: BPE 8-3.4

39. How many different phenotypes can be produced by a pair of codominant alleles?
    a. 1
    b. 2
    c. 3
    d. 4

    ANS: C   DIF: II   OBJ: BPE 8-4.1

40. Which of the following traits is controlled by multiple alleles in humans?
    a. sickle cell anemia
    b. blood type
    c. hemophilia
    d. Huntington's disease

    ANS: B   DIF: I   OBJ: BPE 8-4.1

41. What would be the blood type of a person who inherited an *A* allele from one parent and an *O* allele from the other?
    a. type A
    b. type B
    c. type AB
    d. type O

    ANS: A   DIF: II   OBJ: BPE 8-4.1

42. A change in a gene due to damage or being copied incorrectly is called
    a. evolution.
    b. meiosis.
    c. segregation.
    d. a mutation.

    ANS: D   DIF: I   OBJ: BPE 8-4.2

43. Which of the following describes hemophilia?
    a. multiple-allele trait
    b. dominant trait
    c. sex-linked trait
    d. codominant trait

    ANS: C   DIF: I   OBJ: BPE 8-4.3

44. Both sickle-cell anemia and hemophilia
    a. are caused by genes coding for defective protein.
    b. are seen in homozygous dominant individuals.
    c. provide resistance to malaria infections.
    d. are extremely common throughout the world.

    ANS: A   DIF: I   OBJ: BPE 8-4.3

Biology: Principles and Explorations

45. Genetic counseling is a process that
   a. helps identify parents at risk for having children with genetic defects.
   b. assists parents in deciding whether or not to have children.
   c. uses a family pedigree.
   d. All of the above

   ANS: D   DIF: I   OBJ: BPE 8-4.4

46. Which of the following is an example of gene technology?
   a. A genetic counselor studies a pedigree.
   b. A student studies the colors of flowers in pea plants.
   c. A geneticist explains the inheritance of albinism using a Punnett square.
   d. A physician transfers a normal gene into the DNA of a person with a genetic disease.

   ANS: D   DIF: II   OBJ: BPE 8-4.4

COMPLETION

1. The patterns that Mendel discovered form the basis of _____, the branch of biology that deals with heredity.

   ANS: genetics   DIF: I   OBJ: BPE 8-1.1

2. The passing of traits from parents to offspring is called _____.

   ANS: heredity   DIF: I   OBJ: BPE 8-1.1

3. A reproductive process in which fertilization occurs within a single plant is
   _____ _____.

   ANS: self-pollination   DIF: I   OBJ: BPE 8-1.2

4. The transferring of pollen between plants is called _____
   _____.

   ANS: cross-pollination   DIF: I   OBJ: BPE 8-1.2

5. A(n) _____ cross is a cross that involves one pair of contrasting traits.

   ANS: monohybrid   DIF: I   OBJ: BPE 8-1.3

6. Mendel called the offspring of the P generation the _____ generation.

   ANS: F_1 DIF: I   OBJ: BPE 8-1.3

7. In Mendel's experiments, a trait that disappeared in the F_1 generation but reappeared in the F_2 generation was always a(n) _____ trait.

   ANS: recessive   DIF: II   OBJ: BPE 8-1.4

8. A trait that is not expressed in the F_1 generation resulting from the crossbreeding of two genetically different, true-breeding organisms is called _____.

ANS: recessive   DIF: I   OBJ: BPE 8-2.1

9. Different forms of a particular gene are called _____.

ANS: alleles   DIF: I   OBJ: BPE 8-2.1

10. In heterozygous individuals, only the _____ allele is expressed.

ANS: dominant   DIF: I   OBJ: BPE 8-2.2

11. An organism that has two identical alleles for a trait is called _____.

ANS: homozygous   DIF: I   OBJ: BPE 8-2.2

12. An organism's _____ refers to the set of alleles it has inherited.

ANS: genotype   DIF: I   OBJ: BPE 8-2.2

13. The external appearance of an organism is its _____.

ANS: phenotype   DIF: I   OBJ: BPE 8-2.2

14. The statement that the members of each pair of alleles separate when gametes are formed is known as the law of _____.

ANS: segregation   DIF: I   OBJ: BPE 8-2.3

15. The principle that states that alleles of different genes separate independently of one another during gamete formation is the law of _____ _____.

ANS: independent assortment   DIF: I   OBJ: BPE 8-2.3

In pea plants, tallness (*T*) is dominant to shortness (*t*). Crosses between plants with these traits can be analyzed using a Punnett square similar to the one shown below.

	T	t
T	1	2
t	3	4

16. Refer to the illustration above. The parents shown in the Punnett square could have offspring with a genotypic ratio of _____.

    ANS: 1:2:1   DIF: II   OBJ: BPE 8-3.1

17. Refer to the illustration above. Box 2 and box _____ in the Punnett square represent plants that would be heterozygous for the trait for tallness.

    ANS: 3   DIF: II   OBJ: BPE 8-3.1

18. Refer to the illustration above. The phenotype of the plant that would be represented in box 4 of the Punnett square would be _____.

    ANS: short   DIF: II   OBJ: BPE 8-3.1

19. Refer to the illustration above. The genotype of both parents shown in the Punnett square above is _____.

    ANS: *Tt*   DIF: II   OBJ: BPE 8-3.1

20. If some of the offspring of a test cross have the recessive trait, then the genotype of the individual being tested is _____.

    ANS: heterozygous   DIF: II   OBJ: BPE 8-3.1

21. The likelihood that a specific event will occur is called _____.

    ANS: probability   DIF: I   OBJ: BPE 8-3.3

22. A trait that is determined by a gene that is only found on the X chromosome is said to be _____ _____.

    ANS: sex-linked   DIF: I   OBJ: BPE 8-3.4

23. Identifying patterns of inheritance within a family over several generations is possible by studying a diagram called a(n) _____.

    ANS: pedigree   DIF: I   OBJ: BPE 8-3.4

24. A situation in which two or more alleles influence a phenotype is called
_____.

ANS: codominance   DIF: I   OBJ: BPE 8-4.1

25. A trait controlled by three or more alleles is said to have _____
_____.

ANS: multiple alleles   DIF: I   OBJ: BPE 8-4.1

26. A phenomenon in which a heterozygous individual has a phenotype that is intermediate between
the phenotypes of its two homozygous parents is called _____
_____.

ANS: incomplete dominance   DIF: I   OBJ: BPE 8-4.1

27. A change in an organism's DNA is called a(n) _____.

ANS: mutation   DIF: I   OBJ: BPE 8-4.2

28. A person who is heterozygous for a recessive disorder is called a(n) _____.

ANS: carrier   DIF: I   OBJ: BPE 8-4.2

29. A genetic disorder resulting in defective blood clotting is _____.

ANS: hemophilia   DIF: I   OBJ: BPE 8-4.3

30. Fragile blood cells with an irregular shape that may block blood vessels is a symptom of a
genetic disease known as _____ _____
_____.

ANS: sickle cell anemia   DIF: I   OBJ: BPE 8-4.3

31. _____ technology is making it possible to cure genetic disorders.

ANS: Gene   DIF: I   OBJ: BPE 8-4.4

PROBLEM

1. In tomato plants, tallness is dominant over dwarfness and hairy stems are dominant over hairless stems. True-breeding (homozygous) plants that are tall and have hairy stems are available. True-breeding (homozygous) plants that are dwarf and have hairless stems are also available. Design an experiment to determine whether the genes for height and hairiness of the stem are on the same or different chromosomes. Explain how you will be able to determine from the results whether the genes are on the same or different chromosomes. Write your answer in the space below.

ANS:

The experiment should be designed to produce F_1 plants that are then allowed to pollinate each others' flowers and produce an F_2 generation of plants. If the F_2 generation has four different phenotypes present in approximate proportions of 9/16 tall and hairy, 3/16 tall and hairless, 3/16 dwarf and hairy, and 1/16 dwarf and hairless then the student can conclude that the genes for height and hairiness are on different chromosomes. If the F_2 generation has only two different phenotypes present in approximate proportions of 3/4 tall and hairy and 1/4 dwarf and hairless then the student can conclude that the genes for height and hairiness are on the same chromosome. He could also conclude that the genes are located very close to each other on the chromosome. If the F_2 generation has four different phenotypes with the tall and hairless types composing less than 3/16 of the total number and the dwarf and hairy types composing less than 3/16 of the total number, then the student could conclude that the genes for height and hairiness are on the same chromosome but not located adjacent to each other.

DIF: III   OBJ: BPE 8-3.1

ESSAY

1. Briefly discuss the reasons that Mendel chose the pea plant, *Pisum sativum,* as the organism to study in his experiments.

ANS:

The pea plant, *Pisum sativum,* is an ideal organism for genetic studies for several reasons. There are a number of traits that are easily identified and tracked from generation to generation. Each of these traits has two forms, one of which regularly disappears and reappears in alternate generations. Also, this species is easy to grow and matures quickly. Finally, gametes of both sexes are found in the same flower, so cross-pollination is easy to accomplish by removing the anthers from some flowers and transferring pollen from others to the remaining pistils.

DIF: II   OBJ: BPE 8-1.2

2. Describe pollination in pea plants.

   ANS:
   The reproductive structures of seed plants are located inside the flowers. In pea plants, each flower has both male and female structures. The male reproductive parts, the anthers, produce pollen grains that contain sperm. The female reproductive structure produces the egg. The tip of the female structure is called the stigma. Pollination is the transfer of pollen from anthers to stigma.

   DIF: II   OBJ: BPE 8-1.2

3. In what ways did Mendel's methods help ensure his success in unraveling the mechanics of heredity?

   ANS:
   Mendel's choice of plants to study was fortunate since pea plants displayed several traits in contrasting forms. His use of large numbers of samples allowed the gathering of statistically significant amounts of data. In addition, he kept very careful records and used logical, orderly methods that minimized the possibility of errors.

   DIF: II   OBJ: BPE 8-1.3

4. Describe how genotype and phenotype are related.

   ANS:
   The genetic makeup of an organism is its genotype. The external appearance of an organism is its phenotype. The phenotype of an organism is determined to a large degree by the genotype of the organism. Environmental factors and other factors can influence the phenotype of an organism.

   DIF: II   OBJ: BPE 8-2.2

5. Explain what is meant by homozygous and heterozygous.

   ANS:
   When both alleles of a pair are the same, an organism is said to be homozygous for that characteristic. An organism may be homozygous dominant or homozygous recessive. A pea plant that is homozygous dominant for height will have the genotype TT. A pea plant that is homozygous recessive for height will have the genotype tt. When the two alleles in the pair are not the same—for example, when the genotype is Tt—the organism is heterozygous for that characteristic.

   DIF: II   OBJ: BPE 8-2.2

6. What hypotheses did Gregor Mendel develop based on his observations of pea plants?

ANS:
1. For each inherited trait, an individual has two copies of the gene—one from each parent.
2. There are alternative versions of genes (which Mendel called factors).
3. When two different alleles occur together, one of them may be completely expressed, while the other may have no observable effect on the organism's appearance.
4. When gametes are formed, the alleles for each gene in an individual separate independently of one another. Thus, gametes carry only one allele for each inherited trait. When gametes unite during fertilization, each gamete contributes one allele.

DIF: II   OBJ: BPE 8-2.3

7. Describe Mendel's principle of independent assortment.

ANS:
From his work on pea plants, Mendel concluded that factors for different characteristics are not connected. He stated the principle of independent assortment: Factors for different characteristics are distributed to reproductive cells independently.

DIF: II   OBJ: BPE 8-2.3

8. What are three ways to express the probability of an event that occurs 500 times out of 2,000 total trials?

ANS:
The general formula for probability is $\dfrac{\text{number of one kind of event}}{\text{number of all events}}$

This may be expressed as a ratio ($\dfrac{500}{2,000}$, or $\dfrac{1}{4}$), as a decimal (0.25), or as a percentage (25 percent).

DIF: II   OBJ: BPE 8-3.3

9. In humans, colorblindness is a recessive, sex-linked trait. What is the likelihood that the children of a woman heterozygous for colorblindness and a man with normal color vision will be colorblind? Explain your answer.

ANS:
Since all the female offspring receive the normal allele for vision from the father, all female offspring will have normal color vision, although half of them will receive the recessive allele from the mother and thus be carriers. Since all of the male offspring receive the Y chromosome from the father, it is the X chromosome they receive from the mother that will determine whether or not they are colorblind. Since the mother is heterozygous, male offspring will have a 50 percent chance of being colorblind.

DIF: II   OBJ: BPE 8-3.4

10. Discuss the inheritance pattern that would be seen in a pedigree designed to study a recessive sex-linked characteristic.

ANS:
Sex-linked characteristics are carried on alleles on the X chromosome. As a result, sex-linked recessive traits are rarely seen in a female, unless she is the offspring of an affected male and a female who is a carrier or is affected. Males born to a female who is either a carrier or affected may inherit the sex-linked allele. If the female is affected, both of her X chromosomes will possess the gene under study and the male is sure to inherit it. If she is a carrier, only one of her X chromosomes will possess the sex-linked allele and the male will have a 50-50 chance of inheriting this gene. Since the male has only one X chromosome, he will not have a dominant allele in his genotype to counteract the effect of the sex-linked allele.

DIF: II   OBJ: BPE 8-3.4

11. Describe what is meant by multiple alleles, and give an example.

ANS:
Some traits are determined by more than two alleles. When three or more alleles control a trait, it is said to have multiple alleles. For example, the trait of blood type in humans is determined by multiple alleles.

DIF: II   OBJ: BPE 8-4.1

12. All of the offspring resulting from a cross between a red snapdragon and a white snapdragon are pink. What is the possible explanation for this?

ANS:
Incomplete dominance is the phenomenon that occurs when two or more alleles influence a phenotype. In other words, the offspring displays a trait that is intermediate to a trait exhibited by each parent.

DIF: II   OBJ: BPE 8-4.1

TRUE/FALSE

1. Even though they contain weakened or killed infectious organisms, vaccines can still cause an immune response when injected into an organism.

   ANS: T   DIF: I   OBJ: BPE 9-1.1

2. Even though Avery's experiments clearly indicated that genetic material is composed of DNA, most scientists at that time continued to suspect that proteins were the genetic material.

   ANS: T   DIF: I   OBJ: BPE 9-1.2

3. Most scientists at that time agreed with Avery's experiments because of their extensive knowledge of DNA.

   ANS: F   DIF: I   OBJ: BPE 9-1.2

4. It has been discovered that proteins are the genetic material, rather than DNA, because proteins are more complex than DNA.

   ANS: F   DIF: I   OBJ: BPE 9-1.3

5. Bacteriophage are a type of bacteria that infects viruses.

   ANS: F   DIF: I   OBJ: BPE 9-1.3

6. Hershey and Chase were the first two scientists to prove that genetic material is composed of proteins.

   ANS: F   DIF: I   OBJ: BPE 9-1.3

7. The five-carbon sugar in DNA nucleotides is called ribose.

   ANS: F   DIF: I   OBJ: BPE 9-2.1

8. A nucleotide consists of a sugar, a phosphate group, and a nitrogen base.

   ANS: T   DIF: I   OBJ: BPE 9-2.1

9. Despite years of research, the actual structure of the DNA molecule is still unknown.

   ANS: F   DIF: I   OBJ: BPE 9-2.2

10. Franklin's X-ray diffraction images suggested that the DNA molecule resembled a tightly coiled spring, a shape called a helix.

    ANS: T   DIF: I   OBJ: BPE 9-2.3

11. Chargaff observed that the amount of adenine in an organism always equaled the amount of thymine.

   ANS: T   DIF: I   OBJ: BPE 9-2.3

12. Wilkins and Franklin were the first to suggest that the DNA molecule resembled a tightly coiled helix.

   ANS: T   DIF: I   OBJ: BPE 9-2.3

13. The strands of a DNA molecule are held together by hydrogen bonding between adenine with guanine molecules and cytosine with thymine molecules.

   ANS: F   DIF: I   OBJ: BPE 9-2.4

14. In all living things, DNA replication must occur after cell division.

   ANS: F   DIF: I   OBJ: BPE 9-3.1

15. After replication, the nucleotide sequences in both DNA molecules are identical to each other and to the original DNA molecule.

   ANS: T   DIF: I   OBJ: BPE 9-3.1

16. No two nucleotide sequences in DNA molecules are ever the same.

   ANS: F   DIF: I   OBJ: BPE 9-3.1

17. Before a DNA molecule can replicate itself, it must make itself more compact. This is accomplished by the double helix coiling up on itself.

   ANS: F   DIF: I   OBJ: BPE 9-3.1

18. Helicases unwind the double helix of DNA by breaking the nitrogen bonds that link the hydrogen bases.

   ANS: F   DIF: I   OBJ: BPE 9-3.1

19. The two areas on either end of the DNA where the double helix separates are called replication forks.

   ANS: T   DIF: I   OBJ: BPE 9-3.1

20. DNA polymerases have the ability to check for errors in nucleotide pairings.

   ANS: T   DIF: I   OBJ: BPE 9-3.2

21. Typically, during replication only one error occurs for every 10,000 nucleotides.

    ANS: F   DIF: I   OBJ: BPE 9-3.2

22. Errors in nucleotide sequencing that occur during replication cannot be corrected.

    ANS: F   DIF: I   OBJ: BPE 9-3.2

23. Multiple replication forks tend to slow down replication.

    ANS: F   DIF: I   OBJ: BPE 9-3.3

MULTIPLE CHOICE

1. A vaccine is
   a. a substance that kills bacteria or viruses.
   b. an antibody.
   c. a plasmid that contains disease-causing genes.
   d. a harmless version of a disease-causing microbe.

   ANS: D   DIF: I   OBJ: BPE 9-1.1

2. Griffith's transformation experiments
   a. changed proteins into DNA.
   b. caused non-harmful bacteria to become deadly.
   c. resulted in DNA molecules becoming proteins.
   d. were designed to show the effect of heat on bacteria.

   ANS: B   DIF: I   OBJ: BPE 9-1.1

3. Griffith's experiments showed that
   a. dead bacteria could be brought back to life.
   b. harmful bacteria were hardier than harmless bacteria.
   c. heat caused the harmful and harmless varieties of bacteria to fuse.
   d. genetic material could be transferred between dead bacteria and living bacteria.

   ANS: D   DIF: I   OBJ: BPE 9-1.1

4. Avery's experiments showed that transformation
   a. is prevented by protein-destroying enzymes.
   b. is prevented by DNA-destroying enzymes.
   c. causes protein to become DNA.
   d. is caused by a protein.

   ANS: B   DIF: I   OBJ: BPE 9-1.2

5. Oswald Avery and his research team concluded that
   a. RNA was the genetic material.
   b. protein bases were the genetic material.
   c. DNA and RNA were found in the human nucleus.
   d. DNA was the genetic material.

   ANS: D   DIF: I   OBJ: BPE 9-1.2

6. Using radioactive tracers to determine the interactions of bacteriophages and their host bacteria, Hershey and Chase demonstrated without question that
   a. genes are composed of protein molecules.
   b. DNA and proteins are actually the same molecules located in different parts of cells.
   c. bacteria inject their DNA into the cytoplasm of bacteriophages.
   d. DNA is the molecule that stores genetic information in cells.

   ANS: D   DIF: I   OBJ: BPE 9-1.3

7. All of the following are true of the viruses Hershey and Chase used in their study *except*
   a. they consisted of DNA surrounded by a protein coat.
   b. they injected their DNA into cells.
   c. they destroyed the DNA of the infected bacteria.
   d. they caused infected bacteria to make many new viruses.

   ANS: C   DIF: I   OBJ: BPE 9-1.3

8. The scientist who worked with Martha Chase to prove that genetic material is composed of DNA was
   a. Alfred Hershey.   c. Francis Crick.
   b. Oswald Avery.   d. Rosalind Franklin.

   ANS: A   DIF: I   OBJ: BPE 9-1.3

9. All of the following are true about the structure of DNA except
   a. short strands of DNA are contained in chromosomes inside the nucleus of a cell.
   b. every DNA nucleotide contains a sugar, a phosphate group, and a nitrogen base.
   c. DNA consists of two strands of nucleotides joined by hydrogen bonds.
   d. the long strands of nucleotides are twisted into a double helix.

   ANS: A   DIF: I   OBJ: BPE 9-2.1

10. Molecules of DNA are composed of long chains of
    a. amino acids.   c. monosaccharides.
    b. fatty acids.   d. nucleotides.

    ANS: D   DIF: I   OBJ: BPE 9-2.1

11. Which of the following is *not* part of a molecule of DNA?
    a. deoxyribose   c. phosphate
    b. nitrogen base   d. ribose

    ANS: D   DIF: I   OBJ: BPE 9-2.1

12. A nucleotide consists of
    a. a sugar, a protein, and adenine.
    b. a sugar, an amino acid, and starch.
    c. a sugar, a phosphate group, and a nitrogen base.
    d. a starch, a phosphate group, and a nitrogen base.

    ANS: C   DIF: I   OBJ: BPE 9-2.1

13. The part of the molecule for which deoxyribonucleic acid is named is the
    a. phosphate group.   c. nitrogen base.
    b. sugar.   d. None of the above

    ANS: B   DIF: I   OBJ: BPE 9-2.1

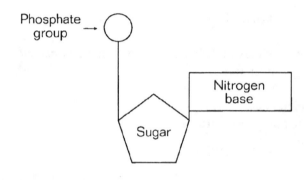

14. The entire molecule shown in the diagram is called a(n)
    a. amino acid.   c. polysaccharide.
    b. nucleotide.   d. pyrimidine.

    ANS: B   DIF: II   OBJ: BPE 9-2.1

15. Purines and pyrimidines are
    a. nitrogen bases found in amino acids.
    b. able to replace phosphate groups from defective DNA.
    c. names of specific types of DNA molecules.
    d. classification groups for nitrogen bases.

    ANS: D   DIF: I   OBJ: BPE 9-2.1

16. Of the four nitrogen bases in DNA, which two are purines and which two are pyrimidines?
    a. adenine—thymine; uracil—cytosine   c. adenine—guanine; thymine—cytosine
    b. adenine—thymine; guanine—cytosine   d. uracil—thymine; guanine—cytosine

    ANS: B   DIF: I   OBJ: BPE 9-2.1

17. Watson and Crick built models that demonstrated that
    a. DNA and RNA have the same structure.
    b. DNA is made of two strands that twist into a double helix.
    c. guanine forms hydrogen bonds with adenine.
    d. thymine forms hydrogen bonds with cytosine.

    ANS: B   DIF: I   OBJ: BPE 9-2.3

18. The scientists credited with establishing the structure of DNA are
    a. Avery and Chargaff.   c. Mendel and Griffith.
    b. Hershey and Chase.   d. Watson and Crick.

    ANS: D   DIF: I   OBJ: BPE 9-2.3

19. X-ray diffraction photographs by Wilkins and Franklin suggested that
    a. DNA and RNA are the same molecules.
    b. DNA is composed of either purines or pyrimidines, but not both.
    c. DNA molecules are arranged as a tightly coiled helix.
    d. DNA and proteins have the same basic structure.

    ANS: C   DIF: I   OBJ: BPE 9-2.3

20. Watson and Crick : DNA
    a. Avery : nucleotides   c. Wilkins and Franklin : DNA
    b. Hershey and Chase : protein d. Chargaff : X-rays

    ANS: C
    (studied)

    DIF: II   OBJ: BPE 9-2.3

21. The amount of guanine in an organism always equals the amount of
    a. protein.   c. adenine.
    b. thymine.   d. cytosine.

    ANS: D   DIF: I   OBJ: BPE 9-2.4

22. During DNA replication, a complementary strand of DNA is made for each original DNA strand. Thus, if a portion of the original strand is CCTAGCT, then the new strand will be
    a. TTGCATG.   c. CCTAGCT.
    b. AAGTATC.   d. GGATCGA.

    ANS: D   DIF: II   OBJ: BPE 9-2.4

23. adenine : thymine
    a. protein : DNA   c. guanine : cytosine
    b. Watson : Crick   d. adenine : DNA

    ANS: C
    (forms a base-pair with)

    DIF: II   OBJ: BPE 9-2.4

24. The attachment of nucleotides to form a complementary strand of DNA
    a. is accomplished by DNA polymerase.
    b. is accomplished only in the presence of tRNA.
    c. prevents separation of complementary strands of RNA.
    d. is the responsibility of the complementary DNA mutagens.

    ANS: A   DIF: I   OBJ: BPE 9-3.1

25. Which of the following is *not* true about DNA replication?
    a. It must occur before a cell can divide.
    b. Two complementary strands are duplicated.
    c. The double strand unwinds and unzips while it is being duplicated.
    d. The process is catalyzed by enzymes called DNA mutagens.

    ANS: D   DIF: I   OBJ: BPE 9-3.1

26. The enzymes responsible for adding nucleotides to the exposed DNA template bases are
    a. replicases.   c. helicases.
    b. DNA polymerases.   d. None of the above

    ANS: B   DIF: I   OBJ: BPE 9-3.1

27. The enzymes that unwind DNA are called
    a. double helixes.   c. forks.
    b. DNA helicases.   d. phages.

    ANS: B   DIF: I   OBJ: BPE 9-3.1

COMPLETION

1. A(n) _____ is a harmless version of a disease-causing microbe that can stimulate a person's immune system to ward off infection by the infectious form of the microbe.

    ANS: vaccine   DIF: I   OBJ: BPE 9-1.1

2. Griffith's experiment showed that live bacteria without capsules acquired the ability to make capsules from dead bacteria with capsules in a process Griffith called _____.

    ANS: transformation   DIF: I   OBJ: BPE 9-1.1

3. The ability of a microorganism to cause disease is referred to as its _____.

    ANS: virulence   DIF: I   OBJ: BPE 9-1.1

4. Avery's prevention of transformation using DNA-destroying enzymes provided evidence that _____ molecules function as the hereditary material.

    ANS: DNA   DIF: I   OBJ: BPE 9-1.2

5. Viruses that infect bacteria are called _____.

   ANS: bacteriophages   DIF: I   OBJ: BPE 9-1.3

6. A DNA subunit composed of a phosphate group, a five-carbon sugar, and a nitrogen-containing base is called a(n) _____.

   ANS: nucleotide   DIF: I   OBJ: BPE 9-2.1

7. The name of the five-carbon sugar that makes up a part of the backbone of molecules of DNA is _____.

   ANS: deoxyribose   DIF: I   OBJ: BPE 9-2.1

8. Watson and Crick determined that DNA molecules have the shape of a(n) _____ _____.

   ANS: double helix   DIF: I   OBJ: BPE 9-2.2

9. Chargaff's observations established the _____ _____ rules, which describe the specific pairing between bases on DNA strands.

   ANS: base pairing   DIF: I   OBJ: BPE 9-2.3

10. Watson and Crick used the X-ray _____ photographs of Wilkins and Franklin to build their model of DNA.

   ANS: diffraction   DIF: I   OBJ: BPE 9-2.3

11. Due to the strict pairing of nitrogen bases in DNA molecules, the two strands are said to be _____ to each other.

   ANS: complementary   DIF: I   OBJ: BPE 9-2.3

12. The process by which DNA copies itself is called _____.

   ANS: replication   DIF: I   OBJ: BPE 9-3.1

13. The enzyme that is responsible for replicating molecules of DNA by attaching complementary bases in the correct sequence is called _____ _____.

   ANS: DNA polymerase   DIF: I   OBJ: BPE 9-3.1

14. Enzymes called _____ are responsible for unwinding the DNA double helix by breaking the hydrogen bonds that hold the complementary strands together.

   ANS: helicases   DIF: I   OBJ: BPE 9-3.1

15. Errors in nucleotide sequences are called _____.

ANS: mutations DIF: I OBJ: BPE 9-3.2

16. Errors in nucleotide sequencing are corrected by enzymes called _____ _____.

ANS: DNA polymerases DIF: I OBJ: BPE 9-3.2

17. The circular DNA molecules in prokaryotes usually contain _____ replicatio forks during replication, while linear eukaryotic DNA contains many more.

ANS: two DIF: I OBJ: BPE 9-3.3

ESSAY

1. Briefly summarize the highlights of the experiments performed by Hershey and Chase that indicated that DNA was probably the genetic material.

ANS:
Hershey and Chase used radioactive labeling methods to tag bacteriophage DNA with 32P and the bacteriophage coat proteins with 35S. They found that the bacteriophages injected the DNA into their host bacterial cells, but that the protein remained on the outside of the cell. It was observed that the genetic material—the DNA—was incorporated into the DNA of the bacteria and provided the code for the production of more phage particles, while the protein was not involved in phage reproduction.

DIF: II OBJ: BPE 9-1.3

2. The DNA molecule is described as a double helix. Describe the meaning of this expression and the general structure of a DNA molecule.

ANS:
DNA molecules are composed of two complementary strands of nucleotides arranged in a patte resembling a spiral staircase. Each nucleotide consists of a sugar molecule, a phosphate group, and one of four possible bases. The double helix arrangement is maintained by the formation of hydrogen bonds between complementary bases. Within the base pair adenine and thymine, as well as within the base pair guanine and cytosine, equal numbers of molecules are present.

DIF: II OBJ: BPE 9-2.2

3. Describe how a molecule of DNA is replicated.

ANS:
To begin the replication process, enzymes called helicases break the hydrogen bonds that hold the two complementary strands of the DNA double helix together, allowing the helix to unwind. The complementary strands are held apart by additional protein molecules. At the replication fork, the point at which the double helix separates, a molecule of DNA polymerase attaches and begins to add nucleotides to the exposed bases according to the base-pairing rules. This continues until the DNA polymerase reaches a nucleotide sequence that signals it to detach, having completed the replication of the DNA strand.

DIF: II   OBJ: BPE 9-3.1

4. How does the number of replication forks in the DNA of prokaryotic cells differ from the the number of replication forks in the DNA of eukaryotic cells?

ANS:
The circular DNA molecules in prokaryotes usually have two replication forks that begin at a single point. In eukaryotic cells, multiple replication forks enable the genome to be replicated quickly.

DIF: II   OBJ: BPE 9-3.3

TRUE/FALSE

1. RNA nucleotides contain the five-carbon sugar ribose.

   ANS: T   DIF: I   OBJ: BPE 10-1.1

2. Only DNA molecules contain the nitrogen base called uracil.

   ANS: F   DIF: I   OBJ: BPE 10-1.1

3. During transcription, the information on a DNA molecule is "rewritten" into an mRNA molecule.

   ANS: T   DIF: I   OBJ: BPE 10-1.2

4. A codon signifies either a specific amino acid or a stop signal.

   ANS: T   DIF: I   OBJ: BPE 10-1.3

5. When a tRNA anticodon binds to an mRNA codon, the amino acid detaches from the tRNA molecule and attaches to the end of a growing protein chain.

   ANS: T   DIF: I   OBJ: BPE 10-1.4

6. Only ribosomal RNA plays a role in translation.

   ANS: F   DIF: I   OBJ: BPE 10-1.4

7. The genetic code is different in nearly all organisms.

   ANS: F   DIF: I   OBJ: BPE 10-1.4

8. It has been discovered that each species of organism has its own unique genetic code for synthesis of its proteins.

   ANS: F   DIF: I   OBJ: BPE 10-1.5

9. Cells regulate gene expression so that each gene will only be transcribed when it is needed.

   ANS: T   DIF: I   OBJ: BPE 10-2.1

10. The operator portion of the *lac* operon controls RNA polymerase's access to lactose-metabolizing genes.

    ANS: T   DIF: I   OBJ: BPE 10-2.1

11. Gene expression is prevented when a repressor binds to the group of genes involved in the same function.

ANS: F　　　　　　DIF: I　　　　　OBJ: BPE 10-2.1

12. A repressor binds to the operator region when lactose is present.

ANS: F　　　　　　DIF: I　　　　　OBJ: BPE 10-2.1

13. Repressor proteins are bound to the DNA in front of each gene, readily allowing transcription to take place as the RNA polymerase moves along that gene.

ANS: F　　　　　　DIF: I　　　　　OBJ: BPE 10-2.1

14. An enhancer is a sequence of nucleotides that, when activated by specific signal proteins, aids in shielding the RNA polymerase binding site of a specific gene.

ANS: F　　　　　　DIF: I　　　　　OBJ: BPE 10-2.2

15. When mRNA leaves the nucleus and enters the cytoplasm, it has a complete set of both introns and exons.

ANS: F　　　　　　DIF: I　　　　　OBJ: BPE 10-2.3

16. Introns are deleted before a gene is transcribed from DNA into mRNA.

ANS: F　　　　　　DIF: I　　　　　OBJ: BPE 10-2.3

17. Introns are the portions of a gene that actually get translated into protein.

ANS: F　　　　　　DIF: I　　　　　OBJ: BPE 10-2.3

18. A point mutation is the failure of a chromosome pair to separate during mitosis.

ANS: F　　　　　　DIF: I　　　　　OBJ: BPE 10-2.4

19. Mutations that result from the substitution of one nitrogen base for another are called deletions.

ANS: F　　　　　　DIF: I　　　　　OBJ: BPE 10-2.4

MULTIPLE CHOICE

1. RNA differs from DNA in that RNA
   a. is single-stranded.
   b. contains a different sugar molecule.
   c. contains the nitrogen base uracil.
   d. All of the above

ANS: D　　　　　　DIF: I　　　　　OBJ: BPE 10-1.1

2. Which of the following is *not* found in DNA?
   a. adenine
   b. cytosine
   c. uracil
   d. None of the above

   ANS: C   DIF: I   OBJ: BPE 10-1.1

3. RNA is chemically similar to DNA except that its sugars have an additional oxygen atom, and the base thymine is replaced by a structurally similar base called
   a. uracil.
   b. alanine.
   c. cytosine.
   d. codon.

   ANS: A   DIF: I   OBJ: BPE 10-1.1

4. In RNA molecules, adenine is complementary to
   a. cytosine.
   b. guanine.
   c. thymine.
   d. uracil.

   ANS: D   DIF: I   OBJ: BPE 10-1.1

5. The function of rRNA is to
   a. synthesize DNA.
   b. synthesize mRNA.
   c. form ribosomes.
   d. transfer amino acids to ribosomes.

   ANS: C   DIF: I   OBJ: BPE 10-1.2

6. During transcription,
   a. proteins are synthesized.
   b. DNA is replicated.
   c. RNA is produced.
   d. translation occurs.

   ANS: C   DIF: I   OBJ: BPE 10-1.2

7. During transcription, the genetic information for making a protein is "rewritten" as a molecule o
   a. messenger RNA.
   b. ribosomal RNA.
   c. transfer RNA.
   d. translation RNA.

   ANS: A   DIF: I   OBJ: BPE 10-1.2

8. Transcription proceeds when RNA polymerase
   a. attaches to a ribosome.
   b. binds to a strand of DNA.
   c. binds to a strand of RNA.
   d. attaches to a promoter molecule.

   ANS: B   DIF: I   OBJ: BPE 10-1.2

9. Transcription is the process by which genetic information encoded in DNA is transferred to a(n)
   a. RNA molecule.
   b. DNA molecule.
   c. uracil molecule.
   d. transposon.

   ANS: A   DIF: I   OBJ: BPE 10-1.2

10. repressor : operator::
    a. promoter : RNA polymerase
    b. promoter : DNA
    c. terminator : RNA polymerase
    d. terminator : DNA

    ANS: C
    (blocks or stops the action of)

    DIF: II   OBJ: BPE 10-1.2

11. Each nucleotide triplet in mRNA that specifies a particular amino acid is called a(n)
    a. mutagen.
    b. codon.
    c. anticodon.
    d. exon.

    ANS: B   DIF: I   OBJ: BPE 10-1.3

Use the diagram below of a strand of an mRNA and the genetic code shown there to answer the following questions:

mRNA: CUCAAGUGCUUC

Genetic Code:

	U	C	A	G	
U	Phe	Ser	Tyr	Cys	U
	Phe	Ser	Tyr	Cys	C
	Leu	Ser	stop	stop	A
	Leu	Ser	stop	Trp	G
C	Leu	Pro	His	Arg	U
	Leu	Pro	His	Arg	C
	Leu	Pro	Gln	Arg	A
	Leu	Pro	Gln	Arg	G
A	Ile	Thr	Asn	Ser	U
	Ile	Thr	Asn	Ser	C
	Ile	Thr	Lys	Arg	A
	Met	Thr	Lys	Arg	G
G	Val	Ala	Asp	Gly	U
	Val	Ala	Asp	Gly	C
	Val	Ala	Glu	Gly	A
	Val	Ala	Glu	Gly	G

12. Refer to the illustration above. What is the portion of the protein molecule coded for by the piece of mRNA shown in the diagram?
    a. Ser—Tyr—Arg—Gly
    b. Val—Asp—Pro—His
    c. Leu—Lys—Cys—Phe
    d. Pro—Glu—Leu—Val

    ANS: C   DIF: II   OBJ: BPE 10-1.3

13. Refer to the illustration above. The anticodons for the codons in the mRNA in the diagram are
    a. GAG—UUC—ACG—AAG.
    b. GAG—TTC—ACG—AAG.
    c. CUC—GAA—CGU—CUU.
    d. CUU—CGU—GAA—CUC.

    ANS: A   DIF: II   OBJ: BPE 10-1.3

Biology: Principles and Explorations
Copyright © by Holt, Rinehart and Winston. All rights reserved.
135

14. Which of the following would represent the strand of DNA from which the mRNA strand in the diagram was made?
   a. CUCAAGUGCUUC
   b. GAGUUCACGAAG
   c. GAGTTCACGAAG
   d. AGACCTGTAGGA

ANS: C   DIF: II   OBJ: BPE 10-1.4

mRNA codons	amino acid
UAU, UAC	tyrosine
CCU, CCC, CCA, CCG	proline
GAU, GAC	aspartic acid
AUU, AUC, AUA	isoleucine
UGU, UGC	cysteine

15. Suppose that you are given a protein containing the following sequence of amino acids: tyrosine, proline, aspartic acid, isoleucine, and cysteine. Use the portion of the genetic code given above to determine which of the possible answers contains a DNA sequence that codes for this amino acid sequence.
   a. AUGGGUCUAUAUACG
   b. ATGGGTCTATATACG
   c. GCAAACTCGCGCGTA
   d. ATAGGGCTTTAAACA

ANS: B   DIF: III   OBJ: BPE 10-1.3

16. Each of the following is a type of RNA *except*
   a. carrier RNA.
   b. messenger RNA.
   c. ribosomal RNA.
   d. transfer RNA.

ANS: A   DIF: I   OBJ: BPE 10-1.4

17. At the very beginning of translation, the first tRNA molecule
   a. binds to the ribosome's A site.
   b. attaches directly to the DNA codon.
   c. connects an amino acid to its anticodon.
   d. attaches to the P site of the ribosome.

ANS: D   DIF: I   OBJ: BPE 10-1.4

18. A ribosome has
   a. one binding site for DNA.
   b. three binding sites used during translation.
   c. four binding sites for tRNA.
   d. no binding sites since the proteins must detach.

ANS: B   DIF: I   OBJ: BPE 10-1.4

19. Transfer RNA
    a. carries an amino acid to its correct codon.
    b. synthesizes amino acids as they are needed.
    c. produces codons to match the correct anticodons.
    d. converts DNA into mRNA.

    ANS: A   DIF: I   OBJ: BPE 10-1.4

20. In order for protein synthesis to occur, mRNA must migrate to the
    a. ribosomes.   c. RNA polymerase.
    b. *lac* operon.   d. heterochromatin.

    ANS: A   DIF: I   OBJ: BPE 10-1.4

21. mRNA : nucleus::
    a. nucleus : protein   c. nucleus : ribosomes
    b. protein : cytoplasm   d. protein : nucleus

    ANS: B
    (is made in the)

    DIF: II   OBJ: BPE 10-1.4

22. A site : tRNA::
    a. codon : mRNA   c. tRNA : amino acid
    b. mRNA : amino acid   d. mRNA : P site

    ANS: C
    (holds)

    DIF: II   OBJ: BPE 10-1.4

23. codon : mRNA::
    a. P site : RNA molecules   c. DNA : protein
    b. ribosome : DNA molecules   d. anticodon : tRNA

    ANS: D
    (is made of)

    DIF: II   OBJ: BPE 10-1.4

24. During translation, the amino acid detaches from the transfer RNA molecule and attaches to the
    end of a growing protein chain when
    a. the ribosomal RNA anticodon binds to the messenger RNA codon.
    b. the transfer RNA anticodon binds to the messenger RNA codon.
    c. a "stop" codon is encountered.
    d. the protein chain sends a signal through the nerve cells to the brain.

    ANS: B   DIF: I   OBJ: BPE 10-1.4

Biology: Principles and Explorations

25. In bacteria, a group of genes that code for functionally related enzymes, their promoter site, and the operator that controls them all function together as a(n)
   a. exon.
   b. intron.
   c. operon.
   d. ribosome.

   ANS: C   DIF: I   OBJ: BPE 10-2.1

26. The function of an operator is to
   a. regulate access of RNA polymerase to specific genes.
   b. turn on and off the molecules of tRNA.
   c. control the process of transcription within the nucleus.
   d. generate amino acids for protein synthesis.

   ANS: A   DIF: I   OBJ: BPE 10-2.1

27. Cells must control gene expression so that
   a. their genes will only be expressed when needed.
   b. their genes will always be expressed.
   c. their genes will never be expressed.
   d. genetic disorders can be corrected.

   ANS: A   DIF: I   OBJ: BPE 10-2.1

28. A repressor protein
   a. prevents DNA synthesis.
   b. blocks movement of RNA polymerase.
   c. attaches to ribosomes during translation.
   d. destroys amino acids before protein synthesis occurs.

   ANS: B   DIF: I   OBJ: BPE 10-2.1

29. The presence of a repressor molecule prevents the action of what enzyme?
   a. DNA polymerase
   b. lactase
   c. RNA polymerase
   d. permease

   ANS: C   DIF: I   OBJ: BPE 10-2.1

30. Refer to the illustration above. To which portion of the *lac* operon does the repressor bind?
   a. regulator
   b. B
   c. C
   d. D

   ANS: C   DIF: II   OBJ: BPE 10-2.1

31. Refer to the illustration above. Where on the *lac* operon does transcription take place?
    a. regulator
    b. B
    c. C
    d. D

    ANS: D   DIF: II   OBJ: BPE 10-2.1

32. Where on the *lac* operon does a repressor molecule bind when lactose is absent?
    a. to the operator
    b. to the promoter
    c. to a structural gene
    d. to the regulator

    ANS: A   DIF: I   OBJ: BPE 10-2.1

33. The *lac* operon is shut off when
    a. lactose is present.
    b. lactose is absent.
    c. glucose is present.
    d. glucose is absent.

    ANS: B   DIF: I   OBJ: BPE 10-2.1

34. Transcription factors are
    a. enhancers.
    b. promoters.
    c. regulatory proteins.
    d. None of the above

    ANS: C   DIF: I   OBJ: BPE 10-2.2

35. The portions of DNA molecules that actually code for the production of proteins are called
    a. mutons.
    b. exons.
    c. introns.
    d. exposons.

    ANS: B   DIF: I   OBJ: BPE 10-2.3

36. The non-coding portions of DNA that are separated from the portions of DNA actually used during transcription are called
    a. mutons.
    b. exons.
    c. introns.
    d. exposons.

    ANS: C   DIF: I   OBJ: BPE 10-2.3

37. Many biologists believe that having the genes of eukaryotic cells interrupted by introns
    a. prevents the code from being copied.
    b. causes severely damaging mutations.
    c. ensures that replication occurs correctly.
    d. provides evolutionary flexibility.

    ANS: D   DIF: I   OBJ: BPE 10-2.3

38. Many thousands of proteins may have arisen from only a few thousand exons because
    a. an exon may be used by many different genes.
    b. there really is no difference between one protein and another.
    c. an exon does not actually code for any meaningful information.
    d. one gene can code for hundreds of different proteins.

    ANS: A   DIF: I   OBJ: BPE 10-2.3

COMPLETION

1. The nitrogen-containing base that is only found in RNA is _____.

   ANS: uracil   DIF: I   OBJ: BPE 10-1.1

2. The enzyme responsible for making RNA is called _____ _____.

   ANS: RNA polymerase   DIF: I   OBJ: BPE 10-1.2

3. A(n) _____ is a sequence of DNA at the beginning of a gene that signals RNA polymerase to begin transcription.

   ANS: promoter   DIF: I   OBJ: BPE 10-1.2

4. Messenger RNA is produced during the process of _____.

   ANS: transcription   DIF: I   OBJ: BPE 10-1.2

5. Transcription and translation are stages in the process of _____ _____.

   ANS: gene expression   DIF: I   OBJ: BPE 10-1.2

6. The first stage of gene expression is called _____.

   ANS: transcription   DIF: I   OBJ: BPE 10-1.2

7. In eukaryotes, gene expression is related to the coiling and uncoiling of _____.

   ANS: DNA   DIF: I   OBJ: BPE 10-1.2

8. During translation, amino acids are brought to the ribosomes by molecules of _____ _____.

   ANS: transfer RNA   DIF: I   OBJ: BPE 10-1.2

9. Nucleotide sequences of tRNA that are complementary to codons on mRNA are called _____.

   ANS: anticodons   DIF: I   OBJ: BPE 10-1.3

10. The sequence of three nucleotides that code for specific amino acids or stop signals in the synthesis of protein is called a(n) _____.

    ANS: codon   DIF: I   OBJ: BPE 10-1.3

11. The information contained in a molecule of messenger RNA is used to make protein during the process of _____.

    ANS: translation   DIF: I   OBJ: BPE 10-1.4

12. The form of ribonucleic acid that carries genetic information from the DNA to the ribosomes is _____.

    ANS: mRNA   DIF: I   OBJ: BPE 10-1.4

13. Cells must regulate gene expression so that genes will only be _____ when the proteins are needed.

    ANS: transcribed   DIF: I   OBJ: BPE 10-2.1

14. A(n) _____ is a cluster of genes in a bacterial cell that codes for proteins with related functions.

    ANS: operon   DIF: I   OBJ: BPE 10-2.1

15. A(n) _____ protein is a molecule that prevents transcription by blocking the path of RNA polymerase along a molecule of DNA.

    ANS: repressor   DIF: I   OBJ: BPE 10-2.1

16. Transcription begins when an enzyme called _____ _____ binds to the beginning of a gene on a region of DNA called a promoter.

    ANS: RNA polymerase   DIF: I   OBJ: BPE 10-2.2

17. Nucleotide segments of a DNA molecule that make up genes and are actually expressed in the phenotype of an organism are called _____.

    ANS: exons   DIF: I   OBJ: BPE 10-2.3

18. Portions of genes that actually get translated into proteins are called _____.

    ANS: exons   DIF: I   OBJ: BPE 10-2.3

19. Mutations that change one nucleotide or just a few nucleotides in a gene are called _____ mutations.

    ANS: point   DIF: I   OBJ: BPE 10-2.4

ESSAY

1. In a particular eukaryotic cell, the DNA fails to uncoil. What effect will this have on gene expression in this cell?

   ANS:
   The degree to which DNA uncoils is an indication of the degree of gene expression. It is the uncoiled DNA that is the site of transcription of DNA into mRNA. Therefore, failure to uncoil will ultimately inhibit or prevent gene expression.

   DIF: II   OBJ: BPE 10-1.2

2. Identify the three types of RNA and briefly describe the function of each.

   ANS:
   Three types of RNA are: messenger RNA (mRNA), transfer RNA (tRNA), and ribosomal RNA (rRNA). Messenger RNA carries hereditary information from the DNA in the nucleus to the site of translation on the ribosomes; tRNA carries amino acids to the ribosomes for assembly into proteins; rRNA is a structural molecule, becoming part of the ribosomes upon which translation occurs.

   DIF: II   OBJ: BPE 10-1.4

3. Genes control cellular activities through a two-step process known as gene expression. Name and discuss the significance of the two steps.

   ANS:
   Information encoded in DNA molecules undergoes *transcription* as RNA polymerase makes an mRNA molecule with nucleotides having a sequence that is complementary to that of one of the original DNA strands. The mRNA molecule leaves the nucleus and associates with a ribosome, where the second step, *translation*, occurs. Translation involves the synthesis of the amino acid sequence of a protein molecule by the combined action of mRNA, tRNA, and rRNA. The sequence of mRNA nucleotides determines the sequence of amino acids in the assembled protein.

   DIF: II   OBJ: BPE 10-1.4

4. Describe the physical structure of the *lac* operon.

   ANS:
   The *lac* operon consists of three segments. These include a promoter, an operator, and three lactose-metabolizing genes. In addition, a regulator gene lies close to the lac operon.

   DIF: II   OBJ: BPE 10-2.1

5. In a mutant strain of Escherichia coli, lactose fails to bind to the repressor on the operator portion of the *lac* operon. What is likely to be the result of this failure?

ANS:
The failure of lactose to bind to and remove the repressor will prevent the *lac* operon from functioning. As a result, RNA polymerase will not transcribe the lactose-metabolizing genes of the *lac* operon, and the enzymes that normally break down lactose will not be produced.

DIF: II   OBJ: BPE 10-2.1

6. In the *lac* operon, how does RNA polymerase affect the expression of the lactose-metabolizing genes, and how is the activity of RNA polymerase controlled?

ANS:
RNA polymerase is needed to transcribe the DNA code into mRNA. As long as the repressor is attached to the operon, the activity of the RNA polymerase is prevented. When lactose binds to and removes the repressor, the RNA polymerase can move to the lactose-metabolizing genes of the *lac* operon, and mRNA can be transcribed.

DIF: II   OBJ: BPE 10-2.1

7. Distinguish between the different types of point mutations.

ANS:
There are three types of point mutations: substitutions, insertions, and deletions. Substitutions involve the replacement of one nucleotide with another. These mutations may not have a serious effect if the new codon codes for the same amino acid as the original. Insertions and deletions, known as frameshift mutations, involve the addition or omission of a single nucleotide, resulting in a shifting of the reading of the triplet code. A shift in the triplet code may result in a nonfunctional protein.

DIF: II   OBJ: BPE 10-2.4

TRUE/FALSE

1. Growing a large number of different cells from one cell is known as cloning.

    ANS: F   DIF: I   OBJ: BPE 11-1.1

2. Manipulating genes for practical purposes is called genetic engineering.

    ANS: T   DIF: I   OBJ: BPE 11-1.1

3. Gene cloning is an efficient way to produce many copies of a specific DNA sequence.

    ANS: T   DIF: I   OBJ: BPE 11-1.1

4. Scientists have used genetic engineering to produce bacteria capable of synthesizing human proteins.

    ANS: T   DIF: I   OBJ: BPE 11-1.1

5. Gene cloning is an efficient means of producing large numbers of different genes.

    ANS: F   DIF: I   OBJ: BPE 11-1.1

6. In bacteria, a circular DNA molecule that replicates independently of the main chromosome is called a plasmid.

    ANS: T   DIF: I   OBJ: BPE 11-1.1

7. In the practice of genetic engineering, scientists directly manipulate genes.

    ANS: T   DIF: I   OBJ: BPE 11-1.1

8. Plasmids are pieces of viral DNA that commonly infect human cells.

    ANS: F   DIF: I   OBJ: BPE 11-1.1

9. DNA ligase can seal the "sticky ends" of a DNA fragment.

    ANS: T   DIF: I   OBJ: BPE 11-1.1

10. Before a foreign gene is inserted into a plasmid, the plasmid is opened with a restriction enzyme

    ANS: T   DIF: I   OBJ: BPE 11-1.2

11. Recombinant DNA is made when a DNA fragment is put into the DNA of a vector.

    ANS: T   DIF: I   OBJ: BPE 11-1.2

12. Restriction enzymes make a straight cut through both strands of DNA.

    ANS: F   DIF: I   OBJ: BPE 11-1.2

13. Gel electrophoresis separates DNA fragments by their size and shape.

    ANS: T   DIF: I   OBJ: BPE 11-1.3

14. In a Southern blot, the DNA from each bacterial colony is isolated and cut into fragments by probes.

    ANS: F   DIF: I   OBJ: BPE 11-1.3

15. Anticoagulants are effective in treating diabetes.

    ANS: F   DIF: I   OBJ: BPE 11-2.1

16. Factor VIII is a protein that promotes blood clotting.

    ANS: T   DIF: I   OBJ: BPE 11-2.1

17. Injection of a particular vaccine can cause the body to produce antibodies that protect against the possibility of future infection by a particular pathogen.

    ANS: T   DIF: I   OBJ: BPE 11-2.2

18. Technological advances have now made it possible to transfer normal genes into the cells of a person who has a genetic disorder.

    ANS: T   DIF: I   OBJ: BPE 11-2.3

19. DNA fingerprinting enables genetic engineers to arrange genes in a particular order on a chromosome.

    ANS: F   DIF: I   OBJ: BPE 11-2.4

20. DNA fingerprint analysis can be used to determine whether two individuals are related.

    ANS: T   DIF: I   OBJ: BPE 11-2.4

21. RFLPs are pieces of DNA that are all the same length.

    ANS: T   DIF: I   OBJ: BPE 11-2.4

22. The effort to catalog, locate, and sequence all the chromosomes of every living organism is called the Human Genome Project.

    ANS: F   DIF: I   OBJ: BPE 11-2.5

23. If a crop is made glyphosate-resistant, treating it with glyphosate will seriously reduce its yield.

ANS: F   DIF: I   OBJ: BPE 11-3.1

24. Despite the potential environmental benefits, genetic engineers have been unable to develop crop plants that are resistant to weedkillers.

ANS: F   DIF: I   OBJ: BPE 11-3.1

25. Genetic engineering techniques can be used to make crops resistant to destructive insects.

ANS: T   DIF: I   OBJ: BPE 11-3.1

26. The tumor-causing Ti plasmid can be transformed into an effective vector for genetic engineering in plants.

ANS: T   DIF: I   OBJ: BPE 11-3.2

27. Genetic engineers have developed a method of infecting cows with milk-producing bacteria to increase the amount of milk produced by the cows.

ANS: F   DIF: I   OBJ: BPE 11-3.2

28. Dairy cattle will produce more milk when genetically engineered growth hormone is added to their food.

ANS: T   DIF: I   OBJ: BPE 11-3.2

29. A transgenic animal is an animal with foreign DNA in its cells.

ANS: T   DIF: I   OBJ: BPE 11-3.3

MULTIPLE CHOICE

1. A strand of DNA formed by the splicing of DNA from two different species is called
   a. determinant RNA.
   b. recombinant DNA.
   c. plasmid DNA.
   d. restriction RNA.

ANS: B   DIF: I   OBJ: BPE 11-1.1

2. Which of the following procedures is *not* a usual step in a genetic engineering experiment?
   a. inducing a mutation in a source chromosome
   b. cleaving DNA with a restriction enzyme
   c. recombining pieces of DNA from different species
   d. cloning and screening target cells

ANS: A   DIF: I   OBJ: BPE 11-1.1

3. "Genetic engineering" refers to the process of
   a.   creating new DNA molecules from nucleotide sequences.
   b.   rearranging nucleotides in a gene of an organism so that new traits appear in the development of an embryo.
   c.   moving genes from a chromosome of one organism to a chromosome of a different organism.
   d.   building a new species by combining genes of different organisms.

   ANS: C   DIF: I   OBJ: BPE 11-1.1

4. Cohen and Boyer transferred a gene from a frog chromosome into the genetic material of a
   a.   different frog.   c.   virus taken from the same frog.
   b.   different chromosome of the same frog.   d.   bacterial cell.

   ANS: D   DIF: I   OBJ: BPE 11-1.1

5. The use of genetic engineering to transfer human genes into bacteria
   a.   is impossible with current technology.
   b.   causes the human genes to manufacture bacterial proteins.
   c.   results in the formation of a new species of organism.
   d.   allows the bacteria to produce human proteins.

   ANS: D   DIF: I   OBJ: BPE 11-1.1

6. Cloning is a process by which
   a.   undesirable genes may be eliminated.
   b.   many identical protein fragments are produced.
   c.   a virus and a bacterium may be fused into one.
   d.   many identical cells may be produced.

   ANS: D   DIF: I   OBJ: BPE 11-1.1

7. Plasmids
   a.   are circular pieces of bacterial DNA.
   b.   can replicate independently of the organism's main chromosome.
   c.   are often used as vectors in genetic engineering experiments.
   d.   All of the above

   ANS: D   DIF: I   OBJ: BPE 11-1.1

8. Recombinant DNA is formed by joining DNA molecules
   a.   from two different species.
   b.   from two chromosomes of the same organism.
   c.   with RNA molecules.
   d.   with proteins from a different species.

   ANS: A   DIF: I   OBJ: BPE 11-1.1

9. plasmid : DNA segment coding for an enzyme ::
   a. DNA ligase : double-stranded DNA
   b. vector : restriction enzyme
   c. cloned cell : DNA ligase
   d. recombinant DNA : DNA from another organism

ANS: D
(contains)

DIF: II   OBJ: BPE 11-1.1

10. Restriction enzymes are specific in their action on
    a. DNA.   c. proteins.
    b. amino acids.   d. chromosomes.

ANS: A   DIF: I   OBJ: BPE 11-1.2

11. Enzymes that cut DNA molecules at specific places
    a. have sticky ends.
    b. are restriction enzymes.
    c. work only on bacterial DNA.
    d. always break the DNA between guanine and adenine.

ANS: B   DIF: I   OBJ: BPE 11-1.2

12. After cloning bacteria that had been exposed to the recombinant DNA, Cohen and Boyer added tetracycline to the culture in order to
    a. kill any contaminating viruses.
    b. kill cells that did not have the recombinant DNA in their genomes.
    c. neutralize any frog genes that might remain.
    d. make the bacterial cells multiply faster.

ANS: B   DIF: I   OBJ: BPE 11-1.2

13. The term *Eco*RI refers to a
    a. restriction enzyme.   c. specific DNA sequence.
    b. bacterial gene.   d. specific mutation.

ANS: A   DIF: I   OBJ: BPE 11-1.2

14. DNA fragments cut by a restriction enzyme, such as the EcoRI enzyme used by Cohen and Boyer, can
    a. pair up and join with any other DNA fragments cut by the same restriction enzyme.
    b. pair only with fragments formed by a complementary restriction enzyme.
    c. combine with any other spliced chromosome.
    d. pair only with DNA from the same species.

ANS: A   DIF: I   OBJ: BPE 11-1.2

15. Radioactive or fluorescent-labeled RNA or single-stranded DNA pieces that are complementary to the gene of interest and are used to confirm the presence of a cloned gene are called
    a. probes.
    b. plasmids.
    c. vaccines.
    d. clones.

    ANS: A   DIF: I   OBJ: BPE 11-1.3

16. A technique that uses radioactively labeled DNA to identify specific genes in a piece of DNA is called the
    a. Northern blot.
    b. Southern vector.
    c. Northern lights.
    d. Southern blot.

    ANS: D   DIF: I   OBJ: BPE 11-1.3

17. A medical condition that can be treated using proteins produced through genetic engineering is
    a. diabetes mellitus type I.
    b. heart attack (treated by dissolving blood clots).
    c. hemophilia (treated by promoting blood clotting).
    d. All of the above

    ANS: D   DIF: I   OBJ: BPE 11-2.1

18. genetic engineering : human health ::
    a. vaccine : anticoagulant
    b. human insulin : diabetes patients
    c. anticoagulant : hemophilia
    d. diabetes : insulin

    ANS: B
    (can benefit)

    DIF: II   OBJ: BPE 11-2.1

19. factor VIII : hemophilia ::
    a. bone marrow gene : diabetes
    b. anticoagulant : diabetes
    c. TNF : viruses
    d. insulin : diabetes

    ANS: D
    (is genetically engineered to treat)

    DIF: II   OBJ: BPE 11-2.1

20. Antibodies
    a. prevent diseases caused by vaccines.
    b. are produced by bacteria that infect animals.
    c. help destroy microbes that invade the body.
    d. cause viruses to infect bacterial cells.

    ANS: C   DIF: I   OBJ: BPE 11-2.2

21. The risk associated with vaccines prepared by injecting killed or weakened pathogenic microbes is that
    a. a few remaining live or unweakened microbes could still cause the disease.
    b. the antibodies that result may not work.
    c. the vaccine protects only against other diseases.
    d. None of the above

    ANS: A   DIF: I   OBJ: BPE 11-2.2

22. Tumor necrosis factor (TNF)
    a. produces antibodies.   c. attacks and kills cancer cells.
    b. is produced by cancer cells.   d. destroys white blood cells.

    ANS: C   DIF: I   OBJ: BPE 11-2.3

23. Transferring normal human genes into human cells that lack them
    a. is impossible at this time.   c. will cause antibodies to kill those cells.
    b. will cause cancer.   d. is called human gene therapy.

    ANS: D   DIF: I   OBJ: BPE 11-2.3

24. Although controversial, DNA fingerprinting has been used in criminal investigations because
    a. criminals leave DNA samples behind them when they touch an object at a crime scene.
    b. DNA analysis is believed to allow investigators to distinguish body cells of different individuals, who are unlikely to have the same DNA.
    c. bacterial DNA on the hands of criminals may provide a clue as to where that person was when the crime was committed.
    d. DNA found on murder weapons is easy to identify.

    ANS: B   DIF: I   OBJ: BPE 11-2.4

25. A genome is
    a. an organism's collection of genes.
    b. a protein fragment.
    c. the nucleotide sequence that makes up a particular gene.
    d. a fragment of DNA added to a chromosome during a gene transfer experiment.

    ANS: A   DIF: I   OBJ: BPE 11-2.5

26. The goal of the Human Genome Project is to
    a. create maps showing where genes are located on human chromosomes.
    b. create maps showing where chromosomes are located on human genes.
    c. treat patients with genetic diseases.
    d. identify people with genetic diseases.

    ANS: A   DIF: I   OBJ: BPE 11-2.5

27. A gene that codes for resistance to glyphosate has been added to the genome of certain plants. These plants will
    a. produce chemicals that kill weeds growing near them.
    b. die when exposed to glyphosate.
    c. convert glyphosate to fertilizer.
    d. survive when glyphosate is sprayed on the field.

    ANS: D   DIF: I   OBJ: BPE 11-3.1

28. The Ti plasmid
    a. contains a gene that causes tumors in plants.
    b. causes tumors in bacterial cultures.
    c. causes uncontrolled reproduction of bacterial cells.
    d. was created in the laboratory by genetic engineering.

    ANS: A   DIF: I   OBJ: BPE 11-3.1

29. For years, genetic engineering in plants was difficult because
    a. the Ti plasmid had not yet been discovered.
    b. plants normally contain few viruses or plasmids that can act as delivery agents.
    c. scientists lacked an appropriate vector to deliver desirable genes.
    d. All of the above

    ANS: D   DIF: I   OBJ: BPE 11-3.1

30. Which of the following is *not* an example of gene technology used in farming?
    a. the use of cow growth hormone produced by bacteria to increase milk production in cows
    b. the development of larger-and faster-growing breeds of livestock
    c. the cloning of human brain cells from selected farm animals
    d. the addition of human genes to farm-animal genes to obtain milk containing human proteins

    ANS: C   DIF: I   OBJ: BPE 11-3.2

31. Ian Wilmut's cloning of Dolly in 1997 was considered a breakthrough in genetic engineering because
    a. scientists thought cloning was impossible.
    b. scientists though only fetal cells could be used to produce clones.
    c. scientists had never before isolated mammary cells.
    d. sheep had never responded well to gene technology procedures.

    ANS: B   DIF: I   OBJ: BPE 11-3.3

COMPLETION

1. The process by which a foreign gene is replicated by insertion into a bacterium is called
   _____ _____.

   ANS: gene cloning   DIF: I   OBJ: BPE 11-1.1

2. The process used to isolate a gene from the DNA of one organism and transfer the gene into the DNA of another is called _____ _____.

   ANS: genetic engineering   DIF: I   OBJ: BPE 11-1.1

3. A(n) _____ is an agent that is used to carry a DNA fragment isolated from one cell into another cell.

   ANS: vector   DIF: I   OBJ: BPE 11-1.1

4. Small circular forms of bacterial DNA are called _____.

   ANS: plasmids   DIF: I   OBJ: BPE 11-1.1

5. Splicing DNA from two different organisms produces a new DNA segment called _____ _____.

   ANS: recombinant DNA   DIF: I   OBJ: BPE 11-1.1

6. Proteins that cut DNA segments into shorter pieces are called _____ _____.

   ANS: restriction enzymes   DIF: I   OBJ: BPE 11-1.1

7. A large number of genetically identical cells grown from a single cell are called _____.

   ANS: clones   DIF: I   OBJ: BPE 11-1.1

8. The process of allowing cells to reproduce in order to obtain a large number of identical cells is called _____.

   ANS: cloning   DIF: I   OBJ: BPE 11-1.1

9. Enzymes that cleave DNA at specific sequences, generating a set of small fragments of DNA, are called _____ _____.

   ANS: restriction enzymes   DIF: I   OBJ: BPE 11-1.2

10. A technique known as _____ _____ can be used to separate molecules in a mixture by subjecting them to an electrical field within a gel.

    ANS: gel electrophoresis   DIF: I   OBJ: BPE 11-1.3

11. The protein _____ is produced by genetic engineering to treat diabetes.

    ANS: insulin   DIF: I   OBJ: BPE 11-1.3

12. _____ are defensive proteins that label infectious microbes for destruction before they can cause disease.

   ANS: Antibodies   DIF: I   OBJ: BPE 11-2.2

13. Transferring normal human genes into human cells that lack them is called
   _____ _____.

   ANS: gene therapy   DIF: I   OBJ: BPE 11-2.3

14. _____ _____ is a method of identifying the sequences of nucleotides in a sample of DNA.

   ANS: DNA fingerprinting   DIF: I   OBJ: BPE 11-2.4

15. The name of the scientific program that has the goals of constructing maps of human chromosomes and determining the DNA sequences of those chromosomes is the
   _____ _____ _____.

   ANS: Human Genome Project   DIF: I   OBJ: BPE 11-2.5

16. The entire collection of genes within the cells of a human is referred to as the
   _____ _____.

   ANS: human genome   DIF: I   OBJ: BPE 11-2.5

17. Crop plants have recently been developed that are resistant to the chemical
   _____, a powerful weedkiller.

   ANS: glyphosate   DIF: I   OBJ: BPE 11-3.1

18. The _____ _____ contains a gene that causes tumors in plants.

   ANS: Ti plasmid   DIF: I   OBJ: BPE 11-3.1

19. Biologists have introduced extra copies of the genes that code for _____
   _____ into the chromosomes of cows and hogs to create leaner, faster-growing animals.

   ANS: growth hormone   DIF: I   OBJ: BPE 11-3.2

20. A(n) _____ _____ was used to fuse mammary cells from one sheep with egg cells without nuclei from a different sheep.

   ANS: electric shock   DIF: I   OBJ: BPE 11-3.3

ESSAY

1. Describe how a human gene may be recombined with an *E. coli* plasmid.

   ANS:
   First the plasmid is removed from the *E. coli* and opened with a restriction enzyme. The human gene is cut with the same restriction enzyme. Then the cut human gene is mixed with the cut plasmid. The sticky ends of the gene and plasmid join resulting in recombinant DNA.

   DIF: II   OBJ: BPE 11-1.1

2. A scientist has produced a bacterium containing a human gene that codes for a useful protein. How can the scientist use gene cloning to produce large quantities of this protein?

   ANS:
   First the scientist should place the bacterium in culture medium to allow the cell to divide. Each new cell produced through division will contain the human gene. As these genes are expressed, the protein will be produced and can be harvested from the culture.

   DIF: II   OBJ: BPE 11-1.1

3. In order to transfer a gene from a member of one species to another, four distinct steps must be followed. Identify, in the correct order, the four steps of a genetic engineering experiment.

   ANS:

   1. The DNA from the source organism and the DNA from the vector are cleaved into fragments with the same restriction enzyme.
   2. Recombinant DNA is then produced by combining the cut source DNA fragment with the cut vector DNA.
   3. The recombined vector DNA is inserted into bacterial cells. The gene is cloned when bacteria are allowed to reproduce.
   4. The cloned target cells are screened to select those cells that contain the desired gene.

   DIF: II   OBJ: BPE 11-1.1

4. A scientist has a long segment of sequenced DNA that contains a gene that he would like to clone. However, the segment of DNA containing the gene is too large to insert into a bacterial plasmid. How might the scientist reduce the size of the fragment containing the gene?

   ANS:
   The scientist could use restriction enzymes to cut the DNA into smaller pieces. By choosing the right restriction enzymes, the scientist could create a smaller segment that still contained the gene to be cloned. This smaller fragment could then be combined with the bacterial plasmid.

   DIF: II   OBJ: BPE 11-1.2

5. Genetic engineering has made it possible for pharmaceutical companies to produce medicines such as insulin and human growth hormone. Give at least two reasons why this is important.

    ANS:
    The production of genetically engineered medicines is important because
    a. large amounts of medicines can be produced.
    b. it is safer—the process eliminates risk of contamination from diseases such as AIDS in human blood products.
    c. it is less expensive.

    DIF: II   OBJ: BPE 11-2.1

6. Explain how a harmless virus might be turned into a vaccine by using genetic engineering.

    ANS:
    A DNA fragment coding for a surface protein of a disease-causing organism is inserted into the genome of a harmless virus. The recombinant virus is allowed to infect the organism that is to be protected. The recipient organism's body will respond by making antibodies that attack the surface protein of the disease-causing organism. If the vaccinated organism is ever exposed to the actual disease-causing organism, the vaccinated organism will immediately produce large amounts of the desired antibody to defend itself.

    DIF: II   OBJ: BPE 11-2.2

    One of the greatest benefits of genetic engineering has been the manipulation of genes in crop plants such as wheat and soybeans. The following item(s) relate to genetic engineering in agriculture.

7. Refer to the paragraph above. Describe how herbicides work and why farmers use them.

    ANS:
    Farmers often apply herbicides (weedkillers) to their crops to get better yields. Herbicides work because they are selective—they kill the weeds but not the crop. Herbicides lower the cost of producing crops since the fields do not have to be weeded and the crop plants grow better. Herbicides also help to prevent soil erosion since the soil does not have to be disturbed to remove weeds.

    DIF: II   OBJ: BPE 11-3.1

8. Refer to the paragraph above. In what ways can genetic engineering affect agriculture?

    ANS:
    Crop plants can be genetically engineered to add favorable characteristics, including improved yields and resistance to herbicides and destructive pests. Genetically engineered growth hormone increases milk production in dairy cows and weight gain in cattle and hogs. Transgenic animals can be cloned and used to make proteins that are useful in medicine.

    DIF: II   OBJ: BPE 11-3.2

9. The Ti plasmid causes tumors to develop in certain types of plants. Using an example, explain how it is possible for this plasmid to be used in a beneficial way in agriculture.

ANS:
Scientists have used genetic engineering techniques to remove the tumor-causing gene from the Ti plasmid. The remaining plasmid can then be used as a vector. A desirable gene, such as a gene for herbicide resistance, can be spliced into the plasmid. Infecting a plant with this altered plasmid results in the injection of the desired gene into the genome of the plant. Thus, the plant now has a new beneficial gene that can be expressed. For example, a plant receiving a gene that provides resistance to the herbicide glyphosate will survive when the weeds around it are treated with the herbicide.

DIF: II   OBJ: BPE 11-3.1

TRUE/FALSE

1. Scientists are unable to calculate the age of the Earth.

    ANS: F   DIF: I   OBJ: BPE 12-1.1

2. Radiometric dating measures the age of an object by measuring the proportions of radioactive isotopes.

    ANS: T   DIF: I   OBJ: BPE 12-1.1

3. The half-life of potassium-40 is 5,700 years.

    ANS: F   DIF: I   OBJ: BPE 12-1.1

4. Radioisotopes are stable elements.

    ANS: F   DIF: I   OBJ: BPE 12-1.1

5. On the early Earth, oxygen was found in the atmosphere millions of years before it was present in the oceans.

    ANS: F   DIF: I   OBJ: BPE 12-1.2

6. The spontaneous origin model states that life developed when molecules of nonliving matter reacted chemically, forming simple organic molecules.

    ANS: T   DIF: I   OBJ: BPE 12-1.2

7. The "primordial soup" model suggests that the ancient oceans were filled with organic molecules that formed as the result of the sun's energy.

    ANS: T   DIF: I   OBJ: BPE 12-1.2

8. Lamarck is credited with developing the bubble model for the origin of life's chemicals.

    ANS: F   DIF: I   OBJ: BPE 12-1.2

9. The origin of cells is clearly understood.

    ANS: F   DIF: I   OBJ: BPE 12-1.3

10. Scientists hypothesize that DNA may have acted as a catalyst in the formation of the first proteins.

    ANS: F   DIF: I   OBJ: BPE 12-1.3

11. Microspheres are tiny vesicles formed by groups of short chains of amino acids.

    ANS: T   DIF: I   OBJ: BPE 12-1.3

12. Scientists think that formation of fatty acids might have been the first step toward cellular organization.

    ANS: F   DIF: I   OBJ: BPE 12-1.3

13. Double-stranded DNA evolved before RNA.

    ANS: F   DIF: I   OBJ: BPE 12-1.4

14. Life began before the mechanism of heredity was developed.

    ANS: F   DIF: I   OBJ: BPE 12-1.4

15. Eukaryotes are characterized by an internal membrane system and a nucleus containing DNA.

    ANS: T   DIF: I   OBJ: BPE 12-1.4

16. The first living things to appear on the Earth were prokaryotes.

    ANS: T   DIF: I   OBJ: BPE 12-2.1

17. The photosynthetic cyanobacteria produced the oxygen in the Earth's atmosphere.

    ANS: T   DIF: I   OBJ: BPE 12-2.1

18. The two major groups of bacteria are eubacteria and cyanobacteria.

    ANS: F   DIF: I   OBJ: BPE 12-2.1

19. Eukaryotes probably descended from bacteria.

    ANS: T   DIF: I   OBJ: BPE 12-2.2

20. Both mitochondria and nuclei are believed to have their beginnings as prokaryotic parasites that invaded the pre-eukaryotic cell.

    ANS: F   DIF: I   OBJ: BPE 12-2.2

21. The theory of endosymbiosis proposes that mitochondria are the descendants of symbiotic aerobic eubacteria.

    ANS: T   DIF: I   OBJ: BPE 12-2.2

22. Mitochondria and chloroplasts each contain DNA unrelated to the nuclear DNA of the cells in which they reside.

    ANS: T   DIF: I   OBJ: BPE 12-2.2

23. Some protists are photosynthetic.

    ANS: T   DIF: I   OBJ: BPE 12-2.3

24. All protists are single-celled.

    ANS: F   DIF: I   OBJ: BPE 12-2.3

25. Multicellularity was not important to the evolution of life on Earth.

    ANS: F   DIF: I   OBJ: BPE 12-2.3

26. Algae are members of the kingdom Plantae.

    ANS: F   DIF: I   OBJ: BPE 12-2.3

27. Multicellular protists evolved independently many different times.

    ANS: T   DIF: I   OBJ: BPE 12-2.3

28. Mass extinctions occur with regularity every 125 million years.

    ANS: F   DIF: I   OBJ: BPE 12-2.4

29. Extinctions increase competition for resources causing a decrease in the population sizes of the surviving species.

    ANS: F   DIF: I   OBJ: BPE 12-2.4

30. Mass extinctions open ecological niches allowing for the invasion of new species which may change the change the face of the ruling class of plants and animals.

    ANS: T   DIF: I   OBJ: BPE 12-2.4

31. Mass extinctions have had a significant impact on the course of evolution of life on Earth.

    ANS: T   DIF: I   OBJ: BPE 12-2.4

32. Ozone was not present approximately 4 billion years ago.

    ANS: T   DIF: I   OBJ: BPE 12-3.1

33. Life on land could not exist without ozone.

    ANS: T   DIF: I   OBJ: BPE 12-3.1

34. Carbon dioxide is an important component of ozone.

    ANS: F   DIF: I   OBJ: BPE 12-3.1

35. Plants and algae developed a mutualistic relationship that allowed them to be the first organism to live on land.

    ANS: F   DIF: I   OBJ: BPE 12-3.2

36. Plants have been on land for more than 1 billion years.

    ANS: F   DIF: I   OBJ: BPE 12-3.2

37. Plants can extract minerals from bare rock.

    ANS: F   DIF: I   OBJ: BPE 12-3.2

38. The evolution of land plants had to take place before the evolution of land animals.

    ANS: T   DIF: I   OBJ: BPE 12-3.2

39. Flight enabled insects to search the Earth's surface for food, mates, and nesting sites.

    ANS: T   DIF: I   OBJ: BPE 12-3.3

40. The first animals to live on land were birds.

    ANS: F   DIF: I   OBJ: BPE 12-3.3

41. Insects evolved from aquatic arthropods.

    ANS: T   DIF: I   OBJ: BPE 12-3.3

42. Insects are the most successful group of organisms on Earth today.

    ANS: T   DIF: I   OBJ: BPE 12-3.3

43. All insects can fly.

    ANS: F   DIF: I   OBJ: BPE 12-3.3

44. Arthropods evolved from insects.

    ANS: F   DIF: I   OBJ: BPE 12-3.3

45. The distinguishing feature of vertebrates is that none of them have jaws.

   ANS: F   DIF: I   OBJ: BPE 12-3.4

46. The first fish to evolve had small, powerful jaws.

   ANS: F   DIF: I   OBJ: BPE 12-3.4

47. Amphibians can lay their eggs on dry land because the eggs are surrounded by a shell that prevents water loss.

   ANS: F   DIF: I   OBJ: BPE 12-3.4

48. Reptiles thrive in dry climates.

   ANS: T   DIF: I   OBJ: BPE 12-3.4

49. Amphibians were able to become successful on land because their skin was watertight.

   ANS: F   DIF: I   OBJ: BPE 12-3.4

MULTIPLE CHOICE

1. So far, the oldest fossils found on Earth are
   a. 200,000 years old.   c. 2 million years old.
   b. 3.5 billion years old.   d. 2 billion years old.

   ANS: B   DIF: I   OBJ: BPE 12-1.1

2. What percentage of potassium-40 remains after 2 half-lives?
   a. 100%   c. 50%
   b. 75%   d. 25%

   ANS: D   DIF: I   OBJ: BPE 12-1.1

3. How long is the half-life of potassium-40?
   a. 1.3 billion years   c. 3.9 billion years
   b. 2.6 billion years   d. 5.2 billion years

   ANS: A   DIF: I   OBJ: BPE 12-1.1

4. As the amount of potassium-40 decreases, the amount of stable isotope formed
   a. decreases.   c. increases then decreases.
   b. increases.   d. remains the same.

   ANS: B   DIF: I   OBJ: BPE 12-1.1

5. Energy used in the formation of the first organic molecules is thought to have come from
   a. water.   c. air.
   b. the sun.   d. fire.

   ANS: B   DIF: I   OBJ: BPE 12-1.2

6. The model stating that organic molecules present in ancient seas lead to the formation of life's building blocks was the
   a. spontaneous origin model.   c. primordial soup model.
   b. bubble model.   d. None of the above

   ANS: C   DIF: I   OBJ: BPE 12-1.2

7. The Lerman bubble model proposes that
   a. ammonia and methane gases were trapped in underwater bubbles.
   b. gases reacted within bubbles producing organic molecules.
   c. organic molecules were released into the air when the bubbles popped.
   d. All of the above

   ANS: D   DIF: I   OBJ: BPE 12-1.2

8. The early molecular catalyst that may have assisted in building the first proteins was
   a. RNA.   c. ATP.
   b. DNA.   d. NADPH.

   ANS: A   DIF: I   OBJ: BPE 12-1.3

9. The first step towards cellular organization may have come in the form of
   a. microsatellites.   c. micrometers.
   b. microspheres.   d. micromolecules.

   ANS: B   DIF: I   OBJ: BPE 12-1.3

10. Cyanobacteria are thought to be the ancestors of
    a. mitochondria.   c. ribosomes.
    b. nuclei.   d. chloroplasts.

    ANS: D   DIF: I   OBJ: BPE 12-2.1

11. Archaebacteria
    a. cause most of the diseases found in people today.
    b. often cause decay.
    c. have ways of producing energy without using oxygen.
    d. are important in the production of cheese and other dairy products.

    ANS: C   DIF: I   OBJ: BPE 12-2.1

12. Biologists separate bacteria into two groups based upon
    a. the composition of their cell walls.
    b. the structure of some of their proteins.
    c. the chemical composition of their cell membranes.
    d. All of the above

    ANS: D   DIF: I   OBJ: BPE 12-2.1

13. The most common living bacteria today are
    a. fungi.   c. archaebacteria.
    b. eubacteria.   d. arthropods.

    ANS: B   DIF: I   OBJ: BPE 12-2.1

14. Cyanobacteria changed the young Earth's atmosphere by producing
    a. carbon dioxide.   c. methane.
    b. ammonia.   d. oxygen.

    ANS: D   DIF: I   OBJ: BPE 12-2.1

15. Cyanobacteria changed the Earth's atmosphere as they carried out the process of
    a. atmospheric bonding.   c. photosynthesis.
    b. nitrogen synthesis.   d. gradualism.

    ANS: C   DIF: I   OBJ: BPE 12-2.1

16. archaebacteria : eukaryotes ::
    a. eubacteria : cyanobacteria   c. eubacteria : archaebacteria
    b. archaebacteria : eubacteria   d. cyanobacteria : eubacteria

    ANS: D
    (are ancestors of)

    DIF: II   OBJ: BPE 12-2.1

17. Eukaryotes may have descended from
    a. eubacteria.   c. cyanobacteria.
    b. archaebacteria.   d. None of the above

    ANS: B   DIF: I   OBJ: BPE 12-2.2

18. Eukaryotes first appeared
    a. 1.5 million years ago.   c. 1.5 billion years ago.
    b. 150 million years ago.   d. 150 billion years ago.

    ANS: B   DIF: I   OBJ: BPE 12-2.2

19. Pre-eukaryotic cells did not contain
    a. mitochondria.   c. DNA.
    b. cell membranes.   d. RNA.

    ANS: C   DIF: I   OBJ: BPE 12-2.2

20. Chloroplasts are thought to be the result of an invasion of pre-eukaryotic cells by
    a. mitochondria.   c. photosynthetic bacteria.
    b. Golgi apparatus.   d. protozoa.

    ANS: C   DIF: I   OBJ: BPE 12-2.2

21. Chloroplasts and mitochondria are both thought to have evolved through the process of
    a. photosynthesis.   c. photophosphorylation.
    b. cellular respiration.   d. endosymbiosis.

    ANS: D   DIF: I   OBJ: BPE 12-2.2

22. Protists evolved from
    a. archaebacteria.   c. eubacteria.
    b. protobacteria.   d. pseudobacteria.

    ANS: A   DIF: I   OBJ: BPE 12-2.3

23. The first eukaryotic kingdom was the Kingdom
    a. Animalia.   c. Protista.
    b. Plantae.   d. Fungi.

    ANS: C   DIF: I   OBJ: BPE 12-2.3

24. The most diverse eukaryotic kingdom is
    a. Protista.   c. Animalia.
    b. Plantae.   d. Fungi.

    ANS: A   DIF: I   OBJ: BPE 12-2.3

25. The oldest known fossils of multicellular organisms were found in rocks that were
    a. 100 million years old.   c. 1.5 billion years old.
    b. 700 million years old.   d. 4 billion years old.

    ANS: B   DIF: I   OBJ: BPE 12-2.3

26. The kingdom that evolved from the protists was the kingdom
    a. Fungi.   c. Animalia.
    b. Plantae.   d. All of the above

    ANS: D   DIF: I   OBJ: BPE 12-2.3

27. Multicellularity
    a. is a relatively recent evolutionary step.
    b. means that an organism is made up of more than one cell.
    c. is found in some protists.
    d. All of the above

    ANS: D   DIF: I   OBJ: BPE 12-2.3

28. All of the major phyla of animals on the Earth today evolved
   a. near the Burgess Shale.
   b. after the five mass extinctions took place.
   c. during the Cambrian period.
   d. prior to the appearance of protists.

   ANS: C   DIF: I   OBJ: BPE 12-2.3

29. The fossil record indicates that the Earth has been host to
   a. 5 mass extinctions.
   b. 4 mass extinctions.
   c. 3 mass extinctions.
   d. 2 mass extinctions.

   ANS: A   DIF: I   OBJ: BPE 12-2.4

30. Two-thirds of all terrestrial life disappeared in the last mass extinction approximately
   a. 440 million years ago.
   b. 360 million years ago.
   c. 245 million years ago.
   d. 65 million years ago.

   ANS: D   DIF: I   OBJ: BPE 12-2.4

31. After a mass extinction, population sizes of remaining species
   a. increase.
   b. decrease.
   c. increases then decrease.
   d. remains the same.

   ANS: A   DIF: I   OBJ: BPE 12-2.4

32. A layer of ozone in the atmosphere was critical to the formation of life on land because
   a. land plants need ozone for photosynthesis.
   b. there is a high concentration of ozone in the oceans.
   c. ozone is necessary in order to produce oxygen.
   d. ozone blocks ultraviolet radiation.

   ANS: D   DIF: I   OBJ: BPE 12-3.1

33. The destruction of the Earth's ozone layer by industrial chemicals is a valid concern because
   a. animals will not have air to breathe.
   b. ultraviolet light damages DNA.
   c. we will be unable to get suntans.
   d. None of the above

   ANS: B   DIF: I   OBJ: BPE 12-3.1

34. Ozone
   a. is composed of three oxygen atoms.
   b. blocks ultraviolet radiation in the upper atmosphere.
   c. made the Earth's surface a safe place to live.
   d. All of the above

   ANS: D   DIF: I   OBJ: BPE 12-3.1

35. The associations between the roots of plants and fungi are known as
   a. powdery mildew.
   b. mycorrhizae.
   c. lichens.
   d. mitochondria.

   ANS: B   DIF: I   OBJ: BPE 12-3.2

36. In mycorrhizae, the fungi provide plants with
   a. food.
   b. energy.
   c. minerals.
   d. All of the above

   ANS: C   DIF: I   OBJ: BPE 12-3.2

37. The first organisms to populate the surface of the land were
   a. bacteria and plants.
   b. plants and animals.
   c. plants and fungi.
   d. bacteria and fungi.

   ANS: C   DIF: I   OBJ: BPE 12-3.2

38. While there was no soil present, plants were able to invade the surface of the ancient Earth because they
   a. were supported by insects.
   b. extracted minerals from protists.
   c. could obtain extra nitrogen from the rocky dust.
   d. formed a partnership with fungi.

   ANS: D   DIF: I   OBJ: BPE 12-3.2

39. mycorrhizae : plant roots ::
   a. mitochondria : eukaryotic cells
   b. Golgi apparatus : nucleus
   c. mitochondria : nucleus
   d. nucleus : mitochondria

   ANS: A
   (are found in)

   DIF: II   OBJ: BPE 12-3.2

40. The first animals to invade the land were the
   a. amphibians.
   b. arthropods.
   c. insects.
   d. monerans.

   ANS: B   DIF: I   OBJ: BPE 12-3.3

41. Insects have been very successful because
   a. they reproduce in large numbers.
   b. they evolved the ability to fly.
   c. some of them can feed on flower nectar.
   d. All of the above

   ANS: D   DIF: I   OBJ: BPE 12-3.3

42. From fossils, we know that insects were the first animals to evolve
   a. pincers on their front legs.
   b. stingers at the end of their tails.
   c. jointed legs.
   d. wings.

   ANS: D   DIF: I   OBJ: BPE 12-3.3

43. Flying insects were able to use the ability to fly to do everything listed below except
    a. patrol the entire surface of the Earth.
    b. search for food, mates, or nesting sites.
    c. develop a mutualistic relationship with fungi.
    d. transport objects long distances.

    ANS: C   DIF: I   OBJ: BPE 12-3.3

44. Lobsters, insects, and spiders are all examples of
    a. amphibians.   c. arthropods.
    b. vertebrates.   d. monerans.

    ANS: C   DIF: I   OBJ: BPE 12-3.3

45. Arthropods have a hard outer skeleton and
    a. a backbone.   c. a four-chambered heart.
    b. hair.   d. jointed appendages.

    ANS: D   DIF: I   OBJ: BPE 12-3.3

46. The most diverse group of animals on Earth is the
    a. reptiles.   c. insects.
    b. mammals.   d. amphibians.

    ANS: C   DIF: I   OBJ: BPE 12-3.3

47. Flying insects feed on flowering plants and
    a. pollinate other plants of the same species.
    b. pollinate other plants of different species.
    c. carry pollen home to the young insects that cannot yet fly.
    d. then, because of their body weight, are unable to fly away.

    ANS: A   DIF: I   OBJ: BPE 12-3.3

48. One major problem faced by organisms moving onto land was
    a. lack of oxygen.
    b. too many competing insects.
    c. body structures that constantly lose water.
    d. All of the above

    ANS: C   DIF: I   OBJ: BPE 12-3.3

49. arthropods : live on land ::
    a. plants : absorb minerals from rocks   c. scorpions : fly
    b. fungi : make food   d. insects : fly

    ANS: D
    (were the first animals to)

    DIF: II   OBJ: BPE 12-3.3

Biology: Principles and Explorations
Copyright © by Holt, Rinehart and Winston. All rights reserved.
167

50. The first vertebrates
    a. had skeletons made of cartilage.
    b. evolved on the land.
    c. were jawless fishes.
    d. resembled amphibians.

    ANS: C   DIF: I   OBJ: BPE 12-3.4

51. Lampreys and hagfishes do not have
    a. a backbone.
    b. jaws.
    c. fins.
    d. bony skeletons.

    ANS: B   DIF: I   OBJ: BPE 12-3.4

52. Vertebrates that are adapted to life both on land and in the water are
    a. reptiles.
    b. arthropods.
    c. bony fish.
    d. amphibians.

    ANS: D   DIF: I   OBJ: BPE 12-3.4

53. Amphibians were able to successfully colonize land because
    a. they can absorb oxygen from the air with lungs.
    b. they have four sturdy limbs.
    c. oxygen-rich blood flows rapidly to the muscles and organs.
    d. All of the above

    ANS: D   DIF: I   OBJ: BPE 12-3.4

54. Reptiles
    a. have watertight skin.
    b. are endotherms.
    c. generally must remain in moist places.
    d. All of the above

    ANS: A   DIF: I   OBJ: BPE 12-3.4

55. Amphibians must lay their eggs in
    a. dry, hot environments.
    b. water or moist environments.
    c. nests in trees.
    d. winter.

    ANS: B   DIF: I   OBJ: BPE 12-3.4

56. lungs : amphibians ::
    a. bony skeleton : reptiles
    b. watertight skin : reptiles
    c. land animal design : protists
    d. circulatory system : reptiles

    ANS: B
    (developed in)

    DIF: II   OBJ: BPE 12-3.4

57. many new reptiles : Permian extinction ::
    a. fish and amphibians : Permian extinction
    b. fish : Cretaceous extinction
    c. Permian extinction : beginning of continental drift
    d. mammals, birds, and small reptiles : Cretaceous extinction

ANS: D
(appeared after)

DIF: II   OBJ: BPE 12-3.4

COMPLETION

1. The study of radioactive decay in rocks indicates that the Earth is about _____
    years old.

    ANS: 4.5 billion   DIF: I   OBJ: BPE 12-1.1

2. Forms of an element that differ in atomic mass are called _____.

    ANS: isotopes   DIF: I   OBJ: BPE 12-1.1

3. _____ are unstable elements that give off energy as they decay, forming stable
    elements.

    ANS: Radioisotopes   DIF: I   OBJ: BPE 12-1.1

4. A(n) _____ _____ is the amount of time required for one
    half the number of radioactive atoms in a sample to decay, forming stable elements.

    ANS: half-life   DIF: I   OBJ: BPE 12-1.1

5. By determining the number of half-lives that have passed since the formation of a rock
    containing radioisotopes and their stable daughter elements, scientists are able to determine the
    approximate _____ of the rock.

    ANS: age   DIF: I   OBJ: BPE 12-1.1

6. _____ _____ is the process through which life developed
    when molecules of nonliving matter reacted chemically during the first 1 billion years of the
    Earth's history.

    ANS: Spontaneous origin DIF: I   OBJ: BPE 12-1.2

7. The goal of each of the models that attempt to explain how life's basic chemicals were formed is
    to explain the development of _____ building blocks.

    ANS: organic   DIF: I   OBJ: BPE 12-1.2

8. Primitive _____ produced the first oxygen in the Earth's atmosphere.

   ANS: cyanobacteria   DIF: I   OBJ: BPE 12-2.1

9. Cyanobacteria produced the _____ that is now present in our atmosphere.

   ANS: oxygen   DIF: I   OBJ: BPE 12-2.1

10. The _____ are the most common bacteria group found on the Earth today.

    ANS: eubacteria   DIF: I   OBJ: BPE 12-2.1

11. The _____ probably were the ancestors of all eukaryotic cells.

    ANS: archaebacteria   DIF: I   OBJ: BPE 12-2.1

12. The theory of _____ is a widely accepted theory that explains the presence o
    mitochondria and chloroplasts in eukaryotic cells.

    ANS: endosymbiosis   DIF: I   OBJ: BPE 12-2.2

13. Both mitochondria and chloroplasts have their own _____.

    ANS: DNA   DIF: I   OBJ: BPE 12-2.2

14. _____ were the first eukaryotes.

    ANS: Protists   DIF: I   OBJ: BPE 12-2.3

15. All of the living things on the Earth today can be grouped into _____
    kingdoms.

    ANS: six   DIF: I   OBJ: BPE 12-2.3

16. Multicellularity allows cells to _____.

    ANS: specialize   DIF: I   OBJ: BPE 12-2.3

17. Having more than one cell is known as _____.

    ANS: multicellularity   DIF: I   OBJ: BPE 12-2.3

18. All of the major phyla on the Earth today evolved during the _____ period.

    ANS: Cambrian   DIF: I   OBJ: BPE 12-2.4

19. The death of all members of many different species is called _____
    _____.

    ANS: mass extinction   DIF: I   OBJ: BPE 12-2.4

20. At the end of the _____ period 250 million years ago, about 96 percent of all
    species of animals became extinct.

    ANS: Permian   DIF: I   OBJ: BPE 12-2.4

21. Refer to the illustration above. The three atoms shown in the diagram make up a molecule of
    _____.

    ANS: ozone   DIF: II   OBJ: BPE 12-3.1

22. Refer to the illustration above. The molecule shown here forms a protective layer in the
    atmosphere that blocks _____ radiation.

    ANS: ultraviolet   DIF: II   OBJ: BPE 12-3.1

23. The Earth's surface is protected from ultraviolet radiation by _____
    molecules.

    ANS: ozone   DIF: I   OBJ: BPE 12-3.1

24. The first terrestrial organisms that were able to fly were the _____.

    ANS: insects   DIF: I   OBJ: BPE 12-3.3

25. Flying insects carry _____ from a flowering plant to other flowers of the same
    species.

    ANS: pollen   DIF: I   OBJ: BPE 12-3.3

26. _____ were the first flying animals.

    ANS: Insects   DIF: I   OBJ: BPE 12-3.3

27. The first animals to successfully invade the land from the sea were _____.

ANS: arthropods   DIF: I   OBJ: BPE 12-3.3

28. Insects were the first animals to evolve _____.

ANS: wings   DIF: I   OBJ: BPE 12-3.3

29. Insects developed important relationships with _____ plants.

ANS: flowering   DIF: I   OBJ: BPE 12-3.3

30. _____ evolved from early, heavily armored jawed fishes.

ANS: Sharks   DIF: I   OBJ: BPE 12-3.4

31. Reptiles evolved from _____.

ANS: amphibians   DIF: I   OBJ: BPE 12-3.4

32. Reptiles thrive in dry climates because both their skin and eggs are largely _____.

ANS: watertight   DIF: I   OBJ: BPE 12-3.4

33. The first vertebrates on land were _____.

ANS: amphibians   DIF: I   OBJ: BPE 12-3.4

34. The large number of marsupials found in Australia and South America can be explained by the movement of the Earth's land masses. This movement is known as _____.

ANS: continental drift   DIF: I   OBJ: BPE 12-3.4

35. Birds and mammals became the dominant vertebrates on land after the _____ extinction.

ANS: Cretaceous   DIF: I   OBJ: BPE 12-3.4

ESSAY

1. On a separate sheet of paper, construct a time table of events relating to the origin and evolution of life on earth. Use information presented in your text which represents scientists' current best estimates of when the relevant events occurred. (Your time scale should be in billions of years.) Illustrate your time table with drawings of cells and organisms that you include. Use descriptions and pictures in your text to help you depict the distinctive features and the environment in which the cells and organisms lived. Include when organic chemicals were first formed, as well as origins for the following in your table: Earth, first cells, first photosynthetic cells, first eukaryotic cells, first multicellular organisms, first animals, first vertebrates, first land plants, first fungi, first land animals, first vertebrates, first mammals, first primates, and first humans.

   ANS:
   Origin of Earth: 4.5 billion years ago
   First formation of organic chemicals: 4 billion years ago
   Origin of the first cells: 3.5 billion years ago (These should be depicted as prokaryotic cells)
   Origin of the first photosynthetic cells: 3 billion years ago (These should be depicted as prokaryotic cells)
   Origin of the first eukaryotic cells: 1.5 billion years ago (These cells should be depicted as containing organelles)
   Origin of the first multicellular organisms: 0.63 billion years ago (These should be depicted as small, aquatic animal-like organisms lacking shells)
   Origin of the first animals: 0.6 billion years ago (These should be depicted as aquatic animals)
   Origin of the first vertebrates: about 0.57 billion years ago (These should be depicted as fishes)
   Origin of the first land plants: 0.4 billion years ago (These should be depicted as green and as having roots)
   Origin of the first fungi: 0.4 billion years ago (These should be depicted in a color other than green and could be shown growing on rock or on plant roots)
   Origin of the first land animals: shortly after 0.4 billion years ago (These should be depicted as arthropods)
   Origin of the first land vertebrates: 0.35 billion years ago (These should be depicted as amphibians)
   Origin of the first mammals: about 0.25 billion years ago (These should be depicted as small, mouse-like animals)
   Origin of the first primates: 0.06 billion years ago (These should be depicted as small, rodent-like animals living in trees)
   Origin of the first humans: 0.005 billion years ago (These should be depicted as upright-walking animals)

   DIF: III   OBJ: BPE 12-1.1

2. Most cells found in organisms on the Earth today are aerobic; that is, they need oxygen. Explain why the first cells could not have been aerobic bacteria.

ANS:
There was no oxygen in the atmosphere of the primitive Earth. Oxygen was found in the atmosphere only after the evolution of the photosynthetic cyanobacteria.

DIF: II   OBJ: BPE 12-2.1

3. Why has there been a burst of evolution after each of the great mass extinctions?

ANS:
The organisms that survive the mass extinctions find themselves in a world of opportunity—an Earth full of food and space that are no longer used by others.

DIF: II   OBJ: BPE 12-2.4

4. The ozone layer in the Earth's atmosphere was discovered less than 40 years ago. Scientists are not certain if the thinning of this layer is part of a natural atmospheric cycle or if the thinning has been caused by the activities of people in industrialized countries. Why do you think many biologists are urging industrialized nations to take steps that may prevent further destruction of the ozone layer?

ANS:
The activities of people might be causing the destruction of the ozone layer, and if so, its thinning will probably be permanent. The ozone layer protects us from harmful ultraviolet light. Ultraviolet light damages DNA, and this may lead to harmful mutations and increased rates of cancer.

DIF: III   OBJ: BPE 12-3.3

5. Why would insects have an ecological advantage over terrestrial animals?

ANS:
Flying allows insects to efficiently search for food, mates, and nesting sites. When competition becomes too great due to high population numbers, flight enables insects to disperse easily to new territories.

DIF: II   OBJ: BPE 12-3.3

6. What characteristic did the first terrestrial animals have that allowed them to survive on land?

ANS:
The first land animals were arthropods, which had hard outer skeletons that prevented them from drying out.

DIF: III   OBJ: BPE 12-3.3

7. Describe the structural innovations that helped amphibians adapt to life on land.

ANS:
A number of adaptations evolved in amphibians that allowed them to live on land. These structural changes included the evolution of lungs and changes in the circulatory system. In addition, amphibians evolved limbs and a skeletal system that allowed the amphibians to walk on land.

DIF: II   OBJ: BPE 12-3.3

TRUE/FALSE

1. Species that have evolved from a common ancestor should have certain characteristics in common.

   ANS: T   DIF: I   OBJ: BPE 13-1.1

2. In his *Essay on the Principle of Population,* Malthus said humans were the only population that could continue to grow in size indefinitely.

   ANS: F   DIF: I   OBJ: BPE 13-1.1

3. Darwin observed that the plants and animals of the Galapagos Islands were the same as those on islands off the coast of Africa with similar environments.

   ANS: F   DIF: I   OBJ: BPE 13-1.1

4. The book *Principles of Geology* by Charles Lyell described how changes in land formations can cause species to evolve.

   ANS: F   DIF: I   OBJ: BPE 13-1.1

5. The inheritance of acquired characteristics was one mechanism of evolution supported by Darwin.

   ANS: F   DIF: I   OBJ: BPE 13-1.2

6. Natural selection can cause the spread of an advantageous adaptation throughout a population.

   ANS: T   DIF: I   OBJ: BPE 13-1.2

7. The two major ideas that Darwin presented in *The Origin of the Species* were that evolution occurred and that natural selection was its mechanism.

   ANS: T   DIF: I   OBJ: BPE 13-1.3

8. The theory of evolution states that species change over time.

   ANS: T   DIF: I   OBJ: BPE 13-1.3

9. Natural selection causes allele frequencies within populations to remain the same.

   ANS: F   DIF: I   OBJ: BPE 13-1.3

10. The fossil record suggests that species have become less complex with time.

   ANS: F   DIF: I   OBJ: BPE 13-2.1

11. The theory of evolution predicts that genes will accumulate more alterations in their nucleotide sequences over time.

    ANS: T   DIF: I   OBJ: BPE 13-2.2

12. Evidence for evolution occurs only in the fossil record.

    ANS: F   DIF: I   OBJ: BPE 13-2.2

13. The human forelimb and the bat forelimb are homologous structures.

    ANS: T   DIF: I   OBJ: BPE 13-2.3

14. Early in development, human embryos and the embryos of all other vertebrates are strikingly similar.

    ANS: T   DIF: I   OBJ: BPE 13-2.3

15. The way an embryo develops is not important in determining the evolutionary history of a species.

    ANS: F   DIF: I   OBJ: BPE 13-2.3

16. Punctuated gradualism refers to the hypothesis that evolution occurs only in short periods of time.

    ANS: F   DIF: I   OBJ: BPE 13-2.4

17. Two hypotheses suggested about the rate at which evolution proceeds are gradualism and punctuated equilibrium.

    ANS: T   DIF: I   OBJ: BPE 13-2.4

18. The environment dictates only the direction and extent of evolution.

    ANS: T   DIF: I   OBJ: BPE 13-3.1

19. The best-known case of industrial melanism involves the American bison.

    ANS: F   DIF: I   OBJ: BPE 13-3.2

20. In industrialized areas, light colored peppered moths were selected for by natural selection mechanisms.

    ANS: F   DIF: I   OBJ: BPE 13-3.2

21. In industrialized areas, light colored moths were eventually replaced by dark colored moths.

    ANS: T   DIF: I   OBJ: BPE 13-3.2

22. The environment selects which organisms will survive and reproduce by presenting challenges that only individuals with particular traits can meet.

   ANS: T   DIF: I   OBJ: BPE 13-3.2

23. When food is plentiful, there is little selective pressure on the beaks of finches.

   ANS: T   DIF: I   OBJ: BPE 13-3.3

24. When food is scarce, there is little selective pressure on the beaks of finches.

   ANS: F   DIF: I   OBJ: BPE 13-3.3

25. When food is scarce, the number of different beak shapes of finches increases.

   ANS: T   DIF: I   OBJ: BPE 13-3.3

26. The accumulation of differences between species or populations is called convergence.

   ANS: F   DIF: I   OBJ: BPE 13-3.4

27. Within populations, divergence leads to speciation.

   ANS: T   DIF: I   OBJ: BPE 13-3.4

MULTIPLE CHOICE

1. Darwin thought that the plants and animals of the Galapagos Islands were similar to those of the nearby coast of South America because
   a. their ancestors had migrated from South America to the Galapagos Islands.
   b. they had all been created by God to match their habitat.
   c. the island organisms had the same nucleotide sequences in their DNA as the mainland organisms.
   d. he found fossils proving that the animals and plants had common ancestors.

   ANS: A   DIF: I   OBJ: BPE 13-1.1

2. Darwin conducted much of his research on
   a. the Samoan Islands.
   b. Manhattan Island.
   c. the Hawaiian Islands.
   d. the Galapagos Islands.

   ANS: D   DIF: I   OBJ: BPE 13-1.1

3. Prior to his voyage on the *Beagle,* Darwin believed in
   a. chromosomal theory.
   b. natural selection.
   c. divine creation.
   d. genetic drift.

   ANS: C   DIF: I   OBJ: BPE 13-1.1

4. Which of the following describes a population?
   a. dogs and cats living in Austin, Texas
   b. four species of fish living in a pond
   c. dogwood trees in Middletown, Connecticut
   d. roses and tulips in a garden

   ANS: C   DIF: I   OBJ: BPE 13-1.1

5. Natural selection is the process by which
   a. the age of selected fossils is calculated.
   b. organisms with traits well suited to their environment survive and reproduce at a greater rate than less well-adapted organisms in the same environment.
   c. acquired traits are passed on from one generation to the next.
   d. All of the above

   ANS: B   DIF: I   OBJ: BPE 13-1.2

6. Natural selection could not occur without
   a. genetic variation in species.   c. competition for unlimited resources.
   b. environmental changes.   d. gradual warming of the Earth.

   ANS: A   DIF: I   OBJ: BPE 13-1.2

7. Natural selection causes
   a. changes in the environment.
   b. plants and animals to produce more offspring than can survive.
   c. changes in the frequency of certain alleles in a population.
   d. All of the above

   ANS: C   DIF: I   OBJ: BPE 13-1.2

8. The process by which a species becomes better suited to its environment is known as
   a. accommodation.   c. adaptation.
   b. variation.   d. selection.

   ANS: C   DIF: I   OBJ: BPE 13-1.3

9. According to Darwin, evolution occurs
   a. by chance.   c. because of natural selection.
   b. during half-life periods of 5,730 years.   d. rapidly.

   ANS: C   DIF: I   OBJ: BPE 13-1.3

10. Organisms well suited to their environment
    a. reproduce at a greater rate than those less suited to the same environment.
    b. are always larger than organisms less suited to that environment.
    c. always live longer than organisms less suited to that environment.
    d. need less food than organisms less suited to that environment.

    ANS: A   DIF: I   OBJ: BPE 13-1.3

11. When Darwin published his theory of evolution, he included all of the following ideas *except*:
    a. the idea that species change slowly over time.
    b. the idea that some organisms become less suited to their environment than others.
    c. Mendel's ideas about genetics.
    d. the idea that some organisms reproduce at a greater rate than others.

    ANS: C   DIF: I   OBJ: BPE 13-1.3

12. The major idea that Darwin presented in his book *The Origin of Species* was that
    a. species changed over time and never competed with each other.
    b. animals changed, but plants remained the same.
    c. giraffes and peppered moths changed constantly.
    d. species changed over time by natural selection.

    ANS: D   DIF: I   OBJ: BPE 13-1.3

The diagrams below represent bones in the limbs of fossil horses and modern horses.

60 million
years ago

modern

13. Refer to the illustration above. The fossils indicate that horse evolution probably has taken place
    a. rapidly.
    b. in only one place on Earth.
    c. gradually.
    d. five times by the process of punctuated equilibrium.

    ANS: C   DIF: II   OBJ: BPE 13-2.1

14. Which of the following are examples of fossils?
    a. shells or old bones
    b. any traces of dead organisms
    c. footprints of human ancestors, insects trapped in tree sap, and animals buried in tar
    d. All of the above

    ANS: D   DIF: I   OBJ: BPE 13-2.1

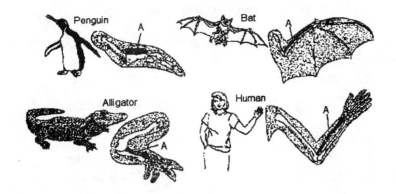

15. Refer to the illustration above. An analysis of DNA from these organisms would indicate that
    a. they have identical DNA.
    b. they all have gill pouches.
    c. their nucleotide sequences show many similarities.
    d. they all have the same number of chromosomes.

    ANS: C   DIF: II   OBJ: BPE 13-2.2

16. Refer to the illustration above. The similarity of these structures suggests that the organisms
    a. have a common ancestor.   c. evolved slowly.
    b. all grow at different rates.   d. live for a long time.

    ANS: A   DIF: II   OBJ: BPE 13-2.3

17. Refer to the illustration above. The bones labeled A are known as
    a. vestigial structures.   c. homologous structures.
    b. sequential structures.   d. fossil structures.

    ANS: C   DIF: II   OBJ: BPE 13-2.3

18. The theory of evolution predicts that
    a. closely related species will show similarities in nucleotide sequences.
    b. if species have changed over time, their genes should have changed.
    c. closely related species will show similarities in amino acid sequences.
    d. All of the above

    ANS: D   DIF: I   OBJ: BPE 13-2.2

19. The occurrence of the same blood protein in a group of species provides evidence that these species
    a. evolved in the same habitat.   c. descended from a common ancestor.
    b. evolved in different habitats.   d. descended from different ancestors.

    ANS: C   DIF: I   OBJ: BPE 13-2.2

20. Evidence for evolution includes all of the following *except*
    a. punctuated sedimentation.
    b. similarities and differences in protein and DNA sequences between organisms.
    c. the fossil record.
    d. homologous structures.

    ANS: A   DIF: I   OBJ: BPE 13-2.3

21. Which of the following is a vestigial structure?
    a. the human tailbone   c. flower color
    b. the bill of a finch   d. fossil cast

    ANS: A   DIF: I   OBJ: BPE 13-2.3

22. Homologous structures in organisms suggest that the organisms
    a. have a common ancestor.   c. have a skeletal structure.
    b. must have lived at different times.   d. are now extinct.

    ANS: A   DIF: I   OBJ: BPE 13-2.3

23. Structures that have reduced in size because they no longer serve an important function are called
    a. inorganic.   c. fossilized.
    b. mutated.   d. vestigial.

    ANS: D   DIF: I   OBJ: BPE 13-2.3

24. A human embryo exhibits all of the following during development *except*
    a. gill pouches.   c. fins.
    b. a bony tail.   d. a coat of fine fur.

    ANS: C   DIF: I   OBJ: BPE 13-2.3

25. vestigial structures : macroevolution ::
    a. homologous structures : common   c. common ancestry : rock
       ancestry
    b. common ancestry : fossils   d. homologous structures : unrelated
                                            species

    ANS: A
    (are evidence of)

    DIF: II   OBJ: BPE 13-2.3

26. The hypothesis that evolution occurs at a slow, constant rate is known as
    a. gradualism.   c. natural selection.
    b. slow motion.   d. adaptation.

    ANS: A   DIF: I   OBJ: BPE 13-2.4

27. The hypothesis that evolution occurs at an irregular rate through geologic time is known as
    a. directional evolution.
    b. directional equilibrium.
    c. punctuated equilibrium.
    d. punctuated evolution.

    ANS: C   DIF: I   OBJ: BPE 13-2.4

28. Populations of the same species living in different places
    a. do not vary.
    b. always show balancing selection.
    c. have a half-life in relation to the size of the population.
    d. become increasingly different as each becomes adapted to its own environment.

    ANS: D   DIF: I   OBJ: BPE 13-3.1

29. Scarcity of resources and a growing population are most likely to result in
    a. homology.
    b. protective coloration.
    c. competition.
    d. convergent evolution.

    ANS: C   DIF: I   OBJ: BPE 13-3.1

30. Since natural resources are limited, all organisms
    a. must migrate to new habitats.
    b. face a constant struggle for existence.
    c. display vestigial structures.
    d. have a species half-life.

    ANS: B   DIF: I   OBJ: BPE 13-3.1

31. A change in the frequency of a particular gene in one direction in a population is called
    a. directional selection.
    b. acquired variation.
    c. chromosome drift.
    d. balancing selection.

    ANS: A   DIF: I   OBJ: BPE 13-3.1

32. struggle for survival : competition ::
    a. time : environment
    b. survival of the fittest : best traits
    c. trait : time
    d. environment : traits

    ANS: B
    (is based on)

    DIF: II   OBJ: BPE 13-3.1

33. Kettlewell found that in industrialized areas light colored peppered moths
    a. were preyed on more often than dark moths.
    b. were preyed on less often than dark moths.
    c. lived longer, healthier lives than dark moths.
    d. were difficult for predators to see.

    ANS: A   DIF: I   OBJ: BPE 13-3.2

34. The Industrial Revolution in Great Britain in the mid to late 1800s
    a. did not affect the allele frequency for color in peppered moths.
    b. was an agent of selection in peppered moth populations.
    c. caused an increase in the number of predators that consume moths.
    d. was an indirect cause of the change in allele frequency in moth populations.

    ANS: D   DIF: I   OBJ: BPE 13-3.2

35. In his experiments with peppered moths, Kettlewell found that
    a. the color of the moths was not important.
    b. birds preferred the flavor of light-colored moths.
    c. moths whose color matched that of the tree trunks were more likely to survive.
    d. coloration was an inherited trait.

    ANS: C   DIF: I   OBJ: BPE 13-3.2

36. dark peppered moth : industrialized areas ::
    a. light peppered moth : unindustrialized areas
    b. dark peppered moth : light tree trunks
    c. light peppered moth : industrialized areas
    d. lack of soot : industrialized areas

    ANS: A
    (escapes predation in)

    DIF: II   OBJ: BPE 13-3.2

37. The finches that Darwin studied differed in the shape of their beaks. According to Darwin, the finches probably
    a. all had a common ancestor.
    b. had been created by design that way.
    c. were descended from similar birds in Africa.
    d. ate the same diet.

    ANS: A   DIF: I   OBJ: BPE 13-3.3

38. Beak shape in finches is affected by
    a. the number of predators in the area.   c. the color of the finch.
    b. the size of the finch.   d. the availability of food.

    ANS: D   DIF: I   OBJ: BPE 13-3.3

39. In order to fit into their habitat, the Galapagos finches had
    a. not changed.   c. evolved.
    b. been created as superior birds.   d. All of the above

    ANS: C   DIF: I   OBJ: BPE 13-3.3

40. The accumulation of differences between species or populations is called
    a. gradualism.
    b. adaptation.
    c. divergence.
    d. cumulative differentiation.

    ANS: C   DIF: I   OBJ: BPE 13-3.4

41. Which of the following statements is *not* true about members of ecological races?
    a. Members of different ecological races are not yet different enough to belong to separate species.
    b. Members of one ecological race cannot interbreed with members of any other such group.
    c. Ecological races often become increasingly different in response to their environment.
    d. Divergence between ecological races occurs because natural selection favors different survival strategies in different environments.

    ANS: B   DIF: I   OBJ: BPE 13-3.4

42. New species form
    a. when ecological races diverge more and more.
    b. because of natural selection.
    c. when members of the same species become adapted to new environments.
    d. All of the above

    ANS: D   DIF: I   OBJ: BPE 13-3.4

43. Populations of the same species that differ genetically because they have adapted to different living conditions are known as
    a. selected populations.
    b. ecological races.
    c. genetic populations.
    d. genetic races.

    ANS: B   DIF: I   OBJ: BPE 13-3.4

COMPLETION

1. A change in species over time is called _____.

    ANS: evolution   DIF: I   OBJ: BPE 13-1.1

2. Charles Darwin sailed for five years on a ship named _____ _____.

    ANS: *H.M.S. Beagle*   DIF: I   OBJ: BPE 13-1.1

3. Darwin's observations led him to doubt the beliefs of divine _____.

    ANS: creation   DIF: I   OBJ: BPE 13-1.1

4. The process by which organisms with traits well suited to an environment survive and reproduce at a greater rate than organisms less suited for that environment is called _____ _____.

   ANS: natural selection   DIF: I   OBJ: BPE 13-1.2

5. Natural selection leads to changes in both the physical appearance and the _____ _____ of a species.

   ANS: genetic makeup   DIF: I   OBJ: BPE 13-1.2

6. Published in 1859, Charles Darwin's book, _____ _____ _____ _____ changed biology forever.

   ANS: *The Origin of Species*   DIF: I   OBJ: BPE 13-1.3

7. A species that has disappeared permanently is said to be _____.

   ANS: extinct   DIF: I   OBJ: BPE 13-1.3

8. The most direct evidence that evolution has occurred comes from _____.

   ANS: fossils   DIF: I   OBJ: BPE 13-2.1

9. Closely related species show more _____ in nucleotide sequences than distantly related species.

   ANS: similarities   DIF: I   OBJ: BPE 13-2.2

10. Homologous structures are similar because they are inherited from a common _____.

    ANS: ancestor   DIF: I   OBJ: BPE 13-2.3

11. Eyes in a blind salamander are an example of a type of organ known as _____

    ANS: vestigial   DIF: I   OBJ: BPE 13-2.3

12. _____ structures are similar because they are inherited from a common ancestor.

    ANS: Homologous   DIF: I   OBJ: BPE 13-2.3

13. _____ is the hypothesis that evolution occurs at a constant rate.

    ANS: Gradualism   DIF: I   OBJ: BPE 13-2.4

14. _____ _____ in species is the raw material for natural selection.

ANS: Genetic variation   DIF: I   OBJ: BPE 13-3.1

15. According to Darwin, the _____ determines the rate at which organisms survive and reproduce.

ANS: environment   DIF: I   OBJ: BPE 13-3.2

16. In response to the darkening of tree trunks by pollution, some peppered moth populations evolved from cream-colored to dark _____.

ANS: gray   DIF: I   OBJ: BPE 13-3.2

17. Dark peppered moths are darker than light peppered moths because dark peppered moths produce more _____.

ANS: melanin   DIF: I   OBJ: BPE 13-3.2

18. Kettlewell concluded that _____ _____ caused industrial melanism in peppered moths.

ANS: natural selection   DIF: I   OBJ: BPE 13-3.2

19. Darwin's observations of finches lead him to believe that there was a close correlation between beak shape and _____ source.

ANS: food   DIF: I   OBJ: BPE 13-3.3

20. The availability of food supply affects the number of different _____ shapes in finches.

ANS: beak   DIF: I   OBJ: BPE 13-3.3

ESSAY

1. Why did Darwin believe that the finches he observed and collected in the Galapagos Islands shared a common ancestor?

ANS:
Although there were differences among these finch species, all the species also had many traits in common. The main similarities among these species led Darwin to conclude that they had a common ancestor.

DIF: II   OBJ: BPE 13-1.1

2. In comparing two species that look very different, how could a comparison of the species' genes contribute to an understanding of their evolutionary relationship?

ANS:
Studying the species' genes would provide much more information than could be obtained by simply observing the physical appearance of the species. If the species had many genes in common, they would likely be more closely related than their physical appearance would suggest. If the species did not have many genes in common, this information would tend to strengthen the argument that the species were not closely related.

DIF: II   OBJ: BPE 13-2.2

3. You are a biologist accompanying some other scientists on an expedition in a region that has not been studied intensively. In your explorations, you come across a colony of small vertebrates that do not look familiar to you. After conducting electronic searches of world wide data bases, you arrive at the tentative conclusion that this organism has never been observed before. Now your job is to determine what kind of vertebrate it is by identifying its closest relatives. Identify three types of data that you would collect and describe how you would use these data to draw your conclusions.

ANS:

a. Analysis of anatomical structures and comparison of these to similar structures of other vertebrates is one type of data that should be collected. For example, the bones composing the forelimb of the organism could be compared to the forelimbs of other vertebrates. Those vertebrates having the greatest number of similar (homologous) anatomical structures to those of your organism could be presumed to be its closest relatives.

b. Analysis of the DNA and/or a protein and comparison of this material to that of other vertebrates could also be studied. For example, DNA hybridization studies could be conducted with the organism and other vertebrates. Or, an analysis of the cytochrome c of the organism in comparison to the cytochrome c of other vertebrates could be done. Those vertebrates having the fewest differences in sequences of DNA and/or proteins from the organism could be presumed to be its closest relatives.

c. Analysis of embryonic development and comparison of structures present at different stages and the pattern of development with the structures and patterns of other vertebrates would be a third type of data collected. For example, an analysis could be made of the persistence of a particular trait until late in embryonic development. This analysis could be compared to the persistence of the same trait in the embryos of other vertebrates. Those vertebrates having the greatest similarity in structures present and pattern of development could be presumed to be its closest relatives.

DIF: III   OBJ: BPE 13-2.3

4. Why is competition among individuals of the same species generally so intense?

ANS:
Individuals of the same species require the same resources for survival. Since resources are generally limited, only those individuals able to secure sufficient amounts of such resources will survive.

DIF: II   OBJ: BPE 13-3.1

5. An agricultural plot of land is sprayed with a very powerful insecticide to destroy harmful insects. Nevertheless, many of the same species of insects are present on the land the following year. How might the theory of evolution account for this phenomenon?

ANS:
A part of the theory of evolution states that genetic variation exists within a species. A small percentage of the insects exposed to the insecticide might have been immune or capable of detoxifying the substance. They survived and produced offspring that were also resistant to the insecticide.

DIF: II   OBJ: BPE 13-3.1

6. What role does the environment play in natural selection?

ANS:
Those organisms that have traits best suited to the environment most successfully survive and reproduce.

DIF: II   OBJ: BPE 13-3.2

7. Suppose that you are a zoologist studying birds on a group of islands. You have just discovered four species of birds that have never before been seen. Each species is on a separate island. The birds are identical to each other except for the shape of their beaks. How can you explain their similarities and differences?

ANS:
It is likely that the four species evolved from a common ancestor, with each species adapting to the conditions on its island. The differences in beak shape may be the result of differences in available food among the islands. Each bird species adapted to the food that was available on its island.

DIF: II   OBJ: BPE 13-3.4

CHAPTER 14—HUMAN EVOLUTION

TRUE/FALSE

1. Fossil evidence indicates that most extinct primate species lived in trees.

    ANS: T   DIF: I   OBJ: BPE 14-1.1

2. The ancient mammals that were the ancestors of the first primates resembled shrews.

    ANS: T   DIF: I   OBJ: BPE 14-1.1

3. Primates all have four fingers.

    ANS: F   DIF: I   OBJ: BPE 14-1.2

4. An opposable thumb is characteristic of anthropoids.

    ANS: T   DIF: I   OBJ: BPE 14-1.2

5. Movable fingers and toes with flattened nails are typical of primates.

    ANS: T   DIF: I   OBJ: BPE 14-1.2

6. Depth perception is a characteristic of most primates.

    ANS: T   DIF: I   OBJ: BPE 14-1.2

7. Today, prosimians can be found in South America, Asia, and Africa.

    ANS: F   DIF: I   OBJ: BPE 14-1.3

8. Fossils of apes have never been found in North and South America.

    ANS: T   DIF: I   OBJ: BPE 14-1.4

9. Apes have larger, more developed brains than monkeys.

    ANS: T   DIF: I   OBJ: BPE 14-1.4

10. Most of the proteins encoded by human genes are very similar or even identical to the corresponding proteins in a chimpanzee.

    ANS: T   DIF: I   OBJ: BPE 14-1.5

11. Human hemoglobin differs from gorilla hemoglobin by two amino acids.

    ANS: T   DIF: I   OBJ: BPE 14-1.5

12. Humans and their closest fossil relatives are known as hominids.

    ANS: T   DIF: I   OBJ: BPE 14-2.1

13. The structure of the ape skeleton makes walking upright for a long period of time difficult for apes.

    ANS: T   DIF: I   OBJ: BPE 14-2.1

14. Apes and humans are classified as hominids.

    ANS: F   DIF: I   OBJ: BPE 14-2.1

15. The arms of a gorilla are longer than its legs.

    ANS: T   DIF: I   OBJ: BPE 14-2.1

16. The oldest hominid skeleton unearthed to date is of the species *Ardipithecus ramidus*.

    ANS: T   DIF: I   OBJ: BPE 14-2.3

17. Increased cranial capacity is an evolutionary trend in the hominid group.

    ANS: T   DIF: I   OBJ: BPE 14-2.3

18. Based on an examination of fossils, australopithecines were taller than modern humans.

    ANS: F   DIF: I   OBJ: BPE 14-2.3

19. The fossil Dart found had a rounded jaw, unlike the pointed jaw of apes.

    ANS: T   DIF: I   OBJ: BPE 14-2.3

20. The fossil that Dart found had a larger brain case than the brain case of an ape of similar age.

    ANS: T   DIF: I   OBJ: BPE 14-2.3

21. Lucy's skeleton revealed that she walked on four legs.

    ANS: F   DIF: I   OBJ: BPE 14-2.3

22. *Homo habilis* evolved from australopithecine ancestors.

    ANS: T   DIF: I   OBJ: BPE 14-3.1

23. *Homo habilis* had a larger brain than *Homo erectus*.

    ANS: F   DIF: I   OBJ: BPE 14-3.2

24. *Homo erectus* had a wider geographical distribution than *Homo habilis.*

   ANS: T   DIF: I   OBJ: BPE 14-3.2

25. *Homo erectus* used stone tools.

   ANS: T   DIF: I   OBJ: BPE 14-3.2

26. The evolutionary history of hominids is clearly established and agreed upon by scientists.

   ANS: F   DIF: I   OBJ: BPE 14-3.3

27. An abundance of hominid fossils have been found in Africa.

   ANS: T   DIF: I   OBJ: BPE 14-3.3

28. Scientists think that early *Homo sapiens* had language capability.

   ANS: T   DIF: I   OBJ: BPE 14-3.3

29. Neanderthals are members of the species *Homo sapiens.*

   ANS: T   DIF: I   OBJ: BPE 14-3.4

30. Neanderthals had larger brains than modern humans.

   ANS: T   DIF: I   OBJ: BPE 14-3.4

MULTIPLE CHOICE

1. Fossil evidence indicates that primates evolved from
   a. the great apes.
   b. arthropods.
   c. small, insect-eating, rodentlike mammals.
   d. small hominids.

   ANS: C   DIF: I   OBJ: BPE 14-1.1

2. The ancient mammals that were the ancestors of the first primates lived about
   a. 5 million years ago.
   b. 80 million years ago.
   c. 5 billion years ago.
   d. 80 billion years ago.

   ANS: B   DIF: I   OBJ: BPE 14-1.1

3. The large eye sockets of early primates indicate that these animals probably
   a. had color vision.
   b. had poor eyesight.
   c. had large eyes to compensate for their inability to judge distance.
   d. were active at night.

   ANS: D   DIF: I   OBJ: BPE 14-1.2

4. In order for an animal to be able to judge distance,
   a. the fields of vision of its eyes must be identical.
   b. it must be able to distinguish colors.
   c. it must be able to walk in an upright position.
   d. the fields of vision of its eyes must slightly overlap.

   ANS: D   DIF: I   OBJ: BPE 14-1.2

5. Two distinctive features of all primates are
   a. binocular vision and grasping hands.   c. binocular vision and a large skull.
   b. grasping hands and feet.   d. large eye sockets and binocular vision.

   ANS: A   DIF: I   OBJ: BPE 14-1.2

6. Primates
   a. have five fingers.   c. suckle their offspring on milk.
   b. have hair.   d. All of the above

   ANS: D   DIF: I   OBJ: BPE 14-1.2

7. The first primates to appear were
   a. australopithecines.   c. gorillas.
   b. prosimians.   d. bonobos.

   ANS: B   DIF: I   OBJ: BPE 14-1.3

8. Monkeys
   a. have smaller eyes than prosimians.   c. and prosimians have binocular vision.
   b. have larger brains than prosimians.   d. All of the above

   ANS: D   DIF: I   OBJ: BPE 14-1.3

9. Which of the following animals has a tail?
   a. gorilla   c. chimpanzee
   b. gibbon   d. lemur

   ANS: D   DIF: I   OBJ: BPE 14-1.3

10. Monkeys are different from prosimians in that they
    a. have color vision and larger brains.   c. have binocular vision.
    b. live in trees.   d. only come out at night.

    ANS: A   DIF: I   OBJ: BPE 14-1.3

11. Apes can be distinguished from monkeys because only
    a. monkeys can climb trees.   c. monkeys have an opposable toe.
    b. apes can be found in Africa.   d. monkeys have a tail.

    ANS: D   DIF: I   OBJ: BPE 14-1.4

12. Modern apes include
    a. orangutans.
    b. gorillas.
    c. chimpanzees.
    d. All of the above

    ANS: D   DIF: I   OBJ: BPE 14-1.4

13. Since DNA sequences in humans and chimpanzees are very similar,
    a. humans must have evolved from chimpanzees.
    b. chimpanzees must have single-stranded DNA.
    c. humans and chimpanzees must have a common ancestor in very recent geologic history.
    d. humans and chimpanzees are the same species.

    ANS: C   DIF: I   OBJ: BPE 14-1.5

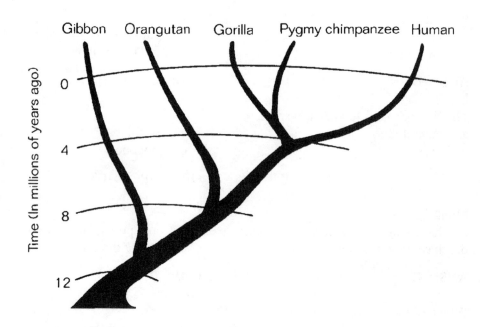

14. Refer to the illustration above. According to the diagram, gorillas evolved
    a. about 3 million years ago.
    b. more than 10 million years ago.
    c. about the same time as modern humans.
    d. after chimpanzees.

    ANS: A   DIF: II   OBJ: BPE 14-1.5

15. Most early hominid fossils have been found in
    a. South America.
    b. Africa.
    c. Australia.
    d. Asia.

    ANS: B   DIF: I   OBJ: BPE 14-2.1

16. In response to environmental changes, human ancestors begain to diverge from the group leadin
    to chimpanzees and bonobos about
    a. 1 million years ago.
    b. 5 to 7 million years ago.
    c. 15–17 million years ago.
    d. None of the above

    ANS: B   DIF: I   OBJ: BPE 14-2.1

17. prosimians : primates ::
    a. primates : hominids
    b. *Ardipithecus* : hominids
    c. *Homo habilis* : hominids
    d. apes : hominids

ANS: B
(were the first)

DIF: II   OBJ: BPE 14-2.1

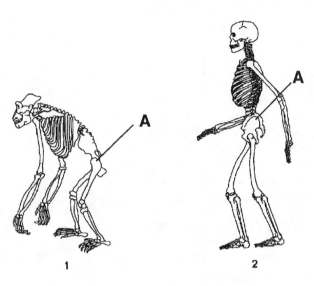

18. Refer to the illustration above. The bone labeled A on both primates is the
    a. pelvis.
    b. femur.
    c. fibula.
    d. spine.

ANS: A   DIF: II   OBJ: BPE 14-2.2

19. Refer to the illustration above. Diagram 2 probably shows the skeleton of a
    a. chimpanzee.
    b. gorilla.
    c. bonobo.
    d. hominid.

ANS: D   DIF: II   OBJ: BPE 14-2.2

20. Refer to the illustration above. By examining the skeletons in the diagram, scientists would
    conclude that both primates
    a. could walk upright on two legs.
    b. had opposable thumbs.
    c. had rather large brains.
    d. All of the above

ANS: D   DIF: II   OBJ: BPE 14-2.2

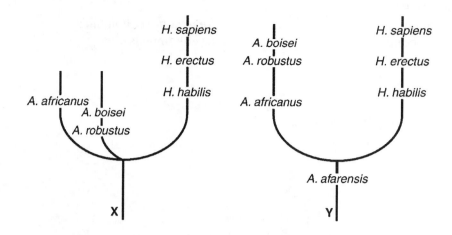

21. By examining the skeletons in the diagram above, scientists conclude that the
    a. gorilla walked upright all of the time.
    b. australopithecine used its arms and legs for walking.
    c. spine of the australopithecine exits at the bottom of the skull.
    d. bowl-shaped pelvis of the gorilla centers its body weight over its legs.

    ANS: C   DIF: II   OBJ: BPE 14-2.2

22. Refer to the illustration above. Which hypothesis is represented by tree X?
    a. An australopithecine is the ancestor of the genus *Homo*.
    b. The genus *Homo* is the ancestor of australopithecines.
    c. *A. africanus* is the ancestor of other australopithecines but not of the genus *Homo*.
    d. The common ancestor of both the australopithecines and the genus *Homo* is unknown.

    ANS: D   DIF: II   OBJ: BPE 14-2.3

23. Refer to the illustration above. Which hypothesis is represented by tree Y?
    a. An australopithecine is the ancestor of the genus *Homo*.
    b. The genus *Homo* is the ancestor of australopithecines.
    c. *A. afarensis* is the ancestor of other australopithecines but not of the genus *Homo*.
    d. The common ancestor of australopithecines and the genus *Homo* is unknown.

    ANS: A   DIF: II   OBJ: BPE 14-2.3

24. Lucy's skeleton revealed that she was bipedal. This means that she
    a. walked using all four limbs.   c. walked on two legs.
    b. lived in trees.   d. crawled along the jungle floor.

    ANS: C   DIF: I   OBJ: BPE 14-2.3

25. An examination of australopithecine fossils indicates that australopithecines
    a. were shorter than modern humans.   c. probably were active during the day.
    b. were bipedal.   d. All of the above

    ANS: D   DIF: I   OBJ: BPE 14-2.4

26. Most scientists agree that the oldest known hominid was
    a. *Homo habilis.*
    b. *Australopithecus afarensis.*
    c. *Australopithecus boisei.*
    d. *Ardipithecus ramidus.*

    ANS: D   DIF: I   OBJ: BPE 14-2.4

27. Which of the following characteristics is most easily inferred from the measurement of a fossil skull's cranial capacity?
    a. intelligence
    b. brain size
    c. cultural development
    d. evolutionary position

    ANS: B   DIF: II   OBJ: BPE 14-2.4

28. *Homo habilis*
    a. is known for its large brain.
    b. used crude stone tools.
    c. lived in Africa.
    d. All of the above

    ANS: D   DIF: I   OBJ: BPE 14-3.1

29. The first member of the genus *Homo* was
    a. *Homo sapiens.*
    b. *Homo erectus.*
    c. *Homo habilis.*
    d. *Homo hominid.*

    ANS: C   DIF: I   OBJ: BPE 14-3.1

30. Evidence of the intelligence of *Homo erectus* includes
    a. the large eye sockets they had.
    b. the written messages they left on cave walls.
    c. finding the tools that they made.
    d. the signs of their primitive agriculture.

    ANS: C   DIF: I   OBJ: BPE 14-3.2

31. *Homo erectus* had a
    a. pair of large eye sockets.
    b. lighter skeleton than other hominids.
    c. written language.
    d. brain almost as large as that of modern humans.

    ANS: D   DIF: I   OBJ: BPE 14-3.2

32. *Homo erectus*
    a. had a large brain.
    b. walked erect.
    c. was larger than *Homo habilis.*
    d. All of the above

    ANS: D   DIF: I   OBJ: BPE 14-3.2

33. Hunting large animals and butchering them using flint and bone tools, as well as living in caves or wooden shelters, are associated with
    a. *H. habilis.*
    b. *A. africanus.*
    c. *A. robustus.*
    d. *H. erectus.*

    ANS: D   DIF: I   OBJ: BPE 14-3.2

34. Fossils of *Homo erectus* were first discovered on the island of
    a. Aruba.
    b. St. Martinique.
    c. Japan.
    d. Java.

    ANS: D   DIF: I   OBJ: BPE 14-3.2

35. When comparing *Homo habilis* and *Homo erectus*, we find that
    a. *Homo habilis* was taller and walked upright.
    b. *Homo habilis* had a larger brain.
    c. *Homo erectus* was taller and walked upright.
    d. *Homo erectus* built houses and grew crops.

    ANS: C   DIF: I   OBJ: BPE 14-3.2

36. orangutan : ape ::
    a. *Homo erectus* : hominid
    b. *Australopithecus* : *Homo*
    c. monkey : ape
    d. hominid : ape

    ANS: A
    (is a type of)

    DIF: II   OBJ: BPE 14-3.2

37. *Homo erectus* were the direct ancestors of
    a. *Homo habilis.*
    b. *Australopithecus.*
    c. *Homo sapiens.*
    d. the genus *Homo.*

    ANS: C   DIF: I   OBJ: BPE 14-3.3

38. *Homo sapiens* appeared in Africa about
    a. 50,000,000 years ago.
    b. 5,000,000 years ago.
    c. 500,000 years ago.
    d. 50,000 years ago.

    ANS: C   DIF: I   OBJ: BPE 14-3.3

39. Scientists infer that early *H. sapiens* had language capability because
    a. prehistoric writings have been found in their caves.
    b. language was essential to maintain social interaction.
    c. the shape of their skulls indicates they could speak.
    d. All of the above

    ANS: C   DIF: I   OBJ: BPE 14-3.4

40. The Neanderthals are noted for
    a. burying their dead.
    b. using several different types of tools.
    c. having a larger brain size than modern humans.
    d. All of the above

    ANS: D   DIF: I   OBJ: BPE 14-3.4

41. Modern humans are most closely related to
    a. *A. boisei.*   c. *A. africanus.*
    b. Neanderthals.   d. *Homo habilis.*

    ANS: B   DIF: I   OBJ: BPE 14-3.4

COMPLETION

1. The group of animals known as _____ includes human beings, apes, and monkeys.

    ANS: primates   DIF: I   OBJ: BPE 14-1.2

2. Front-facing eyes and a reduced snout contribute to a primate's _____ perception.

    ANS: depth   DIF: I   OBJ: BPE 14-1.2

3. Most primate characteristics are adaptations to life in _____.

    ANS: trees   DIF: I   OBJ: BPE 14-1.2

4. Humans belong to the order of mammals called _____.

    ANS: primates   DIF: I   OBJ: BPE 14-1.2

5. A(n) _____ thumb can be bent toward the other fingers.

    ANS: opposable   DIF: I   OBJ: BPE 14-1.2

6. The position of the eyes in primates allows them to have _____ vision.

    ANS: binocular   DIF: I   OBJ: BPE 14-1.2

7. Organisms that are active during the day and sleep at night are said to be _____.

    ANS: diurnal   DIF: I   OBJ: BPE 14-1.3

8. _____ were the first primates and hunted primarily at night.

    ANS: Prosimians   DIF: I   OBJ: BPE 14-1.3

9. Apes first appeared about _____ million years ago.

    ANS: 30   DIF: I   OBJ: BPE 14-1.4

10. Humans and apes share a common _____.

    ANS: ancestor   DIF: I   OBJ: BPE 14-1.5

11. The most complete hominid fossil ever found was that of a female nicknamed _____.

    ANS: Lucy   DIF: I   OBJ: BPE 14-2.4

12. Most researchers think that *Ardipithecus* _____ is the ancestor of all other hominids.

    ANS: *ramidus*   DIF: I   OBJ: BPE 14-2.4

13. _____ _____ is the term used for the human ancestor that made simple tools.

    ANS: *Homo habilis*   DIF: I   OBJ: BPE 14-3.1

14. Java man and _____ man belong to the species *Homo erectus*.

    ANS: Peking   DIF: I   OBJ: BPE 14-3.2

15. The appearance of *Homo* _____ marked the beginnings of an expansion of hominid populations across the globe.

    ANS: *erectus*   DIF: I   OBJ: BPE 14-3.2

16. Modern humans all over the Earth belong to the species _____ _____.

    ANS: *Homo sapiens*   DIF: I   OBJ: BPE 14-3.3

17. The first *Homo sapiens* fossils in Europe were found in the _____ Valley of Germany.

    ANS: Neander   DIF: I   OBJ: BPE 14-3.3

18. Analysis of _____ DNA indicates that *H. sapiens* probably evolved in Africa.

    ANS: mitochondrial   DIF: I   OBJ: BPE 14-3.3

19. Remains of human ancestors known as _____ were first found in modern-day Germany.

ANS: Neanderthals   DIF: I   OBJ: BPE 14-3.4

20. Neanderthals are classified in the species _____ _____.

ANS: *Homo sapiens*   DIF: I   OBJ: BPE 14-3.4

21. Verbal communication is unique to the species _____
_____.

ANS: *Homo sapiens*   DIF: I   OBJ: BPE 14-3.4

ESSAY

1. Describe adaptations of primate vision for living in trees.

ANS:
Good vision is an adaptive trait for tree dwellers. Cones, color-sensitive cells in the eyes, give primates color vision. This allows primates to locate ripe fruit in trees. Front-facing eyes and a reduced snout enable primates to integrate images from both eyes simultaneously and thus perceive depth accurately. Therefore arboreal primates can gauge distances as they leap or swing from branch to branch.

DIF: II   OBJ: BPE 14-1.3

2. Describe the abilities of humans and apes to communicate.

ANS:
Humans have the unique ability to communicate using verbal language. Apes communicate through sounds and gestures; they can also be taught to use certain forms of sign language. However, apes in the wild have not developed any complex, flexible set of signals that can compare to those of human language.

DIF: II   OBJ: BPE 14-1.5

3. Why was the evolution of a large brain important to human evolution?

ANS:
An increased brain size allowed humans to modify their environments as they developed tools, art, symbolic communication, and language.

DIF: II   OBJ: BPE 14-2.2

4. Describe adaptations of the human skeleton for bipedalism.

ANS:
Differences in the pelvic bones of apes and humans correlate with differences in modes of locomotion. The broad shape and muscular attachments of the human pelvis are adaptations for bipedalism. The pelvis supports the internal organs during upright walking. Another adaptation for bipedalism is the shape of the human foot. The bones of the big toe are in alignment with those of the other toes. This causes body weight to be distributed evenly during upright walking.

DIF: II   OBJ: BPE 14-2.2

5. If you were looking for early hominid fossils, where would you search? Why?

ANS:
Africa. The earliest relatives of humans, the chimpanzees and gorillas, lived in Africa.

DIF: II   OBJ: BPE 14-3.3

6. How were Neanderthals similar to modern humans?

ANS:
The bodies of Neanderthals were similar to the bodies of modern humans. In addition, Neanderthals made complex stone tools and shelters, took care of their sick and injured, and buried their dead.

DIF: II   OBJ: BPE 14-3.4

Biology: Principles and Explorations
202

CHAPTER 15—CLASSIFICATION OF ORGANISMS

TRUE/FALSE

1. The Greeks developed the simple system used today for naming organisms.

   ANS: F   DIF: I   OBJ: BPE 15-1.1

2. Carolus Linnaeus simplified the system for naming groups of organisms.

   ANS: T   DIF: I   OBJ: BPE 15-1.1

3. Genus is the basic biological unit in the Linnaean system of classification.

   ANS: F   DIF: I   OBJ: BPE 15-1.2

4. Species is a taxonomic category containing several genera.

   ANS: F   DIF: I   OBJ: BPE 15-1.2

5. Two different organisms can have the same scientific name.

   ANS: F   DIF: I   OBJ: BPE 15-1.2

6. Under the Linnaean system of classification, organisms are grouped based on form and structure.

   ANS: T   DIF: I   OBJ: BPE 15-1.2

7. Linnaeus devised the seven levels into to which different groups of organisms can be classified.

   ANS: F   DIF: I   OBJ: BPE 15-1.3

8. The least inclusive group to which an organism can be assigned is its kingdom.

   ANS: F   DIF: I   OBJ: BPE 15-1.3

9. A species is the smallest taxonomic group into which an organism can be assigned.

   ANS: T   DIF: I   OBJ: BPE 15-1.3

10. Each level of classification contains all organisms that share the same characteristics.

    ANS: T   DIF: I   OBJ: BPE 15-2.1

11. All organisms in the kingdom Animalia are multicellular heterotrophs whose cells lack cell walls.

    ANS: T   DIF: I   OBJ: BPE 15-2.1

12. Dogs and wolves cannot interbreed to produce fertile offspring.

    ANS: F   DIF: I   OBJ: BPE 15-2.2

13. Interbreeding individuals of different species produce a hybrid.

    ANS: T   DIF: I   OBJ: BPE 15-2.2

14. Classification provides strong evidence supporting Darwinian evolution.

    ANS: T   DIF: I   OBJ: BPE 15-2.3

15. All traits are inherited from a common ancestor.

    ANS: F   DIF: I   OBJ: BPE 15-2.3

16. Bat wings and bird wings are examples of analogous structures.

    ANS: F   DIF: I   OBJ: BPE 15-2.3

17. Similar traits that evolve independently are the result of convergent evolution.

    ANS: T   DIF: I   OBJ: BPE 15-2.3

18. Cladistics is used to determine the sequence in which different groups of organisms evolved.

    ANS: T   DIF: I   OBJ: BPE 15-2.4

19. Cladograms are models that show the evolutionary relationship among homologous traits.

    ANS: F   DIF: I   OBJ: BPE 15-2.4

20. On a cladogram, all organisms share all traits.

    ANS: F   DIF: I   OBJ: BPE 15-2.4

21. An out-group is an unrelated organism on a cladogram.

    ANS: F   DIF: I   OBJ: BPE 15-2.4

MULTIPLE CHOICE

1. Linnaeus's two-word system for naming organisms is called
   a. taxonomic evolution.
   b. Genus species.
   c. Greek polynomials.
   d. binomial nomenclature.

   ANS: D   DIF: I   OBJ: BPE 15-1.1

2. Taxonomy is
   a. the study of life.
   b. the science of naming and classifying organisms.
   c. the evolutionary history of a species.
   d. the sequence in which different groups evolved.

   ANS: B   DIF: I   OBJ: BPE 15-1.1

3. All scientific names must have
   a. two Latin words.
   b. the same species name.
   c. different genus names for organisms within the group.
   d. the same common name.

   ANS: A   DIF: I   OBJ: BPE 15-1.2

4. The basic biological unit in the Linnaean system of classification is the
   a. kingdom.   c. genus.
   b. family.   d. species.

   ANS: D   DIF: I   OBJ: BPE 15-1.2

5. An advantage of our scientific naming system is that
   a. common names mean the same in all countries.
   b. Latin names are easy to pronounce.
   c. biologists can communicate regardless of their native languages.
   d. organisms all have the same scientific name.

   ANS: C   DIF: I   OBJ: BPE 15-1.2

6. Under the Linnaean system of classification, plants and animals are sorted into groups based on
   a. number and size.   c. form and size.
   b. form and structure.   d. number and structure.

   ANS: B   DIF: I   OBJ: BPE 15-1.3

7. The largest division that a group of organisms can belong to is
   a. kingdom.   c. genus.
   b. class.   d. species.

   ANS: A   DIF: I   OBJ: BPE 15-1.3

8. Protista is an example of a(n)
   a. kingdom.   c. genus.
   b. class.   d. species.

   ANS: A   DIF: I   OBJ: BPE 15-1.3

9. Similar genera are grouped into a(n)
    a. phylum.   c. family.
    b. class.   d. order.

    ANS: C   DIF: I   OBJ: BPE 15-1.3

10. Species
    a. is a narrowly defined group of   c. has the same meaning as "population."
        organisms.
    b. is a broadly defined group of organisms.   d. None of the above

    ANS: A   DIF: I   OBJ: BPE 15-1.3

11. Each level of classification is based on
    a. specific characteristics.   c. shared characteristics.
    b. general characteristics.   d. All of the above

    ANS: C   DIF: I   OBJ: BPE 15-2.1

12. A biological species
    a. cannot interbreed within the natural population.
    b. is isolated reproductively from other species.
    c. can easily be differentiated from others based on appearance.
    d. interbreed producing infertile offspring.

    ANS: B   DIF: I   OBJ: BPE 15-2.2

13. A hybrid is produced from
    a. interbreeding between same species.
    b. interbreeding between distantly related species.
    c. interbreeding between closely related species.
    d. cannot be produced in plants.

    ANS: C   DIF: I   OBJ: BPE 15-2.2

14. Dogs and wolves are members of
    a. the same family.   c. different species.
    b. the same genus.   d. All of the above

    ANS: D   DIF: I   OBJ: BPE 15-2.2

15. The biological species concept is difficult to apply to
    a. sexually reproducing organisms.   c. organisms that produce pollen.
    b. asexually reproducing organisms. d. organisms that live in groups.

    ANS: B   DIF: I   OBJ: BPE 15-2.2

16. interbreeding : hybrids
    a. water : growth
    b. mitosis : meiosis
    c. natural selection : change
    d. homologous : environment

    ANS: C
    (produces)

    DIF: II   OBJ: BPE 15-2.2

17. Similar features evolved through convergent evolution are called
    a. analogous characters.
    b. homologous characters.
    c. environmental characters.
    d. genetic characters.

    ANS: A   DIF: I   OBJ: BPE 15-2.3

18. Convergent evolution produces similar features in different organisms as the result of
    a. similar environments.
    b. pressure by natural selection.
    c. sharing a common ancestor.
    d. Both (a) and (b)

    ANS: D   DIF: I   OBJ: BPE 15-2.3

19. Analogous structures
    a. have the same form in all organisms.
    b. perform the same function in all organisms.
    c. have the same structure in all organisms.
    d. evolve from a common ancestor.

    ANS: B   DIF: I   OBJ: BPE 15-2.3

20. A model used by evolutionary biologists to represent the evolutionary history among species is called a(n)
    a. phylogeny.
    b. cladogram.
    c. histogram.
    d. parallelogram.

    ANS: B   DIF: I   OBJ: BPE 15-2.4

21. Derived characteristics are traits
    a. shared by all species.
    b. originate in a common ancestor.
    c. are found in closely related species.
    d. are found in distantly related species.

    ANS: C   DIF: I   OBJ: BPE 15-2.4

22. Evolutionary systematics emphasizes the importance of
    a. derived characteristics.
    b. unique characteristics.
    c. shared characteristics.
    d. compared characteristics.

    ANS: B   DIF: I   OBJ: BPE 15-2.4

COMPLETION

1. Aristotle grouped plants and animals according to their _____ similarities.

   ANS: structural   DIF: I   OBJ: BPE 15-1.1

2. _____ developed the current system used for naming organisms.

   ANS: Linnaeus   DIF: I   OBJ: BPE 15-1.1

3. The two-word system for naming organisms is called _____ _____.

   ANS: binomial nomenclature   DIF: I   OBJ: BPE 15-1.2

4. All names assigned to organisms under the Linnaean system are in the _____ language.

   ANS: Latin   DIF: I   OBJ: BPE 15-1.2

5. The unique two-word name for a species is its _____ name.

   ANS: scientific   DIF: I   OBJ: BPE 15-1.2

6. The scientific name of an organism gives biologists a common way of _____ regardless of their native languages.

   ANS: communicating   DIF: I   OBJ: BPE 15-1.2

7. An organism is assigned a(n) _____ based on its major characteristics.

   ANS: genus   DIF: I   OBJ: BPE 15-1.2

8. There are _____ levels of classification.

   ANS: seven   DIF: I   OBJ: BPE 15-1.3

9. Archaebacteria is one of six _____.

   ANS: kingdoms   DIF: I   OBJ: BPE 15-1.3

10. Classes with similar characteristics are assigned to a(n) _____.

    ANS: phylum   DIF: I   OBJ: BPE 15-1.3

11. Each level of classification is based on _____ shared by all the organisms it contains.

ANS: characteristics   DIF: I   OBJ: BPE 15-1.3

12. _____ is a rank system of groups that increase in inclusiveness.

ANS: Taxonomy   DIF: I   OBJ: BPE 15-1.3

13. *Homo habilis, Homo erectus,* and *Homo sapiens* all belong to the same _____.

ANS: genus   DIF: I   OBJ: BPE 15-1.3

14. Biologists may classify organisms based on physical, molecular, or _____ characteristics.

ANS: behavioral   DIF: I   OBJ: BPE 15-2.1

15. A(n) _____ species is a group of actually or potentially interbreeding natural populations that are reproductively isolated from other such groups.

ANS: biological   DIF: I   OBJ: BPE 15-2.2

16. A(n) _____ is produced through breeding closely related species.

ANS: hybrid   DIF: I   OBJ: BPE 15-2.2

17. The formation of a new volcano that divides a population into two populations results in _____ isolation of the newly formed populations.

ANS: reproductive   DIF: I   OBJ: BPE 15-2.2

18. Most species of plants, some mammals, and many fishes are able to form _____ hybrids with one another.

ANS: fertile   DIF: I   OBJ: BPE 15-2.2

19. Making evolutionary connections based on similar _____ can be misleading because not all traits are inherited from a common ancestor.

ANS: traits   DIF: I   OBJ: BPE 15-2.3

20. _____ evolution results in similar characteristics found in different organisms as the result of selection within similar environments.

ANS: Convergent   DIF: I   OBJ: BPE 15-2.3

21. Analogous structures are found in _____ taxa as a result of similar environmental conditions.

    ANS: different   DIF: I   OBJ: BPE 15-2.3

22. Homologous structures are found in organisms that once shared a(n) _____ ancestor.

    ANS: common   DIF: I   OBJ: BPE 15-2.3

23. The evolutionary history of a species is called its _____.

    ANS: phylogeny   DIF: I   OBJ: BPE 15-2.3

24. _____ is a system of taxonomy that reconstructs phylogenies by inferring relationships based on similarities.

    ANS: Cladistics   DIF: I   OBJ: BPE 15-2.4

25. A model developed by taxonomists that diagrams the evolutionary relationships among species i called a(n) _____.

    ANS: cladogram   DIF: I   OBJ: BPE 15-2.4

26. Cladistics is used to determine the _____ in which different groups of organisms evolved.

    ANS: sequence or order   DIF: I   OBJ: BPE 15-2.4

27. Species that have unique characteristics or traits that arose after divergence from other species are said to have _____ traits.

    ANS: derived   DIF: I   OBJ: BPE 15-2.4

28. Animals that appear early on a cladogram do not have all of the same _____ traits as the animals that appear later on the cladogram.

    ANS: derived   DIF: I   OBJ: BPE 15-2.4

29. Unlike cladistics, evolutionary systematics places more _____ on some traits than on others.

    ANS: importance   DIF: I   OBJ: BPE 15-2.4

30. Evolutionary systematics requires _____ information than cladistics.

    ANS: more   DIF: I   OBJ: BPE 15-2.4

ESSAY

1. How did Linnaeus's system of naming organisms simplify and improve the task of naming organisms?

   ANS:
   The polynomial system that existed prior to the Linnaean system of naming organisms produced long and cumbersome names which biologists often changed. Linnaeus gave each organism a two-word Latin name reducing unwieldy names to something more manageable. Because his system has been universally adopted, scientists around the globe can discuss the same organism regardless of their native languages.

   DIF: II   OBJ: BPE 15-1.1

2. Describe the levels of classification in order of increasing inclusiveness.

   ANS:
   The species level is the least inclusive and most specific of all levels containing only those within a species that cannot, generally, interbreed with any organisms outside their own species and contain characteristic molecular, behavioral, as well as morphologic traits. All species with similar characteristics are contained within a genus. All genera with similar characteristics are contained within a family. All families with similar characteristics are contained within an order. All orders with similar characteristics are contained within a class. All classes with similar characteristics are contained within a phylum. All phyla with similar characteristics are contained within a kingdom.

   DIF: II   OBJ: BPE 15-1.3

3. What characteristics do biologists use to classify organisms?

   ANS:
   Taxonomists use physical, molecular, and behavioral characteristics to classify organisms.

   DIF: II   OBJ: BPE 15-2.1

4. A new species of animal is identified in the tropical climate of the northwest coast of Africa. The animal looks similar to a species located in the temperate climate of the southeast coast of North America. How could scientists explain the similarities between the two species?

   ANS:
   Since the organisms have developed in different environments and appear to have similar characteristics, scientists may hypothesize that the species shared a common ancestor in the recent geologic past.

   DIF: II   OBJ: BPE 15-2.3

5. What is the relationship between environment and analogous structures?

ANS:
Analogous structures are physical characteristics shared by organisms from vastly different taxa such as the wings of birds and the wings of insects. While these structures perform similar functions for both groups, these analogous structures do not exist in both groups due to common ancestral origin, but rather exist as a result of convergent evolution. Similar structural characteristics in taxa so distantly related that they may be considered unrelated arise as a result of selective pressure under similar environmental conditions.

DIF: II   OBJ: BPE 15-2.3

6. Compare and contrast cladistics with evolutionary systematics.

ANS:
Both cladistics and evolutionary systematics provide taxonomists with models that may be used to determine phylogenetic relationships between taxonomic groups, particularly species. Cladistics provides evolutionary biologists with an objective tool for organizing taxonomic groups as it weighs all characteristics equally. Evolutionary systematics applies a more subjective view as this approach assigns weights to characteristics based on the importance of the each characteristic to the survival of the organism.

DIF: II   OBJ: BPE 15-2.4

TRUE/FALSE

1. The study of demographics helps predict changes in the size of a population.

   ANS: T   DIF: I   OBJ: BPE 16-1.1

2. Very small populations are less likely to become extinct than larger populations.

   ANS: F   DIF: I   OBJ: BPE 16-1.1

3. Wastes tend to accumulate in the environment as a population reaches the carrying capacity.

   ANS: T   DIF: I   OBJ: BPE 16-1.2

4. Populations of *K*-strategists grow rapidly, while *r*-strategist populations grow slowly.

   ANS: F   DIF: I   OBJ: BPE 16-1.3

5. The Hardy-Weinberg principle states that the proportions of recessive and dominant alleles in a population fluctuate randomly from generation to generation.

   ANS: F   DIF: I   OBJ: BPE 16-2.1

6. Mutations are so common that they are the major cause of changes in allele frequencies within a population.

   ANS: F   DIF: I   OBJ: BPE 16-2.2

7. Natural selection acts on phenotypes, not genotypes.

   ANS: T   DIF: I   OBJ: BPE 16-2.3

8. Natural selection always eliminates any genetic disorders from a population, regardless of the frequency of the gene that is responsible for a disorder.

   ANS: F   DIF: I   OBJ: BPE 16-2.3

9. Directional selection results in the range of phenotypes shifting toward one extreme.

   ANS: T   DIF: I   OBJ: BPE 16-2.4

10. In stabilizing selection, the range of phenotypes becomes wider.

    ANS: F   DIF: I   OBJ: BPE 16-2.4

MULTIPLE CHOICE

1. Which of the following does *not* represent a population?
   a. all the robins in Austin, Texas
   b. all the grass frogs in the pond of Central Park, New York City
   c. all the birds in Chicago, Illinois
   d. all the earthworms in Yosemite National Park

   ANS: C   DIF: I   OBJ: BPE 16-1.1

2. Since individuals in a population usually tend to produce more than one offspring,
   a. populations tend to increase in size.
   b. populations remain stable in size.
   c. individuals tend to die quickly.
   d. the number of individuals declines rapidly.

   ANS: A   DIF: I   OBJ: BPE 16-1.1

3. All of the following are problems arising from inbreeding, *except*
   a. production of a genetically uniform population.
   b. increases in the diversity within a population.
   c. increased chance of homozygous recessive alleles occurring.
   d. reduction of a population's ability to adapt to environmental changes.

   ANS: B   DIF: I   OBJ: BPE 16-1.1

4. Demographic studies of populations must take into consideration
   a. population size.   c. population dispersion.
   b. population density.   d. All of the above

   ANS: D   DIF: I   OBJ: BPE 16-1.1

5. Regarding population dispersion patterns, which of the following is an *improper* pairing?
   a. randomly spaced — chance   c. clumped — clusters
   b. evenly spaced — regular intervals   d. dispersive — randomly distributed

   ANS: D   DIF: I   OBJ: BPE 16-1.1

6. population density : number of individuals in a given area ::
   a. population : an area where organisms live
   b. logistic growth : how populations grow in nature
   c. logistic growth curve : exponential rate of growth
   d. population size : population density

   ANS: B
   (describes)

   DIF: II   OBJ: BPE 16-1.1

7. As a population reaches its carrying capacity, there is an increase in competition for
   a. food.
   b. shelter.
   c. mates.
   d. All of the above

   ANS: D   DIF: I   OBJ: BPE 16-1.2

Population Growth Over Time

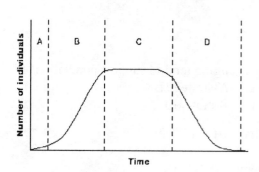

8. Refer to the illustration above. Which time period shows exponential growth of the population?
   a. period A
   b. period B
   c. period C
   d. period D

   ANS: B   DIF: II   OBJ: BPE 16-1.2

9. Refer to the illustration above. During which time period are the birth rate and death rate equal?
   a. period A
   b. period B
   c. period C
   d. period D

   ANS: C   DIF: II   OBJ: BPE 16-1.2

10. Refer to the illustration above. The rate of growth of a population is represented by r. During which time period will $r = 0$?
    a. period A
    b. period B
    c. period C
    d. period D

    ANS: C   DIF: II   OBJ: BPE 16-1.2

11. Refer to the illustration above. The time period during which r (the rate of growth of a population) would have a negative value is
    a. period A.
    b. period B.
    c. period C.
    d. period D.

    ANS: D   DIF: II   OBJ: BPE 16-1.2

12. birth and death rates : constant on exponential growth curve ::
    a. birth rates : equal to death rates
    b. *r*-strategists : equal to *K*-strategists
    c. birth and death rates : not constant on logistic growth curve
    d. exponential models : same as logistic models

    ANS: C
    (are assumed to be)

    DIF: II   OBJ: BPE 16-1.2

13. Environments that are unpredictable and rapidly changing tend to support populations of
    a. *Q*-strategists.   c. *N*-strategists.
    b. *K*-strategists.   d. *r*-strategists.

    ANS: D   DIF: I   OBJ: BPE 16-1.3

14. All of the following are true of *r*-strategists, *except*
    a. early maturation and reproduction.   c. few offspring.
    b. little parental care.   d. offspring are small.

    ANS: C   DIF: I   OBJ: BPE 16-1.3

15. Which of the following is an *r*-strategist?
    a. redwoods   c. whales
    b. dandelions   d. humans

    ANS: B   DIF: I   OBJ: BPE 16-1.3

16. Which of the following is *improperly* paired?
    a. *K*-strategists — reproduce late in life   c. *r*-strategists — reproduce early in life
    b. *K*-strategists — minimal parental care   d. *r*-strategists — mature quickly

    ANS: B   DIF: I   OBJ: BPE 16-1.3

17. bacteria : *r*-strategists ::
    a. gorillas : *K*-strategists   c. annual plants : *K*-strategists
    b. insects : *K*-strategists   d. rhinoceroses : *r*-strategists

    ANS: A
    (are an example of)

    DIF: II   OBJ: BPE 16-1.3

18. In 1908, Hardy and Weinberg independently demonstrated that
    a. *r*- and *K*-strategist populations are actually the same.
    b. recessive alleles replace dominant alleles in a population over long periods of time.
    c. dominant alleles do not replace recessive alleles in a population.
    d. recessive alleles are usually more common than dominant alleles.

    ANS: C   DIF: I   OBJ: BPE 16-2.1

19. Actual proportions of homozygotes and heterozygotes can differ from Hardy-Weinberg predictions because of
   a. the occurrence of mutations.
   b. nonrandom mating among individuals.
   c. genetic drift within the population.
   d. All of the above

   ANS: D   DIF: I   OBJ: BPE 16-2.1

20. The movement of alleles into or out of a population due to migration is called
   a. mutation.
   b. gene flow.
   c. nonrandom mating.
   d. natural selection.

   ANS: B   DIF: I   OBJ: BPE 16-2.2

21. Inbreeding
   a. is a form of random mating.
   b. causes mutations to occur.
   c. increases the proportion of heterozygotes.
   d. increases the proportion of homozygotes.

   ANS: D   DIF: I   OBJ: BPE 16-2.2

22. nonrandom mating : increasing proportion of homozygotes ::
   a. migration of individuals : gene flow
   b. mutation : major change in allele frequencies
   c. Hardy-Weinberg equation : natural selection
   d. inbreeding : frequency of alleles

   ANS: A
   (results in)

   DIF: II   OBJ: BPE 16-2.2

23. homozygous : heterozygous ::
   a. heterozygous : *Bb*
   b. probability : predicting chances
   c. dominant : recessive
   d. factor : gene

   ANS: C
   (is the opposite of)

   DIF: II   OBJ: BPE 16-2.2

24. Natural selection acts
   a. only on heterozygous genotypes.
   b. only on recessive alleles.
   c. on phenotypes that are expressed.
   d. on all mutations.

   ANS: C   DIF: I   OBJ: BPE 16-2.3

25. Directional selection tends to eliminate
    a. both extremes in a range of phenotypes.
    b. one extreme in a range of phenotypes.
    c. intermediate phenotypes.
    d. None of the above; it causes new phenotypes to form.

    ANS: B   DIF: I   OBJ: BPE 16-2.4

26. The range of phenotypes shifts toward one extreme in
    a. stabilizing selection.   c. directional selection.
    b. disruptive selection.   d. polygenic selection.

    ANS: C   DIF: I   OBJ: BPE 16-2.4

COMPLETION

1. A(n) _____ consists of all the individuals of a particular species in a particul
    place.

    ANS: population   DIF: I   OBJ: BPE 16-1.1

2. _____ is the statistical study of all populations.

    ANS: Demography   DIF: I   OBJ: BPE 16-1.1

3. Population density refers to how many _____ are present in a particular
    location.

    ANS: individuals   DIF: I   OBJ: BPE 16-1.1

4. The way in which members of a population are arranged in a given area is referred to as
    _____.

    ANS: dispersion   DIF: I   OBJ: BPE 16-1.1

5. A population _____ is a hypothetical population that has key characteristics
    the real population being studied.

    ANS: model   DIF: I   OBJ: BPE 16-1.2

6. _____ _____ is defined as the difference between the birt
    rate and death rate of a population.

    ANS: Growth rate   DIF: I   OBJ: BPE 16-1.2

7. The _____ _____ is the population size that can be
    sustained by an environment.

    ANS: carrying capacity   DIF: I   OBJ: BPE 16-1.2

8. Species that are _____ -strategists tend to have periods of exponential growth followed by sudden crashes in population size.

    ANS: *r*   DIF: I   OBJ: BPE 16-1.3

9. Small population sizes and slow population growth are typical of organisms that are _____ -strategists.

    ANS: *K*   DIF: I   OBJ: BPE 16-1.3

10. Stable and predictable environments tend to be inhabited by populations of organisms that are _____ -strategists.

    ANS: *K*   DIF: I   OBJ: BPE 16-1.3

11. Alternative versions of genes are called _____.

    ANS: alleles   DIF: I   OBJ: BPE 16-2.1

12. The movement of individuals from one population to another is called _____.

    ANS: migration   DIF: I   OBJ: BPE 16-2.2

13. Migration creates _____ _____.

    ANS: gene flow   DIF: I   OBJ: BPE 16-2.2

14. A characteristic influenced by several genes is called a(n) _____ trait.

    ANS: polygenic   DIF: I   OBJ: BPE 16-2.3

15. _____ selection causes the range of phenotypes to become narrower, increasing the number of individuals with characteristics near the middle of the range.

    ANS: Stabilizing   DIF: I   OBJ: BPE 16-2.4

ESSAY

1. The graph below depicts the growth of a population of fruit flies over time.

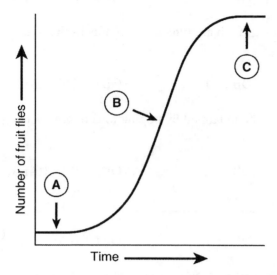

a. Why does the population stop increasing after it reaches the point on the curve labeled C?
b. Would a density-dependent limiting factor have a greater impact on the population at point A, B, or C on the curve? Why?
c. Name one density-independent limiting factor that could affect this population of fruit flies. Would you expect this limiting factor to have a greater impact on the population at any particular point on the curve, and if so, which one?

ANS:

a. The population has reached the carrying capacity of the ecosystem in which it lives. The ecosystem cannot support any more flies than this number.
b. It would have the greatest impact on the population at point C. This is because it is at point on the curve that there is the greatest population density. Density-dependent limiting factors impact populations more as they increase in size.
c. A number of abiotic factors would be suitable answers: temperature extremes (e.g. freezing floods, hurricanes, fires, and volcanic eruptions. Such limiting factors would not be expecte to have a greater impact on the population at any particular point on the curve.

DIF: III   OBJ: BPE 16-1.2

2. Contrast exponential growth with logisitical growth by completing the chart.

Criteria	Exponential Population Growth	Logistic Population Growth
Graph of Growth Rate		
Assumptions		
Birth and death Rates		

ANS:

Criteria	Exponential Population Growth	Logistic Population Growth
Graph of Growth Rate		
Assumptions	unlimited resources	resources limit population growth; stabilizes at the carrying capacity
Birth and death Rates	constant—rates do not change	vary with population size

DIF: II   OBJ: BPE 16-1.2

3. Explain the difference between *r*-strategist and *K*-strategist populations.

ANS:
These two types of populations differ in their rates of maturation and reproduction, the amount of parental care of offspring, and the type of environments that they inhabit. Species that are *r*-strategists mature quickly, reproduce in large numbers, and invest little energy in care of their offspring. This adapts them for unpredictable, rapidly changing environments. *K*-strategists tend to be larger organisms that mature more gradually and exhibit parental care of a smaller number of offspring. *K*-strategists are found in more stable environments.

DIF: II   OBJ: BPE 16-1.3

4. Distinguish between the two types of natural selection acting on polygenic traits.

ANS:
Directional selection tends to eliminate individuals in a population that are at one or the other extreme of the range of phenotypes. Stabilizing selection narrows the range of individuals to those in the middle of the range.

DIF: II   OBJ: BPE 16-2.4

TRUE/FALSE

1. Ecologists call the physical location of a community its habitat.

   ANS: T   DIF: I   OBJ: BPE 17-1.1

2. Ecosystems include only the biotic factors in an area.

   ANS: F   DIF: I   OBJ: BPE 17-1.1

3. A community includes all the species within an area.

   ANS: T   DIF: I   OBJ: BPE 17-1.1

4. Biotic factors in a habitat include all the physical aspects as well as the living organisms.

   ANS: F   DIF: I   OBJ: BPE 17-1.1

5. Biotic factors of a habitat include all abiotic factors.

   ANS: F   DIF: I   OBJ: BPE 17-1.1

6. The number of species living within an ecosystem is a measure of its biodiversity.

   ANS: T   DIF: I   OBJ: BPE 17-1.2

7. The major difference between primary succession and secondary succession is that primary succession occurs only on land and secondary succession occurs in ponds and lakes.

   ANS: F   DIF: I   OBJ: BPE 17-1.3

8. Cutting down trees in a forest alters the habitat of the organisms living in the forest.

   ANS: T   DIF: I   OBJ: BPE 17-1.3

9. When succession takes place in an area where there has been previous growth, it is called secondary succession.

   ANS: T   DIF: I   OBJ: BPE 17-1.3

10. The first organisms to live in a new habitat are large, slow-growing plants.

    ANS: F   DIF: I   OBJ: BPE 17-1.3

11. In a new habitat, pioneer species are eventually replaced by other plant immigrants.

    ANS: T   DIF: I   OBJ: BPE 17-1.3

12. A receding glacier is a good example of secondary succession.

    ANS: F   DIF: I   OBJ: BPE 17-1.3

13. Glaciers, like the ones in Alaska, move very slowly and are good for showing changes that have taken place as time passes.

    ANS: T   DIF: I   OBJ: BPE 17-1.3

14. When an organism dies, the nutrients in its body are released by back into the environment by decomposers.

    ANS: T   DIF: I   OBJ: BPE 17-2.1

15. Decomposers absorb energy from organisms by breaking down living tissue.

    ANS: F   DIF: I   OBJ: BPE 17-2.1

16. The lowest trophic level of any ecosystem is occupied by the producers.

    ANS: T   DIF: I   OBJ: BPE 17-2.1

17. Producers in an ecosystem transfer all of their energy to primary-level consumers.

    ANS: F   DIF: I   OBJ: BPE 17-2.1

18. The source of energy for an organism determines its trophic level.

    ANS: T   DIF: I   OBJ: BPE 17-2.1

19. A trophic level is made up of a group of organisms whose energy sources are the same energy level away from the sun.

    ANS: T   DIF: I   OBJ: BPE 17-2.1

20. Omnivores feed only on primary producers.

    ANS: F   DIF: I   OBJ: BPE 17-2.1

21. Detritivores are especially harmful to an ecosystem.

    ANS: F   DIF: I   OBJ: BPE 17-2.1

22. A food chain is made up of interrelated food webs.

    ANS: F   DIF: I   OBJ: BPE 17-2.2

23. Food chains usually begin with the primary producers.

    ANS: T   DIF: I   OBJ: BPE 17-2.2

24. All organisms in an ecosystem are part of the food web of that ecosystem.

    ANS: T   DIF: I   OBJ: BPE 17-2.2

25. A change in the number of predators in a food web can affect an entire ecosystem.

    ANS: T   DIF: I   OBJ: BPE 17-2.3

26. The number of organisms in a trophic level is always directly proportional to the amount of energy at that level.

    ANS: F   DIF: I   OBJ: BPE 17-2.3

27. Organisms at higher trophic levels tend to be fewer in number than those at lower trophic levels.

    ANS: T   DIF: I   OBJ: BPE 17-2.3

28. Plants release water into the atmosphere through transpiration.

    ANS: T   DIF: I   OBJ: BPE 17-3.1

29. Water and nutrients continue to cycle normally in a forest ecosystem after the trees in the ecosystem have been cut down.

    ANS: F   DIF: I   OBJ: BPE 17-3.1

30. Transpiration is a sun-driven process.

    ANS: T   DIF: I   OBJ: BPE 17-3.1

31. Carbon is returned to the atmosphere by photosynthesis, combustion, and erosion.

    ANS: F   DIF: I   OBJ: BPE 17-3.2

32. Nitrogen gas makes up about 79 percent of the Earth's atmosphere.

    ANS: T   DIF: I   OBJ: BPE 17-3.3

33. During nitrification, decomposers break down the roots of plants to produce nitrates.

    ANS: F   DIF: I   OBJ: BPE 17-3.3

MULTIPLE CHOICE

1. A functioning aquarium displays
   a. a community.
   b. a habitat.
   c. an ecosystem.
   d. All of the above

   ANS: D   DIF: I   OBJ: BPE 17-1.1

2. A group of organisms of different species living together in a particular place is called a
   a. community.
   b. population.
   c. biome.
   d. habitat.

   ANS: A   DIF: I   OBJ: BPE 17-1.1

3. The physical location of an ecosystem in which a given species lives is called a
   a. habitat.
   b. tropical level.
   c. community.
   d. food zone.

   ANS: A   DIF: I   OBJ: BPE 17-1.1

4. Ecology is the study of the interaction of living organisms
   a. with each other and their biotic factors.
   b. and their communities.
   c. with each other and their physical environment.
   d. and the food they eat.

   ANS: C   DIF: I   OBJ: BPE 17-1.1

5. An ecosystem consists of
   a. a community of organisms.
   b. energy.
   c. the soil, water, and weather.
   d. All of the above

   ANS: D   DIF: I   OBJ: BPE 17-1.1

6. All of the following are abiotic factors of a habitat *except*
   a. soil.
   b. plants.
   c. water.
   d. weather.

   ANS: B   DIF: I   OBJ: BPE 17-1.1

7. Biodiversity measures the number of species living within a(n)
   a. ecosystem.
   b. habitat.
   c. organism.
   d. community.

   ANS: A   DIF: I   OBJ: BPE 17-1.2

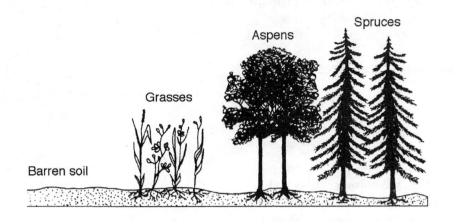

Spruces

Aspens

Grasses

Barren soil

8. Refer to the illustration above. The process shown in the diagram is known as
   a. competitive exclusion.
   b. succession.
   c. symbiosis.
   d. oligotrophy.

   ANS: B   DIF: II   OBJ: BPE 17-1.3

9. Succession is
   a. an organism's ability to survive in its environment.
   b. the number of species living in an ecosystem.
   c. the regular progression of species replacement in an environment.
   d. the transfer of energy through a food chain.

   ANS: C   DIF: I   OBJ: BPE 17-1.3

10. Which of the following types of succession would most likely occur following a forest fire?
    a. primary succession
    b. old field succession
    c. secondary succession
    d. lake succession

    ANS: C   DIF: I   OBJ: BPE 17-1.3

11. Secondary succession occurs
    a. as one generation of organisms replaces the previous one.
    b. as a previously existing community is replaced.
    c. after a new food web is established.
    d. None of the above

    ANS: B   DIF: I   OBJ: BPE 17-1.3

12. When the settlers arrived in New England, many forests were turned into fields. Eventually, some fields were abandoned and then grew back into forests. This is best described as
    a. primary succession.
    b. coevolution.
    c. secondary succession.
    d. niche realization.

    ANS: C   DIF: I   OBJ: BPE 17-1.3

13. primary succession : areas of no previous plant growth ::
    a. new habitat : a climax community
    b. rain forest : a desert
    c. tundra : a desert
    d. secondary succession : abandoned farm fields

    ANS: D
    (occurs in)

    DIF: II   OBJ: BPE 17-1.3

14. When an organism dies, the nutrients in its body
    a. can never be reused by other living things.
    b. are immediately released into the atmosphere.
    c. are released by the action of decomposers.
    d. None of the above

    ANS: C   DIF: I   OBJ: BPE 17-2.1

15. Fungi are
    a. decomposers.   c. omnivores.
    b. scavengers.   d. autotrophs.

    ANS: A   DIF: I   OBJ: BPE 17-2.1

16. A relationship between a producer and consumer is best illustrated by a
    a. snake eating a bird.   c. lion eating a zebra.
    b. fox eating a mouse.   d. zebra eating grass.

    ANS: D   DIF: I   OBJ: BPE 17-2.1

17. Organisms that manufacture organic nutrients for an ecosystem are called
    a. primary consumers.   c. primary producers.
    b. predators.   d. scavengers.

    ANS: C   DIF: I   OBJ: BPE 17-2.1

18. The primary producers in a grassland ecosystem would most likely be
    a. insects.   c. grasses.
    b. bacteria.   d. algae.

    ANS: C   DIF: I   OBJ: BPE 17-2.1

19. cows : herbivores ::
    a. horses : carnivores   c. algae : consumers
    b. plants : producers   d. caterpillars : producers

    ANS: B
    (are examples of)

    DIF: II   OBJ: BPE 17-2.1

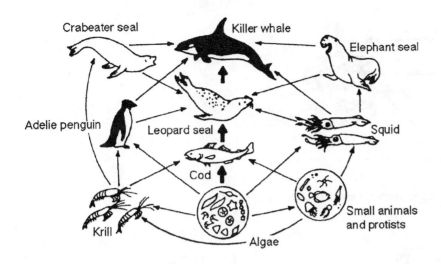

20. Refer to the illustration above. The photosynthetic algae are
    a. producers.
    b. consumers.
    c. parasites.
    d. decomposers.

    ANS: A   DIF: II   OBJ: BPE 17-2.1

21. Refer to the illustration above. The diagram, which shows how energy moves through an ecosystem, is known as a
    a. habitat.
    b. food chain.
    c. food net.
    d. food web.

    ANS: D   DIF: II   OBJ: BPE 17-2.2

22. Refer to the illustration above. Leopard seals are
    a. producers.
    b. omnivores.
    c. herbivores.
    d. carnivores.

    ANS: D   DIF: II   OBJ: BPE 17-2.2

23. Refer to the illustration above. Killer whales feed at the
    a. first and second trophic levels.
    b. second trophic level only.
    c. second and third trophic levels.
    d. third and fourth trophic levels.

    ANS: D   DIF: II   OBJ: BPE 17-2.2

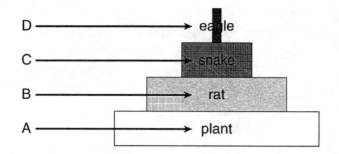

24. Refer to the illustration above. Level A is composed of
    a. carnivores.
    b. herbivores.
    c. producers.
    d. omnivores.

    ANS: C   DIF: II   OBJ: BPE 17-2.2

25. Refer to the illustration above. The diagram shows a(n)
    a. food chain.
    b. community.
    c. food web.
    d. energy pyramid.

    ANS: D   DIF: II   OBJ: BPE 17-2.3

26. Refer to the illustration above. On the pyramid, animals that feed on plant eaters are no lower than
    a. level A.
    b. level B.
    c. level C.
    d. level D.

    ANS: C   DIF: II   OBJ: BPE 17-2.3

27. Refer to the illustration above. How much energy is available to the organisms in level C?
    a. all of the energy in level A plus the energy in level B
    b. all of the energy in level A minus the energy in level B
    c. 10 percent of the energy in level B
    d. 90 percent of the energy in level B

    ANS: C   DIF: II   OBJ: BPE 17-2.3

28. Refer to the illustration above. The diagram represents the decrease in
    a. the number of organisms between lower and higher trophic levels.
    b. available energy between lower and higher trophic levels.
    c. diversity of organisms between lower and higher levels.
    d. All of the above

    ANS: D   DIF: II   OBJ: BPE 17-2.3

29. Food webs are more commonplace than food chains because
    a. many animals that comprise the links in a food chain are migratory.
    b. organisms almost always eat, and are eaten by, many different organisms.
    c. over time, food chains always become food webs.
    d. None of the above

    ANS: B   DIF: I   OBJ: BPE 17-2.2

30. In a food web, which type of organism receives energy from every other type?
    a. producer   c. decomposer
    b. carnivore   d. herbivore

    ANS: C   DIF: I   OBJ: BPE 17-2.2

31. Animals that feed on plants are at least in the
    a. first trophic level.   c. third trophic level.
    b. second trophic level.   d. fourth trophic level.

    ANS: B   DIF: I   OBJ: BPE 17-2.2

32. Which of the following are detritivores?
    a. worms   c. fungi
    b. vultures   d. All of the above

    ANS: D   DIF: I   OBJ: BPE 17-2.2

33. The number of trophic levels in an ecological pyramid
    a. is limitless.
    b. is limited by the amount of energy that is lost at each trophic level.
    c. never exceeds four.
    d. never exceeds three.

    ANS: B   DIF: I   OBJ: BPE 17-2.3

34. In going from one trophic level to the next higher level,
    a. the number of organisms increases.   c. the amount of usable energy decreases.
    b. the amount of usable energy increases.   d. diversity of organisms increases.

    ANS: C   DIF: I   OBJ: BPE 17-2.3

35. The total dry weight of the organisms in an ecosystem is called
    a. trophic level.   c. energy level.
    b. biomass.   d. ecomass.

    ANS: B   DIF: I   OBJ: BPE 17-2.3

36. Because energy diminishes at each successive trophic level, few ecosystems can contain more than
    a. two trophic levels.   c. five trophic levels.
    b. four trophic levels.   d. eight trophic levels.

    ANS: C   DIF: I   OBJ: BPE 17-2.3

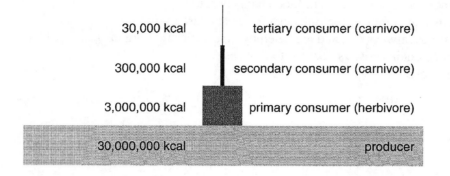

30,000 kcal	tertiary consumer (carnivore)
300,000 kcal	secondary consumer (carnivore)
3,000,000 kcal	primary consumer (herbivore)
30,000,000 kcal	producer

37. Refer to the illustration above. At each trophic level, the energy stored in the organisms in that level is
    a. about one-tenth of the energy in the level below it.
    b. about one-tenth of the energy in the level above it.
    c. 50 percent of of the energy in the level below it.
    d. 100 percent of the energy in the level below it.

    ANS: A   DIF: II   OBJ: BPE 17-2.3

38. Precipitation and evaporation are important components of the
    a. nitrogen cycle.   c. carbon cycle.
    b. water cycle.   d. All of the above

    ANS: B   DIF: I   OBJ: BPE 17-3.1

39. The paths of water, carbon, nitrogen, and phosphorus pass from the non-living environment to living organisms and back to the non-living environment in closed circles called
    a. living cycles.   c. biogeochemical cycles.
    b. environcycles.   d. None of the above

    ANS: C   DIF: I   OBJ: BPE 17-3.1

40. Coal, oil, and natural gas
    a. are formed from decayed plants.
    b. are fossil fuels.
    c. release carbon dioxide when they are burned.
    d. All of the above

    ANS: D   DIF: I   OBJ: BPE 17-3.2

41. Humans are affecting the carbon cycle by
    a. burning fossil fuels.
    b. destroying vegetation that absorbs carbon dioxide.
    c. using electrical labor-saving devices.
    d. All of the above

    ANS: D   DIF: I   OBJ: BPE 17-3.2

42. Which of the following is part of the nitrogen cycle?
    a. conversion of atmospheric nitrogen into usable organic compounds by bacteria
    b. conversion of nitrogen from decaying organisms into ammonia
    c. nitrogen fixation
    d. All of the above

    ANS: D   DIF: I   OBJ: BPE 17-3.3

43. Nitrogen is a component of
    a. proteins.   c. carbohydrates.
    b. fats.   d. water.

    ANS: A   DIF: I   OBJ: BPE 17-3.3

44. denitrification : nitrogen gas in the atmosphere ::
    a. more rain : transformation of rain forests
    b. more transpiration : arid weather
    c. burning fossil fuels : carbon in the atmosphere
    d. combustion : ground water

    ANS: C
    (increases)

    DIF: II   OBJ: BPE 17-3.3

45. ammonification : ammonia ::
    a. denitrification : nitrogen gas   c. nitrification : ammonia
    b. oil : gasoline   d. nitrification : oxygen

    ANS: A
    (produces)

    DIF: II   OBJ: BPE 17-3.3

46. Which of the following is common to the carbon cycle, the nitrogen cycle, *and* the water cycle?
    a. The substance is rearranged into different types of molecules as it moves through its cycle.
    b. The substance must pass through organisms in order to complete its cycle.
    c. The largest reserves of the substance are always in organisms.
    d. The substance is required by all living things and is involved in many processes that occur in all living things.

    ANS: D   DIF: III   OBJ: BPE 17-3.3

COMPLETION

1. An ecosystem consists of the living and _____ environment.

    ANS: nonliving   DIF: I   OBJ: BPE 17-1.1

2. The term _____ is used to describe the physical area in which an organism lives.

   ANS: habitat   DIF: I   OBJ: BPE 17-1.1

3. Ernst Haeckel coined the term _____ to describe the study of how organisms interact with each other and with their environment.

   ANS: ecology   DIF: I   OBJ: BPE 17-1.1

4. The living organisms in a habitat are called _____ factors.

   ANS: biotic   DIF: I   OBJ: BPE 17-1.1

5. The number of species living within an ecosystem is a measure of its _____.

   ANS: biodiversity   DIF: I   OBJ: BPE 17-1.2

6. The sequential replacement of populations in an area that has not previously supported life is called _____ succession.

   ANS: primary   DIF: I   OBJ: BPE 17-1.3

7. The small, fast-growing plants that are the first organisms to live in a habitat are called _____ _____.

   ANS: pioneer species   DIF: I   OBJ: BPE 17-1.3

8. A receding glacier is a good example of _____ _____.

   ANS: primary succession   DIF: I   OBJ: BPE 17-1.3

9. The biological structures of many of the Earth's ecosystems have been determined largely by the ways plants avoid being eaten and the ways by which _____ succeed in eating the plants.

   ANS: herbivores   DIF: I   OBJ: BPE 17-2.1

10. Animals known as _____ eat only primary producers.

   ANS: herbivores   DIF: I   OBJ: BPE 17-2.1

11. An organism that eats a primary consumer is called a(n) _____ consumer.

   ANS: secondary   DIF: I   OBJ: BPE 17-2.1

12. The term _____ is given to the bacteria that break down dead tissue.

   ANS: decomposers   DIF: I   OBJ: BPE 17-2.1

13. The primary productivity of an ecosystem is a measure of the amount of organic material that the _____ organisms in the ecosystem produce.

ANS: photosynthetic   DIF: I   OBJ: BPE 17-2.1

14. In an ecosystem, _____ diminishes at each successive trophic level.

ANS: energy   DIF: I   OBJ: BPE 17-2.1

15. A path of energy through the trophic levels of an ecosystem is called a(n) _____ _____.

ANS: food chain   DIF: I   OBJ: BPE 17-2.2

16. The interrelated food chains in an ecosystem are called a(n) _____ _____.

ANS: food web   DIF: I   OBJ: BPE 17-2.2

17. Decomposers are part of a special class of consumers called _____.

ANS: detritivores   DIF: I   OBJ: BPE 17-2.2

18. An energy pyramid shows the amount of energy contained in the bodies of organisms at each _____ level.

ANS: trophic   DIF: I   OBJ: BPE 17-2.2

19. Every time energy is transferred in an ecosystem, potential energy is lost as _____.

ANS: heat   DIF: I   OBJ: BPE 17-2.3

20. When forests are cut down, both water and nutrient _____ are broken.

ANS: cycles   DIF: I   OBJ: BPE 17-3.1

21. Water that seeps into the soil is called _____ water.

ANS: ground   DIF: I   OBJ: BPE 17-3.1

22. Carbon is returned to the atmosphere by cellular respiration, combustion, and _____.

ANS: erosion   DIF: I   OBJ: BPE 17-3.2

23. The conversion of nitrogen gas to ammonia by the action of bacteria is called
_____ _____.

    ANS: nitrogen fixation.   DIF: I   OBJ: BPE 17-3.3

24. Nitrogen _____ is the absorption and incorporation of nitrogen into plants and animals.

    ANS: assimilation   DIF: I   OBJ: BPE 17-3.3

25. The process of _____ occurs when anaerobic bacteria break down nitrates and release nitrogen gas back into the atmosphere.

    ANS: denitrification   DIF: I   OBJ: BPE 17-3.3

PROBLEM

1. Nitrogen fertilizer is added to soils in virtually all agricultural areas of the world. The use of nitrogen fertilizer greatly increases the amount of food produced. However, it can also affect the ecology of areas near agricultural areas. The data presented in the table below were obtained in an experiment conducted to evaluate the effects of nitrogen fertilizer on grass species diversity. Nitrogen fertilizer was applied yearly to an experimental plot, beginning in 1856.

Year	1856	1872	1949
Total number of grass species	49	15	3
Number of species producing more than 10% of the total dry weight of all species combined	2	3	1
Number of species producing more than 50% of the total dry weight of all species combined	0	1	1
Number of species producing more than 99% of the total dry weight of all species combined	0	0	1

a. Write three conclusions that you can draw from these data.
b. How could this experiment have been designed differently to make it a better experiment?

ANS:
a. The following are some possible conclusions:
   1. The total number of grass species decreased over time and with exposure to nitrogen fertilizer.
   2. At the beginning of the experiment, there was no one dominant species of grass. Over time and with exposure to nitrogen fertilizer, a few species became dominant.
   3. Prolonged use of nitrogen fertilizer encourages the growth of one or a few dominant species.
b. It should have been designed to have a control plot that did not receive nitrogen fertilizer. As the experiment was designed, the effects of nitrogen fertilizer cannot be distinguished from the effects of time.

DIF: III   OBJ: BPE 17-1.2

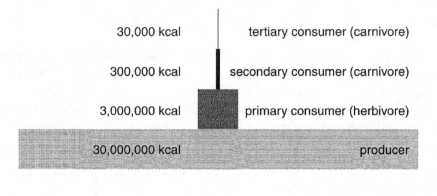

30,000 kcal — tertiary consumer (carnivore)

300,000 kcal — secondary consumer (carnivore)

3,000,000 kcal — primary consumer (herbivore)

30,000,000 kcal — producer

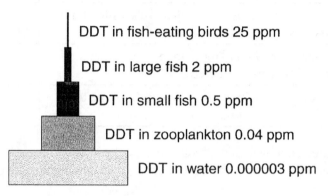

DDT in fish-eating birds 25 ppm

DDT in large fish 2 ppm

DDT in small fish 0.5 ppm

DDT in zooplankton 0.04 ppm

DDT in water 0.000003 ppm

2. The diagram above depicts a typical energy pyramid. It shows how energy is lost as it is transferred from one level to another in the food chain of the pyramid.
The next diagram, shown below, depicts the concentration of DDT, a pesticide, in water and in a number of organisms comprising a food chain.

Explain how DDT and other toxic substances can become concentrated in organisms as it is transferred up through a food chain. Write your answer in the space below.

ANS:
As energy is passed from one level of a food chain to another, only a small amount of it is retained by the next organism up in the food chain. This occurs in part because all energy conversions involve a loss of energy in the form of heat. It is also partly due to the fact that each successive organism in a food chain requires more energy to maintain its body's activities. If there are toxic substances, such as DDT, in an organism's food, it will pass through the organism's body. These substances can be taken up and stored in body tissues. When another organism ingests food containing stored toxins, it can also take up and store the toxins. The toxic substances become increasingly concentrated as they move up through the food chain because each successive organism requires more food energy than the one below it in order to survive.

DIF: III   OBJ: BPE 17-2.3

ESSAY

1. Explain how a change in the habitat of a species affects the entire ecosystem.

   ANS:
   A change in habitat may disturb the interactions of plants and animals in the ecosystem. A drastic change in the factors of a habitat that affects one species can have an effect on the whole ecosystem because it affects the natural cycling of nutrients, food chains, and food webs. This disruption could result in endangerment or extinction of species in the ecosystem.

   DIF: II   OBJ: BPE 17-1.1

2. What is the difference between primary and secondary succession?

   ANS:
   Primary succession is the replacement of species in an area that had not previously supported life, such as bare rock or a sand dune. Secondary succession involves species replacement habitats that have been disrupted due to natural disaster or human activity but that still possess a small amount of soil and vegetation.

   DIF: II   OBJ: BPE 17-1.3

3. Explain how alders can lead to the destruction of a sturdy plant like *Dryas*.

   ANS:
   Alders grow faster than *Dryas*, and dead leaves and fallen branches from them add useable nitrogen to the soil. The added nitrogen allows other trees to invade and develop vigorously. Eventually dense thickets of the trees shade and kill the *Dryas*.

   DIF: II   OBJ: BPE 17-1.3

4. Clover plants, rabbits, and coyotes are some of the organisms that occupy a particular ecosystem. Assign the roles of primary producers, primary consumers, and secondary consumers to these three groups of organisms and explain your answer.

   ANS:
   In this ecosystem, the clover plants are the primary producers. They help manufacture the organic nutrients necessary to sustain the ecosystem. Rabbits are herbivores that consume the primary producers (the clover plants), so they are classified as primary consumers. Coyotes eat the primary consumers (the rabbits), so they are classified as secondary consumers.

   DIF: II   OBJ: BPE 17-2.1

5. Why are decomposers necessary for the continuation of life on Earth?

ANS:
Decomposers release matter from waste materials and dead organisms. Were it not for the action of decomposers, the Earth would eventually be depleted of usable essential matter such as carbon and nitrogen, that organisms need. Without decomposers essential materials would not be recycled.

DIF: II   OBJ: BPE 17-2.1

6. Describe how energy is transferred from one trophic level to another.

ANS:
A portion of the energy available to the organisms at each level of the food chain is stored in the chemical bonds of nutrients that are not used by an organism in order to sustain life. When that organism is eaten by another, the stored chemical energy is transferred to the new organism and used to sustain its life.

DIF: II   OBJ: BPE 17-2.3

7. Why is it cheaper for a farmer to produce a pound of grain than a pound of meat?

ANS:
Animals are on higher trophic levels than plants. Consequently, it takes more energy to produce one pound of meat than to produce several pounds of grain.

DIF: II   OBJ: BPE 17-2.3

8. A plant disease infects most of the vegetation in a particular area, destroying it. How might the destruction of this vegetation affect the animal life in the area?

ANS:
The ecosystem would be seriously disrupted. Herbivores that ate the vegetation would be affected if this was their major source of food. The carnivores in the area would soon die or leave the area because their source of energy—the herbivores—could not remain.

DIF: II   OBJ: BPE 17-2.3

CHAPTER 18—BIOLOGICAL COMMUNITIES

TRUE/FALSE

1. Coevolution is the back-and-forth evolutionary adjustments between the interacting members of an ecosystem.

   ANS: T   DIF: I   OBJ: BPE 18-1.1

2. A change in the number of predators or prey in a food web can alter the entire ecosystem in which they live.

   ANS: T   DIF: I   OBJ: BPE 18-1.2

3. A long-term relationship in which both participating species benefit is known as parasitism.

   ANS: F   DIF: I   OBJ: BPE 18-1.2

4. Predation is an example of a biotic interaction.

   ANS: T   DIF: I   OBJ: BPE 18-1.2

5. Plants and the herbivores that eat them have evolved independently of one another.

   ANS: F   DIF: I   OBJ: BPE 18-1.2

6. Mutualism is a symbiotic relationship in which only one party benefits.

   ANS: F   DIF: I   OBJ: BPE 18-1.3

7. An organism's niche includes its habitat.

   ANS: T   DIF: I   OBJ: BPE 18-2.1

8. An organism's niche is the sum of all its interactions in its environment, including interactions with other organisms.

   ANS: T   DIF: I   OBJ: BPE 18-2.1

9. The total niche an organism is potentially able to occupy within an ecosystem is its realized niche.

   ANS: F   DIF: I   OBJ: BPE 18-2.2

10. When two dissimilar species live together in a close association, they are part of a symbiotic relationship.

    ANS: T   DIF: I   OBJ: BPE 18-2.3

11. The competitive exclusion principle states that competition usually results in the establishment of cooperation between two species.

ANS: F   DIF: I   OBJ: BPE 18-2.3

12. When ecologist Robert Paine removed the sea star from the 15-species ecosystem along the Washington coast, the number of species in the ecosystem fell to eight.

ANS: T   DIF: I   OBJ: BPE 18-2.4

13. When two species compete for limited resources, competitive exclusion is sure to take place.

ANS: F   DIF: I   OBJ: BPE 18-2.4

14. Warm air can hold more moisture than cold air.

ANS: T   DIF: I   OBJ: BPE 18-3.1

15. Climate is not a factor in determining the ecosystem types found in the United States.

ANS: F   DIF: I   OBJ: BPE 18-3.1

16. Biomes characterized by high annual rainfalls are located at high elevations.

ANS: F   DIF: I   OBJ: BPE 18-3.2

17. On land, there are 10 major types of ecosystems, which are called biomes.

ANS: F   DIF: I   OBJ: BPE 18-3.3

18. Some animals of the deciduous forest hibernate during the winter.

ANS: T   DIF: I   OBJ: BPE 18-3.3

19. Permafrost is a characteristic of the taiga.

ANS: F   DIF: I   OBJ: BPE 18-3.3

20. Deserts are most extensive in the interiors of continents.

ANS: T   DIF: I   OBJ: BPE 18-3.3

21. Tropical rain forests have the most fertile soil on Earth.

ANS: F   DIF: I   OBJ: BPE 18-3.3

22. There are three major types of ecosystems found in the ocean.

ANS: T   DIF: I   OBJ: BPE 18-3.4

23. All algae are photosynthetic.

    ANS: F   DIF: I   OBJ: BPE 18-3.4

24. Freshwater habitats are independent of terrestrial habitats.

    ANS: F   DIF: I   OBJ: BPE 18-3.4

MULTIPLE CHOICE

1. The process by which species evolve in response to other living members of their ecosystem is
   called
   a. compromise.   c. coevolution.
   b. parasitism.   d. ecology.

   ANS: C   DIF: I   OBJ: BPE 18-1.1

2. Over millions of years, plants and their pollinators have
   a. coevolved.   c. become parasites.
   b. crossbred.   d. become competitive.

   ANS: A   DIF: I   OBJ: BPE 18-1.1

3. The caterpillars of cabbage butterflies are the only insects that can eat plants of the mustard
   family because they
   a. eat these plants only when young and tender.
   b. have evolved the ability to break down mustard oils into harmless chemicals.
   c. are parasites while in this stage of development.
   d. All of the above

   ANS: B   DIF: I   OBJ: BPE 18-1.2

The diagrams below show different kinds of interactions between species.

The ant keeps predators away from the acacia tree.

Ant ⟶ Acacia

The acacia provides shelter and food for the ant.

1

The cow eats grass.

Cow ⟶ Sheep

The sheep eats same grass.

2

Orchid ⟶ Tree

The tree provides nutrients and a sun-lit location for the orchid living on it.

3

Tapeworm ⟶ Dog

The dog provides nutrients and shelter for the tapeworm living in its intestines.

4

4. Refer to the illustration above. The relationship shown in diagram 4 above is
   a. commensalism.
   b. competition.
   c. mutualism.
   d. parasitism.

   ANS: D   DIF: II   OBJ: BPE 18-1.2

5. Refer to the illustration above. The relationship shown in diagram 1 above is
   a. commensalism.
   b. competition.
   c. mutualism.
   d. parasitism.

   ANS: C   DIF: II   OBJ: BPE 18-1.3

6. Refer to the illustration above. The relationship shown in diagram 3 above is
   a. commensalism.
   b. competition.
   c. mutualism.
   d. parasitism.

   ANS: A   DIF: II   OBJ: BPE 18-1.3

7. Refer to the illustration above. The relationship shown in diagram 2 above is
   a. commensalism.
   b. competition.
   c. mutualism.
   d. parasitism.

   ANS: B   DIF: II   OBJ: BPE 18-2.1

8. Parasites
   a. coevolve with their hosts.
   b. are usually smaller than their hosts.
   c. rarely kill their hosts.
   d. All of the above

   ANS: D   DIF: I   OBJ: BPE 18-1.2

9. A tick feeding on a human is an example of
   a. parasitism.
   b. mutualism.
   c. symbiosis.
   d. predation.

   ANS: A   DIF: I   OBJ: BPE 18-1.2

10. Characteristics that enable plants to protect themselves from herbivores include
    a. thorns and prickles.
    b. sticky hairs and tough leaves.
    c. chemical defenses.
    d. All of the above

    ANS: D   DIF: I   OBJ: BPE 18-1.2

11. The relationship between plants and the bees that pollinate them is an example of
    a. commensalism.
    b. competition.
    c. mutualism.
    d. parasitism.

    ANS: C   DIF: I   OBJ: BPE 18-1.3

12. The relationship between a whale and barnacles growing on its skin is an example of
    a. commensalism.
    b. competition.
    c. mutualism.
    d. parasitism.

    ANS: A   DIF: I   OBJ: BPE 18-1.3

13. The relationship between a clown fish and a sea anemone is known as
    a. parasitism.
    b. competition.
    c. mutualism.
    d. commensalism.

    ANS: D   DIF: I   OBJ: BPE 18-1.3

1	both organisms benefit from the activity of each other
2	one organism benefits and the other organism neither benefits nor suffers harm
3	one organism obtains its nutrients from another; other organism may weaken due to deprivation

14. Refer to the table above. The table represents three types of
    a. competition.
    b. rhythmic patterns.
    c. symbiosis.
    d. secondary succession.

    ANS: C   DIF: II   OBJ: BPE 18-1.3

15. Refer to the table above. Which pair of organisms generally exhibits the type of relationship that corresponds to description 1 in the table?
    a. coyotes and sheep
    b. shrimp and sea cucumbers
    c. parasitic worms and white-tailed deer
    d. ants and aphids

    ANS: D   DIF: II   OBJ: BPE 18-1.3

16. Refer to the table above. The relationship that corresponds to description 2 in the table is known as
    a. parasitism.
    b. commensalism.
    c. mutualism.
    d. predation.

    ANS: B   DIF: II   OBJ: BPE 18-1.3

17. commensalism : one organism ::
    a. parasitism : both organisms
    b. predation : neither organism
    c. competition : both organisms
    d. mutualism : both organisms

    ANS: D
    (benefits)

    DIF: II   OBJ: BPE 18-1.3

18. Which of the following usually results when members of the same species require the same food and space?
    a. primary succession
    b. competition
    c. secondary succession
    d. interspecific competition

    ANS: B   DIF: I   OBJ: BPE 18-2.1

19. Which of the following would not be included in a description of an organism's niche?
    a. its trophic level
    b. the humidity and temperature it prefers
    c. its number of chromosomes
    d. when it reproduces

    ANS: C   DIF: I   OBJ: BPE 18-2.1

20. An organism's niche includes
    a. what it eats.
    b. where it eats.
    c. when it eats.
    d. All of the above

    ANS: D   DIF: I   OBJ: BPE 18-2.1

21. Most ecosystems tend to be complex because
    a. they are found in all climates.
    b. potential competitors in the ecosystem often occupy slightly different niches.
    c. they all contain a wide variety of producers.
    d. of symbiotic relationships within them.

    ANS: B   DIF: I   OBJ: BPE 18-2.1

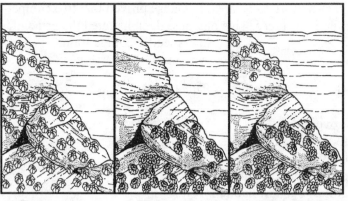

A. The barnacle *Chthamalus stellatus* can live in both shallow and deep water on a rocky coast.

B. The barnacle *Balanus balanoides* prefers to live in deep water.

C. When the two live together, *Chthamalus* is restricted to shallow water.

22. Refer to the illustration above. Since the two species of barnacles attempt to use the same resources, they are
    a. parasitic.
    b. in competition with one another.
    c. mutualistic.
    d. symbiotic.

    ANS: B   DIF: II   OBJ: BPE 18-2.1

23. Refer to the illustration above. Diagram A indicates that the barnacle *Chthamalus stellatus* can live in both shallow and deep water on a rocky coast. This is the barnacle's
    a. competitive niche.
    b. realized niche.
    c. fundamental niche.
    d. exclusive niche.

    ANS: C   DIF: II   OBJ: BPE 18-2.3

24. Refer to the illustration above. Diagram B indicates that the barnacle *Balanus balanoides* prefers to live in deep water. Deep water is the barnacle's
    a. competitive niche.
    b. realized niche.
    c. fundamental niche.
    d. exclusive niche.

    ANS: C   DIF: II   OBJ: BPE 18-2.3

25. Refer to the illustration above. Diagram C indicates that when the two barnacles live together, *Chthamalus* is restricted to shallow water. Shallow water is the barnacle's
    a. competitive niche.
    b. realized niche.
    c. fundamental niche.
    d. exclusive niche.

    ANS: B   DIF: II   OBJ: BPE 18-2.3

26. When two species compete, the niche that each species ultimately occupies is its
    a. competitive niche.
    b. realized niche.
    c. fundamental niche.
    d. exclusive niche.

    ANS: B   DIF: I   OBJ: BPE 18-2.2

27. In his experiments with two species of paramecia, G. F. Gause proved that two competitors cannot coexist on the same limited resources. This outcome demonstrated the principle of
    a. competitive exclusion.
    b. secondary succession.
    c. intraspecific competition.
    d. symbiosis.

    ANS: A   DIF: I   OBJ: BPE 18-2.3

28. If the niches of two organisms overlap,
    a. the organisms may have to compete directly.
    b. the two organisms will always form a symbiotic relationship.
    c. both organisms will disappear from the habitat.
    d. one organism usually migrates to a new habitat.

    ANS: A   DIF: I   OBJ: BPE 18-2.4

29. Sea stars are fierce competitors of marine organisms such as clams and mussels. An ecologist studying an ocean ecosystem performed an experiment in which the sea stars were removed from the ecosystem. After the removal of the sea stars,
    a. the ecosystem became more diverse.
    b. the size of the ecosystem was reduced.
    c. food webs in the ecosystem became more complex.
    d. the number of species in the ecosystem was reduced.

    ANS: D   DIF: I   OBJ: BPE 18-2.4

30. Major ecosystems that occur over wide areas of land are called
    a. communities.
    b. habitats.
    c. biomes.
    d. food chains.

    ANS: C   DIF: I   OBJ: BPE 18-3.1

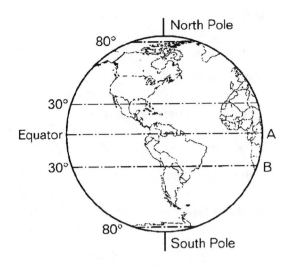

31. Refer to the illustration above. An ecosystem located along latitude A would
    a. have a shorter growing season than an ecosystem on latitude B.
    b. probably contain fewer species than an ecosystem at latitude B.
    c. probably be more diverse than an ecosystem at latitude B.
    d. probably have less rainfall than an ecosystem at latitude B.

    ANS: C   DIF: II   OBJ: BPE 18-3.2

32. Generally, the closer an ecosystem is to the equator,
    a. the longer its growing season.   c. the warmer its temperature.
    b. the greater its diversity.   d. All of the above

    ANS: D   DIF: I   OBJ: BPE 18-3.2

33. Generally, the closer an area is to the equator, the greater the diversity in species. Following are the latitudes of four cities. Which city would you predict to have the greatest diversity of species?
    a. Berlin, Germany (52 degrees 32′ North latitude)
    b. Montreal, Canada (45 degrees 0′ North latitude)
    c. Denver, Colorado (39 degrees 44′ North latitude)
    d. Brisbane, Australia (27 degrees 30′ South latitude)

    ANS: D   DIF: I   OBJ: BPE 18-3.2

34. Which of the following biomes is characterized by evergreen trees and mammals such as moose, bears, and lynx?
    a. taiga   c. temperate deciduous forest
    b. polar   d. tundra

    ANS: A   DIF: I   OBJ: BPE 18-3.2

35. Herds of grazing animals are most likely to be found in a
    a. savanna.   c. deciduous forest.
    b. tropical rain forest.   d. taiga.

    ANS: A   DIF: I   OBJ: BPE 18-3.3

36. The biome that makes up most of the central part of the United States is
    a. rain forest.   c. tundra.
    b. temperate grassland.   d. deciduous forest.

    ANS: B   DIF: I   OBJ: BPE 18-3.3

37. Which of the following animals would most likely be found in a temperate deciduous forest?
    a. monkeys   c. deer
    b. caribou   d. leopards

    ANS: C   DIF: I   OBJ: BPE 18-3.3

38. Tropical ecosystems are more diverse than temperate zone ecosystems because
    a. the growing season in tropical ecosystems never stops.
    b. the climate in tropical ecosystems does not vary much from year to year.
    c. a greater amount of food is produced in tropical ecosystems.
    d. All of the above

    ANS: D   DIF: I   OBJ: BPE 18-3.3

39. Plankton are
    a. a major formation ingredient of most fossil fuels.
    b. found in the deep-water zone of most lakes and oceans.
    c. the base of most aquatic food webs.
    d. usually in the third and fourth trophic levels of ocean ecosystems.

    ANS: C   DIF: I   OBJ: BPE 18-3.4

40. Organisms with light-producing body parts would most likely be found in
    a. the deep-water zone of lakes.   c. open ocean surfaces.
    b. shallow ocean waters.   d. deep ocean waters.

    ANS: D   DIF: I   OBJ: BPE 18-3.4

41. The greatest diversity of life in the ocean is found in
    a. shallow ocean waters.   c. deep ocean waters.
    b. the ocean surface.   d. tidal areas.

    ANS: A   DIF: I   OBJ: BPE 18-3.4

42. Almost all of the Earth's surface water is contained in
    a. ocean ecosystems.   c. tropical rain forests.
    b. freshwater biomes.   d. ponds and lakes.

    ANS: A   DIF: I   OBJ: BPE 18-3.4

43. many fish : shallow ocean water habitat ::
    a. nutrients : deep-sea waters
    b. plankton : deep-sea-water habitat
    c. plankton : open-sea surface habitat
    d. animals producing own light : shallow-ocean-water habitat

    ANS: C
    (live in)

    DIF: II   OBJ: BPE 18-3.4

COMPLETION

1. The back-and-forth evolutionary adjustments between interacting members of an ecosystem are
    called _____.

    ANS: coevolution   DIF: I   OBJ: BPE 18-1.1

2. In a parasitic relationship, the organism that provides benefits to another organism at its own
    expense is called the _____.

    ANS: host   DIF: I   OBJ: BPE 18-1.2

3. The general term for the biotic relationship in which one organism feeds upon another is
    _____.

    ANS: predation   DIF: I   OBJ: BPE 18-1.2

4. A symbiotic relationship in which one organism benefits and another is often harmed but not
    killed is called _____.

    ANS: parasitism   DIF: I   OBJ: BPE 18-1.2

5. _____ occurs as two or more species evolve in response to each other.

    ANS: Coevolution   DIF: I   OBJ: BPE 18-1.2

6. The symbiotic relationship in which one organism benefits and the other neither benefits nor
    suffers harm is called _____.

    ANS: commensalism   DIF: I   OBJ: BPE 18-1.3

7. The term _____ is used to describe a close relationship between two
    dissimilar organisms in which one organism usually benefits.

    ANS: symbiosis   DIF: I   OBJ: BPE 18-1.3

8. A fish called a cleaner wrasse eats the tiny parasites that cling to and feed upon much larger fis Therefore, the cleaner wrasse has a(n) _____ relationship with the larger fis

   ANS: mutualistic   DIF: I   OBJ: BPE 18-1.3

9. A(n) _____ describes the habitat, feeding habits, other aspects of an organism's biology, and its interactions with other organisms and the environment.

   ANS: niche   DIF: I   OBJ: BPE 18-2.1

10. The struggle among organisms for the same limited natural resources is called _____.

   ANS: competition   DIF: I   OBJ: BPE 18-2.1

11. The total niche that an organism is potentially able to use within an ecosystem is called that organism's _____ _____.

   ANS: fundamental niche   DIF: I   OBJ: BPE 18-2.2

12. Local elimination of one competing species is called _____ _____.

   ANS: competitive exclusion   DIF: I   OBJ: BPE 18-2.3

13. The variety of organisms in a community is called _____.

   ANS: biodiversity   DIF: I   OBJ: BPE 18-2.4

14. _____refers to the prevailing weather conditions in any given area.

   ANS: Climate   DIF: I   OBJ: BPE 18-3.1

15. A major biological community that occurs over a large area of land is called a(n) _____.

   ANS: biome   DIF: I   OBJ: BPE 18-3.2

16. Coniferous trees are predominantly found in the _____ biome.

   ANS: taiga   DIF: I   OBJ: BPE 18-3.3

17. The thick, continually frozen layer of ground found in the northern tundra is called _____.

   ANS: permafrost   DIF: I   OBJ: BPE 18-3.3

18. The biome that makes up most of the central part of the continental United States is
    _____ _____ .

    ANS: temperate grasslands   DIF: I   OBJ: BPE 18-3.3

19. Trees that lose their leaves every year are known as _____ .

    ANS: deciduous   DIF: I   OBJ: BPE 18-3.3

20. Elk and moose may live in the _____ , areas that are also the primary source of
    the world's lumber.

    ANS: taiga   DIF: I   OBJ: BPE 18-3.3

21. A(n) _____ is open, windswept ground that is always frozen.

    ANS: tundra   DIF: I   OBJ: BPE 18-3.3

22. _____ _____ _____ are characterized by
    lush vegetation, abundant rain, and year-round warm temperatures.

    ANS: Tropical rain forests   DIF: I   OBJ: BPE 18-3.3

23. A dry grassland known as a(n) _____ is the home of elephants, giraffes, and
    lions, having open, widely spaced trees and seasonal rainfall.

    ANS: savanna   DIF: I   OBJ: BPE 18-3.3

24. _____ ocean waters are small in area but contain most of the ocean's
    diversity.

    ANS: Shallow   DIF: I   OBJ: BPE 18-3.4

PROBLEM

1. The data in the table shown below were taken during a study of an abandoned agricultural field. Scientists counted the number of different kinds of herbs, shrubs, and trees present in the field 1, 25, and 40 years after it had been abandoned.

	Time after abandonment of agricultural field		
	1 year	**25 years**	**40 years**
Number of herb species	31	30	36
Number of shrub species	0	7	19
Number of tree species	0	14	2
Total number of species	31	51	77

    a. In the space below, write three conclusions that you can draw from these data.

    b. Make a prediction of the relative numbers of herbs, shrubs, trees, and of the total number of plant species that you would expect to see 100 years after abandonment of the field.

ANS:
a. The following are some possible conclusions:
1. The total number of plant species present in the field increased over the 40 year time period.
2. The plants that grew initially in the field were all herbs.
3. Over the 40 year time period, the relative proportions of herbs, shrubs, and trees changed. The relative number of herbs decreased while the relative number of shrubs and trees increased.
4. The total number of herbs present did not change significantly over the 40 year time period.

b. It is likely that the total number of species present would be even greater 100 years after abandonment. There would probably be relatively fewer herbs, about the same or relatively more shrubs, and relatively more trees.

DIF: III   OBJ: BPE 18-2.3

ESSAY

1. To control its wild rabbit population, the Australian government introduced the viral disease myxomatosis. At first the virus was very deadly to the rabbits but eventually the rabbit population stabilized. Explain what happened to the rabbit population and why the virus became less virulent.

ANS:
At first the virus was very deadly, so rabbits that survived tended to be resistant to the virus. The virus also became less deadly because viral infections that kill their hosts too quickly are not able to spread to as many other rabbits. The rabbits and virus coevolved.

DIF: II   OBJ: BPE 18-1.1

2. Some species of orchids grow high in the trees of tropical forests. The trees provide the orchids with the support to grow and allow them to capture more sunlight than they would on the forest floor. What form of symbiosis is illustrated by this occurrence? Explain your answer.

ANS:
Commensalism is the form of symbiosis illustrated; in commensalism one organism benefits and the other organism neither benefits nor suffers harm. In this example, the orchids benefit from the presence of the trees, but the trees are not harmed since the orchids neither feed on their tissues nor prevent significant amounts of sunlight from reaching their leaves.

DIF: II   OBJ: BPE 18-1.3

3. Describe the type of biotic interaction called competition.

ANS:
All organisms compete for food, water, space, and other resources. One type of competition occurs between members of the same species, and another type of competition occurs between different species.

DIF: II   OBJ: BPE 18-2.1

4. Which type of organisms are most likely to survive, those that have a narrow ecological niche or those that have a broad niche? Explain.

ANS:
Organisms having broad niches are more likely to survive because they are not likely to depend on a single food source or a single habitat. If one food source becomes scarce, they can turn to another; or if one habitat is destroyed they can move to another. An organism having a narrow niche may depend totally on a single food source or require a specific habitat. If the food source or habitat is disrupted, the organism may not survive.

DIF: II   OBJ: BPE 18-2.4

5. Can two species occupy the same niche? Explain.

ANS:
No two species can have the exact same niche. The principle of competitive exclusion states that if two species are competing for the same resource, the species that uses the resource more efficiently will eventually eliminate the other.

DIF: II   OBJ: BPE 18-2.4

6. Explain and give an example of what is meant by the statement "Climate has an important influence on the type of ecosystem found in an area."

ANS:
The climate of an area refers to the daily atmospheric conditions—the temperature, amount of rainfall, and amount of sunlight in a given area. The physical features of the Earth and amount of solar energy reaching an area influence the climate. Ecosystems vary based on the types of living organisms—plants and animals—that can survive in an area.
Areas receiving large amounts of sunlight and precipitation tend to be warm and moist and support different types of organisms than colder, dry areas. Areas that are warm and dry, such as parts of southern Arizona, promote the growth of fewer plants than areas with heavy rainfall. The plants that survive, such as cacti, have developed structures that promote water conservation. Areas with mild temperatures and heavier rainfall, such as Virginia and North Carolina, promote the growth of dense forests with tall trees that shed their leaves and consume large amounts of water on a daily basis. (Other examples also are acceptable that establish a link between the type of organisms that can survive and the climate.)

DIF: II   OBJ: BPE 18-3.1

7. Why are plankton important in freshwater ecosystems? Are plankton important in land ecosystems as well? Explain.

ANS:
Plankton, a diverse biological community of microscopic organisms, live near the surface of lakes and ponds. Plankton contain photosynthetic organisms that are the base of aquatic food webs. Plankton are important in land ecosystems because these ecosystems are closely connected to freshwater habitats. Many land animals come to water to feed on aquatic animals that rely on plankton or plankton-eating organisms for food.

DIF: II   OBJ: BPE 18-3.4

CHAPTER 19—HUMAN IMPACT ON THE ENVIRONMENT

TRUE/FALSE

1. Acid rain usually has a pH between 8.3 and 9.7.

   ANS: F   DIF: I   OBJ: BPE 19-1.1

2. The phenomenon called acid rain helps many plants to grow stronger and taller.

   ANS: F   DIF: I   OBJ: BPE 19-1.1

3. Most countries have banned the use of CFCs, thus limiting the destruction of the ozone layer.

   ANS: F   DIF: I   OBJ: BPE 19-1.2

4. In the United States, the number of cases of malignant melanoma almost doubled since 1980.

   ANS: T   DIF: I   OBJ: BPE 19-1.2

5. CFCs are the only chemicals that destroy ozone in the atmosphere.

   ANS: F   DIF: I   OBJ: BPE 19-1.2

6. Sources of excess carbon dioxide in the atmosphere include burning of fossil fuels and vegetation.

   ANS: T   DIF: I   OBJ: BPE 19-1.3

7. The world's climate is warming as large amounts of carbon dioxide are released into the atmosphere.

   ANS: T   DIF: I   OBJ: BPE 19-1.4

8. The environment is capable of absorbing any amount of pollution.

   ANS: F   DIF: I   OBJ: BPE 19-2.1

9. The oil spill in 1989 off the coast of Alaska could have been less destructive if the tanker carrying the oil had been loaded no higher than the water line.

   ANS: T   DIF: I   OBJ: BPE 19-2.1

10. Huge oil spills like the one in Alaska account for the vast majority of pollution from oil seepage.

    ANS: F   DIF: I   OBJ: BPE 19-2.1

11. If a lake is polluted with DDT, there will be a higher concentration of it in the water than in large fish in the lake.

    ANS: F   DIF: I   OBJ: BPE 19-2.1

12. The presence of DDT in birds causes thin, fragile eggshells, most of which break during incubation.

    ANS: T   DIF: I   OBJ: BPE 19-2.1

13. There is no benefit to using chemicals in agriculture.

    ANS: F   DIF: I   OBJ: BPE 19-2.1

14. The use of chemicals in agriculture is necessary to meet the needs of an increasingly crowded world, but it must be done intelligently.

    ANS: T   DIF: I   OBJ: BPE 19-2.1

15. Since use of DDT was banned in the United States, it has disappeared from use throughout the world.

    ANS: F   DIF: I   OBJ: BPE 19-2.1

16. Companies in the United States continue to manufacture and export chlorinated hydrocarbons, even though they are banned here.

    ANS: T   DIF: I   OBJ: BPE 19-2.1

17. Because of human efforts in the past decade, the preservation of nonrenewable resources such as topsoil, ground water, and our diverse species are no longer concerns for environmentalists.

    ANS: F   DIF: I   OBJ: BPE 19-2.2

18. About one-half of the earth's tropical rain forests have been destroyed.

    ANS: T   DIF: I   OBJ: BPE 19-2.2

19. The population of the Earth has not changed very much over the last 350 years.

    ANS: F   DIF: I   OBJ: BPE 19-2.3

20. The human birth rate has remained about the same for the last 350 years.

    ANS: T   DIF: I   OBJ: BPE 19-2.3

21. The human population began to increase dramatically in 500 A.D.

    ANS: F   DIF: I   OBJ: BPE 19-2.3

22. The population of every country on the Earth is steadily increasing.

    ANS: F   DIF: I   OBJ: BPE 19-2.4

23. The exploding human population is the single greatest threat to the world's future.

    ANS: T   DIF: I   OBJ: BPE 19-2.4

24. In the early 1990's there was a global increase in efforts to reduce pollution.

    ANS: T   DIF: I   OBJ: BPE 19-3.1

25. There is no way known today to reduce emissions of sulfur dioxide, carbon monoxide, and soot from the air.

    ANS: F   DIF: I   OBJ: BPE 19-3.1

26. Pollution and the economy of the United States are closely related.

    ANS: T   DIF: I   OBJ: BPE 19-3.1

27. The first step toward solving an environmental problem is political action.

    ANS: F   DIF: I   OBJ: BPE 19-3.2

28. Political action is one of the five steps to successfully environmental problems.

    ANS: T   DIF: I   OBJ: BPE 19-3.2

29. There is nothing that an individual can do to affect environmental problems— the problem is just too large and complex.

    ANS: F   DIF: I   OBJ: BPE 19-3.3

30. W.T. Edmondson, at the University of Washington, proved that dumping sewage into Lake Washington was beneficial to the species diversity of the lake.

    ANS: F   DIF: I   OBJ: BPE 19-3.3

31. As demonstrated in Lake Washington, sewage that has been treated and is safe enough to drink is not necessarily "harmless."

    ANS: T   DIF: I   OBJ: BPE 19-3.3

MULTIPLE CHOICE

1. The decrease in species diversity of some lakes in the northeastern United States during this century may best be explained by
   a. global warming.
   b. evolutionary trends.
   c. the destruction of the ozone layer.
   d. acid rain.

   ANS: D   DIF: I   OBJ: BPE 19-1.1

2. Tall smokestacks were placed on power plants because the smoke they produced from the burning of coal contained high concentrations of
   a. ozone.
   b. sulfur.
   c. oxygen.
   d. nitrogen.

   ANS: B   DIF: I   OBJ: BPE 19-1.1

3. A community that is *downwind* from a power plant that burns high-sulfur coal
   a. may experience the effects of acid rain.
   b. is safe since pollution from the plant is dispersed by the wind.
   c. will experience ozone depletion in the surrounding air.
   d. should pump extra oxygen into the air.

   ANS: A   DIF: I   OBJ: BPE 19-1.1

4. In the upper atmosphere, sulfur released from the burning of sulfur-rich coal combines with water vapor to form
   a. sulfur dioxide.
   b. sulfuric acid.
   c. ozone.
   d. All of the above

   ANS: B   DIF: I   OBJ: BPE 19-1.1

5. The destruction of the ozone layer may be responsible for an increase in
   a. cataracts.
   b. melanoma.
   c. cancer of the retina.
   d. All of the above

   ANS: D   DIF: I   OBJ: BPE 19-1.2

6. CFCs in the atmosphere
   a. result in free chlorine.
   b. change oxygen into ozone.
   c. convert sunlight into ozone.
   d. convert ozone into methane.

   ANS: A   DIF: I   OBJ: BPE 19-1.2

7. Chlorofluorocarbons (CFCs) are a problem because they
   a. corrode aerosol cans and release iron oxide into the atmosphere.
   b. are released by air conditioners into the groundwater.
   c. attack ozone molecules in the upper atmosphere.
   d. were once thought to be a hazard, but this now causes unnecessary expense for industry.

   ANS: C   DIF: I   OBJ: BPE 19-1.2

8. CFCs were once
   a. thought to be chemically inert.
   b. used as refrigerants.
   c. used as aerosol propellants.
   d. All of the above

   ANS: D   DIF: I   OBJ: BPE 19-1.2

9. Ozone in the atmosphere
   a. leads to formation of acid precipitation.
   b. combines readily with water vapor.
   c. absorbs harmful radiation from the sun.
   d. All of the above

   ANS: C   DIF: I   OBJ: BPE 19-1.2

10. As a result of the discovery of the ozone hole,
    a. tall smokestacks were placed on power plants.
    b. the production of most CFCs was banned in the United States.
    c. methane has been substituted for nitrous oxides in some chemicals.
    d. large greenhouses were built in Europe, the United States, and Canada.

    ANS: B   DIF: I   OBJ: BPE 19-1.2

11. CFC : ozone ::
    a. ozone : carbon dioxide
    b. ozone : oxygen
    c. acid rain : fish and amphibians
    d. acid rain : carbon dioxide

    ANS: C
    (destroys)

    DIF: II   OBJ: BPE 19-1.2

12. burning fossil fuels : atmospheric carbon dioxide ::
    a. greenhouse effect : CFCs
    b. atmospheric carbon dioxide : global warming
    c. ground level ozone : CO_2
    d. atmospheric carbon dioxide : ozone

    ANS: B
    (increases)

    DIF: II   OBJ: BPE 19-1.3

$$CH_4 + 2O_2 \rightarrow CO_2 + 2H_2O$$

13. Refer to the equation above. Which of the molecules in this reaction poses environmental danger when it is produced in too large a quantity?
    a. CH_4
    b. O_2
    c. CO_2
    d. H_2O

    ANS: C   DIF: II   OBJ: BPE 19-1.3

Biology: Principles and Explorations

14. Refer to the equation above. The continued use of this reaction by humans may contribute to
    a. acid rain.
    b. increased rates of skin cancer.
    c. increases in average temperatures worldwide.
    d. All of the above

    ANS: C   DIF: I   OBJ: BPE 19-1.4

15. The heat-trapping ability of some gases in the atmosphere can be compared to
    a. the melting of snow.   c. condensation due to heating.
    b. the way glass traps heat in a greenhouse. d. heating water on a stove.

    ANS: B   DIF: I   OBJ: BPE 19-1.4

16. Solar energy can be trapped in the atmosphere by
    a. the chemical bonds of carbon dioxide.   c. radiation.
    b. ozone.   d. sunlight.

    ANS: A   DIF: I   OBJ: BPE 19-1.4

17. The greenhouse effect may increase on Earth because
    a. decomposers essential to recycling matter are being destroyed.
    b. too much oxygen is now given off by plants.
    c. increasing carbon dioxide will trap more heat.
    d. the Earth tilts toward the sun in the summer.

    ANS: C   DIF: I   OBJ: BPE 19-1.4

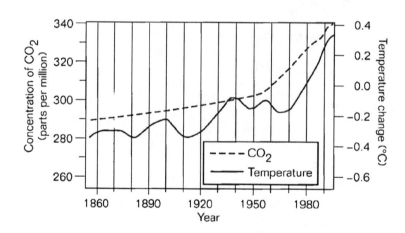

18. Refer to the illustration above. According to the graph,
    a. from 1900 to 1950 the average global temperature constantly increased.
    b. the concentration of CO_2 in the atmosphere has increased at the same steady rate for the past 10 years.
    c. the concentration of CO_2 and the temperature were the same in 1940.
    d. None of the above

    ANS: D   DIF: II   OBJ: BPE 19-1.4

19. Refer to the illustration above. The graph shows
    a. the concentration of CO_2 in the atmosphere from 1860 to the present.
    b. the average global temperature from 1860 to present.
    c. that the concentration of oxygen in the atmosphere has increased since 1860.
    d. Both (a) and (b)

    ANS: D   DIF: II   OBJ: BPE 19-1.4

20. *Exxon Valdez* was
    a. a species of bird that is now extinct.   c. an oil tanker.
    b. a bacteria.   d. the founder of the Sierra Club.

    ANS: C   DIF: I   OBJ: BPE 19-2.1

21. If a large amount of chemicals gets into a river or lake, the species diversity
    a. is usually enhanced.   c. recovers quickly.
    b. recovers, but it takes years.   d. is usually unaffected.

    ANS: B   DIF: I   OBJ: BPE 19-2.1

22. One way to help reduce pollution is to put a tax on the product contributing to the problem. To be fully effective, however, the tax must be
    a. high enough to reflect the actual cost of the pollution.
    b. very low so people will realize that they must donate money to help fight pollution.
    c. so high that no one can afford the product.
    d. the same throughout the world.

    ANS: A   DIF: I   OBJ: BPE 19-2.1

23. The extinction of species
    a. is a problem limited to the tropics.
    b. has been speeded up by the activities of people.
    c. is a problem only where topsoil and ground water are limited.
    d. is not a problem in the twentieth century.

    ANS: B   DIF: I   OBJ: BPE 19-2.2

24. Topsoil and ground water
    a. exist in unlimited quantities in aquifers throughout the world.
    b. are found only on the prairie.
    c. are renewable resources.
    d. are nonreplaceable resources.

    ANS: D   DIF: I   OBJ: BPE 19-2.2

25. Topsoil
    a. is a renewable resource.
    b. is formed from the remains of plants and animals.
    c. forms at the rate of 1 cm each growing season.
    d. forms by the action of water and wind.

    ANS: B   DIF: I   OBJ: BPE 19-2.2

26. All of the following are important environmental problems that must be solved *except*
    a. increasing levels of ocean pollution.
    b. dependence on fossil fuels.
    c. rapid population growth.
    d. coastal devastation by hurricanes.

    ANS: D   DIF: I   OBJ: BPE 19-2.2

27. Water trapped beneath the soil, largely in porous rock,
    a. is called ground water.
    b. is replenished immediately after a heavy rainstorm.
    c. is safe from pollution since it is deep beneath the soil.
    d. will never dry up.

    ANS: A   DIF: I   OBJ: BPE 19-2.2

28. Renewable sources of energy
    a. replenish themselves naturally.
    b. must be created in laboratories.
    c. are manufactured from fossil fuels.
    d. were never utilized until this century.

    ANS: A   DIF: I   OBJ: BPE 19-2.2

29. Destruction of the tropical rain forests
    a. threatens the existence of thousands of species.
    b. provides for more pasture and farmlands.
    c. is done partly because of the need for lumber.
    d. All of the above

    ANS: D   DIF: I   OBJ: BPE 19-2.2

30. If a population is composed of a balance of people of pre-reproductive, reproductive, and post-reproductive age, what will most likely happen to the size of the population?
    a. It will grow steadily.
    b. It will experience no growth for a time and then increase rapidly.
    c. It will decrease steadily.
    d. It will experience no growth for a time and then decrease rapidly.

    ANS: A   DIF: I   OBJ: BPE 19-2.3

31. A population of organisms grows
    a. when there are no natural restrictions except the availability of food.
    b. when the birth rate exceeds the death rate.
    c. only in the absence of predators or natural diseases.
    d. All of the above

    ANS: B   DIF: I   OBJ: BPE 19-2.3

World Population Growth

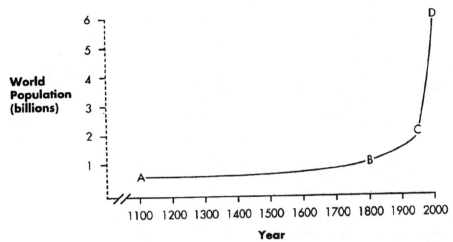

32. Refer to the illustration above. The American Revolution began in 1776. According to the graph, what was the approximate world population at that time?
    a.   500 thousand   c.   1 billion
    b.   1 million   d.   2 billion

    ANS: C   DIF: II   OBJ: BPE 19-2.3

33. Refer to the illustration above. Which letter in the graph indicates the approximate world population in the year 1950?
    a.   letter A   c.   letter C
    b.   letter B   d.   letter D

    ANS: C   DIF: II   OBJ: BPE 19-2.3

34. Refer to the illustration above. Which of the following contributed to the change in world population during the 1900s shown in the graph?
    a.   better sanitation   c.   agricultural improvements
    b.   improved health care   d.   All of the above

    ANS: D   DIF: II   OBJ: BPE 19-2.3

35. Refer to the illustration above. The current rate of population growth will result in a doubling of the world population every 39 years. Based on information in the graph, what will be the approximate world population in the year 2039 if nothing is done to change this rate?
    a.   6 billion   c.   12 billion
    b.   10 billion   d.   24 billion

    ANS: C   DIF: II   OBJ: BPE 19-2.3

Human Population Growth

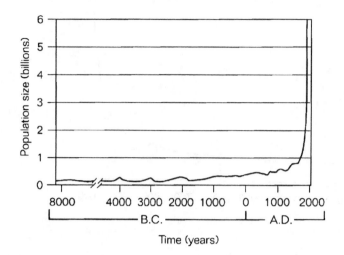

Time (years)

36. Refer to the illustration above. According to the graph,
    a. there were no humans on the Earth around 6000 B.C.
    b. the human population has never decreased in size.
    c. an increase in the food supply was responsible for the increase in the population.
    d. the human population is currently rising dramatically.

    ANS: D   DIF: II   OBJ: BPE 19-2.3

37. Refer to the illustration above. According to the graph, the human population
    a. remained essentially unchanged for thousands of years.
    b. doubled in size from 2000 B.C. to 1000 B.C.
    c. reached 1 billion in 1492.
    d. will stop growing in the year 2000.

    ANS: A   DIF: II   OBJ: BPE 19-2.3

38. Human population growth is most rapid in
    a. Europe.   c. Japan.
    b. the United States.   d. developing countries.

    ANS: D   DIF: I   OBJ: BPE 19-2.4

39. Pollutants produced by the burning of coal include
    a. chlorinated hydrocarbons.   c. carbon monoxide.
    b. carbon dioxide.   d. CFCs.

    ANS: C   DIF: I   OBJ: BPE 19-3.1

40. Which of the following is (are) effective in preventing pollution?
    a. stricter standards   c. better education of the public
    b. higher taxes on polluters   d. All of the above

    ANS: D   DIF: I   OBJ: BPE 19-3.1

41. What is the first step in solving an environmental problem?
    a. risk analysis
    b. political action
    c. assessment
    d. public education

    ANS: C   DIF: I   OBJ: BPE 19-3.2

42. The steps needed to solve environmental problems include
    a. waiting for the affected species to leave an ecosystem that is in trouble.
    b. leaving the problems to United Nations committees to address.
    c. educating the public about the problems and the costs of their solution.
    d. taking any necessary action, regardless of the consequences or adverse effects.

    ANS: C   DIF: I   OBJ: BPE 19-3.2

43. In solving environmental problems, which of the following is *not* a part of public education?
    a. explaining the problem in understandable terms
    b. sending out highly technical brochures that present detailed scientific research and
        complex data so everyone can become an expert on the problem
    c. presenting alternative actions available
    d. explaining the probable costs and results of the various choices

    ANS: B   DIF: I   OBJ: BPE 19-3.2

44. Things that you as an individual can do to contribute to a cleaner environment include
    a. recycling.
    b. using alternative means of transportation.
    c. helping educate the public.
    d. All of the above

    ANS: D   DIF: I   OBJ: BPE 19-3.3

COMPLETION

1. The formation of sulfuric acid in the atmosphere causes _____
    _____.

    ANS: acid rain or acid precipitation   DIF: I   OBJ: BPE 19-1.1

2. The precipitation of sulfur-containing pollutants that lowers the natural pH of lakes and ponds,
    often killing the organisms that live there, is called _____
    _____.

    ANS: acid rain   DIF: I   OBJ: BPE 19-1.1

3. Pollutants called _____ are converted into free chlorine that eventually
    destroys the protective ozone layer.

    ANS: CFCs or chlorofluorocarbons   DIF: I   OBJ: BPE 19-1.2

4. The heat-trapping ability of carbon dioxide, methane, and nitrous oxide in the atmosphere is known as the _____ _____.

   ANS: greenhouse effect   DIF: I   OBJ: BPE 19-1.3

5. Many scientists think that the increased levels of carbon dioxide in the atmosphere are causing global _____.

   ANS: warming   DIF: I   OBJ: BPE 19-1.4

6. A knowledge of _____ is essential to solving our environmental problems.

   ANS: ecology   DIF: I   OBJ: BPE 19-1.4

7. The phenomenon known as the _____ _____ is characterized by a rise in global temperatures resulting from the burning of fossil fuels.

   ANS: greenhouse effect   DIF: I   OBJ: BPE 19-1.4

8. As molecules of pollutants pass up through the trophic levels of the food chain, they become increasingly concentrated in a process called _____ _____.

   ANS: biological magnification   DIF: I   OBJ: BPE 19-2.1

9. If the rate of destruction of the biome known as the _____ _____ _____ remains at its current rate, it is likely that it will be gone within our lifetime.

   ANS: tropical rain forest   DIF: I   OBJ: BPE 19-2.2

10. _____ _____ is water trapped beneath the soil, largely in porous rock.

    ANS: Ground water   DIF: I   OBJ: BPE 19-2.2

11. The reason that _____ resources must be conserved is that they cannot replenish themselves naturally.

    ANS: nonrenewable   DIF: I   OBJ: BPE 19-2.2

12. A great deal of water is found beneath the soil within porous rock reservoirs called _____.

    ANS: aquifers   DIF: I   OBJ: BPE 19-2.2

13. The population of the Earth is expected to exceed _____ billion people by the year 2000.

    ANS: 6   DIF: I   OBJ: BPE 19-2.3

14. The main reason the Earth's human population has increased over the past 350 years is because of a decrease in the _____ rate.

   ANS: death   DIF: I   OBJ: BPE 19-2.3

15. A population of organisms will grow when its _____ _____ exceeds its death rate.

   ANS: birth rate   DIF: I   OBJ: BPE 19-2.3

16. The _____ countries on the Earth are experiencing the greatest increase in population growth.

   ANS: developing   DIF: I   OBJ: BPE 19-2.4

17. The Clean Air Act of 1990 requires that power plants install scrubbers on their smokestacks to restrict _____ emissions.

   ANS: sulfur   DIF: I   OBJ: BPE 19-3.1

18. The economy of much of the industrialized world is based on a system of _____ and demand.

   ANS: supply   DIF: I   OBJ: BPE 19-3.1

19. In order to help solve environmental problems, one must be _____ about the environment.

   ANS: educated or knowledgeable DIF: I   OBJ: BPE 19-3.2

20. The first step in addressing an environmental problem is _____.

   ANS: assessment   DIF: I   OBJ: BPE 19-3.2

21. The fifth and final step in successfully solving any environmental problem is _____-_____.

   ANS: follow-through   DIF: I   OBJ: BPE 19-3.2

22. In solving an environmental problem, predicting positive and negative consequences of environmental intervention is called _____ _____.

   ANS: risk analysis   DIF: I   OBJ: BPE 19-3.2

ESSAY

1. Describe how acid precipitation in the form of rain or snow is formed.

   ANS:
   Sulfur in the smoke from burning sulfur-rich coal is released into the atmosphere. When condensation occurs, sulfuric acid forms from the combination of sulfur and water, and the sulfuric acid is brought back to Earth in the form of acid rain or snow.

   DIF: II   OBJ: BPE 19-1.1

2. John says that his teacher told him that ozone is a type of air pollutant produced by the burning of gasoline in automobiles. It has been determined to be harmful to humans. But he remembers reading that scientists and government officials are concerned about a decrease in the amount of the earth's ozone. Scientists are predicting that a decrease in the ozone layer will be harmful to humans. In the space below, write an explanation for John that will clarify the apparently conflicting pieces of information he has received.

   ANS:
   Ozone pollution from automobiles is released into the lower area of the earth's atmosphere, where it can be breathed in by humans. It can damage lung tissue. The earth's ozone layer is in the upper atmosphere. We do not breathe in this air. However, this higher level ozone layer acts to protect our health by absorbing ultra-violet radiation from the sun. With a depletion of the earth's ozone layer, more ultraviolet radiation would likely reach humans. Ultraviolet radiation causes mutations, some of which can result in cancer.

   DIF: III   OBJ: BPE 19-1.2

3. Describe the greenhouse effect.

   ANS:
   The greenhouse effect causes atmospheric temperatures to increase. The higher temperatures result from increased levels of carbon dioxide in the atmosphere due to the combustion of fossil fuels. The increase in levels of carbon dioxide causes an increase in the ability of the atmosphere to trap heat, thus causing temperatures to rise gradually.

   DIF: II   OBJ: BPE 19-1.4

4. Define biological magnification.

   ANS:
   As molecules of pollutants pass up through the trophic levels of the food chain, they become increasingly concentrated.

   DIF: II   OBJ: BPE 19-2.1

5. Using examples, distinguish between renewable and nonrenewable natural energy resources.

ANS:
Renewable energy sources are readily and naturally replenished. For example, trees are a renewable resource, since new trees may be grown to replace those which are cut down. Nonrenewable resources are gone once they are used up; they cannot be replenished. Fossil fuels such as coal, oil, and natural gas are nonrenewable.

DIF: II   OBJ: BPE 19-2.2

6. Why has our society made it profitable for industries to pollute the environment?

ANS:
Since indirect costs of pollution and environment damage are not included in the price that a consumer pays for a product, far more products are consumed than if indirect costs had been included. By not adding the indirect costs to the price of energy and manufactured goods, our society has made it profitable to pollute.

DIF: II   OBJ: BPE 19-3.1

7. What are the five steps that must be followed in order to successfully solve an environmental problem?

ANS:
In order to solve the problem facing an ecosystem it is necessary to
1. assess the problem by collecting data
2. perform a risk analysis to evaluate the various possible courses of action
3. educate the public about the most feasible course of action and its costs
4. implement a solution through political action
5. follow through on any action taken, to verify that the problem is being effectively addressed and solved.

DIF: II   OBJ: BPE 19-3.2

8. Explain what was happening to Lake Washington in the 1950s because of the "harmless" sewage being dumped into it.

ANS:
The sewage was fertilizing the lake, thus providing an abundance of nutrients which allowed blue-green algae to grow in the water. The bacteria that was decomposing the dead algae was depleting the lake's oxygen and killing the lake.

DIF: II   OBJ: BPE 19-3.3

CHAPTER 20—INTRODUCTION TO THE KINGDOMS OF LIFE

TRUE/FALSE

1. Kingdoms are the most inclusive taxonomic group.

    ANS: T   DIF: I   OBJ: BPE 20-1.1

2. Kingdoms are subgroups of phyla.

    ANS: F   DIF: I   OBJ: BPE 20-1.1

3. Some biologists use five kingdoms into which they organize all living things, but most biologists use six.

    ANS: T   DIF: I   OBJ: BPE 20-1.1

4. All organisms in the kingdoms Plantae and Animalia are multicellular.

    ANS: T   DIF: I   OBJ: BPE 20-1.1

5. Organisms in the kingdoms Archaebacteria, Eubacteria, and Protista can be autotrophic or heterotrophic.

    ANS: T   DIF: I   OBJ: BPE 20-1.1

6. All organisms in the kingdom Animalia have cell walls as part of their structure.

    ANS: F   DIF: I   OBJ: BPE 20-1.1

7. All kingdoms include some unicellular organisms.

    ANS: F   DIF: I   OBJ: BPE 20-1.1

8. All kingdoms include unicellular or multicellular organisms, but never both.

    ANS: F   DIF: I   OBJ: BPE 20-1.1

9. Archaebacteria have cell walls that do not contain peptidoglycan.

    ANS: T   DIF: I   OBJ: BPE 20-1.2

10. Eubacteria and archaebacteria are practically identical in their characteristics.

    ANS: F   DIF: I   OBJ: BPE 20-1.2

11. Biologists group eubacteria mostly by their shape, cell wall, and metabolism.

    ANS: T   DIF: I   OBJ: BPE 20-1.2

12. Some heterotrophic eubacteria are capable of living in the absence of oxygen.

    ANS: T   DIF: I   OBJ: BPE 20-1.2

13. Eubacteria are involved in the recycling of carbon, nitrogen, and phosphorus.

    ANS: T   DIF: I   OBJ: BPE 20-1.2

14. Very salty water will kill all forms of archaebacteria.

    ANS: T   DIF: I   OBJ: BPE 20-1.2

15. Eubacterial genes have no introns.

    ANS: T   DIF: I   OBJ: BPE 20-1.2

16. Archaebacteria are eukaryotes characterized by several unique biochemical characteristics.

    ANS: F   DIF: I   OBJ: BPE 20-1.2

17. The cell walls of archaebacteria do not contain peptidoglycan.

    ANS: T   DIF: I   OBJ: BPE 20-1.2

18. Methanogens are archaebacteria that live in very hot water, such as deep-sea hydrothermal vents.

    ANS: F   DIF: I   OBJ: BPE 20-1.2

19. There are at least three major groups of archaebacteria.

    ANS: T   DIF: I   OBJ: BPE 20-1.2

20. More than half the biomass on Earth is composed of multicelled organisms.

    ANS: F   DIF: I   OBJ: BPE 20-2.1

21. Colonies are one form of aggregates.

    ANS: F   DIF: I   OBJ: BPE 20-2.1

22. Colonies are truly multicellular.

    ANS: F   DIF: I   OBJ: BPE 20-2.1

23. Multicellularity enables cells to specialize in different functions.

    ANS: T   DIF: I   OBJ: BPE 20-2.1

24. Protists usually reproduce asexually, but many can reproduce sexually in times of environment stress.

ANS: T   DIF: I   OBJ: BPE 20-2.2

25. Algae cannot exist in a saltwater environment.

ANS: F   DIF: I   OBJ: BPE 20-2.2

26. Protists all require a microscope to be seen.

ANS: F   DIF: I   OBJ: BPE 20-2.2

27. Some protists can grow to over 300 feet tall.

ANS: T   DIF: I   OBJ: BPE 20-2.2

28. Fungi exist mainly in the form of slender filaments, barely visible with the naked eye.

ANS: T   DIF: I   OBJ: BPE 20-2.3

29. Fungal cells have an exterior wall made of chitin.

ANS: T   DIF: I   OBJ: BPE 20-2.3

30. Septa in fungal walls rarely form a complete barrier.

ANS: T   DIF: I   OBJ: BPE 20-2.3

31. Prior to the 1950s, most scientists believed there were dozens of kingdoms.

ANS: F   DIF: I   OBJ: BPE 20-3.1

32. The members of all six kingdoms have a body type that includes organs and tissues.

ANS: F   DIF: I   OBJ: BPE 20-3.1

33. Plants are multicellular autotrophs.

ANS: T   DIF: I   OBJ: BPE 20-3.2

34. Plants are the primary producers in most terrestrial food webs.

ANS: T   DIF: I   OBJ: BPE 20-3.2

35. Plants differ from one another according to their type of vascular and reproductive structures.

ANS: T   DIF: I   OBJ: BPE 20-3.2

36. Roses, grasses, and oaks are the most common seedless vascular plants.

    ANS: F   DIF: I   OBJ: BPE 20-3.2

37. Animals are the primary producers in most terrestrial food webs.

    ANS: F   DIF: I   OBJ: BPE 20-3.3

38. The vast majority of animals have a backbone.

    ANS: F   DIF: I   OBJ: BPE 20-3.3

39. There are six general categories of animals.

    ANS: T   DIF: I   OBJ: BPE 20-3.3

40. Nonvascular plants lack true roots, stems, and leaves.

    ANS: T   DIF: I   OBJ: BPE 20-3.4

MULTIPLE CHOICE

1. Four of the kingdoms include eukaryotes and the other two include
   a. plants.   c. animals.
   b. fungi.   d. prokaryotes.

    ANS: D   DIF: I   OBJ: BPE 20-1.1

2. Which of the following is *not* a characteristic used to differentiate kingdoms?
   a. cell type   c. nutrition
   b. root system   d. body type

    ANS: B   DIF: I   OBJ: BPE 20-1.1

3. The kingdom that contains both unicellular and multicellular organisms is the kingdom
   a. Protista.   c. Both (a) and (b)
   b. Fungi.   d. None of the above

    ANS: C   DIF: I   OBJ: BPE 20-1.1

4. Some biologists group eubacteria and archaebacteria together in a kingdom called
   a. Protista.   c. Monera.
   b. Animalia.   d. Plantae.

    ANS: C   DIF: I   OBJ: BPE 20-1.2

5. Plantae : pine trees ::
   a. Animalia : humans
   b. mushrooms : Fungi
   c. Eubacteria : euglena
   d. dogs : Animalia

   ANS: A
   (includes)

   DIF: II   OBJ: BPE 20-1.1

6. Eubacteria : prokaryotes ::
   a. Fungi : prokaryotes
   b. Animalia : prokaryotes
   c. Protista : eukaryotes
   d. Archaebacteria : eukaryotes

   ANS: C
   (have the cell type)

   DIF: II   OBJ: BPE 20-1.1

7. Which of the following is *not* a characteristic used to group eubacteria?
   a. shape
   b. color
   c. metabolism
   d. cell wall

   ANS: B   DIF: I   OBJ: BPE 20-1.2

8. Some heterotrophic eubacteria are capable of living in the absence of
   a. water.
   b. soil.
   c. oxygen.
   d. None of the above

   ANS: C   DIF: I   OBJ: BPE 20-1.2

9. Eubacteria are responsible for the recycling of
   a. phosphorus.
   b. iron.
   c. copper.
   d. water.

   ANS: A   DIF: I   OBJ: BPE 20-1.2

10. The major groups of archaebacteria include
    a. methanogens.
    b. thermophiles.
    c. halophiles.
    d. All of the above

    ANS: D   DIF: I   OBJ: BPE 20-1.2

11. Halophiles : salty water ::
    a. Thermophiles : swamps
    b. Methanogens : very cold water
    c. Thermophiles : very hot water
    d. Magiphiles : sand

    ANS: C
    (live in)

    DIF: II   OBJ: BPE 20-1.2

Biology: Principles and Explorations
Copyright © by Holt, Rinehart and Winston. All rights reserved.
276

12. A temporary collection of cells that come together for a period of time and then separate is called a(n)
    a. colony.
    b. aggregation.
    c. tribe.
    d. collection.

    ANS: A   DIF: I   OBJ: BPE 20-2.1

13. The process by which cells become specialized in form and function is called
    a. specialization.
    b. aggregation.
    c. collection.
    d. differentiation.

    ANS: D   DIF: I   OBJ: BPE 20-2.1

14. Multicellular organisms : permanently ::
    a. colonies : temporarily
    b. weight : permanently
    c. aggregations : permanently
    d. aggregations : temporarily

    ANS: D
    (associate)

    DIF: II   OBJ: BPE 20-2.1

15. How many general groups of protists do most biologists recognize?
    a. 1
    b. 6
    c. 16
    d. 20

    ANS: B   DIF: I   OBJ: BPE 20-2.2

16. Non-motile unicellular parasites that form spores and are responsible for malaria are called
    a. flagella.
    b. sporozoans.
    c. autotrophs.
    d. algae.

    ANS: B   DIF: I   OBJ: BPE 20-2.2

17. Which of the following are *not* protists?
    a. fungi
    b. algae
    c. slime molds
    d. diatoms

    ANS: A   DIF: I   OBJ: BPE 20-2.2

18. Amoebas move using extensions of cytoplasm called
    a. flagella.
    b. sporozoans.
    c. forams.
    d. pseudopodia.

    ANS: D   DIF: I   OBJ: BPE 20-2.2

19. Diatoms have double shells made of
    a. cartilage.
    b. calcium.
    c. plankton.
    d. silica.

    ANS: D   DIF: I   OBJ: BPE 20-2.2

20. Slime molds can be found
    a. in deserts.
    b. on the skin of animals.
    c. on forest floors.
    d. All of the above

    ANS: C   DIF: I   OBJ: BPE 20-2.2

21. Strings of connected fungal cells are called
    a. hyphae.
    b. septa.
    c. mushrooms.
    d. zygotes.

    ANS: A   DIF: I   OBJ: BPE 20-2.3

22. Chitin is a tough material found in
    a. crab shells.
    b. insect bodies.
    c. fungal cells.
    d. All of the above

    ANS: D   DIF: I   OBJ: BPE 20-2.3

23. The presence of _____ is a key way in which fungi differ fundamentally from all other multicellular organisms.
    a. hyphae.
    b. septa.
    c. chitin.
    d. zygotes.

    ANS: B   DIF: I   OBJ: BPE 20-2.3

24. All of the following are phyla of fungi *except*
    a. ascomycetes.
    b. fungomycetes.
    c. basidiomycetes.
    d. zygomycetes.

    ANS: B   DIF: I   OBJ: BPE 20-2.3

25. Zygosporangia : zygomycetes ::
    a. mold : bread
    b. mushrooms : basidiomycetes
    c. zygotes : zygomycetes
    d. fungi : ascomycetes

    ANS: B
    (are the sexual reproductive structures of)

    DIF: II   OBJ: BPE 20-2.3

26. Distinct types of cells with a common structure and function are called
    a. organ systems.
    b. organs.
    c. tissues.
    d. bodies.

    ANS: C   DIF: I   OBJ: BPE 20-3.1

27. Tissues organized into specialized structures with specific functions are called
    a. organ systems.
    b. organs.
    c. tissues.
    d. bodies.

    ANS: B   DIF: I   OBJ: BPE 20-3.1

28. The various organs that carry out major body functions are called
    a. organ systems.   c. tissues.
    b. organs.   d. bodies.

    ANS: A   DIF: I   OBJ: BPE 20-3.1

29. The major gas that is released to the atmosphere by plants is
    a. nitrogen.   c. helium.
    b. carbon dioxide.   d. oxygen.

    ANS: D   DIF: I   OBJ: BPE 20-3.1

30. The most common seedless vascular plants are
    a. ferns.   c. fruits.
    b. gymnosperms.   d. pine trees.

    ANS: A   DIF: I   OBJ: BPE 20-3.2

31. Vascular plants that reproduce by making seeds, but that do not produce flowers are called
    a. ferns.   c. fruits.
    b. gymnosperms.   d. pine trees.

    ANS: B   DIF: I   OBJ: BPE 20-3.2

32. Angiosperms produce seeds in
    a. ferns.   c. fruits.
    b. gymnosperms.   d. pine trees.

    ANS: C   DIF: I   OBJ: BPE 20-3.2

33. Most plants are
    a. flowering.   c. seedless.
    b. nonflowering.   d. vascular.

    ANS: D   DIF: I   OBJ: BPE 20-3.2

34. Two-thirds of all named species of animals are
    a. worms.   c. arthropods.
    b. cnidarians.   d. mollusks.

    ANS: C   DIF: I   OBJ: BPE 20-3.3

35. A variety of animals with cylinder-shaped bodies that occur in both aquatic and terrestrial habitats are
    a. worms.   c. arthropods.
    b. cnidarians.   d. mollusks.

    ANS: A   DIF: I   OBJ: BPE 20-3.3

36. Snails, squids, and clams are all examples of
   a. worms.
   b. cnidarians.
   c. arthropods.
   d. mollusks.

   ANS: D   DIF: I   OBJ: BPE 20-3.3

37. Jellyfish, sea anemones, and corals are all examples of
   a. worms.
   b. cnidarians.
   c. arthropods.
   d. mollusks.

   ANS: B   DIF: I   OBJ: BPE 20-3.3

38. The major contributing factor to the success of insects is their high rate of
   a. speed.
   b. metabolism.
   c. breathing.
   d. reproduction.

   ANS: D   DIF: I   OBJ: BPE 20-3.3

39. Primary consumers : primary producers ::
   a. secondary consumers : primary consumers
   b. secondary consumers : primary producers
   c. Both (a) and (b)
   d. None of the above

   ANS: C
   (eat)

   DIF: II   OBJ: BPE 20-3.3

40. The plant tissue that transports water and dissolved nutrients is called
   a. vascular tissue.
   b. spongy tissue.
   c. nervous tissue.
   d. muscle tissue.

   ANS: A   DIF: I   OBJ: BPE 20-3.4

COMPLETION

1. Biologists group organisms in the different kingdoms based on their _____.

   ANS: similarities   DIF: I   OBJ: BPE 20-1.1

2. Two of the kingdoms include prokaryotes, while four of the kingdoms include _____.

   ANS: eukaryotes   DIF: I   OBJ: BPE 20-1.1

3. Eubacteria have strong exterior cell walls made of _____.

   ANS: peptidoglycan   DIF: I   OBJ: BPE 20-1.2

4. Archaebacteria that live in very salty places, like the Great Salt Lake in Utah, are called

    _____.

    ANS: halophiles   DIF: I   OBJ: BPE 20-1.2

5. Archaebacteria that obtain their energy by making methane gas from other organic compounds
    are called _____.

    ANS: methanogens   DIF: I   OBJ: BPE 20-1.2

6. Some thermophiles obtain their energy from elemental _____.

    ANS: sulfur   DIF: I   OBJ: BPE 20-1.2

7. The ribosomal proteins of archaebacteria are very similar to those of eukaryotes and differ from
    those of _____.

    ANS: eubacteria   DIF: I   OBJ: BPE 20-1.2

8. A group of cells that are permanently associated but that do not communicate with one another is
    called a(n) _____ organism.

    ANS: colonial   DIF: I   OBJ: BPE 20-2.1

9. An organism made of a group of cells that are permanently associated and that integrate their
    activities is called a(n) _____ organism.

    ANS: multicellular   DIF: I   OBJ: BPE 20-2.1

10. Eukaryotes that are not fungi, plants, or animals are called _____.

    ANS: protists   DIF: I   OBJ: BPE 20-2.2

11. Photosynthetic protists with unique double shells are called _____.

    ANS: diatoms   DIF: I   OBJ: BPE 20-2.2

12. The tough material that makes up the exterior wall of fungal cells is called

    _____.

    ANS: chitin   DIF: I   OBJ: BPE 20-2.3

13. The two primary decomposers in the biosphere are _____ and

    _____.

    ANS: fungi, bacteria   DIF: I   OBJ: BPE 20-2.3

14. Ascomycetes form sexual spores in special sac-like structures called _____.

    ANS: asci   DIF: I   OBJ: BPE 20-2.3

15. Distinct types of cells with a common structure and function are called _____

    ANS: tissues   DIF: I   OBJ: BPE 20-3.1

16. Tissues organized into specialized structures with specific functions are called _____.

    ANS: organs   DIF: I   OBJ: BPE 20-3.1

17. _____ _____ is a group of specialized cells in plants that transport water and dissolved nutrients.

    ANS: Vascular tissue   DIF: I   OBJ: BPE 20-3.2

18. Seed plants can be divided into two general types, _____ and _____.

    ANS: nonflowering, flowering   DIF: I   OBJ: BPE 20-3.2

19. Animals are multicellular _____.

    ANS: heterotrophs   DIF: I   OBJ: BPE 20-3.3

20. The one attribute that best enables animals to avoid predators and to look for food and mates is _____.

    ANS: movement   DIF: I   OBJ: BPE 20-3.3

21. Sea stars, sea urchins, and sand dollars are all in the group of invertebrates called _____.

    ANS: echinoderms   DIF: I   OBJ: BPE 20-3.3

22. Two-thirds of all named species of animals are _____.

    ANS: arthropods   DIF: I   OBJ: BPE 20-3.3

23. Animal cells differ from plant cells in that animal cells do not contain _____.

    ANS: cell walls (or central vacuoles)   DIF: I   OBJ: BPE 20-3.4

ESSAY

1. Name at least three ways in which biologists study life.

   ANS:
   They live with gorillas, collect fossils, listen to whales, identify bacteria, grow mushrooms and various plants, examine the structure of fruit flies, read messages encoded in the long molecules of heredity, and count how many times a hummingbird's wings beat per second. (These are examples listed in the book, allow credit for other appropriate responses.)

   DIF: II   OBJ: BPE 20-1.1

2. Name the six kingdoms recognized by most biologists.

   ANS:
   The six kingdoms recognized by most biologists are Eubacteria, Archaebacteria, Protista, Fungi, Plantae, and Animalia.

   DIF: II   OBJ: BPE 20-1.1

3. Differentiate between a colonial organism, a multicellular organism, and an aggregation.

   ANS:
   A colonial organism is a group of cells that are permanently associated but in which the cells do not communicate with one another. A multicellular organism is a group of cells that are permanently associated and that integrate their activities. An aggregation is a temporary collection of cells that come together for a period of time and then separate.

   DIF: II   OBJ: BPE 20-2.1

4. How did evolution of multicellularity affect the size in eukaryotes and why?

   ANS:
   Unicellular organisms can only grow to a certain size before there is too little surface area to properly support the cell volume. The evolution of multicellularity enabled eukaryotes to increase in size.

   DIF: II   OBJ: BPE 20-2.1

5. What is meant by "division of labor" in multicellular organisms and how does it help them survive?

   ANS:
   "Division of labor," called differentiation, means that different cells have different and distinct functions. This allows multicellular organisms to have some cells devoted specifically to protection, others devoted to movement, others to reproduction, and still others to feeding.

   DIF: II   OBJ: BPE 20-2.1

6. Why do some biologists place ciliates in a separate kingdom from those using flagella for movement?

ANS:
Because the ciliates, which use a large number of tiny hairlike whips for movement, are so different from other protists, some biologists place them in a separate kingdom.

DIF: II OBJ: BPE 20-2.2

7. How do fungi obtain nutrients?

ANS:
Fungi obtain nutrients by secreting digestive enzymes into their environment and then absorbing the digested organic molecules.

DIF: II OBJ: BPE 20-2.3

8. Describe vertebrates.

ANS:
Vertebrates have an internal skeleton made of bone, a vertebral column (backbone) that surrounds and protects the spinal cord, and a head containing a skull and brain.

DIF: II OBJ: BPE 20-3.3

CHAPTER 21—VIRUSES AND BACTERIA

TRUE/FALSE

1. Although viruses do not consist of cells, biologists consider them to be living because they are capable of reproduction.

   ANS: F   DIF: I   OBJ: BPE 21-1.1

2. A virus can only reproduce by controlling a cell.

   ANS: T   DIF: I   OBJ: BPE 21-1.1

3. Smallpox is caused by bacteria.

   ANS: F   DIF: I   OBJ: BPE 21-1.3

4. Some viruses have a membranous envelope surrounding their protein coat and the envelope helps the viruses gain entry into host cells.

   ANS: T   DIF: I   OBJ: BPE 21-1.3

5. Viruses consist of RNA or DNA surrounded by a coat of protein.

   ANS: T   DIF: I   OBJ: BPE 21-1.3

6. The lytic cycle is a cycle of viral infection, replication, and cell destruction.

   ANS: T   DIF: I   OBJ: BPE 21-1.4

7. During the lysogenic cycle, the viral genome replicates and the host cell is destroyed.

   ANS: F   DIF: I   OBJ: BPE 21-1.4

8. HIV initially infects cells of the nervous system.

   ANS: F   DIF: I   OBJ: BPE 21-1.5

9. An HIV-infected individual can feel healthy and still spread the virus to others.

   ANS: T   DIF: I   OBJ: BPE 21-1.5

10. Bacteria lack nuclei and therefore, also lack genetic material.

   ANS: F   DIF: I   OBJ: BPE 21-2.1

11. Bacterial cells have membrane-bound organelles and chromosomes.

   ANS: F   DIF: I   OBJ: BPE 21-2.1

12. Bacterial cells are usually much larger than eukaryotic cells.

ANS: F   DIF: I   OBJ: BPE 21-2.1

13. Although there are some bacteria that are heterotrophic, the vast majority are autotrophic.

ANS: F   DIF: I   OBJ: BPE 21-2.2

14. Photosynthetic bacteria are present in leguminous plants and convert atmospheric nitrogen into a form that is usable by the plants.

ANS: F   DIF: I   OBJ: BPE 21-2.2

15. *Escherichia coli* is a eukaryotic cell with a rigid cell wall made of peptidoglycan.

ANS: F   DIF: I   OBJ: BPE 21-2.2

16. Tuberculosis is a disease of the respiratory tract caused by a virus.

ANS: F   DIF: I   OBJ: BPE 21-2.4

17. Certain antibiotics have become ineffective against certain strains of bacteria. These bacteria have developed a resistance, which may be passed on from one generation of bacteria to the next.

ANS: T   DIF: I   OBJ: BPE 21-2.4

18. Genetically engineered bacteria are used to produce drugs and other chemicals that benefit humans.

ANS: T   DIF: I   OBJ: BPE 21-2.5

MULTIPLE CHOICE

1. We know viruses are not alive because
   a. they are not cellular.
   b. they cannot make proteins.
   c. they cannot use energy.
   d. All of the above

   ANS: D   DIF: I   OBJ: BPE 21-1.1

2. The study of viruses is a part of biology because
   a. they belong to the kingdom Monera.
   b. they are about to become extinct.
   c. they are living organisms.
   d. they are active inside living cells.

   ANS: D   DIF: I   OBJ: BPE 21-1.1

3. Tobacco mosaic virus
   a. is able to be crystallized.
   b. causes disease in tobacco plants.
   c. is smaller than a bacterium.
   d. All of the above

   ANS: D   DIF: I   OBJ: BPE 21-1.2

4. Viruses
   a. are cellular organisms.
   b. reproduce only in living cells.
   c. have nuclei and organelles.
   d. are surrounded by a polysaccharide coat.

   ANS: B   DIF: I   OBJ: BPE 21-1.3

5. A viral disease that causes painful swelling of a salivary gland is
   a. mumps.
   b. AIDS.
   c. polio.
   d. measles.

   ANS: A   DIF: I   OBJ: BPE 21-1.3

6. Viruses are
   a. photosynthetic.
   b. chemosynthetic.
   c. parasitic.
   d. All of the above

   ANS: C   DIF: I   OBJ: BPE 21-1.3

7. A typical virus consists of
   a. a protein coat and a cytoplasm core.
   b. a carbohydrate coat and a nucleic acid core.
   c. a protein coat and a nucleic acid core.
   d. a polysaccharide coat and a nucleic acid core.

   ANS: C   DIF: I   OBJ: BPE 21-1.3

8. Biologists now know that viruses
   a. are the smallest organisms.
   b. consist of a protein surrounded by a nucleic acid coat.
   c. contain RNA or DNA in a protein coat.
   d. all form the same crystalline shape.

   ANS: C   DIF: I   OBJ: BPE 21-1.3

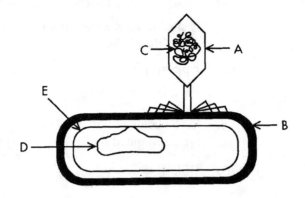

9. Refer to the illustration above. Which structure in the diagram represents RNA?
   a. structure B
   b. structure C
   c. structure D
   d. structure E

   ANS: B   DIF: II   OBJ: BPE 21-1.3

10. A membranous envelope surrounding some viruses may be composed of
    a. lipids.
    b. proteins.
    c. glycoproteins.
    d. All of the above

    ANS: D   DIF: I   OBJ: BPE 21-1.3

11. The capsid of a virus is the
    a. protective outer coat.
    b. cell membrane.
    c. nucleus.
    d. cell wall and membrane complex.

    ANS: A   DIF: I   OBJ: BPE 21-1.3

12. All viruses have
    a. cytoplasm.
    b. ribosomes.
    c. mitochondria.
    d. None of the above

    ANS: D   DIF: I   OBJ: BPE 21-1.3

13. An animal virus enters its host cell by
    a. being injected into the cell.
    b. penetrating a rip in the cell wall.
    c. punching a hole in the cell membrane.
    d. endocytosis across the cell membrane.

    ANS: D   DIF: I   OBJ: BPE 21-1.4

14. The cycle of viral infection, replication, and cell destruction is called the
    a. lysogenic cycle.
    b. metabolic cycle.
    c. lytic cycle.
    d. None of the above

    ANS: C   DIF: I   OBJ: BPE 21-1.4

15. A pathogen is an agent that is
    a.   beneficial to humans.   c.   harmful to living organisms.
    b.   harmful only to plants.   d.   nearly extinct.

    ANS: C   DIF: I   OBJ: BPE 21-1.4

16. viruses : host cells::
    a.   photosynthetic bacteria : chemosynthetic bacteria
    b.   bacteria : viruses
    c.   antibiotics : bacteria
    d.   cyanobacteria : chlorophyll

    ANS: C
    (can kill)

    DIF: II   OBJ: BPE 21-1.4

17. HIV can be transmitted
    a.   through sexual contact.
    b.   through the sharing of nonsterile needles.
    c.   to infants during pregnancy or through breast milk.
    d.   All of the above

    ANS: D   DIF: I   OBJ: BPE 21-1.5

18. It is important to distinguish between Gram-positive and Gram-negative bacteria in diagnosing a
    bacterial infection because
    a.   Gram-negative and gram-positive bacteria differ in their response to different antibiotics.
    b.   Gram-positive bacteria never cause fatal diseases.
    c.   Gram-positive bacteria destroy antibiotics, preventing them from working.
    d.   Gram-positive bacteria do not respond to many antibiotics.

    ANS: A   DIF: I   OBJ: BPE 21-2.1

19. The chromosomes of bacteria
    a.   contain numerous types of organelles.
    b.   are divided into compartments.
    c.   vary in number, depending on the species of bacteria.
    d.   contain a single circular piece of DNA.

    ANS: D   DIF: I   OBJ: BPE 21-2.1

20. Bacteria are the only organisms characterized as
    a.   unicellular.   c.   eukaryotic.
    b.   prokaryotic.   d.   photosynthetic.

    ANS: B   DIF: I   OBJ: BPE 21-2.1

21. One difference between the cells in a human body and bacterial cells is that bacterial cells have
    a. an outer cell wall made up of lipids.
    b. an outer cell wall made up of polysaccharides and proteins.
    c. no DNA.
    d. no ribosomes.

    ANS: B   DIF: I   OBJ: BPE 21-2.1

22. Structures found in eukaryotic cells but not in a bacterial cells are
    a. nuclei.   c. membrane-bound organelles.
    b. linear chromosomes.   d. All of the above

    ANS: D   DIF: I   OBJ: BPE 21-2.1

Organism A   Organism B   Organism C

23. Refer to the illustration above. Which of the diagrams has a shape like the *Bacillus* bacterial genus?
    a. Organism A   c. Organism C
    b. Organism B   d. None of the above

    ANS: B   DIF: II   OBJ: BPE 21-2.1

24. Refer to the illustration above. The shape represented by Organism A in the diagram applies to the bacterial genus
    a. *Streptococcus*, which causes strep throat.
    b. *Leptospira*, which can cause urinary tract infections in humans.
    c. *Bacillus*, which produces antibiotics.
    d. *Penicillium*, which produces penicillin.

    ANS: A   DIF: II   OBJ: BPE 21-2.1

25. Refer to the illustration above. The shape represented by Organism C is called
    a. coccus.   c. bacillus.
    b. spirillum.   d. filamentous.

    ANS: B   DIF: I   OBJ: BPE 21-2.1

26. Which of the following might be found in the cytoplasm of a bacterial cell?
    a. chloroplasts   c. mitochondria
    b. Golgi bodies   d. None of the above

    ANS: D   DIF: I   OBJ: BPE 21-2.1

27. Bacterial cells
    a. have a cell wall only.
    b. have a cell membrane only.
    c. have both a cell membrane and an outer cell wall.
    d. have a cell wall inside their cell membrane.

    ANS: C   DIF: I   OBJ: BPE 21-2.1

28. Bacterial endospores
    a. occur where there is plenty of available food.
    b. allow certain species to survive harsh environmental conditions.
    c. are similar to human tumors.
    d. can cause growth abnormalities in plants.

    ANS: B   DIF: I   OBJ: BPE 21-2.1

29. Bacteria can be classified according to their
    a. type of cell walls.   c. Gram-staining characteristics.
    b. methods of obtaining energy.   d. All of the above

    ANS: D   DIF: I   OBJ: BPE 21-2.2

30. photosynthetic bacteria : sunlight::
    a. chemotrophic bacteria : dead organisms
    b. chemoautotrophic bacteria : inorganic molecules
    c. photosynthesis : nitrification
    d. heterotrophic bacteria : photosynthesis

    ANS: B
    (require)

    DIF: II   OBJ: BPE 21-2.2

31. Nitrogen-fixing bacteria
    a. repair nitrogen-damaged legume roots.
    b. damage the environment by using atmospheric oxygen to produce toxic nitrogen
       compounds.
    c. convert atmospheric nitrogen into ammonia.
    d. convert ammonia in the soil into nitrogen gas.

    ANS: C   DIF: I   OBJ: BPE 21-2.2

32. Cell organelles that *Escherichia coli* and other bacteria have in common with eukaryotes are
    a. chloroplasts.   c. nuclei.
    b. mitochondria.   d. ribosomes.

    ANS: D   DIF: I   OBJ: BPE 21-2.3

33. Bacterial cells such as *Escherichia coli* transfer pieces of genetic material in a process called
    a. binary fission.   c. conjugation.
    b. mitosis.   d. sexual reproduction.

    ANS: C   DIF: I   OBJ: BPE 21-2.3

34. *Escherichia coli* is an example of a bacterium that has short, thin, hairlike projections called
    a. pili.   c. cocci.
    b. cilia.   d. ribosomes.

    ANS: A   DIF: I   OBJ: BPE 21-2.3

35. Bacteria that cause botulism may survive in canned food for a long time because
    a. the can was left open.
    b. some cans may contain viruses that protect the bacteria.
    c. the bacteria may form endospores.
    d. sterilized cans do not have enough oxygen to harm the bacteria.

    ANS: C   DIF: I   OBJ: BPE 21-2.4

36. Alexander Fleming, a British bacteriologist, is credited with the discovery of
    a. photosynthetic bacteria.   c. tuberculosis.
    b. antibodies.   d. penicillin.

    ANS: D   DIF: I   OBJ: BPE 21-2.4

37. Antibiotics
    a. include penicillin, tetracycline, and streptomycin.
    b. may prevent bacteria from making new cell walls.
    c. are very effective treatments for bacterial diseases.
    d. All of the above

    ANS: D   DIF: I   OBJ: BPE 21-2.4

38. Antibiotics are ineffective against viral infections because
    a. viruses are protected inside their host cells.
    b. viruses have enzymes that inactivate the antibiotics.
    c. antibiotics interfere with metabolic processes that viruses do not perform.
    d. viral protein coats block the antibiotics from entering the virus.

    ANS: C   DIF: I   OBJ: BPE 21-2.4

39. Cholera is usually transmitted by
    a. insects.   c. contaminated water.
    b. sexual contact.   d. airborne water droplets.

    ANS: C   DIF: I   OBJ: BPE 21-2.4

40. A bacterial disease carried from rodents to humans by fleas is
    a. tuberculosis.
    b. bubonic plague.
    c. cholera.
    d. Lyme disease.

    ANS: B   DIF: I   OBJ: BPE 21-2.4

41. Lyme disease : ticks::
    a. tuberculosis : food and feces
    b. cholera : human tubercles
    c. typhus : lice
    d. bubonic plague : fleas

    ANS: D
    (is carried by)

    DIF: II   OBJ: BPE 21-2.4

42. Mining companies harvest copper or uranium by using
    a. photosynthetic bacteria.
    b. heterotrophic bacteria.
    c. cyanobacteria.
    d. chemoautotrophic bacteria.

    ANS: D   DIF: I   OBJ: BPE 21-2.5

COMPLETION

1. _____ are segments of nucleic acids contained in a protein coat.

    ANS: Viruses   DIF: I   OBJ: BPE 21-1.1

2. A disease of tobacco plants in which growth is stunted and leaves are blotchy is caused by the
    _____ _____ virus.

    ANS: tobacco mosaic   DIF: I   OBJ: BPE 21-1.2

3. _____ are bacterial viruses with a polyhedral head attached to a helical tail.

    ANS: Bacteriophages   DIF: I   OBJ: BPE 21-1.3

4. The protein coat of a virus is called a(n) _____.

    ANS: capsid   DIF: I   OBJ: BPE 21-1.3

5. All viruses reproduce by taking over the reproductive machinery of a(n)
    _____.

    ANS: cell   DIF: I   OBJ: BPE 21-1.4

6. Microscopic, nucleic acid–containing particles that invade cells of organisms in order to
    reproduce, and often destroy the cells in the process, are called _____.

    ANS: viruses   DIF: I   OBJ: BPE 21-1.4

7. An enzyme called _____ _____ manufactures DNA that is complementary to a virus's RNA.

    ANS: reverse transcriptase   DIF: I   OBJ: BPE 21-1.4

8. The virus that causes AIDS is called _____ _____

    _____.

    ANS: human immunodeficiency virus or HIV

    DIF: I   OBJ: BPE 21-1.5

9. The cell walls of eubacteria are composed of _____, a network of polysaccharide molecules that are linked together with chains of amino acids.

    ANS: peptidoglycan   DIF: I   OBJ: BPE 21-2.1

10. Structurally, bacteria have one of two types of _____ _____ that can be distinguished by the Gram stain.

    ANS: cell walls   DIF: I   OBJ: BPE 21-2.1

11. The procedure used to distinguish between two types of bacterial cell wall structures is called _____ _____.

    ANS: Gram staining   DIF: I   OBJ: BPE 21-2.1

12. Protective coverings that some bacteria may form under harsh conditions are _____.

    ANS: endospores   DIF: I   OBJ: BPE 21-2.1

13. Spiral bacteria are called _____.

    ANS: spirilli   DIF: I   OBJ: BPE 21-2.1

14. Round bacteria are called _____.

    ANS: cocci   DIF: I   OBJ: BPE 21-2.1

15. Rod-shaped bacteria are called _____.

    ANS: bacilli   DIF: I   OBJ: BPE 21-2.1

16. Bacteria that obtain their energy by removing electrons from inorganic molecules, rather than obtaining energy from the sun, are called _____ bacteria.

    ANS: chemoautotrophic   DIF: I   OBJ: BPE 21-2.2

17. Plants that possess nitrogen-fixing bacteria in swellings on their roots are called
_____.

ANS: legumes   DIF: I   OBJ: BPE 21-2.2

18. A species of bacteria that lives in the intestines of many mammals is _____
_____.

ANS: *Escherichia coli*   DIF: I   OBJ: BPE 21-2.3

19. The process in which ammonia is oxidized into nitrate, a form of nitrogen commonly used by plants, is called _____.

ANS: nitrification   DIF: I   OBJ: BPE 21-2.3

20. _____ is a disease of the respiratory tract caused by the bacterium *Mycobacterium tuberculosis.*

ANS: Tuberculosis   DIF: I   OBJ: BPE 21-2.4

21. A(n) _____ is a substance that can be obtained from bacteria or fungi and can be used as a drug to fight pathogenic bacteria.

ANS: antibiotic   DIF: I   OBJ: BPE 21-2.4

22. Mining companies use _____ bacteria to harvest copper or uranium.

ANS: chemoautotrophic   DIF: I   OBJ: BPE 21-2.5

ESSAY

1. A new disease has suddenly appeared and scientists are trying to determine whether the disease agent is a virus or a bacterium. They collect the following information:
   1. The disease can be transmitted through the air.
   2. The disease agent is too small to be seen under a light microscope.
   3. There are no known antibiotics that are effective against the disease.
   4. The genetic material of the disease agent is DNA.
   5. The disease agent cannot be cultured using any known culture medium.
   Is the disease agent most likely a bacterium or a virus? Explain your answer in the space below.

   ANS:
   The disease agent is most likely a virus. Like bacteria, many viruses can be transmitted through the air. Almost all viruses are too small to be seen under a light microscope, although many bacteria are also too small to be seen under a light microscope. Antibiotics are ineffective against viruses, while there are antibiotics that are effective against most bacteria. The genetic material of viruses may be DNA or RNA and the genetic material of bacteria is always DNA. Viruses cannot be cultured on artificial media, while most bacteria can be cultured. Facts 2, 3, and 5 provide the most significant information indicating that the disease agent is a virus.

   DIF: III   OBJ: BPE 21-1.1

2. Viruses are not considered to be living organisms, but they are still studied as part of biology. Explain.

   ANS:
   Viruses are active inside living cells, making them an important part of the study of biology. Although viruses contain genetic material and can evolve as this material changes over time, they are not considered living because they are not cellular, cannot make their own protein, and cannot use energy in metabolic processes.

   DIF: II   OBJ: BPE 21-1.1

3. Explain why viruses are not considered to be living.

   ANS:
   Viruses are segments of nucleic acids contained in a protein coat. Because viruses do not grow, do not maintain homeostasis, and do not metabolize, biologists do not consider viruses to be living.

   DIF: II   OBJ: BPE 21-1.1

4. It has been observed that antibiotics are generally effective against bacterial infections but cannot be used to treat viral infections. Why is this the case?

ANS:
Antibiotics work by interfering with cell wall formation or cellular processes such as protein synthesis. Some antibiotics can cause disruption of the cell membrane. All of these actions can negatively affect the survival of bacteria. However, since viruses do not undergo cellular processes, they are not influenced by the actions of antibiotics. Thus, antibiotic treatment is ineffective against viral infections.

DIF: II   OBJ: BPE 21-2.4

TRUE/FALSE

1. The kingdom Protista contains the eukaryotes that are not plants, animals, or fungi.

   ANS: T   DIF: I   OBJ: BPE 22-1.1

2. The first protists were prokaryotes.

   ANS: F   DIF: I   OBJ: BPE 22-1.1

3. All protists are unicellular.

   ANS: F   DIF: I   OBJ: BPE 22-1.1

4. Some protists live in damp soil.

   ANS: T   DIF: I   OBJ: BPE 22-1.2

5. The major phyla of protists are, for the most part, closely related to each other.

   ANS: F   DIF: I   OBJ: BPE 22-1.3

6. Sexual reproduction allows *Chlamydomonas* to delay development of new organisms until environmental conditions are favorable.

   ANS: T   DIF: I   OBJ: BPE 22-1.4

7. The green alga *Spyrogyra* reproduces sexually by alternation of generations.

   ANS: F   DIF: I   OBJ: BPE 22-1.5

8. Amoebas move by means of pseudopodia.

   ANS: T   DIF: I   OBJ: BPE 22-2.1

9. Diatoms are the only type of protists with shells.

   ANS: F   DIF: I   OBJ: BPE 22-2.2

10. *Paramecium* takes in food through its contractile vacuole.

    ANS: F   DIF: I   OBJ: BPE 22-2.5

11. Disease is one of the greatest effects protists have on humans.

    ANS: T   DIF: I   OBJ: BPE 22-3.1

12. Protists cause disease in humans only.

    ANS: T   DIF: I   OBJ: BPE 22-3.1

13. Amebic dysentery is usually passed from person to person by coughing and sneezing.

    ANS: F   DIF: I   OBJ: BPE 22-3.2

14. Protists cause amebic dysentery, giardiasis, and sleeping sickness.

    ANS: T   DIF: I   OBJ: BPE 22-3.2

15. Malaria is caused by several species of *Plasmodium,* and it is spread by the bite of certain mosquitoes.

    ANS: T   DIF: I   OBJ: BPE 22-3.3

16. Some strains of *Plasmodium* are resistant to all known antimalarial drugs.

    ANS: T   DIF: I   OBJ: BPE 22-3.4

17. Derivatives of quinine, such as chloroquine and primaquine, are used today to treat individuals infected with malaria and to prevent it in healthy individuals.

    ANS: T   DIF: I   OBJ: BPE 22-3.4

MULTIPLE CHOICE

1. A protist may be
   a. unicellular and heterotrophic.
   b. unicellular and autotrophic.
   c. multicellular and autotrophic.
   d. All of the above

   ANS: D   DIF: I   OBJ: BPE 22-1.1

2. The kingdom Protista includes
   a. most of the single-celled eukaryotes.
   b. slime and water molds.
   c. multicellular seaweed.
   d. All of the above

   ANS: D   DIF: I   OBJ: BPE 22-1.1

3. Protists are found almost everywhere there is
   a. water.
   b. carbon monoxide.
   c. methane.
   d. ammonia.

   ANS: A   DIF: I   OBJ: BPE 22-1.2

4. protists : damp soil or sand ::
   a. cells : cilia
   b. protists : oceans
   c. green algae : dry ground
   d. forams : fresh water

   ANS: B
   (live in)

   DIF: II   OBJ: BPE 22-1.2

5. Eukaryotes that lack the features of animals, plants, or fungi are placed in the kingdom
   a. Archaebacteria.
   b. Plantae.
   c. Protista.
   d. Animalia.

   ANS: C   DIF: I   OBJ: BPE 22-1.3

6. You have been given an unknown organism to identify. You find that it is unicellular and has a cell wall. Which of the following *must* it also have?
   a. chloroplasts
   b. asexual reproduction
   c. pseudopodia
   d. one or more flagella

   ANS: B   DIF: II   OBJ: BPE 22-1.3

7. When *Chlamydomonas* reproduces asexually, it divides by mitosis, producing
   a. zygospores.
   b. diploid gametes.
   c. haploid gametes.
   d. zoospores.

   ANS: C   DIF: I   OBJ: BPE 22-1.4

8. Zoospores are
   a. produced as a result of meiosis.
   b. diploid.
   c. produced as a result of mitosis.
   d. all parasitic.

   ANS: C   DIF: I   OBJ: BPE 22-1.4

9. The haploid, gamete-producing phase in the life cycle of some protists is known as the
   a. zygospore generation.
   b. gametophyte generation.
   c. conjugation generation.
   d. sporophyte generation.

   ANS: B   DIF: I   OBJ: BPE 22-1.5

10. The marine green alga *Ulva* reproduces sexually by
    a. alternation of generations.
    b. conjugation.
    c. mitosis.
    d. aggregation.

    ANS: A   DIF: I   OBJ: BPE 22-1.5

11. Pseudopodia are used for
    a. *Paramecium* conjugation.
    b. movement by amoebas.
    c. *Euglena* reproduction.
    d. *Paramecium* mitosis.

    ANS: B   DIF: I   OBJ: BPE 22-2.1

12. Amoebas capture food by
    a. engulfing it.
    b. using cilia.
    c. trapping it with flagella.
    d. taking it into a gullet.

    ANS: A   DIF: I   OBJ: BPE 22-2.1

13. When an individual diatom gets too small because of repeated division, it
    a. grows to full size in its existing shell.
    b. slips out of its shell, grows to full size, and regenerates a new shell.
    c. slips out of its shell, grows to full size, and reinhabits its old shell.
    d. slips out of its shell and lives the rest of its life without a shell.

    ANS: B   DIF: I   OBJ: BPE 22-2.2

14. Algae are
    a. sometimes heterotrophic.
    b. always microscopic in size.
    c. found in both fresh water and salt water.
    d. found only in fresh water.

    ANS: C   DIF: I   OBJ: BPE 22-2.3

15. Zoomastigotes
    a. reproduce sexually and asexually.
    b. are unicellular.
    c. can cause diseases in humans.
    d. All of the above

    ANS: D   DIF: I   OBJ: BPE 22-2.4

16. *Euglena* is an example of a protist that
    a. is both autotrophic and heterotrophic.
    b. is only a parasitic heterotroph.
    c. is always autotrophic.
    d. swims away from light.

    ANS: A   DIF: I   OBJ: BPE 22-2.4

17. dinoflagellates : flagella ::
    a. amoebas : pseudopodia
    b. forams : flagella
    c. ciliates : pseudopodia
    d. amoebas : flagella

    ANS: A
    (have)

    DIF: II   OBJ: BPE 22-2.4

18. The process in which two *Paramecia* come together after meiosis to exchange parts of their genetic material is called
    a. mitosis.
    b. replication.
    c. pollination.
    d. conjugation.

    ANS: D   DIF: I   OBJ: BPE 22-2.5

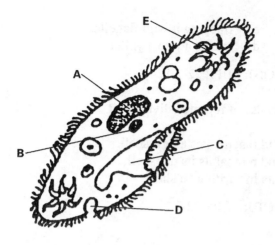

19. Excess water in the body of the *Paramecium* is forced back out by the structure in the diagram labeled
    a. A.
    b. C.
    c. D.
    d. E.

    ANS: D   DIF: II   OBJ: BPE 22-2.5

20. The structure that contains the cell's chromosomes is labeled
    a. A.
    b. B.
    c. C.
    d. E.

    ANS: B   DIF: I   OBJ: BPE 22-2.5

21. Structure E is the
    a. macronucleus.
    b. contractile vacuole.
    c. gullet.
    d. micronucleus.

    ANS: B   DIF: I   OBJ: BPE 22-2.5

22. In the diagram, the structure that contains fragmented chromosomes used in routine cellular functions is labeled
    a. A.
    b. B.
    c. C.
    d. D.

    ANS: A   DIF: II   OBJ: BPE 22-2.5

23. pseudopodia and cilia : locomotion structures ::
    a. nucleus and gullet : eyespots in euglenoids
    b. food and contractile : vacuoles in Paramecia
    c. cilia and pellicle : nuclei in amoebas
    d. "dino" and "zoo" : ciliates

    ANS: B
    (are types of)

    DIF: II   OBJ: BPE 22-3.2

24. In addition to causing disease, protists also affect humans through
    a. their role in the nitrogen cycle.
    b. the diseases they transmit to plants.
    c. the diseases they cause in livestock.
    d. All of the above

    ANS: D   DIF: I   OBJ: BPE 22-3.1

25. Giardiasis is a disease that is spread
    a. by direct person-to-person contact.
    b. through the air.
    c. through contaminated food and water.
    d. by the *Anopheles* mosquito.

    ANS: C   DIF: I   OBJ: BPE 22-3.2

26. African sleeping sickness is spread by
    a. tsetse flies.
    b. mosquitos.
    c. contaminated food.
    d. All of the above

    ANS: A   DIF: I   OBJ: BPE 22-3.2

27. Which of the following are human diseases caused by protists?
    a. amebic dysentery
    b. toxoplasmosis
    c. malaria
    d. All of the above

    ANS: D   DIF: I   OBJ: BPE 22-3.2

28. giardiasis : contaminated water ::
    a. amebic dysentery : mosquito
    b. amebic dysentery : giardiasis
    c. malaria : mosquito
    d. malaria : food contamination

    ANS: C
    (is transmitted by)

    DIF: II   OBJ: BPE 22-3.2

29. The protozoan that causes malaria reproduces in the
    a. intestine of a human.
    b. red blood cells of a mosquito.
    c. red blood cells of a human.
    d. stinger of a mosquito.

    ANS: C   DIF: I   OBJ: BPE 22-3.3

30. Malaria is caused by several species of
    a. *Toxoplasma.*
    b. *Phytophthara.*
    c. *Giardia.*
    d. *Plasmodium.*

    ANS: D   DIF: I   OBJ: BPE 22-3.3

31. The stage in the life cycle of *Plasmodium* in which it lives in mosquitos and is injected into humans is called the
    a. gametophyte.
    b. sporozoite.
    c. sporophyte.
    d. zoospore.

    ANS: B   DIF: I   OBJ: BPE 22-3.3

32. The symptoms of malaria
    a.   include delirium and sweating.
    b.   follow a cycle.
    c.   include severe chills and fever.
    d.   All of the above

    ANS: D   DIF: I   OBJ: BPE 22-3.3

33. Quinine
    a.   can be used to relieve the symptoms of malaria.
    b.   is a cure for malaria.
    c.   was produced in the 1980's using genetic engineering techniques.
    d.   is derived from fungi.

    ANS: A   DIF: I   OBJ: BPE 22-3.4

COMPLETION

1. Two important features that evolved in the protists were sexual reproduction and
   _____.

   ANS: multicellularity   DIF: I   OBJ: BPE 22-1.1

2. Most protists are made up of _____ cell(s).

   ANS: one   DIF: I   OBJ: BPE 22-1.1

3. Most protists live in a(n) _____ environment.

   ANS: water   DIF: I   OBJ: BPE 22-1.2

4. Two of the most important features that evolved among the protists are _____
   reproduction and _____.

   ANS: sexual, multicellularity   DIF: I   OBJ: BPE 22-1.3

Life Cycle of *Chlamydomonas*

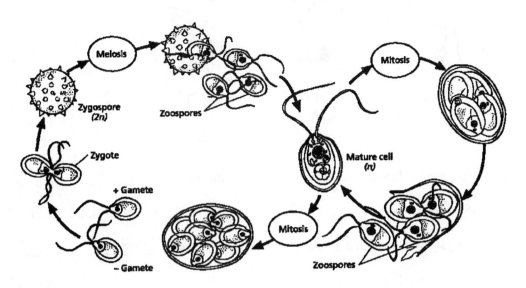

5. Arrow B is pointing to the _____ stage in the life cycle.

    ANS: zygote or zygospore   DIF: I   OBJ: BPE 22-1.4

6. Arrow A is pointing to the _____ stage in the life cycle.

    ANS: zoospore   DIF: I   OBJ: BPE 22-1.4

7. According to the diagram, *Chlamydomonas* reproduces both sexually and

    _____.

    ANS: asexually   DIF: I   OBJ: BPE 22-1.4

8. Some protists undergo sexual reproduction only at times of environmental

    _____.

    ANS: stress   DIF: I   OBJ: BPE 22-1.4

9. *Ulva* is characterized by two distinct multicellular phases: a diploid, spore producing phase
    called the _____ generation and a haploid, gamete-producing phase called the
    _____ generation.

    ANS: sporophyte, gametophyte   DIF: I   OBJ: BPE 22-1.5

A   **B**   **C**

10. The organism shown in diagram A moves by means of _____.

    ANS: pseudopodia   DIF: II   OBJ: BPE 22-2.1

11. The organism shown in diagram C moves by means of _____.

    ANS: a flagellum or flagella   DIF: II   OBJ: BPE 22-2.4

12. The organism shown in diagram B moves by means of _____.

    ANS: cilia   DIF: II   OBJ: BPE 22-2.5

13. Forams have porous shells called _____.

    ANS: tests   DIF: I   OBJ: BPE 22-2.1

14. Diatoms exhibit either radial or _____ symmetry.

    ANS: bilateral   DIF: I   OBJ: BPE 22-2.2

15. The large brown algae that grow along coasts are called _____.

    ANS: kelp   DIF: I   OBJ: BPE 22-2.3

16. _____ are protists that are strict phototrophs.

    ANS: Algae   DIF: I   OBJ: BPE 22-2.3

17. Poisonous "red tides" are caused by population explosions of _____.

    ANS: dinoflagellates   DIF: I   OBJ: BPE 22-2.4

18. A flexible _____ allows a euglenoid to change its shape.

    ANS: pellicle   DIF: I   OBJ: BPE 22-2.4

19. Some protists have _____ that contain light-sensitive pigments.

    ANS: eyespots   DIF: I   OBJ: BPE 22-2.4

20. One of the greatest effects that protists have on humans is that protists cause
    _____.

    ANS: disease   DIF: I   OBJ: BPE 22-3.1

21. Disease-causing protists are transmitted mainly by insects and contaminated
    _____.

    ANS: food or water   DIF: I   OBJ: BPE 22-3.2

22. The stage of *Plasmodium* that lives in mosquitoes and is injected into humans is called the
    _____ ; the second stage of the *Plasmodium* life cycle is called the
    _____.

    ANS: sporozoite, merozoite   DIF: I   OBJ: BPE 22-3.3

23. _____ has been used since the 1600's to relieve the symptoms of malaria.

    ANS: Quinine   DIF: I   OBJ: BPE 22-3.4

ESSAY

1. In what three environments are protists found?

   ANS:
   Protists are found in lakes and oceans; in damp soil, sand, and other moist environments, such as leaf litter; and inside animals or plants.

   DIF: II   OBJ: BPE 22-1.2

2. How do euglenoids illustrate the problems of classifying protists as plants or animals?

   ANS:
   Some species of euglenoids are photosynthetic; others lack chloroplasts and are heterotrophic. Some photosynthetic euglenoids may reduce the size of their chloroplasts and become heterotrophic if kept in a dark environment.

   DIF: II   OBJ: BPE 22-2.4

3. Why is the relationship between a termite and the protozoan *Trichonympha* an example of mutualism?

ANS:
In a mutualistic relationship, both organisms benefit. The protozoan lives in the intestine of the termite, which takes in wood that is digested with the aid of the protozoan. The termite cannot digest wood without the protozoan, and the protozoan would not have a source of food without the termite.

DIF: II   OBJ: BPE 22-2.4

4. Describe how protists can impact the economy of a country without actually causing disease in humans?

ANS:
Protists can cause disease in livestock. The cost of treating the diseased livestock is passed on consumers in the form of higher prices.

DIF: I   OBJ: BPE 22-3.1

5. The diagram below is a generalized sexual life cycle of a protist.

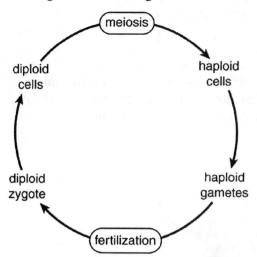

In the space below, redraw this life cycle so that it illustrates the life cycle of the malaria parasite, *Plasmodium*. Indicate which cell types and processes occur in the human host and which occur in the mosquito host. Also indicate where asexual reproduction occurs in this life cycle.

ANS:

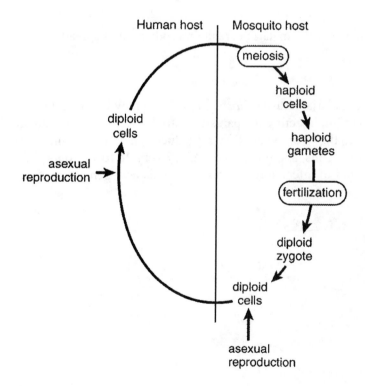

DIF: III   OBJ: BPE 22-3.1

6. After a vacation in the tropics you become seriously ill. Your symptoms include cycles of chills and fever every 48 hours. Why does your doctor suspect malaria?

ANS:
In the second stage of the cycle of *Plasmodium,* merozoites reenter the host's bloodstream, invade red blood cells, and divide rapidly. In about 48 hours the blood cells rupture, releasing merozoites and toxic substances throughout the host's body and initiating a cycle of chills and fever. The cycle repeats itself every 48 hours as new blood cells are infected.

DIF: II   OBJ: BPE 22-3.3

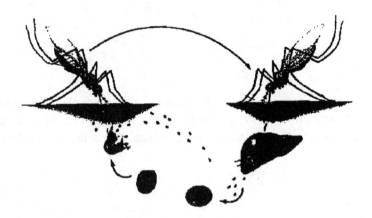

7. Based on the diagram, describe how the malaria parasite reproduces and spreads from person to person.

ANS:
Female mosquitos acquire the malaria parasite *Plasmodium* when they bite infected humans. The mosquito then bites another victim, injecting the parasites into the victim's bloodstream. Once in the blood, the parasites travel to the liver, where they reproduce. They then reenter the bloodstream, penetrate red blood cells, and reproduce again. Every 48 to 72 hours, a new generation of parasites bursts out of infected red blood cells. This new generation then invades other red blood cells.

DIF: II   OBJ: BPE 22-3.3

CHAPTER 23—FUNGI

TRUE/FALSE

1. All fungi are heterotrophic.

   ANS: T   DIF: I   OBJ: BPE 23-1.1

2. The cell walls of fungi are made up of cellulose.

   ANS: F   DIF: I   OBJ: BPE 23-1.1

3. All fungi except yeasts have bodies composed of filaments.

   ANS: T   DIF: I   OBJ: BPE 23-1.2

4. Some fungi are parasites.

   ANS: T   DIF: I   OBJ: BPE 23-1.3

5. Fungi obtain nutrients through photosynthesis.

   ANS: F   DIF: I   OBJ: BPE 23-1.3

6. Hyphae are slender filaments that increase the surface-area-to-volume ratio of a fungus, enabling the fungus to absorb nutrients efficiently from the environment.

   ANS: T   DIF: I   OBJ: BPE 23-1.4

7. Fungal spores are haploid spores formed by meiosis during sexual reproduction.

   ANS: F   DIF: I   OBJ: BPE 23-1.5

8. The classification of organisms in the three phyla of the kingdom Fungi is based on sexual reproductive structure.

   ANS: T   DIF: I   OBJ: BPE 23-2.1

9. Commercial uses for fungi include antibiotics, wine-making, and cheese-making.

   ANS: T   DIF: I   OBJ: BPE 23-2.2

10. Some yeasts can cause diseases in humans.

    ANS: T   DIF: I   OBJ: BPE 23-2.3

11. Sporangia are reproductive structures in which spores form.

    ANS: T   DIF: I   OBJ: BPE 23-2.4

12. The recognizable part of *Amanita muscaria* is the mushroom.

    ANS: T   DIF: I   OBJ: BPE 23-2.5

13. The basidium is a club-shaped nutrient-collecting structure.

    ANS: F   DIF: I   OBJ: BPE 23-2.5

14. Fungi usually form symbiotic associations with animals and bacteria.

    ANS: F   DIF: I   OBJ: BPE 23-3.1

15. Some fungi aid in the transfer of minerals from the soil to the roots of plants.

    ANS: T   DIF: I   OBJ: BPE 23-3.2

16. Lichens have been found all over the world except in arid desert regions.

    ANS: F   DIF: I   OBJ: BPE 23-3.3

MULTIPLE CHOICE

1. Fungi obtain energy
    a. directly from the sun.
    b. from inorganic material in their environment.
    c. by absorbing organic molecules.
    d. from nuclear fusion.

    ANS: C   DIF: I   OBJ: BPE 23-1.1

2. Chitin is found in fungi and in
    a. clam shells.   c. some plant cell walls.
    b. the outer shells of insects.   d. snail shells.

    ANS: B   DIF: I   OBJ: BPE 23-1.1

3. Fungi
    a. do not contain chlorophyll.   c. do not produce their own food.
    b. have cell walls that contain chitin.   d. All of the above

    ANS: D   DIF: I   OBJ: BPE 23-1.1

4. A hypha is a long string of cells divided by
    a. spindle fibers   c. mycorrhizae
    b. an ascus   d. septa

    ANS: D   DIF: I   OBJ: BPE 23-1.2

5. The individual filaments that make up the body of a fungus are called
   a. vascular tissue.
   b. hyphae.
   c. rhizoids.
   d. stem cells.

   ANS: B   DIF: I   OBJ: BPE 23-1.2

6. fungal food : organic molecules ::
   a. pea plant cell wall : chitin
   b. insect exoskeleton : cellulose
   c. fungus cell wall : cellulose
   d. mycelium : hyphae

   ANS: D
   (is composed of)

   DIF: II   OBJ: BPE 23-1.2

7. Fungi obtain food by
   a. photosynthesis.
   b. the nitrogen fixation process in their hyphae.
   c. digesting food externally before absorbing it.
   d. None of the above

   ANS: C   DIF: I   OBJ: BPE 23-1.3

8. Fungi digest food
   a. through photosynthesis.
   b. outside their bodies.
   c. inside their bodies.
   d. All of the above

   ANS: B   DIF: I   OBJ: BPE 23-1.3

9. Fungi are important to an ecosystem as
   a. producers.
   b. regulators.
   c. decomposers.
   d. controllers.

   ANS: C   DIF: I   OBJ: BPE 23-1.4

10. Most fungal spores are formed by
    a. the fusing of hyphae.
    b. the fusing of asci.
    c. mitosis.
    d. None of the above

    ANS: C   DIF: I   OBJ: BPE 23-1.5

11. An economically important use of fungi is
    a. bread making.
    b. the production of antibiotics.
    c. the manufacture of alcoholic beverages.
    d. All of the above

    ANS: D   DIF: I   OBJ: BPE 23-2.2

12. yeasts : bread ::
   a. hyphae : wine-making
   b. aspergillus : soy sauce
   c. molds : drug manufacturing
   d. ascus : making cheeses

   ANS: B
   (are used in making)

   DIF: II   OBJ: BPE 23-2.2

13. The organism illustrated is a(n)
   a. mycorrhizae.
   b. zygomycete.
   c. basidiomycete.
   d. unicellular fungus.

   ANS: D   DIF: II   OBJ: BPE 23-2.3

14. The organism that is illustrated can reproduce
   a. by fission.
   b. by forming buds.
   c. sexually.
   d. All of the above

   ANS: D   DIF: II   OBJ: BPE 23-2.3

15. Mushrooms, puffballs, and shelf fungi are examples of
   a. club fungi.
   b. sac fungi.
   c. molds.
   d. yeasts.

   ANS: A   DIF: I   OBJ: BPE 23-2.3

16. Mushrooms and toadstools are members of the phylum
   a. Ascomycota.
   b. Basidiomycota.
   c. Zygomycota.
   d. Deuteromycota.

   ANS: B   DIF: I   OBJ: BPE 23-2.3

17. An example of a fungus is
   a. a mushroom.
   b. a bread mold.
   c. a yeast.
   d. All of the above

   ANS: D   DIF: I   OBJ: BPE 23-2.3

18. All of the following are true of ascomycetes *except*
    a. they have saclike reproductive cells in which spores grow.
    b. some are truffles.
    c. they are often used in the baking of bread.
    d. they are imperfect fungi.

    ANS: D   DIF: I   OBJ: BPE 23-2.3

19. The group of fungi that includes the molds that often grow on bread is the
    a. ascomycetes.   c. zygomycetes.
    b. basidiomycetes.   d. deuteromycetes.

    ANS: C   DIF: I   OBJ: BPE 23-2.3

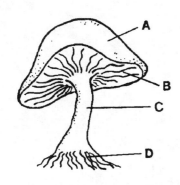

20. Which features characterize the kingdom of which this organism is a member?
    a. eukaryotic, absorbs nutrients   c. autotrophic, ingests nutrients
    b. aquatic, multicellular   d. prokaryotic, photosynthetic

    ANS: A   DIF: II   OBJ: BPE 23-2.3

21. Which structure is responsible for meeting the food requirements of the organism shown?
    a. A   c. C
    b. B   d. D

    ANS: D   DIF: II   OBJ: BPE 23-2.4

22. Zygospores allow molds to
    a. remain dormant until conditions are favorable for their spores.
    b. digest bread.
    c. grow unusually large.
    d. produce antibiotics.

    ANS: A   DIF: I   OBJ: BPE 23-2.4

23. Reproductive structures in which spores form are known as
    a. septa.   c. mycorrhizae.
    b. cnidophores.   d. sporangia.

    ANS: D   DIF: I   OBJ: BPE 23-2.4

Life Cycle of a Mold

24. Structure A is
    a. a rhizoid.
    b. vascular tissue.
    c. a hypha.
    d. a stem.

    ANS: C   DIF: II   OBJ: BPE 23-2.4

25. Structure B is
    a. commensal.
    b. haploid.
    c. embryonic.
    d. diploid.

    ANS: B   DIF: II   OBJ: BPE 23-2.4

26. The process that takes place at C is known as
    a. meiosis.
    b. conjugation.
    c. mitosis.
    d. fusion.

    ANS: D   DIF: II   OBJ: BPE 23-2.4

27. In a symbiotic association, such as a lichen, a fungus provides mineral nutrients to a(n)
    a. animal.
    b. heterotrophic bacterium.
    c. photosynthetic partner.
    d. None of the above

    ANS: C   DIF: I   OBJ: BPE 23-3.1

28. Mycorrhizae
    a. aid in the transfer of minerals from the soil to a plant.
    b. cause a variety of plant diseases.
    c. aid in the transfer of minerals to fungi.
    d. are only found on aquatic fungi.

    ANS: A   DIF: I   OBJ: BPE 23-3.2

29. Some mycorrhizae do not penetrate the host plant but rather wrap around the
    a. stem.   c. root.
    b. cap.   d. gills.

    ANS: C   DIF: I   OBJ: BPE 23-3.2

30. A lichen
    a. consists of a fungus and an alga in a symbiotic relationship.
    b. is a fungus clump.
    c. is found only in temperate climates.
    d. is a mold found on the shady side of trees.

    ANS: A   DIF: I   OBJ: BPE 23-3.3

31. fungus : lichen ::
    a. plant : mycorrhiza   c. septa : hypha
    b. mycelium : hypha   d. mycelium : fungus

    ANS: A
    (is one partner in the relationship with a)

    DIF: II   OBJ: BPE 23-3.3

COMPLETION

1. Unlike plants, fungi lack _____ and cannot carry out photosynthesis.

   ANS: chloroplasts   DIF: I   OBJ: BPE 23-1.1

2. The typical fungus is a eukaryotic heterotroph that has a body consisting of many slender
   filaments called _____.

   ANS: hyphae   DIF: I   OBJ: BPE 23-1.2

3. When hyphae grow, they form a mass called a(n) _____.

   ANS: mycelium   DIF: I   OBJ: BPE 23-1.2

4. Fungi obtain food by _____ organic matter.

   ANS: decomposing   DIF: I   OBJ: BPE 23-1.3

5. Fungi that absorb nutrients in a person's body can cause life-threatening
   _____.

   ANS: infections   DIF: I   OBJ: BPE 23-1.4

6. Fungi reproduce sexually and _____.

   ANS: asexually   DIF: I   OBJ: BPE 23-1.5

7. Most fungal spores are formed by _____.

   ANS: mitosis   DIF: I   OBJ: BPE 21-2.1

8. Chestnut blight is caused by fungi belonging to the phylum called _____.

   ANS: Ascomycota   DIF: I   OBJ: BPE 23-2.3

9. The familiar mushroom belongs to the phyla _____.

   ANS: Basidiomycota   DIF: I   OBJ: BPE 23-2.3

10. Mildews and yeasts are examples of _____.

    ANS: ascomycetes   DIF: I   OBJ: BPE 23-2.3

11. The common name given to unicellular ascomycetes is _____.

    ANS: yeasts   DIF: I   OBJ: BPE 23-2.4

12. A(n) _____ is a saclike structure in which haploid spores are formed.

    ANS: ascus   DIF: I   OBJ: BPE 23-2.4

13. A fungal _____ is a haploid reproductive cell that is capable of developing
    into a new organism.

    ANS: spore   DIF: I   OBJ: BPE 23-2.4

14. Fungi form symbiotic relationships with a(n) _____, such as a plant or an alga.

    ANS: photosynthesizer   DIF: I   OBJ: BPE 23-3.1

15. Certain fungi play important roles in the nutrition of vascular plants by forming symbiotic
    associations with their roots, called _____.

    ANS: mycorrhizae   DIF: I   OBJ: BPE 23-3.2

16. Lichens are able to carry out _____ fixation.

    ANS: nitrogen   DIF: I   OBJ: BPE 23-3.3

17. Lichens are sensitive to _____ such as sulfur dioxide in the atmosphere.

    ANS: pollutants   DIF: I   OBJ: BPE 23-3.3

18. A lichen consists of a fungus and a(n) _____ living together in a symbiotic relationship.

    ANS: alga   DIF: I   OBJ: BPE 23-3.3

ESSAY

1. How does mitosis in a mushroom differ from that in most other eukaryotic organisms?

   ANS:
   Fungi exhibit nuclear mitosis. In most organisms the nuclear membrane breaks down in the early stages of mitosis. In dividing mushroom cells, however, the nuclear envelope remains intact from prophase to anaphase. The spindle fibers form within the nucleus and drag the chromosomes to opposite poles of the nucleus, rather than to opposite poles of the cell. Mitosis is complete when the nuclear envelope pinches in two. This basic difference in the process of cell division suggests that fungi are not closely related to any other organism.

   DIF: II   OBJ: BPE 23-1.1

2. Why are fungi well suited for absorbing food from the environment?

   ANS:
   The mycelium of a fungus can be made of many meters of individual hyphae. This creates a high surface-area-to-volume ratio, which makes a fungus well suited for absorbing food from the environment.

   DIF: II   OBJ: BPE 23-1.3

3. Explain how, under different conditions, either sexual or asexual reproduction might be advantageous to a fungus.

   ANS:
   During periods when the environment is favorable, the rapid asexual formation of spores ensures the quick spread of the species. In periods of environmental stress, sexual reproduction ensures genetic recombination before the hyphae die.

   DIF: II   OBJ: BPE 23-2.4

4. Why are lichens a good indicator of the environment's health?

    ANS:
    Lichens are particularly sensitive to pollutants in the atmosphere because they readily absorb substances dissolved in rain and dew. Lichen are some of the first living organisms to be destroyed by air pollutants and can warn us to curb pollutants before other species are destroyed

    DIF: II   OBJ: BPE 23-3.3

5. Describe the symbiotic relationship that enables a lichen to exist.

    ANS:
    A lichen is a symbiosis between a fungus and a photosynthetic partner such as a green alga, a cyanobacterium, or both. The fungus absorbs minerals and other nutrients from rocks or logs and retains water the photosynthetic partner needs for photosynthesis. Through photosynthesis, the alga produces carbohydrates that the fungus uses for food.

    DIF: II   OBJ: BPE 23-3.3

TRUE/FALSE

1. The surface of a vascular plant is covered by a cuticle in order to reduce water loss.

   ANS: T   DIF: I   OBJ: BPE 24-1.1

2. Land plants have a complex life cycle that involves an alternation of generations between a haploid gametophyte and a diploid sporophyte.

   ANS: T   DIF: I   OBJ: BPE 24-1.1

3. The sporophyte of a nonvascular plant is larger and lives longer than the gametophyte.

   ANS: F   DIF: I   OBJ: BPE 24-1.2

4. The life cycle of nonvascular plants involves alternation of generations.

   ANS: T   DIF: I   OBJ: BPE 24-1.2

5. Seed plants cannot reproduce without a film of water.

   ANS: F   DIF: I   OBJ: BPE 24-1.3

6. A seed is a structure that contains a plant embryo.

   ANS: T   DIF: I   OBJ: BPE 24-1.3

7. The development of flowers did not affect the reproductive efficiency of land plants.

   ANS: F   DIF: I   OBJ: BPE 24-1.3

8. The first flowering plants appeared 10,000 years ago.

   ANS: F   DIF: I   OBJ: BPE 24-1.3

9. Many seeds have appendages that aid in dispersal.

   ANS: T   DIF: I   OBJ: BPE 24-1.3

10. Seeds remain dormant until moisture and temperature conditions favor seedling growth.

    ANS: T   DIF: I   OBJ: BPE 24-1.3

11. Shoots, stems, and rhizoids characterize vascular sporophyte bodies.

    ANS: F   DIF: I   OBJ: BPE 24-1.4

12. Phloem transports water and mineral nutrients.

    ANS: F   DIF: I   OBJ: BPE 24-1.4

13. Pines and all other conifers have needle-like leaves.

    ANS: F   DIF: I   OBJ: BPE 24-2.1

14. Gymnosperm seeds are enclosed in a fruit.

    ANS: F   DIF: I   OBJ: BPE 24-2.1

15. Ferns are characterized by frond and fiddleheads.

    ANS: T   DIF: I   OBJ: BPE 24-2.1

16. The most successful group of gymnosperms belong to the phylum Ginkgophyta.

    ANS: F   DIF: I   OBJ: BPE 24-2.2

17. Angiosperms are the most recently evolved group of plants.

    ANS: T   DIF: I   OBJ: BPE 24-2.2

18. The presence of cones in horsetails groups horsetails with conifers.

    ANS: F   DIF: I   OBJ: BPE 24-2.2

19. Botanically, tomatoes are classified as vegetables.

    ANS: F   DIF: I   OBJ: BPE 24-3.1

20. Botanically, corn kernels are classified as fruits.

    ANS: T   DIF: I   OBJ: BPE 24-3.1

21. Potatoes are a food source rich in protein.

    ANS: F   DIF: I   OBJ: BPE 24-3.1

22. Most of the foods that people eat come directly or indirectly from the fruits of cereals.

    ANS: T   DIF: I   OBJ: BPE 24-3.1

23. The most valuable nonfood product obtained from plants is rubber.

    ANS: F   DIF: I   OBJ: BPE 24-3.2

24. Wood from trees is still a main source of fuel in the United States.

 ANS: F   DIF: I   OBJ: BPE 24-3.2

25. Plant substances are the foundation of modern medicine.

 ANS: T   DIF: I   OBJ: BPE 24-3.3

26. Foxglove is the source of a drug used to treat cardiac disorders.

 ANS: T   DIF: I   OBJ: BPE 24-3.3

27. Paper is made exclusively from wood pulp.

 ANS: F   DIF: I   OBJ: BPE 24-3.4

28. The cotton fibers used to make cloth come from the fruit of a cotton plant.

 ANS: T   DIF: I   OBJ: BPE 24-3.4

MULTIPLE CHOICE

1. The challenges that faced early land plants included
    a.   conserving water.
    b.   reproducing on land.
    c.   absorbing minerals from the rocky surface.
    d.   All of the above

 ANS: D   DIF: I   OBJ: BPE 24-1.1

2. The ancestors of today's land plants were probably
    a.   brown algae.   c.   green algae.
    b.   red algae.   d.   lichens.

 ANS: C   DIF: I   OBJ: BPE 24-1.1

3. The waxy protective covering of a land plant is called a
    a.   cuticle.   c.   rhizome.
    b.   capsule.   d.   stoma.

 ANS: A   DIF: I   OBJ: BPE 24-1.1

4. The cuticle
    a.   helps reduce the evaporation of fluids from a plant.
    b.   is a plant adaptation to an aquatic environment.
    c.   in a reproductive structure in some plants.
    d.   is crucial to plant cell nourishment.

 ANS: A   DIF: I   OBJ: BPE 24-1.1

5. Some land plants developed an internal system of interconnected tubes and vessels called
   a. cuticles.
   b. nonvascular canals.
   c. the circulatory system.
   d. vascular tissues.

   ANS: D   DIF: I   OBJ: BPE 24-1.2

6. The diploid form in a plant's life cycle is called the
   a. sporophyte.
   b. gametophyte.
   c. parental generation.
   d. alternate generation.

   ANS: A   DIF: I   OBJ: BPE 24-1.2

7. The haploid form in a plant's life cycle is called the
   a. sporophyte.
   b. gametophyte.
   c. parental generation.
   d. alternate generation.

   ANS: B   DIF: I   OBJ: BPE 24-1.2

8. A haploid stage following a diploid stage in a plant's life cycle is called
   a. generational recycling.
   b. periodic gametogenesis.
   c. alternating forms.
   d. alternation of generations.

   ANS: D   DIF: I   OBJ: BPE 24-1.2

9. In plants, haploid gametes are produced as a result of
   a. fertilization.
   b. meiosis.
   c. encapsulation.
   d. mitosis.

   ANS: D   DIF: I   OBJ: BPE 24-1.2

10. The seed coat
    a. provides the seed with nourishment.
    b. aids in the dispersal of seeds.
    c. protects the seed from drying out.
    d. causes the seed to reproduce.

    ANS: C   DIF: I   OBJ: BPE 24-1.3

11. The flowers produced by angiosperms help ensure the transfer of gametes by
    a. traveling in the air currents.
    b. bursting open and projecting gametes onto the landscape.
    c. attracting a particular bird, insect, or other animal, which then carries pollen from one flower to another.
    d. All of the above

    ANS: C   DIF: I   OBJ: BPE 24-1.3

12. A flower is a
    a. reproductive structure.
    b. vegetative structure.
    c. photosynthetic structure.
    d. homologous structure.

    ANS: A   DIF: I   OBJ: BPE 24-1.3

13. The dominant generation in vascular plants is the
    a. gametophyte.
    b. gymnosperm.
    c. angiosperm.
    d. sporophyte.

    ANS: D   DIF: I   OBJ: BPE 24-1.4

14. The xylem in a plant
    a. transports food from the leaves.
    b. transports water and minerals.
    c. exchanges carbon dioxide with the atmosphere.
    d. All of the above

    ANS: B   DIF: I   OBJ: BPE 24-1.4

15. What function do fruits produced by angiosperms perform?
    a. provide food for humans and other animals
    b. protect the seeds
    c. disperse the seeds
    d. All of the above

    ANS: D   DIF: I   OBJ: BPE 24-2.1

16. Monocots have
    a. leaves with branching veins.
    b. flower parts in multiples of four or five.
    c. leaves with parallel veins.
    d. two cotyledons.

    ANS: C   DIF: I   OBJ: BPE 24-2.1

17. Flowering plants are classified as monocots or dicots according to the number of their
    a. leaves.
    b. roots.
    c. meristems.
    d. cotyledons.

    ANS: D   DIF: I   OBJ: BPE 24-2.1

18. The primary purpose of the fruit is
    a. to provide nutrition for the seed.
    b. photosynthesis.
    c. seed dispersal.
    d. to permit cross-fertilization.

    ANS: C   DIF: I   OBJ: BPE 24-2.1

19. Mosses, hornworts, and liverworts all possess
    a. fibrous roots.
    b. spore capsules.
    c. tap roots.
    d. green leaves.

    ANS: B   DIF: I   OBJ: BPE 24-2.1

20. Fiddleheads are produced by
    a. wisk ferns.
    b. club mosses.
    c. ferns.
    d. horsetails.

    ANS: C   DIF: I   OBJ: BPE 24-2.1

21. liverworts, hornworts, mosses : nonvascular plants ::
    a. gymnosperms, angiosperms : bryophytes
    b. ferns : mosses
    c. gymnosperms and angiosperms : vascular
    d. bryophytes, liverworts : vascular plants

    ANS: C
    (are)

    DIF: II   OBJ: BPE 24-2.1

22. vascular plants : sporophytes ::
    a. sporophytic plants : gametophytes
    b. gametes : sporophytes
    c. spores : gametes
    d. nonvascular plants : gametophytes

    ANS: D
    (have large)

    DIF: II   OBJ: BPE 24-2.1

23. sporophytes : spores ::
    a. sporophytes : gametophytes
    b. gametophytes : gametes
    c. gametophytes : spores
    d. sporophytes : gametes

    ANS: B
    (produce)

    DIF: II   OBJ: BPE 24-2.1

24. antheridia : sperm ::
    a. rhizoids : gametes
    b. seeds : gametophytes
    c. archegonia : eggs
    d. megaspores : microspores

    ANS: C
    (produce)

    DIF: II   OBJ: BPE 24-2.1

25. gymnosperms : naked seeds ::
    a. pollen : mosses
    b. liverwort : pollen
    c. liverwort : vascular tissue
    d. angiosperms : enclosed seeds

    ANS: D
    (have)

    DIF: II   OBJ: BPE 24-2.1

26. fruit : mature ovary
    a. gametophyte : sporophyte
    b. gymnosperm : angiosperm
    c. cotyledon : food reserve
    d. vascular plant : nonvascular plant

    ANS: C
    (is a)

    DIF: II   OBJ: BPE 24-2.1

27. Which of the following is *not* a nonvascular plant?
    a. moss
    b. hornwort
    c. liverwort
    d. fern

    ANS: D   DIF: I   OBJ: BPE 24-2.2

28. California redwoods are some of the tallest members of the phylum
    a. Ginkgophyta.
    b. Coniferophyta.
    c. Cycadophyta.
    d. Gnetophyta.

    ANS: B   DIF: I   OBJ: BPE 24-2.2

29. Approximately 90 percent of all living plants are
    a. angiosperms.
    b. gymnosperms.
    c. endosperms.
    d. None of the above

    ANS: A   DIF: I   OBJ: BPE 24-2.2

30. Monocots and dicots are subdivisions of
    a. angiosperms.
    b. gymnosperms.
    c. ferns.
    d. mosses.

    ANS: A   DIF: I   OBJ: BPE 24-2.2

31. All of the following are derived from angiosperms and used by humans in their daily lives *except*
    a. food.
    b. textiles.
    c. baker's yeast.
    d. timber.

    ANS: C   DIF: I   OBJ: BPE 24-3.1

32. Potatoes are actually
    a. roots.
    b. tubers.
    c. flowers.
    d. leaves.

    ANS: B   DIF: I   OBJ: BPE 24-3.1

33. Soybeans are a globally important crop because 45 percent of this legume is
    a. protein.
    b. carbohydrate.
    c. fat.
    d. sugar.

    ANS: A   DIF: I   OBJ: BPE 24-3.1

34. More than 70 percent of the world's cultivated farmland is used for growing
    a. fruit.
    b. tubers.
    c. grains.
    d. ferns.

    ANS: C   DIF: I   OBJ: BPE 24-3.1

35. The world's best wheat-growing area is
    a. northern Canada.
    b. southeastern United States.
    c. Mexico.
    d. the Great Plains.

    ANS: D   DIF: I   OBJ: BPE 24-3.1

36. Corn is one of the world's chief foods for
    a. farm animals.
    b. wild animals.
    c. birds.
    d. deer.

    ANS: A   DIF: I   OBJ: BPE 24-3.1

37. Rayon is made from
    a. wood pulp.
    b. root fibers.
    c. leaves of the foxglove.
    d. tea leaves.

    ANS: A   DIF: I   OBJ: BPE 24-3.2

38. Salicin derived from the bark of willow trees is the starting compound used to make
    a. paper.
    b. clothes.
    c. rubber.
    d. aspirin.

    ANS: D   DIF: I   OBJ: BPE 24-3.3

39. Paper-making fibers are obtained from
    a. wood.
    b. cotton.
    c. bamboo.
    d. All of the above

    ANS: D   DIF: I   OBJ: BPE 24-3.4

COMPLETION

1. In leaves, the expansion and contraction of the guard cells regulate the opening and closing of the _____.

    ANS: stomata   DIF: I   OBJ: BPE 24-1.1

2. The surface of a vascular plant is covered by a waxy, waterproof layer called a(n) _____.

    ANS: cuticle   DIF: I   OBJ: BPE 24-1.1

3. One of the first environmental challenges that early land plants had to overcome was finding a way to conserve _____.

ANS: water   DIF: I   OBJ: BPE 24-1.1

4. In alternation of generations, the _____ generation alternates with the diploid generation.

ANS: haploid   DIF: I   OBJ: BPE 24-1.1

5. The sporophyte generation produces spores by the process of _____.

ANS: meiosis   DIF: I   OBJ: BPE 24-1.2

6. The fusion of two gametes results in the production of a(n) _____ sporophyte.

ANS: diploid   DIF: I   OBJ: BPE 24-1.2

7. The haploid form of a plant is known as the _____ generation.

ANS: gametophyte   DIF: I   OBJ: BPE 24-1.2

8. Nonvascular plants transport materials within their bodies through the process of _____.

ANS: diffusion   DIF: I   OBJ: BPE 24-1.2

9. Vascular tissues are specialized cells that move _____, nutrients, and other materials through the plant body.

ANS: water   DIF: I   OBJ: BPE 24-1.2

10. True roots, stems, and leaves are associated with _____ plants.

ANS: vascular   DIF: I   OBJ: BPE 24-1.2

11. The first seed plants appeared about _____ million years ago.

ANS: 380   DIF: I   OBJ: BPE 24-1.3

12. The _____ _____ is the protective cover that surrounds a seed.

ANS: seed coat   DIF: I   OBJ: BPE 24-1.3

13. The seed coat prevents the embryo from drying out, from mechanical injury, and from _____.

ANS: disease   DIF: I   OBJ: BPE 24-1.3

14. In order for seeds to sprout, environmental conditions must be _____.

    ANS: favorable   DIF: I   OBJ: BPE 24-1.3

15. A flower is a(n) _____ structure that produces pollen and seeds.

    ANS: reproductive   DIF: I   OBJ: BPE 24-1.3

16. Appendages on seeds are an important adaptation that aid in _____.

    ANS: dispersal   DIF: I   OBJ: BPE 24-1.3

17. The first flowering plants appeared approximately _____ million years ago.

    ANS: 130   DIF: I   OBJ: BPE 24-1.3

18. Because flowering plants are rooted in the ground and cannot move from place to place, they must disperse their _____ so that their offspring can grow in new environments.

    ANS: seeds   DIF: I   OBJ: BPE 24-1.3

19. A(n) _____ is a specialized structure that develops from an ovule and serves to protect a plant embryo from harsh conditions.

    ANS: seed   DIF: I   OBJ: BPE 24-1.3

20. The tissues that transport water and minerals within a plant make up the _____ system.

    ANS: vascular   DIF: I   OBJ: BPE 24-1.4

21. _____ are zones of actively dividing plant cells that produce plant growth.

    ANS: Meristems   DIF: I   OBJ: BPE 24-1.4

22. In mosses and liverworts, the _____ generation is the dominant generation.

    ANS: gametophyte   DIF: I   OBJ: BPE 24-2.1

23. A rootlike structure that anchors nonvascular plants is called a(n) _____.

    ANS: rhizoid   DIF: I   OBJ: BPE 24-2.1

24. In most vascular plants, the _____ grows within the sporophyte.

    ANS: gametophyte   DIF: I   OBJ: BPE 24-2.1

25. The life cycle of a conifer is characterized by a large _____.

ANS: sporophyte   DIF: I   OBJ: BPE 24-2.1

26. Angiosperms are ultimately the source of much of our _____.

ANS: food   DIF: I   OBJ: BPE 24-2.1

27. Many fruits are spread by _____ that are attracted to sweet, fleshy fruits, which they use for food.

ANS: animals   DIF: I   OBJ: BPE 24-2.1

28. Gymnosperms are pollinated through _____, which makes sexual reproduction possible even during dry conditions.

ANS: wind   DIF: I   OBJ: BPE 24-2.1

29. _____ are seed plants whose seeds do not develop within a sealed container (fruit).

ANS: Gymnosperms   DIF: I   OBJ: BPE 24-2.2

30. A plant that has flower parts that occur in fours or fives or multiples of four or five is a(n) _____.

ANS: dicot   DIF: I   OBJ: BPE 24-2.2

31. A green, hornlike sporophyte growing upward from the gametophyte is typical of _____.

ANS: hornworts   DIF: I   OBJ: BPE 24-2.2

32. A fern is an example of a(n) _____ vascular plant.

ANS: seedless   DIF: I   OBJ: BPE 24-2.2

33. Fruit is a characteristic associated only with _____.

ANS: angiosperms   DIF: I   OBJ: BPE 24-2.2

34. Peas, peanuts, and alfalfa are examples of _____, and are important sources of protein.

ANS: legumes   DIF: I   OBJ: BPE 24-3.1

35. One-third of the world's population depends on _____ as its primary food source.

    ANS: wheat   DIF: I   OBJ: BPE 24-3.1

36. Most of the corn grown in the United States today is grown in a region known as the _____ _____, which includes the states of Iowa, Nebraska, Minnesota, Illinois, and Indiana.

    ANS: Corn Belt   DIF: I   OBJ: BPE 24-3.1

37. Rice is an excellent source of _____.

    ANS: carbohydrates   DIF: I   OBJ: BPE 24-3.1

38. _____ is wood that has been cut into boards and planks.

    ANS: Lumber   DIF: I   OBJ: BPE 24-3.2

39. Wood is an important source of _____ energy in many countries.

    ANS: heat   DIF: I   OBJ: BPE 24-3.2

40. Compounds derived from plants form the foundation of modern _____.

    ANS: medicine   DIF: I   OBJ: BPE 24-3.3

41. The strength and flexibility of plant _____ make them ideal materials for making paper, cloth, and rope.

    ANS: fibers   DIF: I   OBJ: BPE 24-3.4

PROBLEM

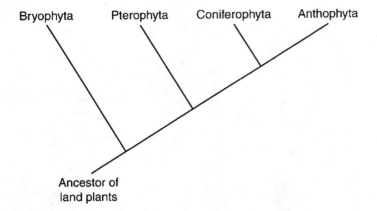

Bryophyta   Pterophyta   Coniferophyta   Anthophyta

Ancestor of
land plants

1. Refer to the illustration above. The cladogram depicts the presumed evolutionary relationships between the major phyla of land plants. The list below consists of paired characteristics found in at least some land plants. For each pair of characteristics, choose the one that is the more evolutionarily advanced of the two. Then complete the cladogram by indicating on it where each of the more advanced characteristics first appeared.

Characteristics:
    cones / flowers
    sporophyte dominant / gametophyte dominant
    waxy cuticle present / waxy cuticle absent
    vascular tissue absent / vascular tissue present
    gametophyte independent of sporophyte / gametophyte dependent on sporophyte
    stomata absent / stomata present
    seeds / spores
    multicellular reproductive structure / unicellular reproductive structure

ANS:
The students' completed cladograms should look like the one shown below. Where two or more evolutionary advancements occur between branch points, their order on the branch is not important.

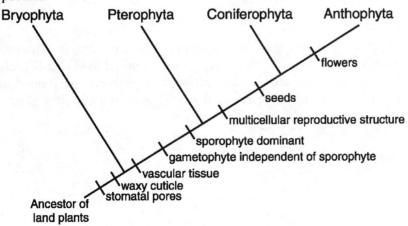

Bryophyta   Pterophyta   Coniferophyta   Anthophyta

flowers

seeds

multicellular reproductive structure

sporophyte dominant

gametophyte independent of sporophyte

vascular tissue

waxy cuticle

stomatal pores

Ancestor of
land plants

Biology: Principles and Explorations

DIF: III   OBJ: BPE 24-2.1

ESSAY

1. What problems were encountered by the first land plants, such as the one in the diagram above?
    What adaptations evolved to solve these problems?

    ANS:
    Before early plants could survive on land, they had to overcome three basic problems: how to
    avoid drying out, how to reproduce on land, and how to obtain minerals from rocky surfaces.
    They were able to avoid drying out by developing a waterproof, waxy coating on the stems.
    Lightweight spores were produced at the tips of the stems, allowing the spores to be distributed
    by wind to other land areas. Once covered in dew, the spores would germinate, enabling the
    plants to reproduce with very little water. Mineral absorption was accomplished through the
    formation of mycorrhizae with fungi.

    DIF: II   OBJ: BPE 24-1.1

2. How is a seed an adaptation for life on land?

    ANS:
    Seeds enable the dispersal of offspring so that they will not have to compete with their parents
    for space, light, and nutrients. Additionally, seeds provide an initial food supply (cotyledons) for
    the embryo. A hard, outer seed coat provides protection from physical injury and drought,
    allowing the embryo to lie dormant for years and then still grow into a healthy plant.

    DIF: II   OBJ: BPE 24-1.3

3. Why is insect pollination more efficient than wind pollination?

ANS:
Insects and plants have coevolved so that certain insects are attracted by particular flowers. A particular insect carries pollen from the flowers of one individual to the flowers of another individual of the same species. Thus, the flowers of insect-pollinated plant species do not need to produce as much pollen as the flowers of wind-pollinated species.

DIF: II   OBJ: BPE 24-1.3

4. Distinguish between legumes and root crops.

ANS:
Legumes, such as peas, soybeans, and other members of the pea family, produce protein-rich seeds in a pod. Root crops, such as potatoes, sweet potatoes, and carrots, produce underground parts that are rich in starch.

DIF: II   OBJ: BPE 24-3.1

TRUE/FALSE

1. Gametophytes produce zygotes and are diploid.

    ANS: F DIF: I OBJ: BPE 25-1.1

2. Mosses are found in all places and in all environments.

    ANS: F DIF: I OBJ: BPE 25-1.1

3. Spores form through mitosis in the spore capsule of mosses.

    ANS: F DIF: I OBJ: BPE 25-1.1

4. Water must be present for fertilization to take place in mosses.

    ANS: T DIF: I OBJ: BPE 25-1.1

5. Water must be present for fertilization to take place in ferns.

    ANS: T DIF: I OBJ: BPE 25-1.2

6. In ferns, sorus is another word for frond.

    ANS: F DIF: I OBJ: BPE 25-1.2

7. Haploid fern spores are produced by gametophytes.

    ANS: F DIF: I OBJ: BPE 25-1.2

8. Adult fern sporophytes are haploid.

    ANS: F DIF: I OBJ: BPE 25-1.2

9. In ferns, a large sporophyte with leaves called fronds alternates with a heart-shaped gametophyt

    ANS: T DIF: I OBJ: BPE 25-1.2

10. Ferns need water to reproduce because their sperm must swim to eggs.

    ANS: T DIF: I OBJ: BPE 25-1.2

11. In ferns, the antheridia and archegonia are produced by different individuals.

    ANS: F DIF: I OBJ: BPE 25-1.2

12. Both mosses and ferns require a thin film of water for gametes to meet.

    ANS: T   DIF: I   OBJ: BPE 25-1.3

13. Unlike mosses, ferns show alternation of generations.

    ANS: F   DIF: I   OBJ: BPE 25-1.3

14. In both mosses and ferns, eggs are formed through mitosis in the antheridia.

    ANS: F   DIF: I   OBJ: BPE 25-1.3

15. In both mosses and ferns, sperm are formed through mitosis in the archegonia.

    ANS: F   DIF: I   OBJ: BPE 25-1.3

16. Mosses and ferns no longer require the presence of a film of water for reproduction.

    ANS: F   DIF: I   OBJ: BPE 25-1.3

17. Gametophytes of seed plants are large and easily viewed with the unaided eye.

    ANS: F   DIF: I   OBJ: BPE 25-2.1

18. In seed plants, gametophytes develop within the tissue of sporophytes.

    ANS: T   DIF: I   OBJ: BPE 25-2.1

19. Sexual reproduction in seed plants involves the transfer of eggs from female reproductive structures of a plant to the male reproductive structures.

    ANS: F   DIF: I   OBJ: BPE 25-2.1

20. Pollination results from the fusion of male and female gametes.

    ANS: F   DIF: I   OBJ: BPE 25-2.1

21. The female gametophyte of a seed plant develops inside an ovule.

    ANS: T   DIF: I   OBJ: BPE 25-2.1

22. A plant embryo is a new sporophyte.

    ANS: T   DIF: I   OBJ: BPE 25-2.2

23. Seeds are a mechanism of survival for plants.

    ANS: T   DIF: I   OBJ: BPE 25-2.2

24. In flowering plants, the embryos of monocots have two cotyledons.

    ANS: F   DIF: I   OBJ: BPE 25-2.2

25. A mature pine tree produces either male or female cones.

    ANS: F   DIF: I   OBJ: BPE 25-2.3

26. Eggs and sperm are produced through mitosis in immature cones.

    ANS: F   DIF: I   OBJ: BPE 25-2.3

27. Gametophytes are physically much larger in conifers than their sporophytes.

    ANS: F   DIF: I   OBJ: BPE 25-2.3

28. In conifers, after pollination, a pollen tube grows from each pollen grain towards the eggs inside the ovule.

    ANS: T   DIF: I   OBJ: BPE 25-2.3

29. Many gymnosperms, such as pine, spruce, and fir trees, produce their seeds in cones.

    ANS: T   DIF: I   OBJ: BPE 25-2.3

30. Pollen is produced in the tip of the stamen, an area called the sepal.

    ANS: F   DIF: I   OBJ: BPE 25-2.4

31. In conifers, flower parts are arranged in four concentric whorls.

    ANS: F   DIF: I   OBJ: BPE 25-2.4

32. The purpose of petals is to attract pollinators such as birds and insects.

    ANS: T   DIF: I   OBJ: BPE 25-2.4

33. The lower portion of the pistil produces pollen.

    ANS: F   DIF: I   OBJ: BPE 25-2.4

34. Incomplete flowers consist of sepals, petals, stamens, and pistil.

    ANS: F   DIF: I   OBJ: BPE 25-2.4

35. Gametophytes develop within flowers.

    ANS: T   DIF: I   OBJ: BPE 25-2.4

36. Virtually all of our food is derived, directly or indirectly, from flowering plants.

    ANS: T   DIF: I   OBJ: BPE 25-2.4

37. Pollen tubes grow through the style toward the ovule.

    ANS: T   DIF: I   OBJ: BPE 25-2.5

38. The flower of angiosperms are ornamental and have no reproductive function.

    ANS: F   DIF: I   OBJ: BPE 25-2.5

39. The fusion of a sperm with two nuclei in the ovule produces the endosperm of a seed.

    ANS: T   DIF: I   OBJ: BPE 25-2.5

40. Double fertilization has great survival value because each new generation carries its own initial source of nutrition.

    ANS: T   DIF: I   OBJ: BPE 25-2.5

41. All plants can only reproduce by sexual reproduction.

    ANS: F   DIF: I   OBJ: BPE 25-3.1

42. Asexual reproduction produces new plants that are genetically different from the parent plant.

    ANS: F   DIF: I   OBJ: BPE 25-3.1

43. Vegetative reproduction requires a plant to have flowers.

    ANS: F   DIF: I   OBJ: BPE 25-3.1

44. In vegetative reproduction, new plants may be generated from stems or roots.

    ANS: T   DIF: I   OBJ: BPE 25-3.1

45. Kalanchoe plants are capable of carrying out both sexual and asexual reproduction.

    ANS: T   DIF: I   OBJ: BPE 25-3.2

46. Kalanchoe plants produce adventitious roots.

    ANS: T   DIF: I   OBJ: BPE 25-3.2

47. Kalanchoe plants do not produce flowers.

    ANS: F   DIF: I   OBJ: BPE 25-3.2

48. Growing new plants from seeds or from vegetative parts is called plant propagation.

ANS: T   DIF: I   OBJ: BPE 25-3.3

MULTIPLE CHOICE

1. The structures on a moss gametophyte in which spores are produced are known as
   a. meristems.   c. cones.
   b. pollen grains.   d. sporangia.

   ANS: D   DIF: I   OBJ: BPE 25-1.1

2. Which of the following statements about moss spores is *not* true?
   a. They are produced by the sporophyte.   c. They are produced in a capsule-like top.
   b. They are dispersed and then germinate. d. They are diploid.

   ANS: D   DIF: I   OBJ: BPE 25-1.1

3. The sporophyte generation in mosses produces spores by
   a. meiosis.   c. sexual reproduction.
   b. mitosis.   d. None of the above

   ANS: A   DIF: I   OBJ: BPE 25-1.1

4. The dominant form of a moss life cycle is the
   a. sporophyte.   c. rhizoid.
   b. gametophyte.   d. zygote.

   ANS: B   DIF: I   OBJ: BPE 25-1.1

5. In which of the following structures do liverworts and mosses produce eggs?
   a. antheridia   c. archegonia
   b. capsules   d. cones

   ANS: C   DIF: I   OBJ: BPE 25-1.1

The diagram below shows the plant life cycle.

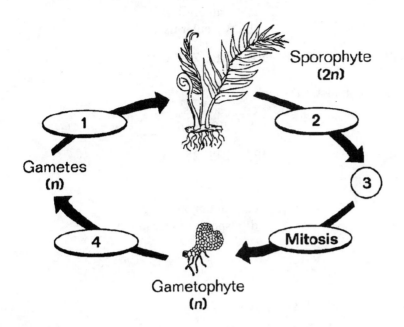

6. At which point in the life cycle does fertilization take place?
   a. 1
   b. 2
   c. 3
   d. 4

   ANS: A   DIF: II   OBJ: BPE 25-1.2

7. The structures produced at 3 are called
   a. sporangia.
   b. archegonia.
   c. spores.
   d. antheridia.

   ANS: C   DIF: II   OBJ: BPE 25-1.2

8. Fern sporophytes consist of rhizomes and
   a. flowers
   b. stems
   c. microgametophytes
   d. fronds

   ANS: D   DIF: I   OBJ: BPE 25-1.2

9. Ferns
   a. are found only in the tropics.
   b. require water for fertilization.
   c. produce diploid spores.
   d. have dominant gametophyte form.

   ANS: B   DIF: I   OBJ: BPE 25-1.2

10. Both mosses and ferns produce
    a. seeds.
    b. fruit.
    c. flowers.
    d. spores.

    ANS: D   DIF: I   OBJ: BPE 25-1.3

11. Unlike mosses, ferns possess
    a. spore capsules.   c. antheridia.
    b. archegonia.   d. vascular tissue.

    ANS: D   DIF: I   OBJ: BPE 25-1.3

12. Both mosses and ferns produce gametes through
    a. mitosis.   c. osmosis.
    b. meiosis.   d. diffusion.

    ANS: A   DIF: I   OBJ: BPE 25-1.3

13. antheridia : sperm ::
    a. rhizoids : gametes   c. archegonia : eggs
    b. seeds : gametophytes   d. sperm : megaspores

    ANS: C
    (produces)

    DIF: II   OBJ: BPE 25-1.3

14. In seed plants, female gametophytes produce
    a. sperm.   c. cells.
    b. eggs.   d. spores.

    ANS: B   DIF: I   OBJ: BPE 25-2.1

15. A male gametophyte of a seed plant develops into a
    a. pollen grain.   c. pollen tube.
    b. spore capsule.   d. seed coat.

    ANS: A   DIF: I   OBJ: BPE 25-2.1

16. A seed coat
    a. protects the seed from injury.   c. protects the seed from disease.
    b. prevents the embryo from dehydration.   d. All of the above

    ANS: D   DIF: I   OBJ: BPE 25-2.2

17. Cotyledons
    a. abosorb sunlight.   c. store nutrients.
    b. produce carbon dioxide. d. store water.

    ANS: C   DIF: I   OBJ: BPE 25-2.2

18. The seeds of monocots have
    a. one embryo and two cotyledons.   c. one embryo and one cotyledon.
    b. two embyos and two cotyledons.   d. two embryos and one cotyledon.

    ANS: C   DIF: I   OBJ: BPE 25-2.2

19. The cotyledons in a seed
   a. protect the embryo.
   b. provide a source of food for the embryo.
   c. develop from the seed coat.
   d. are part of the gametophyte.

   ANS: B   DIF: I   OBJ: BPE 25-2.2

20. The partially developed plant found in seeds is known as a(n)
   a. gametophyte.
   b. spore capsule.
   c. embryo.
   d. sporophyte.

   ANS: C   DIF: I   OBJ: BPE 25-2.2

21. A typical seed contains all of the following *except* a(n)
   a. seed coat.
   b. cotyledon.
   c. embryo.
   d. spore case.

   ANS: D   DIF: I   OBJ: BPE 25-2.2

22. Which of the following were the first land plants to evolve seeds?
   a. angiosperms
   b. gymnosperms
   c. mosses
   d. ferns

   ANS: B   DIF: I   OBJ: BPE 25-2.2

23. The process of transferring pollen from a male cone to a female cone in gymnosperms is called
   a. fertilization.
   b. seed formation.
   c. pollination.
   d. asexual reproduction.

   ANS: C   DIF: I   OBJ: BPE 25-2.3

24. Pines, spruces, and firs are
   a. angiosperms.
   b. gymnosperms.
   c. flowering plants.
   d. sometimes nonvascular.

   ANS: B   DIF: I   OBJ: BPE 25-2.3

25. The tallest trees in the world are a species of
   a. conifers.
   b. dicots.
   c. liverworts.
   d. angiosperms.

   ANS: A   DIF: I   OBJ: BPE 25-2.3

26. In conifers, the diploid condition is resumed following
   a. pollination.
   b. fertilization.
   c. respiration.
   d. sporulation.

   ANS: B   DIF: II   OBJ: BPE 25-2.3

27. sporophytes : spores ::
    a. sporophytes : gametophytes
    b. gametophytes : gametes
    c. gametes : gametophytes
    d. sporophytes : gametes

ANS: B
(produces)

DIF: II   OBJ: BPE 25-2.3

28. The structure indicated at f
    a. supports the anther.
    b. produces pollen.
    c. supports the pistil.
    d. develops into a fruit.

ANS: B   DIF: II   OBJ: BPE 25-2.4

29. The structure labeled c
    a. produces pollen.
    b. contains sperm cells.
    c. is the area where pollen lands on and sticks.
    d. contains meristematic tissue.

ANS: C   DIF: II   OBJ: BPE 25-2.4

30. Removing a flower's stigma would initially affect
    a. fertilization.
    b. seed production.
    c. pollination.
    d. seed dispersal.

ANS: C   DIF: I   OBJ: BPE 25-2.4

31. Pollen is produced in a structure called the
    a. anther.
    b. stigma.
    c. ovary.
    d. pistil.

ANS: A   DIF: I   OBJ: BPE 25-2.4

32. If a plant's flowers are very colorful and produce nectar, the plant is probably pollinated by
    a. water.
    b. wind.
    c. insects.
    d. self-pollination.

ANS: C   DIF: I   OBJ: BPE 25-2.4

33. In angiosperms, immediately following pollination
    a. the seed develops.
    b. an egg cell is formed.
    c. fertilization occurs.
    d. the pollen tube begins to form.

    ANS: D   DIF: I   OBJ: BPE 25-2.5

34. In angiosperms, fertilization
    a. involves the union of the egg and sperm.
    b. may not follow pollination at all.
    c. may not occur until weeks or months after pollination has taken place.
    d. All of the above

    ANS: D   DIF: I   OBJ: BPE 25-2.5

35. During fertilization in flowering plants, one sperm fuses with an egg to form an embryo, and
    another fuses with two nuclei to form nutritive tissue. This event is called
    a. self-pollination.
    b. adaptation.
    c. maximization.
    d. double fertilization.

    ANS: D   DIF: I   OBJ: BPE 25-2.5

36. Angiosperms produce spores that grow into gametophytes through the process of
    a. mitosis.
    b. meiosis.
    c. osmosis.
    d. All of the above

    ANS: B   DIF: I   OBJ: BPE 25-2.5

37. In angiosperms, flowers are
    a. photosynthetic.
    b. autotrophic.
    c. sporophytes.
    d. gametophytes.

    ANS: C   DIF: I   OBJ: BPE 25-2.5

38. Which structure allows plants to reproduce asexually?
    a. rhizome
    b. flower
    c. archegonium
    d. antheridium

    ANS: A   DIF: II   OBJ: BPE 25-3.1

39. The production of offspring genetically identical to the parent plant is the result of
    a. sexual reproduction.
    b. asexual reproduction.
    c. alternation of generation.
    d. double fertilization.

    ANS: B   DIF: I   OBJ: BPE 25-3.1

40. Plantlets are
    a. tiny, new plants that develop at leaf margins.
    b. a means of vegetative reproduction in Kalanchoe.
    c. genetically idenctical to the parent plant.
    d. All of the above

    ANS: D   DIF: I   OBJ: BPE 25-3.2

41. Kalanchoes are succulents, meaning that they
    a. have fleshy leaves and stems to store water.
    b. have a large taproot that stores water.
    c. require a large amount of water from the soil.
    d. have stomata that open only in the daytime.

    ANS: A   DIF: I   OBJ: BPE 25-3.2

42. Large volumes of water are stored in a cell's
    a. Golgi apparatus.   c. cell membrane.
    b. endoplasmic reticulum.   d. central vacuole.

    ANS: D   DIF: I   OBJ: BPE 25-3.2

43. Growing new plants from seed or from vegetative parts is called
    a. sexual reproduction.   c. plant propagation.
    b. double fertilization.   d. binary fission.

    ANS: C   DIF: I   OBJ: BPE 25-3.3

COMPLETION

1. Mosses have a life cycle called _____ _____
   _____.

   ANS: alternation of generations   DIF: I   OBJ: BPE 25-1.1

2. The very tiny liverwort _____ grow from the archegonia under the caps of
   female stalks.

   ANS: sporophytes   DIF: I   OBJ: BPE 25-1.1

3. The gametophytes of _____ plants are larger and more noticeable than the
   sporophytes.

   ANS: nonvascular   DIF: I   OBJ: BPE 25-1.1

4. In ferns, the diploid sporophytes produce spores by _____.

   ANS: meiosis   DIF: I   OBJ: BPE 25-1.2

5. Like the nonvascular plants, the seedless vascular plants can only reproduce sexually when a
   film of _____ covers the gametophyte.

   ANS: water   DIF: I   OBJ: BPE 25-1.3

6. Unlike mosses, ferns have sporophytes that are much _____ than their gametophytes.

   ANS: larger   DIF: I   OBJ: BPE 25-1.3

7. Both mosses and ferns produce eggs within the _____.

   ANS: archegonia   DIF: I   OBJ: BPE 25-1.3

8. Both mosses and ferns produce sperm within the _____.

   ANS: antheridia   DIF: I   OBJ: BPE 25-1.3

9. A male gametophyte of a seed plant develops into a(n) _____
   _____.

   ANS: pollen grain   DIF: I   OBJ: BPE 25-2.1

10. A(n) _____ is a multicellular structure that is part of the sporophyte.

    ANS: ovule   DIF: I   OBJ: BPE 25-2.1

11. The structure labeled A in the diagram above is called the _____
    _____.

    ANS: seed coat   DIF: II   OBJ: BPE 25-2.2

12. The structure labeled X in the diagram above is called the _____.

    ANS: cotyledon   DIF: II   OBJ: BPE 25-2.2

13. A mature pine tree produces both male and female _____.

    ANS: cones   DIF: I   OBJ: BPE 25-2.3

14. _____ occurs when a haploid sperm fuses with a haploid egg, forming a diploid zygote.

   ANS: Fertilization   DIF: I   OBJ: BPE 25-2.3

15.   In conifers, a very large sporophyte that produces cones alternates with tiny gametophytes that form on the _____ of cones.

   ANS: scales   DIF: I   OBJ: BPE 25-2.3

16.   The structure labeled c in the diagram above is called the _____.

   ANS: stigma   DIF: II   OBJ: BPE 25-2.4

17.   The structure labeled f in the diagram above is called the _____.

   ANS: anther   DIF: II   OBJ: BPE 25-2.4

18.   The structure labeled b in the diagram above is called the _____.

   ANS: sepal   DIF: II   OBJ: BPE 25-2.4

19.   The flower in the diagram above is an example of a(n) _____ flower.

   ANS: complete   DIF: II   OBJ: BPE 25-2.4

20.   Flowers are a source of _____ for pollinators.

   ANS: food   DIF: I   OBJ: BPE 25-2.4

21.   The transfer of pollen grains from an anther to a stigma is known as _____.

   ANS: pollination   DIF: I   OBJ: BPE 25-2.5

22.   In angiosperms, seeds develop from the _____ after an egg has been fertilized

   ANS: ovules   DIF: I   OBJ: BPE 25-2.5

23. The seeds of angiosperms are enclosed in _____.

   ANS: fruits   DIF: I   OBJ: BPE 25-2.5

24. The event in which one sperm fertilizes an egg and a second sperm fuses with two nuclei is called _____ _____.

   ANS: double fertilization   DIF: I   OBJ: BPE 25-2.5

25. Many of the structures by which plants reproduce vegetatively are modified _____.

   ANS: stems   DIF: I   OBJ: BPE 25-3.1

26. Bulbs, corms, rhizomes, and tubers are examples of modified stems that allow plants to reproduce _____.

   ANS: vegetatively   DIF: I   OBJ: BPE 25-3.1

27. Kalanchoes and other succulents that fix carbon by a water-conserving pathway are called _____ plants.

   ANS: CAM (crassulacean acid metabolism)

   DIF: I   OBJ: BPE 25-3.2

28. _____ _____ involves taking a small piece of tissue from a plant and placing it on a nutrient-rich medium to produce large numbers of identical plants.

   ANS: Tissue culture   DIF: I   OBJ: BPE 25-3.3

29. _____ involves attaching small stems from one plant to larger stems or roots of another plant.

   ANS: Grafting   DIF: I   OBJ: BPE 25-3.3

ESSAY

1. Compare and contrast nonvascular plants with seedless vascular plants.

   ANS:
   Eggs are produced in archegonia and sperm are produced in antheridia in both nonvascular and seedless vascular plants. Both plant types require the presence of a thin film of water to enable sperm to come into contact with eggs. Unlike vascular plants, nonvascular plants lack organized tissues that move water and nutrients a great distance within the plant body. Additionally, the sporophyte is significantly larger than the gametophyte in vascular plants. This condition is reversed in nonvascular plants.

   DIF: II   OBJ: BPE 25-1.3

2. Describe the function of the seed coat.

   ANS:
   The outside of the seed is covered by a protective seed coat. The seed coat prevents the embryo from drying out and protects the embryo from mechanical injury and disease.

   DIF: II   OBJ: BPE 25-2.2

3. Ouline the processes of pollination and fertilization in gymnosperms.

   ANS:
   Pollen produced by pollen cones are carried by the wind to female cones that have opened, exposing the ovules. After pollen grains land near ovules, slender pollen tubes grow out of the pollen grains and into the ovules. Sperm move through the pollen tubes and enter the ovules. Once inside the ovules, fertilization occurs when sperm fuse with eggs, forming zygotes.

   DIF: II   OBJ: BPE 25-2.3

4. List and describe the location of the parts of a complete flower.

   ANS:
   A complete flower is one that contains all four floral parts. The outermost whorl of the flower is made up of sepals. Proceeding toward the interior, the second whorl is made up of petals. The third whorl is made up of stamens. At the center of the flower is the pistil. Dependent upon the species, a flower may possess more than one pistil.

   DIF: II   OBJ: BPE 25-2.4

5. Describe a unique method of vegetative reproduction in kalanchoe.

ANS:
Tiny new plants called plantlets develop in notches along the leaf margins, fall to the ground, and then grow into new plants.

DIF: II   OBJ: BPE 25-3.3

CHAPTER 26—PLANT STRUCTURE AND FUNCTION

TRUE/FALSE

1. Shoots consist of stems and leaves.

   ANS: T   DIF: I   OBJ: BPE 26-1.1

2. Tracheids and sieve tubes make up a xylem vessel.

   ANS: F   DIF: I   OBJ: BPE 26-1.1

3. The outer protective layer of tissue on a vascular plant is known as the meristem.

   ANS: F   DIF: I   OBJ: BPE 26-1.1

4. The main function of ground tissue is to conduct water and minerals.

   ANS: F   DIF: I   OBJ: BPE 26-1.1

5. In plants, xylem tissue is alive at maturity.

   ANS: F   DIF: I   OBJ: BPE 26-1.1

6. Vascular tissue is found within ground tissue, which makes up the outside of the plant.

   ANS: F   DIF: I   OBJ: BPE 26-1.1

7. The blade of a compound leaf is divided into leaflets.

   ANS: T   DIF: I   OBJ: BPE 26-1.2

8. In monocot stems, the vascular bundles are arranged in a ring.

   ANS: F   DIF: I   OBJ: BPE 26-1.2

9. Herbaceous plants have non-woody stems.

   ANS: T   DIF: I   OBJ: BPE 26-1.2

10. A compound leaf had two or more leaflets.

    ANS: T   DIF: I   OBJ: BPE 26-1.2

11. Cactus spines are modified leaves.

    ANS: T   DIF: I   OBJ: BPE 26-1.2

12. Sapwood contains vessel cells that can conduct water.

    ANS: T   DIF: I   OBJ: BPE 26-1.3

13. Xylem in sapwood cannot conduct water.

    ANS: F   DIF: I   OBJ: BPE 26-1.3

14. Leaflets reduce the surface area of a leaf blade.

    ANS: T   DIF: I   OBJ: BPE 26-1.3

15. The loss of water vapor from a plant can be explained by the pressure-flow model.

    ANS: F   DIF: I   OBJ: BPE 26-2.1

16. The loss of water by transpiration at the leaves helps pull water into the plant at the roots.

    ANS: T   DIF: I   OBJ: BPE 26-2.1

17. The rate of water absorption in roots is influenced by the amount of water lost through transpiration.

    ANS: T   DIF: I   OBJ: BPE 26-2.1

18. Stomata are important regulators in photosynthesis.

    ANS: F   DIF: I   OBJ: BPE 26-2.2

19. When water leaves the guard cells, the guard cells swell which opens the stoma, allowing transpiration to proceed.

    ANS: F   DIF: I   OBJ: BPE 26-2.2

20. Maple flowers develop several weeks after the leaves appear.

    ANS: F   DIF: I   OBJ: BPE 26-2.3

21. Sugars are converted to starch in roots.

    ANS: T   DIF: I   OBJ: BPE 26-2.4

22. In a plant, sugar moves from where it is made to where it is needed, through the lenticels.

    ANS: F   DIF: I   OBJ: BPE 26-2.4

23. The movement of sugar in a plant is called transpiration.

    ANS: F   DIF: I   OBJ: BPE 26-2.4

24. The transport of organic molecules from a leaf to the rest of the plant is called translocation.

ANS: T   DIF: I   OBJ: BPE 26-2.4

MULTIPLE CHOICE

The diagram below shows the stem of a coleus plant.

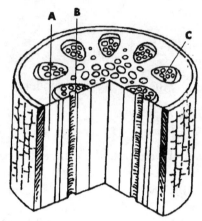

1. Refer to the illustration above. The tissue labeled A in the diagram is called
   a. meristem.
   b. xylem.
   c. phloem.
   d. ground tissue.

   ANS: D   DIF: II   OBJ: BPE 26-1.1

2. Refer to the illustration above. In the diagram, the tissue labeled B, which conducts water and is made of elongated cells that connect end to end, is called
   a. meristem.
   b. xylem.
   c. phloem.
   d. ground tissue.

   ANS: B   DIF: II   OBJ: BPE 26-1.1

3. Refer to the illustration above. In the diagram, the tissue labeled C, which transports sugars from regions where they are made, to regions where they are used, is called
   a. meristem.
   b. xylem.
   c. phloem.
   d. ground tissue.

   ANS: C   DIF: II   OBJ: BPE 26-1.1

4. The conducting cells of phloem are called
   a. tracheids.
   b. sieve tube cells.
   c. sieve plates.
   d. vessel elements.

   ANS: B   DIF: I   OBJ: BPE 26-1.1

5. The phloem in a plant
   a. transports sugars.
   b. transports water and minerals.
   c. exchanges carbon dioxide and oxygen with the atmosphere.
   d. None of the above

ANS: A   DIF: I   OBJ: BPE 26-1.1

The diagram below shows a portion of a plant's vascular system.

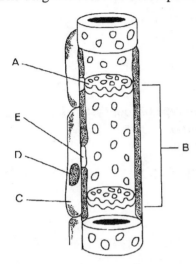

6. Refer to the illustration above. Structure B is known as a
   a. tracheid.   c. vessel element.
   b. companion cell.   d. sieve tube cells.

ANS: D   DIF: II   OBJ: BPE 26-1.1

7. Refer to the illustration above. Structure C is a
   a. tracheid.   c. vessel element.
   b. companion cell.   d. sieve tube member.

ANS: B   DIF: II   OBJ: BPE 26-1.1

8. Refer to the illustration above. Which structure allows the cytoplasm of one cell to connect to the cytoplasm of a neighboring cell and allows substances to pass freely from cell to cell?
   a. A   c. D
   b. C   d. E

ANS: D   DIF: II   OBJ: BPE 26-1.1

9. In xylem tissue, water moves from tracheid to tracheid through
   a. pits.   c. sieve tubes.
   b. vessel elements.   d. companion cells.

ANS: A   DIF: I   OBJ: BPE 26-1.1

10. The ground tissue in plants that is made up of chloroplast-rich cells is called the
    a. vascular bundle.
    b. petiole.
    c. pith.
    d. mesophyll.

    ANS: D   DIF: I   OBJ: BPE 26-1.1

11. vascular tissue: transport of fluids ::
    a. epidermis : support
    b. dermal tissue : storage
    c. dermal tissue : transport of fluids
    d. ground tissue : photosynthesis

    ANS: D
    (functions in)

    DIF: II   OBJ: BPE 26-1.1

12. The large central root of a carrot is an example of which type of root system?
    a. adventitious
    b. aerial
    c. taproot
    d. fibrous

    ANS: C   DIF: I   OBJ: BPE 26-1.2

13. The vascular bundles of dicot stems are arranged
    a. in rings surrounded by ground tissue.
    b. scattered throughout ground tissue.
    c. in piths scattered throughout ground tissue.
    d. in cortex scattered throughout ground tissue.

    ANS: A   DIF: I   OBJ: BPE 26-1.2

14. Leaves with an undivided blade are called
    a. tendrils.
    b. spines.
    c. compound.
    d. simple.

    ANS: D   DIF: I   OBJ: BPE 26-1.2

15. The tissue of the leaf mesophyll that is located directly below the upper epidermis and consists of tightly packed column-shaped cells is the
    a. palisade layer.
    b. cortex.
    c. adventitious layer.
    d. pith.

    ANS: A   DIF: I   OBJ: BPE 26-1.2

16. The outer layers of ground tissue in a stem are known as the
    a. sapwood.
    b. nodes.
    c. pith.
    d. cortex.

    ANS: D   DIF: I   OBJ: BPE 26-1.2

17. Bark contains
    a. xylem and phloem.
    b. sapwood.
    c. phloem and cork cells.
    d. mesophyll.

    ANS: C   DIF: I   OBJ: BPE 26-1.2

Four Different Kinds of Leaves

  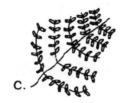 

18. Refer to the illustration above. Which of the leaves is a compound leaf?
    a. leaf a
    b. leaf b
    c. leaf c
    d. leaf d

    ANS: B   DIF: II   OBJ: BPE 26-1.2

19. cuticle : above-ground parts ::
    a. vascular system : plant
    b. sperm : pollen
    c. guard cell : stoma
    d. wax : root system

    ANS: C
    (surrounds)

    DIF: II   OBJ: BPE 26-1.2

The diagram below shows a leaf cross section.

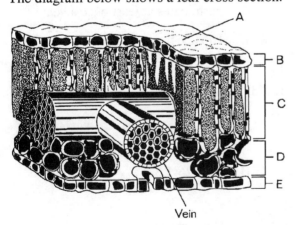

20. Refer to the illustration above. The vein illustrated is made up of
    a. only xylem vessels.
    b. only phloem vessels.
    c. both xylem and phloem vessels.
    d. neither xylem nor phloem vessels.

    ANS: C   DIF: II   OBJ: BPE 26-1.2

21. Refer to the illustration above. The spongy layer is indicated at
    a. B.
    b. C.
    c. D.
    d. E.

    ANS: C   DIF: II   OBJ: BPE 26-1.3

22. Refer to the illustration above. Structure A
    a. is the cuticle.
    b. protects the leaf.
    c. covers the epidermis.
    d. All of the above

    ANS: D   DIF: II   OBJ: BPE 26-1.3

23. The outer layers of ground tissue in a stem are known as the
    a. sapwood.
    b. nodes.
    c. pith.
    d. cortex.

    ANS: D   DIF: I   OBJ: BPE 26-1.2

24. Leaves connect to the stems of plants at the
    a. lateral buds.
    b. pith.
    c. nodes.
    d. internodes.

    ANS: C   DIF: I   OBJ: BPE 26-1.2

25. Garden-pea tendrils are specialized leaves for
    a. photosynthesis.
    b. climbing.
    c. respiration.
    d. absorption.

    ANS: B   DIF: I   OBJ: BPE 26-1.3

26. The ground tissue in the center of roots and stems
    a. turns into meristem.
    b. transports food.
    c. provides support.
    d. germinates at least once a year.

    ANS: C   DIF: I   OBJ: BPE 26-1.3

27. The primary function of root hairs is
    a. to strengthen roots as they grow downward.
    b. to transport food up the stem.
    c. absorption of water and minerals.
    d. water storage.

    ANS: C   DIF: I   OBJ: BPE 26-1.3

28. The root cap
    a. protects the growing root tip.
    b. stores food in the form of starch.
    c. absorbs water.
    d. contains meristematic tissue.

    ANS: A   DIF: I   OBJ: BPE 26-1.3

29. adventitious roots : support ::
    a. fibrous roots : photosynthesis
    b. root hairs : surface area for absorption
    c. cork cells : transport of fluids
    d. lenticels : storage

ANS: B
(provide)

DIF: II   OBJ: BPE 26-1.3

30. leaves : carbon dioxide from the air
    a. leaves : water from the air
    b. roots : light from the air
    c. roots : carbon dioxide from the air
    d. roots : nutrients from the soil

ANS: D
(take in)

DIF: II   OBJ: BPE 26-1.3

31. The movement of water through a plant is caused by
    a. the attraction of water molecules for each other.
    b. capillary action.
    c. transpiration.
    d. All of the above

ANS: D   DIF: I   OBJ: BPE 26-2.1

32. The loss of water by the leaves and stem of a plant is called
    a. translocation.
    b. osmosis.
    c. active transport.
    d. transpiration.

ANS: D   DIF: I   OBJ: BPE 26-2.1

33. The stomata are responsible for
    a. translocation.
    b. leaf growth.
    c. regulating water loss.
    d. the transport of minerals.

ANS: C   DIF: I   OBJ: BPE 26-2.2

34. The guard cells that surround a stoma
    a. have no walls.
    b. swell with water, causing the stoma to open.
    c. shrivel up when opening the stoma.
    d. are responsible for translocation.

ANS: B   DIF: I   OBJ: BPE 26-2.2

35. A commercially valuable tree in North America is the
    a. white ash.
    b. American basswood.
    c. tulip poplar.
    d. sugar maple.

ANS: D   DIF: I   OBJ: BPE 26-2.3

36. The seeds of the sugar maple mature inside fruits that are carried away by
    a. squirrels.
    b. birds.
    c. the wind.
    d. pollinators.

    ANS: C   DIF: I   OBJ: BPE 26-2.3

37. watery solution in sugar maple : sap ::
    a. flower with petals : incomplete
    b. wavy grain pattern : "sapping season"
    c. sugar maple winged fruit : samara
    d. sugar maple wooden design : "bird's eye"

    ANS: C
    (is called)

    DIF: II   OBJ: BPE 26-2.3

38. The transport of food from the leaf to the rest of the plant is called
    a. translocation.
    b. osmosis.
    c. active transport.
    d. transpiration.

    ANS: A   DIF: I   OBJ: BPE 26-2.4

39. One model that explains the movement of sugar in a plant is known as the
    a. transpiration model.
    b. translocation model.
    c. pressure-flow model.
    d. source-sink model.

    ANS: C   DIF: I   OBJ: BPE 26-2.4

Scientists studying the transport of sugars in plants found it difficult to conduct experiments that did not damage the plants they were studying. Some of them decided to use some insects they knew fed on plants. The insects they chose were aphids, which have mouthparts they insert into plants and use to suck out nutrients. Many of these aphids also release excess sugars from the anal end of their digestive tracts. These substances are called "honeydew," because they are released as sugary droplets. The scientists conducted the following experiments:

1. They measured the rate at which "honeydew" was released from aphids feeding on cucumber plants. The average rate was two drops per hour.
2. They froze some aphids and the plant parts they were attached to. They then took cross-sections of the plant parts and examined them using an electron microscope. They found that the tips of the aphids' mouthparts were in individual cells in the phloem tissue.
3. They anesthetized aphids feeding on plants and then cut away the aphids, leaving the mouthparts in place on the plant. They noted that the "honeydew" continued to be released through the mouthparts. The rate at which it was released was measured to be two drops per hour. They also analyzed the "honeydew" and found that it had the same chemical composition as the sugars transported in the plants.

40. Which of the following statements is *not* supported by the data obtained in these experiments?
    a. the contents of the phloem are under pressure
    b. sugars are transported in the phloem of plants
    c. sugars are actively transported into cells of the phloem
    d. some aphids take up more sugars from plants than they can use

    ANS: C   DIF: III   OBJ: BPE 26-2.4

COMPLETION

1. _____ are narrow, elongated, thick-walled cells that taper at each end.

    ANS: Tracheids   DIF: I   OBJ: BPE 26-1.1

2. _____ tissue forms the protective outer layer of a plant.

    ANS: Dermal   DIF: I   OBJ: BPE 26-1.1

3. Some plant cells cannot perform their functions until they have lost most of their _____.

    ANS: organelles   DIF: I   OBJ: BPE 26-1.1

4. Dermal tissue also functions in _____ _____ as well as in the absorption of mineral nutrients.

    ANS: gas exchange   DIF: I   OBJ: BPE 26-1.1

5. The underground stem of a potato that functions in food storage is called a(n) _____.

    ANS: tuber   DIF: I   OBJ: BPE 26-1.2

6. Flexible, soft, and usually green stems are known as _____ stems.

   ANS: herbaceous   DIF: I   OBJ: BPE 26-1.2

7. The two main types of root systems are fibrous root systems and _____ systems.

   ANS: taproot   DIF: I   OBJ: BPE 26-1.2

8. The darker wood in the center of a tree trunk is called _____.

   ANS: heartwood   DIF: I   OBJ: BPE 26-1.2

9. Wood consists primarily of _____ _____ cells.

   ANS: secondary xylem   DIF: I   OBJ: BPE 26-1.2

10. The broad, flat portion of a typical leaf is called the _____.

    ANS: blade   DIF: I   OBJ: BPE 26-1.2

11. Prop roots of corn are also called _____ roots.

    ANS: adventitious   DIF: I   OBJ: BPE 26-1.2

12. In _____ stems, the vascular bundles are arranged in a ring with ground tissue surrounding the ring.

    ANS: dicot   DIF: I   OBJ: BPE 26-1.2

13. The _____ of plants absorb water and minerals necessary for growth.

    ANS: roots   DIF: I   OBJ: BPE 26-1.3

14. As water evaporates from the surface of leaves, more water is _____ up the plant.

    ANS: pulled   DIF: I   OBJ: BPE 26-2.1

15. When the guard cells that surround a stoma fill with water, the stoma _____.

    ANS: opens   DIF: I   OBJ: BPE 26-2.2

16. Changes in _____ _____ within the guard cells cause stoma to open and close.

    ANS: water pressure   DIF: I   OBJ: BPE 26-2.2

17. The loss of water in guard cells causes stomata to _____.

ANS: close   DIF: I   OBJ: BPE 26-2.2

18. Maple trees are _____, which means that they lose their leaves in the fall.

ANS: deciduous   DIF: I   OBJ: BPE 26-2.3

19. The transport of organic molecules from the leaf to the rest of the plant is called
_____.

ANS: translocation   DIF: I   OBJ: BPE 26-2.4

ESSAY

1. Describe the functions of ground tissue in a vascular plant.

    ANS:
    Much of the body of a vascular plant is made up of ground tissue. Ground tissue performs photosynthesis, stores water and carbohydrates, assists in transport, and surrounds and supports the conducting tissues.

    DIF: II   OBJ: BPE 26-1.1

2. Describe how stomata open and close.

    ANS:
    Plants control water loss by opening and closing their stomata. Each stoma is formed by two cells, shaped like two cupped hands, called guard cells. Extra cellulose strands in their cell walls permit the cells to increase in length but not in diameter when the guard cells are swollen with water. The swollen cells curve outward and the stoma opens. When the guard cells lose water, they collapse and the stoma closes.

    DIF: II   OBJ: BPE 26-2.2

3. Define the terms *source* and *sink* in relation to the transportation of organic molecules in the phloem of plants.

    ANS:
    Sugar moves in the phloem of stems. Movement of sugar is from the source, where it is made, to the sink, where it is used or stored.

    DIF: II   OBJ: BPE 26-2.4

4. Compare the movement of sugar and water in a plant.

ANS:
Water only moves upward within the xylem, while sugar moves up and down in the same sieve tube. Water can diffuse freely through a plasma membrane, but sugar cannot.

DIF: II   OBJ: BPE 26-2.4

CHAPTER 27—PLANT GROWTH AND DEVELOPMENT

TRUE/FALSE

1. A plant embryo's shoot develops above the cotyledons, and its roots develop below the cotyledons.

   ANS: T   DIF: I   OBJ: BPE 27-1.1

2. A protective sheath covers the shoot of a bean seed.

   ANS: F   DIF: I   OBJ: BPE 27-1.1

3. The cotyledons of beans are visible above the soil after germination.

   ANS: T   DIF: I   OBJ: BPE 27-1.1

4. The cotyledons of corn are visible above the soil after germination.

   ANS: F   DIF: I   OBJ: BPE 27-1.1

5. Perennials can return from dormancy each year only because they grow anew from seeds left from the previous year.

   ANS: F   DIF: I   OBJ: BPE 27-1.2

6. In order to avoid extinction, all successful plant species must produce flowers and seeds during each and every growing season.

   ANS: F   DIF: I   OBJ: BPE 27-1.2

7. Biennials require two growing seasons to complete their life cycle.

   ANS: T   DIF: I   OBJ: BPE 27-1.2

8. A perennial is a plant that lives for several years even in climates that experience harsh winters.

   ANS: T   DIF: I   OBJ: BPE 27-1.2

9. Secondary tissues result from the extension of apical meristems.

   ANS: F   DIF: I   OBJ: BPE 27-1.3

10. Primary plant growth occurs in apical meristems located at the tips of stems and roots.

    ANS: T   DIF: I   OBJ: BPE 27-1.3

11. Cell division in meristems decreases the length and girth of a plant.

    ANS: F   DIF: I   OBJ: BPE 27-1.3

12. Plants grow in length by adding new cells at the tips of their stems and roots.

    ANS: T   DIF: I   OBJ: BPE 27-1.3

13. Wheat is an important dicot.

    ANS: F   DIF: I   OBJ: BPE 27-1.4

14. Wheat is a type of grass.

    ANS: T   DIF: I   OBJ: BPE 27-1.4

15. Wheat bear fruit called kernels.

    ANS: T   DIF: I   OBJ: BPE 27-1.4

16. Wheat have hollow, jointed stems called culms.

    ANS: T   DIF: I   OBJ: BPE 27-1.4

17. Wheat is a hexaploid plant.

    ANS: T   DIF: I   OBJ: BPE 27-1.4

18. Plant development is considered reversible because cells of certain tissues can produce unspecialized cells that can then differentiate into mature plant tissues.

    ANS: T   DIF: I   OBJ: BPE 27-1.5

19. Like animals, once a plant has matured it stops developing.

    ANS: F   DIF: I   OBJ: BPE 27-1.5

20. Genes guide the development of both plants and animals.

    ANS: T   DIF: I   OBJ: BPE 27-1.5

21. Plants need oxygen to carry out cellular respiration.

    ANS: T   DIF: I   OBJ: BPE 27-2.1

22. Nitrogen is an essential mineral nutrient for plant growth and development.

    ANS: T   DIF: I   OBJ: BPE 27-2.1

23. Because they do not contain bones, plants do not require calcium.

ANS: F   DIF: I   OBJ: BPE 27-2.1

24. Fertilizers only contain nitrogen.

ANS: F   DIF: I   OBJ: BPE 27-2.1

25. A hormone is a chemical messenger that remains at the location at which it was produced.

ANS: F   DIF: I   OBJ: BPE 27-2.2

26. Auxins are produced at root tips.

ANS: F   DIF: I   OBJ: BPE 27-2.2

27. Cytokinins are hormones that slow the aging of some plant organs.

ANS: T   DIF: I   OBJ: BPE 27-2.2

28. The availability of light and nutrients affect the rate of plant growth.

ANS: T   DIF: I   OBJ: BPE 27-2.3

29. Plant shoots show negative gravitropism.

ANS: T   DIF: I   OBJ: BPE 27-2.3

MULTIPLE CHOICE

1. The first sign of germination is the emergence of the embryo's
   a. shoot.
   b. root.
   c. stem.
   d. flowers.

ANS: B   DIF: I   OBJ: BPE 27-1.1

2. Chrysanthemums, daffodils, and irises are examples of
   a. perennials.
   b. annuals.
   c. biennials.
   d. All of the above

ANS: A   DIF: I   OBJ: BPE 27-1.2

3. Annuals complete their life cycles in
   a. one growing season.
   b. two growing seasons.
   c. many growing seasons.
   d. 100 growing seasons.

ANS: A   DIF: I   OBJ: BPE 27-1.2

4. Which of the following is *not* true of biennial plants?
   a. They take two years to complete their life cycle.
   b. Most biennial plants are weeds.
   c. Energy is stored in roots and shoots during the winter.
   d. Flowering usually occurs only during the second growing season.

   ANS: B   DIF: I   OBJ: BPE 27-1.2

5. A plant that completes its life cycle in a single growing season is called a(n)
   a. annual.   c. biennial.
   b. perennial.   d. perpetual.

   ANS: A   DIF: I   OBJ: BPE 27-1.2

6. biennials : two years ::
   a. perennials : more than two years   c. annuals : two years
   b. perennials : less than two years   d. annuals : more than two years

   ANS: A
   (live for)

   DIF: II   OBJ: BPE 27-1.2

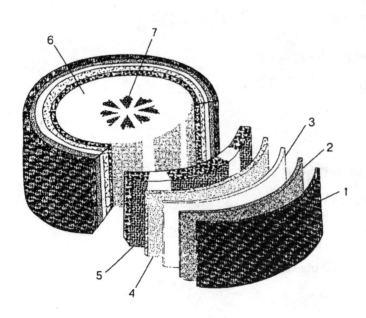

7. Refer to the illustration above. Outer bark is produced by
   a. layer 2.
   b. layer 4.
   c. layer 6.
   d. None of the above; the outer bark is inorganic material that sticks to the surface.

   ANS: A   DIF: II   OBJ: BPE 27-1.3

8. Refer to the illustration above. The cells that produce the secondary xylem are labeled as
    a. layer 2.
    b. layer 3.
    c. layer 4.
    d. layer 5.

    ANS: C   DIF: II   OBJ: BPE 27-1.3

9. Refer to the illustration above. Secondary xylem is indicated by the cells labeled as
    a. layer 1.
    b. layer 3.
    c. layer 5.
    d. layer 7.

    ANS: C   DIF: II   OBJ: BPE 27-1.3

10. Secondary xylem and phloem form from
    a. cork cambium.
    b. vascular cambium.
    c. apical meristems.
    d. bark.

    ANS: B   DIF: I   OBJ: BPE 27-1.3

11. In a woody stem, cork cambium
    a. forms phloem.
    b. forms xylem.
    c. produces the cells of the outer bark.
    d. becomes vascular cambium.

    ANS: C   DIF: I   OBJ: BPE 27-1.3

12. Plants grow in regions of active cell division called
    a. meristems.
    b. xylem.
    c. phloem.
    d. dermal tissue.

    ANS: A   DIF: I   OBJ: BPE 27-1.3

13. During periods of primary growth at apical meristems, stems and roots
    a. become wider.
    b. become longer.
    c. maintain a constant number of cells.
    d. undergo photoperiodism.

    ANS: B   DIF: I   OBJ: BPE 27-1.3

14. Meristems are found
    a. only at the tips of roots.
    b. only at the tips of shoots.
    c. at the tips of roots and shoots.
    d. None of the above

    ANS: C   DIF: I   OBJ: BPE 27-1.3

15. secondary growth : width ::
    a. secondary growth : height
    b. lateral meristem : length
    c. apical meristem : width
    d. primary growth : length

    ANS: D
    (adds)

    DIF: II   OBJ: BPE 27-1.3

16. xylem : inner side of vascular cambium ::
    a. vascular cambium : cork cambium
    b. cork : vascular cambium
    c. phloem : outer side of vascular cambium
    d. phloem : cork cambium

    ANS: C
    (is produced by)

    DIF: II   OBJ: BPE 27-1.3

17. As a member of the grass family, the veins in wheat leaves are
    a. netted.
    b. branching.
    c. absent.
    d. parallel.

    ANS: D   DIF: I   OBJ: BPE 27-1.4

18. Wheat flowers lack
    a. stamens and petals.
    b. stamens and sepals.
    c. sepals and petals.
    d. petals and pistils.

    ANS: C   DIF: I   OBJ: BPE 27-1.4

19. Approximately 85 percent of a wheat kernel is made up of
    a. embryo.
    b. seed coat.
    c. endosperm.
    d. bran.

    ANS: C   DIF: I   OBJ: BPE 27-1.4

20. Plants, like wheat, with many sets of chromosomes are referred to as
    a. haploid.
    b. diploid.
    c. polyploid.
    d. tetraploid.

    ANS: C   DIF: I   OBJ: BPE 27-1.4

21. Plant development is very different from animal development because
    a. a plant continues to develop throughout its life.
    b. plants are more strongly influenced by the environment.
    c. plant development can be reversed.
    d. All of the above

    ANS: D   DIF: I   OBJ: BPE 27-1.5

22. plants : very little movement ::
    a. plant : little influence from the environment
    b. plant : no stimulation from the environment
    c. animals : continual development
    d. animals : movement

    ANS: C
    (are characterized by)

    DIF: II   OBJ: BPE 27-1.5

23. Photosynthesis enables plants to produce most of the organic molecules that they need. This process requires the use of all of the following except
    a. carbon dioxide.   c. light.
    b. water.   d. glucose.

    ANS: D   DIF: I   OBJ: BPE 27-2.1

The diagrams below illustrate an experiment that was performed to better understand how plants grow toward the light. Diagram "A" illustrates the cut tip of a seedling that was put on a block of agar.

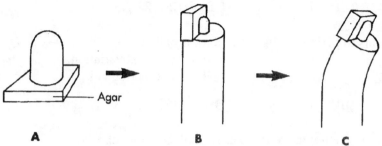

24. Refer to the illustration above. In the diagram, the plant growth hormones that diffused into the agar block from the tip of the seedling are called
    a. meristems.   c. auxins.
    b. gibberellins.   d. herbicides.

    ANS: C   DIF: II   OBJ: BPE 27-2.2

25. Refer to the illustration above. These hormones caused the stem in diagram C to bend by
    a. exerting a cohesive force on the stem.
    b. causing cells to reproduce at a greater rate.
    c. causing cells to elongate.
    d. translocation.

    ANS: C   DIF: II   OBJ: BPE 27-2.2

26. A plant hormone that is produced primarily in root tips is
    a. auxin.   c. ethylene.
    b. cytokinin.   d. gibberellin.

    ANS: B   DIF: I   OBJ: BPE 27-2.2

27. Apical dominance
    a. is caused by gibberellin in terminal buds.
    b. stimulates terminal buds to elongate.
    c. is the inhibition of lateral bud growth by auxin.
    d. results from gardeners cutting terminal buds in growing plants.

    ANS: C   DIF: I   OBJ: BPE 27-2.2

28. Which of the following hormones normally exists in a gaseous state?
    a. auxin
    b. cytokinin
    c. ethylene
    d. gibberellin

    ANS: C   DIF: I   OBJ: BPE 27-2.2

29. All of the following generally cause tropisms in plants *except*
    a. light.
    b. gravity.
    c. touch.
    d. heat.

    ANS: D   DIF: I   OBJ: BPE 27-2.3

30. The response of plants to periods of light and dark is called
    a. seasonal.
    b. daily activity.
    c. nocturnal variation.
    d. photoperiodism.

    ANS: D   DIF: I   OBJ: BPE 27-2.3

31. When vines grow, they often wrap tendrils around objects for support.
    The tendrils wrap because of
    a. phototropism.
    b. gravitropism.
    c. thigmotropism.
    d. chance.

    ANS: C   DIF: I   OBJ: BPE 27-2.3

Newly Germinated Seedling

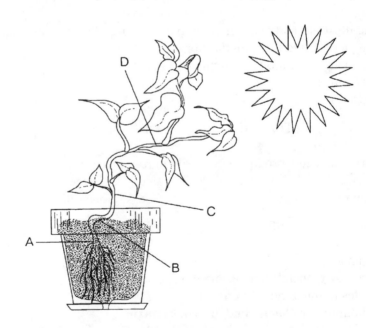

32. Refer to the illustration above. Which part of the plant indicates positive phototropism?
    a. A
    b. B
    c. C
    d. D

    ANS: D   DIF: II   OBJ: BPE 27-2.3

33. Refer to the illustration above. Which part of the plant indicates negative geotropism?
   a. A   c. C
   b. B   d. D

   ANS: C   DIF: II   OBJ: BPE 27-2.3

34. shoots : negative gravitropism ::
   a. light stimulations : gravitropism   c. shoots : negative phototropism
   b. gravity movements : phototropism   d. roots : positive gravitropism

   ANS: D
   (exhibit)

   DIF: II   OBJ: BPE 27-2.3

COMPLETION

1. Resumption of growth by a plant embryo in a seed is called _____.

   ANS: germination   DIF: I   OBJ: BPE 27-1.1

2. Seeds typically enter a period of dormancy before they _____.

   ANS: germinate   DIF: I   OBJ: BPE 27-1.1

3. Plants that may drop some leaves throughout the year but that retain most of their leaves year-round are _____.

   ANS: evergreens   DIF: I   OBJ: BPE 27-1.2

4. Plants that lose their leaves at the end of each growing season, only to grow new ones the following year, are called _____.

   ANS: deciduous   DIF: I   OBJ: BPE 27-1.2

5. A lateral meristem that produces secondary vascular tissue is called the _____
   _____.

   ANS: vascular cambium   DIF: I   OBJ: BPE 27-1.3

6. A lateral meristem that produces the cork cells of the outer bark is called the
   _____ _____.

   ANS: cork cambium   DIF: I   OBJ: BPE 27-1.3

7. Growth that occurs from the formation of new cells at the tip of a plant is called
   _____ _____.

   ANS: primary growth   DIF: I   OBJ: BPE 27-1.3

8. Cell division in the part of the plant called the _____ adds layers of new cells around the outside of a plant's body.

   ANS: lateral meristem or cambium   DIF: I   OBJ: BPE 27-1.3

9. Growth that causes a plant to increase in width is called _____ _____.

   ANS: secondary growth   DIF: I   OBJ: BPE 27-1.3

10. The process by which cells become specialized in form and function is called _____.

    ANS: differentiation   DIF: I   OBJ: BPE 27-1.3

11. Plant tissues that result from primary growth are called _____ _____.

    ANS: primary tissues   DIF: I   OBJ: BPE 27-1.3

12. Plants grow in regions of active cell division at the tips of roots and shoots called _____.

    ANS: meristems   DIF: I   OBJ: BPE 27-1.3

13. The thickening of a plant body by the production of new xylem and phloem is called _____ growth.

    ANS: secondary   DIF: I   OBJ: BPE 27-1.3

14. Bread wheat has three distinct _____ of 14 chromosomes.

    ANS: sets   DIF: I   OBJ: BPE 27-1.4

15. Apical meristems of bread wheat are _____ from being eaten by grazing animals.

    ANS: protected   DIF: I   OBJ: BPE 27-1.4

16. A kernel of wheat's outer layer is called the _____.

    ANS: bran   DIF: I   OBJ: BPE 27-1.4

17. Having many sets of chromosomes is called _____.

    ANS: polyploidy   DIF: I   OBJ: BPE 27-1.4

18. Unlike animal development, plant development is _____ and reversible.

    ANS: continuous   DIF: I   OBJ: BPE 27-1.5

19. Raw materials required by plants are carbon dioxide, water, oxygen, and _____ nutrients.

    ANS: mineral   DIF: I   OBJ: BPE 27-2.1

20. Nitrogen is an important component of proteins, _____ _____, chlorophylls, and coenzymes.

    ANS: nucleic acids   DIF: I   OBJ: BPE 27-2.1

21. ATP contains the mineral nutrient _____.

    ANS: phosphorus   DIF: I   OBJ: BPE 27-2.1

22. The three numbers at the top of a bag of fertilizer indicate the amount of nitrogen, phosphorus, and _____.

    ANS: potassium   DIF: I   OBJ: BPE 27-2.1

23. Inhibition of bud growth along a stem by auxin is called _____ _____.

    ANS: apical dominance   DIF: I   OBJ: BPE 27-2.2

24. A(n) _____ is a chemical produced in one part of an organism and transported to another part of the organism, where it causes a response.

    ANS: hormone   DIF: I   OBJ: BPE 27-2.2

25. _____ is a hormone that stimulates fruits to ripen.

    ANS: Ethylene   DIF: I   OBJ: BPE 27-2.2

26. A plant hormone that causes elongation of plant cells by enabling them to stretch during cell growth is named _____.

    ANS: auxin   DIF: I   OBJ: BPE 27-2.2

27. A growth response in plants in which the direction of growth is determined by the direction from which a stimulus comes is called a(n) _____.

    ANS: tropism   DIF: I   OBJ: BPE 27-2.3

28. The response of plants to periods of light and dark is called _____.

    ANS: photoperiodism   DIF: I   OBJ: BPE 27-2.3

ESSAY

1. While walking through a forest you notice that someone has carved his or her initials into the bark of a tree. The initials are exactly 1.5 meters from the ground. How far from the ground will the initials be next year and the year after that? Why? Discuss growth tissues in plants in your answer.

    ANS:
The initials will be exactly 1.5 meters from the ground no matter how much the tree grows. Meristems (growth tissues) at the tips of roots and shoots enable plants to increase in length. Secondary-growth meristems cause plant bodies to thicken. The initials will get wider but not higher.

    DIF: II   OBJ: BPE 27-1.3

2. Secondary growth adds width to a woody stem. Briefly describe the tissues involved and explain how they increase the stem's diameter.

    ANS:
Lateral meristems called cork and vascular cambia produce tissues that contribute to the diameter of a woody stem. Cork cambium produces cells that become part of the outer bark of the plant. Secondary vascular tissues form on opposite sides of the vascular cambium. Secondary xylem forms on the inner side of the vascular cambium, while secondary phloem forms on the outer surface of the vascular cambium, becoming part of the inner bark.

    DIF: II   OBJ: BPE 27-1.3

3. Describe why plants may be more influenced by environmental factors than are animals.

    ANS:
Since plants cannot move around the way animals can, plants are likely to be intimately tied to their immediate surroundings. As the local environment changes in such aspects as light, humidity, temperature, and nutrient availability, plants may respond physiologically by entering or leaving dormancy, dropping or growing leaves, and so forth. Animals, on the other hand, are able to move to new environments when conditions change, thus reducing the influence of the environment.

    DIF: II   OBJ: BPE 27-1.5

4. Describe how auxin causes a plant to bend toward a light source.

ANS:
The plant hormone auxin causes cells to stretch during growth, resulting in elongation of the cells. Under the influence of light, auxin in the plant's terminal bud moves from the lighted side of a shoot to the unlighted side. Cells in the area of the shoot beneath the auxin begin to lengthen. This uneven growth of the cells in the shoot causes bending toward the light; cells on the unlighted side grow slightly longer than those on the lighted side.

DIF: II   OBJ: BPE 27-2.2

5. Chrysanthemums are short day plants that normally flower in late fall. Suppose that you are a chrysanthemum grower and would like to produce a chrysanthemum crop for harvesting around Mother's Day (the second Sunday in May). What could you change about the way you grow chrysanthemums in order to postpone flowering from late fall until almost summer? Write your answer in the space below.

ANS:
Since chrysanthemums are short day plants, they will flower only when nights are of a certain critical length or longer. There are two different ways that a grower could postpone flowering in these plants as the nights lengthen. First, a grower could provide supplemental lighting for the plants, turning on lights in the evenings, for example, and keeping them on for several hours. This would cause the plants to experience shorter nights than their critical period for flowering. An easier and cheaper method would be to expose the plants to a brief flash of bright light in the middle of each night. This would cause the plants to experience essentially two short nights instead of one long one, and they would not flower.

DIF: III   OBJ: BPE 27-2.2

TRUE/FALSE

1. Without exception, all animals are heterotrophs.

   ANS: T   DIF: I   OBJ: BPE 28-1.1

2. The development of a particular animal's body plan depends on the animal's environment, rather than on its genetic heritage.

   ANS: F   DIF: I   OBJ: BPE 28-1.1

3. In most animal species, the gametes are the only haploid cells in the life cycle.

   ANS: T   DIF: I   OBJ: BPE 28-1.1

4. The majority of animal species are classified as invertebrates.

   ANS: T   DIF: I   OBJ: BPE 28-1.1

5. All animal cells lack cell walls.

   ANS: T   DIF: I   OBJ: BPE 28-1.1

6. Multicellularity enables individual cells to specialize on one life task.

   ANS: T   DIF: I   OBJ: BPE 28-1.1

7. A tissue is a group of dissimilar cells that are organized into a functional unit.

   ANS: F   DIF: I   OBJ: BPE 28-1.1

8. The first animals to evolve in the ancient oceans had bilateral symmetry.

   ANS: F   DIF: I   OBJ: BPE 28-1.2

9. Bilateral symmetry divides an organism into distinct left and right halves.

   ANS: T   DIF: I   OBJ: BPE 28-1.2

10. Jellyfish and echinoderms both exhibit radial symmetry, demonstrating that they are close relatives.

    ANS: F   DIF: I   OBJ: BPE 28-1.2

11. Most radially symmetric animals are aquatic.

    ANS: T   DIF: I   OBJ: BPE 28-1.2

12. The development of a true coelom between the ectoderm and the mesoderm represents a true evolutionary advance over the pseudocoelomate body plan.

    ANS: F   DIF: I   OBJ: BPE 28-1.3

13. All bilaterally symmetric animals have the same internal body plan.

    ANS: F   DIF: I   OBJ: BPE 28-1.3

14. The development of a body cavity did not affect the evolution of organs.

    ANS: F   DIF: I   OBJ: BPE 28-1.3

15. The body cavities of coelomates are located entirely within the ectoderm.

    ANS: F   DIF: I   OBJ: BPE 28-1.3

16. Segmentation occurs in the bodies of higher vertebrates (annelids, arthropods, and echinoderms) but is not present in chordates.

    ANS: F   DIF: I   OBJ: BPE 28-1.4

17. Clues to animal relationships can be found in the fossil record.

    ANS: T   DIF: I   OBJ: BPE 28-1.4

18. Animals are grouped into phyla based on similar body plans.

    ANS: T   DIF: I   OBJ: BPE 28-1.4

19. Anatomy and physiology are never used to determine evolutionary relationships between animal phyla.

    ANS: F   DIF: I   OBJ: BPE 28-1.4

20. Single celled organisms and sponges digest their food within their body cells.

    ANS: T   DIF: I   OBJ: BPE 28-2.1

21. Jellyfish have a well developed respiratory system.

    ANS: F   DIF: I   OBJ: BPE 28-2.1

22. The uptake of carbon dioxide and the release of oxygen is called respiration.

    ANS: F   DIF: I   OBJ: BPE 28-2.1

23. Some terrestrial animals respire with gills.

    ANS: T   DIF: I   OBJ: BPE 28-2.1

24. In a closed circulatory system, a heart pumps fluid containing oxygen and nutrients through a system of blood vessels.

    ANS: T   DIF: I   OBJ: BPE 28-2.1

25. All animals have nerve cells.

    ANS: F   DIF: I   OBJ: BPE 28-2.1

26. An exoskeleton functions in the same way as a hydrostatic skeleton.

    ANS: F   DIF: I   OBJ: BPE 28-2.1

27. A gastrovascular cavity is a digestive tract with two openings, a mouth and an anus.

    ANS: F   DIF: I   OBJ: BPE 28-2.2

28. Unlike blood moved through an open circulatory system, blood in a closed circulatory system never comes into direct contact with a body's tissues.

    ANS: T   DIF: I   OBJ: BPE 28-2.3

29. Unlike blood moved through a closed circulatory system, blood in an open circulatory system never comes into direct contact with a body's tissues.

    ANS: F   DIF: I   OBJ: BPE 28-2.3

30. In a closed circulatory system, oxygen and nutrients are exchanged directly between the cells an the environment.

    ANS: F   DIF: I   OBJ: BPE 28-2.3

31. Gametes are necessary for successful sexual reproduction.

    ANS: T   DIF: I   OBJ: BPE 28-2.4

32. Insects are capable of reproducing asexually.

    ANS: T   DIF: I   OBJ: BPE 28-2.4

33. Female bees are capable of reproducing both sexually and asexually.

    ANS: T   DIF: I   OBJ: BPE 28-2.4

34. Hermaphroditic animals reproduce asexually.

ANS: F   DIF: II   OBJ: BPE 28-2.4

35. Internal fertilization is a sexual reproductive strategy used by most terrestrial animals.

ANS: T   DIF: II   OBJ: BPE 28-2.4

MULTIPLE CHOICE

1. The presence of flight is
   a. observed in at least some species of all kingdoms.
   b. unique to certain animals.
   c. restricted to certain invertebrate species.
   d. blamed for the extinction of pterosaurs.

   ANS: B   DIF: I   OBJ: BPE 28-1.1

2. A most striking characteristic of animals that distinguishes them from the members of the other kingdoms is that members of the animal kingdom
   a. are capable of more complex and rapid movements than members of the other kingdoms.
   b. possess cells with rigid cell walls.
   c. contain choanocytes within their tissues.
   d. include both aquatic and terrestrial species.

   ANS: A   DIF: I   OBJ: BPE 28-1.1

3. All the members of the kingdom Animalia
   a. are heterotrophs.
   b. are multicellular.
   c. have cells without cell walls.
   d. All of the above

   ANS: D   DIF: I   OBJ: BPE 28-1.1

4. Specialized cells
   a. can carry out their tasks more effectively than cells that must do many tasks.
   b. are found only in chordates and echinoderms.
   c. always operate independently of all other cells.
   d. All of the above

   ANS: A   DIF: I   OBJ: BPE 28-1.1

5. The most important advantage to multicellularity is that
   a. organisms can grow to a larger size.
   b. organisms can become a "higher" species.
   c. organisms can produce a larger number of cells.
   d. individual cells can specialize in one life task.

   ANS: D   DIF: I   OBJ: BPE 28-1.1

6. As an animal develops, the ectoderm becomes the
   a. heart.
   b. tissue that lines the gut.
   c. skin and nervous system.
   d. muscle tissue.

   ANS: C   DIF: I   OBJ: BPE 28-1.1

7. animal cells : cell walls ::
   a. grass : roots
   b. asexual reproduction : gametes
   c. tissues : organ
   d. sexual reproduction : diploid

   ANS: B
   (lack)

   DIF: II   OBJ: BPE 28-1.1

A

B

8. Refer to the illustration above. The organism labeled B in the diagram
   a. is asymmetrical.
   b. is bilaterally symmetrical.
   c. exhibits radial symmetry.
   d. has reverse symmetry.

   ANS: C   DIF: II   OBJ: BPE 28-1.2

9. Refer to the illustration above. The organism labeled "A" in the diagram
   a. has no symmetry.
   b. is bilaterally symmetrical.
   c. exhibits radial symmetry.
   d. has reverse symmetry.

   ANS: B   DIF: II   OBJ: BPE 28-1.2

10. Radially symmetrical phyla include all of the following *except*
    a. jellyfish.
    b. comb jellies.
    c. hydra.
    d. sponges.

    ANS: D   DIF: II   OBJ: BPE 28-1.2

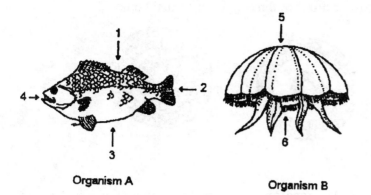

Organism A   Organism B

11. Organism B is
    a. radially symmetrical.
    b. bilaterally symmetrical.
    c. unilaterally symmetrical.
    d. nonsymmetrical.

    ANS: A   DIF: II   OBJ: BPE 28-1.2

12. Refer to the illustration above. The position of the arrow labeled _____ can be referred to as anterior.
    a. 1
    b. 4
    c. 5
    d. 6

    ANS: B   DIF: II   OBJ: BPE 28-1.2

13. Cephalization
    a. is a feature of most invertebrates, including the sponges.
    b. is characterized by the concentration of sensory organs in the anterior end.
    c. occurs in marine protozoa.
    d. results when the brain does not develop properly.

    ANS: B   DIF: I   OBJ: BPE 28-1.2

14. radial symmetry : many axes ::
    a. tissue : cells
    b. blood : circulatory
    c. gills : oxygen
    d. excretion : elimination

    ANS: A
    (is made of)

    DIF: II   OBJ: BPE 28-1.2

The diagrams below are cross sections of three types of animal bodies.

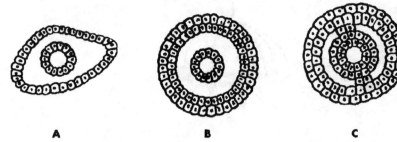

A   B   C

15. Refer to the illustration above. An organism with no body cavity is shown in diagram
    a. A.   c. C.
    b. B.   d. None of the above

    ANS: A   DIF: II   OBJ: BPE 28-1.3

16. Refer to the illustration above. The organism shown in diagram B is a(n)
    a. acoelomate.   c. coelomate.
    b. pseudocoelomate.   d. vertebrate.

    ANS: B   DIF: II   OBJ: BPE 28-1.3

17. Refer to the illustration above. Humans have a body plan similar to that of the organism shown
    in diagram
    a. A.   c. C.
    b. B.   d. None of the above

    ANS: C   DIF: II   OBJ: BPE 28-1.3

18. Refer to the illustration above. Which diagram shows an organism that probably
    has a circulatory system?
    a. A
    b. B
    c. C
    d. None of the organisms illustrated would have a circulatory system.

    ANS: C   DIF: II   OBJ: BPE 28-2.3

19. The acoelomate body type is exemplified by
    a. flatworms.   c. mollusks.
    b. roundworms.   d. annelids.

    ANS: D   DIF: I   OBJ: BPE 28-1.3

20. Roundworms have a fluid-filled cavity between the gut and body wall called a
    a. coelom.   c. digestive system.
    b. pseudocoelom.   d. None of the above

    ANS: B   DIF: I   OBJ: BPE 28-1.3

21. Pseudocoelomates
    a. must move rapidly to enhance diffusion of nutrients.
    b. must be very small or have body shapes with short distances between organs and the body surface.
    c. must have a circulatory system.
    d. All of the above

    ANS: B   DIF: I   OBJ: BPE 28-1.3

22. The evolution of body cavities was important because
    a. fluids within the body cavity aid in circulation of materials from one part of the body to another.
    b. fluids in the cavity make the body rigid and offer resistance to muscles, aiding in movement.
    c. organs are better able to function if they are protected.
    d. All of the above

    ANS: D   DIF: I   OBJ: BPE 28-1.3

23. As animals evolved, the coelom
    a. became the cavity within the digestive tract.
    b. developed between the mesoderm and the endoderm.
    c. became located between the ectoderm and the mesoderm.
    d. developed completely within the mesoderm.

    ANS: D   DIF: I   OBJ: BPE 28-1.3

24. Animals evolved from
    a. plants.   c. heterotrophic protists.
    b. photosynthetic protists.   d. None of the above

    ANS: C   DIF: II   OBJ: BPE 28-1.4

25. Scientists determine evolutionary relationships between animal phyla using evidence from the
    a. fossil record.   c. animal size.
    b. number of offspring.   d. animal behavior.

    ANS: A   DIF: I   OBJ: BPE 28-1.4

26. All of the following groups of invertebrates are coelomates *except*
    a. annelids.   c. mollusks.
    b. echinoderms.   d. nematodes.

    ANS: D   DIF: II   OBJ: BPE 28-1.4

27. Most direct evidence of evolutionary relationships between animal species comes from comparing
    a. anatomy.   c. DNA.
    b. weight.   d. fossils.

    ANS: C   DIF: I   OBJ: BPE 28-1.4

28. The exoskeleton of arthropods is
   a. moist and thin.
   b. hard and encases the body.
   c. internal and made up of bones and cartilage.
   d. None of the above

   ANS: B   DIF: I   OBJ: BPE 28-2.1

29. In some animals, ganglia at the anterior end of the animal serve as a primitive
   a. eye.   c. ear.
   b. brain.   d. mouth.

   ANS: B   DIF: I   OBJ: BPE 28-2.1

30. Single celled organisms digest their food
   a. within their body cavities.   c. outside their body cavities.
   b. within their body cells.   d. with a digestive tract.

   ANS: B   DIF: I   OBJ: BPE 28-2.2

31. Digestion functions as a mechanism for
   a. converting carbon dioxide into oxygen.   c. breaking down food into small molecules.
   b. converting oxygen into ATP.   d. breaking down glucose into ATP.

   ANS: C   DIF: I   OBJ: BPE 28-2.2

32. A gastrovascular cavity is
   a. a digestive cavity with one opening.   c. a digestive tract with one opening.
   b. a digestive cavity with two openings.   d. a digestive tract with two openings.

   ANS: A   DIF: I   OBJ: BPE 28-2.2

33. Oxygen and nutrients are transported around an animal's body by the
   a. digestive system.   c. skeletal system.
   b. nervous system.   d. circulatory system.

   ANS: D   DIF: I   OBJ: BPE 28-2.3

34. In an open circulatory system,
   a. water is drawn into the mantle cavity to provide oxygen to body tissues.
   b. lungs branch into small tubules to provide oxygen to tissues.
   c. wastes are eliminated directly to the environment from tissues.
   d. body tissues are bathed directly in fluid containing oxygen.

   ANS: D   DIF: I   OBJ: BPE 28-2.3

35. Hermaphroditic organisms
    a. reproduce only by asexual means.
    b. produce both eggs and sperm.
    c. have gemmules that are fertilized by amoebocytes.
    d. possess only male amoebocytes.

    ANS: B   DIF: I   OBJ: BPE 28-2.4

36. Asexual reproduction
    a. involves the fusion of gametes.
    b. takes place as the result of fertilization.
    c. produces offspring genetically identical to the parent.
    d. does not occur naturally in some insect populations.

    ANS: C   DIF: II   OBJ: BPE 28-2.4

37. Most terrestrial animals reproduce
    a. sexually using internal fertilization.   c. sexually using external fertilization.
    b. asexually using internal fertilization.   d. asexually using external fertilization.

    ANS: A   DIF: I   OBJ: BPE 28-2.4

COMPLETION

1. Almost all animals have two copies of each chromosome and are therefore

   _____.

   ANS: diploid   DIF: II   OBJ: BPE 28-1.1

2. Flight evolved _____ times among animals groups.

   ANS: four   DIF: I   OBJ: BPE 28-1.1

3. Cells within the _____ eventually develop into three distinct tissue layers.

   ANS: blastula   DIF: I   OBJ: BPE 28-1.1

4. Since animals cannot make their own food, they are said to be _____.

   ANS: heterotrophs   DIF: I   OBJ: BPE 28-1.1

5. Multicellularity allows for _____ of cells.

   ANS: specialization   DIF: I   OBJ: BPE 28-1.1

6. All animals are heterotrophs and are _____.

   ANS: multicellular   DIF: I   OBJ: BPE 28-1.1

7. Since sponges do not have body parts that grow around a central point as do all other animals, the sponges are said to lack _____.

    ANS: symmetry   DIF: I   OBJ: BPE 28-1.2

8. An animal whose body parts are arranged around a central point, like spokes around the hub of wheel, has _____ symmetry.

    ANS: radial   DIF: I   OBJ: BPE 28-1.2

9. A(n) _____ _____ is a term used to describe an animal's shape, symmetry, and internal organization.

    ANS: body plan   DIF: I   OBJ: BPE 28-1.2

10. An animal's body plan is determined by its _____.

    ANS: genes   DIF: I   OBJ: BPE 28-1.2

11. Animals with _____ symmetry have body parts arranged around a central axi

    ANS: radial   DIF: I   OBJ: BPE 28-1.2

12. Distinct right and left halves are characteristic of _____ symmetry.

    ANS: bilateral   DIF: I   OBJ: BPE 28-1.2

13. Cephalization concentrates sensory organs in the _____ end of an animal.

    ANS: anterior   DIF: II   OBJ: BPE 28-1.2

14. Organisms that have left and right halves that mirror each other when divided by an imaginary longitudinal plane are said to have _____ symmetry.

    ANS: bilateral   DIF: I   OBJ: BPE 28-1.2

15. The evolution of a definite head end is called _____.

    ANS: cephalization   DIF: I   OBJ: BPE 28-1.2

16. The _____ is a fluid-filled cavity that develops within the mesoderm of highe invertebrates and vertebrates.

    ANS: coelom   DIF: I   OBJ: BPE 28-1.3

17. An animal without a body cavity is called a(n) _____.

    ANS: acoelomate   DIF: I   OBJ: BPE 28-1.3

18. A(n) _____ tree is a model developed by scientists used to illustrate relationships between animal phyla.

   ANS: phylogenetic   DIF: I   OBJ: BPE 28-1.4

19. Animals without backbones are called _____.

   ANS: invertebrates   DIF: I   OBJ: BPE 28-1.4

20. Animals with backbones are called _____.

   ANS: vertebrates   DIF: I   OBJ: BPE 28-1.4

21. Annelids, arthropods, echinoderms, and chordates all have _____ bodies.

   ANS: segmented   DIF: I   OBJ: BPE 28-1.4

22. Extremely thin projections of tissue that provide a large surface area for gas exchange are called _____.

   ANS: gills   DIF: I   OBJ: BPE 28-2.1

23. The fluid-filled coelom of an earthworm functions as a(n) _____ skeleton.

   ANS: hydrostatic   DIF: I   OBJ: BPE 28-2.1

24. Cellular wastes are removed from a cell through _____.

   ANS: excretion   DIF: I   OBJ: BPE 28-2.1

25. A(n) _____ is a collection of different tissues that work together as a unit to perform a particular function.

   ANS: organ   DIF: I   OBJ: BPE 28-2.1

26. A group of different tissues that are dedicated to one function is called a(n) _____.

   ANS: organ   DIF: I   OBJ: BPE 28-2.1

27. In simple animals, oxygen gas and carbon dioxide are exchanged directly with the _____ by diffusion.

   ANS: environment   DIF: I   OBJ: BPE 28-2.3

28. Male bees develop from unfertilized eggs through _____.

   ANS: parthenogenesis   DIF: I   OBJ: BPE 28-2.4

29. Sexual reproduction produces _____ variation within species.

 ANS: genetic   DIF: II   OBJ: BPE 28-2.4

30. Many aquatic organisms release their gametes into the water where _____ fertilization takes place.

 ANS: external   DIF: I   OBJ: BPE 28-2.4

31. An organism that produces both eggs and sperm is called a(n) _____.

 ANS: hermaphrodite   DIF: I   OBJ: BPE 28-2.4

PROBLEM

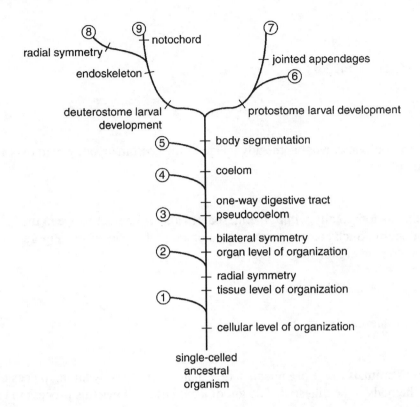

1. Shown above is a possible evolutionary tree of the animal kingdom. Evolutionary innovations are indicated at various positions on this tree. The numbers on the tree indicate positions of various animal phyla. From the list below, select which phylum belongs in each of the numbered positions:

Annelida (Earthworms, etc.)
Arthropoda (Insects, crustaceans, etc.)
Chordata (Vertebrates, etc.)
Cnidaria (Jellyfish, etc.)
Echinodermata (Sea stars, etc.)
Mollusca (Snails, clams, etc.)
Nematoda (Roundworms)
Platyhelminthes (Flatworms)
Porifera (Sponges)

List your answers in the space below.

ANS:
1. Porifera
2. Cnidaria
3. Platyhelminthes
4. Nematoda

5. Mollusca
6. Annelida
7. Arthropoda
8. Echinodermata
9. Chordata

DIF: III   OBJ: BPE 28-1.4

ESSAY

1. From a development point of view, what is the advantage of the coelomate body plan over the pseudocoelomate body plan?

    ANS:
    The development of the coelom totally within the mesoderm allows contact between the mesoderm and the endoderm. Such contact permits development of organ systems more complex than those in pseudocoelomate organisms.

    DIF: II   OBJ: BPE 28-1.3

2. Explain the advantage of internal digestion.

    ANS:
    Internal digestion allows animals to eat organisms larger than themselves by taking pieces of those organisms into the body to be digested. The gut of a cnidarian allows this process to take place. A sponge has no gut and is able to consume only organisms small enough to be absorbed by the cells lining its internal cavity.

    DIF: II   OBJ: BPE 28-2.1

3. Why is external fertilization not a practical reproductive strategy for terrestrial animals?

    ANS:
    External fertilization involves the fertilization of eggs by sperm within the environment. Flagellated sperm require a liquid medium to propel themselves towards eggs and potential fertilization opportunities. On land, gametes would quickly dry out limiting the likelihood of fertilization.

    DIF: II   OBJ: BPE 28-2.4

CHAPTER 29—SIMPLE INVERTEBRATES

TRUE/FALSE

1. Sponges are filter feeders.

   ANS: T   DIF: I   OBJ: BPE 29-1.1

2. Sponge cells are organized into tissues and organs.

   ANS: F   DIF: I   OBJ: BPE 29-1.1

3. Water enters a sponge's body through pores in its body wall.

   ANS: T   DIF: I   OBJ: BPE 29-1.1

4. Most sponges are free-swimming organisms.

   ANS: F   DIF: I   OBJ: BPE 29-1.1

5. Water exits a sponge through its osculum.

   ANS: T   DIF: I   OBJ: BPE 29-1.1

6. Nutrients are transported to the cells of a sponge by choanocytes.

   ANS: F   DIF: I   OBJ: BPE 29-1.2

7. Taxonomists group sponges according to the composition of their bodies.

   ANS: F   DIF: I   OBJ: BPE 29-1.3

8. Sponges have hard exoskeletons encasing their bodies.

   ANS: F   DIF: I   OBJ: BPE 29-1.3

9. Spongin is made of silica spicules.

   ANS: F   DIF: I   OBJ: BPE 29-1.3

10. Sponges cannot reproduce sexually.

    ANS: F   DIF: I   OBJ: BPE 29-1.4

11. Many sponges are hermaphroditic.

    ANS: T   DIF: I   OBJ: BPE 29-1.4

12. Sponges are capable of total regeneration, even from the smallest pieces of their bodies.

    ANS: T   DIF: I   OBJ: BPE 29-1.4

13. Polyps are a body form of cnidarians that are specialized for swimming.

    ANS: F   DIF: I   OBJ: BPE 29-2.1

14. Like sponges, many cnidarians have a layer of mesoglea.

    ANS: T   DIF: I   OBJ: BPE 29-2.1

15. Cells in cnidarians are organized into organs.

    ANS: F   DIF: I   OBJ: BPE 29-2.1

16. Nematocysts are located within cnidocytes.

    ANS: T   DIF: I   OBJ: BPE 29-2.2

17. Cnidarians are characterized by stinging nematocysts.

    ANS: T   DIF: I   OBJ: BPE 29-2.2

18. Cnidarians are easy prey items for predators because they are defenseless.

    ANS: F   DIF: I   OBJ: BPE 29-2.2

19. Nematocysts are used for reproduction.

    ANS: F   DIF: I   OBJ: BPE 29-2.2

The diagram below illustrates the life cycle of the jellyfish.

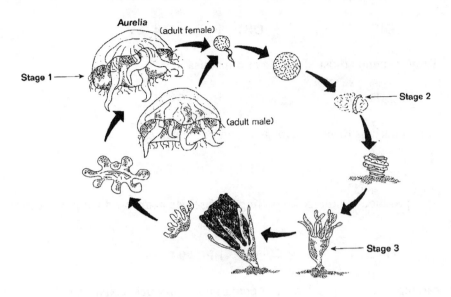

20. *Obelia* is sessile throughout its life cycle.

    ANS: F   DIF: II   OBJ: BPE 29-2.3

21. In its sessile stage, *Obelia* is referred to as a medusa.

    ANS: F   DIF: I   OBJ: BPE 29-2.3

22. In its sessile stage, *Obelia* is referred to as a polyp.

    ANS: T   DIF: I   OBJ: BPE 29-2.3

23. The life cycle of anthozoans includes medusae, planulae, and polyps.

    ANS: F   DIF: I   OBJ: BPE 29-2.4

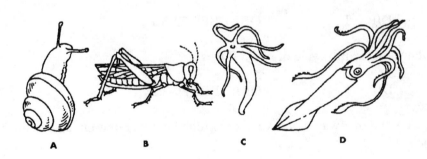

24. Portuguese man-of-war is most closely related to squid.

    ANS: F   DIF: II   OBJ: BPE 29-2.4

25. Portuguese man-of-war and jellyfish belong to different classes of cnidarians.

ANS: T   DIF: I   OBJ: BPE 29-2.4

26. Unlike *Obelia, Aurelia* spends most of its life as a medusa.

ANS: T   DIF: I   OBJ: BPE 29-2.4

27. All three classes of cnidarians have both medusa and polyp stages.

ANS: F   DIF: I   OBJ: BPE 29-2.4

28. Sea anemones can reproduce asexually by pulling themselves apart producing two genetically distinct halves.

ANS: F   DIF: I   OBJ: BPE 29-2.5

29. Although some can reproduce asexually, most cnidarians reproduce sexually.

ANS: T   DIF: I   OBJ: BPE 29-2.5

30. In cnidarians, adult polyps produce gametes.

ANS: F   DIF: I   OBJ: BPE 29-2.5

31. Tapeworms absorb food from their host's intestine directly through their skin.

ANS: T   DIF: I   OBJ: BPE 29-3.1

32. Planarians have a branched digestive tract with both a mouth and an anus.

ANS: F   DIF: I   OBJ: BPE 29-3.1

33. Most flatworms are not parasitic.

ANS: F   DIF: I   OBJ: BPE 29-3.1

34. Snails are the final host in the life cycle of blood flukes.

ANS: F   DIF: I   OBJ: BPE 29-3.2

35. The pseudocoelomates and one-way digestive tract of roundworms represent an evolutionary milestone in animals.

ANS: T   DIF: I   OBJ: BPE 29-3.3

36. Roundworm infestations are common in both plants and animals.

ANS: T   DIF: I   OBJ: BPE 29-3.3

37. Trichinosis is a disease caused by the consumption of undercooked pork containing roundworm larvae.

   ANS: T   DIF: I   OBJ: BPE 29-3.4

38. Hookworm infections are common in Northern Canada.

   ANS: F   DIF: I   OBJ: BPE 29-3.4

39. Humans can avoid trichinosis by wearing shoes when they walk through fields.

   ANS: F   DIF: I   OBJ: BPE 29-3.4

MULTIPLE CHOICE

1. Adult sponges
   a. have body walls with many pores.   c. are active swimmers.
   b. possess true tissues.   d. use stinging cells to capture prey.

   ANS: A   DIF: I   OBJ: BPE 29-1.1

2. Spicules are
   a. flexible protein fibers.
   b. hard needle-like structures in the wall of a sponge.
   c. similar to seeds; a complete sponge can grow from each spicule.
   d. used for taking in food and water.

   ANS: B   DIF: I   OBJ: BPE 29-1.1

3. Sponges
   a. are nonsymmetrical.
   b. lack organization into tissues and organs.
   c. possess cells that are capable of recognizing other sponge cells.
   d. All of the above

   ANS: D   DIF: I   OBJ: BPE 29-1.1

4. Sponges : fewer than three body layers ::
   a. eumetazoans : no body symmetry   c. cnidarians : extracellular digestion
   b. sponges : bilateral symmetry   d. cnidarians : choanocytes

   ANS: C
   (have)

   DIF: II   OBJ: BPE 29-1.1

5. collar cell : trap plankton ::
   a. mesenchyme : wastes
   b. spongin : eat food
   c. spicule : circulate water
   d. amoebocyte : carry nutrients and wastes

   ANS: D
   (function to)

   DIF: II   OBJ: BPE 29-1.1

6. In sponges, currents that draw water through the organism are created by
   a. amoebocytes.   c. gemmules.
   b. choanocytes.   d. spicules.

   ANS: B   DIF: I   OBJ: BPE 29-1.2

7. Cells that move throughout the sponge mesenchyme to deliver food to the organism's cells are
   a. amoebocytes.   c. gemmules.
   b. choanocytes.   d. spicules.

   ANS: A   DIF: I   OBJ: BPE 29-1.2

8. Water leaves the internal cavity of a sponge through the
   a. food vacuoles.   c. mesenchyme.
   b. spicules.   d. osculum.

   ANS: D   DIF: I   OBJ: BPE 29-1.2

9. Choanocytes
   a. are specialized for reproduction.   c. produce cytochrome oxidase.
   b. draw water into the body of a sponge.   d. are parasitic protozoa.

   ANS: B   DIF: I   OBJ: BPE 29-1.2

10. Sponges obtain food
    a. by photosynthesis.
    b. by using their spicules to paralyze protozoa.
    c. by filtering small organisms from the water.
    d. with spongin.

    ANS: C   DIF: I   OBJ: BPE 29-1.2

11. Certain sponges have been harvested because they possess a middle layer
    a. that contains sharp spicules, making them good for scraping paint off surfaces.
    b. that contains a protein called spongin, which holds water and releases it when squeezed.
    c. that is hollow, allowing them to be filled with water.
    d. that is composed of cellulose, which is a water-absorbent substance.

    ANS: B   DIF: I   OBJ: BPE 29-1.3

12. Skeletal support in sponges may be provided by
    a. spicules of calcium carbonate.
    b. spicules of silica.
    c. spongin fibers.
    d. All of the above

    ANS: D   DIF: I   OBJ: BPE 29-1.3

13. The gemmules of sponges
    a. create water currents for feeding.
    b. are equivalent to the sperm cells of higher animals.
    c. are equivalent to the egg cells of higher animals.
    d. are necessary for one form of asexual reproduction.

    ANS: D   DIF: I   OBJ: BPE 29-1.4

14. Self-fertilization is avoided in sponges because
    a. there is no way for sperm to enter the sponge.
    b. the sperm do not possess the enzyme needed to penetrate the egg.
    c. sperm and eggs are not produced at the same time.
    d. None of the above is true; self-fertilization is common in sponges.

    ANS: C   DIF: I   OBJ: BPE 29-1.4

15. Sponges can reproduce
    a. by the budding of new sponges from the parent.
    b. by a breakup of the original parent into fragments that each become a new sponge.
    c. sexually, using the production of sperm and eggs.
    d. All of the above

    ANS: D   DIF: I   OBJ: BPE 29-1.4

16. freshwater sponges : gemmules ::
    a. hermaphrodites : eggs and sperm
    b. gemmules : eggs
    c. gemmules : sperms
    d. amoebocytes : eggs

    ANS: A
    (produce)

    DIF: II   OBJ: BPE 29-1.4

17. Which of the following has radial symmetry?
    a. flatworm
    b. annelid
    c. echinoderm larva
    d. hydra

    ANS: D   DIF: I   OBJ: BPE 29-2.1

18. The cnidarian's inner layer of tissue is specialized for
    a. extracellular digestion.
    b. reproduction.
    c. capturing prey.
    d. All of the above

    ANS: A   DIF: I   OBJ: BPE 29-2.1

19. The outermost tissue layer of a cnidarian is the
    a. ectoderm.
    b. mesoglea.
    c. endoderm.
    d. epidermis.

    ANS: A   DIF: I   OBJ: BPE 29-2.1

20. Many cnidarians have two distinct life stages called
    a. the gametophyte and the sporophyte.
    b. the polyp and the medusa.
    c. egg and adult.
    d. egg and larva.

    ANS: B   DIF: I   OBJ: BPE 29-2.1

21. Nematocysts
    a. contain harpoonlike structures called cnidocytes.
    b. create water currents in sponges.
    c. can spear a sea anemone's prey.
    d. are found in most predatory eumetazoans.

    ANS: C   DIF: I   OBJ: BPE 29-2.2

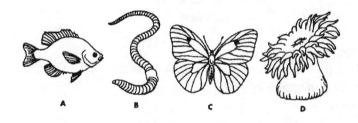

22. Refer to the illustration above. Which organism in the diagrams captures its prey using nematocysts?
    a. organism A
    b. organism B
    c. organism C
    d. organism D

    ANS: D   DIF: II   OBJ: BPE 29-2.2

23. Which of the following is a characteristic associated *only* with cnidarians?
    a. a digestive tract with a single opening
    b. tentacles with stinging cells
    c. choanocytes containing nematocysts
    d. a parasitic life cycle

    ANS: B   DIF: I   OBJ: BPE 29-2.2

24. Reproductive polyps of *Obelia* produce male and female medusa
    a. hydrostatically.
    b. asexually.
    c. colonially.
    d. sexually.

    ANS: B   DIF: I   OBJ: BPE 29-2.3

25. Free-swimming larvae of *Obelia* are called
    a. gametophytes.
    b. polyps.
    c. planulae.
    d. gametes.

    ANS: C   DIF: I   OBJ: BPE 29-2.3

26. *Obelia* spends most of its life cycle in the
    a. polyp stage.
    b. medusa stage.
    c. planulae stage.
    d. free-swimming stage.

    ANS: A   DIF: I   OBJ: BPE 29-2.3

27. *Obelia* : polyp ::
    a. *Hydra* : jellyfish
    b. jellyfish : polyp
    c. *Aurelia* : colony
    d. *Aurelia* : medusa

    ANS: D
    (spend most of life as a)

    DIF: II   OBJ: BPE 29-2.3

28. The phylum Cnidaria includes all of the following *except*
    a. jellyfish.
    b. squids.
    c. sea anemones.
    d. corals.

    ANS: B   DIF: I   OBJ: BPE 29-2.4

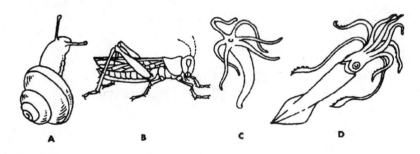

29. Refer to the illustration above. Which organism in the diagrams is most closely related to a jellyfish?
    a. organism A
    b. organism B
    c. organism C
    d. organism D

    ANS: C   DIF: II   OBJ: BPE 29-2.4

30. The hydra is unique among the hydrozoans because it
    a. is an active swimmer.
    b. feeds without tentacles.
    c. is strictly a marine species.
    d. has no medusa stage.

    ANS: D   DIF: I   OBJ: BPE 29-2.4

31. Which of the following is *not* sessile as an adult?
    a. sponge
    b. hydra
    c. sea anemone
    d. Portuguese man-of-war

    ANS: D   DIF: I   OBJ: BPE 29-2.4

32. Sea anemones are
    a. medusae.
    b. polyps.
    c. larvae.
    d. eggs.

    ANS: B   DIF: I   OBJ: BPE 29-2.4

33. Scyphozoans, such as jellyfish, spend most of their lives as
    a. polyps.
    b. medusae.
    c. corals.
    d. parasites.

    ANS: B   DIF: I   OBJ: BPE 29-2.4

34. Anthozoans include organisms known as
    a. jellyfish.
    b. hydras.
    c. Portuguese men-of-war.
    d. sea anemones and corals.

    ANS: D   DIF: I   OBJ: BPE 29-2.4

35. The class of cnidarians that typically live only as polyps is the
    a. Anthozoa.
    b. Hydrozoa.
    c. Scyphozoa.
    d. None of the above

    ANS: A   DIF: I   OBJ: BPE 29-2.4

36. *Hydra* : one polyp ::
    a. class Hydrozoa : jellyfish
    b. Portuguese man-of-war : a colony
    c. Cnidaria : four classes
    d. *Hydra* : medusa stage

    ANS: B
    (is composed of)

    DIF: II   OBJ: BPE 29-2.4

37. Planula larvae of hydrozoans
    a. result from fertilization of eggs by sperm.
    b. swim freely through the water.
    c. settle to the ocean bottom and grow into polyps.
    d. All of the above

    ANS: D   DIF: I   OBJ: BPE 29-2.5

The diagram below illustrates the life cycle of the jellyfish.

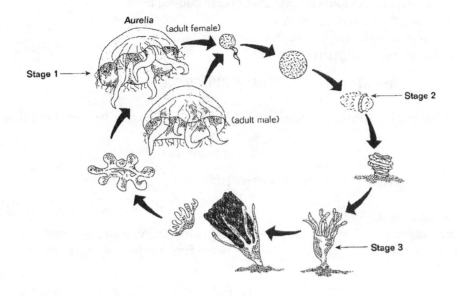

38. Refer to the illustration above. Which stage is called a planula?
    a. stage 1   c. stage 3
    b. stage 2   d. None of the above

    ANS: B   DIF: II   OBJ: BPE 29-2.5

39. Refer to the illustration above. Which of the indicated stages reproduces asexually?
    a. stage 1   c. stage 3
    b. stage 2   d. None of the above

    ANS: C   DIF: II   OBJ: BPE 29-2.5

40. Flatworms can reproduce asexually by
    a. regeneration.   c. producing polyps.
    b. forming larvae.   d. exchanging both sperm and eggs.

    ANS: A   DIF: I   OBJ: BPE 29-3.1

41. Schistosomiasis is a disease caused by a
    a. roundworm.   c. cestode.
    b. trematode.   d. planarian.

    ANS: B   DIF: I   OBJ: BPE 29-3.1

42. Flatworms have no need for circulatory and respiratory systems because
    a. the digestive system performs these functions.
    b. their cells are close to the animal's exterior surface.
    c. the spherical body shape allows diffusion of materials into tissues.
    d. the coelom is bathed in blood and oxygen.

    ANS: B   DIF: I   OBJ: BPE 29-3.1

43. Which of the following statements about tapeworms is *false?*
    a. Tapeworms can infect a person who eats improperly cooked beef.
    b. Tapeworms belong to the genus *Schistosoma.*
    c. Tapeworms can grow to be large in human intestines.
    d. Tapeworms do not have a digestive system.

    ANS: B   DIF: I   OBJ: BPE 29-3.1

44. To avoid being digested by their host, endoparasites have a thick protective covering called the
    a. cell wall.   c. protoplasm.
    b. cilia.   d. tegument.

    ANS: D   DIF: I   OBJ: BPE 29-3.2

45. corals : stonelike outer covering ::
    a. ectoparasites : tegument   c. flatworms : circulatory systems
    b. endoparasites : tegument   d. flatworms : respiratory systems

    ANS: B
    (have)

    DIF: II   OBJ: BPE 29-3.1

46. turbellarians : free living ::
    a. planaria : parasitic   c. cestodes : free living
    b. tapeworms : free living   d. flukes : parasitic

    ANS: D
    (are)

    DIF: II   OBJ: BPE 29-3.1

47. Beef tapeworm larva live in the
    a. retina of infected cattle.   c. intestines of infected cattle.
    b. muscle tissue of infected cattle.   d. mouth of infected cattle.

    ANS: D   DIF: I   OBJ: BPE 29-3.2

48. To which phylum do roundworms belong?
    a. Annelida   c. Platyhelminthes
    b. Nematoda   d. Arthropoda

    ANS: B   DIF: I   OBJ: BPE 29-3.3

49. A type of roundworm that lives a parasitic life is
    a. *Ascaris.*   c. *Trichinella.*
    b. *Necator.*   d. All of the above

    ANS: D   DIF: I   OBJ: BPE 29-3.3

50. The eggs of the roundworm, *Ascaris,* can live for years in
   a. soil.
   b. water.
   c. intestine.
   d. muscle.

   ANS: A   DIF: I   OBJ: BPE 29-3.4

51. *Ascaris* eggs develop into larvae while in human
   a. muscle.
   b. blood.
   c. intestine.
   d. liver.

   ANS: C   DIF: I   OBJ: BPE 29-3.4

52. The nematode *Ascaris lumbricoides* infects humans, spending most of its adult life inside the intestines of its host. To be infected, a person must
   a. consume the nematode's eggs.
   b. walk barefoot on infested soil.
   c. sit on an infested toilet seat.
   d. All of the above

   ANS: A   DIF: I   OBJ: BPE 29-3.4

53. *Necator* : hookworm infestation ::
   a. ribbon worm : human waste
   b. *Trichinella* : trichinosis
   c. *Ascaris* : free swimming
   d. *Ascaris* : proglottids

   ANS: B
   (causes)

   DIF: II   OBJ: BPE 29-3.4

COMPLETION

1. _____ is drawn into a sponge through pores and leaves through the osculum.

   ANS: Water   DIF: I   OBJ: BPE 29-1.1

2. Facing into the internal cavity of a sponge are flagellated collar cells called

   _____.

   ANS: choanocytes   DIF: I   OBJ: BPE 29-1.1

3. Food molecules are carried throughout a sponge's body by _____.

   ANS: amoebocytes   DIF: I   OBJ: BPE 29-1.2

4. Water is moved through the body of a sponge by the action of flagellated cells called

   _____.

   ANS: choanocytes   DIF: I   OBJ: BPE 29-1.2

5. A network of tough protein fibers that provide support in some sponges is called
   _____.

   ANS: spongin   DIF: I   OBJ: BPE 29-1.3

6. Needle-like objects in the middle layers of sponges that make up the skeleton of these organisms
   are called _____.

   ANS: spicules   DIF: I   OBJ: BPE 29-1.3

7. Spicules may be composed of either _____ _____ or
   _____.

   ANS: calcium carbonate, silica DIF: I   OBJ: BPE 29-1.3

8. Food-filled balls of sponge amoebocytes that are involved in asexual reproduction are called
   _____.

   ANS: gemmules   DIF: I   OBJ: BPE 29-1.4

9. The two distinct life stages of cnidarians are the _____ and the
   _____.

   ANS: polyp, medusa   DIF: I   OBJ: BPE 29-2.1

10. A free-floating, gelatinous body form found in some cnidarians is called a(n)
    _____, while an attached body form in these animals is called a(n)
    _____.

    ANS: medusa, polyp   DIF: I   OBJ: BPE 29-2.1

11. Cnidarians have two _____ layers.

    ANS: tissue   DIF: I   OBJ: BPE 29-2.1

12. Hydras attach themselves to their substrate by means of a sticky secretion produced by the area
    called the _____ _____.

    ANS: basal disk   DIF: I   OBJ: BPE 29-2.4

13. The Portuguese man-of-war is a complex colony containing both _____ and
    _____.

    ANS: medusae, polyps   DIF: I   OBJ: BPE 29-2.4

14. Cnidarians that typically have a thick, stalk-like body crowned by tentacles that occur in groups
    of six belong to the class known as the _____.

    ANS: anthozoans   DIF: I   OBJ: BPE 29-2.4

15. A coral is a member of the phylum _____.

    ANS: Cnidaria   DIF: I   OBJ: BPE 29-2.4

16. The _____ is a thick protective cellular covering of the bodies of
    endoparasitic flukes that prevents them from being digested by their hosts.

    ANS: tegument   DIF: I   OBJ: BPE 29-3.1

17. A schistosome is a member of the phylum _____.

    ANS: Platyhelminthes   DIF: I   OBJ: BPE 29-3.1

18. The ability of some animals, such as flatworms, to regrow lost parts of their bodies is called
    _____.

    ANS: regeneration   DIF: I   OBJ: BPE 29-3.1

19. _____ are rectangular body sections of tapeworms.

    ANS: Proglottids   DIF: I   OBJ: BPE 29-3.1

20. The organisms that are the simplest animals with a complete digestive system consisting of a
    tube that is open at both ends are _____ _____.

    ANS: ribbon worms   DIF: I   OBJ: BPE 29-3.3

21. Roundworms are members of the phylum _____.

    ANS: Nematoda   DIF: I   OBJ: BPE 29-3.3

ESSAY

1. Like plants that show an alternation of generations, many cnidarians also exhibit two different
   body forms during their life cycles. Describe these two body forms and their role in cnidarian life
   cycles.

   ANS:
   Polyps are a form that lives attached to a hard surface. They reproduce asexually by budding,
   resulting in the production of either more polyp forms or, in some species, the medusa stage.
   Medusae (or jellyfish) are free-living organisms, swimming or floating in currents. They
   reproduce sexually, producing an embryo that develops into a larva, settles to the bottom of the
   body of water, and grows into a polyp.

   DIF: II   OBJ: BPE 29-2.1

2. Compare the symmetry of body forms observed in the phylum Porifera and the phylum Cnidari

ANS:
The members of the phylum Porifera, the sponges, are asymmetrical. Their bodies are not arranged in any particular way around a central pint or axis. On the other hand, the animals belonging to the phylum Cnidaria, including the jellyfish, hydra, and sea anemones, are radially symmetrical. Their bodies are arranged around a central point.

DIF: II   OBJ: BPE 29-2.1

3. Sea anemones and corals belong to the same group of cnidarians, the class Anthozoa. Distingui between these two groups of organisms.

ANS:
While both types of organisms exist only in polyp forms, their adult structures are different. Se anemones are generally solitary, soft-bodied polyps. Corals, on the other hand, usually live in colonies that are surrounded by a calcium-rich skeleton.

DIF: II   OBJ: BPE 29-2.4

4. A flatworm cannot eat when food is already in its gut. Why?

ANS:
The guts of most flatworms have only one opening. Because they consume their food and excre their wastes through the same opening, two-way movement of material occurs within their guts A flatworm cannot eat when food is already in the gut because newly consumed food would mi with partially digested food and wastes.

DIF: II   OBJ: BPE 29-3.1

5. Describe a major similarity and a major difference between ribbon worms and roundworms.

ANS:
These two types of worms are similar in that both have a complete digestive system consisting digestive tubes that are open at both ends, the mouth and the anus. A major difference between these worms is that ribbon worms are acoelomates, while roundworms are pseudocoelomates.

DIF: II   OBJ: BPE 29-3.3

6. Parasitic lifestyles have evolved independently among different phyla of worms. Using examples, discuss species of worms that are adapted to a parasitic lifestyle.

ANS:
Among the Platyhelminthes, two parasitic worms are schistosomes, which inhabit blood vessels of their hosts, and tapeworms, which live in the intestinal tracts of their hosts. Parasitic nematodes include *Ascaris,* an intestinal parasite of humans and pigs, and *Wuchereria*, the cause of filariasis (elephantiasis) in humans. Leeches, blood-sucking worms of the phylum Annelida, can live off the blood of a variety of hosts.

DIF: II   OBJ: BPE 29-3.4

TRUE/FALSE

1. Mollusks and annelids are believed to be the first animals to develop a true coelom.

    ANS: T   DIF: I   OBJ: BPE 30-1.1

2. Unlike annelids, mollusks have a larval stage called a trochophore.

    ANS: F   DIF: I   OBJ: BPE 30-1.1

3. Mollusks have four distinct body parts: a foot, a head, a visceral mass, and a tail.

    ANS: F   DIF: I   OBJ: BPE 30-1.2

4. Most mollusks are radially symmetrical.

    ANS: F   DIF: I   OBJ: BPE 30-1.2

5. All mollusks have shells.

    ANS: F   DIF: I   OBJ: BPE 30-1.2

6. Mollusks use radula for reproduction.

    ANS: F   DIF: I   OBJ: BPE 30-1.2

7. All mollusk shells are lined with and secreted by a fleshy fold of tissue called the foot.

    ANS: F   DIF: I   OBJ: BPE 30-1.2

8. In terrestrial snails, the mantle cavity functions as a simple lung.

    ANS: T   DIF: I   OBJ: BPE 30-1.3

9. Mollusks must eat constantly because the functioning of their nephridia causes the disposal of useful molecules as well as of waste products.

    ANS: F   DIF: I   OBJ: BPE 30-1.3

10. The digestive system of mollusks is similar to the digestive system of roundworms.

    ANS: T   DIF: I   OBJ: BPE 30-1.3

11. All mollusks utilize gills for respiration.

    ANS: F   DIF: I   OBJ: BPE 30-1.3

12. The circulatory system of octopuses is the same as the circulatory system of snails.

    ANS: F   DIF: I   OBJ: BPE 30-1.3

13. Nephridia are important circulatory organs.

    ANS: F   DIF: I   OBJ: BPE 30-1.3

14. All mollusks carry out sexual reproduction.

    ANS: T   DIF: I   OBJ: BPE 30-1.3

15. Most bivalves have separate sexes, but some are hermaphroditic.

    ANS: T   DIF: I   OBJ: BPE 30-1.4

16. Due to the presence of a shell, all gastropods are capable of living on land for at least a portion of their lives.

    ANS: F   DIF: I   OBJ: BPE 30-1.4

17. Since cephalopods have tentacles, they have no need for a radula.

    ANS: F   DIF: I   OBJ: BPE 30-1.4

18. The eyes of cephalopods are very similar to the compound eyes of insects.

    ANS: F   DIF: I   OBJ: BPE 30-1.4

19. While all but one group of mollusks have open circulatory systems, all annelids possess a closed circulatory system.

    ANS: T   DIF: I   OBJ: BPE 30-2.1

20. The cerebral ganglion of annelids is the equivalent of a primitive brain.

    ANS: T   DIF: I   OBJ: BPE 30-2.1

21. Segmentation is first observed in mollusks.

    ANS: F   DIF: I   OBJ: BPE 30-2.1

22. An earthworm's digestive system is very similar to the digestive system of a roundworm.

    ANS: F   DIF: I   OBJ: BPE 30-2.1

23. All annelids have segmented bodies.

    ANS: T   DIF: I   OBJ: BPE 30-2.1

24. Annelids were the first animals to have a segmented body.

    ANS: T   DIF: I   OBJ: BPE 30-2.1

25. Lungs are present in each annelid segment.

    ANS: F   DIF: I   OBJ: BPE 30-2.2

26. Different regions of an annelid's body specialize for different functions.

    ANS: T   DIF: I   OBJ: BPE 30-2.2

27. Annelids have neither lungs nor gills.

    ANS: T   DIF: I   OBJ: BPE 30-2.2

28. The body cavity in annelids is a true coelom.

    ANS: T   DIF: I   OBJ: BPE 30-2.2

29. An earthworm's crop crushes soil particles thereby breaking them down for further digestion.

    ANS: F   DIF: I   OBJ: BPE 30-2.3

30. In earthworms, food molecules are extracted from soil and absorbed into the bloodstream through the intestinal wall.

    ANS: T   DIF: I   OBJ: BPE 30-2.3

31. All annelids are terrestrial.

    ANS: F   DIF: I   OBJ: BPE 30-2.4

32. *Polychaetes* consume their own weight in soil every day.

    ANS: F   DIF: I   OBJ: BPE 30-2.4

33. Earthworms have parapodia that aid in movement.

    ANS: F   DIF: I   OBJ: BPE 30-2.4

34. Leeches have both setae and parapodia.

    ANS: F   DIF: I   OBJ: BPE 30-2.4

35. Some leeches have become specialized to a parasitic way of life by developing the ability to suc blood from the bodies of other organisms.

    ANS: T   DIF: I   OBJ: BPE 30-2.4

MULTIPLE CHOICE

1. Both mollusks and annelids
   a. have true body cavities.
   b. closed circulatory systems.
   c. well developed respiratory systems.
   d. carry out asexual reproduction.

   ANS: A   DIF: I   OBJ: BPE 30-1.1

2. Which of the following is *not* a member of the phylum Mollusca?
   a. gastropods
   b. echinoderms
   c. cephalopods
   d. bivalves

   ANS: B   DIF: I   OBJ: BPE 30-1.1

3. In addition to a true coelom, mollusks and annelids share
   a. the same type of circulatory system.
   b. a trochophore larval stage.
   c. the same type of respiratory system.
   d. an asexual reproductive stage.

   ANS: B   DIF: I   OBJ: BPE 30-1.1

4. All of the animal phyla that evolved after the mollusks
   a. are vertebrates.
   b. are prokaryotes.
   c. have a coelom.
   d. lack mesoderm.

   ANS: C   DIF: I   OBJ: BPE 30-1.1

5. The evolution of a coelom was significant because
   a. more food could be stored within it.
   b. more wastes could be stored before excretion.
   c. it enabled development of more complex organ systems.
   d. it eliminated the need for a circulatory system.

   ANS: C   DIF: I   OBJ: BPE 30-1.1

6. All of the following are characteristics of mollusks *except*
   a. a pseudocoelomate body plan.
   b. bilateral symmetry.
   c. a complete digestive tract.
   d. an open circulatory system.

   ANS: A   DIF: I   OBJ: BPE 30-1.2

7. A characteristic structure found in many mollusks is the radula, which is involved in
   a. jet propulsion.
   b. opening and closing of the shells.
   c. eating.
   d. reproduction.

   ANS: C   DIF: I   OBJ: BPE 30-1.2

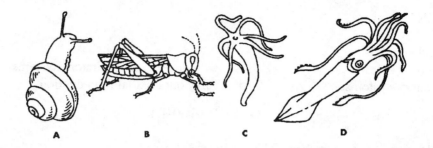

A   B   C   D

8. Refer to the illustration above. Which two organisms in the diagrams possess mantles?
   a. organisms A and C
   b. organisms B and C
   c. organisms A and D
   d. organisms B and D

   ANS: C   DIF: II   OBJ: BPE 30-1.2

9. Which of the following has a true coelom?
   a. flatworm
   b. roundworm
   c. rotifer
   d. mollusk

   ANS: D   DIF: I   OBJ: BPE 30-1.2

10. The foot of the mollusk performs all the following functions *except*
    a. locomotion.
    b. scraping particles of food off the sea bottom.
    c. burrowing into the sand.
    d. capturing prey.

    ANS: B   DIF: I   OBJ: BPE 30-1.2

11. Shells of mollusks
    a. may consist of one or more pieces.
    b. provide protection.
    c. allow for the attachment of muscles.
    d. All of the above

    ANS: D   DIF: I   OBJ: BPE 30-1.2

12. The only cephalopod that has retained its external shell is the
    a. cuttlefish.
    b. nautilus.
    c. octopus.
    d. squid.

    ANS: B   DIF: I   OBJ: BPE 30-1.2

13. mollusks : a mantle ::
    a. a gut with one opening : worms
    b. earthworms : coelom
    c. mollusks : a pseudocoelom
    d. earthworms : pseudocoelom

    ANS: B
    (have)

    DIF: II   OBJ: BPE 30-1.2

14. Small tubules that collect wastes from the coelom of mollusks and discharge them from the body are called
    a. nephridia.
    b. radulae.
    c. bivalves.
    d. spicules.

    ANS: A   DIF: I   OBJ: BPE 30-1.3

15. Among the various species of gastropods, respiration may take place
    a. with gills.
    b. through the skin.
    c. with lungs.
    d. All of the above

    ANS: D   DIF: I   OBJ: BPE 30-1.3

16. Octopuses and squids differ from all other mollusks because octopuses and squids have
    a. closed circulatory systems.
    b. open circulatory systems.
    c. reproduce sexually.
    d. reproduce asexually.

    ANS: A   DIF: I   OBJ: BPE 30-1.3

17. Terrestrial snails are the only mollusks that have
    a. gills.
    b. open circulatory systems.
    c. closed circulatory systems.
    d. primitive lungs.

    ANS: D   DIF: I   OBJ: BPE 30-1.3

18. All mollusks reproduce
    a. sexually.
    b. asexually.
    c. hermaphroditically.
    d. photosynthetically.

    ANS: A   DIF: I   OBJ: BPE 30-1.3

19. All of the following are classes of the phylum Mollusca *except*
    a. bivalves.
    b. cephalopods.
    c. gastropods.
    d. pseudopods.

    ANS: D   DIF: I   OBJ: BPE 30-1.4

20. The only mollusks that have a closed circulatory system are
    a. bivalves.
    b. cephalopods.
    c. chitons.
    d. gastropods.

    ANS: B   DIF: I   OBJ: BPE 30-1.4

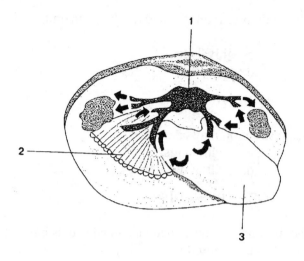

21. Refer to the illustration above. The organism shown in this diagram is a
    a. bivalve.
    b. cephalopod
    c. chiton.
    d. gastropod.

    ANS: A   DIF: II   OBJ: BPE 30-1.4

22. Refer to the illustration above. This organism possesses a(n)
    a. simple lung.
    b. closed circulatory system.
    c. internal beak.
    d. open circulatory system.

    ANS: D   DIF: II   OBJ: BPE 30-1.4

23. Refer to the illustration above. Movement of this organism is dependent upon the structure labeled
    a. 1.
    b. 2.
    c. 3.
    d. None of the above

    ANS: C   DIF: II   OBJ: BPE 30-1.4

24. "Jet propulsion" is the usual means of locomotion in water for
    a. arthropods.
    b. echinoderms.
    c. cephalopods.
    d. annelids.

    ANS: C   DIF: I   OBJ: BPE 30-1.4

25. Adductor muscles are responsible for
    a. moving the valves of bivalves.
    b. extending the feet of mollusks.
    c. pumping the hearts of mollusks.
    d. fanning the gills of aquatic mollusks.

    ANS: A   DIF: I   OBJ: BPE 30-1.4

26. The gills of bivalves are covered with a sticky mucus
    a. because bivalves live in polluted waters.
    b. in order to trap small organisms consumed as food.
    c. to protect them from irritation.
    d. in order to cause water to pass over them more rapidly.

    ANS: B   DIF: I   OBJ: BPE 30-1.4

27. During reproduction in bivalves, fertilization
    a. occurs internally.
    b. occurs externally.
    c. takes place in the mantle cavity.
    d. does not occur, since bivalves are hermaphroditic.

    ANS: B   DIF: I   OBJ: BPE 30-1.4

28. All of the cephalopods
    a. have eight tentacles.   c. have protective shells.
    b. are active predators.   d. are filter feeders.

    ANS: B   DIF: I   OBJ: BPE 30-1.4

29. Jet propulsion in an octopus or squid is the result of
    a. rapid closing of the organism's shell.
    b. strong contractions of the tentacles.
    c. high-pressure "spitting" of fluid from the organism's mouth.
    d. forcefully squeezing water from the siphon.

    ANS: D   DIF: I   OBJ: BPE 30-1.4

30. Which of the following is *correctly* paired?
    a. phylum Platyhelminthes - hydra   c. phylum Mollusca - octopus
    b. phylum Nematoda - planaria   d. phylum Annelida - roundworm

    ANS: C   DIF: I   OBJ: BPE 30-1.4

31. The most significant evolutionary advancement of annelids over mollusks is believed to be
    a. the ability to burrow.   c. segmentation.
    b. the existence of a true coelom. d. cephalization.

    ANS: C   DIF: I   OBJ: BPE 30-2.1

32. Segmented worms are known as
    a. nematodes.   c. planarians.
    b. annelids.   d. arthropods.

    ANS: B   DIF: I   OBJ: BPE 30-2.1

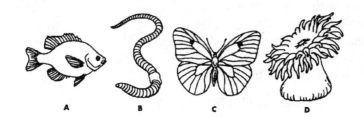

33. Refer to the illustration above. Which two organisms in the diagrams have segmented body plans?
    a. organisms A and C
    b. organisms B and D
    c. organisms A and D
    d. organisms B and C

    ANS: D   DIF: II   OBJ: BPE 30-2.1

34. Coordinated movements of an annelid's body segments are possible because of the
    a. development of an advanced brain.
    b. ventral nerve cord and paired segmental ganglia.
    c. presence of a true coelom in the annelid body.
    d. existence of a complete digestive system.

    ANS: B   DIF: I   OBJ: BPE 30-2.1

35. Of the four basic types of tissue, the tissue that is specialized to transmit and receive messages in the body is
    a. epithelial tissue.
    b. connective tissue.
    c. muscle tissue.
    d. nerve tissue.

    ANS: D   DIF: I   OBJ: BPE 30-2.1

36. The evolution of tremendous diversity in the phylum Annelida is due primarily to
    a. gills.
    b. specialized reproductive organs.
    c. cephalization.
    d. segmented bodies.

    ANS: D   DIF: I   OBJ: BPE 30-2.1

37. true coelom : mollusks and annelids ::
    a. tentacle : annelids
    b. siphon : annelids
    c. valve : annelids
    d. segmentation : annelids

    ANS: D
    (is found in)

    DIF: II   OBJ: BPE 30-2.1

38. The basic body plan of an annelid
    a. consists of joined legs.
    b. is similar to a long tube.
    c. is a tube within a tube.
    d. can be compared to a corkscrew.

    ANS: C   DIF: I   OBJ: BPE 30-2.2

Biology: Principles and Explorations

39. Almost every segment of an annelid
    a. is capable of reproduction.
    b. has a well-developed brain.
    c. has a pseudocoelom.
    d. has excretory organs.

    ANS: D   DIF: I   OBJ: BPE 30-2.2

40. The advantage of a closed circulatory system over an open circulatory system is that
    a. blood moves more efficiently through the tubes of a closed circulatory system.
    b. a closed circulatory system prevents blood from leaking out of the body.
    c. blood is able to be pumped by a muscular heart in a closed circulatory system.
    d. lungs are able to function in animals with a closed circulatory system.

    ANS: A   DIF: I   OBJ: BPE 30-2.2

41. Of the following organs, the one that does *not* exist in annelids is the
    a. heart.
    b. gills.
    c. nephridia.
    d. stomach.

    ANS: B   DIF: I   OBJ: BPE 30-2.2

42. Segmented worms are known as
    a. nematodes.
    b. annelids.
    c. planarians.
    d. arthropods.

    ANS: B   DIF: I   OBJ: BPE 30-2.2

43. The clitellum of an earthworm
    a. contains the heart.
    b. is associated with reproduction.
    c. acts as a primitive respiratory system.
    d. is necessary for movement.

    ANS: B   DIF: I   OBJ: BPE 30-2.2

44. cephalopod motion : siphon ::
    a. annelid motion : siphon
    b. annelid breathing : nephridia
    c. annelid circulation : closed circulatory system
    d. annelid motion : tentacles

    ANS: C
    (is performed by)

    DIF: II   OBJ: BPE 30-2.2

45. The digestive tube of annelids is divided into three regions. Which of the following is *not* among these regions?
    a. crop
    b. intestine
    c. radula
    d. stomach

    ANS: C   DIF: I   OBJ: BPE 30-2.3

46. Earthworms are considered to be beneficial to the environment because
    a. their castings contain nutrients.
    b. they aerate the soil as they move through it.
    c. they break up the soil in which they live.
    d. All of the above

    ANS: D   DIF: I   OBJ: BPE 30-2.4

47. The body of the water leech
    a. has suckers on the front and back.   c. is segmented.
    b. is somewhat flattened.   d. All of the above

    ANS: D   DIF: I   OBJ: BPE 30-2.4

48. Parapodia are involved in all of the following *except*
    a. swimming.   c. burrowing.
    b. gas exchange.   d. reproduction.

    ANS: D   DIF: I   OBJ: BPE 30-2.4

49. Leeches
    a. use suckers to aid in movement.   c. are segmented.
    b. may be parasitic.   d. All of the above

    ANS: D   DIF: I   OBJ: BPE 30-2.4

50. earthworm movement : circular muscles and setae ::
    a. earthworm digestion : circular muscles and setae
    b. earthworm digestion : sperm receptacles
    c. earthworm respiration : gizzard
    d. earthworm respiration : skin

    ANS: D
    (is carried out by)

    DIF: II   OBJ: BPE 30-2.4

51. leeches : blood ::
    a. earthworms : small animals   c. marine worms : small animals
    b. earthworms : blood   d. marine worms : blood

    ANS: C
    (feed on)

    DIF: II   OBJ: BPE 30-2.4

COMPLETION

1. The _____ larva is a distinguishing characteristic of mollusks and annelids.

    ANS: trochophore   DIF: I   OBJ: BPE 30-1.1

2. Annelids and mollusks share a larval stage called a(n) _____.

   ANS: trochophore   DIF: I   OBJ: BPE 30-1.1

3. The body cavity of mollusks develops entirely within the _____ tissue layer.

   ANS: mesoderm   DIF: I   OBJ: BPE 30-1.2

4. An organ known as the _____ is a rasping, tongue-like structure found in some mollusks.

   ANS: radula   DIF: I   OBJ: BPE 30-1.2

5. Constant beating of _____ in the mantle cavity of mollusks causes a continuous stream of water to pass over the gills.

   ANS: cilia   DIF: I   OBJ: BPE 30-1.3

6. A clam's shells close when the pair of _____ _____ contract.

   ANS: adductor muscles   DIF: I   OBJ: BPE 30-1.3

7. Structures in mollusks that function as simple kidneys are called _____.

   ANS: nephridia   DIF: I   OBJ: BPE 30-1.3

8. Water is drawn into the bodies of bivalves through tubes called _____.

   ANS: siphons   DIF: I   OBJ: BPE 30-1.4

9. A tongue-like scraping organ used by gastropods in feeding is called a(n) _____.

   ANS: radula   DIF: I   OBJ: BPE 30-1.4

10. The only living cephalopod that has retained its external shell is the _____.

    ANS: nautilus   DIF: I   OBJ: BPE 30-1.4

11. The foot of cephalopods has been divided into numerous _____.

    ANS: tentacles   DIF: I   OBJ: BPE 30-1.4

12. Snails and slugs belong to the molluscan class _____.

    ANS: Gastropoda   DIF: I   OBJ: BPE 30-1.4

13. Of the major classes of mollusks, the one that contains sessile filter-feeders is the

    _____.

    ANS: bivalves   DIF: I   OBJ: BPE 30-1.4

14. Bristles that exist along the sides of an annelid are called _____.

    ANS: setae   DIF: I   OBJ: BPE 30-2.1

15. A feature of annelids that allowed the development of specialized functions in different parts of the body is _____.

    ANS: segmentation   DIF: I   OBJ: BPE 30-2.1

16. Earthworms belong to the phylum _____.

    ANS: Annelida   DIF: I   OBJ: BPE 30-2.1

17. In one anterior segment of annelids there is a(n) _____
    _____, which is the brain of these organisms.

    ANS: cerebral ganglion   DIF: I   OBJ: BPE 30-2.2

18. Annelids were the first organisms to evolve a body plan based on repeated body

    _____.

    ANS: segments   DIF: I   OBJ: BPE 30-2.2

19. Paired _____ located on each segment increase traction as annelids crawl along.

    ANS: setae   DIF: I   OBJ: BPE 30-2.2

20. _____ are fleshy appendages that may aid in swimming and increase the surface area available for gas exchange.

    ANS: Parapodia   DIF: I   OBJ: BPE 30-2.2

21. The primary respiratory organ of annelids is _____.

    ANS: skin   DIF: I   OBJ: BPE 30-2.2

22. A muscular portion of the annelid digestive system that grinds up organic material is called the

    _____.

    ANS: gizzard   DIF: I   OBJ: BPE 30-2.3

23. The digestive system of annelids has evolved different regions that perform different _____.

   ANS: functions   DIF: I   OBJ: BPE 30-2.3

24. The _____ connects the mouth of the earthworm to its crop.

   ANS: esophagus   DIF: I   OBJ: BPE 30-2.3

25. Leeches are _____ annelids because they feed on the blood of other animals.

   ANS: parasitic   DIF: I   OBJ: BPE 30-2.4

26. The _____ are annelids that are marine and that have many setae and parapodia.

   ANS: polychaetes   DIF: I   OBJ: BPE 30-2.4

27. A mucus cocoon that will contain the eggs and sperm and allow development of an earthworm's offspring is produced by the _____.

   ANS: clitellum   DIF: I   OBJ: BPE 30-2.4

ESSAY

1. Describe the function of nephridia in mollusks.

   ANS:
   The movement of cilia draws coelomic fluid into the nephridia. Useful molecules in this fluid are reabsorbed into the mollusk's body tissues. Wastes are then passed out of the nephridia through a pore that leads into the mantle cavity. The wastes then leave the body.

   DIF: II   OBJ: BPE 30-1.3

2. Distinguish among the three classes of annelids.

   ANS:
   The phylum Annelida is divided into three classes: polychaetes, oligochaetes, and hirudineans. The polychaetes, believed to be the most ancient of the three classes, possess many setae and parapodia on each body segment. Oligochaetes have fewer setae per segment and completely lack parapodia. Hirudineans, the leeches, have neither setae nor parapodia.

   DIF: II   OBJ: BPE 30-2.4

CHAPTER 31—ARTHROPODS

TRUE/FALSE

1. Arthropods are evolutionarily related to annelids.

   ANS: T   DIF: I   OBJ: BPE 31-1.1

2. Arthropods share the property of segmentation with annelids.

   ANS: T   DIF: I   OBJ: BPE 31-1.1

3. Arthropods are divided into subphyla based on the size of the animals.

   ANS: F   DIF: I   OBJ: BPE 31-1.2

4. Because of the presence of fangs, spiders belong to the subphylum Chelicerata.

   ANS: T   DIF: I   OBJ: BPE 31-1.2

5. There are more arthropods on Earth than all of the other animals species combined.

   ANS: T   DIF: I   OBJ: BPE 31-1.2

6. Arthropods may have either an open or a closed circulatory system.

   ANS: F   DIF: I   OBJ: BPE 31-1.3

7. The bodies of arthropods are encased in a shell-like exoskeleton.

   ANS: T   DIF: I   OBJ: BPE 31-1.3

8. Most members of the phylum Arthropoda have open circulatory systems.

   ANS: F   DIF: I   OBJ: BPE 31-1.3

9. The eyes of arthropods are very similar to the eyes of humans.

   ANS: F   DIF: I   OBJ: BPE 31-1.3

10. Each body segment of an arthropod has a set of nephridia.

    ANS: F   DIF: I   OBJ: BPE 31-1.3

11. Arthropods have well developed lungs.

    ANS: F   DIF: I   OBJ: BPE 31-1.3

12. Terrestrial arthropods respire through a network of fine tubes called tracheae.

    ANS: T   DIF: I   OBJ: BPE 31-1.3

13. The exoskeleton of arthropods grows larger as the animal grows.

    ANS: F   DIF: I   OBJ: BPE 31-1.4

14. Arthropods grow through the process of accretion.

    ANS: F   DIF: I   OBJ: BPE 31-1.4

15. Arthropods grow a new exoskeleton periodically throughout their lives.

    ANS: T   DIF: I   OBJ: BPE 31-1.4

16. The anatomy of spiders and insects is essentially identical.

    ANS: F   DIF: I   OBJ: BPE 31-2.1

17. Horseshoe crabs belong to the same subphylum as spiders and mites.

    ANS: T   DIF: I   OBJ: BPE 31-2.1

18. Similar to insects, arachnids have three body parts.

    ANS: F   DIF: I   OBJ: BPE 31-2.1

19. Most arachnids are herbivores.

    ANS: F   DIF: I   OBJ: BPE 31-2.1

20. Arachnids have large, powerful jaws that enable them to capture and hold prey.

    ANS: F   DIF: I   OBJ: BPE 31-2.1

21. Pedipalps enable arachnids to capture and hold prey.

    ANS: T   DIF: I   OBJ: BPE 31-2.1

22. The pedipalps of the brown recluse spider are used to capture and hold prey.

    ANS: F   DIF: I   OBJ: BPE 31-2.2

23. Air enters the book lungs of the brown recluse spider through slits on the top side of the spider's abdomen.

    ANS: F   DIF: I   OBJ: BPE 31-2.2

24. The brown recluse spider gives birth to live young.

    ANS: F   DIF: I   OBJ: BPE 31-2.2

25. The head, thorax, and abdomen of a scorpion are fused into a single, unsegmented body.

    ANS: F   DIF: I   OBJ: BPE 31-2.3

26. Scorpions, spiders, and mites are evolutionarily linked by the presence of chelicerae and pedipalps.

    ANS: T   DIF: I   OBJ: BPE 31-2.3

27. Unlike spiders and scorpions, some mites are herbivorous.

    ANS: T   DIF: I   OBJ: BPE 31-2.3

28. All spider bites pose a greater health risk to humans than tick bites.

    ANS: F   DIF: I   OBJ: BPE 31-2.4

29. More than 50 percent of all named animal species are insects.

    ANS: T   DIF: I   OBJ: BPE 31-3.1

30. Insects were the first animals to evolve wings.

    ANS: T   DIF: I   OBJ: BPE 31-3.1

31. The bodies of all insects are made up of three sections.

    ANS: T   DIF: I   OBJ: BPE 31-3.1

32. All insects have wings.

    ANS: F   DIF: I   OBJ: BPE 31-3.1

33. In insects, the thorax houses the heart and the respiratory organs.

    ANS: F   DIF: I   OBJ: BPE 31-3.1

34. Butterflies undergo incomplete metamorphosis.

    ANS: F   DIF: I   OBJ: BPE 31-3.2

35. Incomplete metamorphosis is a reproductive strategy that reduces competition between parents and offspring.

    ANS: F   DIF: I   OBJ: BPE 31-3.2

36. A complete metamorphosis includes a pupa stage passed inside a chrysalis.

    ANS: T   DIF: I   OBJ: BPE 31-3.2

37. The immature offspring of insects that undergo complete metamorphosis are called nymphs.

    ANS: F   DIF: I   OBJ: BPE 31-3.2

38. The antennae of the grasshopper are sense organs used for both touch and smell.

    ANS: T   DIF: I   OBJ: BPE 31-3.3

39. The grasshopper only has one set of wings.

    ANS: F   DIF: I   OBJ: BPE 31-3.3

40. Except for the number of legs, millipedes and centipedes are basically the same in structure and diet.

    ANS: F   DIF: I   OBJ: BPE 31-3.4

41. Despite the high concentrations often found in the sea, copepods play a very small role in the ocean's food web.

    ANS: F   DIF: I   OBJ: BPE 31-4.1

42. Most crustaceans are aquatic.

    ANS: T   DIF: I   OBJ: BPE 31-4.1

43. Crustaceans range in size from microscopic forms to huge lobsters.

    ANS: T   DIF: I   OBJ: BPE 31-4.1

44. The swimmerets of lobsters and crayfish are attached to their thorax.

    ANS: F   DIF: I   OBJ: BPE 31-4.2

45. The walking legs of crustaceans are attached to both the thorax and the abdomen.

    ANS: T   DIF: I   OBJ: BPE 31-4.2

46. Unlike insects, decapods, like crayfish and lobsters, have two pair of antennae.

    ANS: T   DIF: I   OBJ: BPE 31-4.2

47. Swimmerets on the underside of the abdomen of crustaceans are only used for swimming.

    ANS: F   DIF: I   OBJ: BPE 31-4.2

MULTIPLE CHOICE

1. Both arthropods and annelids have
   a. jointed appendages.
   b. protective exoskeletons.
   c. hydrostatic skeletons.
   d. segmented bodies.

   ANS: D   DIF: I   OBJ: BPE 31-1.1

2. Like annelids, arthropods have
   a. a coelom.
   b. antennae.
   c. eyes.
   d. setae.

   ANS: A   DIF: I   OBJ: BPE 31-1.1

3. A similarity between annelids and arthropods is that they both have
   a. exoskeletons made of chitin.
   b. the ability to fly.
   c. segmented body patterns.
   d. well-developed lungs for respiration.

   ANS: C   DIF: I   OBJ: BPE 31-1.1

4. Evolutionary origin of arthropod circulatory system : mollusks ::
   a. annelid evolution : arthropods
   b. annelid evolution : trilobite
   c. evolution of arthropod segmentation : annelids
   d. evolution of arthropod segmentation : mollusks

   ANS: C
   (is from the)

   DIF: II   OBJ: BPE 31-1.1

5. Spiders, scorpions, and mites belong to the subphylum
   a. Arthropoda.
   b. Crustacea.
   c. Chordata.
   d. Chelicerata.

   ANS: D   DIF: I   OBJ: BPE 31-1.2

6. All of the following are arthropods *except*
   a. spiders.
   b. clam worms.
   c. crabs.
   d. centipedes.

   ANS: B   DIF: I   OBJ: BPE 31-1.2

7. arthropod exoskeleton : muscle attachment ::
   a. antennae : walking or flying
   b. mouthparts : flying or walking
   c. arthropod appendages : walking or chewing
   d. arthropod muscles : impeding water loss

   ANS: C
   (function in)

   DIF: II   OBJ: BPE 31-1.2

8. The exoskeleton of an insect
   a. does not have any muscles attached to it.
   b. is moved by muscles that are attached to the outside of the exoskeleton.
   c. may be modified into large pincers.
   d. is moved only by muscles attached to the wings.

   ANS: C   DIF: I   OBJ: BPE 31-1.3

9. Jointed appendages of arthropods may
   a. become specialized for particular functions.
   b. function in locomotion.
   c. function in feeding.
   d. All of the above

   ANS: D   DIF: I   OBJ: BPE 31-1.3

10. The exoskeleton of arthropods is made of a material called
    a. spongin.   c. chitin.
    b. mesoglea.   d. None of the above

    ANS: C   DIF: I   OBJ: BPE 31-1.3

11. The appendages of arthropods
    a. may serve as walking legs.   c. may be modified into large pincers.
    b. may be modified into antennae.   d. All of the above

    ANS: D   DIF: I   OBJ: BPE 31-1.3

12. Malpighian tubules in insects
    a. remove wastes.   c. carry Malpighian fluid.
    b. carry blood.   d. are important in respiration.

    ANS: A   DIF: I   OBJ: BPE 31-1.3

13. In what way are lobsters similar to spiders?
    a. They both have jointed appendages.   c. They both have segmented bodies.
    b. They both have exoskeletons.   d. All of the above

    ANS: D   DIF: I   OBJ: BPE 31-1.3

14. Characteristics of the arthropods include
    a. segmentation.
    b. a chitinous exoskeleton.
    c. jointed appendages.
    d. All of the above

    ANS: D   DIF: I   OBJ: BPE 31-1.3

15. In order for arthropods to grow larger, they must
    a. grow a new endoskeleton.
    b. grow a new exoskeleton.
    c. add to the old endoskeleton.
    d. add to the old exoskeleton.

    ANS: B   DIF: I   OBJ: BPE 31-1.4

16. Directly behind the chelicerae, spiders have a pair of appendages called the
    a. antennae.
    b. walking legs.
    c. pedipalps.
    d. spinnerets.

    ANS: C   DIF: I   OBJ: BPE 31-2.1

17. Spiders use silk to
    a. trap their prey.
    b. line their nests.
    c. encase captured prey.
    d. All of the above

    ANS: D   DIF: I   OBJ: BPE 31-2.1

18. The appendages that scorpions and spiders use to capture and handle their prey are called
    a. diptera.
    b. walking legs.
    c. palps.
    d. uropods.

    ANS: C   DIF: I   OBJ: BPE 31-2.1

19. Spiders typically have
    a. three body segments and six legs.
    b. two body segments and four legs.
    c. two body segments and eight legs.
    d. None of the above

    ANS: C   DIF: I   OBJ: BPE 31-2.1

20. The small nozzle-like structures used by spiders to produce silk are called
    a. mouthparts.
    b. pedipalps.
    c. spinnerets.
    d. silk nozzles.

    ANS: C   DIF: I   OBJ: BPE 31-2.1

21. spiders : subphylum Chelicerata ::
    a. scorpions : class Crustacea
    b. millipedes : class Crustacea
    c. insects : class Crustacea
    d. lobsters : class Crustacea

    ANS: D
    (belong to)

    DIF: II   OBJ: BPE 31-2.1

22. The excretory system of the brown recluse spider is composed of excretory units called
    a. digestive glands.
    c. Malpighian tubules.
    b. poison glands.
    d. cephalothorax.

    ANS: C   DIF: I   OBJ: BPE 31-2.2

23. In the brown recluse spider the heart is located in the
    a. abdomen.
    c. midgut.
    b. cephalothorax.
    d. chelicera.

    ANS: A   DIF: I   OBJ: BPE 31-2.2

24. arachnid's second pair of appendages : pedipalps ::
    a. arachnid's legs : pincers
    b. arachnid's first pair of appendages : walking legs
    c. spider's first pair of appendages : chelicerae
    d. spider's fangs : pedipalps

    ANS: C
    (use)

    DIF: II   OBJ: BPE 31-2.2

25. Spiders, scorpions, and ticks belong to the class
    a. Isoptera.
    c. Chordata.
    b. Crustacea.
    d. Arachnida.

    ANS: D   DIF: I   OBJ: BPE 31-2.3

26. Lyme disease is transmitted through the bite of a
    a. house mite.
    c. black-widow spider.
    b. deer tick.
    d. scorpion.

    ANS: B   DIF: I   OBJ: BPE 31-2.4

27. Some allergies in humans have been linked to
    a. house mites.
    c. black-widow spiders.
    b. deer ticks.
    d. scorpions.

    ANS: A   DIF: I   OBJ: BPE 31-2.4

28. Most insects
    a. have two pairs of wings and two pairs of legs.
    b. have one set of wings and six pairs of legs.
    c. cannot fly.
    d. have two wings and three pairs of legs.

    ANS: D   DIF: I   OBJ: BPE 31-3.1

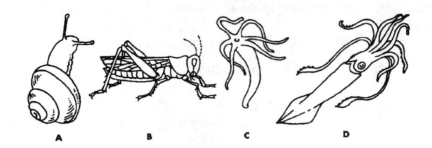

A B C D

29. Refer to the illustration above. Which of the organisms in the diagrams has a chitinous exoskeleton?
   a. organism A
   b. organism B
   c. organism C
   d. organism D

   ANS: B   DIF: II   OBJ: BPE 31-3.1

30. An insect's caste is determined by
   a. its grade.
   b. how much it can eat in its lifetime.
   c. its genes.
   d. its size.

   ANS: C   DIF: I   OBJ: BPE 31-3.1

31. In incomplete metamorphosis, the young insect hatches from the egg as a(n)
   a. adolescent.
   b. chrysalis.
   c. caterpillar.
   d. nymph.

   ANS: D   DIF: I   OBJ: BPE 31-3.2

Life Cycle of a Butterfly

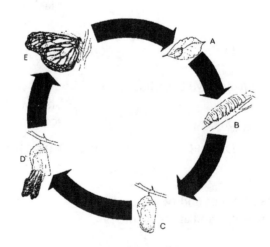

32. Refer to the illustration above. The life cycle shown is an example of
   a. direct development.
   b. complete metamorphosis.
   c. seasonal development.
   d. incomplete metamorphosis.

   ANS: B   DIF: II   OBJ: BPE 31-3.2

Biology: Principles and Explorations

33. Refer to the illustration above. The developmental stage shown in diagram C is known as the
    a. larva.
    c. nymph.
    b. caterpillar.
    d. chrysalis.

    ANS: D   DIF: II   OBJ: BPE 31-3.2

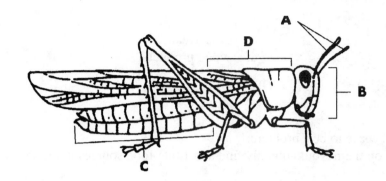

34. Refer to the illustration above. Mandibles are attached to the structure labeled
    a. A.
    c. C.
    b. B.
    d. D.

    ANS: B   DIF: II   OBJ: BPE 31-3.3

35. Refer to the illustration above. The structure labeled C is called the
    a. diptera.
    c. boll.
    b. thorax.
    d. abdomen.

    ANS: D   DIF: II   OBJ: BPE 31-3.3

36. Refer to the illustration above. The structure labeled D is called the
    a. abdomen.
    c. thorax.
    b. orthopterus.
    d. cuticle.

    ANS: C   DIF: II   OBJ: BPE 31-3.3

37. Refer to the illustration above. The structures labeled A are
    a. similar to structures found on spiders.
    c. specialized for sensing the environment.
    b. used to take in air and water.
    d. reproductive organs.

    ANS: C   DIF: II   OBJ: BPE 31-3.3

38. Centipedes
    a. have one pair of legs per segment and eat decaying matter.
    b. have two pairs of legs per segment and are predators.
    c. have two pairs of legs per segment and eat decaying matter.
    d. have one pair of legs per segment and are predators.

    ANS: D   DIF: I   OBJ: BPE 31-3.4

39. The name *millipede* means
   a. "thousand feet."
   b. "hundred feet."
   c. "one foot per millimeter."
   d. None of the above

   ANS: A   DIF: I   OBJ: BPE 31-3.4

40. Millipedes feed mainly on
   a. decayed plants.
   b. other insects.
   c. crustaceans.
   d. wood products.

   ANS: A   DIF: I   OBJ: BPE 31-3.4

41. If all copepods died,
   a. bubonic plague would cease to be a problem.
   b. predators that depend on them would quickly find substitute food sources in the sea and fresh water.
   c. our sources of food from the ocean would disappear.
   d. nothing would change.

   ANS: C   DIF: I   OBJ: BPE 31-4.1

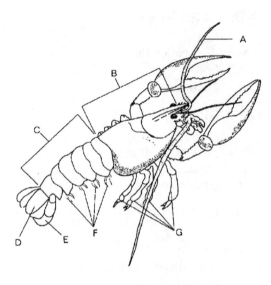

42. Refer to the illustration above. "A flattened, paddle-like appendage" best describes the structure labeled
   a. D.
   b. E.
   c. F.
   d. G.

   ANS: B   DIF: II   OBJ: BPE 31-4.2

43. Refer to the illustration above. The structure labeled C is the
   a. cephalothorax.
   b. tail.
   c. abdomen.
   d. gill case.

   ANS: C   DIF: II   OBJ: BPE 31-4.2

44. Refer to the illustration above. The structure labeled B is covered on top by a shield called the
   a. nauplius.
   b. carapace.
   c. thorax.
   d. ossicle.

   ANS: B   DIF: II   OBJ: BPE 31-4.2

45. Refer to the illustration above. The organism shown is a(n)
   a. insect.
   b. chelicerate.
   c. crustacean.
   d. nymph.

   ANS: C   DIF: II   OBJ: BPE 31-4.2

46. Crabs, lobsters, shrimp, and barnacles are members of the subphylum
   a. Diptera.
   b. Centipeda.
   c. Crustacea.
   d. Arachnida.

   ANS: C   DIF: I   OBJ: BPE 31-4.2

47. Shrimps, lobsters, and crabs are examples of
   a. uropods.
   b. copepods.
   c. hemipods.
   d. decapods.

   ANS: D   DIF: I   OBJ: BPE 31-4.2

48. crayfish : swimmerets for swimming and reproduction ::
   a. lobsters : uropods for reproduction
   b. shrimp : telson for chewing
   c. crabs : telson for eating
   d. crustaceans : gills for breathing

   ANS: D
   (use)

   DIF: II   OBJ: BPE 31-4.2

COMPLETION

1. Arthropods were the first animals to have _____ appendages.

   ANS: jointed   DIF: I   OBJ: BPE 31-1.1

2. The first animals with eyes capable of forming images were the _____.

   ANS: trilobites   DIF: I   OBJ: BPE 31-1.1

3. Arthropods have an external skeleton called a(n) _____.

   ANS: exoskeleton   DIF: I   OBJ: BPE 31-1.2

4. Arthropods such as centipedes that have jaws are called _____.

   ANS: mandibulates   DIF: I   OBJ: BPE 31-1.2

5. A lobster is a member of the phylum _____.

    ANS: Arthropoda   DIF: I   OBJ: BPE 31-1.2

Respiratory Structure of Some Arthropods

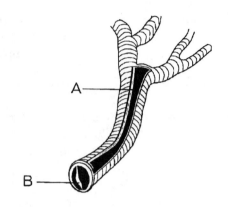

6. Refer to the illustration above. Structure B is called a(n) _____.

    ANS: spiracle   DIF: II   OBJ: BPE 31-1.3

7. Refer to the illustration above. Air from the outside passes into the insect through structure A, which is known as a(n) _____.

    ANS: trachea   DIF: II   OBJ: BPE 31-3.3

8. Insects, millipedes, and centipedes belong to the subphylum _____.

    ANS: Uniramia   DIF: I   OBJ: BPE 31-1.3

9. Bees, spiders, shrimp, and lobsters are all members of the phylum _____.

    ANS: Arthropoda   DIF: I   OBJ: BPE 31-1.3

10. The process whereby arthropods shed and discard their exoskeletons periodically is called molting or _____.

    ANS: ecdysis   DIF: I   OBJ: BPE 31-1.4

11. An arthropod sheds its exoskeleton through the process of _____ which is triggered by the release of specific hormones.

    ANS: molting   DIF: I   OBJ: BPE 31-1.4

12. Many spiders are major _____ of insect pests.

    ANS: predators   DIF: I   OBJ: BPE 31-2.1

13. The mouthparts of the members of the subphylum Chelicerata are modified into
    _____ or pincers.

    ANS: fangs   DIF: I   OBJ: BPE 31-2.1

14. The arachnid body is made up of a(n) _____ and an abdomen.

    ANS: cephalothorax   DIF: I   OBJ: BPE 31-2.1

15. The structures at the end of a spider's abdomen that direct the flow of silk from silk-producing
    glands are called _____.

    ANS: spinnerets   DIF: I   OBJ: BPE 31-2.1

16. Deer ticks may carry the virus that causes _____ _____.

    ANS: Lyme disease   DIF: I   OBJ: BPE 31-2.3

17. Unlike the bite of a spider, the bite of some ticks can transmit _____.

    ANS: disease   DIF: I   OBJ: BPE 31-2.4

18. The mouthparts of insects are _____ for the particular kind of food that the
    insect eats.

    ANS: specialized   DIF: I   OBJ: BPE 31-3.1

19. All insects have _____ pairs of walking legs.

    ANS: three   DIF: I   OBJ: BPE 31-3.1

20. The _____ of different insect species are adapted for different functions.

    ANS: mouthparts   DIF: I   OBJ: BPE 31-3.1

21. The insect body plan is made up of _____ body sections.

    ANS: three   DIF: I   OBJ: BPE 31-3.1

22. Insects that undergo _____ metamorphosis go through a larval and pupal
    stage.

    ANS: complete   DIF: I   OBJ: BPE 31-3.2

23. The name _____ means "hundred feet."

    ANS: centipede   DIF: I   OBJ: BPE 31-3.4

24. _____ are very important crustaceans that link the ocean's photosynthetic li
to the rest of the ocean's food web.

ANS: Copepods DIF: I OBJ: BPE 31-4.1

25. Crustaceans breathe with the aid of _____.

ANS: gills DIF: I OBJ: BPE 31-4.1

26. _____ are the only arthropods with two pairs of antennae.

ANS: Crustaceans DIF: I OBJ: BPE 31-4.2

27. Some decapods have a tail spine called a(n) _____.

ANS: telson DIF: I OBJ: BPE 31-4.2

ESSAY

1. Insects have a relatively hard outer covering, called an exoskeleton, that helps protect against excessive water loss and provides structural support. As an insect grows, it periodically sheds its exoskeleton and replaces it with a larger exoskeleton. This process is called molting. Molting is regulated by at least two hormones. One of these, molting hormone, determines when a molt occurs. A sudden, large production of molting hormone will induce an insect to molt. A second hormone, juvenile hormone, determines the nature of a molt. When juvenile hormone levels are high, an insect molts into another juvenile, or larval, stage. When juvenile hormone levels are low, an insect molts into a pupa or an adult. In the space below, draw a graph showing relative levels of molting and juvenile hormones over the lifespan of an insect that hatches from an egg, has four larval molts, a pupal stage, and an adult stage. Indicate on the time axis when molts occur.

ANS:
The students' graphs should look similar to the following:

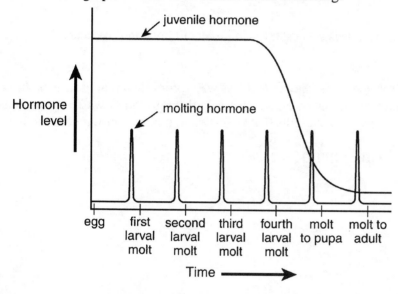

DIF: III   OBJ: BPE 31-1.4

2. Describe the uses of spider silk.

ANS:
Spider silk is used as a safety line, to protect the young, to line burrows, and to trap food.

DIF: II   OBJ: BPE 31-2.1

3. What is the evolutionary advantage of complete metamorphosis in insects?

ANS:
During development, the larva exploits different habitats and food sources than the adult does. Competition between the larva and the adult is eliminated, thus increasing the chance for survival in each stage of the insect life cycle.

DIF: II   OBJ: BPE 31-3.2

4. If a mutation occurred during a crustacean's embryonic development that prevented it from molting, how might the crustacean be affected?

ANS:
Because crustaceans must molt in order to grow, the crustacean would be unable to grow larger than the size it attained before emerging from the egg.

DIF: II   OBJ: BPE 31-4.2

5. Why have crustaceans been less successful than insects in invading the land?

ANS:
The exoskeleton of crustaceans is heavier and less waterproof than that of insects. Insects have efficient excretory and water-balance organs that help them get rid of wastes while conserving water. In addition, crustaceans have gills that are efficient underwater but collapse in air.

DIF: II   OBJ: BPE 31-4.2

TRUE/FALSE

1. An animal whose mouth develops from or near the blastopore is called a protostome.

   ANS: T   DIF: I   OBJ: BPE 32-1.1

2. An animal whose mouth develops from or near the blastopore is called a deuterostome.

   ANS: F   DIF: I   OBJ: BPE 32-1.1

3. Sea stars and tunicates are examples of deuterostomes.

   ANS: T   DIF: I   OBJ: BPE 32-1.1

4. Chordates and echinoderms have a common ancestor.

   ANS: T   DIF: I   OBJ: BPE 32-1.1

5. The hard, spiny skin of an echinoderm is called an exoskeleton.

   ANS: F   DIF: I   OBJ: BPE 32-1.2

6. All echinoderms except the sand dollar display a five-part radial symmetry.

   ANS: F   DIF: I   OBJ: BPE 32-1.2

7. The adult form of all echinoderms exhibits radial symmetry.

   ANS: T   DIF: I   OBJ: BPE 32-1.2

8. None of the echinoderms living in the oceans today are sessile.

   ANS: F   DIF: I   OBJ: BPE 32-1.2

9. In some echinoderms, respiration and waste removal are performed by skin gills.

   ANS: T   DIF: I   OBJ: BPE 32-1.2

10. Sea stars are carnivores and are among the most important predators in many marine ecosystems.

    ANS: T   DIF: I   OBJ: BPE 32-1.2

11. In addition to radial symmetry, echinoderms have a water-vascular system.

    ANS: T   DIF: I   OBJ: BPE 32-1.2

12. The water-vascular system of a sea star function in defense.

    ANS: F   DIF: I   OBJ: BPE 32-1.3

13. Water enters and leaves a sea star through its central disk.

    ANS: F   DIF: I   OBJ: BPE 32-1.3

14. The madreporite functions like a sieve for the water vascular system filtering out large particles.

    ANS: T   DIF: I   OBJ: BPE 32-1.3

15. Chordates are characterized by an exoskeleton that encases the body.

    ANS: F   DIF: I   OBJ: BPE 32-2.1

16. All chordates have a ventral notochord during some stage of embryonic development.

    ANS: F   DIF: I   OBJ: BPE 32-2.1

17. All chordates have a postanal tail at some time in their lives.

    ANS: T   DIF: I   OBJ: BPE 32-2.1

18. All chordates are classified as vertebrates.

    ANS: F   DIF: I   OBJ: BPE 32-2.1

19. Invertebrate chordates do not have notochords.

    ANS: F   DIF: I   OBJ: BPE 32-2.2

20. Tunicates keep the nerve cord, notochord, and postanal tail throughout their lives.

    ANS: F   DIF: I   OBJ: BPE 32-2.3

21. Like tunicates, lancelets are hermaphroditic.

    ANS: F   DIF: I   OBJ: BPE 32-2.3

22. The adult forms of both tunicates and lancelets are sessile.

    ANS: F   DIF: I   OBJ: BPE 32-2.3

MULTIPLE CHOICE

1. In protostomes,
    a. the developmental fate of each cell is determined when the cell first appears.
    b. the initial depression that starts gastrulation becomes the mouth of the adult.
    c. molecules within the egg determine which cells will form which tissues.
    d. All of the above

    ANS: D   DIF: I   OBJ: BPE 32-1.1

2. Embryological evidence suggests that the echinoderms are closely related to the
    a. vertebrates.   c. annelids.
    b. arthropods.   d. arachnids.

    ANS: A   DIF: I   OBJ: BPE 32-1.1

3. In echinoderms and chordates, all the cells of the early embryo
    a. are controlled by molecules within the egg.
    b. form the "first mouth."
    c. fall into four different categories.
    d. are identical.

    ANS: D   DIF: I   OBJ: BPE 32-1.1

4. Echinoderms
    a. are radially symmetrical as larvae and as adults.
    b. have an exoskeleton as adults.
    c. are bilaterally symmetrical as larvae and radially symmetrical as adults.
    d. are radially symmetrical as larvae and bilaterally symmetrical as adults.

    ANS: C   DIF: I   OBJ: BPE 32-1.2

5. The first organisms to develop a hardened endoskeleton were the
    a. echinoderms.   c. arthropods.
    b. annelids.   d. chordates.

    ANS: A   DIF: I   OBJ: BPE 32-1.2

6. The symmetry exhibited by echinoderms is
    a. bilateral.   c. radial.
    b. spherical.   d. mirror image.

    ANS: C   DIF: I   OBJ: BPE 32-1.2

7. Which of the following are echinoderms?
    a. sea stars   c. sea urchins
    b. sand dollars   d. All of the above

    ANS: D   DIF: I   OBJ: BPE 32-1.2

8. The skeleton of an echinoderm is composed of individual plates called
   a. ocelli.
   b. ossicles.
   c. odonata.
   d. isopods.

   ANS: B   DIF: I   OBJ: BPE 32-1.2

9. Which of the following are sessile echinoderms?
   a. feather stars
   b. sand dollars
   c. sea urchins
   d. sea lilies

   ANS: D   DIF: I   OBJ: BPE 32-1.2

10. sea cucumbers : a fused skeleton ::
    a. sea urchins : a five-part body plan
    b. sea urchins : distinct arms
    c. sand dollars : endoskeletons
    d. sea urchins : endoskeletons

    ANS: B
    (lack)

    DIF: II   OBJ: BPE 32-1.2

11. tunicates : in shallow- and deep-water environments
    a. lancelets : buried in mud or sand
    b. lancelets : swimming near the water's surface
    c. tentacles : in sea urchin mouths
    d. ossicles : in lancelets

    ANS: A
    (are found)

    DIF: II   OBJ: BPE 32-1.2

12. Interconnected canals and hollow tube feet work together in sea star's
    a. digestive system.
    b. respiratory system.
    c. circulatory system.
    d. water vascular system.

    ANS: D   DIF: I   OBJ: BPE 32-1.3

13. Each tube foot is connected to a water-filled sac called a(n)
    a. madreporite.
    b. ampulla.
    c. ring canal.
    d. central disk.

    ANS: B   DIF: I   OBJ: BPE 32-1.3

14. All chordates have a supportive rod along their back called the
    a. spinal cord.
    b. pharynx.
    c. notochord.
    d. None of the above

    ANS: C   DIF: I   OBJ: BPE 32-2.1

15. A characteristic shared by all chordates is
    a. a dorsal hollow nerve cord.   c. pharyngeal gill slits.
    b. a notochord.   d. All of the above

    ANS: D   DIF: I   OBJ: BPE 32-2.1

16. The subphylum Vertebrata includes all of the following *except*
    a. fish.   c. reptiles.
    b. lancelets.   d. birds.

    ANS: B   DIF: I   OBJ: BPE 32-2.1

17. Lancelets
    a. are animals that live near the ocean surface.
    b. filter food from water that enters the mouth.
    c. have chordate features only in the larvae stage.
    d. are the first animals that evolved backbones.

    ANS: B   DIF: I   OBJ: BPE 32-2.3

18. Vertebrates, tunicates, and lancelets
    a. are all members of the phylum Chordata.   c. are all marine fish.
    b. all have a backbone in the adult stage.   d. are all terrestrial heterotrophs.

    ANS: A   DIF: I   OBJ: BPE 32-2.3

The tunicates are chordates that lack a vertebral column. They are classified in the subphylum Urochordata. The adult forms of tunicates bear little resemblance to vertebrates and the only major chordate characteristic they retain is the presence of pharyngeal gill slits. Most tunicate larvae, however, have all four chordate characteristics, pharyngeal gill slits, a notochord, a dorsal, hollow nerve cord, and a tail. The diagrams below illustrate the larval and adult forms of a tunicate.

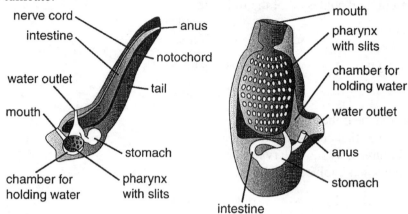

19. Some scientists have hypothesized that the first vertebrates, which were fish, may have evolved from an ancestral tunicate that became sexually mature in the larval form. They suggest that these reproducing larvae were successful and natural selection reinforced the absence of metamorphosis to the adult. Which of the following statements does not support the hypothesis that vertebrates evolved from a sexually mature larval tunicate?
    a. Many invertebrates, tunicate larvae and adults, and the earliest vertebrates are or were filter feeders.
    b. Adult tunicates are sessile and larval tunicates are free-swimming.
    c. The vertebral column of adult vertebrates replaces the notochord present in embryonic vertebrates
    d. Some living urochordates exist only as free-swimming larvae.

    ANS: A   DIF: II   OBJ: BPE 32-2.3

COMPLETION

1. In _____, molecules within the egg usually determine which cells will form which tissues.

    ANS: protostomes   DIF: I   OBJ: BPE 32-1.1

2. In _____, genes within the cells control development, and the first opening in the embryo becomes the anus of the adult.

    ANS: deuterostomes   DIF: I   OBJ: BPE 32-1.1

3. A(n) _____ is an opening to the outside of a gastrula.

   ANS: blastopore   DIF: I   OBJ: BPE 32-1.1

4. All chordates are _____ due to their pattern of early development.

   ANS: deuterostomes   DIF: I   OBJ: BPE 32-1.1

5. The two traits that both chordates and echinoderms share are gene-controlled development and
   _____.

   ANS: endoskeletons   DIF: I   OBJ: BPE 32-1.2

6. Embryological evidence suggests that the echinoderms are closely related to the
   _____.

   ANS: vertebrates   DIF: I   OBJ: BPE 32-1.2

7. Refer to the illustration above. The animals shown are members of the phylum
   _____.

   ANS: Echinodermata   DIF: II   OBJ: BPE 32-1.2

8. Sea cucumbers belong to the phylum _____.

   ANS: Echinodermata   DIF: I   OBJ: BPE 32-1.2

9. A sand dollar is a member of the phylum _____.

   ANS: Echinodermata   DIF: II   OBJ: BPE 32-1.2

10. A fluid-filled system of interconnected internal canals and tube feet in echinoderms is called the
    _____ _____ system.

    ANS: water vascular   DIF: I   OBJ: BPE 32-1.3

11. When water is pumped from an ampulla into a tube foot, the foot _____ outward.

 ANS: expands DIF: I OBJ: BPE 32-1.3

12. During the development of a chordate embryo, a(n) _____ develops along the back of the embryo.

 ANS: notochord DIF: I OBJ: BPE 32-2.1

13. Chordates have a series of _____ _____ that develop in the wall of pharynx.

 ANS: pharyngeal slits DIF: I OBJ: BPE 32-2.1

14. Tunicates and lancelets are examples of _____ chordates.

 ANS: invertebrate DIF: I OBJ: BPE 32-2.2

15. Invertebrate chordates are chordates that lack _____.

 ANS: backbones DIF: I OBJ: BPE 32-2.2

16. Unlike lancelets, tunicates are _____.

 ANS: hermaphrodites DIF: I OBJ: BPE 32-2.3

17. Both tunicates and lancelets are _____ feeders in their adult forms.

 ANS: filter DIF: I OBJ: BPE 32-2.3

ESSAY

1. Using examples, distinguish between protostomes and deuterostomes.

 ANS:
 Protostomes are animals (including acoelomates, pseudocoelomates, annelids, mollusks, and arthropods) in which the blastopore of the embryo becomes the mouth of the organism. Another pattern of embryonic development characterizes coelomates that evolved after the arthropods. In these animals, the anus develops from or near the blastopore. This pattern of development is see in echinoderms and chordates.

 DIF: II OBJ: BPE 32-1.1

2. The phylum Chordata is divided into three subphyla. Briefly describe each of these groups of organisms, and explain why animals in each group are considered chordates.

ANS:
All these subphyla exhibit the four typical chordate features (notochord, dorsal hollow nerve cord, postanal tail, and pharyngeal gill slits) at some time during their life cycle. The Urochordata (tunicates) have larvae that show these characteristics, but the adults do not. Members of Cephalochordata show the features as adults. Members of the subphylum Vertebrata have all the stages throughout the life cycle, but are distinguished from members of the other two subphyla by the possession of a vertebral column (backbone) as well.

DIF: II   OBJ: BPE 32-2.1

3. While lancelets and humans do not resemble each other in appearance, they are both members of the same phylum. Why?

ANS:
Lancelets and humans are chordates. At some time in their life, all chordates have a dorsal hollow nerve chord, a notochord, a postanal tail, and slits in the pharynx that connect the pharynx to the outside.

DIF: II   OBJ: BPE 32-2.3

4. Compare and contrast tunicates and lancelets. How are they alike and how are they different from vertebrates?

ANS:
Tunicates and lancelets are both members of the phylum Chordata, which also includes vertebrates. The tunicates lack a notochord in their adult stage but possess one in their free-swimming, larval state. Tunicates and lancelets differ from vertebrates in several ways. Tunicates are sessile, filter-feeding marine animals and have a plantlike substance, cellulose, in their outer body layer. Tunicates lose the ability to swim once they become adults, and they maintain only one chordate feature, the pharyngeal slit. Lancelets are tiny marine animals that live in shallow water. Lancelets can swim, but they spend most of their time burrowed in the mud or sand. Lancelets retain all four chordate features throughout their lifetime.

DIF: II   OBJ: BPE 32-2.3

5. Why are tunicates classified in the phylum Chordata?

ANS:
Tunicate larvae have a body cavity, nerve cord, and notochord. These are all characteristics possessed by chordates.

DIF: II   OBJ: BPE 32-2.3

TRUE/FALSE

1. All vertebrates have backbones.

    ANS: T   DIF: I   OBJ: BPE 33-1.1

2. All animals have bony skulls.

    ANS: F   DIF: I   OBJ: BPE 33-1.1

3. Both vertebrates and invertebrates have chambered hearts.

    ANS: F   DIF: I   OBJ: BPE 33-1.1

4. Vertebrates have true coeloms and open circulatory systems.

    ANS: F   DIF: I   OBJ: BPE 33-1.1

5. All vertebrates carry out sexual reproduction.

    ANS: T   DIF: I   OBJ: BPE 33-1.1

6. Small, jawed fishes are the first vertebrates for which there is fossil evidence.

    ANS: F   DIF: I   OBJ: BPE 33-1.2

7. The first fishes that appeared in the ancient seas were jawless and toothless.

    ANS: T   DIF: I   OBJ: BPE 33-1.2

8. Jawless fishes were the first vertebrates to evolve.

    ANS: T   DIF: I   OBJ: BPE 33-1.2

9. The first fishes to develop jaws were called spiny fishes and were members of the class Acanthodia.

    ANS: T   DIF: I   OBJ: BPE 33-1.2

10. Sharks and rays have skeletons of bone.

    ANS: F   DIF: I   OBJ: BPE 33-1.2

11. Both sharks and bony fishes evolved in the ancient seas.

    ANS: F   DIF: I   OBJ: BPE 33-1.2

12. Lobe-finned fishes were the ancestors of amphibians.

   ANS: T   DIF: I   OBJ: BPE 33-1.3

13. Fishes and amphibians first appeared on the Earth during the Cambrian period, about 550 million years ago.

   ANS: F   DIF: I   OBJ: BPE 33-1.3

14. A land animal needs stronger bones and muscles than an aquatic animal does because of the increased pull of gravity on terrestrial body structures.

   ANS: T   DIF: I   OBJ: BPE 33-1.4

15. A fish's gills would collapse on land.

   ANS: T   DIF: I   OBJ: BPE 33-1.4

16. Amphibians were the first animals to evolve lungs for gas exchange.

   ANS: T   DIF: I   OBJ: BPE 33-1.4

17. Because of their aquatic nature, frogs and fish have the same kinds of hearts.

   ANS: F   DIF: I   OBJ: BPE 33-1.4

18. Birds, reptiles, and mammals minimize water loss by means of their watertight skins.

   ANS: T   DIF: I   OBJ: BPE 33-2.1

19. Waterproof skin is a reptilian adaptation to life on land.

   ANS: T   DIF: I   OBJ: BPE 33-2.1

20. Lizards appeared in the late Permian period, about 250 million years ago.

   ANS: T   DIF: I   OBJ: BPE 33-2.1

21. The Jurassic period is often referred to as "the golden age of dinosaurs."

   ANS: T   DIF: I   OBJ: BPE 33-2.1

22. Crocodiles have undergone enormous changes since they first appeared 200 million years ago.

   ANS: F   DIF: I   OBJ: BPE 33-2.1

23. The dominant land animals from the middle of the Permian era until the middle of the Triassic era were the therapsids.

    ANS: F   DIF: I   OBJ: BPE 33-2.1

24. Animals in which body temperature is largely determined by the environment are called endothermic.

    ANS: F   DIF: I   OBJ: BPE 33-2.2

25. Reptiles are endotherms.

    ANS: F   DIF: I   OBJ: BPE 33-2.2

26. Though most dinosaurs became extinct 65 million years ago, a few species still live in remote areas.

    ANS: F   DIF: I   OBJ: BPE 33-2.3

27. Mammals have been the dominant land animals on Earth for over 500 million years.

    ANS: F   DIF: I   OBJ: BPE 33-2.3

28. Some skeletons of fossil birds have teeth.

    ANS: T   DIF: I   OBJ: BPE 33-2.4

29. Modern birds have teeth.

    ANS: F   DIF: I   OBJ: BPE 33-2.4

MULTIPLE CHOICE

1. All vertebrates are characterized by
   a. radial symmetry.
   b. bilateral symmetry.
   c. open circulatory system.
   d. exoskeleton.

   ANS: B   DIF: I   OBJ: BPE 33-1.1

2. The backbone of vertebrates provides support and protects the
   a. ventral nerve cord.
   b. backbone.
   c. dorsal nerve cord.
   d. heart.

   ANS: C   DIF: I   OBJ: BPE 33-1.1

3. The internal skeleton of vertebrates
   a. allows vertebrates to grow larger than invertebrates.
   b. plays an important role in the digestive system.
   c. allows vertebrates to carry out asexual reproduction.
   d. plays an important role in mate selection.

   ANS: A   DIF: I   OBJ: BPE 33-1.1

4. The first stage in the evolution of the animal body occurred
   a. over millions of years in the sea.
   b. relatively recently, once organisms emerged from the sea.
   c. among free-floating algae in ancient seas.
   d. on dry land, several hundred million years ago.

   ANS: A   DIF: I   OBJ: BPE 33-1.2

5. The first fishes to appear in the seas were members of the class
   a. Vertebrata.   c. Placodermii.
   b. Chondrichthyes.   d. Agnatha.

   ANS: D   DIF: I   OBJ: BPE 33-1.2

6. The first vertebrates
   a. were jawless fishes.
   b. had thick, bony plates that covered their bodies.
   c. had no well-developed vertebral column.
   d. All of the above

   ANS: D   DIF: I   OBJ: BPE 33-1.2

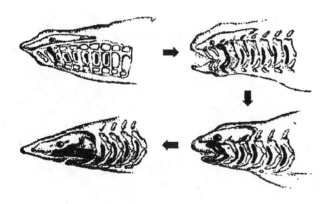

7. Refer to the illustration above. The diagrams show
   a. how a lamprey feeds.   c. the evolution of jaws.
   b. the evolution of gills.   d. the evolution of bony skeletons.

   ANS: C   DIF: II   OBJ: BPE 33-1.2

8. Jaws probably evolved from the
   a. pectoral fins of jawless fishes.
   b. gills slits of sharks and rays.
   c. paired pelvic fins of jawless fishes.
   d. gill arches of jawless fishes.

   ANS: D   DIF: I   OBJ: BPE 33-1.2

9. The word *agnatha* means
   a. "bony fish."
   b. "without jaws."
   c. "without vertebral column."
   d. "early fish."

   ANS: B   DIF: I   OBJ: BPE 33-1.2

10. The earliest jawed fishes were the
    a. acanthodians.
    b. Agnathans.
    c. chondrichthyes.
    d. placoderms.

    ANS: A   DIF: I   OBJ: BPE 33-1.2

11. placoderms : armor ::
    a. bony fishes : cartilaginous skeleton
    b. sharks : no teeth
    c. lampreys : jaws
    d. sharks and bony fishes : streamlined bodies

    ANS: D
    (have)

    DIF: II   OBJ: BPE 33-1.2

12. bony fishes : stronger muscles ::
    a. bony fishes : lungs
    b. sharks : bony skeleton
    c. sharks : ray fins
    d. sharks : rows of teeth

    ANS: D
    (have)

    DIF: II   OBJ: BPE 33-1.2

13. Amphibians probably evolved from
    a. ruby-throated hummingbirds.
    b. lobed-finned fishes.
    c. crested lizards.
    d. therapsids.

    ANS: B   DIF: I   OBJ: BPE 33-1.3

14. Some type of skeletal support
    a. exists in all animals, whether they are aquatic or terrestrial.
    b. was necessary for animals to leave aquatic environments.
    c. is present primarily in land vertebrates.
    d. evolved first in reptiles.

    ANS: B   DIF: I   OBJ: BPE 33-1.4

15. The earliest known land vertebrate
    a. was a coelacanth.
    b. was an amphibian.
    c. lacked bones in its legs.
    d. was a now-extinct reptile.

    ANS: B   DIF: I   OBJ: BPE 33-1.4

16. Amphibians must have thin, moist skin
    a. to allow easier gas exchange.
    b. because thin, moist skin cannot be eaten by a predator.
    c. so that they can slip easily into tight places.
    d. to resist water loss.

    ANS: A   DIF: I   OBJ: BPE 33-1.4

17. Gas exchange is necessary in all animals because
    a. oxygen is needed to break down food molecules.
    b. carbon dioxide is a waste product that must be eliminated.
    c. there is more oxygen in the environment than in animal bodies.
    d. All of the above

    ANS: D   DIF: I   OBJ: BPE 33-1.4

18. In amphibians, gases are exchanged through lung breathing and through the
    a. heart.
    b. air bladder.
    c. tracheids.
    d. skin.

    ANS: D   DIF: I   OBJ: BPE 33-1.4

19. All of the following evolved from early reptiles *except*
    a. fish.
    b. birds.
    c. dinosaurs.
    d. mammals.

    ANS: A   DIF: I   OBJ: BPE 33-2.1

20. Therapsids replaced amphibians as the dominant vertebrate form by the end of the
    a. Permian.
    b. Pennsylvanian.
    c. Cretaceous.
    d. Devonian.

    ANS: A   DIF: I   OBJ: BPE 33-2.1

21. Dinosaurs dominated over all other land vertebrates for approximately
    a. 1.5 million years.
    b. 15 million years.
    c. 150 million years.
    d. 1500 million years.

    ANS: C   DIF: I   OBJ: BPE 33-2.1

22. Dinosaurs were more successful than their competitors, thecodonts, because dinosaurs were
    a. larger.
    b. faster.
    c. smaller.
    d. slower.

    ANS: B   DIF: I   OBJ: BPE 33-2.1

23. Ectothermic animals
    a. produce their own heat.
    b. are found among mammals.
    c. absorb heat from their environment.
    d. are characterized by the presence of feathers.

    ANS: C   DIF: I   OBJ: BPE 33-2.2

24. Endothermic animals
    a. have bodies whose metabolisms maintain a constant internal temperature.
    b. have body temperatures that are not stable.
    c. are found among reptiles.
    d. are cold-blooded.

    ANS: A   DIF: I   OBJ: BPE 33-2.2

25. Early reptiles evolved into
    a. lizards.   c. mammals.
    b. birds.   d. All of the above

    ANS: D   DIF: I   OBJ: BPE 33-2.3

26. The most ancient surviving group of reptiles are the
    a. rhynchocephalians.   c. lizards.
    b. snakes.   d. turtles.

    ANS: D   DIF: I   OBJ: BPE 33-2.3

27. Mammals arose from early reptiles called
    a. mesosaurs.   c. therapsids.
    b. ichthyosaurs.   d. pterosaurs.

    ANS: C   DIF: I   OBJ: BPE 33-2.3

28. Mammals reached their maximal diversity during the
    a. Jurassic period.   c. Triassic period.
    b. Permian period.   d. Tertiary period.

    ANS: D   DIF: I   OBJ: BPE 33-2.3

29. The most widely accepted hypothesis to explain the mass extinction of dinosaurs proposes
    a. a massive volcanic eruption.
    b. sunspots that disrupted the Earth's weather.
    c. that the Earth cooled in an ice age 65 million years ago.
    d. that the Earth was struck by a meteorite that caused thick dust clouds.

    ANS: D   DIF: I   OBJ: BPE 33-2.3

30. Scientific evidence suggests that birds arose from
    a. mammals.
    b. amphibians.
    c. reptiles.
    d. protozoa.

    ANS: C   DIF: I   OBJ: BPE 33-2.4

31. Relationships among the families of modern birds are mostly inferred from studies of
    a. fossils.
    b. bones.
    c. feathers.
    d. DNA.

    ANS: D   DIF: I   OBJ: BPE 33-2.4

32. amphibians : reptiles ::
    a. land : jaw
    b. feathers : scales
    c. reptiles : birds
    d. mammals : birds

    ANS: C
    (preceded)

    DIF: II   OBJ: BPE 33-2.4

33. bird : hollow bones ::
    a. *Compsognathus* : feathers
    b. reptile : hollow bones
    c. *Archaeopteryx* : feathers
    d. bird : dinosaur forelimbs

    ANS: C
    (has)

    DIF: II   OBJ: BPE 33-2.4

COMPLETION

1. In most vertebrates, the _____ completely replaces the notochord found in invertebrate chordates.

    ANS: backbone   DIF: I   OBJ: BPE 33-1.1

2. The backbone provides _____ for and protects the dorsal nerve cord.

    ANS: support   DIF: I   OBJ: BPE 33-1.1

3. All vertebrates have a(n) _____ circulatory system.

    ANS: closed   DIF: I   OBJ: BPE 33-1.1

4. The tissues of vertebrates are organized into _____.

    ANS: organs   DIF: I   OBJ: BPE 33-1.1

5. A backbone provides a central axis for _____ attachment.

   ANS: muscle   DIF: I   OBJ: BPE 33-1.1

   Cross Section of the Head of a Jawless Fish

6. The structure labeled C is pointing to the _____ _____.

   ANS: gill slits   DIF: II   OBJ: BPE 33-1.2

7. The structure labeled B is pointing to the _____ _____.

   ANS: gill arches   DIF: II   OBJ: BPE 33-1.2

8. Structure A is the _____.

   ANS: skull   DIF: II   OBJ: BPE 33-1.2

9. Fishes evolved paired _____ which provided finer control of movement through water while in pursuit of prey.

   ANS: fins   DIF: I   OBJ: BPE 33-1.2

10. A key evolutionary innovation in fishes was the development of _____.

    ANS: jaws   DIF: I   OBJ: BPE 33-1.2

11. _____ were jawed fishes with massive armored heads.

    ANS: Placoderms   DIF: I   OBJ: BPE 33-1.2

12. Lobe-finned fishes evolved _____, which let them extract oxygen from the air.

    ANS: lungs   DIF: I   OBJ: BPE 33-1.3

13. Amphibians were able to leave their aquatic environments due to the development of _____ as the site of gas exchange.

    ANS: lungs   DIF: I   OBJ: BPE 33-1.4

14. Walking around on land requires a greater expenditure of _____ necessitating a change in the heart of amphibians.

    ANS: energy   DIF: I   OBJ: BPE 33-1.4

15. All of the continents were once joined together in a single supercontinent called _____.

    ANS: Pangaea   DIF: I   OBJ: BPE 33-2.1

16. Adaptations in dinosaurs that allowed them to live their entire life cycle on land include changes which made their bodies _____.

    ANS: watertight   DIF: I   OBJ: BPE 33-2.1

17. Unlike amphibians, reptiles did *not* need to return to _____ in order to reproduce.

    ANS: water   DIF: I   OBJ: BPE 33-2.1

18. Reptiles replaced _____ as the dominant land vertebrate by the end of the Permian.

    ANS: amphibians   DIF: I   OBJ: BPE 33-2.1

19. Fishes, amphibians, and reptiles, whose body temperatures change as the temperature of their surroundings changes, are _____.

    ANS: ectotherms   DIF: I   OBJ: BPE 33-2.2

20. Reptiles, whose body temperature changes with the temperature of their surroundings, are known as _____.

    ANS: ectotherms   DIF: I   OBJ: BPE 33-2.2

21. While the cause of the mass extinction is still unknown, the extinction of dinosaurs opened ecological niches for _____.

    ANS: mammals   DIF: I   OBJ: BPE 33-2.3

22. The _____ are the direct ancestors of the mammals.

    ANS: therapsids   DIF: I   OBJ: BPE 33-2.3

23. Mammals reached their greatest diversity in the late _____ period.

    ANS: Tertiary   DIF: I   OBJ: BPE 33-2.3

24. *Archaeopteryx* shared many features with small _____.

    ANS: therapods   DIF: I   OBJ: BPE 33-2.4

25. The teeth of *Archaeopteryx* are a feature associated with _____.

    ANS: reptiles   DIF: I   OBJ: BPE 33-2.4

26. The feathers of *Archaeopteryx* are a feature associated with _____.

    ANS: birds   DIF: I   OBJ: BPE 33-2.4

27. Unlike the bones of birds, the bones of *Archaeopteryx* are believed to have been _____.

    ANS: solid   DIF: I   OBJ: BPE 33-2.4

ESSAY

1. Describe how jaws are thought to have evolved.

    ANS:
    Scientists think that jaws evolved from one or more of the gill arches that support the pharynx in agnathans.

    DIF: II   OBJ: BPE 33-1.2

2. In what way are amphibians not fully adapted to life on land?

    ANS:
    The eggs of amphibians are not watertight, so amphibians must return to water to reproduce.

    DIF: II   OBJ: BPE 33-1.4

3. Why were reptiles able to become the dominant animals on Earth?

    ANS:
    Earth began a long, dry period 320 million years ago. Because of reptiles' watertight skin and eggs, they were better suited to these conditions than amphibians were.

    DIF: II   OBJ: BPE 34-1.2

4. Birds live in the Arctic, but reptiles do not. Offer an explanation for this fact.

ANS:
Reptiles are ectothermic and cannot survive extreme temperatures. Birds are endothermic and can adapt to some extremes.

DIF: II   OBJ: BPE 33-2.2

TRUE/FALSE

1. Members of the class Osteichthyes have skeletons of cartilage.

   ANS: F   DIF: I   OBJ: BPE 34-1.1

2. In modern fishes, gas exchange takes place through membranes of their gills.

   ANS: T   DIF: I   OBJ: BPE 34-1.1

3. All fishes have an internal skeleton.

   ANS: T   DIF: I   OBJ: BPE 34-1.1

4. All fishes have a bony skeleton.

   ANS: F   DIF: I   OBJ: BPE 34-1.1

5. Almost all fishes have single-loop circulation.

   ANS: T   DIF: I   OBJ: BPE 34-1.1

6. In fishes, oxygenated blood passes from the gills to the heart and then to the rest of the body.

   ANS: F   DIF: I   OBJ: BPE 34-1.2

7. Fish are the only vertebrates that use gills as adults to carry out respiration.

   ANS: T   DIF: I   OBJ: BPE 34-1.2

8. During countercurrent flow, water flows over the gills of fish in the same direction that blood within their gills flows.

   ANS: F   DIF: I   OBJ: BPE 34-1.2

9. In a fish, countercurrent flow prevents a steady supply of oxygen from reaching the gill filaments.

   ANS: F   DIF: I   OBJ: BPE 34-1.2

10. The gills of bony fishes are the most efficient respiratory organs known.

    ANS: T   DIF: I   OBJ: BPE 34-1.2

11. The tube heart of fishes is an efficient pump of blood.

    ANS: F   DIF: I   OBJ: BPE 34-1.3

12. Fish need a stronger pump than a tubular heart provides due to the capillaries in the gills, which create resistance to the flow of blood.

    ANS: T   DIF: I   OBJ: BPE 34-1.3

13. The heart of a fish is very similar to that of a crocodile.

    ANS: F   DIF: I   OBJ: BPE 34-1.3

14. Contractions of the fish's heart ventricle pumps blood towards the gills.

    ANS: T   DIF: I   OBJ: BPE 34-1.3

15. The sinus venosus acts like a collection chamber in the fish heart.

    ANS: T   DIF: I   OBJ: BPE 34-1.3

16. Since they live in salt water, marine fishes do not have a problem maintaining the proper balance of water and salt in their bodies.

    ANS: F   DIF: I   OBJ: BPE 34-1.4

17. Minimizing water loss is a key evolutionary challenge in some fishes.

    ANS: T   DIF: I   OBJ: BPE 34-1.4

18. Nephridia are complex organs in fish that regulate the body's salt and water balance.

    ANS: F   DIF: I   OBJ: BPE 34-1.4

19. In fish, excess water and bodily wastes leave the kidneys in the form of uric acid.

    ANS: F   DIF: I   OBJ: BPE 34-1.4

20. Marine fishes excrete large amounts of dilute urine.

    ANS: F   DIF: I   OBJ: BPE 34-1.4

21. Marine fishes excrete small amounts of concentrated urine.

    ANS: T   DIF: I   OBJ: BPE 34-1.4

22. Fishes carry out both asexual and sexual reproduction.

    ANS: F   DIF: I   OBJ: BPE 34-1.5

23. Most fishes have external fertilization.

    ANS: T   DIF: I   OBJ: BPE 34-1.5

24. Some fishes give birth to live young.

    ANS: T   DIF: I   OBJ: BPE 34-1.5

25. Bony fishes have a swim bladder.

    ANS: T   DIF: I   OBJ: BPE 34-2.1

26. In order to fill their swim bladders, bony fishes have to come to the surface to gulp air.

    ANS: F   DIF: I   OBJ: BPE 34-2.1

27. All fishes have cartilaginous skeletons.

    ANS: F   DIF: I   OBJ: BPE 34-2.1

28. Lampreys and hagfish represent jawless fishes.

    ANS: T   DIF: I   OBJ: BPE 34-2.1

29. Lampreys and hagfish have scaled bodies and multiple paired fins.

    ANS: T   DIF: I   OBJ: BPE 34-2.1

30. Lampreys are also known as "vultures of the sea."

    ANS: F   DIF: I   OBJ: BPE 34-2.1

31. The skeletons of sharks and rays are made up of cartilage.

    ANS: T   DIF: I   OBJ: BPE 34-2.1

32. The scales and teeth of sharks are very similar in structure.

    ANS: T   DIF: I   OBJ: BPE 34-2.1

33. Modern fishes gulp air to fill their swim bladders.

    ANS: F   DIF: I   OBJ: BPE 34-2.1

34. The fins of yellow perch are used to draw water into the mouth and over the gills.

    ANS: F   DIF: I   OBJ: BPE 34-2.2

35. Movements of the opercula draw water into the yellow perch's mouth.

    ANS: T   DIF: I   OBJ: BPE 34-2.2

36. The structure of the digestive system of yellow perch is very similar to that of all vertebrates.

    ANS: T   DIF: I   OBJ: BPE 34-2.2

37. Bony fishes must remain swimming in order to respire.

    ANS: F   DIF: I   OBJ: BPE 34-2.3

38. A bony fish must swim forward with its mouth open to move water over its gills.

    ANS: F   DIF: I   OBJ: BPE 34-2.3

39. The lateral line system of bony fishes acts as a specialized sensory system.

    ANS: T   DIF: I   OBJ: BPE 34-2.3

40. Because their skins are watertight, amphibians can live anywhere on dry land.

    ANS: F   DIF: I   OBJ: BPE 34-3.1

41. In amphibians, the blood that is pumped from the heart to the body is completely oxygenated.

    ANS: F   DIF: I   OBJ: BPE 34-3.1

42. Frog eggs must be laid in a wet or moist environment.

    ANS: T   DIF: I   OBJ: BPE 34-3.1

43. In most amphibians, fertilization takes place externally.

    ANS: T   DIF: I   OBJ: BPE 34-3.1

44. The skin of most amphibians functions as a respiratory organ.

    ANS: T   DIF: I   OBJ: BPE 34-3.1

45. Unlike fish, pulmonary veins carry oxygenated blood to the hearts of amphibians.

    ANS: T   DIF: I   OBJ: BPE 34-3.1

46. A frog must remain in water in order to stay moist.

    ANS: F   DIF: I   OBJ: BPE 34-3.1

47. Caecilians are tropical amphibians with four legs and a tail.

    ANS: F   DIF: I   OBJ: BPE 34-3.2

48. Frogs and toads are in the only order of herbivorous amphibians.

    ANS: F   DIF: I   OBJ: BPE 34-3.2

49. Anurans are found in desert as well as mountain environments.

    ANS: T   DIF: I   OBJ: BPE 34-3.2

50. Unlike frog and toad larvae, salamanders of the order Urodela do not undergo a dramatic metamorphosis.

    ANS: T   DIF: I   OBJ: BPE 34-3.2

51. Caecilians are found in every environment on the Earth.

    ANS: F   DIF: I   OBJ: BPE 34-3.2

52. Leopard frogs only hear well when under water.

    ANS: F   DIF: I   OBJ: BPE 34-3.3

53. The eyelids of frogs protect the eyes from dust.

    ANS: T   DIF: I   OBJ: BPE 34-3.3

MULTIPLE CHOICE

1. All fishes have a(n)
   a.   internal skeleton.
   b.   external skeleton.
   c.   cartilaginous skeleton.
   d.   bony skeleton.

    ANS: A   DIF: I   OBJ: BPE 34-1.1

2. Seahorses are
   a.   horses.
   b.   fishes.
   c.   lizards.
   d.   salamanders.

    ANS: B   DIF: I   OBJ: BPE 34-1.1

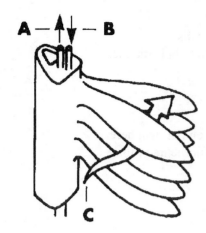

3. Refer to the illustration above. The structure shown in the diagram is a
   a. lung.   c. gill.
   b. lateral line.   d. trachea.

   ANS: C   DIF: II   OBJ: BPE 34-1.2

4. Refer to the illustration above. In the diagram, which arrow indicates the direction of water flow?
   a. arrow A
   b. arrow B
   c. arrow C
   d. None of the arrows show the direction of water flow.

   ANS: C   DIF: II   OBJ: BPE 34-1.2

5. Refer to the illustration above. In which of the following organisms might you expect to find the structure illustrated in the diagram?
   a. frog   c. bird
   b. spider   d. goldfish

   ANS: D   DIF: II   OBJ: BPE 34-1.2

6. The concurrent flow of water and blood found in the gills of fishes
   a. allows blood and water to flow in the same direction.
   b. ensures that oxygen diffuses into the blood over the whole length of the blood vessels in the gills.
   c. results in an uneven supply of oxygen reaching the blood vessels in the gills.
   d. inhibits the diffusion of oxygen and carbon dioxide between the blood and the water.

   ANS: B   DIF: I   OBJ: BPE 34-1.2

7. When the blood enters the gill filaments
   a. its carbon dioxide content is low and oxygen content is high.
   b. its carbon dioxide content is low and oxygen content is low.
   c. its carbon dioxide content is high and oxygen content is high.
   d. its carbon dioxide content is high and oxygen content is low.

   ANS: D   DIF: I   OBJ: BPE 34-1.2

8. Generally, fishes obtain oxygen
   a. through their skin.
   b. with lungs.
   c. with gills.
   d. through their mantles.

   ANS: C   DIF: I   OBJ: BPE 34-1.2

9. folds : lung ::
   a. fire : wood
   b. fish : gill filaments
   c. oxygen : atmosphere
   d. gill filaments : gills

   ANS: D
   (increase the surface area of the)

   DIF: II   OBJ: BPE 34-1.2

10. A collection chamber that reduces the resistance of blood flow into the heart of a fish is called the
    a. sinus venosus.
    b. ventricle.
    c. conus arteriosus.
    d. atrium.

    ANS: A   DIF: I   OBJ: BPE 34-1.3

11. Oxygenated blood moves from the gills to the
    a. heart.
    b. sinus venosus.
    c. body.
    d. conus arteriosus.

    ANS: C   DIF: I   OBJ: BPE 34-1.3

12. The chamber that pumps blood to the lungs is the
    a. sinus venosus.
    b. conus arteriosus.
    c. atrium.
    d. ventricle.

    ANS: D   DIF: I   OBJ: BPE 34-1.3

13. The concentration of the urine an animal produces depends primarily on
    a. the time of the year.
    b. the size of the organism.
    c. the environment in which the animal lives.
    d. the diet of the organism.

    ANS: C   DIF: I   OBJ: BPE 34-1.4

14. To make up for water loss in the bodies of marine fishes, they
    a. drink a lot of water.
    b. actively pump excess ions into their bodies.
    c. take in water through osmosis.
    d. actively take in salts from their environment.

    ANS: A   DIF: I   OBJ: BPE 34-1.4

15. freshwater fish kidney : dilute urine ::
    a. nephron : kidney
    b. marine fish kidney : concentrated urine
    c. milk : kitten
    d. salt water intake : absorption

ANS: B
(produces)

DIF: II   OBJ: BPE 34-1.4

16. The eggs of sharks are
    a. covered by a watertight outer covering.
    b. fertilized internally.
    c. released from the body before fertilization.
    d. fertilized externally.

ANS: B   DIF: I   OBJ: BPE 34-1.5

17. Eggs and sperm released near each other into the surrounding waters occurs during the process of
    a. growth.
    b. development.
    c. accretion.
    d. spawning.

ANS: D   DIF: I   OBJ: BPE 34-1.5

18. Lampreys and hagfishes have
    a. jaws.
    b. paired fins.
    c. a rigid skeleton.
    d. a notochord through all stages of their life cycle.

ANS: D   DIF: I   OBJ: BPE 34-2.1

19. The living agnathans are the
    a. lampreys and sharks.
    b. sharks and rays.
    c. hagfishes and coelacanths.
    d. lampreys and hagfishes.

ANS: D   DIF: I   OBJ: BPE 34-2.1

20. Lampreys are
    a. autotrophs.
    b. mutualistic organisms.
    c. parasites.
    d. amphibians.

ANS: C   DIF: I   OBJ: BPE 34-2.1

21. *Chondrichthyes* means
    a. bony fish.
    b. gilled fish.
    c. big fish.
    d. cartilage fish.

ANS: D   DIF: I   OBJ: BPE 34-2.1

22. Cartilaginous fishes have all of the following *except*
    a.   spiracles.
    b.   internal fertilization.
    c.   a swim bladder.
    d.   gill slits.

    ANS: C   DIF: I   OBJ: BPE 34-2.1

23. jaws : lampreys ::
    a.   cartilage : shark
    b.   fins : jawed fishes
    c.   teeth : jaws
    d.   paired fins : jawless fishes

    ANS: D
    (are absent in)

    DIF: II   OBJ: BPE 34-2.1

Three Types of Fish

24. Refer to the illustration above. Fish A in the diagram
    a.   has skin covered by overlapping structures called scales.
    b.   has many small scales embedded in the skin.
    c.   feeds parasitically on other fish.
    d.   does not have a lateral line system.

    ANS: B   DIF: II   OBJ: BPE 34-2.1

25. Fish C in the diagram
    a.   has skin covered by overlapping structures called scales.
    b.   has many small scales embedded in the skin.
    c.   feeds parasitically on other fish.
    d.   does not have a lateral line system.

    ANS: C   DIF: II   OBJ: BPE 34-2.1

26. Refer to the illustration above. Fish B in the diagram
    a.   has skin covered by overlapping structures called scales.
    b.   has many small scales embedded in the skin.
    c.   feeds parasitically on other fish.
    d.   does not have a lateral line system.

    ANS: A   DIF: II   OBJ: BPE 34-2.2

27. In most bony fishes,
    a. internal fertilization takes place.
    b. external fertilization takes place.
    c. internal development takes place.
    d. All of the above

    ANS: B   DIF: I   OBJ: BPE 34-2.1

28. A critical difference between bony fishes and sharks is
    a. the presence of a swim bladder in most bony fishes.
    b. the presence of a lateral line system in sharks.
    c. that most sharks have color vision.
    d. All of the above

    ANS: A   DIF: I   OBJ: BPE 34-2.1

29. Which of the following is *not* an order of fish?
    a. Osteichthyes
    b. Chondrichthyes
    c. Urodela
    d. Agnatha

    ANS: C   DIF: I   OBJ: BPE 34-2.1

30. The two major groups of bony fishes are the lobe-finned fishes and the
    a. lungfishes.
    b. ray-finned fishes.
    c. coelacanths.
    d. placoderms.

    ANS: B   DIF: I   OBJ: BPE 34-2.3

31. Members of the class Osteichthyes
    a. have skeletons made of bone.
    b. do not have jaws.
    c. include the rays and skates.
    d. All of the above

    ANS: A   DIF: I   OBJ: BPE 34-2.3

32. The coelacanth is a
    a. lungfish.
    b. cartilaginous fish.
    c. ray-finned fish.
    d. lobe-finned fish.

    ANS: D   DIF: I   OBJ: BPE 34-2.3

33. The swim bladder
    a. stores air for breathing.
    b. contains antibodies.
    c. is found in all amphibians.
    d. allows fishes to become more buoyant.

    ANS: D   DIF: I   OBJ: BPE 34-2.3

34. The operculum
    a. is part of the skeletal system.
    b. is an adaptation for rapid swimming.
    c. covers the gills in fish.
    d. None of the above

    ANS: C   DIF: I   OBJ: BPE 34-2.3

35. The gills of bony fishes
    a. give them buoyancy.
    b. are found in a single chamber behind the operculum.
    c. are composed of scales.
    d. are housed in chambers on each side of the head.

    ANS: D   DIF: I   OBJ: BPE 34-2.3

External Structure of a Bony Fish

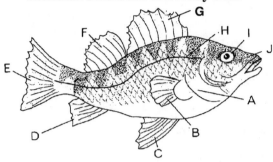

36. Refer to the illustration above. In order to move forward, the fish uses the fin(s) labeled
    a. B.   c. E.
    b. C.   d. F.

    ANS: C   DIF: II   OBJ: BPE 34-2.3

37. Refer to the illustration above. The structure labeled A, which draws water into the mouth of the
    fish, is the
    a. pharynx.   c. gills.
    b. esophagus.   d. operculum.

    ANS: D   DIF: II   OBJ: BPE 34-2.3

Structures of the Lateral Line of a Fish

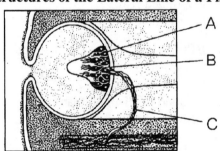

38. Refer to the illustration above. The structure labeled C is a
    a. cilium.   c. supporting cell.
    b. scale.   d. nerve.

    ANS: D   DIF: II   OBJ: BPE 34-2.3

39. lateral line : motion detector ::
    a. swim bladder : roof on a house
    b. operculum : wheel
    c. operculum : water pump
    d. fin : microwave oven

    ANS: C
    (is a)

    DIF: II   OBJ: BPE 34-2.3

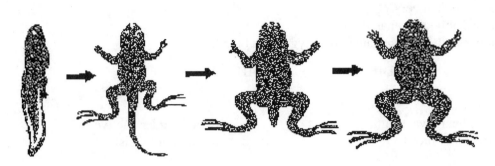

40. The process illustrated in the diagram is
    a. amniocentesis.
    b. metamorphosis.
    c. evolution.
    d. synapsis.

    ANS: B   DIF: II   OBJ: BPE 34-3.1

41. Although adapted to land, toads must have access to a watery environment in order to
    a. obtain food.
    b. excrete wastes.
    c. reproduce.
    d. All of the above

    ANS: C   DIF: I   OBJ: BPE 34-3.1

42. Amphibians must reproduce in water or moist places because their eggs
    a. are fertilized externally.
    b. have a jelly-like coating that is freely permeable to water.
    c. will dry out if removed from moisture.
    d. All of the above

    ANS: D   DIF: I   OBJ: BPE 34-3.1

43. In amphibians, gases are exchanged through lung breathing and through the
    a. heart.
    b. air bladder.
    c. lateral line system.
    d. skin.

    ANS: D   DIF: I   OBJ: BPE 34-3.1

44. Toads, like frogs,
    a. must live in moist areas.
    b. return to the water to reproduce.
    c. have long tails as adults.
    d. belong to the order Urodela.

    ANS: B   DIF: I   OBJ: BPE 34-3.1

45. During metamorphosis in frogs,
    a. lungs replace gills.
    b. limbs develop.
    c. the tail disappears.
    d. All of the above

    ANS: D   DIF: I   OBJ: BPE 34-3.1

46. The amphibian heart
    a. pumps only deoxygenated blood.
    b. has four chambers.
    c. pumps only oxygenated blood.
    d. pumps both deoxygenated and oxygenated blood.

    ANS: D   DIF: I   OBJ: BPE 34-3.1

47. reptile : dry ::
    a. amphibian : watertight
    b. terrestrial : moist
    c. swim bladder : active
    d. amphibian : moist

    ANS: D
    (skin is)

    DIF: II   OBJ: BPE 34-3.1

48. Amphibians without tails are classified in the order
    a. Apoda.
    b. Anura.
    c. Urodela.
    d. Hydrodela.

    ANS: B   DIF: I   OBJ: BPE 34-3.2

49. Newts and salamanders are amphibians of the order
    a. Apoda.
    b. Anura.
    c. Urodela.
    d. Gymnophiona.

    ANS: C   DIF: I   OBJ: BPE 34-3.2

50. Amphibians that have slender bodies and no limbs are classified as
    a. anurans.
    b. caecilians.
    c. salamanders.
    d. newts.

    ANS: B   DIF: I   OBJ: BPE 34-3.2

51. Adult frogs, like other amphibians, are
    a. herbivores.
    b. omnivores.
    c. parasites.
    d. carnivores.

    ANS: D   DIF: I   OBJ: BPE 34-3.3

52. tympanic membrane : hearing ::
    a. cloaca : breathing
    b. frog teeth : chewing food
    c. frog tongue : vocalization
    d. frog tongue : catching prey

    ANS: D
    (is for)

    DIF: II   OBJ: BPE 34-3.3

53. Because of their tympanic membrane, leopard frogs can hear well in
    a. both water and air.
    b. water but not in air.
    c. air but not in water.
    d. None of the above

    ANS: A   DIF: I   OBJ: BPE 34-3.3

COMPLETION

1. During _____ -loop circulation, blood is pumped from the heart to the capillaries in the gills, and then to the rest of the body before the blood returns to the heart.

    ANS: single   DIF: I   OBJ: BPE 34-1.1

2. The vertebral column surrounds the _____ _____ in fishes.

    ANS: spinal cord   DIF: I   OBJ: BPE 34-1.1

3. The process of _____ is responsible for the exchange of gases across respiratory membranes.

    ANS: diffusion   DIF: I   OBJ: BPE 34-1.2

4. Each gill in a fish is made up of rows of gill _____ that are stacked on top of one another.

    ANS: filaments   DIF: I   OBJ: BPE 34-1.2

5. The tiny _____ in the fish's gills create resistance to the flow of blood.

    ANS: capillaries   DIF: I   OBJ: BPE 34-1.3

6. In fishes, the tube pump of early chordates is replaced with a(n) _____ -pump heart.

    ANS: chamber   DIF: I   OBJ: BPE 34-1.3

7. Marine bony fish lose water continuously by _____ to the saltier water in which they swim.

    ANS: osmosis   DIF: I   OBJ: BPE 34-1.4

8. A kidney is made up of individual units called _____ that filter the blood.

    ANS: nephrons   DIF: II   OBJ: BPE 34-1.4

9. For most fishes, fertilization takes place _____.

    ANS: externally   DIF: I   OBJ: BPE 34-1.5

10. Lampreys and hagfishes that are found on the Earth today are descendants of the armored _____.

    ANS: ostracoderms   DIF: I   OBJ: BPE 34-2.1

11. Lampreys are _____ on other living fish.

    ANS: parasitic   DIF: I   OBJ: BPE 34-2.1

12. The mineral _____ _____ strengthens the cartilaginous skeletons of sharks and rays.

    ANS: calcium carbonate   DIF: I   OBJ: BPE 34-2.1

13. Yellow perch produce _____ during their breeding season in the spring.

    ANS: gametes   DIF: I   OBJ: BPE 34-2.2

14. Within the brain of the perch, the _____ _____ receives sensory information from the eyes.

    ANS: optic lobe   DIF: I   OBJ: BPE 34-2.2

15. The _____ are the most advanced of the ray-finned bony fishes.

    ANS: teleosts   DIF: I   OBJ: BPE 34-2.3

16. The _____ _____ gives most bony fishes buoyancy.

    ANS: swim bladder   DIF: I   OBJ: BPE 34-2.3

17. Amphibians achieve more efficient circulation than fishes because of their _____ -loop circulatory system.

    ANS: double   DIF: I   OBJ: BPE 34-3.1

18. The changes that transform a tadpole into an adult frog are called _____.

    ANS: metamorphosis   DIF: I   OBJ: BPE 34-3.1

19. In some species of amphibians, a(n) _____ partly or completely divides the atrium into right and left halves.

   ANS: septum   DIF: I   OBJ: BPE 34-3.1

20. Frogs and toads are amphibians of the class _____.

   ANS: Anura   DIF: I   OBJ: BPE 34-3.2

21. Salamanders and _____ are amphibians with a distinct head, tail, and limbs.

   ANS: newts   DIF: I   OBJ: BPE 34-3.2

22. In frogs, the eardrum is called the _____ _____.

   ANS: tympanic membrane   DIF: I   OBJ: BPE 34-3.3

ESSAY

1. Why is maintaining water balance a different process for freshwater fish than for marine fish?

   ANS:
   Sea water has a much higher salt concentration than the cells of marine fish, so marine fish continually lose water by osmosis. Marine fish must drink a lot of water and excrete only small amounts of urine. Freshwater fish continually take in water by osmosis and excrete large amounts of diluted urine.

   DIF: II   OBJ: BPE 34-1.4

2. How is the body design of bony fishes and sharks better adapted for swimming than the body design of primitive fishes?

   ANS:
   Most bony fishes and sharks have streamlined bodies that are well adapted for movement through the water. The head acts as a wedge that cleaves the water, and the body tapers back to the tail, allowing the fish to slip through the water with minimal resistance. In addition, sharks and bony fishes have an assortment of movable fins that aid their swimming.

   DIF: II   OBJ: BPE 34-2.1

3. Explain the importance of the swim bladder to bony fishes.

   ANS:
   The swim bladder is a gas-filled sac that gives the fishes active control of their buoyancy. By regulating the amount of gas in the swim bladder, bony fishes can remain at different depths without expending energy through swimming.

   DIF: II   OBJ: BPE 34-2.3

4. Why are amphibians found near water?

ANS:
Most amphibians pass through a larval stage in water before moving to land, and most amphibians return to water to lay their eggs. Also, the lack of a watertight skin limits many amphibians to a moist environment.

DIF: II   OBJ: BPE 34-3.1

CHAPTER 35—REPTILES AND BIRDS

TRUE/FALSE

1. Lizards and snakes are found on every continent of the Earth.

    ANS: F   DIF: I   OBJ: BPE 35-1.1

2. Modern reptiles are classified by the number of membranes found in their eggs.

    ANS: F   DIF: I   OBJ: BPE 35-1.1

3. Both reptiles and birds lay amniotic eggs.

    ANS: T   DIF: I   OBJ: BPE 35-1.1

4. Many reptiles regulate their temperature by their behavior.

    ANS: T   DIF: I   OBJ: BPE 35-1.2

5. A reptile's high metabolism causes most reptiles to be endothermic.

    ANS: F   DIF: I   OBJ: BPE 35-1.2

6. Reptilian body temperature is mostly determined by the temperature of their environment.

    ANS: T   DIF: I   OBJ: BPE 35-1.2

7. Reptiles have dry, largely watertight skin and lay watertight eggs.

    ANS: T   DIF: I   OBJ: BPE 35-1.3

8. Most land animals reproduce by external fertilization.

    ANS: F   DIF: I   OBJ: BPE 35-1.3

9. Reptiles must return to the water in order to reproduce.

    ANS: F   DIF: I   OBJ: BPE 35-1.3

10. Ovoviviparous reptiles carry their eggs in their bodies throughout development, and their young are born alive.

    ANS: T   DIF: I   OBJ: BPE 35-1.3

11. The majority of reptiles are oviparous.

    ANS: T   DIF: I   OBJ: BPE 35-1.3

12. The surviving reptiles include crocodiles and alligators, turtles, the tuatara, and snakes.

    ANS: T   DIF: I   OBJ: BPE 35-2.1

13. Turtles generally live on land, while tortoises generally live in the water.

    ANS: F   DIF: I   OBJ: BPE 35-2.1

14. A special sense organ in the tail of the timber rattlesnake helps it locate and capture prey.

    ANS: F   DIF: I   OBJ: BPE 35-2.2

15. The ages of a rattlesnake can be accurately determined by counting the number of rings on its rattle.

    ANS: F   DIF: I   OBJ: BPE 35-2.2

16. An organ located in the roof of the rattlesnake's mouth helps it track prey.

    ANS: T   DIF: I   OBJ: BPE 35-2.2

17. Crocodiles care for their young, after the young hatch, in ways similar to birds.

    ANS: T   DIF: I   OBJ: BPE 35-2.3

18. Because of their small sizes, most birds are exothermic.

    ANS: F   DIF: I   OBJ: BPE 35-3.1

19. Birds do not have bladders.

    ANS: T   DIF: I   OBJ: BPE 35-3.1

20. Feathers may be specialized for flight.

    ANS: T   DIF: I   OBJ: BPE 35-3.2

21. Down feathers cover the body of adult birds.

    ANS: F   DIF: I   OBJ: BPE 35-3.2

22. A bird's skeleton is more rigid than the skeleton of a reptile.

    ANS: T   DIF: I   OBJ: BPE 35-3.2

23. When birds fly they use a considerable amount of metabolic energy.

    ANS: T   DIF: I   OBJ: BPE 35-3.2

24. Birds meet their increased need for oxygen with lungs that have a larger surface area than the lungs of reptiles.

    ANS: F   DIF: I   OBJ: BPE 35-3.3

25. Birds have a three-chambered heart.

    ANS: F   DIF: I   OBJ: BPE 35-3.3

26. The way that air that passes through the lungs of birds is similar to the way that air passes through the lungs of reptiles.

    ANS: F   DIF: I   OBJ: BPE 35-3.3

27. Oxygen-rich and oxygen-poor blood mix in the heart of birds.

    ANS: F   DIF: I   OBJ: BPE 35-3.3

28. The shape of a bird's beak is a strong indicator of its food source.

    ANS: T   DIF: I   OBJ: BPE 35-3.4

29. The feet of birds are adaptations to specific types of environments.

    ANS: T   DIF: I   OBJ: BPE 35-3.4

MULTIPLE CHOICE

1. Reptiles are
   a. ectothermic.   c. ergothermic.
   b. endothermic.   d. None of the above

   ANS: A   DIF: I   OBJ: BPE 35-1.1

2. The skin of a reptile is
   a. moist and watertight.   c. dry and nearly watertight.
   b. moist and thin.   d. dry and watertight.

   ANS: D   DIF: I   OBJ: BPE 35-1.1

3. Reptiles respire through
   a. gills.   c. skin.
   b. lungs.   d. trachaea.

   ANS: B   DIF: I   OBJ: BPE 35-1.1

4. Reptiles have
   a. internal fertilization.
   b. endothermic metabolism.
   c. concurrent flow.
   d. cartilaginous skeletons.

   ANS: A   DIF: I   OBJ: BPE 35-1.1

5. Amphibian : moist ::
   a. ball : square
   b. oxygen : liquid
   c. reptile : scaly
   d. lung : primitive

   ANS: C
   (skin is)

   DIF: II   OBJ: BPE 35-1.1

6. One disadvantage of endothermy is that it
   a. limits the size of an organism.
   b. requires that the organism consume a relatively great amount of food.
   c. impedes circulation.
   d. limits the organism to temperate climates.

   ANS: B   DIF: I   OBJ: BPE 35-1.2

7. The geographical range of reptiles is limited by
   a. length of day.
   b. moisture.
   c. temperature.
   d. topography.

   ANS: C   DIF: I   OBJ: BPE 35-1.2

8. Reptiles are least active
   a. at sunset.
   b. at noon.
   c. at 4 PM.
   d. at sunrise.

   ANS: D   DIF: I   OBJ: BPE 35-1.2

9. Which of the following is a reptilian adaptation to living on land?
   a. external fertilization
   b. endothermic temperature regulation
   c. respiration through gills
   d. the amniotic egg

   ANS: D   DIF: I   OBJ: BPE 35-1.3

10. External fertilization is not common on land because
    a. both the sperm and egg are at risk of drying out.
    b. sexual reproduction takes place more readily in rivers, lakes, and oceans.
    c. most of the surface area of the Earth is covered by water.
    d. All of the above

    ANS: A   DIF: I   OBJ: BPE 35-1.3

11. Reptiles, except for alligators and crocodiles, have a heart that has
    a. two atria and two ventricles.
    b. two atria and one partially divided ventricle.
    c. one atrium and two partially divided ventricles.
    d. two atria and two partially divided ventricles.

    ANS: B   DIF: I   OBJ: BPE 35-1.3

12. Which of the following is usually characteristic of reproduction in a terrestrial environment?
    a. external fertilization   c. water-permeable eggs with no shells
    b. internal fertilization   d. None of the above

    ANS: B   DIF: I   OBJ: BPE 35-1.3

13. During internal fertilization,
    a. a sperm is deposited directly inside an egg that is floating in a pond.
    b. males and females need not be present at the site of fertilization at the same time.
    c. a male deposits sperm directly into the female.
    d. a female deposits eggs into a nest and the male covers them with sperm.

    ANS: C   DIF: I   OBJ: BPE 35-1.3

14. Some animals are oviparous. This means their young
    a. are nourished by placenta.
    b. are born live from eggs that hatch within the mother's body.
    c. hatch from eggs laid outside the mother's body.
    d. continue to develop in the mother's pouch.

    ANS: C   DIF: I   OBJ: BPE 35-1.3

15. Which of the following statements is *not* a true statement providing evidence for the hypothesis that birds evolved from a dinosaur ancestor?
    a. Some dinosaurs had feathers.
    b. Some dinosaurs were endothermic.
    c. The collarbone of certain dinosaurs is well-developed, as it is in birds.
    d. The pubic bone of certain dinosaurs is directed towards the tail end of the animal, as it is in birds.

    ANS: C   DIF: II   OBJ: BPE 35-1.3

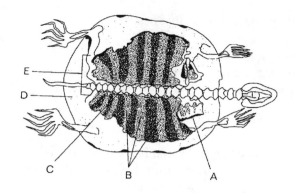

16. Refer to the illustration above. The pectoral girdle is labeled
    a. A.
    b. B.
    c. C.
    d. D.

    ANS: A   DIF: II   OBJ: BPE 35-2.1

17. Refer to the illustration above. In a turtle,
    a. the ribs are reduced or missing.
    b. the shells are made of calcified cartilage.
    c. the vertebrae are fused to the ventral shell.
    d. None of the above

    ANS: D   DIF: I   OBJ: BPE 35-2.1

18. Unlike other reptiles, turtles and tortoises
    a. live only in water.
    b. are prehistoric.
    c. are endangered.
    d. do not have teeth.

    ANS: D   DIF: I   OBJ: BPE 35-2.1

19. Which of the following is true of snakes?
    a. They lack limbs.
    b. They lack movable eyelids.
    c. They lack external ears.
    d. All of the above

    ANS: D   DIF: I   OBJ: BPE 35-2.1

20. The tuatara
    a. represents the last species of reptiles to have evolved.
    b. has a four-chambered heart.
    c. represents the last surviving species of a group of reptiles that appeared more than 225 million years ago.
    d. is found throughout the world except in the Antarctic.

    ANS: C   DIF: I   OBJ: BPE 35-2.1

21. Snakes are reptiles of the order
    a. Squamata.
    b. Chelonia.
    c. Crocodilia.
    d. Rhynchocephalia.

    ANS: A   DIF: I   OBJ: BPE 35-2.1

22. The heat-sensing organs between the eyes and nostril on each side of the head of a rattlesnake are the
    a. tracheal organs.
    b. Jacobson's organs.
    c. thermal organs.
    d. pit organs.

    ANS: D   DIF: I   OBJ: BPE 35-2.2

23. A rattlesnake can detect prey at night using its
    a. rattle.
    b. eye.
    c. pit organ.
    d. venom.

    ANS: C   DIF: I   OBJ: BPE 35-2.2

24. The fangs of a rattlesnake are used for
    a. reproduction.
    b. predation.
    c. respiration.
    d. chewing.

    ANS: B   DIF: II   OBJ: BPE 35-2.2

25. rattlesnake pit organ : heat ::
    a. cat's whisker : light
    b. crocodile eye : heat
    c. earthquake seismograph : chemicals
    d. human ear : sound

    ANS: D
    (detects)

    DIF: II   OBJ: BPE 35-2.2

26. Unlike other living reptiles, crocodilians
    a. are viviparous.
    b. have a three-chambered heart.
    c. care for their young after hatching.
    d. have a synapsid skull.

    ANS: C   DIF: I   OBJ: BPE 35-2.3

27. Birds retain many reptilian features, including
    a. teeth.
    b. a long bony tail.
    c. scales on their feet and lower legs.
    d. None of the above

    ANS: C   DIF: I   OBJ: BPE 35-3.1

28. A bird's crop
    a. temporarily stores food.
    b. is the first chamber of its stomach.
    c. is critical for flight.
    d. often contains small stones that the bird has swallowed.

    ANS: A   DIF: I   OBJ: BPE 35-3.1

29. Birds excrete most of their nitrogenous wastes as
    a. urea.   c. uric acid.
    b. ammonia.   d. urine.

    ANS: C   DIF: I   OBJ: BPE 35-3.1

30. Birds are different from reptiles in that they
    a. are endothermic.
    b. have feathers, rather than scales, covering their bodies.
    c. have four-chambered hearts.
    d. All of the above

    ANS: D   DIF: I   OBJ: BPE 35-3.1

31. Feathers
    a. evolved as a deterrent to insects.
    b. replaced fur as the body covering of birds.
    c. are found on all birds and some mammals.
    d. replaced scales as the body covering of birds.

    ANS: D   DIF: I   OBJ: BPE 35-3.2

32. The bones of birds
    a. are composed primarily of keratin.   c. are found sparingly throughout the body.
    b. are solid.   d. are thin and hollow.

    ANS: D   DIF: I   OBJ: BPE 35-3.2

33. A bird's skeleton
    a. is composed of thin, hollow bones.   c. is composed of many fused bones.
    b. is more rigid than a reptile's.   d. All of the above

    ANS: D   DIF: I   OBJ: BPE 35-3.2

34. The skeletons of birds are
    a. lightweight and inflexible.   c. solid and inflexible.
    b. lightweight and flexible.   d. solid and flexible.

    ANS: A   DIF: I   OBJ: BPE 35-3.2

35. Barbs appear on a bird's
    a. feet.   c. feathers.
    b. beak.   d. wings.

    ANS: C   DIF: I   OBJ: BPE 35-3.2

36. The power for flight comes from
    a. strong wing muscles.   c. strong shoulder muscles.
    b. strong breast muscles.   d. strong back muscles.

    ANS: B   DIF: I   OBJ: BPE 35-3.2

37. A bird's heart has
    a. one chamber.
    b. two chambers.
    c. three chambers.
    d. four chambers.

    ANS: D   DIF: I   OBJ: BPE 35-3.3

38. Bird respiration is very efficient because
    a. bird lungs are small and hollow.
    b. only one lung functions at a time.
    c. of a special set of blood vessels.
    d. birds' system of air sacs permits air to flow in only one direction through the lungs.

    ANS: D   DIF: I   OBJ: BPE 35-3.3

39. The amount of oxygen a lung can absorb depends primarily on
    a. its thickness.
    b. its position in the body of an animal.
    c. its internal surface area.
    d. the diameter of the bronchioles in the lung.

    ANS: C   DIF: I   OBJ: BPE 35-3.3

40. The body temperature of a bird is approximately
    a. 41 degrees C.
    b. 41 degrees F.
    c. 37 degrees C.
    d. 37 degree F.

    ANS: A   DIF: I   OBJ: BPE 35-3.3

41. To increase their respiratory efficiency, birds have
    a. two-way air flow.
    b. four-way air flow.
    c. one-way air flow.
    d. three-way air flow.

    ANS: C   DIF: I   OBJ: BPE 35-3.3

42. Talons would most likely be found among birds that
    a. eat seeds.
    b. capture their prey.
    c. live in water.
    d. drink the nectar of flowers.

    ANS: B   DIF: I   OBJ: BPE 35-3.4

COMPLETION

1. Modern reptiles differ from amphibians in that they have _____ skin.

   ANS: watertight   DIF: I   OBJ: BPE 35-1.1

2. Shelled eggs with membranes that surround the embryo and provide an aquatic environment for the development of reptiles and birds are called _____ eggs.

   ANS: amniotic   DIF: I   OBJ: BPE 35-1.1

3. A reptile's body temperature is largely determined by the temperature of its
   _____.

   ANS: environment   DIF: I   OBJ: BPE 35-1.1

4. Reptilian limbs are positioned to support _____ body weight than are the
   limbs of amphibians.

   ANS: more or greater   DIF: I   OBJ: BPE 35-1.1

5. A reptile's body temperature is largely determined by the _____ of its
   environment.

   ANS: temperature   DIF: I   OBJ: BPE 35-1.2

6. Reptiles must _____ during winter months in temperate climates.

   ANS: hibernate   DIF: I   OBJ: BPE 35-1.2

7. The inner surface of reptile lungs consists of small chambers called _____.

   ANS: alveoli   DIF: I   OBJ: BPE 35-1.3

8. Refer to the illustration above. Diagram III represents the heart of a(n) _____.

   ANS: reptile   DIF: II   OBJ: BPE 35-1.3

9. Refer to the illustration above. The structure labeled B is a(n) _____.

   ANS: ventricle   DIF: II   OBJ: BPE 35-1.3

10. Refer to the illustration above. The structure labeled A is a(n) _____.

    ANS: atrium   DIF: II   OBJ: BPE 35-1.3

11. Reptiles have dry, largely _____ skin.

    ANS: watertight or waterproof   DIF: I   OBJ: BPE 35-1.3

12. _____ fertilization reduces the risk that gametes will dry out.

   ANS: Internal   DIF: I   OBJ: BPE 35-1.3

13. The lower (ventral) portion of a tortoise's shell is called the _____.

   ANS: plastron   DIF: I   OBJ: BPE 35-2.1

14. Turtles and tortoises lack _____ but have jaws.

   ANS: teeth   DIF: I   OBJ: BPE 35-2.1

15. The _____ is the dorsal part of a turtle shell.

   ANS: carapace   DIF: I   OBJ: BPE 35-2.1

16. Tuataras are _____ reptiles that are most active at low temperatures.

   ANS: lizardlike   DIF: I   OBJ: BPE 35-2.1

17. Refer to the illustration above. Structure C, which is analogous to the taste buds found in other vertebrates, is called _____ _____.

   ANS: Jacobson's organs   DIF: II   OBJ: BPE 35-2.2

18. Refer to the illustration above. Structure B is a(n) _____.

   ANS: fang   DIF: II   OBJ: BPE 35-2.2

19. Refer to the illustration above. Structure A is the _____ gland.

   ANS: venom   DIF: II   OBJ: BPE 35-2.2

20. Unlike other living reptiles, _____ care for their young after hatching.

    ANS: crocodilians   DIF: I   OBJ: BPE 35-2.3

21. Feathers are modified _____ scales.

    ANS: reptilian   DIF: I   OBJ: BPE 35-3.1

22. Birds, like mammals, are _____.

    ANS: endothermic   DIF: I   OBJ: BPE 35-3.1

23. An adult bird's body is covered by _____ feathers.

    ANS: contour   DIF: I   OBJ: BPE 35-3.1

24. Refer to the illustration above. Structure B is called the _____, or keel of the _____.

    ANS: breastbone, sternum   DIF: II   OBJ: BPE 35-3.2

25. Refer to the illustration above. Structure A is known as the wishbone or _____.

    ANS: collarbone   DIF: II   OBJ: BPE 35-3.2

26. The breastbone of birds are greatly enlarged and bear prominent _____.

    ANS: keels   DIF: I   OBJ: BPE 35-3.2

27. The fused _____ of birds helps to absorb the stresses of flight.

    ANS: collarbone   DIF: I   OBJ: BPE 35-3.2

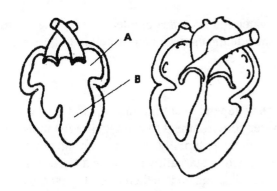

28. Refer to the illustration above. Diagram II represents the heart of a(n) _____.

     ANS: bird or mammal   DIF: II   OBJ: BPE 35-3.3

29. Over the course of vertebrate evolution, the _____ _____
    has become reduced in size. It has become the pacemaker in the hearts of birds and mammals.

     ANS: sinus venosus   DIF: I   OBJ: BPE 35-3.3

30. The amount of oxygen delivered to body cells is increased in birds through
    _____ - way air flow.

     ANS: one   DIF: I   OBJ: BPE 35-3.3

31. The avian heart has a completely divided _____.

     ANS: septum   DIF: I   OBJ: BPE 35-3.3

32. The feet of carnivorous birds are _____ for seizing prey.

     ANS: curved   DIF: I   OBJ: BPE 35-3.4

33. The beaks of ducks are _____ for shoveling through water and mud.

     ANS: flat   DIF: I   OBJ: BPE 35-3.4

ESSAY

1. Why isn't external fertilization an effective way to reproduce on dry land?

     ANS:
     External fertilization takes place outside the body of either parent. This form of fertilization is
     less common on dry land because both the egg and sperm are at risk of drying out and dying.

     DIF: II   OBJ: BPE 35-1.3

2. As reptiles evolved, many were able to leave water and become completely terrestrial animals. Amphibians, however, are not totally free of the aquatic environment. Explain two reasons why these statements are true.

ANS:
Amphibians must remain near water because they depend on a thin, moist skin for oxygen and carbon dioxide exchange. They also need a watery environment to keep their eggs moist, and to enable sperm to swim to the eggs, which are fertilized externally. Reptiles, on the other hand evolved lungs and a scaly skin, that is impermeable to water, allowing them a terrestrial existence. Also, reptiles have evolved internal fertilization and shelled eggs so that they can reproduce on land.

DIF: II   OBJ: BPE 35-1.3

3. Support the statement "Crocodiles resemble birds far more than they resemble living reptiles."

ANS:
Crocodiles are the only living reptiles that, like birds, care for their young. They are also the onl living reptiles that have a four-chambered heart like that of birds. In many other anatomical features, crocodiles differ from all other living reptiles and resemble birds.

DIF: II   OBJ: BPE 35-1.3

4. What improvements in jaw design have contributed to the success of snakes and lizards as predators?

ANS:
The lower jaw of snakes and lizards is loosely connected to the skull. This loose connection allows the mouth to open to accommodate large prey. In addition, the loss of the lower arch of bone below the lower opening in the skull of lizards makes room for large muscles to move the jaws.

DIF: II   OBJ: BPE 35-2.2

5. Flying requires a great amount of energy. What adaptations in the respiratory systems of birds allow them to meet their high energy needs?

ANS:
In order to release large amounts of energy, birds must have a constant supply of oxygen. Birds have a system of air sacs that maintain a constant one-way flow (and supply of oxygen) to the lungs. In addition, the network of lung capillaries is arranged across the air flow at a 90° angle. Blood leaving a bird's lung can contain more oxygen than exhaled air does.

DIF: II   OBJ: BPE 35-3.3

6. The right and left sides of a bird's heart are completely separated, so oxygen-rich blood is never mixed with oxygen-poor blood. Why is this complete separation necessary for birds?

ANS:
Birds need blood with a high oxygen content because flight requires large amounts of energy. The oxygen is used during cellular respiration.

DIF: II   OBJ: BPE 35-3.3

TRUE/FALSE

1. Hair evolved from reptilian scales.

    ANS: F   DIF: I   OBJ: BPE 36-1.1

2. Mammals have greater geographic distribution than reptiles or amphibians.

    ANS: T   DIF: I   OBJ: BPE 36-1.1

3. Hair may serve as camouflage.

    ANS: T   DIF: I   OBJ: BPE 36-1.1

4. Mammals have hair on their bodies and the ability to produce milk.

    ANS: T   DIF: I   OBJ: BPE 36-1.1

5. The primary function of hair is camouflage.

    ANS: F   DIF: I   OBJ: BPE 36-1.1

6. The whiskers of animals are stiff hairs that serve a sensory function.

    ANS: T   DIF: I   OBJ: BPE 36-1.1

7. The structure of a mammal's jaw and teeth usually reveals its diet.

    ANS: T   DIF: I   OBJ: BPE 36-1.2

8. The incisors of a rodent continue to grow throughout its lifetime.

    ANS: T   DIF: I   OBJ: BPE 36-1.2

9. Ectotherms have a higher metabolic rate than endotherms.

    ANS: F   DIF: I   OBJ: BPE 36-1.3

10. Alveoli decrease the surface area of mammalian lungs.

    ANS: F   DIF: I   OBJ: BPE 36-1.3

11. The name "grizzly" comes from silver-tipped hairs that are often sprinkled over the grizzly bear's head and back.

    ANS: T   DIF: I   OBJ: BPE 36-1.4

12. The hump atop a grizzly bear's back is a knot of strong muscles that power the forelimbs.

   ANS: T   DIF: I   OBJ: BPE 36-1.4

13. Grizzly bears are not able to eat plant material because they do not have a way of digesting the cellulose in plant material.

   ANS: F   DIF: I   OBJ: BPE 36-1.4

14. Like reptiles, monotremes are oviparous.

   ANS: T   DIF: I   OBJ: BPE 36-2.1

15. Marsupials are egg-laying mammals.

   ANS: F   DIF: I   OBJ: BPE 36-2.1

16. Egg-laying mammals nourish their young after birth with milk.

   ANS: T   DIF: I   OBJ: BPE 36-2.1

17. The offspring of placental mammals receive nourishment through the placenta throughout development.

   ANS: T   DIF: I   OBJ: BPE 36-2.1

18. Monotremes are mammals that carry their young in pouches.

   ANS: F   DIF: I   OBJ: BPE 36-2.1

19. The gestation period in marsupials is far shorter than the gestation period in placental mammals.

   ANS: T   DIF: I   OBJ: BPE 36-2.1

20. All mammals reproduce by internal fertilization.

   ANS: T   DIF: I   OBJ: BPE 36-2.1

21. Monotremes are egg-laying mammals.

   ANS: T   DIF: I   OBJ: BPE 36-2.1

22. Most species of mammals are placental.

   ANS: T   DIF: I   OBJ: BPE 36-2.1

23. During its development, the embryo of a placental mammal is nourished by the mother through unique structure called the placenta.

ANS: T   DIF: I   OBJ: BPE 36-2.1

24. The eggs of monotremes most closely resemble those of amphibians.

ANS: F   DIF: I   OBJ: BPE 36-2.1

25. Marsupials have internal fertilization and external development.

ANS: F   DIF: I   OBJ: BPE 36-2.1

26. Marsupials are incompletely developed at birth.

ANS: T   DIF: I   OBJ: BPE 36-2.1

27. Monotremes are found on every continent on Earth.

ANS: F   DIF: I   OBJ: BPE 36-2.2

28. Marsupials are abundant in North America.

ANS: F   DIF: I   OBJ: BPE 36-2.2

29. Whales are examples of mammals that do not have any hair.

ANS: F   DIF: I   OBJ: BPE 36-2.3

30. Because they can fly, bats are no longer classified as mammals.

ANS: F   DIF: I   OBJ: BPE 36-2.3

31. Animals of the order Cetacea are the only mammals that live entirely in the water.

ANS: T   DIF: I   OBJ: BPE 36-2.3

32. All ungulates chew their cud.

ANS: F   DIF: I   OBJ: BPE 36-2.3

33. Artiodactyls, such as giraffes, have stomachs with storage chambers where microbes aid in the digestion of plant materials.

ANS: T   DIF: I   OBJ: BPE 36-2.3

MULTIPLE CHOICE

1. Hair may
   a. serve as insulation.
   b. have a sensory function.
   c. be a defensive weapon.
   d. All of the above

   ANS: D   DIF: I   OBJ: BPE 36-1.1

2. The primary component of the claws, fingernails, hooves, and hair of mammals is
   a. nucleic acid.
   b. keratin.
   c. lipids.
   d. ivory.

   ANS: B   DIF: I   OBJ: BPE 36-1.1

3. hair : insulation ::
   a. endothermy : keeping mammals warm in hot weather
   b. synapsid opening : swallowing
   c. diaphragm : helping to draw air into lungs
   d. complex teeth : breathing

   ANS: C
   (is for)

   DIF: II   OBJ: BPE 36-1.1

Coyote's Skull

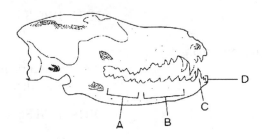

4. Refer to the illustration above. The teeth labeled A are called
   a. premolars.
   b. incisors.
   c. molars.
   d. canines.

   ANS: C   DIF: II   OBJ: BPE 36-1.2

5. Refer to the illustration above. The teeth labeled C are called
   a. premolars.
   b. incisors.
   c. molars.
   d. canines.

   ANS: D   DIF: II   OBJ: BPE 36-1.2

6. Refer to the illustration above. The teeth primarily used for biting and cutting are labeled
   a. A.
   b. B.
   c. C.
   d. D.

   ANS: D   DIF: II   OBJ: BPE 36-1.2

7. Refer to the illustration above. The fact that the coyote is a predator can be inferred from
   a. the shape of the skull.
   b. the position of the eye sockets.
   c. the length of the jawbone.
   d. the shape of the teeth.

   ANS: D   DIF: II   OBJ: BPE 36-1.2

8. A deer has
   a. long, sharp canine teeth.
   b. large, flat molars with ridged surfaces.
   c. small, sharp molars.
   d. All of the above

   ANS: B   DIF: I   OBJ: BPE 36-1.2

9. Carnivorous mammals have
   a. large, flat molars.
   b. short, square canine teeth.
   c. long, sharp canine teeth.
   d. poor vision.

   ANS: C   DIF: I   OBJ: BPE 36-1.2

10. Mammals, as well as birds, have
    a. teeth.
    b. a four-chambered heart.
    c. air sacs.
    d. All of the above

    ANS: B   DIF: I   OBJ: BPE 36-1.3

11. A four-chambered heart is characteristic of
    a. ectotherms.
    b. reptiles.
    c. amphibians.
    d. endotherms.

    ANS: D   DIF: I   OBJ: BPE 36-1.3

12. The sheet of muscle at the bottom of the rib cage of mammals is called the
    a. secondary palate.
    b. metabolic sheet.
    c. diaphragm.
    d. placenta.

    ANS: C   DIF: I   OBJ: BPE 36-1.3

13. gills : fish ::
    a. skin : reptile
    b. blood vessels : circulation
    c. tree : plant
    d. lungs : mammal

    ANS: D
    (are used to absorb O_2 in)

    DIF: II   OBJ: BPE 36-1.3

14. During the winter grizzly bears
    a. sleep in underground dens.
    b. have a slower metabolism.
    c. obtain energy from stored fat.
    d. All of the above

    ANS: D   DIF: I   OBJ: BPE 36-1.4

15. Half of the energy in milk comes from
    a. keratin.
    b. carbohydrates.
    c. protein.
    d. fat.

    ANS: D   DIF: I   OBJ: BPE 36-1.5

16. The time when the mothers of young mammals stop nursing their young is called
    a. the gestation period.
    b. reproduction.
    c. weaning.
    d. None of the above

    ANS: C   DIF: I   OBJ: BPE 36-1.5

17. Unlike reptiles, mammalian young are dependent on parental care for
    a. food.
    b. protection.
    c. learning.
    d. All of the above

    ANS: D   DIF: I   OBJ: BPE 36-1.5

18. Mammals whose offspring remain inside the mother until development is complete are called
    a. placental mammals.
    b. monotremes.
    c. marsupials.
    d. All of the above

    ANS: A   DIF: I   OBJ: BPE 36-2.1

19. The offspring of marsupial mammals
    a. hatch from eggs.
    b. remain inside their mother until development is complete.
    c. are born early and complete their development in their mother's pouch.
    d. All of the above

    ANS: C   DIF: I   OBJ: BPE 36-2.1

20. The placental mammals are animals that
    a. nurse their young with milk.
    b. have body hair.
    c. give birth to live young.
    d. All of the above

    ANS: D   DIF: I   OBJ: BPE 36-2.1

21. Mammals that lay eggs are
    a. placental mammals.
    b. pouched mammals.
    c. monotremes.
    d. semi-pouched mammals.

    ANS: C   DIF: I   OBJ: BPE 36-2.1

22. Egg-laying mammals are
    a. oviparous.
    b. viviparous.
    c. ovoviviparous.
    d. None of the above

    ANS: A   DIF: I   OBJ: BPE 36-2.1

23. Which of the following is *not* an advantage of the eggs of placental mammals over those of reptiles?
    a. protection from predators
    b. protection from overheating or freezing
    c. a protective shell forms around the egg
    d. further nourishment can be provided to the offspring

    ANS: C   DIF: I   OBJ: BPE 36-2.1

24. The function of the placenta in certain mammals is to
    a. hold the embryo in place, preventing premature loss.
    b. carry nutrition to and remove wastes from the embryo during development.
    c. surround and protect the embryo like a shell.
    d. maintain a constant internal temperature.

    ANS: B   DIF: I   OBJ: BPE 36-2.1

25. Which of the following characteristics is *not* associated with marsupial mammals?
    a. pouch
    b. shelled egg
    c. milk-fed young
    d. internal fertilization

    ANS: B   DIF: I   OBJ: BPE 36-2.1

26. The major difference between marsupials and placentals is
    a. their ability to maintain a steady body temperature.
    b. their teeth.
    c. their pattern of embryonic development.
    d. the size of their eggs.

    ANS: C   DIF: I   OBJ: BPE 36-2.1

27. Offspring remain inside the mother until development is essentially complete in
    a. placental mammals.
    b. monotremes.
    c. marsupials.
    d. All of the above

    ANS: A   DIF: I   OBJ: BPE 36-2.1

28. The duckbill platypus and two species of echidnas are the only living
    a. monotremes.
    b. marsupials.
    c. placental mammals.
    d. reptiles.

    ANS: A   DIF: I   OBJ: BPE 36-2.2

29. Kangaroos and opossums are
    a. marsupials.
    b. monotremes.
    c. macroscelidea.
    d. placentals.

    ANS: A   DIF: I   OBJ: BPE 36-2.2

30. Today all monotremes and most marsupials live in Australia and New Guinea. This limited distribution is due to
    a. predation by other mammals.
    b. continental drift.
    c. inability of these animals to survive in cold climates.
    d. All of the above

    ANS: B   DIF: I   OBJ: BPE 36-2.2

31. monotremes : Australia and New Guinea ::
    a. placentals : Australia
    b. Virginia opossums : North America
    c. placentals : New Guinea
    d. marsupials : Central America

    ANS: B
    (live only in)

    DIF: II   OBJ: BPE 36-2.2

32. Bat wings
    a. are covered with feathers.
    b. can be used only for gliding.
    c. are leathery membranes of skin.
    d. are modified hind limbs.

    ANS: C   DIF: I   OBJ: BPE 36-2.3

33. The sounds that bats emit
    a. help them navigate.
    b. help them capture their prey.
    c. are too high pitched to be heard by humans.
    d. All of the above

    ANS: D   DIF: I   OBJ: BPE 36-2.3

34. Bats
    a. are all exclusively carnivores.
    b. fly only by gliding.
    c. always emerge only at night.
    d. use sound to help them navigate.

    ANS: D   DIF: I   OBJ: BPE 36-2.3

35. Seals and walruses belong to the order
    a. Cetacea.
    b. Pinnipedia.
    c. Proboscidea.
    d. Insectivora.

    ANS: B   DIF: I   OBJ: BPE 36-2.3

36. Dugongs and sea cows are
    a. toothless mammals.
    b. hoofed mammals.
    c. sirenians.
    d. marine hunters.

    ANS: C   DIF: I   OBJ: BPE 36-2.3

37. A dog is a member of the order
    a. Rodentia.
    b. Insectivora.
    c. Carnivora.
    d. Cetacea.

    ANS: C   DIF: I   OBJ: BPE 36-2.3

38. The storage chamber in an ungulate's stomach is called a(n)
    a. rumen.
    b. cud.
    c. trunk.
    d. hyrax.

    ANS: A   DIF: I   OBJ: BPE 36-2.3

39. The nostrils of marine mammals are located on their
    a. noses.
    b. backs.
    c. heads.
    d. tails.

    ANS: C   DIF: I   OBJ: BPE 36-2.3

40. Scientists hypothesize that whales are probably descendants of
    a. sharks.
    b. land mammals.
    c. arthropods.
    d. reptiles.

    ANS: B   DIF: I   OBJ: BPE 36-2.3

41. The front limbs of cetaceans have been modified into
    a. hair.
    b. tails.
    c. baleens.
    d. flippers.

    ANS: D   DIF: I   OBJ: BPE 36-2.3

COMPLETION

1. It is usually possible to determine a mammal's _____ by examining its teeth.

   ANS: diet   DIF: I   OBJ: BPE 36-1.2

2. An animal that maintains a high, nearly constant body temperature through metabolism is said t
   be _____.

   ANS: endothermic   DIF: I   OBJ: BPE 36-1.3

3. Mammals characteristically have a _____ -looped circulatory system.

   ANS: double   DIF: I   OBJ: BPE 36-1.3

4. Alveoli in the lungs of mammals greatly increase the _____
_____ through which gas exchange takes place.

   ANS: surface area   DIF: I   OBJ: BPE 36-1.3

5. Female mammals have _____ _____ that secrete milk.

   ANS: mammary glands   DIF: I   OBJ: BPE 36-1.5

6. Milk contains water to prevent _____.

   ANS: dehydration   DIF: I   OBJ: BPE 36-1.5

7. The period of time between fertilization and birth in placentals and marsupials is known as the
_____ _____.

   ANS: gestation period   DIF: I   OBJ: BPE 36-2.1

8. Marsupial animals complete their development in the mother's _____.

   ANS: pouch   DIF: I   OBJ: BPE 36-2.1

9. Scientists think that _____ are more closely related to the early mammals than
are any other living mammals.

   ANS: monotremes   DIF: I   OBJ: BPE 36-2.1

10. Mice and humans belong to a group of mammals in which the young receive nutrition from the
mother through a structure called a(n) _____.

   ANS: placenta   DIF: I   OBJ: BPE 36-2.1

11. All monotremes live in _____ and New Guinea.

   ANS: Australia   DIF: I   OBJ: BPE 36-2.2

12. _____ are the only mammals capable of powered flight.

   ANS: Bats   DIF: I   OBJ: BPE 36-2.3

13. _____ in the stomachs of ungulates aid in the digestion of plant materials.

   ANS: Microbes   DIF: I   OBJ: BPE 36-2.3

14. Instead of hair as a source of insulation, marine mammals have a layer of
_____ which protects them from cold ocean water.

   ANS: blubber   DIF: I   OBJ: BPE 36-2.3

15. Seals are members of the order _____.

ANS: Pinnipedia   DIF: I   OBJ: BPE 36-2.3

16. Members of Cetacea have _____ bodies and front limbs modified into flippers.

ANS: streamlined   DIF: I   OBJ: BPE 36-2.3

ESSAY

1. List the unique characteristics of mammals.

ANS:
Mammals have hair and are endothermic. Female mammals have mammary glands that produce milk to nourish their young until the offspring are able to feed on their own.

DIF: II   OBJ: BPE 36-2.1

2. Why do scientists think monotremes are more closely related to the early mammals than are any other living mammals?

ANS:
Monotremes, like reptiles, lay eggs and have a cloaca. In addition, monotreme shoulders and forelimbs resemble those of reptiles.

DIF: I   OBJ: BPE 36-2.1

CHAPTER 37—ANIMAL BEHAVIOR

TRUE/FALSE

1. Scientists ask "how" questions about behavior as a way of studying the triggers of specific animal behaviors.

    ANS: T   DIF: I   OBJ: BPE 37-1.1

2. "Why" questions ask questions about the purpose of a specific behavior.

    ANS: T   DIF: I   OBJ: BPE 37-1.1

3. There is no connection between observed behavior and natural selection.

    ANS: F   DIF: I   OBJ: BPE 37-1.2

4. Over time, traits that provide a survival advantage become less common.

    ANS: F   DIF: I   OBJ: BPE 37-1.2

5. Natural selection favors traits that improve the likelihood that an individual will survive and reproduce.

    ANS: T   DIF: I   OBJ: BPE 37-1.2

6. A trait or behavior ensures the survival of the species.

    ANS: F   DIF: I   OBJ: BPE 37-1.2

7. Web-building spiders learn to build webs from their parents.

    ANS: F   DIF: I   OBJ: BPE 37-1.3

8. In classical conditioning, the animal associates a related response with a stimulus.

    ANS: F   DIF: I   OBJ: BPE 37-1.3

9. Some animal behaviors are genetic.

    ANS: T   DIF: I   OBJ: BPE 37-1.4

10. Genetic behaviors can never be modified by experience.

    ANS: F   DIF: I   OBJ: BPE 37-1.4

11. Animal behaviors have both genetic and learned components.

    ANS: T   DIF: I   OBJ: BPE 37-1.4

12. Innate behavior cannot be modified by learning.

ANS: F   DIF: I   OBJ: BPE 37-1.4

13. The bright coloration of male stickleback fish during breeding season is an example of a displa of territorial behavior.

ANS: F   DIF: I   OBJ: BPE 37-2.1

14. Defensive behavior is a strategy for locating, obtaining, and consuming food.

ANS: F   DIF: I   OBJ: BPE 37-2.1

15. Monarch butterflies that fly thousands of kilometers in search of suitable seasonal environment are displaying migratory behavior.

ANS: T   DIF: I   OBJ: BPE 37-2.1

16. Each species has a unique set of courtship signals.

ANS: T   DIF: I   OBJ: BPE 37-2.1

17. Animals use signals to influence the behavior of other animals.

ANS: T   DIF: I   OBJ: BPE 37-2.2

18. Not all animals are capable of communicating.

ANS: F   DIF: I   OBJ: BPE 37-2.2

19. Because chimpanzees cannot talk, they cannot communicate with members of their own or othe troops.

ANS: F   DIF: I   OBJ: BPE 37-2.2

20. Sexual selection does not influence the evolution of species.

ANS: F   DIF: I   OBJ: BPE 37-2.3

21. Sexual selection is a mechanism driving evolution.

ANS: T   DIF: I   OBJ: BPE 37-2.3

MULTIPLE CHOICE

1. Scientists who question the reason a behavior exists are asking
   a. a "how" question.
   b. a "why" question.
   c. about the evolution of behavior.
   d. Both (b) and (c)

   ANS: D   DIF: I   OBJ: BPE 37-1.1

2. Natural selection favors
   a. traits that benefit the species.
   b. traits that benefit the individual.
   c. traits that benefit the group.
   d. traits that benefit the order.

   ANS: B   DIF: I   OBJ: BPE 37-1.2

3. Innate animal behaviors are influenced by
   a. genes.
   b. age.
   c. reasoning.
   d. experience.

   ANS: A   DIF: I   OBJ: BPE 37-1.3

4. Learned animal behaviors are influenced by
   a. genes.
   b. age.
   c. reasoning.
   d. experience.

   ANS: D   DIF: I   OBJ: BPE 37-1.3

5. Trial-and-error learning is an example of
   a. classical conditioning.
   b. operant conditioning.
   c. seasonal conditioning.
   d. simple conditioning.

   ANS: B   DIF: I   OBJ: BPE 37-1.3

6. For classical conditioning
   a. a related response is associated with a stimulus.
   b. a related stimulus is associated with a response.
   c. an unrelated response is associated with a stimulus.
   d. an unrelated stimulus is associated with a response.

   ANS: B   DIF: I   OBJ: BPE 37-1.3

7. Learning that can occur only during a specific period early in the life of an animal is called
   a. operant.
   b. classical.
   c. reasoning.
   d. imprinting.

   ANS: D   DIF: I   OBJ: BPE 37-1.3

8. Pavlov : classical conditioning ::
   a. dog : meat powder
   b. trial : error
   c. rat : box
   d. Skinner : operant conditioning

   ANS: D
   (founded)

   DIF: II   OBJ: BPE 37-1.3

9. When Konrad Lorenz raised a group of newly hatched goslings, the goslings showed
   a. operant conditioning.
   b. reasoning.
   c. imprinting.
   d. classic conditioning.

   ANS: C   DIF: I   OBJ: BPE 37-1.4

10. Behavior that causes animals to locate, obtain, and consume food is called ____ behavior.
    a. foraging
    b. territorial
    c. migratory
    d. defensive

    ANS: A   DIF: I   OBJ: BPE 37-2.1

11. The hognose snake that flips onto its back and pretends to be dead is displaying ____ behavior
    a. foraging
    b. territorial
    c. migratory
    d. defensive

    ANS: D   DIF: I   OBJ: BPE 37-2.1

12. An example of an animal signal is
    a. sound.
    b. posture.
    c. movement.
    d. All of the above

    ANS: D   DIF: I   OBJ: BPE 37-2.2

13. Animal signals have been shaped by
    a. photoperiod.
    b. natural selection.
    c. classical conditioning.
    d. reasoning.

    ANS: B   DIF: I   OBJ: BPE 37-2.2

14. The purpose of animal signals is to
    a. stimulate a response in another animal.
    b. obtain food.
    c. travel to a more suitable environment.
    d. learn a new behavior.

    ANS: A   DIF: I   OBJ: BPE 37-2.2

15. Sexual selection is a(n)
    a. innate behavior.
    b. evolutionary mechanism.
    c. behavioral signal.
    d. genetic trait.

    ANS: B   DIF: I   OBJ: BPE 37-2.3

COMPLETION

1. A(n) _____ is an action performed in response to a stimulus.

   ANS: behavior   DIF: I   OBJ: BPE 37-1.1

2. Investigations into the circumstance that trigger a specific behavior are usually outlined in _____ questions.

   ANS: "how"   DIF: I   OBJ: BPE 37-1.1

3. Natural selection is a process by which _____ change in response to their environment.

   ANS: populations   DIF: I   OBJ: BPE 37-1.2

4. Actions that are repeated generation after generation without being learned are called _____ _____ pattern behavior.

   ANS: fixed action   DIF: I   OBJ: BPE 37-1.3

5. Genetically-programmed behavior is often called _____ behavior.

   ANS: innate   DIF: I   OBJ: BPE 37-1.3

6. Dogs that salivate in response to a bell have probably undergone _____ conditioning.

   ANS: classical   DIF: I   OBJ: BPE 37-1.3

7. _____ is the development of behaviors through experience.

   ANS: Learning   DIF: I   OBJ: BPE 37-1.3

8. The ability to analyze a problem and think of a possible solution is called _____.

   ANS: reasoning   DIF: I   OBJ: BPE 37-1.3

9. Learning that can occur only during a specific period early in the life of an animal and cannot be changed once learned is called _____.

   ANS: imprinting   DIF: I   OBJ: BPE 37-1.4

10. _____ behavior is observed in many bird species that have regular seasonal movements.

    ANS: Migratory   DIF: I   OBJ: BPE 37-2.1

11. Animals use signals to _____ with other animals.

   ANS: communicate   DIF: I   OBJ: BPE 37-2.2

12. Natural selection has shaped animal signals so that they reach the intended receiver
    _____.

   ANS: efficiently   DIF: I   OBJ: BPE 37-2.2

13. Native human language is a _____ signal.

   ANS: learned   DIF: II   OBJ: BPE 37-2.2

14. Mate selection based on the presence of desirable traits is called _____
    selection.

   ANS: sexual   DIF: I   OBJ: BPE 37-2.3

ESSAY

1. Why would it be advantageous for predators to learn the courtship signals of their prey?

   ANS:
   If predators learned the courtship signals of their prey, they could potentially locate their prey
   more efficiently during the prey's breeding season.

   DIF: II   OBJ: BPE 37-2.1

TRUE/FALSE

1. The four basic types of tissue in the body are epithelial, muscle, nervous, and connective.

    ANS: T   DIF: I   OBJ: BPE 38-1.2

2. Cartilage is a type of connective tissue.

    ANS: T   DIF: I   OBJ: BPE 38-1.2

3. The smooth muscle that is found in the stomach walls is an example of voluntary muscle.

    ANS: F   DIF: I   OBJ: BPE 38-1.2

4. The three basic types of muscle are skeletal muscle, smooth muscle, and cardiac muscle.

    ANS: T   DIF: I   OBJ: BPE 38-1.2

5. The excretory system filters metabolic wastes from the bloodstream and controls the concentration of body fluids.

    ANS: T   DIF: I   OBJ: BPE 38-1.3

6. Organs working together form an organ system.

    ANS: T   DIF: I   OBJ: BPE 38-1.3

7. Ectothermy is the primary factor that enables the human body to maintain homeostasis.

    ANS: F   DIF: I   OBJ: BPE 38-1.4

8. The hip attachment of the bones is called the pectoral girdle and the shoulder attachment is called the pelvic girdle.

    ANS: F   DIF: I   OBJ: BPE 38-2.1

9. The majority of the bones of the skeleton are part of the axial skeleton.

    ANS: F   DIF: I   OBJ: BPE 38-2.1

10. Yellow bone marrow is contained in the shaft of the long bones.

    ANS: T   DIF: I   OBJ: BPE 38-2.2

11. The Haversian canals of long bones are filled with yellow marrow.

    ANS: F   DIF: I   OBJ: BPE 38-2.3

12. The chances of developing osteoporosis later in life are greatly reduced by a mineral-rich diet and regular exercise throughout life.

    ANS: T   DIF: I   OBJ: BPE 38-2.4

13. Osteoporosis is the painful inflammation of freely movable joints.

    ANS: F   DIF: I   OBJ: BPE 38-2.4

14. The bones of the knee are connected by semimovable joints.

    ANS: F   DIF: I   OBJ: BPE 38-2.5

15. The shoulder joint is an example of a ball-and socket joint.

    ANS: T   DIF: I   OBJ: BPE 38-2.5

16. Extensor muscles cause bones to bend at a joint, while flexors cause them to straighten.

    ANS: F   DIF: I   OBJ: BPE 38-3.1

17. Moving a muscle requires three sets of muscles working in opposition.

    ANS: F   DIF: I   OBJ: BPE 38-3.1

18. A sarcomere is composed of filaments called myofibrils.

    ANS: F   DIF: I   OBJ: BPE 38-3.2

19. Actin and myosin are proteins that enable muscles to contract.

    ANS: T   DIF: I   OBJ: BPE 38-3.2

20. When a muscle fiber contracts, the sarcomeres relax.

    ANS: F   DIF: I   OBJ: BPE 38-3.2

21. The total amount of force a muscle exerts during contraction depends on how many muscle fibers contract.

    ANS: T   DIF: I   OBJ: BPE 38-3.2

22. The binding of myosin heads to actin filaments during a muscle contraction causes the sarcomere to lengthen.

    ANS: F   DIF: I   OBJ: BPE 38-3.2

23. Aerobic exercise increases skeletal muscle size and strength.

    ANS: F   DIF: I   OBJ: BPE 38-3.3

24. Resistance exercises, such as chin-ups, use the most efficient pathway of producing ATP within the body.

    ANS: F   DIF: I   OBJ: BPE 38-3.3

25. The distribution of melanin in the epidermis of the skin determines the color of an individual.

    ANS: T   DIF: I   OBJ: BPE 38-4.1

26. The dermis is a dead layer of skin that is nonfunctional.

    ANS: F   DIF: I   OBJ: BPE 38-4.2

27. Each hair on your head grows indefinitely.

    ANS: F   DIF: I   OBJ: BPE 38-4.3

28. Nails are produced by specialized epidermal cells.

    ANS: T   DIF: I   OBJ: BPE 38-4.3

29. Sweat glands in the dermis help remove excess body heat.

    ANS: T   DIF: I   OBJ: BPE 38-4.4

30. Acne is caused by excessive sweating.

    ANS: F   DIF: I   OBJ: BPE 38-4.4

31. Most skin cancers result from mutations in the melanin-producing cells.

    ANS: F   DIF: I   OBJ: BPE 38-4.4

MULTIPLE CHOICE

1. From the smallest functional units to the largest, the body is organized as follows:
   - a. cell, system, organ, tissue, body.
   - b. organ, cell, tissue, system, body.
   - c. system, organ, tissue, cell, body.
   - d. cell, tissue, organ, system, body.

    ANS: D   DIF: I   OBJ: BPE 38-1.1

2. Tissue that is specialized to cover the inner and outer surfaces of the internal organs is called
   a. epithelial tissue.
   b. connective tissue.
   c. muscles tissue.
   d. nerve tissue.

   ANS: A   DIF: I   OBJ: BPE 38-1.2

3. Tightly connected cells that are arranged in flat sheets are characteristic of
   a. epithelial tissue.
   b. connective tissue.
   c. muscle tissue.
   d. nerve tissue.

   ANS: A   DIF: I   OBJ: BPE 38-1.2

4. Blood, bone, and cartilage are examples of
   a. three different tissue types found in the body.
   b. connective tissue.
   c. epithelial tissue.
   d. organs of the body.

   ANS: B   DIF: I   OBJ: BPE 38-1.2

5. Connective tissue includes
   a. tendons.
   b. blood.
   c. fat.
   d. All of the above

   ANS: D   DIF: I   OBJ: BPE 38-1.2

6. The three types of muscle tissues are
   a. skeletal, smooth, and cardiac.
   b. skeletal, voluntary, and cardiac.
   c. smooth, cardiac, and involuntary.
   d. skeletal, cardiac, and ridged.

   ANS: A   DIF: I   OBJ: BPE 38-1.2

7. Smooth muscle
   a. can change the diameter of blood vessels.
   b. moves food through the digestive tract.
   c. is not under conscious control.
   d. All of the above

   ANS: D   DIF: I   OBJ: BPE 38-1.2

8. Smooth muscles can be found
   a. attached to the skeleton.
   b. in the wrist bones.
   c. at the knee joint.
   d. in internal organs.

   ANS: D   DIF: I   OBJ: BPE 38-1.2

9. Muscle tissue functions to move
   a. blood.
   b. food in the digestive tract.
   c. bones.
   d. All of the above

   ANS: D   DIF: I   OBJ: BPE 38-1.2

10. Organs that work together form
    a. connective tissues.
    b. tissue systems.
    c. organ systems.
    d. All of the above

    ANS: C   DIF: I   OBJ: BPE 38-1.3

11. The heart and the blood vessels are separate organs that form the
    a. skeletal system.
    b. circulatory system.
    c. reproductive system.
    d. digestive system.

    ANS: B   DIF: I   OBJ: BPE 38-1.3

12. Which of the following would likely occur if endothermy were disrupted?
    a. Body temperature could not be maintained.
    b. Strenuous physical activity would be difficult.
    c. Enzymes would be inactivated.
    d. All of the above

    ANS: D   DIF: I   OBJ: BPE 38-1.4

13. The heart and lungs are protected by the
    a. pectoral girdle.
    b. pelvic girdle.
    c. rib cage.
    d. periosteum.

    ANS: C   DIF: I   OBJ: BPE 38-2.1

14. Of the following, the structure that is *not* part of the axial skeleton is the
    a. backbone.
    b. pectoral girdle.
    c. rib cage.
    d. skull.

    ANS: B   DIF: I   OBJ: BPE 38-2.1

15. A person with a broken pelvic girdle would probably be unable to
    a. walk.
    b. turn his or her head.
    c. raise his or her arm.
    d. bend his or her wrist.

    ANS: A   DIF: I   OBJ: BPE 38-2.1

16. Yellow marrow
    a. provides internal support to spongy bone.
    b. produces red blood cells.
    c. is found only in lower vertebrates.
    d. consists mainly of fat that stores energy

    ANS: D   DIF: I   OBJ: BPE 38-2.2

17. The type of bone that provides the greatest strength for support is
    a. spongy bone.
    b. chitinous bone.
    c. compact bone.
    d. marrow bone.

    ANS: C   DIF: I   OBJ: BPE 38-2.2

18. The periosteum is the tough exterior membrane that surrounds bones and which contains
    a. blood vessels.
    b. osteocytes.
    c. spongy bone.
    d. red bone marrow.

    ANS: A   DIF: I   OBJ: BPE 38-2.2

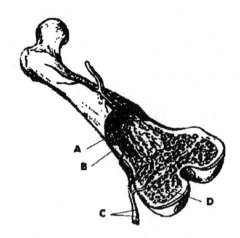

19. Refer to the illustration above. In the diagram, the compact bone is labeled
    a. A.
    b. B.
    c. C.
    d. D.

    ANS: B   DIF: II   OBJ: BPE 38-2.2

20. Refer to the illustration above. In the diagram, the material labeled A, which fills the center and spaces at ends and produces blood cells, is known as
    a. exocrine material.
    b. cartilage.
    c. bone marrow.
    d. spongy bone.

    ANS: C   DIF: II   OBJ: BPE 38-2.2

21. Refer to the illustration above. The structure labeled C in the diagram is a
    a. nerve.
    b. blood vessel.
    c. muscle.
    d. ligament.

    ANS: B   DIF: II   OBJ: BPE 38-2.2

22. compact bone : periosteum ::
    a. periosteum : compact bone
    b. compact bone : spongy bone
    c. spongy bone : marrow
    d. marrow : compact bone

    ANS: D
    (is found inside)

    DIF: II   OBJ: BPE 38-2.2

23. In an embryo, the skeleton is originally made of
    a. red and yellow marrow.
    b. calcium phosphate.
    c. cartilage.
    d. osteopores.

    ANS: C   DIF: I   OBJ: BPE 38-2.3

24. Bone cells that become embedded within the concentric layers of bone tissue are
    a. osteocytes.
    b. periosteal cells.
    c. red marrow cells.
    d. yellow marrow cells.

    ANS: A   DIF: I   OBJ: BPE 38-2.3

25. Osteocytes trapped within the spaces in the bone surrounding them
    a. are called marrow cells.
    b. are provided with food and oxygen by Haversian canals.
    c. receive nutrients directly from the cells of the surrounding cartilage.
    d. eventually become osteoblasts as the bone matures.

    ANS: B   DIF: I   OBJ: BPE 38-2.3

26. Bone loss may be slowed by
    a. calcium.
    b. regular exercise.
    c. a balanced diet.
    d. All of the above

    ANS: D   DIF: I   OBJ: BPE 38-2.4

27. Women are more susceptible than men to the effects of osteoporosis because
    a. their bones are smaller than those of men.
    b. they lose calcium during the child-bearing years.
    c. sex hormone production declines during menopause.
    d. All of the above

    ANS: D   DIF: I   OBJ: BPE 38-2.4

28. The loss of bone density that may occur in the later years of life is called
    a. menopause.
    b. bone replacement.
    c. bone fractures.
    d. osteoporosis.

    ANS: D   DIF: I   OBJ: BPE 38-2.4

29. The point where two or more bones meet is called a
    a. sprain.
    b. joint.
    c. point of intersection.
    d. growth region.

    ANS: B   DIF: I   OBJ: BPE 38-2.5

A   B   C   D

30. Refer to the illustration above. The joint shown in diagram A is an example of a
    a. suture joint.   c. pivot joint.
    b. ball-and-socket joint.   d. plant joint.

    ANS: B   DIF: II   OBJ: BPE 38-2.5

31. Refer to the illustration above. The joint shown in diagram D would most likely be found in the
    a. shoulder.   c. knee.
    b. elbow.   d. wrist.

    ANS: C   DIF: II   OBJ: BPE 38-2.5

32. Refer to the illustration above. Which of the diagrams shows a joint that allows bones to "glide"
    over each other?
    a. A   c. C
    b. B   d. D

    ANS: C   DIF: II   OBJ: BPE 38-2.5

33. Refer to the illustration above. The elbow is a hinge joint that allows your hand to turn over. It is
    shown in diagram
    a. A.   c. C.
    b. B.   d. D.

    ANS: B   DIF: II   OBJ: BPE 38-2.5

34. Tendons connect
    a. bone to bone.   c. muscle to muscle.
    b. muscle to bone.   d. cartilage to bone.

    ANS: B   DIF: I   OBJ: BPE 38-3.1

35. A muscle can
    a. push a bone.
    b. pull a bone.
    c. both push and pull a bone simultaneously.
    d. sometimes push and sometimes pull a bone.

    ANS: B   DIF: I   OBJ: BPE 38-3.1

36. Muscles that function by bending joints, such as the biceps, are categorized as
    a. flexors.
    b. abductors.
    c. extensors.
    d. adductors.

    ANS: A   DIF: I   OBJ: BPE 38-3.1

37. Muscle cells are able to exert force by
    a. converting ADP and organic phosphate into ATP.
    b. interfering with the forces of gravity and friction.
    c. rapidly relaxing the muscle fibers.
    d. pulling on surrounding tissues.

    ANS: D   DIF: I   OBJ: BPE 38-3.1

38. A muscle's insertion
    a. is located on a bone that remains stationary when the muscle contracts.
    b. moves away from the origin during muscle contraction.
    c. is attached to the bone by a ligament.
    d. None of the above

    ANS: D   DIF: I   OBJ: BPE 38-3.1

39. The origin of a muscle
    a. is at the opposite end of the muscle from the insertion.
    b. is located on a bone that remains stationary when the muscle contracts.
    c. does not move when the muscle contracts.
    d. All of the above

    ANS: D   DIF: I   OBJ: BPE 38-3.1

40. flexors : bend ::
    a. immovable joints : bend
    b. slightly movable joints : be immovable
    c. extensors : straighten
    d. sutures : move a great deal

    ANS: C
    (causes a joint to)

    DIF: II   OBJ: BPE 38-3.1

41. The functional unit of muscle contraction is called the
    a. myofibril.
    b. sarcomere.
    c. muscle fiber.
    d. myosin filament.

    ANS: B   DIF: I   OBJ: BPE 38-3.2

42. Actin and myosin
    a. are found in the sarcomeres.
    b. are proteins.
    c. interact during muscle contraction.
    d. All of the above

    ANS: D   DIF: I   OBJ: BPE 38-3.2

43. Repeating units of myosin and actin filaments bound by two Z lines are
    a. muscles.
    c. sarcomeres.
    b. myofibrils.
    d. extensors.

    ANS: C   DIF: I   OBJ: BPE 38-3.2

44. The total amount of force that a muscle can exert
    a. is determined by the strength of the nerve impulse that caused the contraction.
    b. depends on the total number of individual muscle fibers that have been stimulated.
    c. is dependent upon the weight of the object being moved.
    d. correlates to the number of Z lines contained within the sarcomeres of the muscle.

    ANS: B   DIF: I   OBJ: BPE 38-3.2

45. sarcomere contractions : ATP ::
    a. Z lines : actin and myosin
    b. actin and myosin : sarcomeres
    c. muscle forces : number of Z lines
    d. muscle forces : muscle fibers contracting

    ANS: D
    (depend on)

    DIF: II   OBJ: BPE 38-3.2

46. Aerobic activities
    a. increase muscle size and strength.
    b. produce ATP more efficiently than glycolysis.
    c. use up glycogen stores quickly.
    d. prevent myosin and actin linkages in muscles.

    ANS: B   DIF: I   OBJ: BPE 38-3.3

47. If you want to increase your cardiovascular endurance, the best type of exercise is
    a. anaerobic.
    c. resistance.
    b. aerobic.
    d. None of the above

    ANS: B   DIF: I   OBJ: BPE 38-3.3

48. If you want to increase the size and strength of your muscles, the best type of exercise is
    a. anaerobic.
    c. resistance.
    b. aerobic.
    d. None of the above

    ANS: C   DIF: I   OBJ: BPE 38-3.3

49. It has been known for a long time that muscle contraction requires ATP. Scientists have discovered that ATP is required to release the attachments between actin and myosin in the many cycles of attachment, release, and reattachment that result in sliding of these filaments past each other. Which of the following phenomena is explained by this specific role of ATP?
    a. muscle fatigue
    b. stiffening of a body after death (rigor mortis)
    c. opposing pairs of muscles functioning as flexors and extensors
    d. muscle sprain

    ANS: B   DIF: II   OBJ: BPE 38-3.3

50. The skin performs all of the following *except*
    a. protection.   c. control of body temperature
    b. sensation of heat.   d. production of gametes.

    ANS: D   DIF: I   OBJ: BPE 38-4.1

51. The thin outer layer of the skin is
    a. the dermis.   c. the fatty layer.
    b. the epidermis.   d. connective skin.

    ANS: B   DIF: I   OBJ: BPE 38-4.1

52. The functions of the skin include
    a. defense against microbes.   c. prevention of dehydration.
    b. regulation of body temperature. d. All of the above

    ANS: D   DIF: I   OBJ: BPE 38-4.1

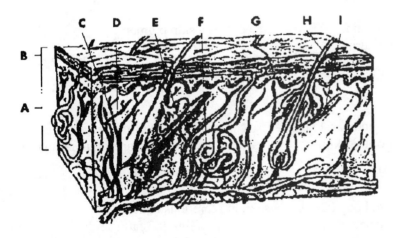

53. Refer to the illustration above. Which of the structures in the diagram are composed mainly of *dead* cells?
    a. structures A and F
    b. structures B and H
    c. structures C and D
    d. Skin is a living organ that does not have any dead cells.

    ANS: B   DIF: II   OBJ: BPE 38-4.1

54. Refer to the illustration above. The structure labeled E in the diagram
    a. often is responsible for the formation of acne.
    b. is found in adults and teenagers.
    c. may be affected by high levels of sex hormones.
    d. All of the above

    ANS: D   DIF: II   OBJ: BPE 38-4.1

55. Refer to the illustration above. Skin receives nutrients, eliminates wastes, and helps regulate
    body temperature by using which of the following structures?
    a. I   c. F
    b. G   d. D

    ANS: B   DIF: II   OBJ: BPE 38-4.2

56. Refer to the illustration above. The structure labeled F in the diagram
    a. is often responsible for the formation of acne.
    b. helps regulate body temperature.
    c. is a reservoir for excess blood cells.
    d. is only found in teenagers.

    ANS: B   DIF: II   OBJ: BPE 38-4.2

57. Refer to the illustration above. The portion of the skin labeled A in the diagram is
    a. the dermis.   c. composed mainly of connective tissue.
    b. sensitive to heat and cold.   d. All of the above

    ANS: A   DIF: II   OBJ: BPE 38-4.2

58. Keratin
    a. is a strong, fibrous protein.   c. is a skin pigment.
    b. fills dead cells in the dermis.   d. All of the above

    ANS: A   DIF: I   OBJ: BPE 38-4.1

59. The dermis of the skin is
    a. composed of corneal and basal layers.   c. the location of melanocytes.
    b. the innermost layer of the skin.   d. involved in temperature regulation.

    ANS: D   DIF: I   OBJ: BPE 38-4.2

60. Sweat glands contribute to body odor because their secretions contain
    a. carbohydrates and nucleic acids.   c. proteins and fatty acids.
    b. water.   d. All of the above

    ANS: C   DIF: I   OBJ: BPE 38-4.2

61. Keratin
    a. is a waterproof protein.   c. is a skin pigment.
    b. fills dead cells in the dermis.   d. All of the above

    ANS: A   DIF: I   OBJ: BPE 38-4.3

62. Hair and nails are produced by the cells of the
    a. dermis.
    b. subcutaneous level.
    c. subcutaneous glands.
    d. epidermis.

    ANS: D   DIF: I   OBJ: BPE 38-4.3

63. Goose bumps are caused by
    a. excessive oil production.
    b. tiny muscles in the dermis.
    c. the loss of keratin from the dermis.
    d. None of the above

    ANS: B   DIF: I   OBJ: BPE 38-4.3

64. specialized epidermal cells : nails ::
    a. "half-moon area" : hair
    b. keratin : melanocytes
    c. melanocytes : keratin
    d. hair follicles : hair

    ANS: D
    (produce)

    DIF: II   OBJ: BPE 38-4.3

65. Overexposure to sunlight may cause all of the following *except*
    a. mutations in the skin cells.
    b. premature aging of the skin.
    c. acne.
    d. skin cancer.

    ANS: C   DIF: I   OBJ: BPE 38-4.4

66. A skin disorder caused by blockage of oil glands is called
    a. acne.
    b. carcinoma.
    c. osteoporosis.
    d. psoriasis.

    ANS: A   DIF: I   OBJ: BPE 38-4.4

67. The most dangerous skin cancers are called
    a. malignant keratomas.
    b. malignant melanomas.
    c. third-degree sunburn.
    d. acne.

    ANS: B   DIF: I   OBJ: BPE 38-4.4

68. The most effective way to reduce the risk of skin cancer includes
    a. using a sunscreen.
    b. increasing exposure to the sunlight gradually.
    c. minimizing exposure to sunlight.
    d. All of the above

    ANS: C   DIF: I   OBJ: BPE 38-4.5

COMPLETION

1. _____ tissue joins, supports, and protects other types of tissue.

   ANS: Connective   DIF: I   OBJ: BPE 38-1.2

2. All organs of the body contain epithelial, connective, muscle, and _____ tissues.

   ANS: nerve   DIF: I   OBJ: BPE 38-1.2

3. _____ tissue can be classified as smooth, skeletal, or cardiac.

   ANS: Muscle   DIF: I   OBJ: BPE 38-1.2

4. _____ muscle is found in the walls of many internal organs.

   ANS: Smooth   DIF: I   OBJ: BPE 38-1.2

5. The _____ system is the primary organ system which functions by breaking down food into nutrients that can be used by the body.

   ANS: digestive   DIF: I   OBJ: BPE 38-1.3

6. The excretory system includes the kidneys, _____ _____, ureters, and the _____.

   ANS: urinary bladder, urethra   DIF: I   OBJ: BPE 38-1.3

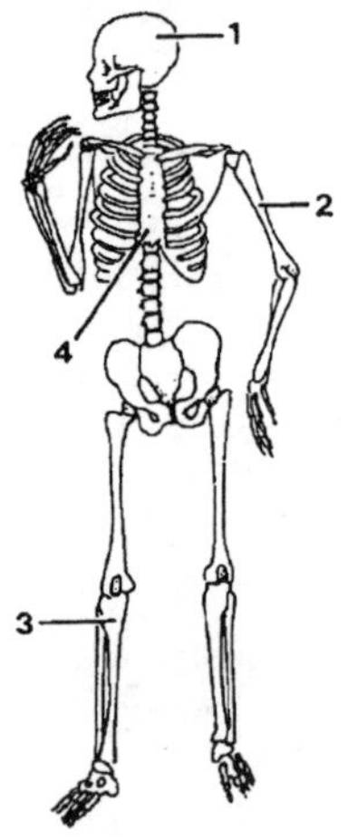

7. Refer to the illustration above. The bones labeled _____ and _____ are part of the appendicular skeleton.

   ANS: 2 and 3   DIF: II   OBJ: BPE 38-2.1

Biology: Principles and Explorations
Copyright © by Holt, Rinehart and Winston. All rights reserved.
524

8. Refer to the illustration above. The bones labeled _____ and _____ are part of the axial skeleton.

ANS: 1 and 4   DIF: II   OBJ: BPE 38-2.1

9. The bones of the skull and backbone are part of the _____ skeleton.

ANS: axial   DIF: I   OBJ: BPE 38-2.1

10. The heart and lungs are protected by the _____ _____.

ANS: rib cage   DIF: I   OBJ: BPE 38-2.1

11. The bones of the arms, legs, pectoral girdle, and pelvic girdle make up the _____ skeleton.

ANS: appendicular   DIF: I   OBJ: BPE 38-2.1

12. The rib cage is formed by curved ribs extending from the backbone and joining together in the front at the bone called the _____.

ANS: sternum or breastbone   DIF: I   OBJ: BPE 38-2.1

13. The bone _____ inside long bones is important in blood cell production and fat storage.

ANS: marrow   DIF: I   OBJ: BPE 38-2.2

14. _____ is a membrane that surrounds individual bones.

ANS: Periosteum   DIF: I   OBJ: BPE 38-2.2

15. _____ bone is dense—almost solid—and provides a great deal of support.

ANS: Compact   DIF: I   OBJ: BPE 38-2.2

16. The loss of bone density that occurs in the later years of life is known as _____.

ANS: osteoporosis   DIF: I   OBJ: BPE 38-2.4

17. The junction of two bones is called a(n) _____.

ANS: joint   DIF: I   OBJ: BPE 38-2.5

18. _____ _____ is a painful degeneration of movable joints caused by attacks on the joints by cells of the immune system.

ANS: Rheumatoid arthritis   DIF: I   OBJ: BPE 38-2.5

19. _____ are muscles that cause limbs to bend toward each other at a joint.

    ANS: Flexors   DIF: I   OBJ: BPE 38-3.1

20. Moving a bone requires the cooperation of two sets of _____.

    ANS: muscles   DIF: I   OBJ: BPE 38-3.1

21. Muscles that function to straighten a joint are called _____.

    ANS: extensors   DIF: I   OBJ: BPE 38-3.1

22. Strips of dense connective tissue that attach muscles to bones are called _____.

    ANS: tendons   DIF: I   OBJ: BPE 38-3.1

23. Repeating units of actin and myosin filaments are called _____.

    ANS: sarcomeres   DIF: I   OBJ: BPE 38-3.2

24. _____ exercises are the most effective form of exercises to increase the size of your skeletal muscles.

    ANS: Resistance   DIF: I   OBJ: BPE 38-3.3

25. The outermost layer of the skin is called the _____.

    ANS: epidermis   DIF: I   OBJ: BPE 38-4.1

26. The outer layer of the skin that contains both living and nonliving cells is called the _____.

    ANS: epidermis   DIF: I   OBJ: BPE 38-4.1

27. The brown pigment, _____, is responsible for most skin color.

    ANS: melanin   DIF: I   OBJ: BPE 38-4.1

28. Hairs grow from specialized epidermal structures called hair _____.

    ANS: follicles   DIF: I   OBJ: BPE 38-4.3

29. Acne is caused by overactive _____ _____ and hormones.

    ANS: oil glands   DIF: I   OBJ: BPE 38-4.4

30. The most common type of skin cancers are _____, which originate in the skin cells that do not produce pigments.

    ANS: carcinomas   DIF: I   OBJ: BPE 38-4.4

31. Overexposure to _____ rays may result in the mutations in skin cells that can cause skin cancer.

    ANS: ultraviolet   DIF: I   OBJ: BPE 38-4.5

ESSAY

1. Connective tissue plays many different roles in the human body. It is crucial for providing structural support for the body. It provides protection for internal organs. It facilitates the movements of body parts. It functions in the transport of substances throughout the body. It serves a storage function for certain kinds of molecules. It also plays a vital role in enabling the body to defend itself against invading organisms or other foreign substances.

In the space below or on a separate sheet of paper, write a short essay that first identifies the connective cell types discussed in your text. Next, distinguish these cell types from each other by their physical characteristics and by the type of matrix that is produced between the cells. Finally, relate the physical characteristics and the type of intercellular matrix to the specific function(s) that each of these cell types performs.

ANS:
Answers will vary and may include the following information:

Bone is a type of connective tissue that contains cells embedded in a matrix of collagen fibers that are coated with calcium salts. This makes bone fairly rigid and thus well-suited for providing structural support. It also provides protection of internal organs. For example, the skull protects the brain, the rib cage protects the heart and lungs, and the pelvic girdle protects organs of the reproductive, digestive, and excretory systems. Most of the human skeleton is composed of bone. Cartilage is a kind of connective tissue that contains cells embedded in a matrix of protein fibers. These fibers make cartilage strong yet flexible. Cartilage provides some structural support, particularly in young humans and at stress points between adjacent bones. Ligaments and tendons are both kinds of connective tissue that contain cells embedded in a matrix of collagen fibers. Ligaments connect bones to each other at joints and tendons attach muscles to bones. Both thus help the body make skeletal movements. Fibroblasts are connective tissue cells that produce collagen and secrete it. This collagen is then used as the intercellular matrix of the other types of connective tissue that contain collagen. Blood is a kind of connective tissue that contains cells embedded in a matrix of water. Blood is the medium in which oxygen, nutrients, wastes, hormones, antibodies, and many other chemicals are transported to and from the cells of the body. Some of the blood cells function as part of the immune system and other cells that defend our bodies against invading organisms and foreign substances. Some of these cells, such as macrophages, ingest and destroy any such harmful agent. Others of these cells, many of the lymphocytes, are involved in attacks against specific harmful agents. Adipose tissue is a kind of connective tissue that contains cells embedded in a matrix of mostly collagen fibers. The cells store fat as an energy reserve for our bodies.

DIF: III   OBJ: BPE 38-1.2

2. Give an example of each of the following types of tissue, and briefly describe its functions: epithelial tissue, muscle tissue, connective tissue, and nerve tissue.

ANS:
Epithelial tissues, such as skin, are generally flat sheets of cells that protect the body from damage and control water loss in the tissues that they cover. Muscle tissue moves the body structures (skeletal muscle) and moves materials through the body (cardiac and smooth muscle). Connective tissue defends the body from invaders (white blood cells), sequesters materials (fat, melanin), and supports the body (bone and cartilage). Nerve tissues (brain, spinal cord) carry information, in the form of electrical impulses, throughout the body.

DIF: II   OBJ: BPE 38-1.2

3. List the three types of muscle tissue, and give the function of each.

ANS:
The three types of muscle tissue are skeletal muscle, cardiac muscle, and smooth muscle. Skeletal muscle moves bones, and cardiac muscle pumps blood through the body. Smooth muscle moves food through the body and performs other internal functions including changing blood vessel diameter, opening and closing bronchioles, and causing uterine contractions during labor.

DIF: II   OBJ: BPE 38-1.2

4. How does maintaining a relatively warm body temperature (endothermy) help humans?

ANS:
Endothermy permits the body to maintain its activity at all times and in many different places, regardless of the temperature of the surroundings. In addition, endothermy allows the body to sustain strenuous activity. Ectotherms, by contrast, are limited to short periods of exertion.

DIF: II   OBJ: BPE 38-1.4

5. Why is it essential for the body to maintain homeostasis?

ANS:
A stable fluid environment is necessary for multicellular organisms. Any extreme change in extracellular fluid can have very serious effects on the activities inside cells. If factors such as pH level, ion concentration, and sugar level vary outside the range that cells require, death may result.

DIF: II   OBJ: BPE 38-1.4

6. List five types of freely movable joints in your body, and give a location for each.

ANS:
Ball-and-socket joints are found in the shoulders and hip. Pivot joints enable heads to rotate and are found at the top of spines. Gliding joints are found in wrists and ankles. Saddle joints function at the base of thumbs. The knees, elbows, and knuckles provide examples of hinge joints.

DIF: II   OBJ: BPE 38-2.5

7. Using examples, describe the three basic types of joints and their primary functions.

ANS:
Immovable joints are very tight joints that hold adjacent bones together, permitting little or no movement. The cranial bones of the skull are held together by virtually immovable joints called sutures. Limited mobility is permitted by slightly movable joints, the second basic type of joint. In these joints, a bridge of cartilage joins two bones together, as in the joints between the vertebrae of the spine. The third type of joint is the freely movable joint. These joints allow the greatest degree of movement; they are found between bones that are held together by ligaments.

DIF: II   OBJ: BPE 38-2.5

8. What is a ligament? What does it mean to say that a ligament is sprained? Explain.

ANS:
A ligament is a tough connective tissue that joins one bone to another. Although ligaments are very elastic, there is a limit to how far they can stretch. When a ligament is stretched too far, the injury that results is called a sprain.

DIF: II   OBJ: BPE 38-2.5

9. Describe the contraction of muscle according to the sliding filament theory.

ANS:
Myosin and actin filaments lie in parallel lines. along the length of a myofibril in units called sarcomeres. The myosin heads touch the adjacent actin filaments. When a muscle contracts, the myosin heads attach to the actin filaments, and when the heads bend inward, they pull the actin filaments along with them, toward each other. As the actin filaments move toward each other along the myosin filament, they pull their Z lines with them, thus shortening the sarcomere. As sarcomeres are shortened along the entire muscle fiber, the entire muscle contracts. ATP is used as the myosin head detaches from the binding site and snaps back into its original position

DIF: II   OBJ: BPE 38-3.2

10. The skin is composed of three layers. What are they, and what do they do?

ANS:
The outermost layer of the skin is the epidermis. This layer is responsible for protection from the environment. The epidermis produces new cells from its deepest layer (the basal layer) that move upward to become the corneal layer. Accessory structures, such as hair and nails, are produced by cells of the epidermis. The middle and thickest, layer of the skin is called the dermis, which is the major framework of the skin. This layer provides structural support and is a matrix for nerve endings, blood vessels, and the specialized cells of the skin. The subcutaneous layer is the innermost layer of the skin. This is a layer of fat-rich cells that act as shock absorbers, provide insulation, and store vitamins.

DIF: II   OBJ: BPE 38-4.1

11. How does the skin help regulate body temperature?

ANS:
Nerves in the skin sense heat, providing stimuli that dilate or constrict blood vessels. When the temperature in the environment is high, blood vessels dilate, allowing body heat to escape. Also, the skin produces sweat through its sweat glands, and the evaporation of sweat has a cooling effect on the body. When the temperature of the environment is low, blood vessels in the skin contract, reducing heat loss.

DIF: II   OBJ: BPE 38-4.2

12. What are three functions of the blood vessels in the dermis? Explain.

ANS:
The blood vessels in the dermis provide nutrient-rich blood to nourish skin cells, to carry away cellular waste products, and to regulate body temperature. Blood radiates heat into the air as it passes near the surface of the skin. If the body becomes too hot, these blood vessels enlarge, allowing more blood to flow through the dermis near the body surface.

DIF: II   OBJ: BPE 38-4.2

13. What causes acne? Can it be prevented or controlled?

ANS:
Acne is caused by several factors including hormones, and an increase in oil production by glands during adolescence. Excessive oil production can clog the oil glands, causing a buildup of oil, dirt, and bacteria. While acne cannot be prevented, the conditions associated with it may be controlled with proper skin care.

DIF: II   OBJ: BPE 38-4.4

TRUE/FALSE

1. Nutrients are transported to all cells in the body through blood vessels.

   ANS: T   DIF: I   OBJ: BPE 39-1.1

2. Arteries contain valves that prevent the backward flow of blood.

   ANS: F   DIF: I   OBJ: BPE 39-1.2

3. The innermost layer of an artery is a layer of elastic, smooth muscle tissue.

   ANS: F   DIF: I   OBJ: BPE 39-1.2

4. Blood vessels in the body include arteries, veins, and capillaries.

   ANS: T   DIF: I   OBJ: BPE 39-1.2

5. The lymphatic system returns fluids from around cells back to the blood vessels.

   ANS: T   DIF: I   OBJ: BPE 39-1.3

6. When a platelet encounters a damaged blood vessel, it releases fibrin, which causes a clot to form.

   ANS: F   DIF: I   OBJ: BPE 39-1.4

7. Blood plasma is composed primarily of water.

   ANS: T   DIF: I   OBJ: BPE 39-1.4

8. New red blood cells are produced by stem cells in the bone marrow.

   ANS: T   DIF: I   OBJ: BPE 39-1.4

9. Red blood cells are responsible for the production of antibodies.

   ANS: F   DIF: I   OBJ: BPE 39-1.4

10. A person with type AB blood can donate blood to a person with any blood type.

    ANS: F   DIF: I   OBJ: BPE 39-1.5

11. Type O blood contains neither A nor B antigens.

    ANS: T   DIF: I   OBJ: BPE 39-1.5

12. Systemic circulation carries blood from the heart to the rest of the body.

    ANS: T   DIF: I   OBJ: BPE 39-2.1

13. The upper chambers of the heart are called the ventricles.

    ANS: F   DIF: I   OBJ: BPE 39-2.2

14. The superior vena cava drains blood from the head and neck.

    ANS: T   DIF: I   OBJ: BPE 39-2.2

15. Blood from the left ventricle flows into the aorta.

    ANS: T   DIF: I   OBJ: BPE 39-2.2

16. Contraction of the heart is initiated by a cluster of cardiac muscle cells called the sinoatrial node.

    ANS: T   DIF: I   OBJ: BPE 39-2.3

17. Blood pressure is measured with a device called a sphygmomanometer.

    ANS: T   DIF: I   OBJ: BPE 39-2.4

18. The systolic pressure tells how much pressure is exerted when the heart relaxes.

    ANS: F   DIF: I   OBJ: BPE 39-2.4

19. A stroke occurs when an area of the heart muscle dies.

    ANS: F   DIF: I   OBJ: BPE 39-2.5

20. The smallest bronchioles end in clusters of air sacs called alveoli, where gases are exchanged in the lungs.

    ANS: T   DIF: I   OBJ: BPE 39-3.1

21. When the diaphragm and the rib muscles contract, exhalation occurs.

    ANS: F   DIF: I   OBJ: BPE 39-3.2

22. Breathing is regulated mainly by response to the level of carbon dioxide detected in the blood.

    ANS: T   DIF: I   OBJ: BPE 39-3.3

23. The majority of carbon dioxide in the blood is attached to hemoglobin molecules inside red blood cells.

    ANS: F   DIF: I   OBJ: BPE 39-3.4

24. Asthma is a respiratory disease in which the alveoli of the lungs become narrowed.

   ANS: F   DIF: I   OBJ: BPE 39-3.5

MULTIPLE CHOICE

1. The human circulatory system
   a. helps maintain a constant body temperature.
   b. carries cells that help protect the body from disease.
   c. helps the body maintain homeostasis.
   d. All of the above

   ANS: D   DIF: I   OBJ: BPE 39-1.1

2. Which type of blood vessel is both strong and elastic?
   a. capillary   c. vein
   b. artery   d. venule

   ANS: B   DIF: I   OBJ: BPE 39-1.2

3. An artery has a much thicker muscle layer than
   a. a vein.   c. a venule.
   b. a capillary.   d. All of the above

   ANS: D   DIF: I   OBJ: BPE 39-1.2

4. The smallest and most numerous blood vessels in the body are the
   a. venules.   c. arteries.
   b. veins.   d. capillaries.

   ANS: D   DIF: I   OBJ: BPE 39-1.2

5. An artery
   a. usually carries oxygen-rich blood.
   b. has thin, slightly elastic walls.
   c. has valves that prevent blood from flowing backward.
   d. All of the above

   ANS: A   DIF: I   OBJ: BPE 39-1.2

6. If a blood vessel has valves, it probably is a(n)
   a. vein.   c. venule.
   b. artery.   d. capillary.

   ANS: A   DIF: I   OBJ: BPE 39-1.2

7. Vessels that carry blood away from the heart are called
   a. veins.   c. arteries.
   b. capillaries.   d. venules.

   ANS: C   DIF: I   OBJ: BPE 39-1.2

8. The fluid between cells is transported to the bloodstream by the
   a. renal circulation.
   b. hepatic portal circulation.
   c. respiratory system.
   d. lymphatic system.

   ANS: D   DIF: I   OBJ: BPE 39-1.3

9. Mature red blood cells
   a. can live for about a year.
   b. are the largest cells in the blood.
   c. promote clotting.
   d. do not have a nucleus.

   ANS: D   DIF: I   OBJ: BPE 39-1.4

10. Infections generally result in an increase in the number of
    a. white blood cells.
    b. red blood cells.
    c. platelets.
    d. alveoli.

    ANS: A   DIF: I   OBJ: BPE 39-1.4

11. The iron-containing molecule in red blood cells is called
    a. plasma.
    b. ferric oxide.
    c. hemoglobin.
    d. carbonic acid.

    ANS: C   DIF: I   OBJ: BPE 39-1.4

12. Red blood cells
    a. transport respiratory gases.
    b. combat bacterial infection.
    c. destroy viruses.
    d. transport cholesterol.

    ANS: A   DIF: I   OBJ: BPE 39-1.4

13. Defending the body against bacterial infection and invasion by foreign substances is a function of
    a. red blood cells.
    b. plasma.
    c. platelets.
    d. white blood cells.

    ANS: D   DIF: I   OBJ: BPE 39-1.4

14. An abnormality involving the platelets would probably affect the process of
    a. breathing.
    b. locomotion.
    c. fighting bacterial infections.
    d. blood clotting.

    ANS: D   DIF: I   OBJ: BPE 39-1.4

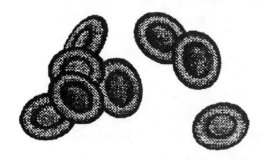

15. Refer to the illustration above. The cells shown in the diagram are
    a. filled with plasma.   c. red blood cells.
    b. platelets.   d. white blood cells.

    ANS: C   DIF: II   OBJ: BPE 39-1.4

16. Refer to the illustration above. The cells shown in the diagram
    a. can live for at least a year.
    b. are the largest cells in the circulatory system.
    c. promote clotting.
    d. contain hemoglobin.

    ANS: D   DIF: II   OBJ: BPE 39-1.4

17. vitamins, salts, and proteins : plasma solutes ::
    a. arteries and veins : lymphatic vessels
    b. erythrocytes, leukocytes, and platelets : blood cells
    c. platelets and megakaryocytes : leukocytes
    d. lymphocytes and macrophages : erythrocytes

    ANS: B
    (are different types of)

    DIF: II   OBJ: BPE 39-1.4

18. A person with antigen A on their red blood cells can give blood to someone with blood type(s)
    a. A and AB.   c. only AB
    b. B and AB.   d. only O

    ANS: A   DIF: I   OBJ: BPE 39-1.5

19. Pulmonary circulation flows to and from the
    a. stomach.   c. intestines.
    b. liver.   d. lungs.

    ANS: D   DIF: I   OBJ: BPE 39-2.1

20. The heart chamber that receives blood from the venae cavae is the
    a. left atrium.
    b. right atrium.
    c. left ventricle.
    d. right ventricle.

    ANS: B   DIF: I   OBJ: BPE 39-2.2

21. The ventricles are
    a. the upper chambers of the heart.
    b. the chambers of the heart that pump blood to the lungs and to the rest of the body.
    c. the chambers of the heart that receive blood from the lungs and the rest of the body.
    d. lower chambers of the heart that contract separately.

    ANS: B   DIF: I   OBJ: BPE 39-2.2

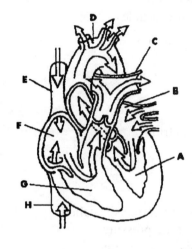

22. Refer to the illustration above. The vessels indicated by C in the diagram carry deoxygenated blood. The vessels are
    a. the pulmonary arteries.
    b. the pulmonary veins.
    c. parts of the aorta.
    d. part of the atria.

    ANS: A   DIF: II   OBJ: BPE 39-2.2

23. Refer to the illustration above. The chamber in the diagram indicated by F is
    a. the right atrium.
    b. the left atrium.
    c. the right ventricle.
    d. the left ventricle.

    ANS: A   DIF: II   OBJ: BPE 39-2.2

24. Refer to the illustration above. In the diagram, the aorta is indicated by
    a. C.
    b. D.
    c. G.
    d. H.

    ANS: B   DIF: II   OBJ: BPE 39-2.2

25. Refer to the illustration above. In the diagram, blood in chamber A
    a. is full of oxygen.
    b. is returning from the vena cavae.
    c. is oxygen poor.
    d. has very little plasma.

    ANS: A   DIF: II   OBJ: BPE 39-2.2

26. Blood entering the right atrium
    a. is full of oxygen.
    b. is returning from the lungs.
    c. is deoxygenated.
    d. is low in plasma and platelets.

    ANS: C   DIF: I   OBJ: BPE 39-2.2

27. Oxygenated blood from the lungs is received by the
    a. left ventricle.
    b. right atrium.
    c. left atrium.
    d. right ventricle.

    ANS: C   DIF: I   OBJ: BPE 39-2.2

28. The pacemaker responsible for starting a heartbeat
    a. is located in the brain.
    b. squeezes the ventricles shut.
    c. is a small bundle of cells at the entrance to the right atrium.
    d. is in the aorta.

    ANS: C   DIF: I   OBJ: BPE 39-2.3

29. The force exerted against the arterial walls when the heart contracts is called
    a. hypertension.
    b. systolic pressure.
    c. diastolic pressure.
    d. arterial relaxation.

    ANS: B   DIF: I   OBJ: BPE 39-2.4

30. Normal blood measure in millimeters of mercury is
    a. 145/95.
    b. 130/100.
    c. 120/80.
    d. 100/50.

    ANS: C   DIF: I   OBJ: BPE 39-2.4

31. The pressure exerted on the inner walls of the arteries when the heart relaxes between beats is the ____ pressure.
    a. systolic.
    b. diastolic.
    c. barometric.
    d. residual.

    ANS: B   DIF: I   OBJ: BPE 39-2.4

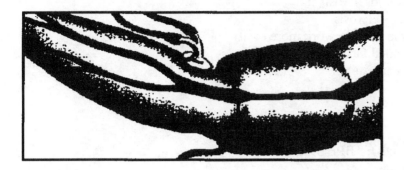

32. Refer to the illustration above. In the diagram, what is being measured?
    a. cholesterol.
    b. heartbeat.
    c. blood pressure.
    d. oxygen concentration of the blood.

    ANS: C   DIF: II   OBJ: BPE 39-2.4

33. blood pressure : sphygmomanometer ::
    a. heart electrical impulse : blood pressure device
    b. heart electrical impulse : heart muscle contractor
    c. heart electrical impulse : electrocardiogram
    d. diastolic pressure : pressure in the left ventricle

    ANS: C
    (is measured with a[n])

    DIF: II   OBJ: BPE 39-2.4

34. A heart attack can result from the blockage of a blood vessel because of
    a. iron deposits.
    b. hypothyroidism.
    c. plaque build-up.
    d. excessive hemoglobin.

    ANS: C   DIF: I   OBJ: BPE 39-2.5

35. A condition known as atherosclerosis results in
    a. increased circulation to the heart.
    b. larger muscles.
    c. a narrowing of the inner walls of blood vessels.
    d. a widening of inner walls of blood vessels.

    ANS: C   DIF: I   OBJ: BPE 39-2.5

36. Hypertension is another name for what condition?
    a. anemia
    b. stroke
    c. high blood pressure
    d. heart murmur

    ANS: C   DIF: I   OBJ: BPE 39-2.5

37. cholesterol buildup : atherosclerosis ::
    a. iron buildup : atherosclerosis
    b. arteriosclerosis : the heart to work more easily
    c. low intake of saturated fats : heart attacks
    d. atherosclerosis : heart attacks

    ANS: D
    (causes)

    DIF: II   OBJ: BPE 39-2.5

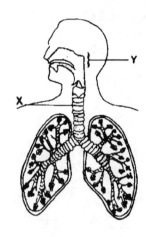

38. Refer to the illustration above. The structure labeled "X" is the
    a. epiglottis.   c. trachea.
    b. pharynx.   d. larynx.

    ANS: C   DIF: II   OBJ: BPE 39-3.1

39. During swallowing, the air passage of the pharynx is covered by the
    a. larynx.   c. trachea.
    b. epiglottis.   d. bronchi.

    ANS: B   DIF: I   OBJ: BPE 39-3.1

40. Alveoli in the lungs are connected to the bronchi by a network of tiny tubes called
    a. arterioles.   c. capillaries.
    b. venules.   d. bronchioles.

    ANS: D   DIF: I   OBJ: BPE 39-3.1

41. The actual exchange of gases occurs at the site of the
    a. trachea.   c. larynx.
    b. nasal passageway.   d. alveoli.

    ANS: D   DIF: I   OBJ: BPE 39-3.1

42. Each alveolus
    a. contains many air sacs.
    b. attaches directly to the larynx.
    c. is surrounded by capillaries.
    d. is a large air sac.

    ANS: C   DIF: I   OBJ: BPE 39-3.1

43. bronchiole : alveoli ::
    a. alveoli : bronchi
    b. bronchi : larynx
    c. larynx : pharynx
    d. bronchi : bronchioles

    ANS: D
    (transports air to the)

    DIF: II   OBJ: BPE 39-3.1

44. When the diaphragm and rib cage muscles relax,
    a. the chest cavity enlarges.
    b. inhalation occurs.
    c. exhalation occurs.
    d. it is impossible to breathe.

    ANS: C   DIF: I   OBJ: BPE 39-3.2

45. The dome-shaped muscle below the chest cavity is called the
    a. soleus.
    b. biceps.
    c. diaphragm.
    d. popliteus.

    ANS: C   DIF: I   OBJ: BPE 39-3.2

46. Which of the following occurs as air rushes into the lungs from the environment to equalize air pressure?
    a. inhalation
    b. contraction
    c. exhalation
    d. None of the above

    ANS: A   DIF: I   OBJ: BPE 39-3.2

47. The breathing center in the brain is *most* sensitive to the
    a. concentration of oxygen.
    b. concentration of carbon dioxide in the lungs.
    c. concentration of carbon dioxide in the blood.
    d. amount of oxygen in the cells.

    ANS: C   DIF: I   OBJ: BPE 39-3.3

48. Gas exchange occurs when
    a. oxygen in the alveoli diffuses into the blood in the capillaries.
    b. oxygen binds with hemoglobin in the red blood cells.
    c. the red blood cells give up oxygen to the cells of the body tissues.
    d. All of the above

    ANS: D   DIF: I   OBJ: BPE 39-3.4

49. Carbon dioxide is transported in the blood in all of the following ways *except*
    a. dissolved in plasma.
    b. combined with hemoglobin.
    c. as bicarbonate ions.
    d. by white blood cells.

    ANS: D   DIF: I   OBJ: BPE 39-3.4

50. A respiratory disease in which airways in the lungs become narrow because of sensitivity to certain stimuli is called
    a. asthma.
    b. bronchitis.
    c. emphysema.
    d. alveolar reduction.

    ANS: A   DIF: I   OBJ: BPE 39-3.5

COMPLETION

1. The _____ system transports oxygen, carbon dioxide, food molecules, hormones, and other material to and from the cells of the body.

    ANS: circulatory   DIF: I   OBJ: BPE 39-1.1

2. _____ are the blood vessels that connect the arteries to the veins.

    ANS: Capillaries   DIF: I   OBJ: BPE 39-1.2

3. The diagram below shows two human blood vessels, A and B, connected by a capillary bed, C. Blood pressure is higher in vessel B than in vessel A. The arrows indicate the direction of diffusion of O_2 and CO_2.

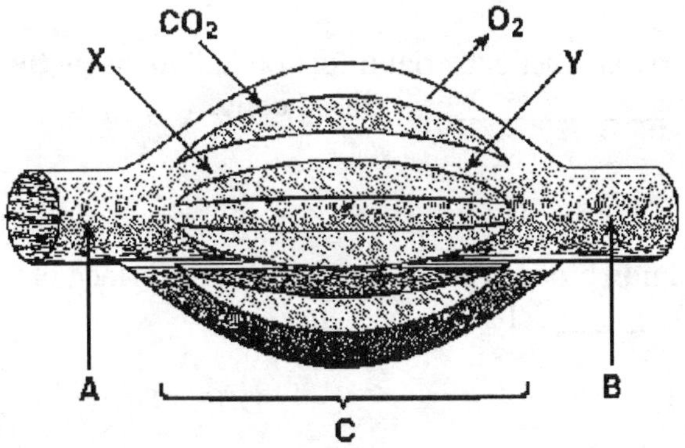

a. What type of blood vessel is vessel A? _____
b. What type of blood vessel is vessel B? _____
c. Does this diagram show part of the systemic circuit or part of the pulmonary circuit of the human circulatory system? _____
d. In which location, X or Y, will the concentration of O_2 in the blood be higher? _____
e. Name one other substance typically found in blood that would move out of a capillary bed into body tissues along with the O_2 shown in the diagram: _____
f. Name one other substance typically found in blood that would move into a capillary bed from body tissues along with the CO_2 shown in the diagram: _____

ANS:
a. vein
b. artery
c. systemic circuit
d. "Y"
e. food molecule, water, vitamin, ion, hormone, white blood cell are possible answers
f. wastes or ammonia are possible answers

DIF: III   OBJ: BPE 39-1.2

4. Excess fluids and proteins in the body are returned to the blood by a system of vessels called the _____ system.

ANS: lymphatic   DIF: I   OBJ: BPE 39-1.3

5. The major function of _____ is to assist in the blood clotting process.

ANS: platelets   DIF: I   OBJ: BPE 39-1.4

6. The primary role of hemoglobin in the blood is to carry _____.

ANS: oxygen   DIF: I   OBJ: BPE 39-1.4

7. The iron-containing molecule in red blood cells is called _____.

ANS: hemoglobin   DIF: I   OBJ: BPE 39-1.4

8. Defending the body against bacterial infection and invasion by other foreign substances is the function of _____ blood cells.

ANS: white   DIF: I   OBJ: BPE 39-1.4

9. Antigens determining blood type are carried on the surface of _____ _____ cells.

ANS: red blood   DIF: I   OBJ: BPE 39-1.5

10. The flow of blood from the heart to all parts of the body except the lungs is part of the system of circulation called the _____ circulation.

ANS: systemic   DIF: I   OBJ: BPE 39-2.1

11. The largest vein in the human body is the _____ _____.

ANS: vena cava   DIF: I   OBJ: BPE 39-2.2

12. The _____ node starts each contraction of the heart.

ANS: sinoatrial   DIF: I   OBJ: BPE 39-2.3

13. Systolic pressure is caused by contraction of the heart's _____.

ANS: ventricles   DIF: I   OBJ: BPE 39-2.4

14. The condition that results when blood pressure is consistently higher than normal is called _____.

ANS: hypertension   DIF: I   OBJ: BPE 39-2.4

15. A(n)_____ _____ occurs when an area of the heart muscle dies and stops working.

ANS: heart attack   DIF: I   OBJ: BPE 39-2.5

16. The _____ is a long, straight tube that carries air from the back of the throat to the lungs.

ANS: trachea   DIF: I   OBJ: BPE 39-3.1

17. When you swallow, the _____ prevents food from entering the trachea.

ANS: epiglottis   DIF: I   OBJ: BPE 39-3.1

18. When the diaphragm and the rib muscles contract, enlarging the chest cavity, _____ occurs.

    ANS: inhalation   DIF: I   OBJ: BPE 39-3.2

19. Breathing is regulated mainly by response to the level of _____ _____ detected in the blood.

    ANS: carbon dioxide   DIF: I   OBJ: BPE 39-3.3

20. Hemoglobin in red blood cells binds to both oxygen and _____ _____.

    ANS: carbon dioxide   DIF: I   OBJ: BPE 39-3.4

21. _____ is a disease in which the lung tissue loses its elasticity.

    ANS: Emphysema   DIF: I   OBJ: BPE 39-3.5

ESSAY

1. Describe how oxygen is transported in the blood.

    ANS:
    Red blood cells are filled with hemoglobin, which is an iron-containing protein that gives blood its red color. Oxygen easily binds to the hemoglobin iron, making red blood cells efficient oxygen carriers that circulate throughout the body as they flow with the plasma.

    DIF: I   OBJ: BPE 39-1.4

2. Describe the antibody-antigen interactions that take place when an Rh⁻ person who has blood type B receives blood from an Rh⁺ person who has blood type AB.

    ANS:
    An Rh⁻ person who has blood type B has only blood antigen B. A person having this antigen would produce antibodies to antigens A and Rh. An Rh⁺ person who has blood type AB has blood antigens Rh, A, and B. When these antigens enter the recipient's blood, antibodies to the A and Rh will produce clumping of the red blood cells. The B antigen of the donor's blood will not cause clumping because the recipient does not produce antibodies to this antigen.

    DIF: II   OBJ: BPE 39-1.5

3. Every living cell in the human body must have an energy supply. Cells take up glucose or a related chemical and break it down inside the mitochondria to get ATP. ATP is the form of energy that cells use for their various activities. The breakdown of glucose occurs in the process of aerobic respiration. A summary of this process is shown in the following equation (note that this is not a balanced equation):

$$C_6H_{12}O_6 + O_2 \leftrightarrow CO_2 + H_2O + ATP$$

O_2, which is a gas, is consumed in this process and CO_2, also a gas, is produced. Trace the pathway of a molecule of O_2 from the location where it enters the human body, across any cell membranes it must pass, until it reaches a muscle cell in the right leg. Then, trace the pathway of a molecule of CO_2 from inside that muscle cell, where it is produced in aerobic respiration, until it leaves the body. Write your answer in the space below or on a separate sheet of paper.

ANS:
The O_2 molecule would enter the body through one of the nostrils, pass through the pharynx, the trachea, one of the two bronchi, and then enter a bronchiole in the lung. It would then move into an alveolus and then move across a cell membrane of the alveolus and enter the blood. Once in the blood, the O_2 would move across the cell membrane into a red blood cell. It would then be transported in the blood leaving the lungs in the pulmonary vein, which takes blood to the heart. The O_2 in blood would enter the heart in the left atrium, move to the left ventricle, and then be forced out of the heart into the aorta. The O_2 in blood would then be transported into smaller arteries, still smaller arterioles, and finally a capillary bed in the muscle in the right leg. The O_2 would then move out of the red blood cell, across its cell membrane, and across a cell membrane to enter a muscle cell. A CO_2 molecule produced by aerobic respiration in this muscle cell would leave the cell by moving across its cell membrane. It would then enter the blood. In the blood, it would most likely move across the cell membrane of a red blood cell and remain in its cytoplasm. The CO_2 in blood would then be transported into venules, and then into veins, until it returned to the vena cava. From the vena cava, it would reenter the heart. The CO_2 in blood would enter the right atrium of the heart, move to the right ventricle, and then be forced out of the heart into the pulmonary artery. From there, it would be transported to one of the lungs. In a lung, the CO_2 would move out of the red blood cell by moving across its cell membrane. It would then move across a cell membrane of an alveolus. From the alveolus, the CO_2 would pass through a bronchiole, a bronchus, the trachea, the pharynx, and then leave the body through one of the nostrils.

DIF: III   OBJ: BPE 39-2.1

4. Do arteries carry oxygenated blood or deoxygenated blood? Explain.

ANS:
An artery is a blood vessel that carries blood away from the heart. Most arteries carry oxygenated blood, but some arteries carry deoxygenated blood. The pulmonary arteries, which carry blood from the heart to the lungs, carry deoxygenated blood that has been returned to the heart from the rest of the body. The arteries that carry blood from the heart to the rest of the body carry oxygenated blood that has been returned to the heart from the lungs.

DIF: II   OBJ: BPE 39-2.2

5. How is air moved in and out of the lungs from the environment?

ANS:
When the diaphragm and rib muscles contract, the diaphragm moves downward and the rib cage moves up and outward. This expands the chest cavity, lowering the air pressure in the lungs and causing air to flow in. When the diaphragm and the rib muscles relax, the diaphragm moves upward and the rib cage moves down and inward. This reduces the size of the chest cavity, increasing the pressure of the air in the lungs and causing air to flow out.

DIF: II   OBJ: BPE 39-3.2

6. Carbon dioxide (CO_2) dissolves poorly in plasma. While it can be carried by hemoglobin, the ability of red blood cells to transport it on hemoglobin is limited. Thus, seventy percent of the CO_2 that leaves the body is carried out in a third way. Explain what happens.

ANS:
With the help of an enzyme, the remaining 70 percent of carbon dioxide combines with water in the blood to form carbonic acid (H_2CO_3) inside red blood cells. Because carbonic acid is unstable, hydrogen (H^+) and bicarbonate (HCO_3^-) ions quickly form. When the blood reaches the lungs, chemical reactions occur that reverse the process, releasing carbon dioxide. The carbon dioxide diffuses from the blood into the alveoli in the lungs. It is then exhaled with water vapor.

DIF: II   OBJ: BPE 39-3.4

7. Asthma and emphysema are two diseases that cause problems with normal respiratory function. Briefly describe what each disease does to a person.

ANS:
Asthma is a respiratory disease in which certain airways in the lungs become constricted because of sensitivity to certain stimuli. The narrowing of the airways reduces the efficiency of respiration, which decreases the amount of oxygen reaching body cells.

Emphysema (often the result of cigarette smoking) causes lung alveoli to lose their elasticity. This loss of elasticity makes it difficult to release air during exhalation and also greatly reduces the efficiency of gas exchange in the lungs. Severely affected individuals must breathe from tanks of pure oxygen in order to live.

DIF: II   OBJ: BPE 39-3.5

TRUE/FALSE

1. Nutrients are needed by the body for repair and maintenance.

   ANS: T   DIF: I   OBJ: BPE 40-1.1

2. Water is one of the five basic classes of nutrients.

   ANS: F   DIF: I   OBJ: BPE 40-1.1

3. Vitamins, minerals, and lipids are not classified as nutrients because of their method of absorption.

   ANS: F   DIF: I   OBJ: BPE 40-1.1

4. Excess calories that the body takes in are metabolized to produce heat energy.

   ANS: F   DIF: I   OBJ: BPE 40-1.2

5. Carbohydrates are obtained mostly from oils, margarine, and butter.

   ANS: F   DIF: I   OBJ: BPE 40-1.2

6. Proteins are the body's main source of fuel.

   ANS: F   DIF: I   OBJ: BPE 40-1.2

7. Calcium is an example of a trace element that is required by the body.

   ANS: F   DIF: I   OBJ: BPE 40-1.2

8. Proteins consist of mainly simple sugars bonded together.

   ANS: F   DIF: I   OBJ: BPE 40-1.2

9. USDA food guide pyramid recommends that grains should be eaten in greater amounts than meats.

   ANS: T   DIF: I   OBJ: BPE 40-1.3

10. Obesity is described as being 10 percent heavier than your ideal body weight.

    ANS: F   DIF: I   OBJ: BPE 40-1.4

11. Determining the taste of food is one of the major functions of the digestive system.

    ANS: F   DIF: I   OBJ: BPE 40-2.1

12. In the first stage of digestion, proteins are broken down by pepsins in the stomach.

    ANS: F   DIF: I   OBJ: BPE 40-2.2

13. The rectum is the final section of the digestive tract.

    ANS: T   DIF: I   OBJ: BPE 40-2.2

14. Almost all lipids are broken down in the small intestine.

    ANS: T   DIF: I   OBJ: BPE 40-2.2

15. Some nutrients are absorbed in the large intestine.

    ANS: T   DIF: I   OBJ: BPE 40-2.2

16. The synthesis of hydrochloric acid (HCl) in the stomach is regulated by the hormone ulcerin.

    ANS: F   DIF: I   OBJ: BPE 40-2.2

17. During emulsification, bile salts break down large fat globules into smaller fat droplets.

    ANS: T   DIF: I   OBJ: BPE 40-2.3

18. Bile salts are made by the small intestine.

    ANS: F   DIF: I   OBJ: BPE 40-2.4

19. Bile is a chemical secreted by the small intestine.

    ANS: F   DIF: I   OBJ: BPE 40-2.4

20. The liver stores fat-soluble nutrients and regulates the levels of food molecules in the blood.

    ANS: T   DIF: I   OBJ: BPE 40-2.4

21. The liver is part of the digestive system.

    ANS: T   DIF: I   OBJ: BPE 40-2.4

22. Urea is a highly toxic nitrogenous waste.

    ANS: F   DIF: I   OBJ: BPE 40-3.1

23. The skin can be considered an excretory organ.

    ANS: T   DIF: I   OBJ: BPE 40-3.1

24. The kidneys filter out toxins, urea, water, and mineral salts from the blood.

    ANS: T   DIF: I   OBJ: BPE 40-3.1

25. Nitrogenous waste is removed from the blood by a process called filtration.

    ANS: T   DIF: I   OBJ: BPE 40-3.2

26. The blood-cleaning units of the kidneys are called nephrons.

    ANS: T   DIF: I   OBJ: BPE 40-3.2

27. The first stage of urine formation is called reabsorption.

    ANS: F   DIF: I   OBJ: BPE 40-3.3

28. The ureter is a muscular sac that stores urine.

    ANS: F   DIF: I   OBJ: BPE 40-3.4

29. When kidneys are damaged by disease or injury, the blood must be filtered artificially by hemodialysis.

    ANS: T   DIF: I   OBJ: BPE 40-3.5

30. Dialysis is a permanent solution to kidney failure.

    ANS: F   DIF: I   OBJ: BPE 40-3.5

MULTIPLE CHOICE

1. Which of the following are considered nutrients?
   a. lipids
   b. proteins
   c. Both (a) and (b)
   d. None of the above

   ANS: C   DIF: I   OBJ: BPE 40-1.1

2. Nutrients provide the body with the energy and materials it needs for
   a. growth.
   b. maintenance.
   c. repair.
   d. All of the above

   ANS: D   DIF: I   OBJ: BPE 40-1.1

3. Vitamin K
   a. is stored in fatty tissue.
   b. assists with blood clotting.
   c. is found in green, leafy vegetables.
   d. All of the above

   ANS: D   DIF: I   OBJ: BPE 40-1.2

4. Vitamins are organic compounds that
   a. help activate enzymes during chemical reactions.
   b. provide energy for metabolism.
   c. help form cell membranes.
   d. are not obtained from food.

   ANS: A   DIF: I   OBJ: BPE 40-1.2

5. Excess calories and fat in the diet
   a. lead to obesity.
   b. cause heart disease.
   c. increase the risk of diabetes and heart disease.
   d. All of the above

   ANS: D   DIF: I   OBJ: BPE 40-1.2

6. Most of the body's energy needs should be supplied by dietary
   a. carbohydrates.   c. vitamins.
   b. fats.   d. proteins.

   ANS: A   DIF: I   OBJ: BPE 40-1.2

7. Brain cells and red blood cells receive most of their energy directly from
   a. proteins.   c. glucose.
   b. cellulose.   d. deoxyribose.

   ANS: C   DIF: I   OBJ: BPE 40-1.2

8. Excessive amounts of vitamins such as vitamins A, D, E, and K
   a. lead to excellent health.
   b. can be harmful.
   c. present no problem since they are not stored in the body.
   d. prevent beriberi.

   ANS: B   DIF: I   OBJ: BPE 40-1.2

9. All essential amino acids
   a. must be obtained from the foods we eat.   c. are found in gelatin.
   b. are made in our body.   d. None of the above

   ANS: A   DIF: I   OBJ: BPE 40-1.2

10. carbohydrates : energy ::
    a. proteins : insulation for nerve tissue   c. fats : protein
    b. amino acids : enzymes   d. fats : muscle

    ANS: B
    (are used to produce)

    DIF: II   OBJ: BPE 0-1.2

11. vitamins : minute amounts ::
    a. B vitamins : scurvy
    b. vitamin D deficiency : pellagra
    c. vitamin C deficiency : rickets
    d. trace elements : minute amounts

    ANS: D
    (are required in)

    DIF: II   OBJ: BPE 40-1.2

12. The food guide pyramid was developed by the
    a. USDA
    b. USAF
    c. FDA
    d. CDC

    ANS: A   DIF: I   OBJ: BPE 40-1.3

13. According to the USDA food guide pyramid, a person should obtain the most servings per day from
    a. fruits.
    b. breads, cereals, rice, and pasta.
    c. fats, oils, and sweets.
    d. milk, yogurt, and cheese.

    ANS: B   DIF: I   OBJ: BPE 40-1.3

14. The nutritional guide that lists the number of servings needed by your body daily from each food group is in the shape of a
    a. football.
    b. circle.
    c. square.
    d. pyramid.

    ANS: D   DIF: I   OBJ: BPE 40-1.3

15. The final function of the digestive system is
    a. absorption.
    b. ingestion.
    c. elimination.
    d. peristalsis.

    ANS: C   DIF: I   OBJ: BPE 40-2.1

16. The function of the digestive system is to
    a. chemically break down food.
    b. mechanically break apart food.
    c. absorb nutrient materials.
    d. All of the above

    ANS: D   DIF: I   OBJ: BPE 40-2.1

17. The first portion of the small intestine is the
    a. colon.
    b. esophagus.
    c. duodenum.
    d. rectum.

    ANS: C   DIF: I   OBJ: BPE 40-2.2

18. The wavelike contractions of muscle that move food through the digestive system are called
    a. peristalsis.
    b. voluntary contractions.
    c. mechanical digestion.
    d. involuntary digestion.

    ANS: A   DIF: I   OBJ: BPE 40-2.2

19. The pharynx is
    a. located in the colon.
    b. located in the back of the throat.
    c. also called the voice box.
    d. None of the above

    ANS: B   DIF: I   OBJ: BPE 40-2.2

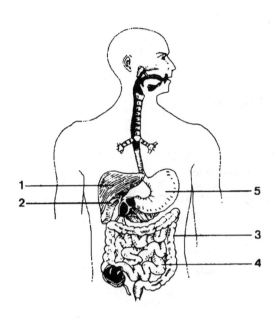

20. What is the name of structure 5?
    a. liver
    b. stomach
    c. duodenum
    d. ileum

    ANS: B   DIF: II   OBJ: BPE 40-2.2

21. Most of the end products of digestion are absorbed into the circulatory system from which
    structure?
    a. structure 1
    b. structure 2
    c. structure 3
    d. structure 4

    ANS: D   DIF: II   OBJ: BPE 40-2.2

22. Which of the following provides a passage for both food and air?
    a. esophagus
    b. trachea
    c. pharynx
    d. duodenum

    ANS: C   DIF: I   OBJ: BPE 40-2.2

23. Enzymes in saliva begin the chemical digestion of
    a. fat.
    b. protein.
    c. carbohydrates.
    d. vitamins.

    ANS: C   DIF: I   OBJ: BPE 40-2.2

24. Pepsin and hydrochloric acid in the stomach begin the digestion of
    a. protein.
    b. starch.
    c. fats.
    d. carbohydrates.

    ANS: A   DIF: I   OBJ: BPE 40-2.2

25. Bile
    a. breaks down globules of fat into tiny droplets.
    b. is stored in the liver.
    c. is produced by the gall bladder.
    d. All of the above

    ANS: A   DIF: I   OBJ: BPE 40-2.2

26. Fat molecules are broken down into fatty acids by
    a. emulsifiers.
    b. amylases.
    c. sphincters.
    d. lipases.

    ANS: D   DIF: I   OBJ: BPE 40-2.2

27. small intestine : large intestine ::
    a. large intestine : small intestine
    b. stomach : large intestine
    c. esophagus : stomach
    d. small intestine : esophagus

    ANS: C
    (delivers food to the)

    DIF: II   OBJ: BPE 40-2.2

28. pancreas : enzymes for small intestine ::
    a. stomach : saliva
    b. stomach : proteins from amino acids
    c. liver : bile salts
    d. liver : hydrochloric acid

    ANS: C
    (produces)

    DIF: II   OBJ: BPE 40-2.2

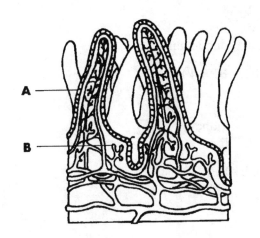

A ——

B ——

29. Structure A in the above diagram is a
    a. villus.
    b. nephron.
    c. ureter.
    d. urethra.

    ANS: A   DIF: II   OBJ: BPE 40-2.3

30. This structure is found in the
    a. kidney.
    b. esophagus.
    c. small intestine.
    d. tongue.

    ANS: C   DIF: II   OBJ: BPE 40-2.3

31. This structure allows for an increase in
    a. nutrient absorption area.
    b. mechanical digestion.
    c. acid production.
    d. bile production.

    ANS: A   DIF: II   OBJ: BPE 40-2.3

32. Structure B in the above diagram is
    a. a passageway for bile to flow into the stomach.
    b. a capillary.
    c. found only in the duodenum.
    d. a nephron.

    ANS: B   DIF: II   OBJ: BPE 40-2.3

33. The villi of the small intestine allow for an increase in the rate of
    a. nutrient absorption.
    b. cellulose digestion.
    c. acid production.
    d. bile production.

    ANS: A   DIF: I   OBJ: BPE 40-2.3

34. Most of the enzymes and chemicals secreted by the upper end of the small intestine come from
    a. villi.
    b. saliva.
    c. the liver and pancreas.
    d. the large intestine.

    ANS: C   DIF: I   OBJ: BPE 40-2.4

35. Bile, which emulsifies fat globules, is produced by the
    a. pancreas.   c. liver.
    b. gallbladder.   d. duodenum.

    ANS: C   DIF: I   OBJ: BPE 40-2.4

36. Urea is formed in the
    a. cells.   c. kidneys.
    b. lungs.   d. liver.

    ANS: C   DIF: I   OBJ: BPE 40-3.1

37. The kidneys play a major role in maintaining
    a. the proper breathing rate.
    b. the proper glucose levels in the blood.
    c. homeostasis by removing urea, water, and other wastes from the blood.
    d. the concentration of digestive enzymes in the blood.

    ANS: C   DIF: I   OBJ: BPE 40-3.1

38. Ammonia is converted to urea because
    a. urea is less toxic to the body.
    b. urea can be converted to a nutrient.
    c. the nitrogen wastes in the urea can be recycled and do not need to be excreted.
    d. All of the above

    ANS: A   DIF: I   OBJ: BPE 40-3.1

39. The filtrate removed from the blood by the kidneys might contain
    a. salts, amino acids, glucose, and urea.   c. fat, urea, and water.
    b. ammonia, red blood cells, and minerals. d. salts, urea, and plasma.

    ANS: A   DIF: I   OBJ: BPE 40-3.2

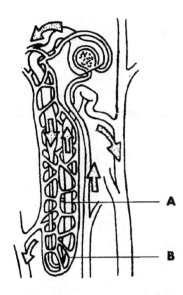

A

B

40. The structure shown in the diagram above is known as a
    a. villus.   c. ureter.
    b. nephron.   d. urethra.

    ANS: B   DIF: II   OBJ: BPE 40-3.2

41. At the location labeled B,
    a. filtration is taking place.
    b. water and solutes are moving back into the blood.
    c. red blood cells are moving out of the blood.
    d. red blood cells are forced back into the blood.

    ANS: A   DIF: II   OBJ: BPE 40-3.2

42. The structure shown in the diagram above is the basic unit of the
    a. esophagus.   c. kidney.
    b. pancreas.   d. liver.

    ANS: C   DIF: II   OBJ: BPE 40-3.2

43. The basic functional unit of the kidney is the
    a. villus.   c. ureter.
    b. nephron.   d. urethra.

    ANS: B   DIF: I   OBJ: BPE 40-3.2

44. Urine, when compared with the initial filtrate, contains
    a. more glucose.
    b. less water, fewer minerals, and more urea.
    c. decomposed red blood cells.
    d. concentrated amino acids.

    ANS: B   DIF: I   OBJ: BPE 40-3.3

45. The first stage of urine formation is called
   a. filtration.
   b. bladder inflation.
   c. reabsorption.
   d. nephrosis.

   ANS: A   DIF: I   OBJ: BPE 40-3.3

46. Which of the following filtrates is *not* reabsorbed in significant quantities back into the bloodstream by the nephrons?
   a. glucose
   b. ions
   c. urea
   d. water

   ANS: C   DIF: I   OBJ: BPE 40-3.3

47. Urine leaves the body through the
   a. ureter.
   b. urethra.
   c. bladder.
   d. intestine.

   ANS: B   DIF: I   OBJ: BPE 40-3.4

48. ureter : urinary bladder ::
   a. urinary bladder : ureter
   b. urethra : urinary bladder
   c. urinary bladder : urethra
   d. urethra : ureter

   ANS: C
   (empties into the)

   DIF: II   OBJ: BPE 40-3.4

49. Hemodialysis simulates the filtering action of the
   a. urethra.
   b. pancreas.
   c. liver.
   d. kidneys.

   ANS: D   DIF: I   OBJ: BPE 40-3.5

50. A kidney dialysis machine
   a. reduces blood volume.
   b. increases the volume of the blood.
   c. removes wastes from the blood.
   d. oxygenates the patient's blood.

   ANS: C   DIF: I   OBJ: BPE 40-3.5

COMPLETION

1. A(n) _____ is a substance needed by the body for growth, energy, repair, and maintenance.

   ANS: nutrient   DIF: I   OBJ: BPE 40-1.1

2. A(n) _____ is a unit of energy that indicates the amount of energy contained in food.

   ANS: calorie   DIF: I   OBJ: BPE 40-1.2

3. The amino acids that humans are unable to manufacture are called _____ amino acids.

ANS: essential   DIF: I   OBJ: BPE 40-1.2

4. The _____ _____ _____ was developed by the USDA as a source of information regarding nutrition.

ANS: food guide pyramid   DIF: I   OBJ: BPE 40-1.3

5. A person who is more than 20 percent heavier than the average person of the same sex and height is said to be _____.

ANS: obese   DIF: I   OBJ: BPE 40-1.4

6. Breaking food into molecules small enough for the body to absorb is a major function of the _____ system.

ANS: digestive   DIF: I   OBJ: BPE 40-2.1

7. The mouth, esophagus, stomach, small intestine, and large intestine are the main organs of the _____ system.

ANS: digestive   DIF: I   OBJ: BPE 40-2.2

8. _____ is the process whereby fat globules are broken down into tiny fat droplets.

ANS: Emulsification   DIF: I   OBJ: BPE 40-2.2

9. Starches are broken down into sugar molecules by enzymes called _____.

ANS: amylases   DIF: I   OBJ: BPE 40-2.2

10. When the stomach lining is weakened by bacteria and acid, the result is a(n) _____.

ANS: ulcer   DIF: I   OBJ: BPE 40-2.2

11. The large intestine is also known as the _____.

ANS: colon   DIF: I   OBJ: BPE 40-2.2

12. Hydrochloric acid is secreted by cells that line the inside of the _____.

ANS: stomach   DIF: I   OBJ: BPE 40-2.2

13. Digestion is completed in the _____, where most nutrients are absorbed.

    ANS: small intestine   DIF: I   OBJ: BPE 40-2.2

14. Pepsin and hydrochloric acid in the stomach begin the digestion of _____.

    ANS: proteins   DIF: I   OBJ: BPE 40-2.2

15. Indigestible material such as fiber is briefly stored and compacted in the
    _____ _____.

    ANS: large intestine   DIF: I   OBJ: BPE 40-2.3

16. Most absorption of nutrients occurs in the _____ intestine.

    ANS: small   DIF: I   OBJ: BPE 40-2.3

17. The _____ sends enzymes through a duct into the first part of the small
    intestine.

    ANS: pancreas   DIF: I   OBJ: BPE 40-2.4

18. The liver secretes _____, which aids in the emulsification of fats.

    ANS: bile   DIF: I   OBJ: BPE 40-2.4

19. In the liver, ammonia is converted to a much less toxic nitrogen waste called
    _____.

    ANS: urea   DIF: I   OBJ: BPE 40-3.1

20. Each kidney contains over 1 million blood-cleaning units called _____.

    ANS: nephrons   DIF: I   OBJ: BPE 40-3.2

21. The renal tubule empties into a larger tube called a(n) _____
    _____.

    ANS: collecting duct   DIF: I   OBJ: BPE 40-3.3

22. Urine produced in the kidneys passes into the bladder through tubes called
    _____.

    ANS: ureters   DIF: I   OBJ: BPE 40-3.4

23. _____ _____ is a procedure for filtering the blood using a
    machine.

    ANS: Kidney dialysis   DIF: I   OBJ: BPE 40-3.5

PROBLEM

1. The graph below shows the progress of digestion as carbohydrates, fats, and proteins pass through the human digestive tract. The horizontal axis indicates the relative distance along the digestive tract, from the mouth to the anus. The vertical axis indicates the percentage of undigested food remaining as the food moves down through the digestive tract. The percentages of undigested carbohydrate, fat, and protein are shown separately, but they are identified only as A, B, and C. Correctly identify which of the graph lines shows carbohydrate digestion, which shows fat digestion, and which shows protein digestion.

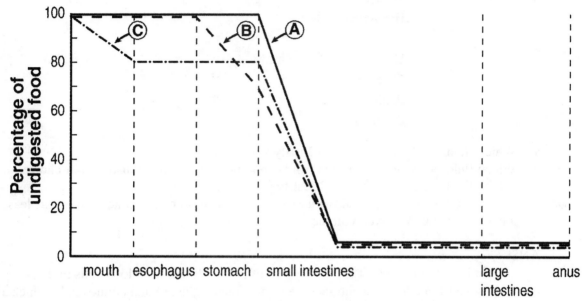

Distance along digestive tract

[Note: Values are approximate.]

ANS:
A is fat, B is protein, and C is carbohydrate.

DIF: III   OBJ: BPE 40-2.2

2. The table below shows the composition of three different body fluids taken from a person. These are identified as fluids A, B, and C. A number of substances are listed in the far left column of the table. The presence of one of these substances in a fluid is indicated by a + in the appropriate column. The absence of one of these substances from a fluid is indicated by a –.

Substance	Fluid A	Fluid B	Fluid C
Water	+	+	+
Blood cells	–	–	+
Proteins	–	–	+
Hormones	–	–	+
Amino acids	+	–	+
Urea	+	+	+
Glucose	+	–	+
Sodium	+	+	+
Other ions	+	+	+

a. Which fluid, A, B, or C, is blood? Justify your choice.
b. Which fluid, A, B, or C, is filtrate from nephrons of the kidney? Justify your choice.
c. Which fluid, A, B, or C, is urine? Justify your choice.
d. Which fluid, A, B, or C, would you expect to be the most concentrated? (have the least amount of water in a given volume)

ANS:
a. C must be blood because it is the only one of the fluids that has blood cells in it.
b. A must be filtrate in the nephrons because it contains glucose and amino acids, which are reabsorbed from the filtrate before urine leaves the body. A could not be blood because it does not contain blood cells.
c. B must be urine because it contains only water, urea, sodium, and other ions. Both blood and nephron filtrate would contain additional substances.
d. B

DIF: III   OBJ: BPE 40-3.1

ESSAY

1. What are the five basic types of nutrients found in food and beverages?

ANS:
Carbohydrates, lipids, proteins, vitamins, and minerals.

DIF: II   OBJ: BPE 40-1.1

2. What are the four major functions of the digestive system?

ANS:
Taking in food, breaking the food down into molecules small enough for the body to absorb, taking up the small molecules, and getting rid of undigested molecules and waste.

DIF: II   OBJ: BPE 40-1.1

3. A strict vegetarian diet consumes no meat or other foods derived from animals, such as eggs or milk. What dietary problems might a strict vegetarian encounter?

ANS:
Individual plant foods may not contain sufficient amounts of all of the essential amino acids. Strict vegetarians must carefully plan their diet so that plant foods lacking or low in some amino acids are eaten with other plant foods that are high in those amino acids. A strict vegetarian who simply abstains from all animal-derived foods may show symptoms of vitamin B_{12} deficiency.

DIF: II   OBJ: BPE 40-1.2

4. Describe the chemical phase of digestion that occurs in the mouth.

ANS:
In the mouth, salivary glands release saliva, which is a mixture of water, mucus, and the enzyme salivary amylase. The salivary amylase begins the chemical digestion of starch.

DIF: II   OBJ: BPE 40-2.2

5. The structure of proteins makes it difficult for the body to digest them. How does the body solve the problem of digesting proteins?

ANS:
Almost all proteins are chains of amino acids that are either folded into tight balls or wound together into tough fibers. Enzymes cannot get at the individual protein chains. The human body solves this problem by carrying out protein digestion in two steps. First, hydrochloric acid in the stomach is used to unfold large proteins into single strands; then pepsin, an enzyme secreted by the stomach, cuts the single protein strands into smaller chains of amino acids. Enzymes in the small intestine complete the breakdown of proteins into amino acids.

DIF: II   OBJ: BPE 40-2.2

6. Identify the major wastes excreted by humans, and briefly describe how each is eliminated from the body.

ANS:
The major waste products excreted by humans are carbon dioxide, urea, salts, nitrogen wastes, and water. Carbon dioxide and some water are excreted by the lungs during exhalation. The kidneys remove water, urea, salts, and other substances from the blood. The skin excretes water salts, and small amounts of nitrogen wastes.

DIF: II   OBJ: BPE 40-3.1

7. Explain how the kidneys play a role in maintaining homeostasis in the body.

ANS:
The kidneys regulate the amounts of substances like salts, minerals, and other chemicals that are retained in the blood or excreted in the urine. In addition, the kidneys regulate the concentration of substances in the blood by adjusting the total amount of water in the body to keep the concentration nearly constant. Kidneys also remove urea and other waste products from the body.

DIF: II   OBJ: BPE 40-3.1

CHAPTER 41—THE BODY'S DEFENSES

TRUE/FALSE

1. The most dangerous enemies of humans are large animals, including other humans.

   ANS: F   DIF: I   OBJ: BPE 41-1.1

2. Certain bacteria, viruses, fungi, and protists can pose a serious threat to humans.

   ANS: T   DIF: I   OBJ: BPE 41-1.1

3. The immune system consists of cells and tissues found throughout the body.

   ANS: T   DIF: I   OBJ: BPE 41-1.1

4. The mechanisms used by the body to detect and destroy pathogens can be specific or nonspecific.

   ANS: T   DIF: I   OBJ: BPE 41-1.1

5. Secretions of sweat and oil glands make the skin extremely basic, allowing it to be an effective barrier to infection.

   ANS: F   DIF: I   OBJ: BPE 41-1.1

6. Most pathogens can readily pass through mucous membranes.

   ANS: F   DIF: I   OBJ: BPE 41-1.1

7. Skin acts as one of the first of the immune system's nonspecific defenses against pathogens.

   ANS: T   DIF: I   OBJ: BPE 41-1.1

8. Fevers above 103°F can have beneficial effects when the body is defending itself against pathogens.

   ANS: F   DIF: I   OBJ: BPE 41-1.2

9. When pathogens enter the body through a wound, they trigger an inflammatory response.

   ANS: T   DIF: I   OBJ: BPE 41-1.2

10. During the inflammatory response, red blood cells engulf foreign substances.

    ANS: F   DIF: I   OBJ: BPE 41-1.2

11. Interferon provides a specific defense against pathogens.

    ANS: F   DIF: I   OBJ: BPE 41-1.3

12. The complement system consists of about 20 different proteins that circulate in the blood and become active when they encounter certain pathogens.

    ANS: T   DIF: I   OBJ: BPE 41-1.3

13. Natural killer cells attack cells that have been infected by microbes, but not the microbes themselves.

    ANS: T   DIF: I   OBJ: BPE 41-1.4

14. Helper T cells are a type of macrophage.

    ANS: F   DIF: I   OBJ: BPE 41-2.1

15. Antigens are substances that the immune system recognizes as foreign.

    ANS: T   DIF: I   OBJ: BPE 41-2.2

16. Killer T cells and B cells are activated by interleukin-2, which is secreted by helper T cells.

    ANS: T   DIF: I   OBJ: BPE 41-2.4

17. The body possesses millions of different types of T cells, each of which bears unique receptor molecules that can recognize millions of different foreign proteins.

    ANS: T   DIF: I   OBJ: BPE 41-2.4

18. Killer T cells are able to recognize and attack virus-infected cells because the infected cells have been coated with a protein called interleukin-2.

    ANS: F   DIF: I   OBJ: BPE 41-2.4

19. B cells function by attacking and destroying body cells that have been infected by viruses.

    ANS: F   DIF: I   OBJ: BPE 41-2.4

20. Sneezing and shaking hands are not among the ways diseases are transmitted.

    ANS: F   DIF: I   OBJ: BPE 41-3.1

21. Meat, poultry, and eggs are potentially hazardous foods because they can be infected with pathogens.

    ANS: T   DIF: I   OBJ: BPE 41-3.1

22. Once you have developed the symptoms of a contagious disease, you probably cannot transmit it to anyone else.

   ANS: F   DIF: I   OBJ: BPE 41-3.1

23. Koch's postulates are used to kill certain pathogens.

   ANS: F   DIF: I   OBJ: BPE 41-3.2

24. The first exposure to a pathogen results in a much faster immune response than the second exposure to the same pathogen.

   ANS: F   DIF: I   OBJ: BPE 41-3.3

25. If a pathogen that has already been defeated is encountered again, memory cells produce antibodies against it.

   ANS: T   DIF: I   OBJ: BPE 41-3.3

26. Vaccination triggers an immune response against the pathogen without symptoms of infection.

   ANS: T   DIF: I   OBJ: BPE 41-3.4

27. Type I diabetes is an autoimmune disease affecting the thyroid gland.

   ANS: F   DIF: I   OBJ: BPE 41-4.1

28. AIDS is a disorder of the immune system.

   ANS: T   DIF: I   OBJ: BPE 41-4.2

29. Any person who is HIV-positive has the disease called AIDS.

   ANS: F   DIF: I   OBJ: BPE 41-4.2

30. AIDS patients often succumb to infections or cancers that are rare in healthy individuals.

   ANS: T   DIF: I   OBJ: BPE 41-4.2

31. The AIDS virus may remain dormant for ten years or longer.

   ANS: T   DIF: I   OBJ: BPE 41-4.3

32. HIV can be transmitted through kissing.

   ANS: F   DIF: I   OBJ: BPE 41-4.3

33. Anyone infected with HIV must be an intravenous-drug user.

   ANS: F   DIF: I   OBJ: BPE 41-4.3

MULTIPLE CHOICE

1. A disease-causing agent is called a(n)
   a. interferon.
   b. pathogen.
   c. infection.
   d. fungi.

   ANS: B   DIF: I   OBJ: BPE 41-1.1

2. The body's first line of defense against infection includes all of the following *except*
   a. skin.
   b. mucous membranes.
   c. acids in the stomach.
   d. interleukin-1.

   ANS: D   DIF: I   OBJ: BPE 41-1.1

3. The skin repels pathogens
   a. by functioning as a barrier.
   b. by producing antibodies.
   c. with sweat, which contains the enzyme lysozyme.
   d. Both (a) and (c)

   ANS: D   DIF: I   OBJ: BPE 41-1.1

4. Mucous membranes
   a. cover all body's surfaces.
   b. line internal body surfaces that are in contact with the environment.
   c. produce antibodies to combat infection.
   d. secrete sweat, which has antibacterial enzymes.

   ANS: B   DIF: I   OBJ: BPE 41-1.1

5. Mucous membranes
   a. are moist epithelial layers that are impermeable to most pathogens.
   b. line the nasal passages, mouth, lungs, digestive tract, urethra, and vagina.
   c. contain glands that secrete mucus, a sticky fluid that traps pathogens.
   d. All of the above

   ANS: D   DIF: I   OBJ: BPE 41-1.1

6. The first line of defense against infection includes
   a. mucous membranes.
   b. neutrophils.
   c. killer T cells.
   d. antibodies.

   ANS: A   DIF: I   OBJ: BPE 41-1.1

7. All of the following possess mucous membranes *except* the
   a. digestive tract.
   b. surface of the skin.
   c. nasal passages.
   d. vagina.

   ANS: B   DIF: I   OBJ: BPE 41-1.1

8. Mucus is produced by the cells lining the walls of the bronchi and bronchioles
   a. only when a person has a severe respiratory infection.
   b. to allow oxygen to diffuse into the blood more efficiently.
   c. as a lubricant for the expulsion of food that might go "down the wrong tube".
   d. to protect against microbes that might be inhaled.

   ANS: D   DIF: I   OBJ: BPE 41-1.1

9. The stomach is involved in defense against infection by
   a. regurgitating any pathogen that might be swallowed.
   b. secreting mucus that is carried away by cilia.
   c. secreting acid that destroys potential pathogens that are swallowed.
   d. sending potential pathogens to the liver for destruction.

   ANS: C   DIF: I   OBJ: BPE 41-1.1

10. Which of the following is a nonspecific defense against pathogens?
    a. B cells
    b. antibodies
    c. helper T cells
    d. the inflammatory response

    ANS: D   DIF: I   OBJ: BPE 41-1.2

11. When the inflammatory response is triggered,
    a. damaged or infected cells release chemical alarm signals.
    b. more fluid than normal leaks from capillaries near the injury, and swelling results.
    c. white blood cells attack invading pathogens.
    d. All of the above

    ANS: D   DIF: I   OBJ: BPE 41-1.2

12. When a puncture wound becomes infected,
    a. damaged cells release chemicals that promote the immune response.
    b. the temperature around the wound increases.
    c. white blood cells move into the injured area.
    d. All of the above

    ANS: D   DIF: I   OBJ: BPE 41-1.2

13. Moderate fevers (below 39°C or 103°F)
    a. damage essential proteins in your body.
    b. inhibit the growth of pathogens and stimulate macrophage action.
    c. occur late in the disease process after the pathogen is almost eliminated.
    d. require emergency treatment.

    ANS: B   DIF: I   OBJ: BPE 41-1.2

14. The redness and swelling associated with an inflammatory response is caused by
    a. secretion of antibodies.
    b. dilation (expansion) of local blood vessels.
    c. complement activity.
    d. natural killer cells destroying bacteria.

    ANS: B   DIF: I   OBJ: BPE 41-1.2

15. redness and swelling : the inflammatory response ::
    a. increased blood flows : AIDS
    b. inflammatory response : membrane attack complex
    c. neutrophils : autoimmune disease
    d. temperature increase : temperature response

    ANS: D
    (is/are part of)

    DIF: II   OBJ: BPE 41-1.2

16. The protein that causes nearby cells to produce and enzyme that prevents viruses from making proteins and RNA is called
    a. interferon.
    b. complement.
    c. mucous.
    d. MAC.

    ANS: A   DIF: I   OBJ: BPE 41-1.3

17. White blood cells that ingest invading microbes and cellular debris resulting from microbial attacks are called
    a. macrophages.
    b. neutrophils
    c. natural killer cells.
    d. complement cells.

    ANS: A   DIF: I   OBJ: BPE 41-1.4

18. Which of the following engulfs foreign cells?
    a. helper T cell
    b. B cell
    c. macrophage
    d. antibody

    ANS: C   DIF: I   OBJ: BPE 41-1.4

19. Neutrophils are responsible for
    a. ingesting individual microbes.
    b. destroying viruses.
    c. secreting toxic chemicals that kill bacteria.
    d. producing antibodies.

    ANS: C   DIF: I   OBJ: BPE 41-1.4

20. neutrophils : releasing chemicals ::
    a. macrophages : releasing chemicals
    b. natural killer cells : releasing chemicals
    c. natural killer cells : puncturing their membranes
    d. macrophages : puncturing their membranes

    ANS: C
    (kill bacteria by)

    DIF: II   OBJ: BPE 41-1.4

21. All of the following are white blood cells that are involved in immune responses *except*
    a. B cells.   c. macrophages.
    b. T cells.   d. megakaryocytes.

    ANS: D   DIF: I   OBJ: BPE 41-2.1

22. Which of the following pairs is *incorrectly* associated?
    a. killer T cells-attack and kill infected cells
    b. helper T cells-activate killer T cells and B cells
    c. B cells-engulf cells that are infected with microbes
    d. macrophages-consume pathogens and infected cells

    ANS: C   DIF: I   OBJ: BPE 41-2.1

23. bacteria and viruses : pathogens ::
    a. B cells and T cells : mucous membrane cells
    b. helper T cells and killer T cells : skin cells
    c. killer T cells and macrophages : pathogens
    d. killer T cells and B cells : white blood cells

    ANS: D
    (are two kinds of)

    DIF: II   OBJ: BPE 41-2.1

24. Once stimulated by antigens on the surface of macrophages, helper T cells may
    a. stimulate killer T cells to attack viruses directly.
    b. stimulate B cells to divide and develop into plasma cells.
    c. repair macrophages.
    d. cause fever.

    ANS: B   DIF: I   OBJ: BPE 41-2.3

25. The role of helper T cells in immune responses is to
    a. secrete interleukin-1.
    b. stimulate macrophages to initiate an "alarm signal."
    c. initiate the activities of neutrophils.
    d. activate two different types of immune system cells.

    ANS: D   DIF: I   OBJ: BPE 41-2.3

26. Killer T cells recognize cells that have been infected by viruses
    a. only after the infected cells have been ingested by macrophages.
    b. because the infected cells have viral proteins on their surfaces.
    c. when the infected cells have been coated with complement.
    d. at the same time that neutrophils release their toxins into damaged tissue.

    ANS: B   DIF: I   OBJ: BPE 41-2.4

27. When B cells encounter a pathogen, they
    a. secrete interleukin-2, which stimulates killer T cells.
    b. divide and produce large amounts of antibody.
    c. initiate an inflammatory response.
    d. attack the cell by making a hole in its membrane.

    ANS: B   DIF: I   OBJ: BPE 41-2.4

28. The Y-shaped molecule that is produced by plasma cells upon exposure to a specific antigen and
    can bind to that antigen is called a(n)
    a. helper T cell.   c. a B cell.
    b. macrophage.   d. antibody.

    ANS: D   DIF: I   OBJ: BPE 41-2.4

29. macrophages : helper T cells ::
    a. killer T cells : macrophages
    b. helper T cells : killer T cells and B cells
    c. B cells : killer T cells and macrophages
    d. mucous membranes cells : helper T cells and B cells

    ANS: B
    (activate)

    DIF: II   OBJ: BPE 41-2.4

30. Ways you can avoid becoming ill include
    a. staying at home and only interacting with your family.
    b. taking lots of different medications before you get sick.
    c. washing your hands often.
    d. eating only vegetables.

    ANS: C   DIF: I   OBJ: BPE 41-3.1

31. Which of the following is *not* one of Koch's postulates?
    a. When the isolated pathogen is injected into the healthy animal, the animal must develop the disease.
    b. The pathogen must be found in an animal with the disease and not in a healthy animal.
    c. The healthy animal must be shown to be susceptible to the pathogen before it is injected with the disease.
    d. The pathogen must be isolated from the sick animal and grown in a laboratory culture.
    e. None of the above

    ANS: C   DIF: I   OBJ: BPE 41-3.2

32. A few B cells that have encountered a pathogen
    a. become killer T cells.
    b. are ingested by macrophages.
    c. have viral protein on their cell membrane surface.
    d. become memory cells.

    ANS: D   DIF: I   OBJ: BPE 41-3.3

33. B cells
    a. sometimes remain in the blood for years.   c. are stimulated by helper T cells.
    b. secrete antibodies.   d. All of the above

    ANS: D   DIF: I   OBJ: BPE 41-3.3

34. After the initial immune response subsides, B cells that continue to patrol body tissues
    a. are called helper T cells.   c. become memory cells.
    b. develop into phagocytes.   d. cannot react to the original antigen.

    ANS: C   DIF: I   OBJ: BPE 41-3.3

35. Secondary exposure to a pathogen
    a. results in very rapid production of antibodies.
    b. stimulates memory cells to divide quickly.
    c. may result in destruction of the pathogen before the person knows he or she is infected.
    d. All of the above

    ANS: D   DIF: I   OBJ: BPE 41-3.3

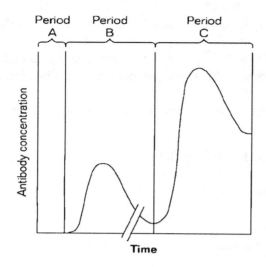

Period A   Period B   Period C

Antibody concentration

Time

36. During which time period would the first antibodies to the pathogen be produced?
    a. Period A
    b. Period B
    c. Period C
    d. None of the above.

    ANS: B   DIF: II   OBJ: BPE 41-3.3

37. Which time period would be characterized by the most rapid division of B cells?
    a. Period A
    b. Period B
    c. Period C
    d. None of the above

    ANS: C   DIF: II   OBJ: BPE 41-3.3

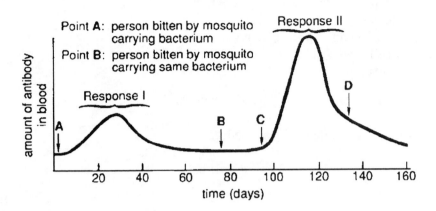

Point **A**: person bitten by mosquito carrying bacterium

Point **B**: person bitten by mosquito carrying same bacterium

38. The most likely reason for Response II being greater than Response I in the graph above is
    a. more bacteria entered at point C than at point A.
    b. memory cells were produced in Response I.
    c. antibodies from Response I were still in the blood.
    d. macrophages increased their production of antibodies.

    ANS: B   DIF: II   OBJ: BPE 41-3.3

39. John and James are identical twins. During the summer following their fifteenth birthday, they went on a vacation and stayed in a cabin with two of their cousins. One of the cousins came down with chicken pox in the middle of the vacation. Chicken pox is caused by a virus. Two weeks later, John came down with chicken pox. James, however, never developed any symptoms of the disease. Which of the following is the best explanation for the different responses John and James had to exposure to the same disease?
    a. John and James are not really identical twins. James inherited an immunity to chicken pox but John did not.
    b. Even though John and James are identical twins, they produce different kinds of immune system cells. James had killer T cells that could recognize and destroy chicken pox viruses, while John did not.
    c. James had been exposed to chicken pox at an earlier age and developed the disease. His body produced memory cells that protected him from further infections of the disease. John did not get exposed to chicken pox at an earlier age.
    d. James had a cold at the time he was exposed to the chicken pox virus. The cold virus stimulated his body to produce lots of B cells, which were then also able to recognize and bind to the chicken pox viruses. John did not have a cold at the time he was exposed to the chicken pox.

    ANS: C   DIF: II   OBJ: BPE 41-3.3

40. Vaccines are effective in preventing disease because they
    a. interfere with the release of suppressor T cells.
    b. are antibodies directed against specific pathogens.
    c. contain specific B cells and T cells.
    d. trigger antibody formation.

    ANS: D   DIF: I   OBJ: BPE 41-3.4

41. All vaccines are produced from killed or weakened
    a. phagocytes.   c. helper T cells.
    b. pathogens.   d. B cells.

    ANS: B   DIF: I   OBJ: BPE 41-3.4

42. Autoimmune diseases occur when
    a. cells release antihistamine.
    b. a person is infected with HIV.
    c. the body manufactures "anti-self" antibodies.
    d. a person receives a blood transfusion of the wrong type.

    ANS: C   DIF: I   OBJ: BPE 41-4.1

43. An autoimmune disease in which the immune system attacks the insulating material surrounding
    nerve cells in the brain, in the spinal cord, and in the nerves leading from the eyes to the brain is
    a. multiple sclerosis.   c. Graves' disease.
    b. rheumatoid arthritis.   d. lupus erythematosus.

    ANS: A   DIF: I   OBJ: BPE 41-4.1

44. Which of the following is *not* an autoimmune disease?
    a. systemic lupus erythematosus
    b. multiple sclerosis
    c. Type I diabetes
    d. Graves' disease
    e. influenza

    ANS: E   DIF: I   OBJ: BPE 41-4.1

45. Which of the following statements describes the actions of HIV?
    a. HIV attacks and cripples the immune system.
    b. HIV invades macrophages and helper T cells.
    c. HIV kills large numbers of helper T cells.
    d. All of the above

    ANS: D   DIF: I   OBJ: BPE 41-4.2

46. Scientists think that practically everyone infected with HIV who is *not* treated
    a. can be cured with vaccines.
    b. will die of AIDS within one year of diagnosis with the virus.
    c. will live a normal life if they don't smoke and if they eat a balanced diet.
    d. will eventually develop AIDS.

    ANS: D   DIF: I   OBJ: BPE 41-4.2

47. A person infected with HIV may
    a. develop the disease called AIDS.
    b. have viruses reproducing in helper T cells.
    c. be more susceptible to a variety of pathogens.
    d. All of the above

    ANS: D   DIF: I   OBJ: BPE 41-4.2

48. HIV causes AIDS by attacking and destroying
    a. helper T cells.   c. neutrophils.
    b. B cells.   d. antibodies.

    ANS: A   DIF: I   OBJ: BPE 41-4.2

49. The debilitating effects of AIDS are due to inability of the immune system to
    a. activate B cells and killer T cells.   c. recognize and destroy infected cells.
    b. produce antibodies against pathogens.   d. All of the above

    ANS: D   DIF: I   OBJ: BPE 41-4.2

50. HIV can be transmitted
    a. through sexual intercourse with an infected person.
    b. by breastfeeding.
    c. by sharing contaminated hypodermic needles and syringes.
    d. All of the above

    ANS: D   DIF: I   OBJ: BPE 41-4.3

51. A misdirected immune system response against a nonpathogenic antigen is called a(n)
    a. autoimmune disease.   c. allergic reaction.
    b. secondary immune reaction.   d. vaccination reaction.

    ANS: C   DIF: I   OBJ: BPE 41-4.4

52. Which of the following is true about the release of histamine from cells in the nasal passages?
    a. It occurs during an allergic reaction.
    b. It causes nearby capillaries to swell.
    c. It may cause increased secretion by mucous membranes.
    d. All of the above

    ANS: D   DIF: I   OBJ: BPE 41-4.4

53. asthma attacks : narrowing of breathing passages ::
    a. antibodies : release of histamines
    b. allergy-causing antigens : release of histamines
    c. allergy-causing antigens : release of macrophages
    d. antihistamines : capillary swelling

    ANS: B
    (cause)

    DIF: II   OBJ: BPE 41-4.4

COMPLETION

1. Defense mechanisms used by the body to prevent infection can be either
    _____ or specific.

    ANS: nonspecific   DIF: I   OBJ: BPE 41-1.1

2. Most epithelia layers that line internal body surfaces and that are barriers to many pathogens are
    called _____ _____.

    ANS: mucous membranes   DIF: I   OBJ: BPE 41-1.1

3. The _____ acts as a barrier to keep foreign organisms and viruses out of the
    body.

    ANS: skin   DIF: I   OBJ: BPE 41-1.1

4. Moderate _____, occurring in the early phases of an infection and caused by
    the release of interleukin-1, inhibits the growth of pathogens and stimulates macrophage action.

    ANS: fever   DIF: I   OBJ: BPE 41-1.2

5. At the site of a splinter, redness, swelling, and an increase in temperature would be signs of a(n)
    _____ response.

    ANS: inflammatory   DIF: I   OBJ: BPE 41-1.2

6. The ring-shaped structure of proteins that ruptures the cell membrane of pathogens is called a(n)
    _____ _____ _____.

    ANS: membrane attack complex (MAC)

    DIF: I   OBJ: BPE 41-1.3

7. The _____ _____ consists of about 20 different proteins
    that circulate in the blood and become active when they encounter certain pathogens.

    ANS: complement system   DIF: I   OBJ: BPE 41-1.3

8. _____ are white blood cells that travel throughout the body, killing bacteria one at a time by ingesting them.

   ANS: Macrophages   DIF: I   OBJ: BPE 41-1.4

9. Immune surveillance by _____ _____ cells is one of the body's most potent defenses against cancer.

   ANS: natural killer   DIF: I   OBJ: BPE 41-1.4

10. A substance that triggers an immune response is called a(n) _____.

   ANS: antigen   DIF: I   OBJ: BPE 41-2.2

11. The proteins that cover white blood cells of the immune system and bind to specific antigens are called _____ proteins.

   ANS: receptor   DIF: I   OBJ: BPE 41-2.2

12. Cells that release special defense proteins into the blood are called _____ cells.

   ANS: plasma   DIF: I   OBJ: BPE 41-2.4

13. An "alarm signal" is emitted by macrophages in the form of a protein called _____, which activates helper T cells.

   ANS: interleukin-1   DIF: I   OBJ: BPE 41-2.4

14. Interleukin-2 is produced by _____ _____ cells.

   ANS: helper T   DIF: I   OBJ: BPE 41-2.4

15. B cells produce proteins called _____ that can mark pathogens for destruction.

   ANS: antibodies   DIF: I   OBJ: BPE 41-2.4

16. To help prevent illnesses caused by bacteria found in potentially hazardous foods (such as meat, poultry, and eggs) these foods should always be _____ thoroughly.

   ANS: cooked   DIF: I   OBJ: BPE 41-3.1

17. The German physician who established a procedure for diagnosing causes of infection was _____ _____.

   ANS: Robert Koch   DIF: I   OBJ: BPE 41-3.2

18. The four-step procedure used by biologists as a guide to identify pathogens is called
_____ _____.

ANS: Koch's postulates   DIF: I   OBJ: BPE 41-3.2

19. After a primary exposure to a pathogen, the bloodstream contains _____ cell
that can be specifically recalled to defend against that particular pathogen.

ANS: memory   DIF: I   OBJ: BPE 41-3.3

20. _____ is the process by which a dead or disabled pathogen (or proteins from
that pathogen) is introduced into the body so that an immune response results without an actual
infection.

ANS: Vaccination   DIF: I   OBJ: BPE 41-3.4

21. Resistance to a particular disease is called _____.

ANS: immunity   DIF: I   OBJ: BPE 41-3.4

22. The branch of science that deals with antigens, antibodies and immunity is called
_____.

ANS: immunology   DIF: I   OBJ: BPE 41-3.4

23. The English doctor who discovered the principles of vaccination was _____
_____.

ANS: Edward Jenner   DIF: I   OBJ: BPE 41-3.4

24. The process whereby viruses mutate over time and produce new antigens that your immune
system does not recognize is called _____ _____.

ANS: antigen shifting   DIF: I   OBJ: BPE 41-3.4

25. A disease in which the body's immune system does not recognize its own body cells as being
part of "self" is called a(n) _____ disease.

ANS: autoimmune   DIF: I   OBJ: BPE 41-4.1

26. _____ causes AIDS.

ANS: HIV   DIF: I   OBJ: BPE 41-4.2

27. You can become infected with HIV if you receive HIV-infected _____
_____ cells, which are present in many body fluids.

ANS: white blood   DIF: I   OBJ: BPE 41-4.3

28. _____ is a chemical released from mast cells during an allergic reaction.

ANS: Histamine   DIF: I   OBJ: BPE 41-4.4

29. A(n) _____ is a misdirected immune system response against a nonpathogenic antigen.

ANS: allergy   DIF: I   OBJ: BPE 41-4.4

ESSAY

1. Describe three components of the first line of defense that the body uses to prevent infections.

ANS:
The skin prevents a pathogen from entering the body. In addition, oils and sweat produced by glands in the skin makes the skin's surface acidic and create a environment unfavorable to pathogens. Tears and saliva are other forms of chemicals that defend the body. Mucous membranes line internal body surfaces that are exposed to the environment. They secrete mucus, which is a sticky substance for trapping pathogens. Once pathogens are trapped, cilia lining the respiratory tract sweep them up to the pharynx, where they are swallowed and travel to the stomach. The stomach contains acid that destroys the pathogens. Sweat also contains the enzyme lysozyme, which digests bacterial cell walls.

DIF: II   OBJ: BPE 41-1.1

2. Imagine a potential pathogen has been able to get through the skin, the first line of body defense. What four steps does the body use as a second line of defense to prevent the pathogen from initiating a major infection?

ANS:
There are four steps that serve as a second line of defense against infection. (1) Cells such as macrophages, neutrophils, and natural killer cells can destroy invading microbes or cells that have been invaded by the microbes. (2) Complement consists of proteins that interact when they encounter cell membranes of bacteria or fungi, causing the membranes to puncture, thus destroying them. (3) Localized infection initiates an inflammatory response that suppresses infection and speeds healing. (4) Fever is initiated by macrophages that send a message to the brain, resulting in an elevation of body temperature. This temperature increase interferes with the ability of bacteria to grow and reproduce.

DIF: II   OBJ: BPE 41-1.2

3. How do white blood cells recognize antigens?

ANS:
The white blood cells are covered with receptor proteins that bind to specific antigens. When the cell encounters an antigen, it attacks the antigen if the receptor protein matches the antigen.

DIF: II   OBJ: BPE 41-2.2

4. Briefly describe how a cell that has been infected by a virus can be recognized and destroyed.

    ANS:
    Macrophages contact infected cells and release an "alarm signal" called interleukin-1. This protein activates helper T cells that secrete another protein, interleukin-2. This substance, in turn, stimulates killer T cells, which bind to the infected cell using surface receptor molecules that recognize traces of viral protein on the surface of the infected cell. This interaction causes damage to the cell membrane of the infected cell, resulting in its destruction.

    DIF: II   OBJ: BPE 41-2.4

5. What are the five ways you can get infectious diseases?

    ANS:
    Person-to-person contact, air, food, water, and animal bites.

    DIF: II   OBJ: BPE 41-3.1

6. Describe the experiment by Koch that led to his postulates.

    ANS:
    Koch isolated bacteria from a cow with anthrax and then infected a healthy cow with bacteria. The healthy cow developed anthrax and had the same bacteria as the first cow had.

    DIF: II   OBJ: BPE 41-3.2

7. What is the function of memory cells in an immune response?

    ANS:
    Some memory cells provide lifelong protectin against previously encountered pathogens. If a pathogen appears again, memory cells activate antibody production against that pathogen.

    DIF: II   OBJ: BPE 41-3.3

8. Describe Jenner's observations regarding smallpox and cowpox, his experiment, and the results.

    ANS:
    Jenner observed that milkmaids who had cowpox, a mild form of smallpox, rarely became infected with smallpox. He proposed that cowpox provided protection against smallpox, and to test his hypothesis, he infected healthy people with cowpox. As he predicted, many of the people he infected with cowpox never developed smallpox when they were exposed to the smallpox virus. Because the viruses that cause smallpox and cowpox are similar, Jenner's patients who were infected with cowpox, the milder form, mounted an immune response that later prevented smallpox infection.

    DIF: II   OBJ: BPE 41-3.4

9. HIV is a fatal infection, but victims are not always killed by the virus itself. They generally die from other diseases that a healthy individual can resist. Explain why this is true.

ANS:
The human immunodeficiency virus (HIV) disables the immune system of the infected person, making the individual susceptible to other pathogens. HIV destroys the immune system by attacking helper T cells, without which the immune system is unable to stimulate B cells or killer T cells.

DIF: II   OBJ: BPE 41-4.2

10. Do insects like mosquitos and ticks transmit HIV? Explain.

ANS:
Insects like mosquitos and ticks to not transmit HIV because they do not carry infected white blood cells.

DIF: II   OBJ: BPE 41-4.3

11. If HIV has been found in saliva, why is it unlikely that you can catch it by kissing someone who is infected?

ANS:
Saliva usually contains too few HIV particles to cause an infection.

DIF: II   OBJ: BPE 41-4.3

TRUE/FALSE

1. The elongated extension of a neuron that conducts nerve impulses is called an axon.

   ANS: T   DIF: I   OBJ: BPE 42-1.1

2. The cells of the nervous system that conduct electrical signals are called nerve cells, or neurons.

   ANS: T   DIF: I   OBJ: BPE 42-1.1

3. Many neurons have a fatty outer layer called a myelin sheath wraps around the axon.

   ANS: T   DIF: I   OBJ: BPE 42-1.1

4. Myelin sheaths slow down nerve impulses.

   ANS: F   DIF: I   OBJ: BPE 42-1.1

5. The potential of a resting neuron is positive.

   ANS: F   DIF: I   OBJ: BPE 42-1.2

6. When a neuron is not conducting a nerve impulse, the neuron is said to be at rest.

   ANS: T   DIF: I   OBJ: BPE 42-1.2

7. Neurons communicate with other cells by using neurotransmitters at synapses.

   ANS: T   DIF: I   OBJ: BPE 42-1.4

8. Neurotransmitters are chemical messengers that carry nerve impulses across the synaptic cleft.

   ANS: T   DIF: I   OBJ: BPE 42-1.4

9. A neurotransmitter may either excite or inhibit the cell it stimulates.

   ANS: T   DIF: I   OBJ: BPE 42-1.4

10. The peripheral nervous system carries all the messages back and forth between the central nervous system and the rest of the body.

    ANS: T   DIF: I   OBJ: BPE 42-2.1

11. The spinal cord and the brain make up the peripheral nervous system.

    ANS: F   DIF: I   OBJ: BPE 42-2.1

12. Motor neurons that conduct impulses to skeletal muscles under our conscious control make up the limbic system.

    ANS: F   DIF: I   OBJ: BPE 42-2.1

13. Most of the activity of the cerebrum occurs in the cerebral cortex.

    ANS: T   DIF: I   OBJ: BPE 42-2.2

14. The spinal cord is a dense cable of nervous tissue that runs through the vertebral column.

    ANS: T   DIF: I   OBJ: BPE 42-2.3

15. The spinal cord links the brain to the central nervous system (CNS).

    ANS: F   DIF: I   OBJ: BPE 42-2.3

16. Some activity in the somatic nervous system, such as spinal reflexes, is involuntary.

    ANS: T   DIF: I   OBJ: BPE 42-2.4

17. A spinal reflex is a self-protective motor response.

    ANS: T   DIF: I   OBJ: BPE 42-2.4

18. Spinal reflexes are usually slow because they involve the spinal cord and the peripheral nervous system.

    ANS: F   DIF: I   OBJ: BPE 42-2.4

19. The peripheral motor neurons that regulate smooth muscles are part of the autonomic nervous system.

    ANS: T   DIF: I   OBJ: BPE 42-2.5

20. Emotions are controlled by the sympathetic division of the autonomic nervous system.

    ANS: F   DIF: I   OBJ: BPE 42-2.5

21. The sympathetic division decreases blood pressure, heart rate, and breathing rate.

    ANS: F   DIF: I   OBJ: BPE 42-2.5

22. Pain receptors are located throughout all tissues and organs except the brain.

    ANS: T   DIF: I   OBJ: BPE 42-3.1

23. Most of the pain receptors in the body are located in the brain.

   ANS: F   DIF: I   OBJ: BPE 42-3.1

24. Processing sites for sensory systems tend to be localized in specific regions of the cerebrum.

   ANS: T   DIF: I   OBJ: BPE 42-3.2

25. Photoreceptors that produce sharp images are called rods.

   ANS: F   DIF: I   OBJ: BPE 42-3.3

26. Rods are receptor cells that respond to bright light.

   ANS: F   DIF: I   OBJ: BPE 42-3.3

27. Most visual processing takes place in the temporal lobe.

   ANS: F   DIF: I   OBJ: BPE 42-3.3

28. Your ears help you maintain your balance.

   ANS: T   DIF: I   OBJ: BPE 42-3.4

29. We hear by detecting vibrations in the ground.

   ANS: F   DIF: I   OBJ: BPE 42-3.4

30. Taste buds located in the tongue are stimulated when a chemical dissolved in saliva binds to taste cells in the taste buds.

   ANS: T   DIF: I   OBJ: BPE 42-3.5

31. Chemicals in the air stimulate olfactory receptors.

   ANS: T   DIF: I   OBJ: BPE 42-3.5

32. The sense of smell affects the enjoyment of food.

   ANS: T   DIF: I   OBJ: BPE 42-3.5

33. Cocaine acts by causing dopamine reuptake.

   ANS: F   DIF: I   OBJ: BPE 42-4.1

34. Addiction to psychoactive drugs is a physiological response because addiction involves interactions of drug molecules with neurons and synapses.

   ANS: T   DIF: I   OBJ: BPE 42-4.2

35. Enkephalins are natural pain relievers released by the body in response to pain and stress.

ANS: T DIF: I OBJ: BPE 42-4.3

36. Narcotics mimic the action of enkephalins.

ANS: T DIF: I OBJ: BPE 42-4.3

37. Alcohol is able to change the structure of a neuron's membrane, changing the shape of receptor proteins.

ANS: T DIF: I OBJ: BPE 42-4.3

38. Nicotine mimics the action of the neurotransmitter acetylcholine.

ANS: T DIF: I OBJ: BPE 42-4.3

MULTIPLE CHOICE

1. "Antennae" that extend from a neuron and that receive information from other cells are called
   a. axons.
   b. cell bodies.
   c. synapses.
   d. dendrites.

   ANS: D DIF: I OBJ: BPE 42-1.1

2. Nodes of Ranvier
   a. strengthen axons.
   b. slow nerve impulses.
   c. occur in malfunctioning axons.
   d. are gaps in the myelin sheath.

   ANS: D DIF: I OBJ: BPE 42-1.1

3. The myelin sheath
   a. transmits impulses from one neuron to another.
   b. insulates synapses.
   c. nourishes neurons.
   d. insulates axons.

   ANS: D DIF: I OBJ: BPE 42-1.1

4. unmyelinated axon : slow nerve impulses ::
   a. neuron : being composed of many axons
   b. nerve impulse : not traveling through axons
   c. myelinated axon : fast nerve impulses
   d. dendrite : sending information

   ANS: C
   (has the characteristic of)

   DIF: II OBJ: BPE 42-1.1

5. synapse : two neurons ::
    a. neuron : two cell bodies
    b. cell body : two axons
    c. synapse : cell body and axon
    d. axon : cell body and synapse

    ANS: D
    (is located between)

    DIF: II   OBJ: BPE 42-1.1

6. Which of the following statements about the resting potential of a neuron is *true*?
    a. There are many times more sodium ions outside the neuron than inside.
    b. Sodium ions are in balance inside and outside the neuron.
    c. There are fewer potassium ions inside the neuron than outside.
    d. There are equal amounts of potassium and sodium ions inside and outside the neuron.

    ANS: A   DIF: I   OBJ: BPE 42-1.2

7. After an action potential, the sodium-potassium pump helps
    a. rebuild axon fibers.
    b. restore the resting potential.
    c. cause a stimulus.
    d. All of the above

    ANS: B   DIF: I   OBJ: BPE 42-1.3

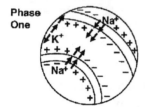 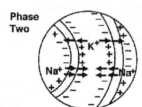 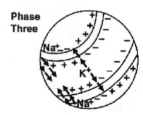

8. Refer to the illustration above. When a neuron is at rest,
    a. sodium ions are most concentrated inside the cell.
    b. potassium ions are most concentrated inside the cell.
    c. the outside of the cell is negatively charged.
    d. All of the above

    ANS: B   DIF: II   OBJ: BPE 42-1.3

9. Refer to the illustration above. The diagrams indicate that a nerve impulse
    a. moves from the inside to the outside of an axon.
    b. moves from the outside to the inside of an axon.
    c. is the movement of an action potential along an axon.
    d. moves slowly.

    ANS: C   DIF: II   OBJ: BPE 42-1.3

10. Refer to the illustration above. When an impulse moves down the axon,
    a. sodium ions first rush out of the cell.
    b. a small part of the axon momentarily reverses its polarity.
    c. the resting potential of the cell does not change.
    d. potassium ions are pumped into the axon.

    ANS: B   DIF: II   OBJ: BPE 42-1.3

11. Neurotransmitters are
    a. electrical impulses.
    b. found only in neurons with myelin sheaths.
    c. released at synapses.
    d. produced by muscles.

    ANS: C   DIF: I   OBJ: BPE 42-1.4

12. Some neurotransmitters cross a synapse and open sodium channels in the membrane of a
    postsynaptic neuron, causing
    a. inhibition of impulses in the neuron.   c. initiation of an impulse in the neuron.
    b. the death of the neuron.   d. the formation of receptors in the neuron.

    ANS: C   DIF: I   OBJ: BPE 42-1.4

13. When a neurotransmitter is released from a presynaptic neuron, the neurotransmitter may
    a. become an enzyme in the space between the neurons.
    b. bind to membrane receptor proteins on the membrane of the postsynaptic neuron.
    c. cover the membrane of the axon.
    d. cause the cell body of the postsynaptic neuron to enlarge.

    ANS: B   DIF: I   OBJ: BPE 42-1.4

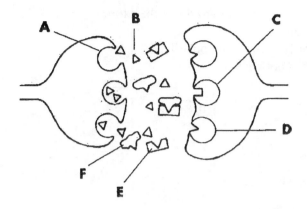

14. Refer to the illustration above. If neurotransmitters could not be cleared out of a synapse after transmitting a message,
    a. a postsynaptic neuron would continue to be stimulated for an indefinite period of time.
    b. the presynaptic neuron could not pass on its impulse.
    c. the postsynaptic neuron would not be stimulated.
    d. None of the above

    ANS: A   DIF: II   OBJ: BPE 42-1.4

15. Refer to the illustration above. In the diagram, label B indicates a
    a. neurotransmitter molecule.   c. receptor protein.
    b. neuromodulator molecule.   d. drug molecule.

    ANS: A   DIF: II   OBJ: BPE 42-4.2

16. Refer to the illustration above. Which labeled object in the diagram would be responsible for removing neurotransmitters from the synaptic cleft?
    a. B   c. E
    b. C   d. F

    ANS: C   DIF: II   OBJ: BPE 42-4.2

17. Refer to the illustration above. The effect of the neurotransmitter might be prolonged by the presence of molecule
    a. B.   c. E.
    b. D.   d. F.

    ANS: D   DIF: II   OBJ: BPE 42-4.2

18. Refer to the illustration above. When a drug blocks removal of a neurotransmitter from a synaptic cleft for a prolonged period,
    a. the postsynaptic neuron is overstimulated.
    b. the number of receptors on the postsynaptic neuron decreases.
    c. the only way to maintain normal functioning of the nerve pathway is to continue taking the drug.
    d. All of the above

    ANS: D   DIF: II   OBJ: BPE 42-4.2

19. The central nervous system consists of
    a. the brain and spinal cord.   c. the spinal cord only.
    b. spinal nerves only.   d. the brain only.

    ANS: A   DIF: I   OBJ: BPE 42-2.1

20. The peripheral nervous system
    a. is not linked to the central nervous system.
    b. provides pathways to and from the central nervous system.
    c. consists of the cerebellum and spinal cord.
    d. is composed of only motor neurons.

    ANS: B   DIF: I   OBJ: BPE 42-2.1

21. Information is carried from the central nervous system to a muscle or gland by
    a. sensory neurons.   c. motor neurons.
    b. sensory receptors.   d. None of the above

    ANS: D   DIF: I   OBJ: BPE 42-2.1

22. Motor neurons transmit messages
    a. to the brain.
    b. to the spinal cord.
    c. from the spinal cord to the brain.
    d. from the central nervous system to a muscle or gland.

    ANS: D   DIF: I   OBJ: BPE 42-2.1

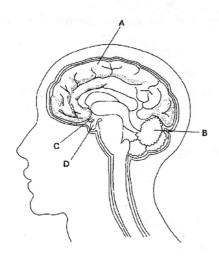

23. Refer to the illustration above. Structure "B" in the diagram is the
    a. spinal cord.   c. cerebellum.
    b. brain stem.   d. cerebrum.

    ANS: C   DIF: II   OBJ: BPE 42-2.2

24. Refer to the illustration above. In the diagram, hunger and thirst are regulated by structure
    a. A.   c. C.
    b. B.   d. D.

    ANS: D   DIF: II   OBJ: BPE 42-2.2

25. Refer to the illustration above. The cerebrum is labeled
    a. A.   c. C.
    b. B.   d. D.

    ANS: A   DIF: II   OBJ: BPE 42-2.2

26. Sensory neurons transmit messages
    a. from the central nervous system to a muscle or gland.
    b. from the brain to the spinal cord.
    c. to the spinal cord or brain.
    d. All of the above

    ANS: C   DIF: I   OBJ: BPE 42-2.2

27. Gray matter consists of
    a. cell bodies of neurons.   c. myelin.
    b. only synapses.   d. axons.

    ANS: A   DIF: I   OBJ: BPE 42-2.3

28. The spinal cord is linked to the peripheral nervous system through
    a. spinal nerves
    b. the thalamus
    c. interneurons
    d. All of the above

    ANS: A   DIF: I   OBJ: BPE 42-2.3

29. A reflex
    a. may involve two or three neurons.
    b. is not under conscious control.
    c. is not learned.
    d. All of the above

    ANS: D   DIF: I   OBJ: BPE 42-2.4

30. When the ligament below the patella is tapped, the quadriceps contracts, the hamstrings _____ and the leg rapidly extends.
    a. contract
    b. relax
    c. extend
    d. None of the above

    ANS: B   DIF: I   OBJ: BPE 42-2.4

31. The peripheral nervous system connects the brain and the _____ to the rest of the body.
    a. patella
    b. thalamus
    c. arms
    d. brain

    ANS: D   DIF: I   OBJ: BPE 42-2.5

32. The autonomic nervous system controls
    a. reflexes.
    b. voluntary movement.
    c. involuntary functions of the internal organs.
    d. locomotion.

    ANS: C   DIF: I   OBJ: BPE 42-2.5

33. The division of the autonomic nervous system that keeps you breathing when you fall asleep is the _____ division.
    a. somatic
    b. central
    c. sympathetic
    d. parasympathetic

    ANS: D   DIF: I   OBJ: BPE 42-2.5

34. Which of these is *not* a lobe of the brain?
    a. occipital
    b. parietal
    c. auditory
    d. temporal

    ANS: C   DIF: I   OBJ: BPE 42-3.2

35. How many lobes are there in the brain?
    a. 2
    b. 4
    c. 6
    d. 8

    ANS: B   DIF: I   OBJ: BPE 42-3.2

36. The layer of photoreceptors and neurons at the back of the eye is called the
    a. retina.
    b. cochlea.
    c. iris.
    d. optic nerve.

    ANS: A   DIF: I   OBJ: BPE 42-3.3

37. Dim-light vision is detected by the
    a. cones.
    b. lens.
    c. cornea.
    d. rods.

    ANS: D   DIF: I   OBJ: BPE 42-3.3

38. pupil : amount of light entering the eye ::
    a. pupil : point of focus on the retina
    b. cornea : shape of the lens
    c. lens : point of focus on the retina
    d. retina : movement of iris

    ANS: C
    (adjusts)

    DIF: II   OBJ: BPE 42-3.3

39. Sensory receptors essential for balance are located in the
    a. eyes.
    b. eardrum.
    c. cochlea of the inner ear.
    d. semicircular canals.

    ANS: D   DIF: I   OBJ: BPE 42-3.4

40. Hair cells in the semicircular canals detect
    a. motion of the head.
    b. loudness.
    c. light.
    d. sounds.

    ANS: A   DIF: I   OBJ: BPE 42-3.4

41. Ears
    a. function to detect sounds.
    b. help maintain your balance.
    c. detect only internal stimuli.
    d. Both (a) and (b)

    ANS: D   DIF: I   OBJ: BPE 42-3.4

42. Specialized receptors that enable hearing are found in the
    a. cornea.
    b. semicircular canals.
    c. cochlea.
    d. cerebellum.

    ANS: C   DIF: I   OBJ: BPE 42-3.4

43. When we hear,
    a. sound waves enter the ear canal and strike the eardrum.
    b. the membrane in the cochlea moves.
    c. the auditory nerve carries nerve impulses to the brain.
    d. All of the above

    ANS: D   DIF: I   OBJ: BPE 42-3.4

44. Chemoreceptors that detect odors are called _____ receptors.
    a. auditory
    b. olfactory
    c. cone
    d. cochlea

    ANS: B   DIF: I   OBJ: BPE 42-3.5

45. Psychoactive drugs, such as cocaine,
    a. affect the central nervous system by changing the activity of synapses.
    b. are usually not addictive.
    c. include only illegal drugs.
    d. All of the above

    ANS: A   DIF: I   OBJ: BPE 42-4.1

46. Cocaine acts by
    a. preventing dopamine reuptake.
    b. affecting the limbic system, causing euphoria.
    c. overstimulating postsynaptic neurons.
    d. All of the above

    ANS: D   DIF: I   OBJ: BPE 42-4.1

47. Narcotics affect the nervous system's control of pain perception by
    a. blocking dopamine reabsorption.   c. inhibiting dopamine production.
    b. mimicking cocaine.   d. mimicking enkephalins.

    ANS: D   DIF: I   OBJ: BPE 42-4.3

48. Nicotine in tobacco causes pleasurable feelings by
    a. blocking dopamine reabsorption.
    b. mimicking the action of acetylcholine.
    c. inhibiting a neurotransmitter similar to dopamine.
    d. mimicking enkephalins.

    ANS: B   DIF: I   OBJ: BPE 42-4.3

49. The effects of alcohol on the human body include
    a. changes to the cell membrane of nerve cells.
    b. altered transmission of nerve signals.
    c. impaired coordination.
    d. All of the above

    ANS: D   DIF: I   OBJ: BPE 42-4.3

COMPLETION

1. A(n) _____ is a cell that conducts electrical signals.

    ANS: neuron   DIF: I   OBJ: BPE 42-1.1

2. Cytoplasmic extensions called _____ allow a neuron to receive information simultaneously from many different sources.

   ANS: dendrites   DIF: I   OBJ: BPE 42-1.1

3. Some axons are surrounded by an insulating structure called a(n) _____ _____.

   ANS: myelin sheath   DIF: I   OBJ: BPE 42-1.1

4. The electrical charge across the membrane of a neuron is caused primarily by different concentrations of _____ and _____ ions inside and outside the cell.

   ANS: sodium, potassium   DIF: I   OBJ: BPE 42-1.2

5. Messages are carried across synapses by signal molecules called _____.

   ANS: neurotransmitters   DIF: I   OBJ: BPE 42-1.4

6. The junction of a neuron with another cell is called a(n) _____.

   ANS: synapse   DIF: I   OBJ: BPE 42-1.4

7. The part of the nervous system that does not include the spinal cord and brain is known as the _____ nervous system.

   ANS: peripheral   DIF: I   OBJ: BPE 42-2.1

8. Nerves that control breathing, swallowing, heartbeat, and the diameter of the blood vessels are found in the _____ _____.

   ANS: brain stem   DIF: I   OBJ: BPE 42-2.2

9. The thalamus, hypothalamus, and cells deep within the cerebral cortex of the brain make up the _____ system, which helps regulate emotions.

   ANS: limbic   DIF: I   OBJ: BPE 42-2.2

10. A sudden, involuntary movement in response to a stimulus is called a(n) _____.

   ANS: reflex   DIF: I   OBJ: BPE 42-2.4

11. The _____ division of the autonomic nervous system regulates involuntary functions during routine conditions.

   ANS: parasympathetic   DIF: I   OBJ: BPE 42-2.5

12. The two divisions of the autonomic nervous system are the parasympathetic division and the _____ division.

    ANS: sympathetic   DIF: I   OBJ: BPE 42-2.5

13. Sensory receptors that respond to tissue damage are called _____ receptors.

    ANS: pain   DIF: I   OBJ: BPE 42-3.1

14. Specialized neurons that detect sensory stimuli are called _____ receptors.

    ANS: sensory   DIF: I   OBJ: BPE 42-3.1

15. Sensory neurons leading from each sense organ to the brain come together at a common region in the _____ _____.

    ANS: cerebral cortex   DIF: I   OBJ: BPE 42-3.2

16. The _____ is the light-sensing portion of the eye.

    ANS: retina   DIF: I   OBJ: BPE 42-3.3

17. When light enters the eye, it activates photoreceptors called _____ and _____.

    ANS: rods, cones   DIF: I   OBJ: BPE 42-3.3

18. When light enters the eye, it first passes through the _____.

    ANS: cornea   DIF: I   OBJ: BPE 42-3.3

19. Auditory processing takes place in the _____ lobe of the brain.

    ANS: temporal   DIF: I   OBJ: BPE 42-3.3

20. The _____ is a small, snail-shaped structure of the inner ear lined with hair cells.

    ANS: cochlea   DIF: I   OBJ: BPE 42-3.4

21. The specialized sensory receptors found in the cochlea are called _____ cells.

    ANS: hair   DIF: I   OBJ: BPE 42-3.4

22. Olfactory receptors are located in the roof of the _____ passage.

    ANS: nasal   DIF: I   OBJ: BPE 42-3.5

23. A(n) _____ _____ is a globular cluster of cells specialize to detect the four basic types of chemicals found in foods.

ANS: taste bud   DIF: I   OBJ: BPE 42-3.5

24. Psychoactive drugs that decrease the activity of the central nervous system are called

_____.

ANS: depressants   DIF: I   OBJ: BPE 42-4.1

25. Exposure to large amounts of a psychoactive drug over a prolonged period of time may cause a change in the functioning of synapses. The result of such exposure is called

_____.

ANS: addiction   DIF: I   OBJ: BPE 42-4.2

26. Neurotransmitters released by the human body in response to pain are called

_____.

ANS: enkephalins   DIF: I   OBJ: BPE 42-4.3

PROBLEM

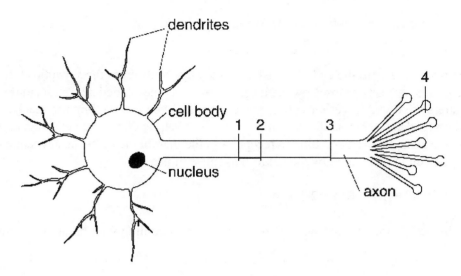

1. Refer to the illustration above. At the locations labeled 1, 3, and 4, the inside of the neuron is negatively charged compared to the outside. At the location labeled 2, the inside of the neuron is positively charged.
    a. Which numbered location(s) on the neuron is(are) at the resting potential?
    b. Which numbered location(s) on the neuron is(are) showing an action potential?
    c. At which numbered location(s) on the neuron is the cell membrane permeable to sodium ions?
    d. At which numbered location(s) on the neuron are sodium-potassium pumps actively pumping these ions?
    e. What happens when an action potential reaches location "4" on the neuron?

    ANS:
    a. 1, 3, and 4
    b. 2
    c. 2
    d. 1
    e. Neurotransmitters are released from the cell.

    DIF: III   OBJ: BPE 42-1.3

ESSAY

1. How is a signal from one neuron transmitted to another neuron?

    ANS:
    When a nerve impulse gets to the end of an axon, its message must cross the synaptic cleft. Messages are carried across synapses by chemical signal molecules called neurotransmitters. Neurotransmitters are found in vesicles at the end of axons. When a nerve impulse reaches an axon's end, the vesicles release neurotransmitters into the synaptic cleft. The neurotransmitters diffuse across the synaptic cleft and bind to receptors in the membrane of the postsynaptic cell. The postsynaptic cell is stimulated by the neurotransmitter molecules.

    DIF: II   OBJ: BPE 42-1.4

2. What part of the peripheral nervous system prevents you from holding your breath indefinitely? Explain.

    ANS:
    The autonomic nervous system carries messages to muscles and glands that usually work without our noticing, and enables the nervous system to maintain homeostasis within the body. We have involuntary control over some functions, such as breathing, that are regulated by the autonomic nervous system. Any voluntary control of the autonomic nervous system that endangers life disturbs the homeostasis of the brain tissue, causing unconsciousness. Then the autonomic nervous system takes over and restores normal functioning—in this case, breathing.

    DIF: II   OBJ: BPE 42-2.5

3. Explain why addiction to psychoactive drugs has a physiological basis.

    ANS:
    Some drugs cause excessive amounts of neurotransmitter to be present in synapses for long periods of time. This results in a decreased number of receptors on the postsynaptic membrane and a less sensitive nerve pathway. The only way a person who is addicted can maintain normal functioning of the nerve pathway is to continue taking the drug.

    DIF: II   OBJ: BPE 42-4.2

4. Describe the action of cocaine at the synapse and the effects of long-term use on receptors.

    ANS:
    Cocaine prevents the reabsorption of dopamine from the synaptic cleft. The trapped dopamine repeatedly stimulates postsynaptic neurons. The postsynaptic neurons adjust to the presence of cocaine by decreasing the number of dopamine receptors. This causes these neurons to become less sensitive, requiring more and more cocaine for stimulation.

    DIF: II   OBJ: BPE 42-4.2

CHAPTER 43—HORMONES AND THE ENDOCRINE SYSTEM

TRUE/FALSE

1. Hormones are substances secreted by cells that act to regulate the activity of other cells in the body.

    ANS: T   DIF: I   OBJ: BPE 43-1.1

2. Hormones must travel through the bloodstream to reach the cell on which they must act.

    ANS: F   DIF: I   OBJ: BPE 43-1.1

3. The same hormone can tell different cells to perform different actions.

    ANS: T   DIF: I   OBJ: BPE 43-1.1

4. An endocrine gland secretes its product directly into the blood.

    ANS: T   DIF: I   OBJ: BPE 43-1.2

5. The pancreas is both an endocrine and an exocrine gland.

    ANS: T   DIF: I   OBJ: BPE 43-1.2

6. Organs and glands that produce most of the hormones in the body make up the endocrine system.

    ANS: T   DIF: I   OBJ: BPE 43-1.2

7. Although hormones are slow-acting, their effects tend to last for a long time.

    ANS: T   DIF: I   OBJ: BPE 43-1.3

8. Prostaglandins function much as hormones do in that they regulate cellular activities.

    ANS: F   DIF: I   OBJ: BPE 43-1.4

9. Amino-acid-based hormones are fat-soluble, while steroid hormones are water-soluble.

    ANS: F   DIF: I   OBJ: BPE 43-2.1

10. Hormones travel throughout the body in the bloodstream and can affect any cell.

    ANS: F   DIF: I   OBJ: BPE 43-2.1

11. Amino-acid-based hormones pass through the cell membrane.

    ANS: F   DIF: I   OBJ: BPE 43-2.2

12. Steroid hormones act from outside the cell by means of second messengers.

    ANS: F   DIF: I   OBJ: BPE 43-2.3

13. Steroid hormones directly genes in their target cells.

    ANS: T   DIF: I   OBJ: BPE 43-2.3

14. When sufficient levels of testosterone are present in a male's bloodstream, production is inhibited by a negative-feedback system.

    ANS: T   DIF: I   OBJ: BPE 43-2.4

15. In females, luteinizing hormone (LH) causes the release of an egg from the ovary.

    ANS: T   DIF: I   OBJ: BPE 43-3.1

16. Antidiuretic hormone causes the muscles of the uterus to contract during childbirth.

    ANS: F   DIF: I   OBJ: BPE 43-3.1

17. The ovary is the source of follicle-stimulating hormone (FSH).

    ANS: F   DIF: I   OBJ: BPE 43-3.1

18. A goiter is the result of futile attempts by the thyroid gland to make thyroid hormones when the person is suffering from an iodine deficiency.

    ANS: T   DIF: I   OBJ: BPE 43-3.2

19. The adrenal cortex produces steroid hormones, and the adrenal medulla produces amino-acid-based hormones.

    ANS: T   DIF: I   OBJ: BPE 43-3.3

20. The inability of cells to take up glucose from blood is called diabetes mellitus.

    ANS: T   DIF: I   OBJ: BPE 43-3.4

21. Estrogens stimulate the development of secondary sex female sex characteristics.

    ANS: T   DIF: I   OBJ: BPE 43-3.5

MULTIPLE CHOICE

1. Hormones are
   a. chemicals that stimulate nerve cells during times of stress.
   b. the same as electrical nerve impulses.
   c. released into the bloodstream or the fluid around cells.
   d. neurons along which messages travel.

   ANS: C   DIF: I   OBJ: BPE 43-1.1

2. Hormones are essential to maintaining homeostasis mainly because
   a. they catalyze specific chemical reactions in brain cells.
   b. the body requires them for digesting food.
   c. they cause specific responses in specific cells.
   d. they act faster than nerve impulses.

   ANS: C   DIF: I   OBJ: BPE 43-1.1

3. Which of the following is a function of hormones?
   a. react to stimuli from outside the body
   b. coordinate the production and use of energy
   c. maintain nutrition and metabolism
   d. regulate growth and reproduction
   e. All of the above

   ANS: D   DIF: I   OBJ: BPE 43-1.1

4. All endocrine glands secrete hormones
   a. directly into the bloodstream or fluid around cells.
   b. that go to the pituitary gland.
   c. that affect every cell near the gland.
   d. that are lipid molecules.

   ANS: A   DIF: I   OBJ: BPE 43-1.2

5. Which of the following organs contain(s) cells that have an endocrine function?
   a. brain   c. small intestine
   b. stomach   d. All of the above

   ANS: D   DIF: I   OBJ: BPE 43-1.2

6. Nearly instantaneous responses to changes in the environment
   a. are impossible.
   b. result from activation of the endocrine system.
   c. involve the activity of the nervous system.
   d. require messages from the pituitary gland.

   ANS: C   DIF: I   OBJ: BPE 43-1.3

7. A disadvantage of nervous signals, which is *not* true of hormonal messages, is that
   a. nerve transmissions reach many cells at once.
   b. nerve cells send messages at a much slower rate than do hormones.
   c. the effects of nervous signals last for only a short time.
   d. they take a long time to reach their target cell.

   ANS: C   DIF: I   OBJ: BPE 43-1.3

8. Modified fatty acids that tend to accumulate in areas of tissue disturbance or injury are
   a. endorphins.   c. neuromodulators.
   b. enkephalins.   d. prostaglandins.

   ANS: D   DIF: I   OBJ: BPE 43-1.4

9. All of the following are hormonelike chemical signal molecules *except*
   a. steroids.   c. neurotransmitters.
   b. neuropeptides.   d. prostaglandins.

   ANS: A   DIF: I   OBJ: BPE 43-1.4

10. Prostaglandins
    a. are transported throughout the body through the blood.
    b. are produced by the hypothalamus.
    c. act locally.
    d. are not considered hormones since they function very differently from them.

    ANS: C   DIF: I   OBJ: BPE 43-1.4

11. In order for a hormone to work
    a. it must reach its target cell.   c. Both (a) and (b)
    b. it must bind to a receptor protein.   d. None of the above

    ANS: D   DIF: I   OBJ: BPE 43-2.1

12. When a hormone binds to a receptor,
    a. the receptor protein changes shape.
    b. the activity or amounts of enzymes in the cell eventually change.
    c. the chemical reactions inside the cell eventually change.
    d. All of the above

    ANS: D   DIF: I   OBJ: BPE 43-2.1

13. endocrine glands : hormones ::
    a. neurons : neurotransmitters   c. all cells : neurotransmitters
    b. neurons : hormones   d. all cells : hormones

    ANS: A
    (produce)

    DIF: II   OBJ: BPE 43-2.1

14. When an amino-acid-based hormone acts on a target cell
    a. it binds to a receptor in the plasma of the cell
    b. it passes through the cell membrane
    c. it eventually results in the activation of a "second messenger."
    d. the hormone is converted to a steroid.

    ANS: C   DIF: I   OBJ: BPE 43-2.2

15. If an amino-acid-based hormone acts as a "first messenger," then a molecule of _____ acts as a "second messenger."
    a. steroid hormone   c. receptor protein
    b. cyclic AMP   d. glucagon

    ANS: B   DIF: I   OBJ: BPE 43-2.2

16. Which of the following is an example of an amino-acid-based hormone?
    a. receptor protein   c. glycogen
    b. estrogen   d. glucagon

    ANS: D   DIF: I   OBJ: BPE 43-2.2

17. Amino-acid-based hormones
    a. send messages from outside the cell.
    b. are carried into the cell by channel proteins.
    c. combine with steroid hormones in order to activate cells.
    d. cannot dissolve in polar molecules.

    ANS: A   DIF: I   OBJ: BPE 43-2.2

18. Since steroid hormones are fat soluble, they
    a. attach only to fat receptor molecules.
    b. cannot enter the target cell.
    c. activate only fat cells.
    d. pass through the cell membranes of their target cells.

    ANS: D   DIF: I   OBJ: BPE 43-2.3

19. A substance that functions by affecting the activities of genes in a target cell is a(n)
    a. carbohydrate.   c. amino-acid-based hormone
    b. steroid hormone.   d. second messenger.

    ANS: B   DIF: I   OBJ: BPE 43-2.3

20. A hormone receptor protein found inside the cytoplasm of a cell may
    a. attach to cyclic AMP.   c. synthesize DNA.
    b. combine with a steroid hormone.   d. act as a second messenger.

    ANS: B   DIF: I   OBJ: BPE 43-2.3

21. amino-acid-based hormones : cell membrane receptors ::
     a. receptor proteins : DNA   c. steroid hormones : DNA
     b. cyclic AMP : steriod hormones   d. amino-acid-based hormones : RNA

     ANS: C
     (act on the)

     DIF: II   OBJ: BPE 43-2.3

22. The organ that plays a role in feedback by removing hormones from the blood and breaking them
     down is the
     a. pancreas.   c. liver.
     b. kidney.   d. small intestine.

     ANS: C   DIF: I   OBJ: BPE 43-2.4

23. Hormones produced by the pituitary gland
     a. are regulated by secretions from the hypothalamus.
     b. control the activity of other endocrine glands.
     c. are produced as the result of stimulation by releasing hormones.
     d. All of the above.

     ANS: D   DIF: I   OBJ: BPE 43-3.1

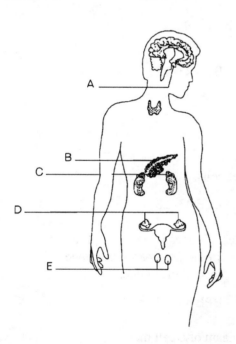

24. The pituitary gland is indicated in the diagram above by gland
     a. A.   c. C.
     b. B.   d. D.

     ANS: A   DIF: II   OBJ: BPE 43-3.1

25. Growth hormone is produced by gland
    a. A.   c. C.
    b. B.   d. D.

    ANS: A   DIF: II   OBJ: BPE 43-3.1

26. The gland in the above diagram that is stimulated during emergency situations (causing the "flight-or-fight" response) is gland
    a. A.   c. C.
    b. B.   d. D.

    ANS: C   DIF: II   OBJ: BPE 43-3.3

27. Diabetes mellitus is associated with a defect in the functioning of gland
    a. A.   c. C.
    b. B.   d. D.

    ANS: B   DIF: I   OBJ: BPE 43-3.4

28. In the diagram above, the gland that produces the hormone insulin is gland
    a. A.   c. C.
    b. B.   d. D.

    ANS: B   DIF: II   OBJ: BPE 43-3.4

29. Development and maintenance of female sexual characteristics are mainly stimulated by secretions of gland
    a. A.   c. C.
    b. B.   d. D.

    ANS: D   DIF: II   OBJ: BPE 43-3.5

30. Testosterone is produced by gland
    a. A.   c. E.
    b. B.   d. All of the above

    ANS: C   DIF: II   OBJ: BPE 43-3.5

31. Until recently, the pituitary gland was called the "master gland." The name is no longer used because
    a. it was recently discovered that the pituitary gland does not not actually do anything.
    b. the hypothalamus is responsible for controlling the activity of the pituitary gland.
    c. the pituitary gland controls the hypothalamus, which in turn controls the other glands.
    d. hormones of the other endocrine glands of the body activate the pituitary gland.

    ANS: B   DIF: I   OBJ: BPE 43-3.1

32. Scientists once thought that the pituitary gland was the regulatory center of the endocrine system. They now think that a structure in the brain, they hypothalamus, acts as this regulatory center. Which of the following does not provide information supporting this new conclusion?
   a.   The hypothalamus can send nerve signals to other parts of the brain.
   b.   The hypothalamus produces and secretes hormones.
   c.   Hormones produced by the hypothalamus stimulate or inhibit the release of other hormones by the pituitary gland.
   d.   Blood vessels have been found that connect the hypothalamus with the pituitary gland.

   ANS: A   DIF: II   OBJ: BPE 43-3.1

33. The posterior lobe of the pituitary gland
   a.   secretes releasing hormones that stimulate the anterior lobe of the pituitary gland.
   b.   produces and secretes certain steroid hormones.
   c.   stores and releases hormones made in the hypothalamus.
   d.   is responsible for producing and secreting seven amino-acid-based hormones.

   ANS: C   DIF: I   OBJ: BPE 43-3.1

34. All of the following are produced by the pituitary gland *except*
   a.   prolactin.   c.   oxytocin.
   b.   growth hormone.   d.   parathyroid hormone.

   ANS: D   DIF: I   OBJ: BPE 43-3.1

35. Which of the following are mismatched?
   a.   oxytocin-hypothalamus   c.   glucagon-pancreas
   b.   insulin-pancreas   d.   calcitonin-pituitary gland

   ANS: D   DIF: I   OBJ: BPE 43-3.2

36. The body's normal metabolic rate is regulated by
   a.   thyroid hormones.   c.   metaboloxin.
   b.   epinephrine.   d.   prolactin.

   ANS: A   DIF: I   OBJ: BPE 43-3.2

37. Thyroid hormones
   a.   stimulate cell metabolism and growth.
   b.   slow growth of their target cells.
   c.   stimulate synthesis of DNA.
   d.   bind to receptor molecules on the target cell's surface.

   ANS: A   DIF: I   OBJ: BPE 43-3.2

38. When the level of calcium in the blood drops,
    a. one should immediately drink at least two eight-ounce glasses of milk.
    b. the parathyroid glands secrete a hormone that causes the release of calcium from the bone into the blood.
    c. the thyroid gland releases calcium into the blood.
    d. All of the above

    ANS: B   DIF: I   OBJ: BPE 43-3.2

39. Excessive production of thyroid hormones by the thyroid gland is the cause of the disease called
    a. hypothyroidism.   c. hyperthyroidism.
    b. diabetes mellitus.   d. gigantism.

    ANS: C   DIF: I   OBJ: BPE 43-3.2

40. Low levels of thyroid hormones cause the disease known as
    a. hypothyroidism.   c. Graves' disease.
    b. diabetes mellitus.   d. gigantism.

    ANS: A   DIF: I   OBJ: BPE 43-3.2

41. In adults, hypothyroidism can cause
    a. nervousness.   c. increased blood sugar.
    b. weight loss.   d. lack of energy.

    ANS: D   DIF: I   OBJ: BPE 43-3.2

42. parathyroid gland : PTH ::
    a. thyroid gland : thyroid hormones   c. pituitary gland : insulin
    b. pancreas : estrogen   d. adrenal gland : FSH

    ANS: A
    (secretes)

    DIF: II   OBJ: BPE 43-3.2

43. A goiter can result from a lack of
    a. iodine.   c. vasopressin.
    b. insulin.   d. sodium ions.

    ANS: A   DIF: I   OBJ: BPE 43-3.2

44. Parathyroid hormone is important for survival because it
    a. stimulates the body's metabolic rate.
    b. regulates the amount of calcium in the blood.
    c. causes the heart to contract and pump blood.
    d. increases the excretion of calcium by the kidneys.

    ANS: B   DIF: I   OBJ: BPE 43-3.2

45. epinephrine : initial reaction to stress ::
    a. norepinephrine : milk production
    b. aldosterone : readiness to "fight"
    c. aldosterone : readiness for "flight"
    d. PTH : blood calcium level

ANS: D
(regulates the body's)

DIF: II   OBJ: BPE 43-3.3

46. increase in blood-glucose level : glucagon release ::
    a. calcitonin production : low blood-calcium level
    b. PTH production : high blood-calcium level
    c. hyperthyroidism : overproduction of thyroid hormones
    d. hypothyroidism : overproduction of thyroid hormones

ANS: C
(is caused by)

DIF: II   OBJ: BPE 43-3.3

47. aldosterone and PTH : fluid retrieval from the body ::
    a. cortisol and adrenaline : loss of sodium and potassium
    b. cortisol and PTH : loss of potassium
    c. epinephrine and norepinephrine : initial response to stress
    d. epinephrine and norepinephrine : potassium ions to be excreted in urine

ANS: C
(regulate)

DIF: II   OBJ: BPE 43-3.3

48. All of the following are steroid hormones *except*
    a. progesterone.   c. epinephrine.
    b. estrogen.   d. testosterone.

ANS: C   DIF: I   OBJ: BPE 43-3.3

49. Which of the following are mismatched?
    a. oxytocin-uterus   c. parathyroid hormone-bones
    b. antidiuretic hormone-kidneys   d. insulin-hypothalamus

ANS: D   DIF: I   OBJ: BPE 43-3.4

50. The islets of Langerhans in the pancreas are responsible for
    a. production of epinephrine and norepinephrine.
    b. making hormones that regulate blood sugar levels.
    c. regulating calcium levels in the blood and in the bones.
    d. controlling the amount of iodine that reaches the thyroid gland.

    ANS: B   DIF: I   OBJ: BPE 43-3.4

51. An increase in which hormone raises the blood sugar level?
    a. glucagon   c. oxytocin
    b. insulin   d. vasopressin

    ANS: A   DIF: I   OBJ: BPE 43-3.4

52. In a person with diabetes mellitus, even though blood glucose levels may be high,
    a. glycogen is stored in large quantities.   c. cells do not receive glucose.
    b. insulin levels still increase.   d. None of the above

    ANS: C   DIF: I   OBJ: BPE 43-3.4

53. Individuals with Type II diabetes
    a. require daily injections of insulin.
    b. suffer from an autoimmune disorder that attacks the islets of Langerhans.
    c. have an abnormally low number of insulin receptors on their cell membranes.
    d. exhibit especially low levels of insulin in their blood.

    ANS: C   DIF: I   OBJ: BPE 43-3.4

54. The hormone that seems to be released as a response to darkness is
    a. melatonin.   c. oxytocin.
    b. calcitonin.   d. testosterone.

    ANS: A   DIF: I   OBJ: BPE 43-3.5

COMPLETION

1. Hormones regulate growth, development, behavior, and _____.

    ANS: reproduction   DIF: I   OBJ: BPE 43-1.1

2. _____ glands deliver substances through ducts.

    ANS: Exocrine   DIF: I   OBJ: BPE 43-1.2

3. _____ are nonendocrine molecules, such as endorphins and enkephalins, that affect cells near the nerve cells that produce them.

    ANS: Neuropeptides   DIF: I   OBJ: BPE 43-1.4

4. _____ are a group of neuropeptides that are thought to regulate emotions and influence pain.

   ANS: Endorphins   DIF: I   OBJ: BPE 43-1.4

5. Hormones affect only the appropriate _____ cells.

   ANS: target   DIF: I   OBJ: BPE 43-2.1

6. Cyclic AMP is a molecule that amplifies the effect of a hormone by acting as a(n) _____ _____ in cells that are activated by amino-acid-base hormones.

   ANS: "second messenger"   DIF: I   OBJ: BPE 43-2.2

7. _____ hormones activate specific genes within a target cell.

   ANS: Steroid   DIF: I   OBJ: BPE 43-2.3

8. Fat-soluble lipid hormones, similar in structure to cholesterol, are called _____ hormones.

   ANS: steroid   DIF: I   OBJ: BPE 43-2.3

9. _____ _____ _____ hormones remain outside their target cells, while _____ hormones carry out their function from within their target cells.

   ANS: Amino-acid-based; steroid   DIF: I   OBJ: BPE 43-2.3

10. A steroid hormone can combine with a receptor protein in the cytoplasm to form a(n) _____-_____ complex, which enters the nucleus of a cell and binds to DNA.

    ANS: hormone-receptor   DIF: I   OBJ: BPE 43-2.3

11. A baby nursing on a mother's breast stimulates the release of oxytocin which in turn stimulates the release of milk from the mother's mammary glands. This type of feedback is an example of _____ feedback.

    ANS: positive   DIF: I   OBJ: BPE 43-2.4

12. The _____, a portion of the brain, controls much of the endocrine activity of the body by regulating the secretions of the pituitary gland.

    ANS: hypothalamus   DIF: I   OBJ: BPE 43-3.1

13. The gland that stores oxytocin is the _____ _____.

    ANS: posterior pituitary   DIF: I   OBJ: BPE 43-3.1

14. The glands responsible for regulating blood levels of calcium and phosphate ions are the
    _____ glands.

    ANS: parathyroid   DIF: I   OBJ: BPE 43-3.2

15. High levels of calcium in the blood stimulate the production of _____, a
    hormone that causes more calcium to be deposited in bone tissue, thus lowering the
    blood-calcium level.

    ANS: calcitonin   DIF: I   OBJ: BPE 43-3.2

16. A hormone that increases the body's metabolic rate is produced by the _____
    gland.

    ANS: thyroid   DIF: I   OBJ: BPE 43-3.2

17. A swollen thyroid gland is called a(n) _____.

    ANS: goiter   DIF: I   OBJ: BPE 43-3.2

18. The _____ glands secrete a hormone that regulates the level of calcium in the
    bloodstream.

    ANS: parathyroid   DIF: I   OBJ: BPE 43-3.2

19. _____ is a steroid hormone that is produced by the adrenal glands in response
    to stress.

    ANS: Cortisol   DIF: I   OBJ: BPE 43-3.3

20. Secretion of cortisol during stressful times causes an increase of _____ in the
    bloodstream.

    ANS: glucose   DIF: I   OBJ: BPE 43-3.3

21. The frequently prescribed medication prednisone, used as an anti-inflammatory agent, is a
    derivative of the hormone _____.

    ANS: cortisol (or hydrocortisone)   DIF: I   OBJ: BPE 43-3.3

22. Epinephrine and norepinephrine are produced by the _____ glands.

    ANS: adrenal   DIF: I   OBJ: BPE 43-3.3

23. A condition that results from the inability of cells to take glucose from blood and tissue fluids is called _____ _____.

    ANS: diabetes mellitus   DIF: I   OBJ: BPE 43-3.4

24. A hormone that enables the cells of certain tissues to take in glucose molecules is _____.

    ANS: insulin   DIF: I   OBJ: BPE 43-3.4

25. Ovaries and testes secrete hormones that regulate _____.

    ANS: reproduction   DIF: I   OBJ: BPE 43-3.5

26. Melatonin is secreted by the _____ _____.

    ANS: pineal gland   DIF: I   OBJ: BPE 43-3.5

27. The hormones that stimulate male secondary sex characteristics are produced in the _____.

    ANS: testes   DIF: I   OBJ: BPE 43-3.5

ESSAY

1. Describe the advantages that hormonal messages have over messages of the nervous system.

    ANS:
    Hormones spread to many cells via the bloodstream or extracellular fluid, rather than being directed to individual cells as nerve impulses are. Although hormones travel throughout the body, they also exhibit specificity; they have a shape that allows them to interact only with specific receptors on specific target cells. Since the same receptor molecule may be found on different kinds of cells in different organs, hormonal effects exhibit flexibility, which is the ability to achieve different effects in different tissues. Hormones also affect more long-term changes whereas nervous system messages affect changes of shorter duration.

    DIF: II   OBJ: BPE 43-1.3

2. Why does a hormone affect only a target cell?

    ANS:
    Only target cells have receptors that bind the hormone.

    DIF: II   OBJ: BPE 43-2.1

3. Glucagon, a hormone produced by the pancreas, cannot enter its target cells, but it causes an increase in glucose in the bloodstream. Explain how this hormone works.

ANS:
Glucagon attaches to a target cell in the liver by binding to a protein receptor on the cell's surface. This binding causes an enzyme to produce cyclic AMP, a "second messenger" that activates certain enzymes within the target cell. These enzymes break down glycogen to glucose molecules, which then moves from the cell to the bloodstream.

DIF: II   OBJ: BPE 43-2.2

4. Compare the action mechanisms of amino acid-based and steroid hormones.

ANS:
Amino-acid-based hormones attach to receptor proteins on the surface of a target cell, causing the production of a second messenger within the cell. The second messenger in turn activates enzymes within the cell. Steroid hormones enter the cell, where they combine with receptor proteins in the cytoplasm or nucleus. The combined hormone and receptor molecules enter into the cell's nucleus, where they activate specific genes.

DIF: II   OBJ: BPE 43-2.3

5. Differentiate between negative and positive feedback with respect to control of hormones.

ANS:
In positive feedback high levels of a hormone stimulate the output of even more hormone. In negative feedback a change in one direction of the amount of a hormone stimulates the control mechanism to counteract any further change in the same direction.

DIF: II   OBJ: BPE 43-2.4

6. Explain why the cells of a patient with diabetes mellitus starve due to lack of glucose even though blood glucose levels are higher than normal.

ANS:
In a patient with diabetes mellitus, the pancreas does not make enough insulin. Insulin stimulates the cells to take up glucose from the bloodstream. In the absence of insulin, even though there may be plenty of glucose in the blood, cells are unable to take it up. Therefore, the cells cannot conduct cellular respiration, and they starve.

DIF: II   OBJ: BPE 43-3.4

7. Even though the function of the pineal gland is not yet known, it has been implicated in several activities and disorders. Name one activity or disorder.

ANS:
Answers may include establishing daily biorhythms, mood disorders such as seasonal affective disorder syndrome, and a variety of aspects of sexual development.

DIF: II   OBJ: BPE 43-3.5

Biology: Principles and Explorations
616

CHAPTER 44—REPRODUCTION AND DEVELOPMENT

TRUE/FALSE

1. Sperm are produced and mature in the testes.

   ANS: F   DIF: I   OBJ: BPE 44-1.1

2. Testosterone is produced by the testes.

   ANS: T   DIF: I   OBJ: BPE 44-1.1

3. The urethra is the tube that carries semen during ejaculation.

   ANS: T   DIF: I   OBJ: BPE 44-1.4

4. Semen contains sugars to provide energy for sperm cells.

   ANS: T   DIF: I   OBJ: BPE 44-1.4

5. An ovum is a mature egg cell.

   ANS: T   DIF: I   OBJ: BPE 44-2.1

6. The fallopian tubes are the organs responsible for producing eggs.

   ANS: F   DIF: I   OBJ: BPE 44-2.1

7. The uterus is a pear-shaped organ made of three muscular layers.

   ANS: F   DIF: I   OBJ: BPE 44-2.2

8. The entrance to the uterus is known as the cervix.

   ANS: T   DIF: I   OBJ: BPE 44-2.2

9. Luteinizing hormone (LH) causes the maturation of eggs.

   ANS: T   DIF: I   OBJ: BPE 44-2.3

10. The ovary is the source of follicle-stimulating hormone (FSH).

    ANS: F   DIF: I   OBJ: BPE 44-2.3

11. The lining of the uterus begins to thicken and become spongy in preparation to receive the embryo in the four or five days after an egg is released from the ovary.

    ANS: F   DIF: I   OBJ: BPE 44-2.3

12. Fertilization usually takes place in the fallopian tubes.

     ANS: T   DIF: I   OBJ: BPE 44-3.1

13. By the time the zygote reaches the uterus, it is a hollow ball of cells called a blastocyst.

     ANS: T   DIF: I   OBJ: BPE 44-3.1

14. The implantation of an embryo into the uterine lining is called fertilization.

     ANS: F   DIF: I   OBJ: BPE 44-3.1

15. Immediately after fertilization, a human embryo rapidly increases in size.

     ANS: F   DIF: I   OBJ: BPE 44-3.1

16. In the placenta, fetal blood mixes directly with maternal blood.

     ANS: F   DIF: I   OBJ: BPE 44-3.2

17. No treatment is necessary for syphilis, gonorrhea, and chlamydia because the body will cure these diseases naturally over a period of time.

     ANS: F   DIF: I   OBJ: BPE 44-4.1

18. Pelvic inflammatory disease, or PID, is one of the most common causes of infertility in women.

     ANS: T   DIF: I   OBJ: BPE 44-4.1

19. Genital herpes is a sexually transmitted disease caused by a virus.

     ANS: T   DIF: I   OBJ: BPE 44-4.2

20. Symptoms of genital herpes include periodic outbreaks of painful blisters in the genital region and flulike aches and fever.

     ANS: T   DIF: I   OBJ: BPE 44-4.2

21. Like HIV, herpes simplex virus can be passed from mother to fetus during pregnancy or birth.

     ANS: T   DIF: I   OBJ: BPE 44-4.2

22. In its early stage, genital herpes can be cured by the use of antibiotics.

     ANS: F   DIF: I   OBJ: BPE 44-4.3

MULTIPLE CHOICE

1. Sperm and eggs are both
    a. haploid.
    b. diploid.
        c. tetraploid.
        d. None of the above

    ANS: A   DIF: I   OBJ: BPE 44-1.1

2. The testes
    a. produce sperm.
    b. produce male hormones.
        c. are suspended in the scrotum.
        d. All of the above

    ANS: D   DIF: I   OBJ: BPE 44-1.1

3. Production of sperm and testosterone is regulated by luteinizing hormone and follicle-stimulating hormone, which are produced by the
    a. testes.
    b. hypothalamus.
        c. bulbourethral gland.
        d. pituitary gland.

    ANS: D   DIF: I   OBJ: BPE 44-1.1

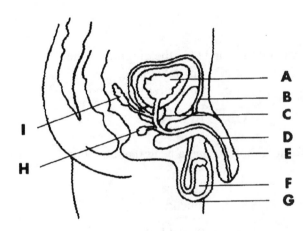

4. Refer to the illustration above. Sperm are produced in
    a. A.
    b. C.
        c. F.
        d. H.

    ANS: C   DIF: II   OBJ: BPE 44-1.1

5. Refer to the illustration above. The structure that connects the epididymis to the urethra is labeled
    a. A.
    b. H.
        c. I.
        d. B.

    ANS: D   DIF: II   OBJ: BPE 44-1.2

6. Refer to the illustration above. The tube that carries urine during excretion and semen during ejaculation is labeled
   a. A.   c. B.
   b. H.   d. D.

   ANS: D   DIF: II   OBJ: BPE 44-1.2

7. Refer to the illustration above. The scrotum is indicated by label
   a. A.   c. G.
   b. E.   d. H.

   ANS: C   DIF: II   OBJ: BPE 44-1.2

8. Refer to the illustration above. The bulbourethral gland is indicated by label
   a. A.   c. D.
   b. B.   d. H.

   ANS: D   DIF: II   OBJ: BPE 44-1.2

9. Refer to the illustration above. The prostate gland is indicated by label
   a. A.   c. D.
   b. C.   d. H.

   ANS: B   DIF: II   OBJ: BPE 44-1.2

10. Refer to the illustration above. The structure labeled C in the diagram is the
    a. urinary bladder.   c. prostate gland.
    b. scrotal sac.   d. bulbourethral gland.

    ANS: C   DIF: II   OBJ: BPE 44-1.4

11. A sperm cell consists of a tail used for locomotion, and a head that contains ____ that help the sperm cell penetrate an egg cell.
    a. semen.   c. enzymes.
    b. RNA.   d. mucus.

    ANS: C   DIF: I   OBJ: BPE 44-1.3

12. The midpiece of a sperm cell contains many ____ that supply sperm with the energy needed to propel themselves through the female reproductive system.
    a. nuclei.   c. tubules.
    b. mitochondria.   d. heads

    ANS: B   DIF: I   OBJ: BPE 44-1.3

13. The process by which sperm leave the male's body is called
    a. secretion.   c. diffusion.
    b. ejaculation.   d. locomotion.

    ANS: B   DIF: I   OBJ: BPE 44-1.4

14. In which of the following ways are mature human sperm and eggs similar?
    a. They both have the same number of chromosomes in their nuclei.
    b. They are both the same size.
    c. They are both equipped with a flagellum that provides motility.
    d. They are both produced after ovulation.

    ANS: A   DIF: I   OBJ: BPE 44-2.1

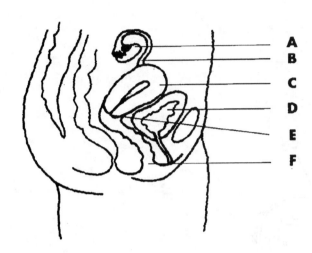

15. Refer to the illustration above. Eggs mature in the structure labeled
    a. A.   c. D.
    b. F.   d. E.

    ANS: A   DIF: II   OBJ: BPE 44-2.1

16. Refer to the illustration above. The structure labeled C in the diagram is
    a. a fallopian tube.   c. the uterus.
    b. the urethra.   d. a ureter.

    ANS: C   DIF: II   OBJ: BPE 44-2.2

17. Refer to the illustration above. Fertilization usually occurs in the structure labeled
    a. A.   c. C.
    b. F.   d. B.

    ANS: D   DIF: II   OBJ: BPE 44-2.2

18. A female gamete is called a(n)
    a. sperm.   c. fallopian.
    b. ovum.   d. follicles.

    ANS: B   DIF: I   OBJ: BPE 44-2.1

19. Eggs are produced in the
    a. ovaries.
    b. fallopian tubes.
    c. uterus.
    d. vagina.

    ANS: A   DIF: I   OBJ: BPE 44-2.1

20. ovary : egg production ::
    a. ovary : sperm production
    b. female reproductive system : sperm production
    c. testes : sperm production
    d. ovary : fertilization

    ANS: C
    (is the location of)

    DIF: II   OBJ: BPE 44-2.1

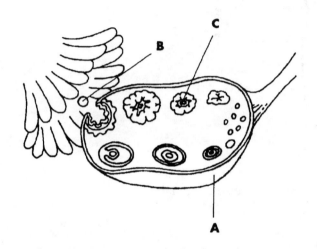

21. Refer to the illustration above. The structure labeled C in the diagram is a(n)
    a. immature follicle.
    b. follicle beginning to break down.
    c. mature egg.
    d. immature egg.

    ANS: B   DIF: II   OBJ: BPE 44-2.1

22. Refer to the illustration above. In the diagram, the structure labeled B is
    a. a sperm cell.
    b. a follicle.
    c. an egg cell.
    d. the cervix.

    ANS: C   DIF: II   OBJ: BPE 44-2.1

23. Refer to the illustration above. The structure labeled A in the diagram is
    a. a follicle.
    b. an egg cell.
    c. the uterus.
    d. an ovary.

    ANS: D   DIF: II   OBJ: BPE 44-2.2

24. The muscular structure in which the fetus develops is the
    a. vagina.
    b. fallopian tube.
    c. cervix.
    d. uterus.

    ANS: D   DIF: I   OBJ: BPE 44-2.2

25. The fallopian tubes
    a. secrete estrogen.
    b. produce eggs.
    c. are tubes that extend from the ovaries to each side of the uterus, through which the egg travels.
    d. All of the above

    ANS: C   DIF: I   OBJ: BPE 44-2.2

26. The entrance to the uterus is called the
    a. vagina.
    b. clitoris.
    c. cervix.
    d. diaphragm.

    ANS: C   DIF: I   OBJ: BPE 44-2.2

27. The ruptured follicle left in the ovary after ovulation develops into a
    a. corpus luteum.
    b. zygote.
    c. chorion.
    d. cervix.

    ANS: A   DIF: I   OBJ: BPE 44-2.3

28. If no embryo arrives after the uterus has prepared to receive it,
    a. birth will occur later than the usual nine months.
    b. the lining of the uterus stays intact in preparation for another embryo.
    c. the lining of the uterus is expelled from the body in menstrual blood.
    d. None of the above

    ANS: C   DIF: I   OBJ: BPE 44-2.3

29. Menopause is the time at which
    a. adult sex characteristics first appear.
    b. eggs are produced.
    c. menstruation begins.
    d. females cease to release eggs.

    ANS: D   DIF: I   OBJ: BPE 44-2.3

30. During implantation,
    a. the follicle matures.
    b. the embryo implants in the uterine wall.
    c. the sperm reaches the egg.
    d. menstruation occurs.

    ANS: B   DIF: I   OBJ: BPE 44-3.1

31. The attachment of an embryo into the uterine wall is known as
    a. implantation.
    b. development.
    c. labor.
    d. fertilization.

    ANS: A   DIF: I   OBJ: BPE 44-3.1

32. Cells produced by division of the fertilized egg give rise to the
    a. embryo.
    b. placenta.
    c. umbilical cord.
    d. All of the above

    ANS: A   DIF: I   OBJ: BPE 44-3.1

33. Embryonic cells are organized into the major organ systems
    a. during the sixth month.
    b. by the end of the first trimester.
    c. during the second trimester.
    d. just before birth.

    ANS: B   DIF: I   OBJ: BPE 44-3.2

34. The embryo is formed
    a. in the ovary.
    b. during the third trimester of pregnancy.
    c. at fertilization.
    d. when the fertilized egg divides.

    ANS: D   DIF: I   OBJ: BPE 44-3.2

35. The structure that exchanges substances between mother and fetus is the
    a. yolk sac.
    b. fallopian tube.
    c. placenta.
    d. mature follicle.

    ANS: C   DIF: I   OBJ: BPE 44-3.2

36. During the fetal period,
    a. the mother's blood flows to the fetus through the umbilical cord.
    b. the infant's lungs absorb oxygen from the amniotic fluid.
    c. digestion occurs independently of the mother.
    d. the blood of the fetus absorbs oxygen and gets rid of carbon dioxide through the placenta.

    ANS: D   DIF: I   OBJ: BPE 44-3.2

37. Pregnancy is often divided into three 3-month periods known as
    a. quarters.
    b. fetal development.
    c. trimesters.
    d. ovarian cycles.

    ANS: C   DIF: I   OBJ: BPE 44-3.2

38. Drinking alcohol, smoking, or using other drugs during pregnancy can cause
    a. birth defects in babies.
    b. small or sick babies.
    c. mental retardation.
    d. All of the above

    ANS: D   DIF: I   OBJ: BPE 44-3.3

39. Sexually transmitted diseases such as gonorrhea and chlamydia, which are caused by bacteria,
    a. are almost always incurable.
    b. are a direct result of viral infections in a fetus.
    c. can usually be treated with antibiotics.
    d. None of the above

    ANS: C   DIF: I   OBJ: BPE 44-4.1

40. Gonorrhea can be acquired
    a. by sharing glassware and dishes with infected persons.
    b. through sexual contact with infected persons.
    c. by swimming in infected swimming pools.
    d. through poor personal hygiene habits.

    ANS: B   DIF: I   OBJ: BPE 44-4.1

41. Pelvic inflammatory disease, or PID, is usually caused by
    a. HIV.   c. gonorrhea or chlamydia.
    b. syphilis.   d. All of the above

    ANS: C   DIF: I   OBJ: BPE 44-4.1

42. gonorrhea infection in females : no symptoms ::
    a. gonorrhea infection : warts   c. chlamydia infection: chancre
    b. syphilis infection : pus discharge d. genital herpes : fever blisters

    ANS: D
    (is usually characterized by)

    DIF: II   OBJ: BPE 44-4.1

43. AIDS is caused by
    a. HPV.   c. HSV.
    b. HIV.   d. CMV.

    ANS: B   DIF: I   OBJ: BPE 44-4.2

44. Sexually transmitted diseases may be
    a. caused by bacteria.
    b. caused by a virus.
    c. passed from the mother to her baby before or during birth.
    d. All of the above

    ANS: D   DIF: I   OBJ: BPE 44-4.2

45. The most common sexually transmitted disease in the United States that is caused by bacteria is
    a. gonorrhea.   c. syphilis.
    b. AIDS.   d. chlamydia.

    ANS: D   DIF: I   OBJ: BPE 44-4.3

46. Pelvic inflammatory disease (PID) is the one of the most common causes of _____ in women.
    a. embryonic developmental problems   c. abortions
    b. prolonged labor   d. infertility

    ANS: D   DIF: I   OBJ: BPE 44-4.3

COMPLETION

1. In the testes, sperm are produced in tubes called _____
   _____.

   ANS: seminiferous tubules   DIF: I   OBJ: BPE 44-1.1

2. The testes are suspended in a sac called the _____.

   ANS: scrotum   DIF: I   OBJ: BPE 44-1.1

3. As sperm cells move into the urethra, they mix with fluids secreted by three glands: the seminal vesicles, the prostate gland, and the _____ glands.

   ANS: bulbourethral   DIF: I   OBJ: BPE 44-1.4

4. The _____ gland secretes an alkaline fluid that neutralizes the acids in the female reproductive system.

   ANS: prostate   DIF: I   OBJ: BPE 44-1.3

5. The immature eggs found in a female at birth are arrested in the _____ stage of the first meiotic division.

   ANS: prophase   DIF: I   OBJ: BPE 44-2.1

6. The lower opening of the uterus is called the _____.

   ANS: cervix   DIF: I   OBJ: BPE 44-2.2

7. The release of an egg from an ovary is called _____.

   ANS: ovulation   DIF: I   OBJ: BPE 44-2.3

8. Clusters of cells that surround an immature egg are called _____.

   ANS: follicles   DIF: I   OBJ: BPE 44-2.3

9. The _____ cycle of the female is usually about 28 days long.

   ANS: menstrual   DIF: I   OBJ: BPE 44-2.3

10. The part of the female reproductive system that is lost each month as menstrual flow is the lining of the _____.

    ANS: uterus   DIF: I   OBJ: BPE 44-2.3

11. The entry of an embryo into the uterine wall is called _____.

ANS: implantation   DIF: I   OBJ: BPE 44-3.1

12. The passageway joining the ovary and the uterus is the _____
_____, where fertilization takes place.

ANS: fallopian tube   DIF: I   OBJ: BPE 44-3.1

13. Cleavage produces a ball of cells called the _____.

ANS: blastocyst   DIF: I   OBJ: BPE 44-3.1

14. The period of rapid division of an egg immediately after fertilization is called
_____.

ANS: cleavage   DIF: I   OBJ: BPE 44-3.1

15. Nutrients, oxygen, and wastes are transferred between the mother and embryo through the
_____.

ANS: placenta   DIF: I   OBJ: BPE 44-3.2

16. Following implantation, a membrane called the _____ encloses the embryo.

ANS: amnion   DIF: I   OBJ: BPE 44-3.2

17. Syphilis usually begins with the appearance of a painless ulcer called a(n)
_____.

ANS: chancre   DIF: I   OBJ: BPE 44-4.1

18. _____ is the most common bacterial STD in the United States.

ANS: Chlamydia   DIF: I   OBJ: BPE 44-4.1

19. AIDS is caused by a virus called _____.

ANS: HIV   DIF: I   OBJ: BPE 44-4.2

20. Gonorrhea and chlamydia can usually be cured with _____.

ANS: antibiotics   DIF: I   OBJ: BPE 44-4.3

PROBLEM

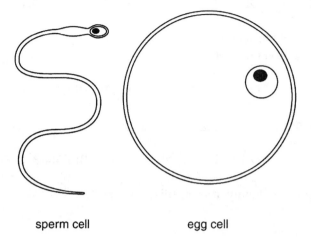

sperm cell   egg cell

1. Refer to the illustration above and write your answers in the space below.
   a. Describe three ways in which these two cells differ from each other.
   b. Relate the differences you noted in part "a" of this question to the activities carried out by these two cells.
   c. Identify one way in which these two cells differ from each other that cannot be seen using a microscope.
   d. Identify one thing that these two cells have in common with each other that cannot be seen using a microscope.
   e. Which part(s) of the sperm cell will enter the egg cell and become part of the zygote?

ANS:
Answers may include the following:
a.
   1. The egg cell is much larger than the sperm cell.
   2. The sperm cell has a flagellum while the egg cell does not.
   3. The sperm cell has much less cytoplasm in it than the egg cell does.
   4. The sperm cell has distinct head and tail ends.
b.
   1. The egg cell contains the organelles and food reserves that the zygote will need in order for it to divide and develop into an embryo. The sperm cell carries mostly mitochondria that enable the cell to move, but no food reserves (these are supplied in the semen).
   2. Sperm cells are deposited in the vagina of the human female and must swim up into a fallopian tube in order to reach an egg. The egg cell does not have to move itself; it is propelled down the fallopian tube to the uterus by cilia.
   3. The sperm cell must swim a long distance inside the female reproductive tract. Sperm carry mitochondria which provide the energy to swim.
   4. The head end of the sperm cell contains the nucleus, which will enter the egg cell. The tail end of the sperm cell propels it in the female reproductive tract.
c. The sperm cell has completed meiosis while the egg cell has not; the sperm cell developed after puberty, while the egg cell began development when the woman carrying the egg was an embryo herself.
d. They are both haploid cells; they both have 23 chromosomes.

e.   Only the nucleus will enter the egg.

DIF: II   OBJ: BPE 44-2.1

ESSAY

1.   Describe the structure of a sperm cell and explain how it is adapted for its function.

ANS:
A sperm cell consists of a head with very little cytoplasm, a midpiece, and a long tail. Digestive enzymes in the head enable a sperm cell to penetrate an egg. The midpiece contains mitochondria that supply the tail with ATP. The ATP supply the energy that the sperm cell needs to swim through a female's reproductive system to an egg. Swimming is accomplished by rapid movement of the tail, which is a powerful flagellum. The head contains genetic information.

DIF: II   OBJ: BPE 44-1.3

2.   Why must so many sperm be ejaculated for fertilization to take place?

ANS:
Although millions of sperm may be ejaculated, sperm are very small and must travel a long distance to reach the egg. The sperm must enter the uterus through the opening of the cervix and travel to the fallopian tube, where fertilization occurs. Usually only one of the fallopian tubes contains an egg. Most sperm never reach an egg cell because most die in the female reproductive tract.

DIF: II   OBJ: BPE 44-1.4

3.   Describe the path of an unfertilized egg from the place where it is produced to the site where it leaves the body with menstrual flow.

ANS:
An egg is produced and stored in the ovaries. When the egg matures, the follicle, which has formed around the egg, moves to the wall of the ovary, ruptures, and releases the egg. Tiny fingerlike projections that are part of the fallopian tube draw the egg from the ovary to the fallopian tube. The egg moves through the fallopian tube to the uterus, and then enters the uterus. If the egg has not been fertilized, it disintegrates in the uterus, and, along with the thickened lining of the uterus, is shed as a bloody discharge at menstruation.

DIF: II   OBJ: BPE 44-2.2

4.   Describe the effect of estrogen on the uterine lining and on the pituitary gland.

ANS:
Estrogen causes the uterine lining to thicken. Estrogen stimulates the anterior pituitary to release luteinizing hormone (LH), which in turn causes the maturation of the ovum.

DIF: II   OBJ: BPE 44-2.3

5. What are the functions of the placenta?

ANS:
The placenta exchanges substances between the mother and the developing fetus. The mother's body must carry out the processes of digestion, respiration, and excretion for the fetus. Oxygen and nutrients pass from the mother to the fetus, and waste products pass from the fetus to the mother, through the placenta.

DIF: II   OBJ: BPE 44-3.2

6. Describe the development that occurs in a fetus from the end of the first trimester to the end of the third trimester.

ANS:
By the end of the first trimester, all of the major body organs have differentiated, and the sex of the fetus has been established. During the second and third trimesters, the fetus grows rapidly as its organs finish developing and become functional. By the end of the third trimester, the fetus is able to exist outside its mother's body.

DIF: II   OBJ: BPE 44-3.2

7. Explain why the first trimester of pregnancy is such a critical time of development.

ANS:
Most of the major developmental events occur during early pregnancy. For example, the embryo grows rapidly, membranes that protect and nourish the embryo develop, and organ formation begins. Substances, including drugs and pathogens, can diffuse through the placenta. Exposure to mutagens or drugs at this stage can cause serious damage to the embryo.

DIF: II   OBJ: BPE 44-3.3

8. Julie was about 6 weeks pregnant. She was very excited about having a baby, as was her husband. However, her husband, Jim, was very concerned about Julie's habit of drinking several alcoholic drinks every day. Jim told her that he thought she should stop drinking because it could affect the health of their baby. Julie told him "the alcohol can't possibly hurt the baby. The baby has a completely separate circulatory system from mine, so alcohol in my blood can't even get into the baby." What error has Julie made in her reasoning?

ANS:
Julie mistakenly believes that her circulatory system is completely separate from her baby's. While it is true that the mother's blood does not flow directly into the baby, many substances flow from the mothers blood into the baby's through the placenta. Substances such as nutrients and oxygen are vital for the embryo's survival and growth. Substances such as alcohol can cause great harm to the developing baby.

DIF: III   OBJ: BPE 44-3.3

9. List two sexually transmitted diseases that are caused by viruses and two that are caused by bacteria. Explain the cures for these diseases.

ANS:
Genital herpes, AIDS, genital warts, and hepatitis B are caused by viruses. Gonorrhea, syphilis, and chlamydia are caused by bacteria. There is no cure for AIDS or genital herpes, although antiviral drugs can temporarily eliminate the blisters caused by genital herpes. The sexually transmitted bacterial diseases can usually be cured with antibiotics but serious consequences can result if treatment is not started early during the infection.

DIF: II   OBJ: BPE 44-4.3